PRACTICAL. USEFUL. G...

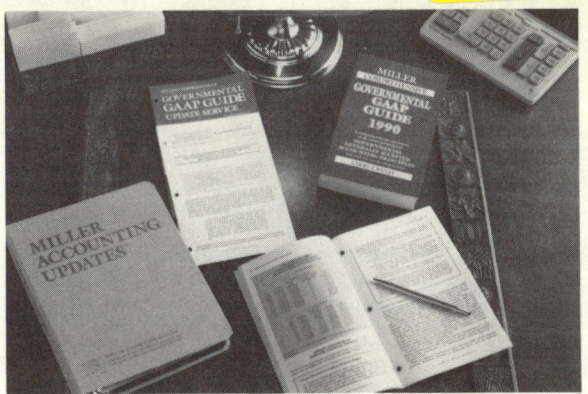

1990 HBJ MILLER
GOVERNMENTAL GAAP GUIDE UPDATE SERVICE

Thank you for choosing the *1990 HBJ Miller Governmental GAAP Guide*. We believe you'll find it to be the most useful and up-to-date *Governmental GAAP Guide* available.

As a valued *Governmental GAAP Guide* buyer, we would like to extend a special offer to you. You can become a member of the *1990 Governmental GAAP Guide Update Service* for only $70.00—a savings of $40.00 off the regular subscription price of $110.00.

The *Governmental GAAP Guide Update Service* is the perfect complement to your *Governmental GAAP Guide*. As a member of this service, you can look forward to receiving timely, accurate interpretations of GASB pronouncements throughout the year, as well as Interpretations, Technical Bulletins, and insightful Commentaries on important governmental accounting issues. You will also receive a handsome, cloth-covered binder filled with many of the important updates from 1989.

Order your *1990 Governmental GAAP Guide Update Service* today and begin receiving your update bulletins immediately.

1990 HBJ MILLER GOVERNMENTAL GAAP GUIDE UPDATE SERVICE

Yes, I accept your special offer to become a member of the *1990 Governmental GAAP Guide Update Service*. I understand that my subscription does not include a *1990 Governmental GAAP Guide*.

☐ My payment of $70 is enclosed. (Make checks payable to Harcourt Brace Jovanovich.)

Charge my ☐ Visa ☐ MasterCard ☐ American Express

Card # _____ Exp. Date _____

Card Signature _____

☐ Bill me ☐ Bill my firm

NAME _____
COMPANY _____
ADDRESS _____
CITY _____ ST _____ ZIP _____

☐ Please send me more information.

I understand that my reference will be kept up-to-date through annual subscription renewal shipped automatically on a 30-day approval basis.

Signature _____

Prices are US only and subject to change without notice.

GG90

1990 HBJ MILLER
GOVERNMENTAL GAAP GUIDE UPDATE SERVICE

Order your subscription today. Simply complete and detach the card below and drop it in the mail to receive the best governmental accounting information available.

NO POSTAGE NECESSARY IF MAILED IN THE UNITED STATES

BUSINESS REPLY MAIL
FIRST CLASS PERMIT NO. 201313 SAN DIEGO, CA

POSTAGE WILL BE PAID BY ADDRESSEE

HBJ Miller Accounting Publications, Inc.
465 South Lincoln Drive
Troy, MO 63379-9900

MILLER
COMPREHENSIVE
GOVERNMENTAL GAAP GUIDE™
1990

A comprehensive interpretation
of all current promulgated
**GOVERNMENTAL
GENERALLY ACCEPTED
ACCOUNTING PRINCIPLES**
FOR STATE AND LOCAL GOVERNMENTS

LARRY P. BAILEY, Ph.D., C.P.A.

MILLER ACCOUNTING PUBLICATIONS, INC.
A SUBSIDIARY OF

HBJ

Harcourt Brace Jovanovich, Publishers
SAN DIEGO   NEW YORK   LONDON

> This publication is designed to provide accurate and authoritative information in regard to the subject matter covered. It is sold with the understanding that the publisher is not engaged in rendering legal, accounting, or other professional service.

The publisher has not sought nor obtained approval of this publication from any other organization, profit or non-profit, and is solely responsible for its contents.

Miller Comprehensive Governmental GAAP Guide
is a trademark of Harcourt Brace Jovanovich, Inc.

Copyright © 1989, 1988, 1987, 1986 by Harcourt Brace Jovanovich, Inc.

All rights reserved. No part of this publication may be reproduced or transmitted in any form or by any means, electronic or mechanical, including photocopy, recording, or any information storage and retrieval system, without permission in writing from the publisher.

Requests for permission to make copies of any part of the work should be mailed to: Permissions, Harcourt Brace Jovanovich, Publishers, Orlando, Florida 32887

ISBN: 0-15-601802-0 (hardcover)
ISBN: 0-15-601801-2 (softcover)
ISSN: 0891-6918

Printed in the United States of America

To

Rufus Wixon
Professor Emeritus
Wharton School

TABLE OF CONTENTS

Basic Governmental Accounting Concepts and Standards

Overview of Governmental Generally Accepted Accounting Principles	1.01
Basic Foundation of Governmental Generally Accepted Accounting Principles	2.01
Basis of Accounting and Measurement Focus of Governmental Funds	3.01
The Governmental Reporting Entity	4.01
Governmental Financial Reporting	5.01
Budgetary Accounting and Reporting	6.01
Financial Statement Terminology and Classification	7.01

Governmental Accounts and Transactions

Revenues	10.01
Special Assessments	11.01
Expenditures	20.01
Assets	30.01
Deposit and Investment Portfolio Disclosures and Reverse Repurchase Agreements	31.01
Liabilities	40.01
Claims, Judgments, and Special Termination Benefits	41.01
Compensated Absences	42.01
Leases	43.01
Pension Disclosures	50.01
Certain Postretirement Benefits	51.01

Governmental Funds and Account Groups

General and Special Revenue Funds	60.01
Capital Projects Funds	61.01
Debt Service Funds	62.01

Table of Contents

Proprietary Funds	64.01
Fiduciary Funds	65.01
Pension Trust Funds	66.01
General Long-Term Debt Account Group	67.01
General Fixed Assets Account Group	68.01

Special Governmental Units and Agencies

Hospitals	80.01
Colleges and Universities	81.01
Certain Nonprofit Organizations	82.01

Appendix

Illustration of Comprehensive Annual Financial Report	90.01

Topical Index

Topical Index	95.01

PREFACE

Governmental accounting has seldom received the attention commercial accounting has enjoyed over the past half century. This imbalance changed dramatically in 1984 with the creation of the Governmental Accounting Standards Board (GASB). After considerable debate, the GASB was granted equal status with the Financial Accounting Standards Board, and both organizations are now subject to oversight review by the Financial Accounting Foundation. The role of the GASB was further enhanced when the American Institute of Certified Public Accountants (AICPA) modified its Code of Professional Conduct by agreeing to accept pronouncements of the GASB and the National Council on Governmental Accounting (NCGA) as authoritative support for generally accepted accounting principles for the preparation of financial statements of state and local governments.

In the past, few publications have attempted to describe governmental generally accepted accounting principles and the analyses that have been done have appeared in a variety of disparate publications. The purpose of the *Governmental GAAP Guide* (or *Gvt-GAAP Guide* for short) is to provide a single book that discusses all the promulgated accounting principles applicable to financial reporting by state and local governments. The *Gvt-GAAP Guide* provides a thorough analysis of GASB Statements, GASB Interpretations, GASB Technical Bulletins, NCGA Statements, NCGA Interpretations, and certain AICPA SOPs and Accounting and Audit Guides. These original pronouncements have been analyzed and restated in straightforward language to allow those responsible for the preparation or audit of governmental financial statements to better understand the original promulgations. Major topics are cross-referenced to the original pronouncements in the Literature Reference sections at the end of each chapter to make the guide a practical research tool.

The *Gvt-GAAP Guide* is organized into four main sections. The first section (Basic Governmental Accounting Concepts and Standards) describes the fundamental concepts and principles that provide the foundation for financial reporting by governmental units. Those familiar with these concepts may want to skip this introductory section, but the basics are here for those who need them. Specific accounting and reporting standards are reviewed in the

Preface

next section of the book (Governmental Accounts and Transactions), and in the third section (Governmental Funds and Account Groups), they are discussed as they apply to governmental funds and account groups. In the final section (Special Governmental Units and Agencies), the accounting and reporting standards applicable to special governmental units or agencies are delineated. Thus, the organizational strategy of the book is to provide a description of general concepts and principles (sections one and two), and then illustrate the application of these concepts and principles in the context of a specific reporting unit (sections three and four).

The preparation of this book was made possible by the efforts of a number of dedicated people. Jane Mayrhofer typed the original manuscript and was instrumental in completing the project on time. The quality of the book was improved by the comprehensive reviews of Rhett Harrell (Touche Ross), Raymond Poteau (Philadelphia College of Textiles), and Bruce Leauby (Rider College). In addition, Paul Amidei (Harcourt Brace Jovanovich) coordinated the project and provided encouragement at critical stages during its development, and Mary Larkin (Harcourt Brace Jovanovich) provided valuable editorial commentary and support during the latter phase of the project.

While the individuals mentioned above played an important role in the preparation of the *Gvt-GAAP Guide*, any errors or omissions are the responsibility of the author. The *Gvt-GAAP Guide* will evolve over time as new pronouncements are issued, and as we strive to better explain governmental accounting and reporting standards. If you have suggestions you believe will improve the quality of the material, please let me know.

Larry P. Bailey
Rider College
Lawrenceville, NJ 08648

CROSS-REFERENCE

ORIGINAL PRONOUNCEMENTS TO COMPREHENSIVE GOVERNMENTAL GAAP GUIDE CHAPTERS

This locator provides instant cross-reference between an original pronouncement and the chapter(s) in this publication where such pronouncement appears. Original pronouncements are listed chronologically on the left and the chapter(s) in which the pronouncement appears in the *Governmental GAAP Guide* on the right.

GOVERNMENTAL ACCOUNTING STANDARDS BOARD STATEMENTS

> GASB Statements are issued by the Governmental Accounting Standards Board under the authority of Rule 203 of the AICPA's Code of Professional Conduct. Rule 203 states in part that an AICPA member "shall not express an opinion that financial statements are presented in conformity with generally accepted accounting principles if such statements contain any departure from an accounting principle promulgated by the body designated . . ." by the AICPA Council. Members of the AICPA should be prepared to justify any departures from the Rules of Conduct of the Code of Professional Conduct. Unless otherwise specified, GASB Statements apply to financial reports of all state and local governmental entities, including public benefit corporations and authorities, public employee retirement systems, and governmental utilities, hospitals, colleges, and universities.

ORIGINAL PRONOUNCEMENT	GOV'T GAAP GUIDE REFERENCE
GASB Statement-1 (1984) Authoritative Status of NCGA Pronouncements and AICPA Industry Audit Guide	Overview of Governmental Generally Accepted Accounting Principles, p. **1.07**
GASB Statement-2 (1986) Financial Reporting of Deferred Compensation Plans Adopted under the Provisions of Internal Revenue Code Section 457	Fiduciary Funds, p. **65.23**
GASB Statement-3 (1986) Deposits with Financial Institutions, Investments (including Repurchase Agreements), and Reverse Repurchase Agreements	Deposit and Investment Portfolio Disclosures and Reverse Repurchase Agreements, p. **31.01**
GASB Statement-4 (1986) Applicability of FASB Statement-87, "Employers' Accounting for Pensions," to State and Local Governmental Employers	Pension Trust Funds, p. **66.01**

Cross-Reference

GASB Statement-5 (1986)
Disclosure of Pension Information by Public
Employee Retirement Systems and State and
Local Governmental Employers   Pension Disclosures, p. **50.01**

GASB Statement-6 (1987)
Accounting and Financial Reporting for Special Assessments   Special Assessments, p. **11.01**

GASB Statement-7 (1987)
Advance Refundings Resulting in Defeasance
of Debt   Liabilities, p. **40.15**

GASB Statement-8 (1988)
Applicability of FASB Statement No. 93, Recognition of Depreciation by Not-for-Profit Organizations, to Certain State and Local Governmental Entities
        Colleges and Universities, p. **81.12**
        Certain Nonprofit Organizations, p. **82.17**

GOVERNMENTAL ACCOUNTING STANDARDS BOARD INTERPRETATIONS

> GASB Interpretations are issued by the Governmental Accounting Standards Board under the authority of Rule 203 of the AICPA's Code of Professional Conduct. Rule 203 states in part that an AICPA member "shall not express an opinion that financial statements are presented in conformity with generally accepted accounting principles if such statements contain any departure from an accounting principle promulgated by the body designated . . ." by the AICPA Council. Members of the AICPA should be prepared to justify any departures from the Rules of Conduct of the Code of Professional Conduct. Unless otherwise specified, GASB Interpretations apply to financial reports of all state and local governmental entities, including public benefit corporations and authorities, public employee retirement systems, and governmental utilities, hospitals, colleges, and universities.

ORIGINAL PRONOUNCEMENT   GOV'T GAAP GUIDE REFERENCE

GASB Interpretation-1 (1984)
Demand Bonds Issued by State and Local
Governmental Entities   Liabilities, p. **40.08**

GOVERNMENTAL ACCOUNTING STANDARDS BOARD TECHNICAL BULLETINS

> GASB Technical Bulletins are issued by the Governmental Accounting Standards Board but are not issued under the authority of Rule 203 of the AICPA's Code of Professional Conduct. The GASB has authorized its staff to prepare Technical Bulletins to respond to governmental accounting issues on a timely basis. Technical Bulletins are not voted on formally by the GASB; however, a Technical Bulletin will not be issued if a majority of the members of the GASB object to its issuance.

Cross-Reference

ORIGINAL PRONOUNCEMENT

GASB Technical Bulletin 84-1 (1984)
Purpose and Scope of GASB Technical Bulletins and Procedures for Issuance

GASB Technical Bulletin 87-1 (1987)
Applying Paragraph 68 of GASB Statement 3

GOV'T GAAP GUIDE REFERENCE

Overview of Governmental Generally Accepted Accounting Principles, p. **1.06**

Deposit and Investment Portfolio Disclosures and Reverse Repurchase Agreements, p. **31.15**

GOVERNMENTAL ACCOUNTING STANDARDS BOARD EXPOSURE DRAFTS AND DISCUSSION MEMORANDA

> Exposure Drafts and Discussion Memoranda are published by the Governmental Accounting Standards Board. Discussion Memoranda are published to provide a general framework for the discussion of a governmental accounting issue. Exposure Drafts provide a tentative position with respect to governmental accounting issues. These publications are not official promulgations. Exposure Drafts and Discussion Memoranda are included in the Gvt-GAAP Guide for informational purposes only.

ORIGINAL PRONOUNCEMENT

GOV'T GAAP GUIDE REFERENCE

EXPOSURE DRAFTS

Measurement Focus and Basis of Accounting—Governmental Fund Operating Statements

Reporting Cash Flows of Proprietary and Nonexpendable Trust Funds and Governmental Entities that Use Proprietary Fund Accounting

Basis of Accounting and Measurement Focus of Governmental Funds, p. **3.16**

Governmental Financial Reporting, p. **5.56**

DISCUSSION MEMORANDA

Measurement Focus of Governmental Business-Type Activities

The Financial Reporting Entity

Accounting and Financial Reporting for Capital Assets of Governmental Entities

Accounting and Financial Reporting for Risk Management Activities

Basis of Accounting and Measurement Focus of Governmental Funds, p. **3.35**

The Governmental Reporting Entity, p. **4.19**

Assets, p. **30.16**

Claims, Judgments, and Special Termination Benefits, p. **41.13**

GOVERNMENTAL GAAP GUIDE / **xiii**

Cross-Reference

Capital Reporting—Capital Transactions of
Governmental Funds and Related Capital
Debt
                              Capital Projects Fund, p. **61.39**
                              Debt Service Funds, p. **62.41**

GOVERNMENTAL ACCOUNTING STANDARDS BOARD CONCEPTS STATEMENTS

> GASB Concepts Statements are issued by the Governmental Accounting Standards Board; however, Concepts Statements do not establish generally accepted accounting principles for state and local governmental entities. Concepts Statements identify concepts that will be used by the GASB in establishing future governmental accounting and reporting standards.

ORIGINAL PRONOUNCEMENT   GOV'T GAAP GUIDE REFERENCE

GASB Concepts Statement-1 (1987)
Objectives of Financial Reporting   Basic Foundation of Governmental Generally Accepted Accounting Principles, p. **2.02**

NATIONAL COUNCIL ON GOVERNMENTAL ACCOUNTING STATEMENTS

> NCGA Statements were issued by the National Council on Governmental Accounting until 1984, when the GASB assumed the role of promulgating accounting principles for state and local governments. GASB-1 concluded that NCGA Statements not otherwise superseded are considered authoritative support for determining generally accepted accounting principles for state and local governments.

ORIGINAL PRONOUNCEMENT   GOV'T GAAP GUIDE REFERENCE

NCGA Statement-1 (1980)
Governmental Accounting and Financial Reporting Principles
- Generally Accepted Accounting Principles and Legal Compliance   Basic Foundation of Governmental Generally Accepted Accounting Principles, p. **2.18**
- Fund Accounting   Basic Foundation of Governmental Generally Accepted Accounting Principles, p. **2.25**
- Fixed Assets   General Fixed Assets Account Group, p. **68.01**
- Long-Term Liabilities   General Long-Term Debt Account Group, p. **67.01**
- Basis of Accounting   Basis of Accounting and Measurement Focus of Governmental Funds, p. **3.01**
- The Budget and Budgetary Accounting   Budgetary Accounting and Reporting, p. **6.01**
- Classification and Terminology   Financial Statement Terminology and Classification, p. **7.01**
- Annual Financial Reporting   Governmental Financial Reporting, p. **5.01**
- Supplemental and Special Purpose Reporting   Governmental Financial Reporting, p. **5.27**

Cross-Reference

NCGA Statement-2 (1980)
Grant, Entitlement, and Shared Revenue Accounting and Reporting by State and Local
Governments				Revenues, p. **10.06**

NCGA Statement-3 (1982)
Defining the Governmental Reporting Entity		The Governmental Reporting Entity, p. **4.01**

NCGA Statement-4 (1982)
Accounting and Financial Reporting Principles for Claims and Judgments and Compensated Absences		Claims, Judgments, and Special Termination Benefits, p. **41.01**

NCGA Statement-5 (1983)
Accounting and Financial Reporting Principles for Lease Agreements of State and Local
Governments				Leases, p. **43.01**

NCGA Statement-6 (effective date deferred)
Pension Accounting and Financial Reporting:
Public Employee Retirement Systems and
State and Local Government Employers		Pension Trust Funds, p. **66.01**

NCGA Statement-7 (1984)
Financial Reporting for Component Units
Within the Governmental Reporting Entity		The Governmental Reporting Entity, p. **4.02**

NATIONAL COUNCIL ON GOVERNMENTAL ACCOUNTING INTERPRETATIONS

> NCGA Interpretations were issued by the National Council on Governmental Accounting until 1984, when the GASB assumed the role of promulgating accounting principles for state and local governments. GASB-1 concluded that NCGA Interpretations not otherwise superseded are considered authoritative support for determining generally accepted accounting principles for state and local governments.

ORIGINAL PRONOUNCEMENT			GOV'T GAAP GUIDE REFERENCE

NCGA Interpretation-1
Superseded with the issuance of NCGA-1		No reference

NCGA Interpretation-2 (1980)
Segment Information for Enterprise Funds	Proprietary Funds, p. **64.40**

NCGA Interpretation-3 (1981)
Revenue Recognition—Property Taxes		Revenues, p. **10.03**

NCGA Interpretation-4
Superseded with the issuance of NCGA-6		No reference

Cross-Reference

NCGA Interpretation-5 (1982)
Authoritative Status of "Governmental Accounting, Auditing, and Financial Reporting" (1968)

Overview of Governmental Generally Accepted Accounting Principles, p. **1.09**

NCGA Interpretation-6 (1982)
Notes to the Financial Statements Disclosure

Governmental Financial Reporting, p. **5.30**

NCGA Interpretation-7 (1983)
Clarification as to the Application of the Criteria in NCGA-3 Defining the Governmental Reporting Entity

The Governmental Reporting Entity, p. **4.02**

NCGA Interpretation-8 (1983)
Certain Pension Matters

Pension Trust Funds, p. **66.01**

NCGA Interpretation-9 (1984)
Certain Fund Classifications and Balance Sheet Accounts

Assets, p. **30.05**
Liabilities, p. **40.04** and **40.14**

NCGA Interpretation-10 (1984)
State and Local Government Budgetary Reporting

Budgetary Accounting and Reporting, p. **6.04**

NCGA Interpretation-11 (1984)
Claim and Judgment Transactions for Governmental Funds

Claims, Judgments, and Special Termination Benefits, p. **41.08**

NATIONAL COUNCIL ON GOVERNMENTAL ACCOUNTING CONCEPTS STATEMENTS

> NCGA Concepts Statements were issued by the National Council on Governmental Accounting until 1984, when the GASB assumed the role of promulgating accounting principles for state and local governments. NCGA Concepts Statement-1 was superseded by the issuance of GASB Concepts Statement-1; however, the GASB concluded that NCGA Concepts Statement-1 is nonetheless a useful source for understanding the role of financial reporting by governmental entities.

ORIGINAL PRONOUNCEMENT   GOV'T GAAP GUIDE REFERENCE

NCGA Concepts Statement-1 (1982)
Objectives of Accounting and Financial Reporting for Governmental Units

Basic Foundation of Governmental Generally Accepted Accounting Principles, p. **2.08**

AICPA STATEMENTS OF POSITION

> Statements of Position are issued by the American Institute of Certified Public Accountants, but these pronouncements do not establish accounting principles enforceable under Rule 203 of the AICPA's Code of Professional Conduct. SOPs should be considered in determining what constitutes generally accepted accounting principles as defined in Statement on Auditing Standards-5 ("Present Fairly in Conformity With Generally Accepted Accounting Principles" in the Independent Auditor's Report). Members of the AICPA should be prepared to justify departures from recommendations contained in SOPs.

ORIGINAL PRONOUNCEMENT	GOV'T GAAP GUIDE REFERENCE
SOP 74-8 (1974) Financial Accounting and Reporting by Colleges and Universities	Colleges and Universities, p. **81.01**
SOP 75-3 (1975) Accrual of Revenues and Expenditures by State and Local Governmental Units	Revenues, p. **10.05**
SOP 77-2 (1977) Accounting for Interfund Transfers of State and Local Governmental Units	Financial Statement Terminology and Classification, p. **7.05**
SOP (Auditing) (no numeric reference) (1978) Clarification of Accounting, Auditing, and Reporting Practices Relating to Hospital Malpractice Loss Contingencies	Hospitals, p. **80.01**
SOP 78-1 (1978) Accounting by Hospitals for Certain Marketable Equity Securities	Hospitals, p. **80.01**
SOP 78-7 (1978) Financial Accounting and Reporting by Hospitals Operated by a Governmental Unit	Hospitals, p. **80.01**
SOP 78-10 (1978) Accounting Principles and Reporting Practices for Certain Nonprofit Organizations	Certain Nonprofit Organizations, p. **82.01**
SOP 81-2 (1981) Reporting Practices Concerning Hospital-Related Organizations	Hospitals, p. **80.01**
SOP 85-1 (1985) Financial Reporting for Not-for-Profit Health Care Entities for Tax-Exempt Debt and Certain Funds Whose Use Is Limited	Hospitals, p. **80.01**
SOP 87-1 (1987) Accounting for Asserted and Unasserted Medical Malpractice Claims of Health Care Providers and Related Issues	Hospitals, p. **80.01**

Cross-Reference

SOP 87-2 (1987)
Accounting for Joint Costs of Informational Materials and Activities for Not-for-Profit Organizations that Include a Fund-Raising Appeal. Certain Nonprofit Organizations, p. **82.14**

AICPA INDUSTRY AUDIT GUIDES
AICPA AUDIT AND ACCOUNTING GUIDES

> Industry Audit Guides and Audit and Accounting Guides are issued by the American Institute of Certified Public Accountants, but these pronouncements do not establish accounting principles enforceable under Rule 203 of the AICPA's Code of Professional Ethics. Industry Audit Guides and Audit and Accounting Guides should be considered in determining what constitutes generally accepted accounting principles as defined in Statement on Auditing Standards-5 ("Present Fairly in Conformity With Generally Accepted Accounting Principles" in the Independent Auditor's Report). Members of the AICPA should be prepared to justify departures from recommendations contained in these pronouncements.

ORIGINAL PRONOUNCEMENT	GOV'T GAAP GUIDE REFERENCE
Industry Audit Guides	
Hospital Audit Guide (1980)	Hospitals, p. **80.01**
Audits of Colleges and Universities (1975)	Colleges and Universities, p. **81.01**
Audit and Accounting Guides	
Audits of Certain Nonprofit Organizations (1981)	Certain Nonprofit Organizations, p. **82.01**
Audits of State and Local Governmental Units (1986)	Overview of Governmental Generally Accepted Accounting Principles, p. **1.10**

Basic Governmental Accounting Concepts and Standards

OVERVIEW OF GOVERNMENTAL GENERALLY ACCEPTED ACCOUNTING PRINCIPLES

In 1968, the National Committee on Governmental Accounting (subsequently the name was changed to the National Council on Governmental Accounting (NCGA)) published *Governmental Accounting, Auditing, and Financial Reporting* (1968 GAAFR), which included most of the NCGA's prior publications at that time. The 1968 GAAFR, through general acceptance, established generally accepted accounting principles for state and local governmental units. The AICPA endorsed these principles in 1974 when it issued an audit guide entitled *Audits of State and Local Governmental Units* (ASLGU). Since that time, the AICPA has issued Statements of Positions (SOPs) that further clarified and modified governmental accounting standards.

The NCGA, in 1979, issued NCGA-1 (Governmental Accounting and Financial Reporting Principles), which was a restatement of accounting principles established in the 1968 GAAFR and the AICPA's ASLGU and SOPs. The following year, the Government Finance Officers Association (GFOA) published *Governmental Accounting, Auditing, and Financial Reporting* (1980 GAAFR), which was not considered authoritative but rather provided illustrations and explanations of governmental generally accepted accounting principles.

The Financial Accounting Standards Board (FASB) did not promulgate accounting principles that specifically addressed governmental accounting principles and reporting standards; however, in 1980, it did issue Financial Accounting Concepts Statement-4 (FASB:CS-4) (Objectives of Financial Reporting by Nonbusiness Organizations) which discussed the broad area of financial reporting by nonprofit organizations. Even with the issuance of the concepts statement, there was significant disagreement as to whether the FASB had the authority to promulgate accounting principles for state and local governments. After much discussion, the profession resolved the problem by establishing the Governmental Accounting Standards Board (GASB) in April 1984.

Authoritative Sources of Governmental Accounting Principles

APB Statement-4 (Basic Concepts and Accounting Principles Underlying Financial Statements of Business Enterprises) defines generally accepted accounting principles as conventions, rules, and procedures necessary to describe accepted accounting practice at a particular time. The importance of reporting entities following generally accepted accounting principles in the preparation of their financial statements is embodied in Rule 203 of the AICPA's Code of Professional Conduct, which states:

> A member shall not express an opinion that financial statements are presented in conformity with generally accepted accounting principles if such statements contain any departure from an accounting principle promulgated by the body designated by Council to establish such principles which has a material effect on the statements taken as a whole, unless the member can demonstrate that due to unusual circumstances the financial statements would otherwise have been misleading. In such cases his report must describe the departure, the approximate effects thereof, if practicable, and the reasons why compliance with the principles would result in a misleading statement.

The AICPA Council has designated the FASB as the body to establish accounting principles (applicable to both profit and nonprofit organizations), and the GASB as the body to establish accounting principles for state and local governments.

The Financial Accounting Foundation (FAF) has agreed that the GASB has the authority to issue generally accepted accounting principles for state and local governmental units. Thus, the GASB establishes accounting principles for state and local governments, and the FASB establishes accounting principles for all other reporting entities, including nonprofit organizations other than state and local governments.

The specific relationship of pronouncements made by the GASB and the FASB was addressed by an audit interpretation issued by the AICPA in December 1984. SAS-5 (The Meaning of "Present Fairly in Conformity with Generally Accepted Accounting Principles" in the Independent Auditor's Report—as amended by SAS-43) identifies a hierarchy of authoritative literature that should be considered in determining whether a particular principle is generally accepted. The SAS Interpretation (December 1984) states that the hierarchy to be followed for governmental accounting principles is the one established in the FAF's agreement, which is reproduced below:

(a) Pronouncements of the Governmental Accounting Standards Board
(b) Pronouncements of the Financial Accounting Standards Board
(c) Pronouncements of bodies composed of expert accountants that follow a due process procedure, including broad distribution of proposed accounting principles for public comment, for the intended purpose of establishing accounting principles or describing existing practices that are generally accepted
(d) Practices or pronouncements that are widely recognized as being generally accepted because they represent prevalent practice in a particular industry or the knowledgeable application to specific circumstances of pronouncements that are generally accepted
(e) Other accounting literature

Based on the hierarchy described above, if a GASB (or NCGA) pronouncement has not addressed an accounting issue, FASB promulgations must be looked to for possible guidance in determining generally accepted accounting principles. If neither the FASB nor the GASB has addressed the accounting issue, material that meets the criteria established by hierarchy levels (c) and (d) must be considered. The SAS Interpretation (December 1984) states that an auditor must be prepared to justify a conclusion that is inconsistent with accounting principles established by categories (c) and (d). If the first four categories in the hierarchy do not address the accounting issue, other accounting literature (category (e)) must be reviewed.

> **OBSERVATION:** *The five-category hierarchy developed above is very similar to the hierarchy initially identified in SAS-5 (The Meaning of "Present Fairly in Conformity with Generally Accepted Accounting Principles" in the Independent Auditor's Report), which described the authoritative sources of accounting principles for business enterprises. While the GASB hierarchy does not elaborate on other accounting literature sources (category (e)), SAS-5 concluded that the category (as it applies to accounting principles for business enterprises) includes such items as FASB Statements for Financial Accounting Concepts, APB Statements, AICPA Issues Papers, pronouncements of other professional associations or regulatory agencies, and accounting textbooks and articles.*

Some entities in the public sector, such as hospitals, colleges, and public authorities, may be subject to accounting principles issued by both the GASB and the FASB. When these entities separately issue general purpose financial statements, they should observe FASB pronouncements unless the GASB has issued a pronouncement applicable to the public sector entity. On the other hand, these entities must observe GASB pronouncements when their financial statements are included in combined general purpose financial statements of the state or local government. If an issue has been addressed by an AICPA SOP but neither the GASB nor the FASB has addressed the issue, the SOP standards should be observed. In general, when the GASB has not issued a pronouncement that applies to a particular transaction or activity and the FASB has done so, the FASB promulgation is *presumed* to apply.

The establishment of generally accepted accounting principles for state and local governments is complicated by a factor not present in the promulgation of accounting principles for business enterprises. Some state and local laws do not recognize GASB or FASB pronouncements as the basis for preparing their governmental financial statements. For example, a governmental unit through its charter or constitution may require that a reporting entity prepare its budget and financial statements on a cash basis. Although the governmental unit will probably maintain its accounting records on a non-GAAP basis for legal compliance purposes, it must adopt a supplementary accounting system that will enable it to report on a GAAP basis.

The GASB Rule-Making Process

The GASB has established a due process for the promulgation of governmental generally accepted accounting principles that encourages participation by parties interested in a particular accounting issue. Once a governmental accounting issue has been identified, the due process will generally consist of the following stages:

- Discussion Memorandum
- Exposure Draft
- Standard Setting

Discussion Memorandum Stage The GASB technical staff researches an issue and discusses the issue with a task force appointed by the GASB chairman. The task force consists of individuals representing a variety of interested parties, including user groups, state and local governments, and academia. In order to provide a basis for broad discussion within the profession, a Discussion Memorandum is issued by the GASB staff. The Discussion Memorandum identifies the issue, discusses possible solutions, and describes their advantages and disadvantages. At this stage, the GASB and its technical staff take no position as to the preferred solution.

Exposure Draft Stage The GASB technical staff receives responses from interested parties based on the description of the issue contained in the Discussion Memorandum. In addition, public hearings on the issue are usually held where participants can present their views orally and respond to questions raised by members of the GASB. When the GASB reaches its tentative solution to the issue, it issues an Exposure Draft for public comment.

Standard Setting Stage After receiving comments on the Exposure Draft, the GASB may hold another public hearing. Once the GASB reaches a consensus on the accounting issue, it promulgates a standard that becomes part of generally accepted accounting principles for state and local governments.

The due process described above is observed for major governmental accounting issues. If the issue is limited in scope, a Discussion Memorandum may not be prepared.

GASB Pronouncements

The GASB may express its position on a particular governmental accounting topic by issuing one or more of the following pronouncements:

- GASB Statement
- GASB Interpretation
- GASB Technical Bulletin

GASB Statement Major governmental accounting issues are addressed by the issuance of a GASB Statement only after all aspects of the due process described in the previous section have occurred.

GASB Interpretation Issues of lesser scope are addressed through the issuance of an Interpretation. An Interpretation is subject to due process, although the procedures are not as formal as those applicable to the promulgation of a Statement. Interpretations are directly voted upon by the GASB and if accepted by a majority of its members become part of governmental generally accepted accounting principles.

GASB Technical Bulletin The GASB recognizes that under certain circumstances it may not be necessary to follow the somewhat lengthy due process associated with the issuance of a Statement or an Interpretation. In 1984, the GASB authorized its staff to provide timely guidance on some governmental accounting issues by preparing a Technical Bulletin Series. The nature and purpose of GASB Technical Bulletins were addressed in GASB Technical Bulletin 84-1 (Purpose and Scope of GASB Technical Bulletins and Procedures for Issuance), which was issued in October 1984.

Technical Bulletin 84-1 concluded that a Technical Bulletin, rather than a Statement or Interpretation, may be issued under the following general criteria:

- The guidance is not expected to cause a major change in accounting practice for a significant number of entities.
- The administrative cost involved in implementing the guidance is not expected to be significant for most affected entities.
- The guidance does not conflict with a broad fundamental principle or create a novel accounting practice.

Due process is followed before a Technical Bulletin is issued. Before an initial draft of a Technical Bulletin is released to the public for comment, members of the GASB are furnished with a copy. If a majority of the members do not object to the initial draft, the proposed Technical Bulletin is released to interested parties. Responses from the interested parties are given to the GASB for its consideration at a public meeting. If a majority of the GASB members do not object to the proposed Technical Bulletin, it will be issued as a formal Technical Bulletin. Each Technical Bulletin is published with a legend that reads, "The GASB has reviewed this Technical Bulletin and a majority of its members do not object to its issuance."

Current Status of Pre-GASB Pronouncements

Prior to the establishment of the GASB, a number of NCGA and AICPA pronouncments concerning governmental accounting and reporting issues were outstanding. The status of these publications is summarized below.

GASB-1 In July 1984, the GASB issued GASB-1 (Authoritative Status of NCGA Pronouncements and AICPA Industry Audit Guides), which identified certain pre-GASB pronouncements as the basis for accounting principles. The GASB concluded that the following pronouncements constitute generally accepted accounting principles for state and local governments until "altered, amended, supplemented, revoked or superseded by subsequent GASB pronouncements."

NCGA Pronouncements

NCGA-1—Governmental Accounting and Financial Reporting Principles (effective for fiscal years ending after June 30, 1980)

NCGA-2—Grant, Entitlement, and Shared Revenue Accounting and Reporting by State and Local Governments (effective for fiscal years ending after June 30, 1980)

NCGA-3—Defining the Governmental Reporting Entity (effective for fiscal years ending after December 31, 1982)

NCGA-4—Accounting and Financial Reporting Principles for Claims and Judgments and Compensated Absences (effective for fiscal years beginning after December 31, 1982)

NCGA-5—Accounting and Financial Reporting Principles for Lease Agreements of State and Local Governments (effective for fiscal years beginning after June 30, 1983)

NCGA-6—Pension Accounting and Financial Reporting: Public Employee Retirement Systems and State and Local Government Employers (effective date extended indefinitely)

NCGA-7—Financial Reporting for Component Units Within the Governmental Reporting Entity (effective for fiscal years ending after June 30, 1984)

NCGA Interpretation-2—Segment Information for Enterprise Funds (effective for fiscal years ending after September 30, 1980)

NCGA Interpretation-3—Revenue Recognition—Property Taxes (effective for years beginning after September 30, 1981)

NCGA Interpretation-5—Authoritative Status of "Governmental Accounting, Auditing, and Financial Reporting" (1968) (effective upon issuance in March 1982)

NCGA Interpretation-6—Notes to the Financial Statements Disclosure (effective for years beginning after December 31, 1982)

NCGA Interpretation-7—Clarification as to the Application of the Criteria in NCGA-3 Defining the Governmental Reporting Entity (effective upon issuance in September 1983)

NCGA Interpretation-8—Certain Pension Matters (effective for fiscal years ending after December 31, 1983)

NCGA Interpretation-9—Certain Fund Classifications and Balance Sheet Accounts (effective for fiscal years ending after June 30, 1984)

NCGA Interpretation-10—State and Local Government Budgetary Reporting (effective for fiscal years ending after June 30, 1984)

NCGA Interpretation-11—Claim and Judgment Transactions for Governmental Funds (effective upon issuance in April 1984)

AICPA Pronouncements

Industry Audit Guide, Audits of State and Local Governmental Units (published 1974)

SOP 75-3—Accrual of Revenues and Expenditures by State and Local Governmental Units (the vacation and sick pay portion of this pronouncement was superseded by NCGA-4) (published 1975)

SOP 77-2—Accounting for Interfund Transfers of State and Local Governmental Units (published 1977)

SOP 78-7—Financial Accounting and Reporting by Hospitals Operated by a Governmental Unit (published 1978)

SOP 80-2—Accounting and Financial Reporting by Governmental Units (published 1980)

In addition to the pronouncements listed above, GASB-1 identified NCGA Concepts Statement-1 (NCGA:CS-1) (Objectives of Accounting and Financial Reporting for Governmental Units (1982)) as continuing to be in force; however, it must be noted that NCGA:CS-1 does not establish generally accepted accounting principles for state and local governmental units.

> **OBSERVATION:** *GASB-1 was not subjected to the due process as described earlier. As part of the compromise reached among the organizations that created the GASB, the Financial Accounting Foundation's by-laws were amended so that proposed GASB Statement(s) that deal with the authoritative status of NCGA and AICPA pronouncements would not have to follow due process.*

Before GASB-1 was issued, certain NCGA pronouncements had been superseded by action taken by the NCGA. These superseded publications are listed below:

- NCGA Interpretation-1, 1980 GAAFR, and the AICPA Guide (issued 1976, superseded by NCGA-1)
- NCGA Interpretation-4, Accounting and Financial Reporting for Public Employee Retirement Systems and Pension Trust Funds (issued 1982, repealed effective June 30, 1983)

Governmental Accounting, Auditing, and Financial Reporting (1968 GAAFR) As noted earlier, the 1968 GAAFR was a codification of previously published NCGA pronouncements. Subsequently, NCGA-1 was issued as a restatement of the 1968 GAAFR and also incorporated relevant portions of the AICPA's *Audits of State and Local Governmental Units* (ASLGU). In 1982, NCGA Interpretation-5 officially stated that the 1968 GAAFR had been superseded. NCGA Interpretation-5 also concluded that while the pronouncement had been superseded, "to the extent that material contained in the 1968 GAAFR is consistent with the principles of such Statements and Interpretations, such material may be considered illustrations of these principles."

Governmental Accounting, Auditing, and Financial Reporting (1980 GAAFR) The 1980 GAAFR was published by the Government Finance Officers Association; unlike the 1968 GAAFR, it did not establish or interpret accounting prinicples for state and local governments. The purpose of the 1980 GAAFR was to provide interested parties with guidance for the implementation of NCGA-1. NCGA Interpretation-5 concludes that the material in the 1980 GAAFR can be considered illustrations of NCGA Statements and Interpretations, as long as they are consistent with generally accepted accounting principles as established by NCGA pronouncements.

ASLGU Audit Guide GASB-1 specifically notes that the AICPA Audit Guide published in 1974, insofar as it addresses governmental accounting issues, establishes generally accepted accounting principles. The AICPA revised its Audit Guide in 1986. The new publication, unlike the earlier guide, does not address accounting issues but rather focuses on the application of generally accepted auditing standards to the examination of financial statements issued by state and local governmental units.

> **OBSERVATION:** *Although the second edition of the 1974 Audit Guide includes SOP 75-3, SOP 77-2, and SOP 78-7, these pronouncements continue in force even though the 1974 Audit Guide has been superseded. GASB-1 separately lists the three SOPs, as well as a fourth SOP not included in the Audit Guide, as authoritative sources of generally accepted accounting principles. Also, the revised audit guide (1986) did not supersede portions of the previous audit guide (1974) that addressed accounting issues.*

Other AICPA Audit Guides As noted earlier, certain public sector entities may be subject to accounting promulgations issued by both the GASB and the FASB. When general purpose financial statements are separately issued by the entity, FASB pronouncements must be observed in the absence of a specific GASB pronouncement. When the public sector entity's financial statements are included in a state and local government's general purpose financial statements, GASB pronouncements must be followed. Thus, the FASB is responsible for establishing accounting and reporting standards for all nonprofit organizations other than state and local governments.

To date, the AICPA has issued three audit guides that address accounting issues of nonprofit organizations that might be included as part of a state and local governmental reporting entity:

- Audits of Colleges and Universities (1975)
- Hospital Audit Guide (1980)
- Audits of Certain Nonprofit Organizations (1981)

While these three guides are not publications of the FASB, they were identified as preferable accounting principles for purposes of justifying a change in accounting principle (FASB-32—Specialized Accounting and Reporting Principles and Practices in AICPA Statements of Position and Guides on Accounting and Auditing Matters).

NCGA-6 Reporting by pension funds is an unsettled question for state and local governmental units. In 1981, NCGA-6 (Pension Accounting and Financial Reporting: Public Employee Retirement Systems and State and Local Government Employers) was issued to supersede NCGA Interpretation-4 (Accounting and Financial Reporting for Public Employee Retirement Systems and Pension Trust Funds). FASB-35 (Accounting and Reporting for Defined Benefit Plans) was issued in 1980. Some of the accounting principles established by NCGA-6 and FASB-35 are inconsistent. In order to allow a period of time for resolving the conflict the effective date for implementing NCGA-6 was indefinitely extended by NCGA Interpretation-8 (Certain Pension Matters), and in a similar fashion the effective date for FASB-35 as it applies to state and local governments was indefinitely extended by FASB-75 (Deferral of the Effective Date of Certain Accounting Requirements for Pension Plans of State and Local Governmental Units).

Until the pension reporting conflict is resolved, GASB-1 accepts the following pronouncements as acceptable accounting and reporting principles for public employee retirement systems:

- NCGA-1 (The related material contained in the 1968 GAAFR may be considered illustrative of the principles of NCGA-1, to the extent such material is consistent with the statement.)
- NCGA-6
- FASB-35

Preferred Accounting Practices for State Governments In 1983, the State Government Accounting Project of the Council of State Governments published a research report entitled *Preferred Accounting Practices for State Governments* (PAPSG). The project was a joint effort of the Council of State Governments and the NCGA, and was partially funded by a National Science Foundation Grant. The seven-year research project had the following objectives:

Phase I— Determine current accounting practices of the 50 states

Phase II—Analyze the findings of Phase I and develop a relevant and accepted State Government Accounting Principles and Preferred Practices document

While the NCGA established three task forces to review the suggested practices identified by the PAPSG, it never issued a pronouncement establishing the authoritative status of the publication. With the replacement of the NCGA by the GASB as the standard-setting authority, PAPSG's status was never formalized. Further, the pronouncement was not referred to as an authoritative source of governmental generally accepted accounting principles in GASB-1.

> *OBSERVATION: Although GASB-1 does not establish PAPSG as one of the pronouncements that constitutes generally accepted accounting principles, presumably the document would be part of the hierarchy of governmental generally accepted accounting principles referred to earlier. Specifically, hierarchy level (d) states that practices or pronouncements that are widely recognized as being generally accepted because they represent prevalent practice in a particular industry or the knowledgeable application to specific circumstances of pronouncements that are generally accepted may constitute GAAP.*

FASB pronouncements When the GASB or its predecessor the NCGA have not addressed a governmental accounting or reporting issue, pronouncements of the FASB and its predecessors establish governmental generally accepted accounting principles. Thus, in determining accounting principles for state and local governmental units, consideration must be given to FASB Statements, FASB Interpretations, and FASB Technical Bulletins.

> *OBSERVATION: In some instances, the adaptation of accounting principles established for business enterprises to the government sector can create problems due to the unique characteristics of governmental fund accounting. For example, footnote 6 of NCGA-1 notes that FASB-13 (Accounting for Leases) is applicable to financial reporting by governmental units. The adaptation of FASB-13 to the governmental accounting sector did not result in the consistent treatment of similar transactions. Thus, the NCGA found it necessary to issue NCGA-5 (Accounting and Financial Reporting Principles for Lease Agreements of State and Local Governments) to "clearly define the accounting and financial reporting requirements for lease agreements of state and local governments."*

ASB pronouncements Pronouncements by the Auditing Standards Board and its predecessor are applicable to audits of state and local governments. In general, when a public accounting firm examines the financial statements of a state or local government, generally accepted auditing standards must be observed. Rule 202 of the Code of Professional Conduct, which is reproduced below, explicitly requires that a member of the AICPA observe generally accepted auditing standards in the conduct of an examination.

> A member who performs auditing, review, compilation, management advisory, tax, or other professional services shall comply with standards promulgated by bodies designated by Council.

Additional audit guidelines and standards may be established by some state agencies. These additional requirements do not replace ASB pronouncements. Rather, in the conduct of examinations the auditor must comply with both generally accepted auditing standards and additional audit guidelines and standards established by state agencies.

The Compliance Issue

Over the past several years, research studies have indicated that there is a higher level of noncompliance with generally accepted accounting principles in the public sector than in the private sector. Some of the suggested reasons for the higher noncompliance rate are:

- The SEC lacks the legislative authority to mandate reporting standards for financial statements prepared by state and local governmental units.
- The SEC cannot discipline public accounting firms associated with financial statements of state or local governmental units that do not comply with generally accepted accounting principles.
- The right of a third-party to sue a state or local government based on errors or omissions in financial statements is an unsettled issue.

Another factor that may have previously reduced the level of compliance with generally accepted accounting principles is that the AICPA had not designated the GASB as the body authorized to promulgate accounting principles in the area of governmental accounting. As noted earlier, Rule 203 of the Code of Professional Conduct was amended in 1986 and now grants the GASB the authority to promulgate accounting principles for state and local governments.

The GFOA has encouraged improvements in financial reporting by governmental units by establishing the Certificate of Achievement for Excellence in Financial Reporting Program (Certificate). The program is voluntary, whereby a reporting unit submits its Comprehensive Annual Financial Report (CAFR) for review by a special committee of the GFOA. In order to earn the Certificate, the following standards must be observed:

- CAFR must be submitted along with additional explanations that are not required by generally accepted accounting principles or law.
- CAFR must be examined by an independent auditor who conducts the examination in accordance with generally accepted auditing standards.
- Standardized terminology and formats must be observed in the preparation of the information.
- Information must be presented in a manner that minimizes ambiguities and misleading inferences.
- Information must be published on a timely basis.
- The spirit of full disclosure must be demonstrated in the preparation of the information.

Once the special committee's review of the CAFR is completed, confidential review comments are given to the reporting entity.

The review process is performed annually but it is not performed concurrently with the audit of the financial statements. Thus, the Certificate covers only the CAFR for the previous, not the current, accounting period.

Accounting Standards for the Federal Government

Pronouncements by the GASB and the FASB are not applicable to financial statements prepared by the federal government and its agencies. Accounting principles at the federal level are established by the U.S. Comptroller General. The *Governmental GAAP Guide* does not discuss financial reporting by the federal government.

LITERATURE REFERENCES

Material in this chapter is based on the following authoritative pronouncements, which are grouped according to the major headings used within the chapter. A dual reference (both paragraph and page number) is used for NCGA-1 and NCGA-2 because the original pronouncements do not use paragraph numbers.

Authoritative Sources of Governmental Accounting Principles
APB STATEMENT 4   *Basic Concepts and Accounting Principles Underlying Financial Statements of Business Enterprises,* ¶138.
AICPA CODE OF PROFESSIONAL CONDUCT   *Rule 203.*
AICPA AUDITING INTERPRETATION—AN INTERPRETATION OF SAS-5   *The Meaning of "Present Fairly in Conformity with Generally Accepted Accounting Principles" in the Independent Auditor's Report,* December 1984.
NCGA-1   *Governmental Accounting and Financial Reporting Principles,* pp. 5 and 13/¶¶ 13 and 88.

The GASB Rule-Making Process
GASB TECHNICAL BULLETIN 84-1   *Purpose and Scope of GASB Technical Bulletins and Procedures for Issuance.*

Current Status of Pre-GASB Pronouncements
GASB-1   *Authoritative Status of NCGA Pronouncements and AICPA Industry Audit Guide.*
NCGA INTERPRETATION-5   *Authoritative Status of Governmental Accounting, Auditing, and Financial Reporting (1968),* ¶¶ 3-4.
FASB-32   *Specialized Accounting and Reporting Principles and Practices in AICPA Statements of Position and Guides on Accounting and Auditing Matters,* ¶ 10.
AICPA CODE OF PROFESSIONAL CONDUCT   *Rule 202.*

BASIC FOUNDATION OF GOVERNMENTAL GENERALLY ACCEPTED ACCOUNTING PRINCIPLES

NCGA-1 concludes that financial statements of a state or local government should be prepared in accordance with generally accepted accounting principles. In many respects, however, accounting principles for financial reporting by governmental entities and accounting principles for financial reporting by business enterprises are not the same. The inconsistencies between the two bodies of accounting rules are the result of fundamental differences between a governmental entity and a business enterprise. These differences have had a significant effect on the basic foundation of governmental accounting and financial reporting standards.

The existence of different accounting rules for governmental entities and business enterprises complicates governmental financial reporting because a governmental entity must often report on both business-type activities and governmental-type activities. Broadly speaking, business-type activities must be accounted for in conformity with commercial accounting rules while governmental-type activities must be accounted for in conformity with governmental accounting rules. The need for governmental financial reporting to satisfactorily present both types of fundamentally different activities makes it difficult to establish a single set of financial reporting objectives and a well-defined body of accounting principles for state and local governments.

The purpose of this chapter is to describe the objectives of governmental financial reporting and to identify the basic governmental generally accepted accounting principles.

OBJECTIVES OF FINANCIAL REPORTING

Three authoritative pronouncements are concerned with identifying objectives of financial reporting for nonbusiness entities. In 1987, the GASB addressed the issue of financial reporting objectives by issuing GASB Concepts Statement-1 (GASB:CS-1) (Objectives of Financial Reporting). Previously, the NCGA had addressed the topic by issuing NCGA Concepts Statement-1 (NCGA:CS-1) (Objectives of Accounting and Financial Reporting for Governmental Units). In addition, financial reporting objectives for nonbusiness entities is discussed in FASB Concepts Statement-4 (FASB:CS-4) (Objectives of Financial Reporting by Nonbusiness Organizations). While these three publications are authoritative pronouncements in that they provide guidance on the establishment of accounting and reporting standards, they do not constitute generally accepted accounting principles.

The establishment of objectives for financial reporting by governmental units provides a framework for the promulgation of governmental accounting and reporting standards. The framework can be useful during the due process period employed by the GASB to resolve accounting issues, and ultimately should provide guidance for the issuance of GASB Statements, Interpretations, and Technical Bulletins. In addition, governmental objectives should provide guidance for governmental accountants and auditors who must resolve numerous compliance problems not specifically addressed by a formal pronouncement. If the standard-setting body, the governmental financial officers, and the community of practicing governmental accountants have a common understanding of the objectives of governmental accounting, the overall quality of financial reporting should be enhanced.

GASB Concepts Statement-1

The purpose of financial reporting by state and local governmental entities is to provide information to facilitate decision making by various user groups. GASB:CS-1 identifies the following primary user groups of governmental financial reports:

- Citizens of the governmental entity
- Direct representatives of the citizens (legislatures and oversight bodies)
- Investors, creditors, and others who are involved in the lending process

Although not specifically identified in the above listing, GASB:CS-1 concludes that intergovernmental grantors and other users have informational needs similar to the three primary user groups. On the other hand, managers in the executive branch are not considered a primary user group because they have access to a considerable amount of internal financial information not generally made available to other user groups.

Basic Foundation of Governmental Generally Accepted Accounting Principles

The financial reporting objectives identified by the GASB in GASB:CS-1 are to be used as a framework for establishing accounting and reporting standards for general purpose financial statements (GPFS); however, the framework may also be used by the GASB to establish standards for financial information presented outside of the GPFS. In addition, the financial reporting standards are also applicable to general purpose financial information presented in special purpose financial reports prepared by state and local governmental entities.

Although the governmental-type activities and the business-type activities conducted by a governmental entity can differ significantly, the GASB concluded that financial reporting objectives identified in GASB:CS-1 are applicable to both types of activities. This conclusion is applicable to business-type activities presented in separate financial reports or presented as part of the governmental entity's GPFS. Although financial reporting objectives are applicable to both governmental-type and business-type activities, the GASB does recognize that a specific objective may vary in its application to a particular reporting situation depending upon the business-type activity and the user group that is evaluating the activity. For example, both creditors and a legislative body may be interested in a business-type activity, but creditors may be more concerned with the ability of the activity to generate cash flow from operations to service future debt requirements while the legislature may be more concerned with the likelihood that future operations may require subsidies from general revenues.

> **OBSERVATION:** *Currently, many accounting principles promulgated by the FASB are applicable to business-type activities conducted by a governmental entity. The FASB uses FASB Concepts Statement-1 (FASB:CS-1) (Objectives of Financial Reporting by Business Enterprises) as a framework for formulating accounting and reporting standards for business enterprises. The financial reporting objectives identified in FASB:CS-1 are different from those identified in GASB:CS-1. Thus, accounting principles applicable to business-type activities of a governmental entity may be based on two different conceptual frameworks and may not lead to a single set of consistent accounting and financial reporting standards.*

GASB:CS-1 identifies accountability as the *paramount* objective of financial reporting by state and local governments. Accountability is based on the transfer of responsibility for resources or actions from

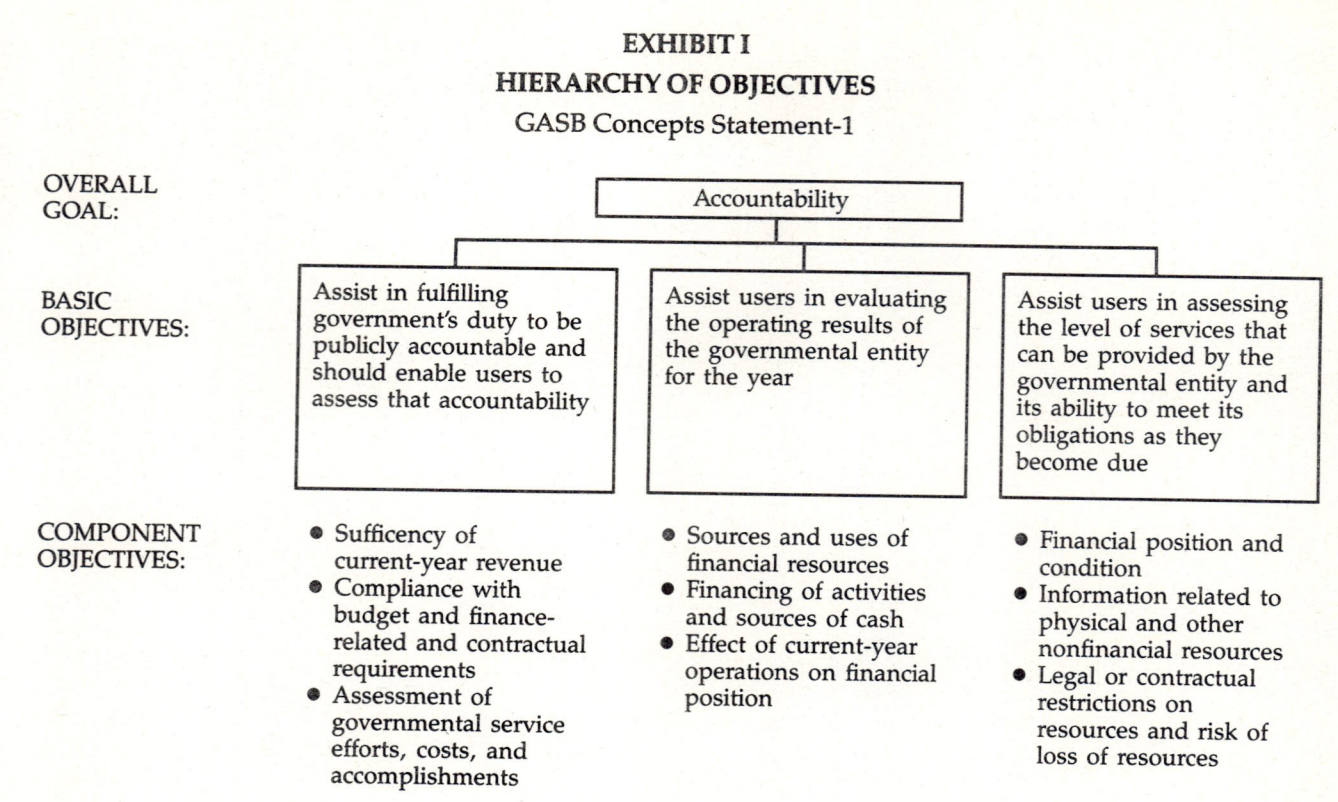

EXHIBIT 1
HIERARCHY OF OBJECTIVES
GASB Concepts Statement-1

OVERALL GOAL: Accountability

BASIC OBJECTIVES:

- Assist in fulfilling government's duty to be publicly accountable and should enable users to assess that accountability
- Assist users in evaluating the operating results of the governmental entity for the year
- Assist users in assessing the level of services that can be provided by the governmental entity and its ability to meet its obligations as they become due

COMPONENT OBJECTIVES:

Under first basic objective:
- Sufficiency of current-year revenue
- Compliance with budget and finance-related and contractual requirements
- Assessment of governmental service efforts, costs, and accomplishments

Under second basic objective:
- Sources and uses of financial resources
- Financing of activities and sources of cash
- Effect of current-year operations on financial position

Under third basic objective:
- Financial position and condition
- Information related to physical and other nonfinancial resources
- Legal or contractual restrictions on resources and risk of loss of resources

the citizenry to another party, such as the management of a governmental entity. Financial reporting should communicate adequate information to user groups to enable them to assess the performance of those parties that have been empowered to act in the place of the citizenry.

The GASB concluded (1) that accountability is a more important concept in governmental financial reporting than in business enterprise financial reporting and (2) that all governmental financial reporting objectives are derived from the accountability concept. The objectives of governmental financial reporting identified in GASB:CS-1 are summarized in Exhibit I. In addition to the overall objective of accountability, GASB:CS-1 identified the following as objectives of governmental financial reporting:

- Financial reporting should assist in fulfilling government's duty to be publicly accountable and should enable users to assess that accountability.
- Financial reporting should assist users in evaluating the operating results of the governmental entity for the year.
- Financial reporting should assist users in assessing the level of services that can be provided by the governmental entity and its ability to meet its obligations as they become due.

The GASB noted that although accountability is referred to only in the first objective, *accountability is implicit in all of the listed objectives.*

Assessment of accountability The assessment of accountability is fulfilled in part when financial reporting enables user groups to determine to what extent current-period expenditures are financed by current-period revenues. This reporting objective is based on the concept of *interperiod equity* which argues that the citizenry that benefits from an expenditure should pay for the expenditure. Financial reporting should provide a basis for determining whether during a budgetary period (1) a surplus was created (a benefit to the future citizenry), (2) a deficit was incurred (a burden to the future citizenry), (3) a surplus from a previous budgetary period was used to finance current expenditures (a benefit to the current citizenry), (4) a deficit from a previous budgetary period was satisfied with current revenues (a burden to the current citizenry), or (5) current and only current expenditures were financed by using current and only current revenues (a balanced budget).

OBSERVATION: *Unlike the federal government, most state and local governments must operate under a balanced budget concept; however, the definition of a balanced budget from an operational perspective is often subject to various interpretations and manipulations.*

Financial reporting by a state or local government should provide a basis for user groups to determine whether (1) the governmental entity obtained and used resources consistent with the legally adopted budget and (2) finance-related legal or contractual requirements have been met. A budget reflects a myriad of public policies adopted by a legislative body and generally has the fcrce of law as its basis for authority. The legally adopted budget is an important document in establishing and assessing the accountability of those responsible for the management of a governmental entity. While finance-related legal or contractual requirements are not as fundamental as the legally adopted budget, they nonetheless provide a basis for accountability, and financial reporting should demonstrate that accountability has or has not been achieved with respect to the requirements.

Assessing accountability of the management of a governmental entity encompasses qualitative analysis (economy, efficiency, and effectiveness) as well as quantitative analysis. GASB:CS-1 concludes that accountability relates to service efforts, costs, and accomplishments. Financial reporting, when combined with other information, may enable user groups, for example, to determine whether certain efforts should be funded or whether elected officials should be continued in office. The information used to measure the economy, efficiency, and effectiveness of a governmental entity should be based upon objective criteria. Such information may be used to compare a governmental entity's current operating results with its prior period operating results or with other governmental entities' current operating results.

OBSERVATION: *The establishment of objective criteria as a basis for generating information about the economy, efficiency, and effectiveness of a governmental entity is an extremely difficult, if not impossible, task. For years, researchers have attempted to develop objective criteria, with very limited results. The GASB recognized this limitation when it concluded that such methods are not generally available; however, the GASB believes "that for a government to fulfill its duty to be publicly accountable, information on service efforts, costs and accomplishments, and physical and other nonfinancial resources needs to be reported."*

Evaluation of operating results Financial reporting should enable user groups to evaluate the operations of a state or local governmental entity. One aspect of operations evaluation is concerned with presenting information about sources and uses of financial resources. With respect to financial resource outflows, financial information presentations should identify all outflows and classify them by function (public health, public safety, etc.) and purpose (adult education, crime prevention, etc.). All financial resource inflows should be presented and identified by source (grants, bond proceeds, etc.) and type (taxes, fees, etc.). Resource inflows and outflows should be presented in a manner that enables user groups to determine the extent to which inflows are sufficient to finance outflows. In addition, nonrecurring inflows and outflows of resources should be disclosed in the financial report.

GASB:CS-1 also concludes that in order to evaluate operating results, financial reporting should enable user groups to determine how a governmental entity financed its activities and met its cash requirements.

> *OBSERVATION: To some extent, this component objective overlaps with the previous component objective (identification of sources and types of resource inflows); however, the objective of determining how cash requirements were met may require the preparation of a specific cash flow analysis.*

Another element used in evaluating operations is the ability of the financial reporting to provide a basis for determining whether results of current operations improved or worsened the governmental entity's financial position as of the end of the current budgetary period.

Assessment of potential for providing services and ability to meet obligations Financial reporting should provide information concerning the financial position and condition of a state or local governmental entity. Resources should be described as current or noncurrent, and contingent liabilities should be disclosed. In order to assess the ability of an entity to raise resources from taxation, disclosure should include tax limitations, burdens, and sources. Likewise, the viability of issuing debt to raise revenues would require that an entity disclose debt limitations.

Disclosures in a financial report should enable user groups to assess current and long-term capital needs of the governmental entity. To this end, descriptions of physical and other nonfinancial resources with lives that extend beyond the current budgetary period should be included in the financial report. Such descriptions should include information that can be used to determine the service potential of such assets.

> **OBSERVATION:** *Although the GASB endorsed disclosures concerning service potential of physical and other nonfinancial resources, it recognized that conventional financial reporting methods have not yet been adequately developed to satisfy this financial reporting objective.*

Finally, in order to assess the ability of a governmental entity to meet its obligations, the legal and contractual restrictions on resources and the potential loss of an entity's resources should be disclosed in the financial report.

NCGA Concepts Statement-1

GASB:CS-1 supersedes NCGA:CS-1; however, the GASB concluded that NCGA:CS-1 is nonetheless a useful source for understanding the role of financial reporting by governmental entities.

NCGA:CS-1 identifies a hierarchy of objectives for governmental accounting and financial reporting. These objectives are divided into three categories, namely, the overall goal, the basic objectives, and the component objectives. The hierarchy of objectives is summarized in Exhibit II.

The principal objective, referred to as the overall goal of governmental accounting and financial reporting, is to (1) "provide financial information useful for making economic, political, and social decisions, and demonstrating accountability and stewardship and (2) provide information useful for evaluating managerial and organizational performance." It is important to note that the second part of the objective is not limited to financial information. NCGA:CS-1 concludes that financial reporting and the preparation of financial statements are not synonymous, and that financial reporting is not limited to "simply enumerating things that accountants have done in the past." For example, there may be a need to report nontraditional information, such as demographic statistics, in order to make available

Basic Foundation of Governmental Generally Accepted Accounting Principles

EXHIBIT II
HIERARCHY OF OBJECTIVES
NCGA Concepts Statement-1

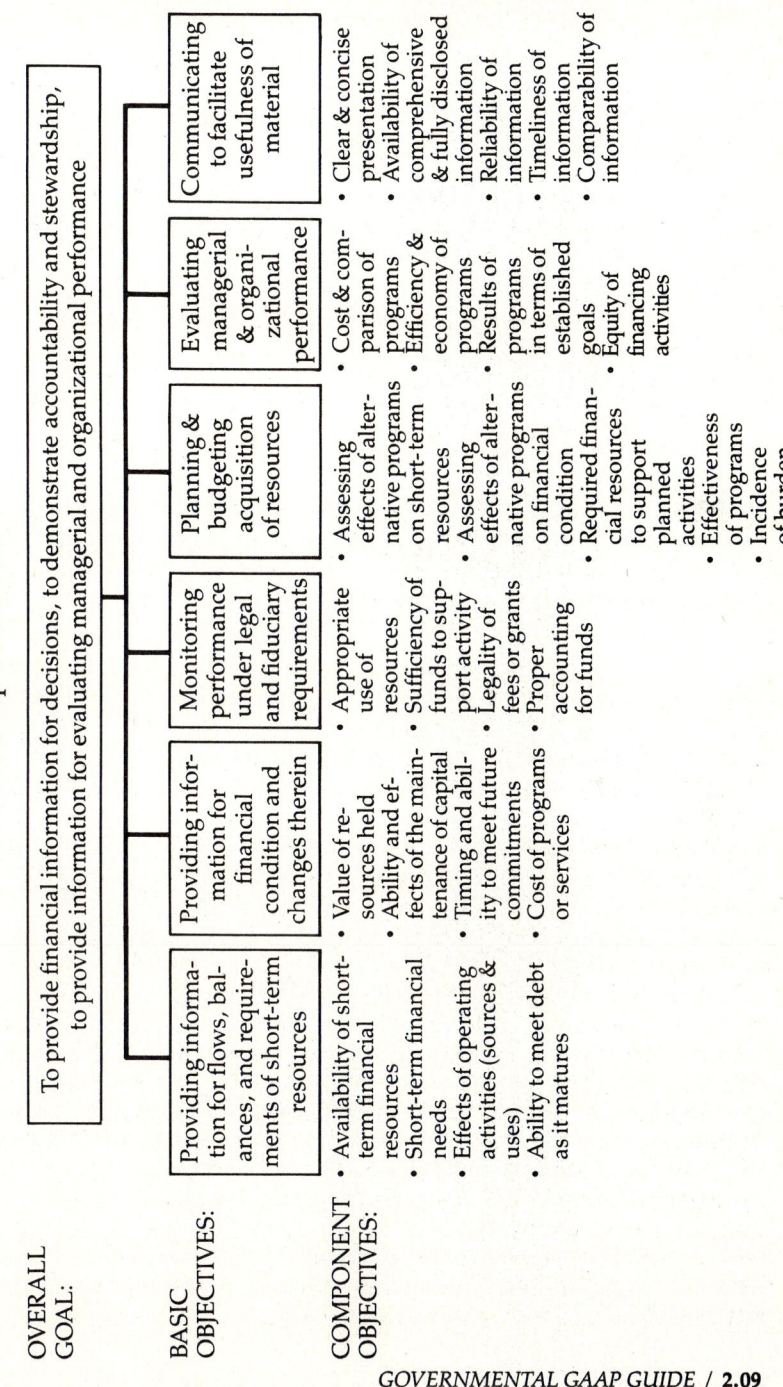

OVERALL GOAL: To provide financial information for decisions, to demonstrate accountability and stewardship, to provide information for evaluating managerial and organizational performance

BASIC OBJECTIVES:

Providing information for flows, balances, and requirements of short-term resources	Providing information for financial condition and changes therein	Monitoring performance under legal and fiduciary requirements	Planning & budgeting acquisition of resources	Evaluating managerial & organizational performance	Communicating to facilitate usefulness of material

COMPONENT OBJECTIVES:

- Availability of short-term financial resources
- Short-term financial needs
- Effects of operating activities (sources & uses)
- Ability to meet debt as it matures

- Value of resources held
- Ability and effects of the maintenance of capital
- Timing and ability to meet future commitments
- Cost of programs or services

- Appropriate use of resources
- Sufficiency of funds to support activity
- Legality of fees or grants
- Proper accounting for funds

- Assessing effects of alternative programs on short-term resources
- Assessing effects of alternative programs on financial condition
- Required financial resources to support planned activities
- Effectiveness of programs
- Incidence of burden

- Cost & comparison of programs
- Efficiency & economy of programs
- Results of programs in terms of established goals
- Equity of financing activities

- Clear & concise presentation
- Availability of comprehensive & fully disclosed information
- Reliability of information
- Timeliness of information
- Comparability of information

GOVERNMENTAL GAAP GUIDE / 2.09

to user groups information sufficient to achieve the overall goal of governmental financial reporting.

The following six basic objectives are derived from the overall goal of governmental accounting and financial reporting:

- To provide financial information useful for determining and forecasting the flows, balances, and requirements of short-term financial resources of the governmental unit
- To provide financial information useful for determining and forecasting the financial condition of the governmental unit
- To provide financial information useful for monitoring performance under terms of legal, contractual, and fiduciary requirements
- To provide information useful for planning and budgeting, and for forecasting the impact of the acquisition and allocation of resources on the achievement of operational objectives
- To provide information useful for evaluating managerial and organizational performance
- To communicate the relevant information in a manner that best facilitates its use

Short-term financial resources Financial reporting should enable the user to determine and forecast the flows, balances, and amounts of resources required for current transactions, such as maturing obligations and operating expenditures. Information should be disclosed in a manner that accurately portrays the entity's liquidity needs and its current liquidity position. Also, users need information that allows them to forecast the effect of future operating activity (such as sources of revenues and planned expenditures) on short-term financial resources. In general, the financial material presented should enable the user to make an informed decision on whether the governmental unit can meet its current obligations.

Financial condition Users need to determine and forecast the governmental entity's financial condition and changes in the financial condition. Financial condition refers to the net asset position (total assets minus total liabilities) of the reporting unit and is concerned with the measurement of assets and liabilities in order to determine net equity. As assets are consumed, the net worth of the entity is reduced. Financial reporting should disclose "whether the value and service potential of physical resources have been maintained during a period" and the possible impact of replacing service capacity that has expired.

Basic Foundation of Governmental Generally Accepted Accounting Principles

>**OBSERVATION:** *NCGA:CS-1 discusses the idea of consumption of physical resources without referring to the concept of depreciation. Presumably, this approach was taken because depreciation is not reflected in a governmental fund and therefore the objective identified by NCGA:CS-1 appears to be in direct conflict with generally accepted accounting principles (see Principle 7, which is discussed later in this chapter) for state and local governmental units.*

Also, liability determination has an impact upon net worth, and financial reporting should enable the user to estimate the *present value*, as well as the timing, of future commitments. Valuation of liabilities to be considered range from amounts due to vendors to estimated liabilities resulting from pension plans.

NCGA:CS-1 points out that determining and forecasting the cost of programs is a component objective in assessing the broader objective of measuring or projecting an entity's financial condition. For this reason, the entity should disclose information about the financial condition and cost of operating units such as a hospital or transportation authority. Also, the full cost of programs should be disclosed, not just the cost of using current resources.

>**OBSERVATION:** *Again, NCGA:CS-1 does not explicitly refer to depreciation but obviously the idea of full cost would require the recognition of depreciation and other amortizations; however, the examples referred to in this "component" objective are units that would be considered a proprietary fund, not a governmental fund. Depreciation is recognized in proprietary funds.*

Legal, contractual, and fiduciary requirements In many instances, a governmental entity may be restricted in the manner in which it expends funds. Financial reporting should enable users to determine whether legal, contractual, and fiduciary requirements have been met by the organization. In general, the government must demonstrate that resources held for the benefit of the public were properly used, and an accounting for the use of the resources must be made.

A broad aspect of the legal requirement is the reporting of revenues and expenditures in a manner that demonstrates whether the government operated at a deficit or surplus for the year. Financial reporting should *accurately* portray the results of operating and financing activities during the accounting period.

Finally, it may be necessary to receive a fee or make a reimbursement to another entity based on the cost of a program or service for the period. The reported financial information should allow the user to determine whether the contractual commitment for the reimbursement has been observed.

Planning and budgeting A budget for a governmental unit, unlike a business enterprise, is a legal document resulting from a budgetary process that involves many interested parties including the legislative body, taxpayers, and special interest groups. The governmental entity's manner of reporting should facilitate the forecasting of the effects of program alternatives on the unit's short-term financial resources and its overall financial condition. Such information is useful at the planning stage when choices among alternative programs must be made. Assessing the cost implications of alternative programs and expected financial resources available during the budget period is an important element of sound financial management and the financial reporting system should contribute to the achievement of this goal.

Cost should not be the only consideration when selecting program alternatives. The budgetary process should disclose how effective a program alternative will be in achieving the stated social and economic goals of the governmental unit. Although it may be difficult to quantify the effects of expended funds, a process for measuring the expected success of programs should be part of the budgetary system. Finally, the budgetary process should enable a user to predict specifically who will finance the cost of government during the forthcoming fiscal period (the incidence of burden).

Organizational and managerial performance Financial reporting should provide a basis for evaluating the operations of the government. The measurement of governmental performance is tremendously complicated by the lack of profit motive. In a business enterprise, success is, to a significant degree, measured in terms of net profit. No similar measurement basis is available for the overall operations of a state or local governmental unit. Nonetheless, to some extent, governmental operations can be evaluated by properly reporting the cost of activities. The cost information should be developed and reported in a manner that allows comparison with (a) established criteria, (b) similar activities performed by other governmental entities, and (c) cost incurred in previous accounting periods.

In addition to determining the cost of services, financial reporting should provide a basis for evaluating the efficiency, economy, and effectiveness of governmental activities. Efficiency and economy of operations do not attempt to measure the achievement of goals but are nevertheless useful in evaluating the performance of lower-level management personnel. Effectiveness refers to the success of the governmental unit in attaining its social and economic goals, and is a broader measure of performance.

Also, financial reporting should be developed to determine whether the cost of government is distributed equitably among the parties who must finance its operations.

> **OBSERVATION:** *Determining organizational and managerial performance presents the accounting profession with a challenge. There is a need to develop measures of performance that can be used to evaluate governmental operations. Also, the concept of equitable distribution of financing governmental operations is highly subjective. NCGA:CS-1 recognized the need for research in these areas but concluded that the objectives of financial reporting as they relate to performance evaluation are valid even if the measurement tools are not well developed.*

Communication Once reliable and relevant financial information is generated by the financial accounting system, it must be communicated in a manner that enhances its usefulness. The information should be clear and concise, readily accessible and presented on a timely basis. In addition, the usefulness of information is increased when it is sufficiently comprehensive and is presented in a format that enables a comparison to be made with other entities and with other time periods.

FASB Concepts Statement-4

In 1980, the FASB, as part of its conceptual framework project, issued FASB:CS-4, which discusses the objectives of nonbusiness organizations. Implicitly, FASB:CS-4 identifies a hierarchy of financial reporting objectives of nonbusiness organizations. For purposes of discussion, although not specifically labeled as such in the FASB:CS-4, the objectives are categorized as the overall goal, the basic objectives, and component objectives. This categorization is done to provide a basis for comparison between GASB:CS-1, NCGA:CS-1, and FASB:CS-4. The hierarchy is summarized in Exhibit III.

Basic Foundation of Governmental Generally Accepted Accounting Principles

EXHIBIT III
HIERARCHY OF OBJECTIVES
FASB Concepts Statement-4

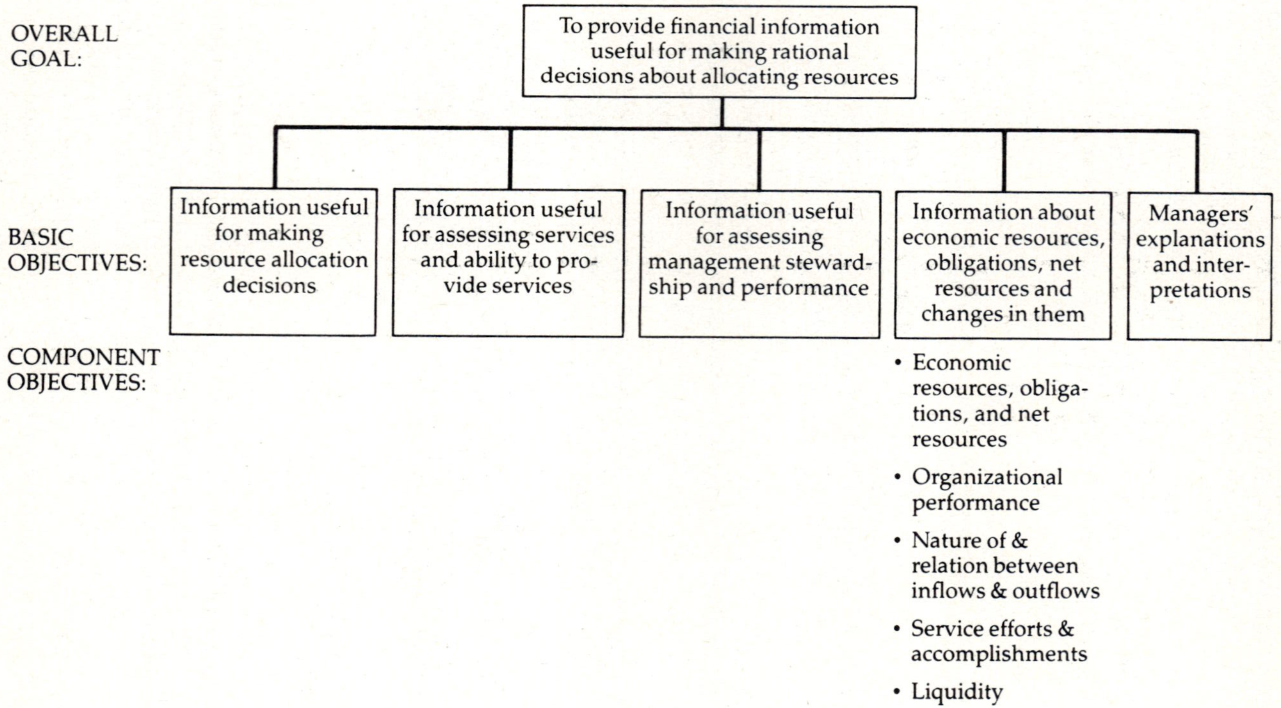

OVERALL GOAL: To provide financial information useful for making rational decisions about allocating resources

BASIC OBJECTIVES:
- Information useful for making resource allocation decisions
- Information useful for assessing services and ability to provide services
- Information useful for assessing management stewardship and performance
- Information about economic resources, obligations, net resources and changes in them
- Managers' explanations and interpretations

COMPONENT OBJECTIVES:
- Economic resources, obligations, and net resources
- Organizational performance
- Nature of & relation between inflows & outflows
- Service efforts & accomplishments
- Liquidity

2.14 / GOVERNMENTAL GAAP GUIDE

OBSERVATION: *There is some question whether FASB:CS-4 is applicable to financial reporting by governmental units. FASB:CS-4 was issued before the roles of the FASB and GASB (and the NCGA) were clearly defined. FASB:CS-4 is inconsistent in its own position on the matter based on the following statements: (1) ". . .the Board has deferred a final decision on whether the objectives set forth in this Statement should apply to general purpose external financial reporting by state and local governmental units." (para. 3); (2) ". . . On the basis of its study to date, the Board is aware of no persuasive evidence that objectives in this Statement are inappropriate for general purpose external financial reports of governmental units." (para. 66). With respect to this question of authority, the GASB in an appendix to GASB:CS-1 noted that "pronouncements of the GASB rank above pronouncements of the FASB in the hierarchy of generally accepted accounting principles applicable to state and local governmental entities."*

The overall objective of financial reporting is concerned with "information that is useful to resource providers and other users in making rational decisions about allocating resources to nonbusiness organizations." Financial reporting, as defined in FASB:CS-4, covers more than simply preparing financial statements and includes communicating information relative to an entity's assets and obligations. Significantly, FASB:CS-4 takes the position that financial reporting does not include reporting information concerning the measurement of the quality of goods and services provided by the governmental entity when the information is not the result of market-determined exchange prices. In this respect, the scope of financial reporting as envisioned by FASB:CS-4 is not as broad as the scope of financial reporting identified in NCGA:CS-1.

The following five basic objectives support the overall goal of financial reporting established in FASB:CS-4:

- Financial reporting by nonbusiness organizations should provide information that is useful to present and potential resource providers and other users in making rational decisions about the allocation of resources to those organizations.
- Financial reporting should provide information to help present and potential resource providers and other users in assessing the service that a nonbusiness organization provides and its ability to continue to provide those services.
- Financial reporting should provide information that is useful to present and potential resource providers and other users in

assessing how managers of a nonbusiness organization have discharged their stewardship responsibilities and about other aspects of their performance.
- Financial reporting should provide information about the economic resources, obligations, and net resources of an organization and the effects of transactions, events, and circumstances that change resources and interests in those resources.
- Financial reporting should include explanations and interpretations to help users understand financial information provided.

Resource allocation decisions Financial reporting should provide information that will enable users to make rational decisions concerning the allocation of resources. The information presented should be comprehensible to those users who have an understanding of the role of financial reporting in the context of a nonprofit environment. This does not imply that information should not be presented simply because it is difficult to understand. Also, there are constraints on the ability of an organization to supply financial information. For example, information is generally subject to cost/benefit analysis whereby only material that has a benefit greater than its cost should be developed and presented.

Assessing services provided User groups need information that will allow them to assess services provided by the nonprofit organization, as well as the ability to continue to provide services in the future. Due to the lack of information directly related to future activities, financial information about past service performances should be useful for both assessing services rendered and the ability to render future services. In general, such information should provide a basis for determining whether the nonprofit organization was successful in achieving its operational goals. To a great extent, the ability of an organization to provide future services is dependent upon its ability to attract resources. In turn, the ability to attract resources is dependent upon the success of providing services in the past.

Assessing management Financial reporting should allow user groups to determine whether resources supplied to the nonprofit organization were properly used. Any use of resources that violated statutory or contractual constraints should be disclosed. Also, financial reporting should provide a basis for determining whether managers used resources in an efficient and effective manner. FASB:CS-4 emphasizes the point that the lack of a profit motive and the existence of numerous exogenous factors make it difficult to evaluate management based on financial information supplied to user groups.

Economic resources and obligations Information about an entity's resources and obligations enables a user to assess the ability of the entity to generate cash flow and predict the demands on cash flows during a forthcoming period. Also, specific restrictions on the use of resources should be presented because the disclosure facilitates the analysis of expected cash flows that are available for designated services or programs. The financial reporting of changes in the net resources position of the organization can provide a basis for measuring organizational performance. The change in the net resources position can, in part, be summarized by reporting the inflows and outflows of resources for a period. Flows of resources during the period should be presented in a manner so that operational flows and nonoperational flows can be distinguished. FASB:CS-4 observes that accrual accounting is the best basis for measuring net resources and summarizing the change in net resources for a period.

Disclosures with respect to service efforts and accomplishments can provide a basis for the measurement of performance by the nonprofit organization. Service efforts relate to how resources were utilized during the period and are usually expressed in terms of dollars spent for wages, materials, and so forth. Determining accomplishments of the organization is far more difficult. FASB:CS-4 recognizes this limitation by concluding that "in the absence of measures suitable for financial reporting, information about service accomplishments may be furnished by managers' explanations and sources other than financial reporting."

Finally, financial reporting of net resources should provide information about an organization's liquidity position. Disclosures, such as sources and dispositions of liquid assets and increases and decreases of debt, should be made. Most users are interested in the liquidity position of a nonprofit entity.

Comments made by managers All financial reporting systems include rules and conventions that in some instances may not create information that conveys the *true* financial position or summary of activities of an organization. For this reason, managers should have the opportunity to present their explanations in order to enhance the understanding of the financial information. Such explanations and interpretations may include comments about the need for estimates or the occurrence of an unusual event.

BASIC GOVERNMENTAL ACCOUNTING PRINCIPLES

Objectives for financial reporting should be the basis for determining specific accounting principles to be used by a governmental entity. There are twelve basic principles of accounting and reporting applicable to state and local governments. These principles are reproduced as stated in NCGA-1.

Principle 1 — Accounting and Reporting Capabilities

A governmental accounting system must make it possible both: (a) to present fairly and with full disclosure the financial position and results of financial operations of the funds and account groups of the governmental unit in conformity with generally accepted accounting principles; and (b) to determine and demonstrate compliance with finance-related legal and contractual provisions.

Principle 2 — Fund Accounting Systems

Governmental accounting systems should be organized and operated on a fund basis. A fund is defined as a fiscal and accounting entity with a self-balancing set of accounts recording cash and other financial resources, together with all related liabilities and residual equities or balances, and changes therein, which are segregated for the purpose of carrying on specific activities or attaining certain objectives in accordance with special regulations, restrictions, or limitations.

Principle 3 — Types of Funds

The following types of funds should be used by state and local governments:

GOVERNMENTAL FUNDS

1. *The General Fund* — to account for all financial resources except those required to be accounted for in another fund.
2. *Special Revenue Funds* — to account for the proceeds of specific revenue sources (other than special assessments, expendable trusts, or for major capital projects) that are legally restricted to expenditure for specified purposes.

3. *Capital Projects Funds* — to account for financial resources to be used for the acquisition or construction of major capital facilities (other than those financed by proprietary funds, Special Assessment Funds, and Trust Funds).
4. *Debt Service Funds* — to account for the accumulation of resources for, and the payment of, general long-term debt principal and interest.

PROPRIETARY FUNDS

5. *Enterprise Funds* — to account for operations (a) that are financed and operated in a manner similar to private business enterprises where the intent of the governing body is that the costs (expenses, including depreciation) of providing goods or services to the general public on a continuing basis be financed or recovered primarily through user charges; or (b) where the governing body has decided that periodic determination of revenues earned, expenses incurred, and/or net income is appropriate for capital maintenance, public policy, management control, accountability, or other purposes.
6. *Internal Service Funds* — to account for the financing of goods or services provided by one department or agency to other departments or agencies of the governmental unit, or to other governmental units, on a cost-reimbursement basis.

FIDUCIARY FUNDS

7. *Trust and Agency Funds* — to account for assets held by a governmental unit in a trustee capacity or as an agent for individuals, private organizations, other governmental units, and/or other funds. These include (a) Expendable Trust Funds, (b) Nonexpendable Trust Funds, (c) Pension Trust Funds, and (d) Agency Funds.

Principle 4 — Numbers of Funds

Governmental units should establish and maintain those funds required by law and sound financial administration. Only the minimum number of funds consistent with legal and operating requirements should be established, however, since unnecessary funds result in inflexibility, undue complexity, and inefficient financial administration.

Principle 5 — Accounting for Fixed Assets and Long-Term Liabilities

A clear distinction should be made between (a) fund fixed assets and general fixed assets and (b) fund long-term liabilities and general long-term debt.
  a. Fixed assets related to specific Proprietary Funds or Trust Funds should be accounted for through those funds. All other fixed assets of a governmental unit should be accounted for through the General Fixed Assets Account Group.
  b. Long-term liabilities of Proprietary Funds, and Trust Funds should be accounted for through those funds. All other unmatured general long-term liabilities of the governmental unit should be accounted for through the General Long-Term Debt Account Group.

Principle 6 — Valuation of Fixed Assets

Fixed assets should be accounted for at cost or, if the cost is not practicably determinable, at estimated cost. Donated fixed assets should be recorded at their estimated fair value at the time received.

Principle 7 — Depreciation of Fixed Assets

(a) Depreciation of general fixed assets should not be recorded in the accounts of governmental funds. Depreciation of general fixed assets may be recorded in cost accounting systems or calculated for cost finding analyses; and accumulated depreciation may be recorded in the General Fixed Assets Account Group. (b) Depreciation of fixed assets accounted for in a proprietary fund should be recorded in the accounts of that fund. Depreciation is also recognized in those Trust Funds where expenses, net income, and/or capital maintenance are measured.

Principle 8 — Accrual Basis in Governmental Accounting

The modified accrual or accrual basis of accounting, as appropriate, should be utilized in measuring financial position and operating results.
  a. *Governmental fund* revenues and expenditures should be recognized on the modified accrual basis. Revenues should be recognized in the accounting period in which they become available and measurable. Expenditures should be recognized in the accounting period in which the fund liability is incurred, if measurable, except for unmatured interest on general long-term

Basic Foundation of Governmental Generally Accepted Accounting Principles

debt and on special assessment indebtedness secured by interest-bearing special assessment levies, which should be recognized when due.

b. *Proprietary fund* revenues and expenses should be recognized on the accrual basis. Revenues should be recognized in the accounting period in which they are earned and become measurable; expenses should be recognized in the period incurred, if measurable.

c. *Fiduciary fund* revenues and expenses or expenditures (as appropriate) should be recognized on the basis consistent with the fund's accounting measurement objective. Nonexpendable Trust and Pension Trust Funds should be accounted for on the accrual basis; Expendable Trust Funds should be accounted for on the modified accrual basis. Agency Fund assets and liabilities should be accounted for on the modified accrual basis.

d. *Transfers* should be recognized in the accounting period in which the interfund receivable and payable arise.

Principle 9 — Budgeting, Budgetary Control, and Budgetary Reporting

(a) An annual budget(s) should be adopted by every governmental unit. (b) The accounting system should provide the basis for appropriate budgetary control. (c) Budgetary comparisons should be included in the appropriate financial statements and schedules for governmental funds for which an annual budget has been adopted.

Principle 10 — Transfer, Revenue, Expenditure, and Expense Account Classification

(a) Interfund transfers and proceeds of general long-term debt issues should be classified separately from fund revenues and expenditures or expenses. (b) Governmental fund revenues should be classified by fund and source. Expenditures should be classified by fund, function (or program), organization unit, activity, character, and principal classes of objects. (c) Proprietary fund revenues and expenses should be classified in essentially the same manner as those of similar business organizations, functions, or activities.

Principle 11 — Common Terminology and Classification

A common terminology and classification should be used consistently throughout the budget, the accounts, and the financial reports of each fund.

Principle 12 — Interim and Annual Financial Reports

(a) Appropriate interim financial statements and reports of financial position, operating results, and other pertinent information should be prepared to facilitate management control of financial operations, legislative oversight, and, where necessary or desired, for external reporting purposes. (b) A comprehensive annual financial report covering all funds and account groups of the reporting entity—including introductory section; appropriate combined, combining, and individual fund statements; notes to the financial statements; schedules; narrative explanations; and statistical tables—should be prepared and published. The reporting entity is the oversight unit and all other component units combined in accordance with NCGA principles. (c) General purpose financial statements of the reporting entity may be issued separately from the comprehensive annual financial report. Such statements should include the basic financial statements and notes to the financial statements that are essential to fair presentation of financial position and results of operations (and changes in financial position of Proprietary Funds and similar Trust Funds). (d) A component unit financial report covering all funds and account groups of a component unit—including introductory section; appropriate combined, combining, and individual fund statements; notes to the financial statements; schedules; narrative explanations; and statistical tables—may be prepared and published, as necessary. (e) Component unit financial statements of a component unit may be issued separately from the component unit financial report. Such statements should include the basic financial statements and notes to the financial statements that are essential to the fair presentation of financial position and results of operations (and changes in financial position of Proprietary Funds and similar Trust Funds).

The first four principles of accounting provide the basic foundation for governmental accounting and are discussed in the remainder of this chapter. Other principles are discussed in subsequent chapters.

Compliance with Generally Accepted Accounting Principles

Unlike financial statements of a business enterprise, financial statements prepared by a governmental unit must comply with certain legal and contractual requirements as well as with generally accepted accounting principles. This dual requirement is established by Principle 1 (Accounting and Reporting Capabilities).

NCGA-1 describes generally accepted accounting principles as "uniform minimum standards of and guidelines to financial accounting and reporting," and concludes that these principles must be observed in order to provide a basis for comparison of governmental units. Generally accepted accounting principles are applicable to the preparation of comprehensive annual financial reports (CAFR) and general purpose financial statements presented separately.

The design of an accounting system for a governmental entity is affected by generally accepted accounting principles and legal and contractual requirements. An entity's constitution, charter, or grant regulations may dictate the manner in which information is to be presented. Likewise, the entity's operating budget may impose certain reporting requirements that affect the design of the information system. Restrictions imposed by legal and contractual requirements cannot be ignored, and management of the reporting entity must be able to demonstrate through the financial reporting system that the established requirements have been observed by the state or local government. Often these legal and contractual requirements create the need for the establishment of separate funds to account for assets and report on specific activities for the accounting period.

Often there are differences between the presentation of information in accordance with generally accepted accounting principles and in accordance with legal requirements. For example, generally accepted accounting principles may require that a transaction be accounted for on an accrual basis but the legal basis may require that the cash method be observed. A similar problem is encountered when funds, such as grants and shared revenues, are received from another governmental unit. Often the funds are made available with specific requirements as to how the funds are to be spent and the method of accounting and reporting the expenditures. NCGA-2 (Grant, Entitlement, and Shared Revenue Accounting by State and Local Governments) concludes that the accounting system must be capable of producing financial statements or supporting schedules that comply both with generally accepted accounting principles and the reporting requirements imposed by the grant. When conflicts between the two exist, there is no need to maintain separate books for each basis. The problem is usually resolved by maintaining the records on a basis consistent with legal requirements. Supplementary data not integrated with the general ledger must also be maintained in order to convert the legal basis information to a basis consistent with generally accepted accounting principles.

If financial statements are not modified to reflect generally accepted accounting principles, these differences must be disclosed in the financial statements. On the other hand, when financial statements are prepared in accordance with generally accepted accounting principles but do not demonstrate compliance with the required legal basis, it will be necessary to present supplementary schedules to satisfy legal requirements. Alternatively, a special report prepared on the legal basis may be presented as a supplement to the general purpose financial statements.

> **OBSERVATION:** *NCGA-1 concluded that generally accepted accounting principles and legal compliance reporting should be equally observed in the preparation of financial statements; however, the AICPA Industry Audit Guide (Audits of State and Local Governmental Units) concluded that where there is a conflict between the two, generally accepted accounting principles take precedence in the preparation of the financial statements.*

Fund Accounting

The entity concept is fundamental in accounting for a business enterprise. APB Statement-4 (Basic Concepts and Accounting Principles Underlying Financial Statements of Business Enterprises) makes two observations about the accounting entity: (a) accounting information pertains to entities, which are circumscribed areas of interest, and, (b) in financial accounting the entity is the specific business enterprise. In governmental accounting, there is no single accounting entity that encompasses all of the activities of the governmental entity. Because of various legal restrictions imposed by constitutions, charters, and the like, resources and related activities often have to be accounted for on an individual basis. These accounting and fiduciary requirements are met by use of fund accounting principles. Thus, in governmental accounting the accounting entity is each individual fund, not the overall reporting entity.

Principle 2 (Fund Accounting Systems) states that the fund basis must be used in accounting for governmental units and defines a fund as follows:

> A fund is defined as a fiscal and accounting entity with a self-balancing set of accounts recording cash and other financial resources, together with all related liabilities and residual equities or balances, and changes therein, which are

segregated for the purpose of carrying on specific activities or attaining certain objectives in accordance with special regulations, restrictions, or limitations.

The governmental unit is comprised of numerous funds which follow the basic accounting model that states, Assets = Liabilities + Fund Balance. The definition of assets and liabilities for a governmental fund is no different from the definitions used in commercial accounting; however, the fund balance concept does not represent the owners' interest in the government's net assets. Since there are no owners of a state or local government, fund balance is simply the arithmetic difference between total assets and total liabilities of the fund.

The basic accounting model is self-contained for each fund. For example, there may be transactions between funds of a single governmental unit that create debtor/creditor relationships. In this circumstance interfund receivables and payables are created, and their balances must be appropriately reflected in each fund's balance sheet. Although each fund must be accounted for separately, this does not necessarily require the physical segregation of assets and liabilities. An accounting system using an appropriately coded chart of accounts could achieve autonomous accounting for each fund without physically segregating the net assets of each fund.

Governmental funds can be classified several ways. They may be classified based on the manner in which they were created, such as by law, charter, or other action. This type of classification is useful in that it may determine the degree of discretion that can be exercised over the fund by the chief executive or the legislative body. In addition, classification by fund type can be useful in controlling activity in the fund and determining whether legal restrictions have been followed. Principle 3 (Types of Funds) identifies eight fund types that are divided into three categories, namely (1) governmental funds, (2) proprietary funds and (3) fiduciary funds.

Governmental funds This category includes General, Special Revenue, Special Assessment, Capital Projects, and Debt Service Funds. These funds are referred to as expendable funds because the measurement focus is on the flow of current financial resources rather than the measurement of net profit. Revenues and expenditures are recognized on a modified accrual basis. Only assets available for achieving the objective of the specific governmental fund and liabilities that will utilize available assets of the fund are presented in the governmental fund. Thus, the balance sheet emphasizes the accounting for currently available assets and current liabilities, and fixed assets are not accounted for in a governmental fund. Current liabilities are defined as "obligations whose liquidation is reasonably expected to require the use of existing resources properly classifiable as current assets, or the creation of current liabilities" (ARB-43 — Restatement and Revision of Accounting Research Bulletins). This definition is applicable to current liabilities of a governmental fund.

An example of financial statements of a governmental fund (General Fund) is found in Exhibit IV.

EXHIBIT IV
General Fund Financial Statements

Centerville, New Jersey
General Fund
Balance Sheets
June 30, 19X5 and 19X4

	19X5	19X4
ASSETS		
Cash	$100,000	$75,000
Taxes receivable (net of allowances for uncollectable taxes)	250,000	215,000
Due from other funds	50,000	20,000
Inventory	10,000	8,000
Total assets	$410,000	$318,000
LIABILITIES AND FUND BALANCE		
Liabilities		
Vouchers payable	$340,000	$250,000
Contracts payable	10,000	15,000
Deferred revenue	5,000	12,000
Total liabilities	355,000	277,000
Fund balance		
Reserved for encumbrances	30,000	25,000
Reserved for inventory	10,000	8,000
Unreserved	15,000	8,000
Total fund balance	55,000	41,000
Total liabilities and fund balance	$410,000	$318,000

(continued next page)

EXHIBIT IV (continued)

Centerville, New Jersey
General Fund
Statements of Revenues, Expenditures, and
Changes in Fund Balance
For Years Ended June 30, 19X5 and 19X4

	19X5	*19X4*
Revenues		
Property taxes	$700,000	$550,000
Gross receipts taxes	150,000	100,000
Fines	30,000	40,000
Other	20,000	10,000
Total revenues	900,000	700,000
Expenditures		
General government	400,000	350,000
Health and welfare	150,000	120,000
Public safety	250,000	170,000
Sanitation	50,000	50,000
Total expenditures	850,000	690,000
Excess (Deficiency) of revenues over expenditures	50,000	10,000
Other financing sources (uses)		
Operating transfers out	(34,000)	(15,000)
Excess (Deficiency) of revenues over expenditures and other uses	16,000	(5,000)
Fund balance at beginning of year	41,000	50,000
Increase in reserve for inventory	(2,000)	(4,000)
Fund balance at end of year	$55,000	$41,000

Proprietary funds Included in this category, which is referred to as nonexpendable funds, are Enterprise Funds and Internal Service Funds. The measurement focus for these funds is a determination of net profit from operations which includes an accounting for all cost allocations (including depreciation) associated with the fund. The cost of services rendered by the fund are financed through user charges (Enterprise Fund) or interfund charges (Internal Service Fund). The accrual method as used by business enterprises is the basis of accounting for proprietary funds. The only differences are that a proprietary fund does not have an owners' equity section on its balance sheet and the fund is not subject to income taxes. Thus, all assets related to the fund, including fixed assets, and all liabilities of the fund, including long-term liabilities, are reported by a proprietary fund. The set of financial statements must include a statement of changes in financial position as well as a balance sheet and a statement of revenues, expenses, and changes in fund retained earnings.

An example of financial statements of a proprietary fund (Enterprise Fund) is presented in Exhibit V.

EXHIBIT V
Proprietary Fund Financial Statements

Centerville, New Jersey
Centerville Parking Authority
Balance Sheets
June 30, 19X5 and 19X4

	19X5	19X4
ASSETS		
Current assets		
Cash	$40,000	$25,000
Supplies	10,000	15,000
Due from other funds	30,000	35,000
Prepaid expenses	10,000	5,000
Total current assets	90,000	80,000
Property, plant and equipment		
Land	300,000	200,000
Buildings	600,000	480,000
Equipment	50,000	40,000
	950,000	720,000
Less: Accumulated depreciation	200,000	150,000
Net property, plant and equipment	750,000	570,000
Total assets	$840,000	$650,000
LIABILITIES AND FUND EQUITY		
Liabilities		
Current liabilities		
Vouchers payable	$20,000	$30,000
Contracts payable	10,000	20,000
Accrued expenses	10,000	25,000
Current portion of long-term debt	30,000	25,000
Total current liabilities	70,000	100,000

(continued on next page)

EXHIBIT V (continued)

Long-term debt		
Revenue bonds	470,000	230,000
General obligation bonds	100,000	150,000
Total long-term debt	570,000	380,000
Total liabilities	640,000	480,000
Fund equity		
Contributed capital		
City contributions	100,000	100,000
Customer contributions	50,000	50,000
Total contributed capital	150,000	150,000
Retained earnings		
Appropriated	10,000	5,000
Unappropriated	40,000	15,000
Total retained earnings	50,000	20,000
Total fund equity	200,000	170,000
Total liabilities and fund equity	$840,000	$650,000

Centerville, New Jersey
Centerville Parking Authority
Statements of Revenues, Expenses, and Changes in Retained Earnings
For Years Ended June 30, 19X5 and 19X4

	19X5	19X4
Revenues		
Parking fees	$750,000	$600,000
Miscellaneous	50,000	34,000
Total revenues	800,000	634,000
Operating expenses		
Salaries and wages	575,000	500,000
Depreciation	50,000	30,000
Other	100,000	70,000
Total expenses	725,000	600,000
Operating income	75,000	34,000
Other expenses		
Interest	45,000	25,000
Net income	30,000	9,000
Retained earnings, beginning of year	20,000	11,000
Retained earnings, end of year	$50,000	$20,000

(continued on next page)

EXHIBIT V (continued)

Centerville, New Jersey
Centerville Parking Authority
Statements of Changes in Financial Position
For Years Ended June 30, 19X5 and 19X4

	19X5	19X4
Sources of working capital		
From operations		
Net income	$30,000	$9,000
Add: Expenses not using working capital		
Depreciation expense	50,000	30,000
	80,000	39,000
Other sources		
Issuance of debt	220,000	100,000
Total sources	300,000	139,000
Applications of working capital		
Purchase of fixed assets	230,000	100,000
Maturing of current portion of long-term debt	30,000	25,000
Total applications	260,000	125,000
Increase in working capital	$40,000	$14,000

Centerville, New Jersey
Schedule of Working Capital Changes
For Years Ended June 30, 19X5 and 19X4

| | Effect of Changes in Current Items on Working Capital Increase (Decrease) ||
	19X5	19X4
Current assets		
Cash	$15,000	$5,000
Supplies	(5,000)	4,000
Due from other funds	(5,000)	(9,000)
Prepaid expenses	5,000	2,000
Current liabilities		
Vouchers payable	10,000	8,000
Contracts payable	10,000	10,000
Accrued expenses	15,000	(3,000)
Current portion of long-term debt	(5,000)	(3,000)
Increase in working capital	$40,000	$14,000

Fiduciary funds This classification includes Expendable Trust Funds, Nonexpendable Trust Funds, Pension Trust Funds, and Agency Funds. The same accounting method used for governmental funds (modified accrual) is used for Expendable Trust Funds and Agency Funds. Nonexpendable Trust Funds and (generally) Pension Trust Funds, like proprietary funds, use the accrual method. The financial statements presented earlier illustrating a governmental fund and a proprietary fund provide the appropriate formats for fiduciary funds, except that an Agency Fund does not include an activity statement.

Group of Accounts

Fixed assets and long-term debt are ordinarily not accounted for in a governmental fund. These items are recorded in the General Fixed Assets Account Group or the General Long-Term Debt Account Group.

General Fixed Assets Account Group This account group is not a fund. It is simply an account where long-lived assets that are not available to finance current operations are recorded. The account is self-balancing and the following entry is made when fixed assets are acquired.

Name Of Fixed Asset (Such As Building)	X	
Investment In General Fixed Asset		
(Source Of Investment)		X

When the asset is disposed of, the entry is reversed. Fixed assets of a proprietary fund and a Nonexpendable Trust Fund are recorded in those funds and not in the General Fixed Assets Account Group. (For a comprehensive discussion of accounting for fixed assets, see Chapter 68.)

An example of a financial statement for the General Fixed Assets Account Group is illustrated below.

Centerville, New Jersey
Statement of General Fixed Assets
(By Source)
June 30, 19X5

General fixed assets
  Land $2,000,000
  Buildings 5,000,000
  Equipment 1,000,000
    Total $8,000,000

Investment in general fixed assets (Source)
  General fund $1,000,000
  Special assessment fund 500,000
  Capital projects fund 6,000,000
  Donations 500,000
    Total $8,000,000

General Long-Term Debt Account Group This account, which is not a fund, provides a place to record long-term debt that will not require the use of current resources. When long-term debt is issued, the following entry is made:

Amount To Be Provided For Payment Of Debt	X	
Bonds Payable		X

As funds are accumulated to pay the debt in the Debt Service Fund, the following entry is made in the General Long-Term Debt Account Group:

Amount Available In Debt Service Fund For Bond Repayment	X	
Amount To Be Provided For Payment Of Debt		X

When the debt is actually paid, the transaction is recorded as follows:

Bonds Payable	X	
Amount Available In Debt Service Fund For Bond Repayment		X

Long-term debt for Enterprise Funds and Special Assessment Funds are recorded in those funds and not in the General Long-Term Debt Account Group. (For a comprehensive discussion of accounting for long-term debt, see Chapter 67.)

An example of a financial statement for the General Long-Term Debt Account Group is presented below.

Centerville, New Jersey
Statement of General Long-Term Debt
June 30, 19X5

Amounts available and to be provided for bonds payable		
Amount to be provided	$600,000	
Amount available in debt service fund	400,000	$1,000,000
Serial bonds payable		
Amount to be provided	1,700,000	
Amount available in debt service fund	300,000	2,000,000
Total		$3,000,000
General long-term obligations		
Bonds payable, 7%, due 12/31/X9		$1,000,000
Serial bonds, 9%, due in the amount of $100,000 every six months beginning 9/1/X5		2,000,000
Total		$3,000,000

Number of Funds

Principle 4 (Number of Funds) states that the actual number of funds used by a governmental unit should be kept to a minimum in order to avoid the creation of an inefficient financial system. In general, the number of funds established must be sufficient to meet operational needs and legal restrictions imposed on the organization. For example, only one General Fund should be maintained. In some circumstances it may be possible to account for restricted resources in the General Fund, and still meet imposed legal requirements. Also, there may be no need to establish a Special Revenue Fund unless specifically required by law.

Basic Foundation of Governmental Generally Accepted Accounting Principles

LITERATURE REFERENCES

Material in this chapter is based on the following authoritative pronouncements which are grouped according to the major headings used within the chapter. A dual reference (both paragraph and page number) is used for NCGA-1 and NCGA-2 because the original pronouncements do not use paragraph numbers.

Introduction
NCGA-1   *Governmental Accounting and Financial Reporting Principles*, p. 5/ ¶ 11.

GASB Concepts Statement-1
GASB:CS-1   *Objectives of Financial Reporting.*

NCGA Concepts Statement-1
GASB-1   *Authoritative Status of NCGA Pronouncements and AICPA Industry Audit Guide*, ¶¶ 8 and 12.
NCGA:CS-1   *Objectives of Accounting and Financial Reporting for Governmental Units.*

FASB Concepts Statement-4
FASB:CS-4   *Objectives of Financial Reporting by Nonbusiness Organizations*, ¶¶ 3, 11, 23, 33-55, and 66.

Basic Governmental Accounting Principles
NCGA-1   *Governmental Accounting and Financial Reporting Principles*, pp. 2-4 (no paragraph reference has been established for the original pronouncement in this section of the pronouncement).

Compliance with Generally Accepted Accounting Principles
NCGA-1   *Governmental Accounting and Financial Reporting Principles*, pp. 4, 5, 7, 13, and 17/¶¶ 2-13, 15, 21, 23, 88, and 125.
NCGA-2   *Grant, Entitlement, and Shared Revenue Accounting by State and Local Governments*, p. 1/¶ 1.
AICPA AUDIT GUIDE (1978)   *Audits of State and Local Governmental Units*, p. 12.

Fund Accounting
APB STATEMENT-4   *Basic Concepts and Accounting Principles Underlying Financial Statements of Business Enterprises*, ¶ 116.
NCGA-1   *Governmental Accounting and Financial Reporting Principles*, pp. 6-7/ ¶¶ 17-19, 21-22 and 24-25.
NCGA-4   *Accounting and Financial Reporting Principles for Claims and Judgments and Compensated Absences*, ¶¶ 33, 35, and 36.

Group of Accounts
NCGA-1   *Governmental Accounting and Financial Reporting Principles,* pp. 8-9/ ¶¶ 33-39 and 41-46.

Number of Funds
NCGA-1   *Governmental Accounting and Financial Reporting Principles,* p. 8/¶¶ 30 and 31.
NCGA Interpretation-9   *Certain Fund Classifications and Balance Sheet Accounts,* ¶ 10.

BASIS OF ACCOUNTING AND MEASUREMENT FOCUS OF GOVERNMENTAL FUNDS

NCGA:CS-1 (Objectives of Accounting and Financial Reporting for Governmental Units) concludes that the overall goal of governmental accounting and financial reporting is to "(1) provide financial information useful for making economic, political, and social decisions, and demonstrating accountability and stewardship and (2) provide information useful for evaluating managerial and organizational performance." While most interested observers may agree with the overall goal, the implementation of the goal is the subject of much debate. An important element in the implementation of the overall goal is the selection of a basis of accounting and a measurement focus for governmental funds. As discussed below, the selection of a basis of accounting and measurement focus has a significant effect on the establishment of specific accounting principles for state and local governments.

BASIS OF ACCOUNTING

An entity's accounting basis determines when transactions and economic events are reflected in its financial statements. NCGA-1 (Governmental Accounting and Financial Reporting Principles) states that basis of accounting refers to "when revenues, expenditures, expenses, and transfers—and the related assets and liabilities—are recognized in the accounts and reported in the financial statements." All operating transactions are the result of expected or unexpected asset flows (usually, but not exclusively cash flows). Due to specific contractual agreements and accepted business practices, commitments that create eventual resource flows may not coincide with the actual flow of resources. For example, goods may be purchased on one date, consumed on another date, and paid for on still a third date. The accounting basis determines when the economic consequences of transactions and events are reflected in financial statements.

Generally, accounting transactions and events may be recorded on a cash basis, accrual basis, or modified accrual basis.

Basis of Accounting and Measurement Focus of Governmental Funds

Cash Basis

When a strict cash basis is used by an organization, revenues and expenditures are recognized as cash is received and disbursed. The balance sheet reflects only a balance in cash and the fund balance accounts, while the activity statement would simply summarize cash receipts and cash disbursements for the period. NCGA-1 concludes that the cash method is not an appropriate basis for accounting and reporting by governmental organizations.

> ***OBSERVATION:*** *Caution must be used when generalizing about the basis of accounting that should be used to account for a specific revenue. The basic rule is that revenue that is both measurable and available should be accrued, and this rule should be applied by each governmental unit to its various sources of revenue. For example, while income taxes are usually accounted for on a cash basis, it is suggested in the AICPA's Audits of State and Local Governmental Units (1986) that some states are using historical experience, including advanced mathematical and statistical techniques, to estimate the amount of receivable or payable (refunds) that should be accrued for income taxes at the end of a fiscal period.*

Although the cash basis cannot be used as a comprehensive basis of accounting for state and local governments, the cash method is used to account for certain transactions. For example, miscellaneous revenues, such as fines and parking fees and self-assessed taxes such as gross receipts taxes and income taxes, generally should be recorded on a cash basis.

Accrual Basis

FASB:CS-1 describes accrual accounting in the following manner:

> Accrual accounting attempts to record the financial effects on an enterprise of transactions and other events and circumstances that have cash consequences for an enterprise in the periods in which those transactions, events, and circumstances occur rather than only in the periods in which cash is received or paid by the enterprise. Accrual accounting is concerned with the process by which cash expended on resources and activities is returned as more (or perhaps less) cash to the enterprise, not just with the beginning and end of that process.

The essential elements of the accrual accounting method include the (1) deferral of expenditures and the subsequent amortization of the deferred costs (prepaid expenses, supplies, etc.), (2) deferral of revenues until they are earned (property taxes received in advance), (3) capitalization of certain expenditures and the subsequent depreciation of the capitalized costs (depreciation of cost of machinery), and (4) accrual of revenues that have been earned and expenses that have been incurred. In governmental accounting the accrual method is recognized as the superior accounting basis, and there is an attempt generally to reflect the fundamental concepts of accrual accounting where appropriate.

The acceptance of the accrual basis as the preferred accounting basis should not be confused as being synonymous with the need to measure income for a period. The determination of net profit is not an objective of governmental fund accounting. Nonetheless, the accrual basis can be used by an entity without the need to reflect amortization, including depreciation and other allocations, in its financial statements. In general, amortization is an allocation process and is not a fundamental concept of accrual accounting.

> **OBSERVATION:** *The contention that the broad concept of amortization is not part of accrual accounting is made in NCGA-1 (page 12); however, this conclusion is certainly not universally accepted. FASB:CS-6 (Elements of Financial Statements) states that accrual accounting attempts to recognize noncash events and circumstances as they occur and involves not only accruals but also deferrals, including allocations and amortizations (paragraph 141).*

Modified Accrual Basis

Both the AICPA Audit Guide (Audits of State and Local Governmental Units) and NCGA-1 conclude that governmental revenues and expenditures should be recorded on the modified accrual basis. The modified accrual basis is a mixture of both cash and accrual basis concepts.

Revenues, including funds received from other governmental units and the issuance of debt, should be recorded when they are *susceptible to accrual*. In order for revenue to be considered susceptible to accrual it must be both measurable and available to finance current expenditures of the fund. Revenue is considered available when it is collectible during the current period, and the actual collection will occur either (1) during the current period or (2) after the end of the period but in time to pay current year-end liabilities. Generally, property taxes, grants, and interfund transfers are accounted for on a modified accrual basis while income taxes, gross receipts taxes, and sales taxes are recorded on a cash basis. These are generalizations, and the basis of accounting for a specific revenue is subject to the measurable and available criteria interpreted in the context of each fund.

> *OBSERVATION:* There is no explicit definition of "measurable" in the pronouncements, but the term undoubtedly refers to the ability to quantify the amount of revenue expected to be collected. Thus, "measurable" can be interpreted as the ability to provide a reasonable estimate of actual cash flow. NCGA-1 does make an implicit reference to "measurable" when it states that revenue may be recognized when collectibility is assured or losses can be reasonably estimated (page 11).

Expenditures, for the most part, are recorded on an accrual basis because they are measurable when they are incurred. Expenditures include salaries, wages, and other operating expenditures, payments for supplies, transfers to other funds, capital outlays for fixed assets, and payments for the service of debt. Although most expenditures are recorded on an accrual basis (timing emphasis), as described below, the measurement focus of a governmental fund significantly affects what items are to be considered expenditures in the governmental fund. Thus, expenditures for a governmental fund cannot be equated to expenses of a business enterprise.

MEASUREMENT FOCUS

The second critical element in the establishment of generally accepted accounting principles for governmental funds is the selection of a measurement focus. Unlike the selection of an accounting basis, which is concerned with the timing of transactions and events, a measurement focus identifies what transactions and events should be recorded. The measurement focus is concerned with the inflow and outflow of resources that affect an entity. The balance sheet should reflect those resources that are available to meet current obligations and to be used in the delivery of goods and services in subsequent periods. The activity statement for the period should summarize those resources received and those consumed during the current period. Although there are a number of measurement focuses, the understanding of the current measurement focus for governmental funds is enhanced by contrasting the following three measurement focuses:

- Flow of economic resources
- Flow of total financial resources
- Flow of current financial resources

Flow of Economic Resources (Accrual Basis)

The flow of economic resources refers to all of the assets available to the governmental unit for the purpose of providing goods and services to the public. When the flow of economic resources and the accrual basis of accounting are combined, they provide the foundation for generally accepted accounting principles used by business enterprises. Thus, this approach would recognize the deferral and capitalization of expenditures and the deferral of revenues.

When the flow of economic resources is applied on an accrual basis for a governmental fund, all assets and liabilities, both current and long-term, would be presented in the fund's balance sheet. The key differences between this approach and the current governmental model are summarized below:

- Fixed assets would be recorded in the fund's balance sheet net of accumulated depreciation and not in the General Fixed Assets Account Group.
- Long-term debt would be recorded in the fund's balance sheet and not in the General Long-Term Debt Account Group.
- The fund balance would represent the net assets (total assets minus total liabilities) available to the fund and not the net assets available to pay future expenditures or existing debts arising from operations.

The activity statement would include all costs of providing goods and services during the period. These costs would include depreciation, the cost of inventories consumed during the period, and other operating expenditures. On the activity statement, revenues earned during the period would be matched with the total cost of the particular segment (fund) of government. There would also be a smoothing effect on the activity statement. For example, expenditures would not include the full cost of purchasing depreciable property during the period and revenues would not include the proceeds from the issuance of long-term debt.

Flow of Total Financial Resources (Modified Accrual Basis)

The flow of total financial resources refers to all of the monetary assets and monetary liabilities that arise from operations. Financial resources would not include liabilities resulting from financing activities. Nonmonetary assets, such as prepaid expenses and supplies, would be treated as expenditures when they are incurred and not when they are consumed. Furthermore, the cost of depreciable property would be treated as a current expenditure and would not be capitalized and depreciated. Revenues would be recorded when they are earned irrespective of when they are expected to be received. For example, a grant from another governmental unit would be recognized as revenue even though a "noncurrent" receivable would be recorded because the grant is not expected to be received until fifteen months after the date of the balance sheet. Likewise, expenditures would be recorded when incurred, and the expected payment date would be irrelevant. For example, pension expenditures would be recognized in the current period on a present value basis even though actual payments might be deferred for several years.

When the measurement focus is the flow of total financial resources, the balance sheet does not present only net assets available to pay future expenditures or existing debts arising from operations. All monetary assets and monetary liabilities are presented.

Flow of Current Financial Resources (Modified Accrual Basis)

The flow of current financial resources applied on a modified accrual basis is a narrow interpretation of what constitutes assets and liabilities for an accounting entity. Revenues, and the resulting assets, are accrued at the end of the year only if the revenues are earned and the receivables are expected to be collected in time to pay for liabilities in existence at the end of the period. Expenditures, and the related liabilities, are accrued when they are expected to be paid out of revenues recognized during the current period. In order to determine which revenues and expenditures should be accrued, an arbitrary date after the end of the year must be established. For example, revenues and expenditures may be accrued at the end of the year only if a cash flow occurs within forty-five, sixty, or some other number of days after the date of the balance sheet.

When the measurement focus is the flow of current financial resources, prepayments, purchases of supplies, and capital expenditures are not recorded as deferred costs but rather as current expenditures. Thus, the activity statement reflects only those expenditures that were made during the current period and ignores cost allocations that might arise from expenditures incurred prior to the current period.

The balance sheet under the flow of current financial resources approach reflects only those assets available to pay future expenditures or existing debts arising from operations.

The following table contrasts the three measurement focuses.

ACCOUNTING TREATMENT

	Flow of Economic Resources	Flow of Total Financial Resources	Flow of Current Financial Resources
Supplies	Capitalized and amortized as goods are consumed	Treated as an expenditure when goods are acquired	Treated as an expenditure when goods are acquired
Prepayments	Capitalized and amortized as goods are consumed	Treated as an expenditure when goods are acquired	Treated as an expenditure when goods are acquired
Current and noncurrent receivables arising from operations	Recorded when earned	Recorded when earned	Recorded when earned and realizable within an arbitrary number of days of the date of the balance sheet
Property, plant and equipment	Capitalized and depreciated over economic life of asset	Treated as an expenditure when the asset is paid for	Treated as an expenditure when the asset is paid for

Basis of Accounting and Measurement Focus of Governmental Funds

	ACCOUNTING TREATMENT		
	Flow of Economic Resources	Flow of Total Financial Resources	Flow of Current Financial Resources
Current and noncurrent liabilities arising from operations	Recorded when incurred	Recorded when incurred	Recorded when incurred and payable within an arbitrary number of days of the date of the balance sheet

Basis of Accounting/Measurement Focus Illustration

The differences and similarities of the flow of economic resources (accrual basis), the flow of total financial resources (modified accrual basis), and the flow of current financial resources (modified accrual basis) are illustrated in the following example.

Fiscal Year:
  Ended June 30, 19X5 (for simplicity it is assumed that this is the first year of operations for the fund)

	(000)
Revenues:	
Billed during year	$30,000
Collected during year (one-half of the remaining balance is expected to be collected within 60 days of the year-end and the remainder within 180 days)	26,000
Salaries:	
Paid during year	9,000
Payable at the end of year and expected to be paid within 30 days	1,000
Property, Plant & Equipment:	
Purchased equipment on July 1, 19X4, at a cost of $20,000, estimated four-year life, no salvage value, straight-line method for depreciation	20,000
Noncurrent Note Payable:	
Equipment purchased was financed by issuing a 10% note whereby all interest and principal are paid four years from date of issuance	20,000
Supplies:	
Purchased during year	8,000
Consumed during year	6,000
Paid during year (balance to be paid 90 days after year-end date)	7,000
Pension:	
Present value of expected future expenditures (normal cost)	5,000
Amount funded during year	3,000

The financial statements for the governmental fund based on the three measurement focuses are presented as follows:

Fund Name
Statement of Revenues, Expenditures, and Changes in Fund Balance
For Year Ended June 30, 19X5
(amounts in thousands of dollars)

	Flow of economic resources	Flow of total financial resources	Flow of current financial resources (60-day assumption*)
Revenues	$30,000	$ 30,000	$28,000
Expenditures:			
Capital Outlays		20,000	
Salaries	10,000	10,000	10,000
Depreciation	5,000		
Interest	2,000	2,000	
Supplies	6,000	8,000	7,000
Pensions	5,000	5,000	3,000
Total	28,000	45,000	20,000
Excess of revenues over (under) expenditures	2,000	(15,000)	8,000
Fund balance 7/1/X4			
Fund balance 6/30/X5	$ 2,000	$(15,000)	$ 8,000

Fund Name
Balance Sheet
June 30, 19X5
(amounts in thousands of dollars)

	Flow of economic resources	Flow of total financial resources	Flow of current financial resources (60-day assumption*)
ASSETS			
Current assets			
Cash	$ 7,000	$ 7,000	$ 7,000
Receivables	4,000	4,000	2,000
Supplies	2,000		
Total	13,000	11,000	9,000
Fixed assets			
Equipment	20,000	A	A
Acc. Depr.	(5,000)		
Net book value	15,000		
Total assets	$28,000	$11,000	$ 9,000

Basis of Accounting and Measurement Focus of Governmental Funds

LIABILITIES AND FUND BALANCE			
Current liab.			
Accts. Payable	$1,000	$1,000	B
Salaries Payable	1,000	1,000	1,000
Total	2,000	2,000	1,000
Noncurrent liabilities			
Notes payable (including interest)	22,000	22,000	
Pensions payable	2,000	2,000	B
Total	24,000	24,000	
Total liabilities	26,000	26,000	1,000
Fund balance	2,000	(15,000)	8,000
Total liabilities and fund balance	$28,000	$11,000	$9,000

*It is assumed that assets must be realizable within 60 days of the end of the fiscal year in order to be considered available to finance current expenditures.
  A Would be recorded in the General Fixed Assets Account Group.
  B Would be recorded in the Long-Term Debt Account Group.

Conventional Accounting Basis/Measurement Focus

As suggested earlier, the accounting basis used in governmental financial reporting is the modified accrual method. The measurement focus used approximates the flow of current financial resources. Some of the applications of the modified accrual basis/flow of current financial resources to a governmental fund are briefly summarized below.

Property tax revenues Revenues from property taxes are recognized on a modified accrual basis when they are measurable and available. Property taxes that have been assessed during the current period but have not been collected at the end of the period are considered available when they are expected to be collected within 60 days of the end of the period. On the balance sheet, the property taxes receivable account should be reduced by the estimated allowance of uncollectible accounts. Property taxes received in advance of the year they are levied should be treated as deferred revenue.

Taxpayer assessed revenues Certain revenues, such as gross receipts taxes and income taxes, are assessed by the taxpayer rather than by the state or local government. Self-assessed taxes should generally be recorded on a cash basis, although taxes collected and held by an agent for the government, such as a retailer in the case of a gross receipts tax, should be recognized as revenue even though actual remittance of the tax has been delayed.

Grants, entitlements, and shared revenues Generally, grants are recognized as revenue when the actual expenditure financed by the grant is made. In contrast, entitlements and shared revenues may be recorded at the date of receipt, although they may be accrued at an earlier date if they are both measurable and available. The availability criterion would be met if all of the regulations associated with the entitlement or shared revenue program have been observed by the state or local government.

Sales tax revenues The cash basis is used to account for sales tax revenues. If sales taxes have been collected by a retailer but the receipt of the revenue from the retailer at the end of the period has been delayed, the revenue should be recognized before the cash is received. Sales taxes collected by retailers but due to be paid to the governmental unit after the end of the period should not be accrued for the current period.

Other revenues Miscellaneous revenues such as recreational fees, fines, charges for services, and parking fees should be recorded on a cash basis.

Operating expenditures NCGA-1 defines expenditures as reductions in net financial resources of a fund and concludes that most expenditures and operating transfers should be recorded when the related liability is incurred. Expenses are different from expenditures. FASB:CS-6 (Elements of Financial Statements) defines expenses as "outflows or other using up of assets or incurrences of liabilities (or a combination of both) during a period from delivering or producing goods, rendering services, or carrying out other activities that constitute the entity's ongoing major or central operations." Although the recognition of depreciation is an expense because it represents the consumption of an asset, it is not an expenditure as applied to fund accounting because it does not result in a reduction of net financial resources. On the other hand, an actual payment for the purchase of a fixed asset is considered an expenditure to be reported on the fund's activity statement since net financial resources are decreased, but the payment does not represent an expense because there was no net asset consumption.

Basis of Accounting and Measurement Focus of Governmental Funds

Inventories   A governmental fund may account for inventories on a purchase basis or a consumption basis. Under the purchase method, inventories are treated as expenditures when acquired, while under the consumption method an expenditure is recognized as the goods are used. If inventories are material they must be reported in the balance sheet under both methods.

Prepayments   Payments for prepaid goods and services such as insurance and rent may be treated either as a current period expenditure or allocated between or among accounting periods.

Encumbrances   Executory contracts that are outstanding at the end of the year represent commitments of the governmental fund, but they are not treated as current expenditures or outstanding liabilities. For example, a purchase order for goods may have been sent to a vendor, but as of the balance sheet date the goods have not been received. A liability does not exist until title to the goods passes, but the encumbrance system provides control over the executory contract and similar transactions. The recording of the encumbrances is part of the governmental fund's budgetary accounting system and is used for budgetary control and cash management.

Expenditures for servicing long-term debt   Interest on general obligation long-term debt is not accrued as an expenditure. Expenditures for maturing principal and interest are recorded as expenditures when they are due and payable. Although this approach is based on the cash method rather than the modified accrual method, it prevents an inconsistency between budgetary financial statements and financial statements prepared on a GAAP basis. An item is treated as an expenditure in the budgetary financial statements when it is appropriated, and appropriation occurs in the year the cash payment is expected to be made. If the GAAP basis financial statements reflected accrued interest and the current portion of the principal, it is possible that the accrual would be made in one budgetary period but the payment would be made in another.

Debt proceeds   The accounting for the proceeds of debt depends upon whether the debt is short term or long term. For short-term debt, the governmental fund responsible for the debt records a liability, since current financial resources will be used to service the debt. When the debt is long term, the governmental fund records the proceeds as a financing source which is reported on its activity statement. The long-term liability is recorded in the General Long-Term Debt Account Group.

Claims, judgments, and compensated absences FASB-5 (Accounting for Contingencies) concludes that a liability for a loss contingency should be recorded when (1) it is probable that an asset has been impaired or a liability incurred and (2) the loss can be reasonably estimated. NCGA-4 (Accounting and Financial Reporting for Claims and Judgments and Compensated Absences) concludes that these criteria should be applied to claims and judgments of a governmental fund; however, only the amount of the claim or judgment that will be paid out of the fund's available financial resources should be recorded as a current expenditure. The balance (noncurrent portion) of the claim or judgment is reported in the General Long-Term Debt Account Group. In a similar fashion, accounting standards established in FASB-43 (Accounting for Compensated Absences) should be used to account for employee compensated absences of a governmental fund. When the criteria in FASB-43 are met, the current part of the liability should be recorded directly in the governmental fund. The portion of the liability that will not be paid from (expendable) available financial resources of the governmental fund should be reported in the General Long-Term Debt Account Group.

Capital leases Criteria established by FASB-13 (Accounting for Leases—as amended and interpreted) must be used to determine whether a lease agreement should be capitalized. If the lease is capitalized, the resulting asset is recorded in the General Fixed Assets Account Group and not in the (lessee) governmental fund. The liability associated with the capitalized lease is recorded in the General Long-Term Debt Account Group. If the state or local government is the lessor and the criteria established by FASB-13 are met, only the portion of the receivable available to finance current operations should be recognized as revenue or other financing source. Availability means that the receivable will be realized after the end of the period but in time to pay liabilities outstanding at the balance sheet date.

Pensions Reporting by pension funds is an unsettled question for state and local governmental units because both the NCGA and the FASB have issued authoritative statements covering the issue. Until the pension issue is resolved, GASB-1 (Authoritative Status of NCGA Pronouncements and AICPA Industry Audit Guide) identifies the following pronouncements as acceptable accounting and reporting standards for public employee retirement systems and state and local governmental employers:

Basis of Accounting and Measurement Focus of Governmental Funds

- NCGA-1 (The related material contained in the 1968 GAAFR may be considered as illustrative of the principles of NCGA-1, to the extent such material is consistent with the statement.)
- NCGA-6 (Pension Accounting and Financial Reporting: Public Employee Retirement Systems and State and Local Government Employers)
- FASB-35 (Accounting and Reporting by Defined Benefit Pension Plans)

Operating transfers   Transfers between funds that do not represent loans, reimbursements, or quasi-external transactions are treated as operating transfers. Interfund transfers are recorded in the governmental fund's activity statement but they must be distinguished from revenues (transfer-in) and expenditures (transfer-out).

Proprietary Funds

NCGA-1 concludes that in the absence of specific GASB pronouncements, the same generally accepted accounting principles used by a business enterprise should be used by an Enterprise Fund and Internal Service Fund. Thus, the accrual basis of accounting is used for proprietary funds, and the measurement focus is the determination of net income (flow of economic resources).

Fiduciary Funds

Accounting for Expendable Trust Funds parallels accounting for governmental funds (modified accrual basis/approximate flow of current financial resources). Pension Trust Funds and Nonexpendable Trust Funds are accounted for in a manner similar to proprietary funds (accrual basis/flow of economic resources).

LITERATURE REFERENCES

Material in this chapter is based on the following authoritative pronouncements, which are grouped according to the major headings used within the chapter. A dual reference (both paragraph and page number) is used for NCGA-1 and NCGA-2 because the original pronouncements do not use paragraph numbers.

Introduction
NCGA:CS-1   *Objectives of Accounting and Financial Reporting for Governmental Units*, ¶ 13.

Basis of Accounting
NCGA-1   *Governmental Accounting and Financial Reporting Principles*, p. 11/¶ 58.

Cash Basis
NCGA-1   *Governmental Accounting and Financial Reporting Principles*, pp. 11-12/¶¶ 59, 60, and 67.
SOP 75-3   *Accrual of Revenues and Expenditure By State and Local Governmental Units*, p. 166 (as reproduced in AICPA Audit Guide).

Accrual Basis
FASB:CS-1   *Objectives of Financial Reporting by Business Enterprises*, ¶ 44.
NCGA-1   *Governmental Accounting and Financial Reporting Principles*, pp. 11-12/¶¶ 60 and 71.
FASB:CS-6   *Elements of Financial Statements*, ¶¶ 139-142.

Modified Accrual Basis
AICPA AUDIT GUIDE   *Audits of State and Local Governmental Units, (1978)*, p. 13.
NCGA-1   *Governmental Accounting and Financial Reporting Principles*, pp. 10-12/¶¶ 57, 61-63, 69, and 70.

Measurement Focus
GASB DISCUSSION MEMORANDUM   *Measurement Focus and Basis of Accounting—Governmental Funds (nonauthoritative).*
NCGA-1   *Governmental Accounting and Financial Reporting Principles*, p. 9/ ¶ 39.

Conventional Accounting Basis/Measurement Focus
NCGA INTERPRETATION-3   *Revenue Recognition—Property Taxes*, ¶¶ 7 and 8.
NCGA-1   *Governmental Accounting and Financial Reporting Principles*, pp. 12, 15, and 16/¶¶ 67, 70, 72, 73 and 105.
AICPA AUDIT GUIDE   *Audits of State and Local Governmental Units (1978)*, p. 14.
NCGA-2   *Grant, Entitlement, and Shared Revenue Accounting by State and Local Governments*, p. 2/¶ 11.
SOP 75-3   *Accrual of Revenues and Expenditures By State and Local Governmental Units*, pp. 166 and 167 (as reproduced in AICPA Audit Guide, 1978).
FASB:CS-6   *Elements of Financial Statements*, ¶ 80.
NCGA-4   *Accounting and Financial Reporting Principles for Claims and Judgments and Compensated Absences*, ¶¶ 7, 14, 16, 25 and 26.
FASB-5   *Accounting for Contingencies*, ¶ 8.

NCGA-5 *Accounting and Financial Reporting Principles for Lease Agreements of State and Local Governments,* ¶¶ 13 and 14.

Proprietary Funds
NCGA-1 *Governmental Accounting and Financial Reporting Principles,* p. 6/ ¶ 18.

Fiduciary Funds
NCGA-1 *Governmental Accounting and Financial Reporting Principles,* p. 6/ ¶ 18.

APPENDIX

MEASUREMENT FOCUS AND BASIS OF ACCOUNTING (EXPOSURE DRAFT—REVISED AUGUST 1989)

In December 1987, the GASB issued an Exposure Draft entitled "Measurement Focus and Basis of Accounting—Governmental Funds." After considerable public debate, the GASB revised the Exposure Draft in August 1989 and changed the title to "Measurement Focus and Basis of Accounting—Governmental Fund Operating Statements." The change in title reflects a somewhat more narrow scope, although the revised Exposure Draft (hereinafter referred to as the proposed Statement), if adopted, would have a significant impact on governmental generally accepted accounting principles.

The proposed Statement addresses the related accounting issues of measurement focus and basis of accounting for governmental funds (General Fund, Special Revenue Funds, Debt Service Funds, and Capital Projects Funds), certain aspects of account groups, and Expendable Trust Funds. This Appendix discusses the tentative conclusions reached in the proposed Statement.

The proposed Statement does not address the following specific accounting and reporting issues:

- Pension expenditures
- Other post-employment benefits
- Special termination benefits
- Claims and judgments and related insurance transactions

- Capital improvement special assessment transactions
- Intergovernmental grants, entitlements, and shared revenues
- Operating expenditures resulting from nonexchange transactions
- Debt service expenditures on general long-term capital debt

The above eight topics are the subjects of various other GASB research projects and will be addressed in later Exposure Drafts. Nonetheless, the GASB takes the position that the measurement focus and basis of accounting discussed in the proposed Statement will provide the accounting framework for future Exposure Drafts concerning the eight topics listed. Also, the GASB's tentative strategy is to have a single effective date for the measurement focus and basis of accounting statement and the other eight statements.

Measurement Focus/Basis of Accounting

Measurement focus is concerned with *what* events and transactions should be captured by the governmental accounting model. Basis of accounting is concerned with *when* events and transactions should be processed through the governmental accounting model.

The proposed Statement establishes the flow of financial resources as the measurement focus and accrual accounting as the accounting basis for governmental funds. The proposed Statement defines financial resources as "cash, claims to cash (for example, debt securities of another entity and accounts and taxes receivable), claims to goods or services (for example, prepaid items), consumable goods (for example, supplies inventories), and marketable securities of another entity obtained or controlled as a result of past transactions or events."

> **OBSERVATION:** *The GASB's definition of financial resources has been broadened from the original definition to include consumable goods and marketable equity securities. Even with the broader definition, the definitional approach has been to list examples rather than provide a general description that could be used to classify specific assets. It is likely that the definition selected by the GASB will lead to a variety of interpretations by preparers of financial statements resulting in a less than uniform classification of governmental assets. For example, prepayments are classified as claims to goods and services. Likewise, it could be argued that capital assets such as buildings and equipment represent claims to goods based on*

the basic concepts related to property rights. The GASB, however, does not classify capital assets as a financial resource. Accountants would agree that capital assets are not financial resources, yet capital assets could be considered financial resources based on the GASB's definition. Also, there is no requirement that a financial resource must be collected within a specific period (for example one year) in order to be classified as a financial asset. Are quantities of supplies that will last three years financial resources? Certainly the amount of supplies that will be consumed in the second and third year will not be relevant to the state or local governmental unit's budgeting requirements for the current fiscal year.

The measurement focus is directed to activities related to changes in financial resources and related liabilities. The flow of financial resources measurement focus enables governmental entities to demonstrate the relationship of financial resources obtained and claims incurred during an accounting period. By analyzing the governmental entity's operating statement, a user can draw a conclusion concerning interperiod equity. For example, if a governmental entity's inflow of financial resources was less than claims against those financial resources for an accounting period (a deficit), it is obvious that the current-year citizens are shifting the burden for financing current expenditures to citizens of a subsequent accounting period(s). By using the flow of financial resources in preparing governmental financial statements, a user can refer to the entity's balance sheet to determine what financial resources are available to finance operations, incur capital expenditures, or service debt in future periods.

The accrual basis of accounting requires that (1) assets be recorded when they are obtained or controlled by an entity and (2) liabilities be recorded when incurred. When the accrual basis of accounting and the flow of financial resource measurement focus are combined, the governmental accounting model can be expressed as follows:

Financial Assets = Fund Liabilities + Fund Balance

Therefore, while resources may be available to a governmental entity in one period but realized (consumed or converted to cash) in another period, the financial asset would be reflected in the period in which it is obtained or controlled by the entity rather than during the period in which it is realized. Fund liabilities are obligations incurred during a period that are claims against financial resources.

The application of measurement focus and basis of accounting described in the proposed Statement to specific governmental transactions and events are discussed below.

Revenues

Governmental revenues are derived from (1) nonexchange transactions or events and (2) exchange transactions. Revenues related to nonexchange transactions or events, such as taxes, fines and donations should be recognized when the governmental entity's net financial resources (financial assets less fund liabilities) are increased. The receipt of cash is not a necessary condition for revenue recognition. Revenues related to exchange transactions, such as user fees and investment earnings, should be recognized when earned. Revenue is considered earned when the governmental unit has completed its obligation with respect to the revenue contract or commitment. Appropriate allowance accounts should be established to properly report the estimated amount of revenue and related receivable.

When cash is collected before revenue recognition criteria are satisfied, deferred revenue (fund liability) should be recognized.

Specific revenue recognition criteria are dependent upon the source of the revenue and are summarized below.

Taxes

In determining when taxes should be recognized as revenue, the GASB concluded that all of the following criteria must be satisfied:

- Occurrence criterion
- Demand criterion
- Acknowledgment or affirmation criterion

Occurrence criterion A prerequisite to the recognition of tax revenue is that a transaction or event must have taken place as the basis for determining that a tax amount is due. The transaction or event may occur on a particular date or may occur over a period of time. For example, a sales tax is based on the occurrence of a specific sale of goods or services covered by the tax. On the other hand, an income tax is based on the earnings of an individual or business organization over

Basis of Accounting and Measurement Focus of Governmental Funds

a specific period of time. Similarly, a property tax is based on the ownership of taxable property for a specific period of time.

Demand criterion The second criterion that must be satisfied before tax revenue can be recognized requires that the governmental unit demand that the tax be paid. That is, a specific due date for payment must be established. The GASB points out that there is a difference between the period during which the taxable transaction or event occurs and the tax due date. The time period allowed for the taxpayer to calculate the amount of taxes owed is referred to as an "administrative lead time." For example, a sales tax may be based on sales activity for a particular quarter even though a retailer does not have to submit a tax payment until 30 days after the end of the quarter. The period during which the taxable transaction or event occurs, not the due date of the tax, is the relevant date for determining revenue recognition.

Acknowledgement or affirmation criterion In addition to the occurrence of a taxable event or transaction and the existence of a tax due date, there must be some action taken either by the governmental unit or the taxpayer that confirms the existences of the tax amount due. Either the taxpayer (acknowledgment) or the governmental entity (affirmation) may confirm the existence of the tax. For example, a taxpayer acknowledges a tax through the payment of the tax or conceding that a tax is owed. On the other hand, a governmental entity affirms a tax by assessing a tax against a particular individual.

Taxes that are recognized but not paid may result in interest charges to the taxpayer. Such charges should be accrued based on the expiration of time.

Amounts received from taxpayers that are expected to be refunded should be reported as a liability of the governmental entity.

Sales taxes With respect to the demand criterion, if an administrative lead time is allowed, sales tax revenue is recognized when the due date is within one month of the end of the period. Furthermore, the acknowledgment criterion (paying the taxes or reporting a liability to the governmental unit) or the affirmation criterion (billing the taxpayer) must occur before the governmental unit's financial statements are issued. Once a date for the acknowledgment criterion and the affirmation criterion are established, the same dates must be used consistently from period to period.

Sales taxes that are due more than one month after the end of the period but are based on sales that occurred during the period and were received within one month of the end of the period should be recognized as revenue for the period.

A sales tax refund liability established at the end of each period should be based on known data such as claims filed but unpaid and historical trend information adjusted for changes in the sales tax law, if any.

> **OBSERVATION**: *Sales tax criteria discussed above should not be used as revenue recognition guidance for shared revenues funded by sales taxes. The accounting for shared revenues is part of a GASB research project on intergovernmental transfers and nonexchange program expenditures.*

Income taxes With respect to an administrative lead time, income taxes for individuals and businesses are considered to be demanded if the due date is within one month of the end of the period. The acknowledgment criterion (paying the taxes or reporting a liability to the governmental unit) or the affirmation criterion (billing the taxpayer) must occur before the governmental unit's financial statements are issued. Once a date for the acknowledgment criterion and the affirmation criterion are established, the same date must be used consistently from period to period.

Income tax withholdings and estimated payments that are due more than one month after the end of the period but are based on earnings that occurred during the period and were received within one month of the end of the period should be recognized as revenue for the period.

An income tax refund liability established at the end of each period should be based on known data such as claims filed but unpaid, and historical trend information adjusted for changes in the sales tax law, if any.

Taxpayer-assessed taxes administered or collected by another government Some taxpayer-assessed taxes, such as income taxes and sales taxes, may be administered or collected by another government. To account for such taxes the same revenue recognition criteria described earlier for taxpayer-assessed taxes should be used, unless the governmental unit that eventually receives the taxes does not have sufficient information to follow the criteria. When sufficient information is not available, revenue from taxpayer-assessed taxes administered or collected by another government should include the following:

- Cash received during the period (less the first month's receipts)
- Cash received within one month of the end of the period

A governmental entity should include as revenue cash received more than one month after the end of the period but before the financial statements are issued if such receipts meet revenue recognition criteria. Once a date is established for determining which receipts after the end of the period are considered revenue, that date should be used consistently from period to period.

Property (or ad valorem) taxes Property taxes are levied for a specific budget period. In general, property taxes should be recognized as revenue in the period levied if revenue recognition criteria are satisfied. The demand criterion date is the due date (last date before penalties and interest begin to accrue on unpaid amount). The affirmation criterion is satisfied when the governmental unit bills taxpayers. In addition, the following guidelines should be observed in recognizing property tax revenue:

- Taxes due after the budgetary period in which they are levied should be considered revenue in the period due.
- Taxes due after the budgetary period in which they are levied but received during that budgetary period should be considered revenue in the period received.
- Taxes received before the budgetary period in which they are levied should be considered deferred revenue.
- Taxes that are due before the budgetary period in which they are levied should be recognized as a receivable and deferred revenue on the date they become due.

The governmental entity should disclose its property tax calendar, including levy dates, lien dates, due dates, and past-due or delinquent dates.

Other taxes Taxes not specifically addressed in the proposed Statement should apply the general and specific guidelines discussed for sales, income, and property taxes in determining when such taxes should be recognized as revenue.

Other Nonexchange Revenues

Included in nonexchange revenues are fines, fees (other than user fees), and donations. In general, other nonexchange revenues should be recognized when the event that gave rise to the item occurs and when the governmental entity has an *enforceable legal claim* to the item.

Fines Fines arise from violations of laws and regulations (transaction or event criterion). The demand criterion and acknowledgment/affirmation criterion are satisfied when the collection of the fine is legally enforceable. The proposed Statement lists the following as actions that satisfy the legally enforceable criterion:

- Expiration date for challenging a court summons whereby a fine is automatically imposed.
- Fine is paid before court date.
- Fine is imposed by a court.

Fees Nonexchange fees may result from a specific event or may apply to a period of time. When the fee is for a particular event, revenue should be recognized when the governmental entity has an enforceable legal claim to the fee or has no obligation to refund a previously paid fee.

When the fee is based on a period of time, such as a driver's license fee, the fee should be allocated as revenue over the period of time covered by the fee. The proposed Statement does allow such fees to be recognized at the date collected or due assuming there is no material difference between the allocation method and the nonallocation method.

Donations Revenue from donations of financial resources should be recognized when an enforceable right to receive an asset exists and it is probable that the donated asset will be received.

Revenue from the donation of capital assets should be recorded as revenue only if the governmental entity intends to sell the asset immediately. The intent to sell must be supported by an actual sale or a contract to sale before the issuance of the financial statements. The capital asset should be presented in the fund reporting the revenue until transfer of title occurs.

Donation revenue from the receipt of financial resources and capital assets should be recorded based on the fair value of the donated asset.

Gifts of capital assets that are not intended for immediate sale should be recorded in the General Fixed Asset Account Group. If the capital asset is subsequently sold, the sales price of the asset should be reported as an other financing source.

Other nonexchange revenues administered or collected by another government Other nonexchange revenues administered or collected by another governmental entity should be recognized as revenue using the same criteria as used to measure other nonexchange revenues unless the governmental unit that eventually receives the taxes does not have sufficient information to follow the criteria. When sufficient information is not available, revenue from other nonexchange items administered or collected by another government should be based on cash received each period.

Exchange Revenues

A governmental entity may receive a variety of revenues from exchange transactions or events. These revenues include user fees, investment-related transactions, and operating leases. In general, revenues based on exchanges should be recognized when earned; that is, when the governmental entity has completed its responsibilities with respect to the exchange transaction.

User fees User fees are based on exchange transactions or events whereby a citizen buys a specific good or service from a governmental entity. User fees arise from a variety of activities, including golf fees and building inspection charges. A governmental entity should record user fees as revenue based on the delivery of the good or service. Fees received before the good or service is delivered should be recorded as deferred revenue. Services or goods that are delivered before the fee is received or billed should be accrued.

Investment gains, losses, and income Interest and dividends on investment securities should be recognized in the period in which they are earned. Thus, interest should be accrued using either the effective interest method or the straight line interest method if there is no material difference between the application of the effective interest method and the straight line method. On the other hand, dividends should be recognized as revenue based on the dividend declaration date.

Gains and losses realized from the sale of investments should be reported in the governmental entity's operating statement based on the date an investment is sold.

Investments in equity securities should be reported at cost. Investment in debt securities should be reported either at cost or at amortized cost. Investments in equity and debt securities should be written down to market (lower of cost or market) in *either* of the following circumstances:

- The decline below cost is considered to be other than temporary.
- The decline below cost is considered to be temporary but it is probable that the loss will be realized before the value of the security increases to its original cost.

Any loss resulting from the application of the lower of cost or market method should be reported on the governmental entity's operating statement. Subsequent recoveries of prior-period write-downs should not be recognized, and the carrying value of the investment becomes the adjusted cost basis. If the security is sold, the amount of the gain or loss is the difference between the sales price and the adjusted cost basis of the security.

Investments in mutual funds should be reported at redemption value as determined by the mutual fund. Changes in the redemption value during the period (net of contributions and withdrawals) should be reported as investment income based on the date the mutual fund posts the amounts to the governmental entity's account.

While cost or amortized cost is the fundamental reporting basis for investments, there are exceptions. The proposed Statement notes that these exceptions generally arise when "assets are specifically associated with liabilities to individuals, private organizations, and other governments and those liabilities are measured using another valuation method." An example would be pooled investments managed by a state government for its local governmental units where the valuation method is mandated in the agreement between the parties. In this case, the local governmental unit should present its investments in the investment pool using the same valuation method employed by the investment pool.

Investments may be held by one fund while the investment or the proceeds from the sale of investments may belong to another fund. As described below, the specific accounting for such investment gains or losses and investment income is dependent on whether the movement of the assets to another fund is based on a legal or contractual provisions:

- When the transfer of the asset is mandated based on a legal or contractual provision, investment gains or losses and investment income should be recorded by the transferring fund and the amount of the transfer should be recorded as an operating transfer.
- When the legal or contractual provisions simply state that investment gains or losses and investment income become the assets of another fund, the other fund (ultimate recipient fund) should record investment gains or losses and investment income, and no transfer should be recorded by any of the funds.
- When assets relating to investment gains or losses and investment income become assets of another fund based on reasons other than legal or contractual, the fund reporting the investment in its balance sheet should report investment gains or losses and investment income and eventual transfers should be recorded as operating transfers.

Operating leases When a governmental entity enters into a lease agreement, criteria established by FASB-13 (Accounting for Leases, as amended) should be used to determine whether the lease is an operating or capital lease. With respect to operating leases of capital assets, lease revenue (for the lessor) and lease expenditure (for the lessee) should be recognized based on the terms of the lease's contract if any one of the following conditions is satisfied:

- Lease payments are made on a level-payment basis.
- Lease payments are made on another systematic and rational basis that reflects the consumption of the benefits derived from the lease property.
- Lease payments increase over the lease term to reflect anticipated increases in the value of the property and the combined lease payments are consistent with the present and anticipated future rental value of the property.

When none of the above conditions is satisfied, the lessor should recognize revenue and the lessee should recognize an expenditure equal to the fair rental value of the capital asset for the period. Under this circumstance, the lessor should record a receivable based on the interest method using the implicit interest rate used (by the lessor) to finance the lessee's cash flow.

Other Financing Sources

Proceeds from the issuance of long-term debt used to finance the acquisition of capital assets and certain nonrecurring projects and activities that have long-term economic benefit, interfund operating transfers, premiums on general long-term capital debt, and the sale or (capital) lease of capital assets should be reported as other financing sources on the governmental entity's statement of operations.

Capital Leases and Sales of Capital Assets

When a governmental entity leases property to another party and the lease qualifies as a capital lease as defined by FASB-13, proceeds from the transaction should be reported as an other financing source based on the inception date of the lease. Likewise, proceeds from the sale of capital assets should be reported as an other financing source based on the date the asset is sold. With respect to the sale of a capital asset, the effective interest method (as described in APB-21, Interest on Receivables and Payables) should be used to recognize interest income related to deferred installment payments, if any.

Residual Equity Transfers In

A residual equity transfer in is presented on the governmental entity's statement of changes in fund balance. Such transfers are characterized as nonrecurring or nonroutine transfers of equity between funds.

Expenditures

In general, expenditures should be reported on a governmental entity's statement of operations when transactions or events that result in claims against financial resources have occurred. Governmental expenditures may be classified as operating expenditures, capital expenditures, or debt service expenditures.

Operating Expenditures

Operating expenditures include all expenditures recognized by a governmental entity other than capital expenditures, debt service expenditures, operating transfers out, and residual equity transfers out. Furthermore, operating expenditures may arise from either exchange or nonexchange transactions or events.

Operating expenditures arise from exchange transactions or events when another party must provide a service or a good to the governmental entity as part of an explicit or implied contract. For example, payroll expenditures and payments for supplies are exchange transactions. Accrual accounting should be used to account for operating expenditures related to exchange transactions or events. Thus, operating expenditures are recorded when a cash payment or other consideration is made or a liability is incurred.

> *OBSERVATION: Operating expenditures arise from nonexchange transactions and events when another party is not required to provide a service or good to the governmental entity. Such operating expenditures include payments to other governmental units and to citizens for basic necessities such as food and housing allowances. The proposed Statement does not address nonexchange expenditures; however, the GASB has instituted a research project that is reviewing the issue and expects to include the results of that project in a separate statement.*

Prepaid items Prepayments should be capitalized and amortized as operating expenditures over the periods in which the related good or service is consumed.

Supplies inventories Inventories should be capitalized and amortized as operating expenditures over the periods in which the supplies are consumed.

Compensated absences The proposed Statement adopts, for the most part, the accounting and reporting standards established by FASB-43 (Accounting for Compensated Absences) to measure compensated absences granted by a governmental entity. Thus, if all of the following conditions are satisfied, a governmental entity must recognize an expenditure for compensated absences (except for sick leave):

- Employer's obligation relating to employees' rights to receive compensation for future absences is attributable to employees' services already rendered.
- Obligation relates to rights that vest or accumulate.
- Payment of the compensation is probable.
- Amount can be reasonably estimated.

If all of the conditions exist, except for the fourth criterion (subject to reasonable estimation), that fact must be disclosed in the financial statements.

> **OBSERVATION**: *The GASB included accounting for compensated absences in the proposed Statement but another research project of the GASB will reconsider how to recognize and measure compensated absences expenditures. It is expected that the standards that will result from the reconsideration will be established before the effective date of the proposed Statement discussed in this Appendix.*

Special criteria apply to compensated absences for sick leave. *Earned sick leave* should be accrued if all of the following conditions are satisfied:

- The sick leave vests.
- Employer's obligation relating to sick leave is attributable to employee services already rendered.
- Payment for the sick leave is probable.
- Amount can be reasonably estimated.

If all of the conditions exist, except for the fourth criterion (subject to reasonable estimation), that fact must be disclosed in the financial statements.

When earned sick leave is based on accumulating nonvesting rights, the governmental entity must not accrue the expenditure, but rather the expenditure is recognized when the leave is taken by the employee.

> *OBSERVATION: The proposed Statement differs from FASB-43 in that the latter pronouncement allows an entity to either accrue nonvesting sick leave benefits as they are earned or when the sick leave is taken by the employee.*

The proposed Statement also establishes accounting standards for a specific type of compensated absence, namely sabbatical leaves. Expenditures for sabbatical leaves should be accrued when the four criteria for compensated absences for other than sick leave (as discussed earlier) are satisfied and the leave provides compensated unrestricted time off based on prior service. On the other hand, there should be no expenditure accrual for sabbatical leaves if either of the following conditions exists:

- The sabbatical leave is granted so that the employee can perform research or provide public service.
- The sabbatical leave is granted so that an employee can gain additional training resulting in the enhancement of the reputation of or benefit to the governmental employer.

In computing the expenditure accrual for compensated absences, the pay or salary scale in effect as of the date of the current balance sheet should be used. The accrual should not include any amount related to fringe benefits associated with the future compensated absences.

Operating leases Expenditures related to a lessee involved in an operating lease was discussed earlier in conjunction with operating lease income for lessors.

Capital expenditures A capital expenditure should be recognized when the capital asset is acquired. For purchased capital assets, the expenditure recognition would occur when the asset is acquired. For constructed capital assets, the expenditure would be recorded as the asset is constructed. The capital expenditure is recorded in the governmental entity's statement of operations. The capital asset is reported in the entity's GFAAG.

Capital assets acquired as an in-substance purchase through a lease agreement should be accounted for in a manner prescribed by FASB-13.

Capital assets acquired through an installment contract should be accounted for in a manner prescribed by APB-21.

> **OBSERVATION:** *In the previous Exposure Draft, the GASB had recommended that donated capital assets be recorded as both a capital expenditure and revenue. The proposed Statement prohibits this approach and simply requires that the donated capital asset be recorded in the General Fixed Asset Accounting Group.*

Debt service expenditures Expenditures for servicing debt reported in the governmental entity's GLTDAG should be recognized when due (maturity date). Thus, the accrual basis is not applicable to interest expenditures on general long-term debt. When funds have been transferred to a Debt Service Fund during the fiscal year in anticipation of making debt service payments shortly after the end of the period, it is acceptable to accrue interest in the Debt Service Fund in the year that the transfer is made.

Expenditures for servicing debt reported in specific governmental funds (operating debt) are subject to accrual and should be recognized as expenditures based on the passage of time. Any premium or discount related to operating debt should be amortized using the effective interest method. The repayment of the principal portion of operating debt should be treated as a reduction to the specific governmental fund's debt and not as a debt service expenditure.

> **OBSERVATION:** *The standards described above for debt service expenditures on long-term capital debt are a continuation of current standards; however, the GASB is studying the recognition and measurement of debt service expenditures in its capital reporting project.*

Other Financing Uses

Interfund operating transfers out should be reported as other financing uses on the governmental entity's statement of operations. In addition, claims on financial resources arising from refunding general long-term capital debt and discount created when general long-term capital debt is issued should be classified as other financing uses.

Residual Equity Transfers Out

A residual equity transfer out is presented on the governmental entity's statement of changes in fund balance. Such transfers are characterized as nonrecurring or nonroutine transfers of equity between funds.

Debt

Accounting for a governmental entity's debt depends on whether the debt is considered to be general long-term capital debt or operating debt.

General Long-Term Capital Debt

Debt that is issued to acquire capital assets (including long-term vendor financing such as capital leases and installment purchases) or to finance certain nonrecurring projects or activities that have long-term economic benefit is referred to as general long-term capital debt. General long-term capital debt should be presented in the governmental entity's GLTDAG. The capital asset acquired through the financing arrangement may be for the governmental entity or may be for another governmental entity (for example, capital grants). Although GLTDAG includes, for the most part, long-term instruments, it may also include debt issued that matures within one year or less if both of the following conditions are satisfied:

- At least part of the short-term debt is expected to be replaced by other debt.
- The time period covered by all of the debt (the debt originally issued and the replacement debt) extends beyond one year.

In order for debt to be classified as general long-term capital debt it does not have to be issued before the related capital asset is acquired. Debt issued after the acquisition of the related capital asset may be classified in the GLTDAG if it can be demonstrated that the intent of issuing the debt was to finance the previously acquired capital asset.

Professional judgment must be used to demonstrate intent; however, if intent cannot be adequately demonstrated the debt can nonetheless be considered general long-term capital debt if (1) the debt was issued within one year of the acquisition of the capital asset and (2) the intent of issuing the debt was to finance the acquisition of the capital asset.

Debt issuance The face amount of general long-term capital debt should be reported as an other source of financing. Discount or premium, if any, should be reported as an other source (premium) or use (discount) of financing. Issuance costs and out-of-pocket costs should be reported as expenditures and should not be netted against the proceeds of the issuance of the debt to determine the amount of the other financing source to be reported.

Debt should be presented at its face amount in the GLTDAG and classified as to type of debt (term bonds, serial bonds, capitalized leases, etc.). Balancing accounts should be presented showing the amounts available in Debt Service Funds for principal repayment and amounts to be provided.

Deep discount debt Deep discount debt (where the stated interest rate is less than seventy-five percent of the effective interest rate) reported in GLTDAG should be reported at an amount net of the discount (for financial reporting purposes either the face amount of the debt less the unamortized discount or a single net amount may be presented). The discount should be amortized using the effective interest method; however, the effect of the amortization should be shown only in the GLTDAG and should not be used to compute annual interest expenditures on the entity's statement of operations. A note to the financial statements should disclose the following with respect to deep discount debt:

- Stated interest rate
- Effective interest rate
- Face amount of debt (if not reported on the balance sheet)

Long-term vendor financing Capital leases and installment purchases used to acquire capital assets should be reported in the governmental entity's GLTDAG.

Debt extinguishment/defeasance General long-term capital debt may be extinguished, defeased (legally or in-substance), or refunded at maturity. When new debt is used to extinguish or defease existing debt, the face amount of the new debt should be reported as an other financing source. Payments made to retire the old debt should be classified as follows:

- Payments made from the proceeds of the new debt should be classified as an other financing use.
- Payments made from other resources should be classified as a debt service expenditure.

Operating Debt

Debt that is issued for purposes other than the financing of capital assets (including infrastructure assets) or certain nonrecurring projects or activities that have long-term economic benefit is referred to as operating debt. Operating debt is reported in a specific governmental fund rather than in the governmental entity's GLTDAG. Operating debt includes revenue anticipation notes, tax anticipation notes, and debt that is issued to finance operations.

Debt issuance Operating debt should be reported in the specific governmental fund (the fund that received the proceeds) as a liability rather than as an other source of financing. The debt should be reported net of discounts or premiums, if any. Issuance costs and out-of-pocket costs should be reported as an expenditure, rather than netted against the carrying value of the debt.

Long-term vendor financing Long-term notes issued to financing operations should be accounted for in a manner consistent with the standards established by APB-21. Essentially, long-term vendor notes must carrying a reasonable interest rate, otherwise a reasonable effective interest rate must be imputed and the original transaction must be recorded at its fair value.

Debt extinguishment/defeasance Extinguishments, defeasances, and refundings of operating debt should be accounted for in accordance with GASB-7 (Advance Refundings Resulting in Defeasance of Debt), except a gain or loss (difference between the carrying value of the debt and the cost to retire the debt) should be recognized on the governmental entity's statement of operations.

Proceeds from a single refunding debt issuance may be used to extinguish, defease, or refund debt reported in the GLTDAG and in governmental funds. In this case, an appropriate allocation should be observed between the two types of debt outstanding and the accounting standards applicable to each type of debt (general long-term capital debt and operating debt) should be followed.

Expendable Trust Funds

The measurement focus and basis of accounting described in the proposed Statement are applicable to Expendable Trust Funds.

> *OBSERVATION: Presently, there is an inconsistency in the standards with respect to fixed assets and long-term liabilities of an Expendable Trust Fund. Fixed assets and long-term liabilities are both reported in the Expendable Trust Fund rather than in the governmental entity's account groups even though they do not represent expendable resources of the fund or claims against current expendable resources. The proposed Statement would rectify this inconsistency because of the change in the measurement focus of a governmental fund.*

Effective Date

The proposed Statement would be applicable to financial statements for periods beginning after June 15, 1993. Early application of the standards established by the proposed Statement is not permitted because the GASB continues to research a number of related topics. These latter topics are expected to result in statements that will have the same effective date as the proposed Statement discussed in this Appendix.

APPENDIX
MEASUREMENT FOCUS FOR GOVERNMENTAL BUSINESS-TYPE ACTIVITIES (DISCUSSION MEMORANDUM)

As discussed earlier in this chapter, governmental business type activities are accounted for using the same measurement focus and basis of accounting used by a commercial enterprise (flow of economic resources and accrual basis). The previous Appendix discussed the GASB Exposure Draft that proposes both a new measurement focus and basis of accounting for governmental-type activities. There has also been an interest in the appropriateness of the measurement focus and basis of accounting for business-type activities conducted by a governmental entity. This Appendix discusses recent developments with respect to business-type activities.

In September 1988, the GASB issued a Discussion Memorandum entitled "Measurement Focus of Governmental Business-Type Activities or Entities." The Discussion Memorandum raises the fundamental issues of what activities should be classified as governmental business-type activities and which measurement focus should be used to account for governmental business-type activities. The issues presented in the GASB Discussion Memorandum are summarized below.

Business-Type Activities

NCGA Statement-1 describes the circumstances under which Enterprise Funds should be used to account for activities of a governmental entity.

> . . . to account for operations (a) that are financed and operated in a manner similar to private business enterprises—where the intent of the governing body is that the costs (expenses, including depreciation) of providing goods or services to the general public on a continuing basis be financed or recovered primarily through user charges; or (b) where the governing body has decided that periodic determination of revenues earned, expenses incurred, and/or net income is appropriate for capital maintenance, public policy, management control, accountability, or other purposes (paragraph 26).

In practice, the application of the above criteria has resulted in noncomparable financial reporting, where one governmental entity may account for a specific activity in an Enterprise Fund while another entity may account for a similar activity in the General Fund or a Special Revenue Fund.

Opponents of the current criteria argue that the phrase *intent of the governing body* allows too much discretion in determining which governmental activities are of a business-type. Likewise, the second part of the description allows the governmental entity to identify governmental business-type activities when it decides that periodic determination of net income is appropriate.

As a possible resolution to the problem of defining governmental business-type activities, the Discussion Memorandum identifies the following alternative definitions:

- Any governmental activity for which there are a significant number of private business enterprise counterparts
- Any governmental activity that charges a fee or fees for services where the revenues generated by those fees are other than incidental
- Any governmental activity that charges a fee or fees for services where the revenues generated by those fees are other than incidental and management's pricing policy is to recoup costs (including depreciation) and maintain capital

Significant number of business counterparts Under this definition, the number of governmental activities that would be considered business-type would increase. The definition does not require the employment of a user fee or the existence of specific management intent. For this reason, many of the activities accounted for currently in governmental funds would be reported in an Enterprise Fund or similar fund. Opponents of the use of a "specific number" criterion believe that (1) excessive judgment would have to be used by management and (2) the results of identifying governmental business-type activities would not be uniform.

Fees not incidental This definition of governmental business-type activities is not as broad as the previous definition (significant number); nonetheless, it is likely that governmental functions not currently accounted for in an Enterprise Fund would meet the definition of a business-type activity under the nonincidental fee criterion. For example, some activities currently accounted for in Special Revenue Funds would have to be accounted for in Enterprise Funds. Opponents argue that many activities that are based on a fee are heavily subsidized and the purpose of the fee is not to maintain capital or to cover all operating costs.

Fees not incidental/full cost recovery The most restrictive definition identified in the Discussion Memorandum requires that activities are business-type only when a nonincidental fee is charged and the purpose of the pricing policy is to recover all costs, including depreciation and similar charges. Thus, only those activities that are self-sustaining would be accounted for in an Enterprise Fund under this definition. Opponents of this definition argue that the identification of a pricing policy is too judgmental and that objective criteria are not available to classify activities as governmental-type or business-type.

In addition to the three alternative definitions discussed above, the Discussion Memorandum points out that governmental business-type activities may be presented in alternative ways. For example, governmental business-type activities could be presented in a governmental fund using the measurement focus for governmental activities; however, relevant information presented on another measurement focus could be presented as supplementary information. A second presentation alternative is to use the measurement focus for governmental funds when governmental business-type activities are presented in general purpose financial statements, but use another measurement focus if governmental business-type activities are presented in separately issued financial statements.

Measurement Focus

Once governmental business-type activities are defined, it is necessary to identify which measurement focus should be used to account for the activities. The Discussion Memorandum emphasizes that more than one measurement focus could be established. That is, as alluded to earlier, a *primary* measurement focus could be used to present the governmental business-type activities in specific financial statements, while a *secondary* measurement focus could be used to present such activities as supplementary information.

The two alternatives discussed in the Discussion Memorandum are the flow of total financial resources measurement focus and the flow of economic resources measurement focus.

Financial resources As noted in the previous Appendix, the GASB has tentatively identified the flow of financial resources as the measurement focus that will be used for governmental-type activities. If the same measurement focus were adopted for governmental business-type activities, the financial statements for all funds would be comparable and consolidated (or combined) financial statements for the governmental entity could be prepared. Under current reporting standards, the financial statements cannot be aggregated because one group of funds (governmental funds) uses the flow of expendable resources and another group of funds (proprietary funds) uses the flow of economic resources.

Economic resources Those who support the flow of economic resources measurement focus for governmental business-type activities argue that the financial statements should reflect the results of utilizing all of the economic resources employed by a governmental entity. Only with the computation and presentation of net income, it is argued, can an entity be adequately evaluated with respect to resources employed. In short, the need for comparability of all financial information presented in the governmental financial statements should not overshadow the usefulness of the information being presented.

The critical evaluation of the current measurement focus used to account for governmental business-type activities is only one of several GASB projects that are interrelated. The other projects include the identification of a measurement focus for governmental-type activities and the accounting for capital assets. To some extent, these projects, as well as other projects, are part of the GASB's ambitious drive to significantly modify the current governmental accounting model.

THE GOVERNMENTAL REPORTING ENTITY

The fund is the basic unit for establishing accountability for activities specifically established by laws, regulations, and other governmental mandates. Each fund consists of self-balancing accounts, including accounts for the fund's assets, liabilities, and residual fund balance. A governmental unit's activities may be reflected in a number of governmental funds, proprietary funds, fiduciary funds, and account groups. In addition, agencies, authorities, and other governmental entities with their various funds may be created by a state or local government. Ultimately, overall financial statements of the state or local government must be prepared, which raises the question as to which funds should be included in these broad-based financial statements. The initial step in resolving this question is concerned with the conceptual definition of a reporting entity.

The definition of the reporting unit must be carefully considered because the inadvertent inclusion or exclusion of a governmental unit can distort the reporting entity's financial statements. NCGA-3 (Defining the Governmental Reporting Entity) concludes that criteria for defining the reporting entity are needed for the following reasons:

- They provide a basis for (1) comparing one governmental unit with another governmental unit and (2) comparing the same governmental unit over two or more reporting periods (Comparability Objective).
- They discourage the arbitrary inclusion/exclusion of governmental components from the reporting entity's financial statements (Comprehensiveness Objective).
- They facilitate the evaluation of elected officials' performances for all relevant governmental operations (Responsibility and Control Objectives).

> **OBSERVATION:** *The criteria for defining a reporting entity in NCGA-3 appear to be biased in that they tend to favor the inclusion rather than the exclusion of a unit in the reporting entity. For this reason, a preparer of governmental financial statements should be cautious in excluding units from the reporting entity when applying these very broad criteria.*

THE REPORTING ENTITY

The identification of the governmental reporting entity begins with the elected legislative body, such as a state legislature or a city council. The particular state or local government prepares an overall financial statement which includes all component units referred to as the Comprehensive Annual Financial Report (CAFR), which includes the following broad categories:

- Introductory Section
- Financial Section
  - Auditor's Report
  - General Purpose Financial Statements (including notes to the financial statements)
  - Combining and Individual Fund Statements
  - Supplemental Information
- Statistical Section

A fundamental assumption is that all governmental activities are ultimately responsible to an elected body, and most activities will be reported in a state or local government's CAFR. Ideally, the activity should be reported in the financial statements of the *lowest level of legislative authority*. In some instances, it may be necessary for representatives of different levels of government to jointly agree where a particular activity should be reported.

The reporting entity may consist of an oversight unit and component units, which are defined in NCGA-7 (Financial Reporting for Component Units Within the Governmental Reporting Entity) as follows:

> *Oversight Unit*   The component unit which has the ability to exercise the basic criterion of oversight responsibility (as defined in NCGA-3) over component units. Typically, an oversight unit is the primary unit of government directly responsible to the chief executive and the elected legislative body.
>
> *Component Unit*   A separate governmental unit, agency or nonprofit corporation which, pursuant to the criteria in NCGA-3, is combined with other component units to constitute the reporting entity.

The financial statements of the oversight unit and the component units that are considered to be part of the reporting entity constitute the CAFR. In some instances it may be appropriate for a component unit to issue its own financial report, which is called the Component Unit Financial Report (CUFR).

NCGA-3 established the criteria to be used in determining whether a governmental unit should be combined with the oversight unit to form the reporting entity. These guidelines can be grouped into basic criteria and other criteria.

Basic Criteria

A component unit should be part of the reporting entity when it is overseen by and, thus, to some degree controlled by the governmental unit directly responsible to the chief executive and the legislative body. To determine what constitutes oversight responsibility, the following characteristics of the relationship between the oversight component and the potential component unit should be evaluated:

- Financial interdependency
- Selection of governing authority
- Designation of management
- Ability to significantly influence operations
- Accountability for fiscal matters

> *OBSERVATION: To determine whether a governmental unit should be part of a reporting entity requires the evaluation of all relevant factors and the application of the five criteria established by NCGA-3; however, a positive response to the financial interdependency criterion may be sufficient to warrant the inclusion of the unit in the reporting entity while it may take more than one positive response to the other four criteria to justify inclusion of the unit.*

Financial interdependency Although oversight responsibility is generally suggested by more than one of the five characteristics listed above, the most important indication of a dependent relationship between the oversight and component units is financial interdependency. Financial interdependency suggests that the potential component unit either creates a financial burden or a financial benefit for the oversight component. If the oversight unit is ultimately financially responsible for a component unit's deficit, this relationship would indicate a financial interdependency. The same interdependency would be suggested when the oversight unit is entitled to any surplus that may arise from the potential component unit's operations. In addition, it is likely that a component unit would be considered part of the reporting entity when the oversight unit directly guarantees the debt of the component unit or indirectly guarantees the debt through a "moral commitment" to pay.

Selection of governing authority Every component unit has a governing authority that is responsible for the activities it conducts. When an elected official appoints the governing authority, it must be determined whether the component unit should be part of the reporting entity. A key ingredient in making this determination depends upon whether the appointment is authoritative. NCGA-3 defines an authoritative appointment as "one where the elected official maintains a significant continuing relationship with the appointed official with respect to carrying out important public functions." The following situations would generally suggest that the oversight component unit has oversight responsibility with respect to the component unit and should be included in the reporting entity. In the cases below, a city or county is the reporting entity:

- A mayor appoints, with city council approval, the governing board of a public housing authority that uses federal funds to subsidize public housing.
- A city appoints the governing board of a public corporation which receives title to properties owned by the city in order to facilitate urban renewal within the city.
- A county flood control district created by the state legislature is governed by the same county board that governs the county itself.
- A city creates a nonprofit corporation that provides EDP services for a fee to the city and other governmental entities, and all members of the corporation's board are appointed by the mayor.

On the other hand, the following relationships would suggest that the potential component unit should not be considered part of the reporting entity:

- A city's school system is separately chartered by the state legislature and its board, the governing authority, is elected by the public.

- A nonprofit corporation administers a museum that is on land owned by a city. Contributing members of the museum elect its governing board.
- An industrial development corporation created by the city council is governed by a board appointed by the mayor although a member of the board cannot be removed by the mayor or city council without just cause.
- A city owns all the operating assets of a mass transit corporation created by the state legislature and a majority of the corporation's governing board is appointed by the governor while the other members are appointed by the mayor.
- A finance corporation is created by the state legislature to assist a financially distressed city. The corporation's governing board of the finance corporation is appointed by the governor of the state.

> **OBSERVATION:** *As might be expected in applying the five criteria established by NCGA-3, often some of the criteria may suggest inclusion of the unit in the reporting entity while others will suggest exclusion. For example, in the above illustration it is suggested that the application of the "selection of governing authority" criterion would suggest a finance corporation created by the state to assist a financially distressed city would not be part of the city's reporting entity because the governing board was appointed by the governor of the state; however, as discussed later in this chapter, the unit was included in the reporting entity due to the special financial relationship between the finance corporation and the city. Thus, the application of the criteria must be evaluated in the context of the overall relationship of the potential oversight unit and component unit. Professional judgment, not the narrow application of the guidelines, must govern.*

Designation of management When the management of a component unit is appointed by and held accountable to another unit that is included in the reporting entity, the component unit should also be part of the reporting entity. If the relationship between the potential oversight unit and the component unit does not include the appointment authority or the authority is more of a ceremonial function, a closer analysis of the relationship must be made. The analysis should, in effect, determine whether there are indications of an employer—employee relationship between the two entities. The following relationships would suggest that the oversight function does exist between two units, and the component unit should be considered to be part of the reporting entity:

- A city creates an urban renewal corporation, appoints its governing board, and approves the board's selection of corporate executives.
- A county flood control district created by the state legislature is governed by the same board that governs the county itself, and the flood control district's management reports to a district director that is appointed by the county's governing body.
- The majority of the board of directors of a state-created mass transit corporation operating within a city are appointed by the state and the remaining members are appointed by the mayor, but the city's mayor approves the selection of all corporate executives.

The following situations would suggest that the unit be excluded from the reporting entity:

- A city school system is administered by a school board elected by the public, and the school board is responsible for the hiring of school district personnel.
- A mayor appoints the members of the governing board of a public housing authority, but the governing board hires the authority's executives.
- A city-created industrial corporation's board is appointed by the mayor, but the board hires corporate executives that staff the various operating departments of the corporation.

> **OBSERVATION:** *While NCGA-3 identifies the financial interdependency criterion as the most "significant manifestation of oversight responsibility," it does not rank the other four criteria as to importance; howerver, the "designation of management" criterion is probably the weakest argument for including a unit in a reporting entity.*

Ability to significantly influence operations Oversight responsibility can be demonstrated when a potential component unit's operations can be significantly influenced by another unit. Specific examples of influence would include budgetary authority over the component unit, control over the component unit's properties, and the ability to function as the contracting authority for the unit. The following circumstances would generally suggest that the subordinate unit should be part of the reporting entity:

- A city's public housing authority's governing board authorizes subsidy contracts pursuant to regulations established by the U.S. Department of Housing and Urban Development; however, the city council must approve contracts that exceed a specified amount.
- A city creates a separate nonprofit corporation that provides EDP services to the city and other governmental entities, and sales to the city account for 90 percent of the corporation's total revenue.

The following relationships suggest that the ability to significantly influence operations does not exist and that the potential component unit should not be part of the reporting entity:

- A city's school board has the right of eminent domain and the authority to acquire equipment without approval from the city.
- A nonprofit corporation administers a city's museum, and the museum's governing body determines the use of museum properties and approves contracts for the acquisition of goods and services.
- A city's industrial development corporation's governing body is appointed by the mayor, but the city has no responsibility for the routine operations of the corporation.
- A city owns all of the operating assets of a mass transit authority. The governor appoints the majority of the authority's governing board and the board determines the services to be provided and has the authority to enter into various contracts.

Accountability for fiscal matters A component unit should be part of the reporting entity when "absolute authority over all funds is vested within the jurisdiction of either a constitutional officer, a management official, or a governing authority that is within the entity." The inclusion of the component unit in the reporting entity is not as certain when (1) there is no absolute authority over all funds of the unit or (2) there is a direct relationship between the oversight unit and the potential component unit but there is a lack of governing authority over, or management responsibility for, the potential component unit. In the latter two circumstances, judgment must be used to determine whether to include the potential component unit. Factors to be considered in this analysis are (1) budgetary authority, (2) responsibility for surpluses or deficits, (3) fiscal management, and (4) revenue characteristics.

Budgetary authority Accountability for fiscal matters would be suggested when the oversight unit has powers such as the approval of authorizations for budgetary appropriations or the approval of amendments to the budget. The following examples would suggest that the component unit should be included in the reporting entity:

- A city's school system, which is administered by a separately elected school board, must submit its annual budget to the city council for approval.
- A city creates an urban renewal corporation which is administered by a governing board. But the mayor and city council must review and approve the corporation's annual budget, and changes in the budget during the year must also be approved.

Surplus/deficit An indication of accountability for fiscal matters can be analyzed by determining whether the oversight unit is entitled to any operating surplus or responsible for financing deficits. If the oversight unit must be consulted in determining the disposition of an operating surplus, there is a suggestion of fiscal accountability. On the other hand, when the oversight unit has no responsibility to fund operating deficits, the accountability-for-fiscal-matters argument is weakened.

Fiscal management Another factor that should be considered when evaluating the component unit is the oversight unit's involvement in the component unit's fiscal management. Fiscal management would include such elements as responsibility for the collection and disbursement of funds, the ownership of assets, and the authority to require an audit of the accounts.

Revenue characteristics The component unit's source of revenues should be analyzed to determine whether the source is a public levy or charge, in which case there is a presumption that the unit should be included in the reporting entity. NCGA-3 defines a public levy as follows:

Public The origin of authority for making the levy or charge lies with elected officials of the entity, or persons appointed by these elected officials, or there exists a delegation, but not an abrogation, of the power to levy or charge; the authority or power would include the ability to determine the nature and type of tax imposed for the fee collected.

Levy or charge The imposition of a monetary payment, the proceeds of which are applicable to and for the benefit of the citizens served by the level of government imposing the levy or charge. The power to levy would include the determination of terms of the levy and establishment of the method of administration.

The following revenue characteristics would suggest that the component unit's revenue is derived from a public levy or charge:

- A city's school system, which is administered by a separately elected school board, gets its funding from taxes levied and collected by the city.
- A nonprofit corporation administers a city's museum, and although the museum's source of funding includes gifts and endowments, it also includes visitors' fees and a tax levied by the city.
- A city creates a separate nonprofit corporation that provides EDP services to the city and other governmental entities, and the city establishes the billing rate at 15 percent above the cost of providing the service.

In contrast to the traits described above, the revenue characteristics described below would suggest that the potential component unit be excluded from the reporting entity:

- A city creates an urban renewal corporation, but the source of operating revenues is grants provided by the federal government.
- An industrial development corporation created by the city finances its operations through fees charged to commercial enterprises.

The criteria (financial interdependency, selection of governing authority, designation of management, ability to significantly influence operations and accountability for fiscal matters) require the exercise of judgment to determine the scope of the reporting entity.

Often some of the basic criteria will suggest inclusion of a component unit while the other basic criteria will suggest exclusion. All five criteria must be reviewed from a broad perspective to arrive at a final decision.

> **OBSERVATION:** *Not all governmental units are applying the five basic criteria described above to determine the financial reporting scope of governmental entities. In the Council of State Governments' research report entitled* Preferred Accounting Practices for State Governments, *it is noted that "in almost all cases general purpose reports issued by states were based on statutory authority and included those component parts of the state which were the bookkeeping responsibility of the office issuing the report." The research report recommends that state statutes, which vary significantly from state to state, should not be used as the basis for defining the state reporting entity.*

> **OBSERVATION:** *A single unit of government may consist of several independently elected officials. The activities under the control of these officials may be autonomous because they may, for example, have their own revenue source. In this circumstance, a positive response to only one criterion may strongly suggest that the independent activity under the control of the elected official be included in the state or local governmental reporting entity. An example may be an independently elected state auditor, county sheriff, or local tax collector.*

Other Criteria

In most instances, the use of the five basic criteria is sufficient to properly define the reporting entity. There may be situations in which the application of the basic criteria has suggested that oversight responsibility does not exist but the unit should nonetheless be included in the reporting entity. Under this circumstance, criteria other than basic oversight criteria, namely scope of public service and special financing relationships, must be evaluated to ensure that the financial statements of the reporting entity are not misleading.

Scope of public service When the degree of oversight responsibility is relatively minor between the oversight unit and the potential component unit, the scope of the public service performed may be of such a nature that the unit should not be excluded from the reporting entity. This may occur when either (1) the activity is for the benefit of the reporting entity or its residents or (2) the activity is performed in the geographical area of the reporting entity and generally available to the citizens of the reporting entity. The following situations would suggest that the component unit be included in the reporting entity's financial statements even when only partial oversight responsibility exists:

- A city's school system is administered by a school board elected by the public but the educational services are available only to city residents.
- A city's urban renewal authority's basic objectives are to return properties to the public tax rolls and provide employment for the city's residents.
- A city creates a separate nonprofit corporation that provides EDP services mainly to the city in order to acquire facilities and hire personnel outside the normal conditions imposed on a governmental agency.

Special financial relationships There may be special financial relationships between the reporting entity and another entity that override the exclusion of the other unit from the reporting entity because of the lack of any degree of oversight responsibility. For example, a special state-created authority may have been established to provide financing for a financially distressed city. Even though the city has no oversight responsibility, the state-created authority should be included in the city's financial statements in order to adequately portray the financial condition of the city.

> **OBSERVATION:** As noted earlier, a fundamental assumption of governmental financial reporting is that all governmental functions are ultimately responsible to elected officials and presumably must be a component part of financial statements directly related to the governmental unit under the control of elected officials. Thus, a dilemma arises when it is concluded that a governmental unit not controlled by elected officials is not part of an oversight unit. Is it possible that an activity is beyond the oversight responsibility of elected officials at all levels of government? This does not appear likely, but the issue is not addressed in the governmental standards. NCGA-3 and NCGA-7 present nine illustrations of potential component units and all but two are concluded to be part of an oversight unit. Of the two not considered to be part of an oversight unit, one appears

to be a nonprofit organization (museum) that would report on an independent basis, and the other one is an industrial development corporation. It is hard to understand how an industrial development corporation created by a governmental unit would not ultimately fall under its domain.

Evaluation of Criteria

All relevant information concerning the basic criteria and other criteria should be gathered as a starting point in the determination of whether to include a potential component unit in the reporting entity. Relationships between the oversight unit and the potential component unit may be complex, *but the substance of the relationship, not the legal basis of the relationship,* should be the foundation for the final determination.

After the relevant information has been gathered and the relationships properly described, the criteria are evaluated without ranking them in terms of importance. No one criterion is more important than another criterion. In some instances, only a single criterion may have been met, but the criterion is so significant in a particular situation that the unit should nevertheless be part of the reporting entity. It is even possible that none of the criteria have been met but in order to avoid the distortion of the reporting entity's financial statements, the component unit should be included. Thus, the criteria form only a framework for evaluation, and the final decision is always based on professional judgment applied in the context of a specific relationship.

> **OBSERVATION:** There is an apparent inconsistency with respect to the ranking of criteria. NCGA-3 (paragraph 10) states that the most significant manifestation of oversight is financial interdependency. However, NCGA Interpretation-7 (paragraph 11) concludes that the criteria are not ranked, and no one criterion outweighs any other.

The criteria used in determining whether a potential component unit should be part of a reporting entity are summarized in Exhibit I.

Disclosures

The scope of the reporting entity and the criteria used to define the reporting entity should be described in a note to the financial statements. Also, the component units included in the reporting entity and the criteria used to justify the inclusion of the component units should be disclosed in a note. An example of a note describing the reporting entity is illustrated in Exhibit II.

When a unit is excluded from the reporting entity and some of the criteria suggested that the unit be included, the specific reason for exclusion must be disclosed. Exhibit III presents an example of a note to the financial statements that describes why a potential component unit was not included in the reporting entity.

> **OBSERVATION:** *Also, it is probably a good rule of thumb to discuss in the notes to the financial statements any governmental entity that contains the name of the reporting entity even though it satisfies none of the inclusion criteria.*

NCGA-7 notes that a component unit may use accounting principles and reporting standards that are generally acceptable but are not in accordance with governmental generally accepted accounting principles. If it is concluded that the inclusion of the component unit would distort the presentation of a fund type's financial statements, the component unit may be presented in a separate column (discrete presentation) of the reporting entity's financial statements. Under this circumstance, a note to the reporting entity's financial statements should explain the component unit's accounting policies and its relationship with the oversight entity.

> **OBSERVATION:** *A strong argument can be made that this provision of NCGA-7 is applicable only under very restrictive circumstances. The GASB structural agreement in 1984 concluded that the GASB is authorized to establish accounting and reporting standards for state and local governments while the FASB is responsible for establishing accounting and reporting standards for all other entities. When the financial statements of entities such as utilities, authorities, hospitals, colleges and universities, and pension plans are included in a state or local government's financial statements, GASB pronouncements are more authoritative than FASB pronouncements. Apparently, the only circumstances under which the provision of NCGA-7 would prevail would be when a GASB (or NCGA) pronouncement has not addressed an accounting or reporting issue but the issue has been addressed by the FASB, or through practice an accounting principle or standard different from nonpromulgated governmental generally accepted accounting principles has gained general acceptance.*

The Governmental Reporting Entity

EXHIBIT I
REPORTING ENTITY CRITERIA

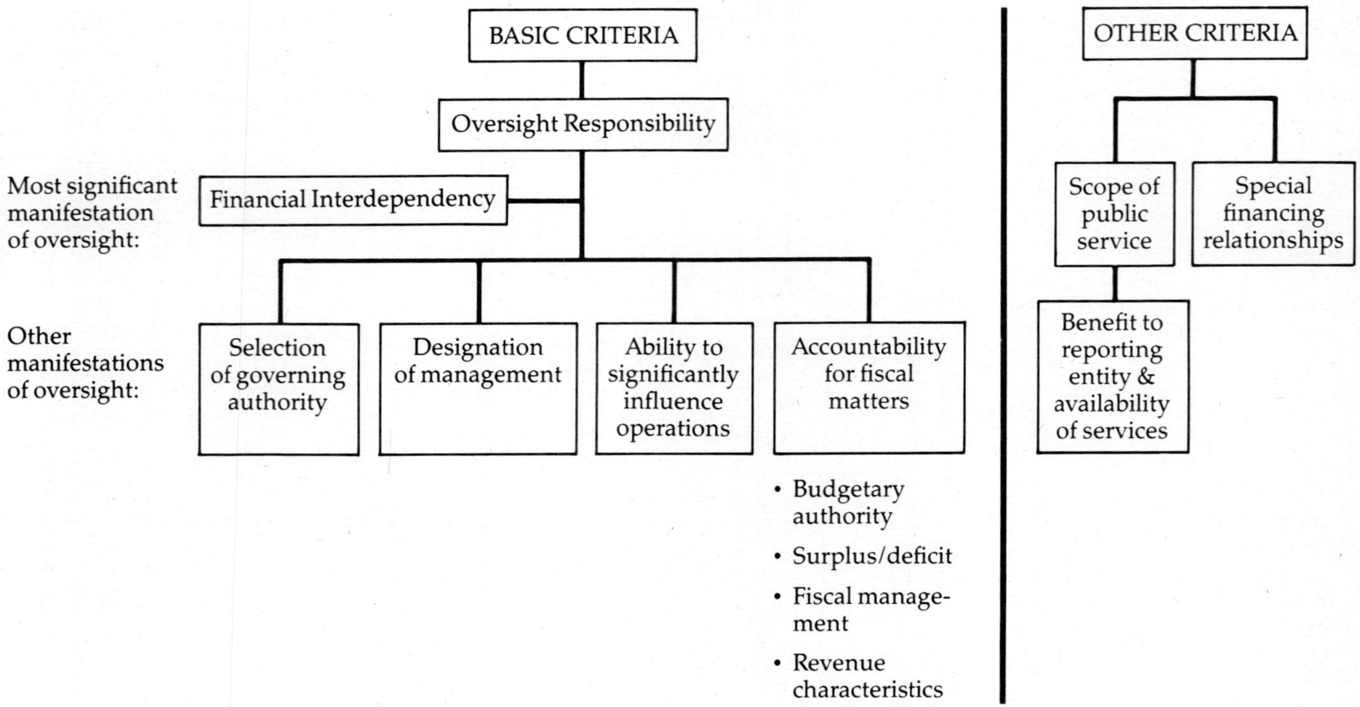

OTHER CRITERIA
- Special financing relationships
- Scope of public service
- Benefit to reporting entity & availability of services

BASIC CRITERIA

Oversight Responsibility

Most significant manifestation of oversight:
- Financial Interdependency

Other manifestations of oversight:
- Selection of governing authority
- Designation of management
- Ability to significantly influence operations
- Accountability for fiscal matters
  - Budgetary authority
  - Surplus/deficit
  - Fiscal management
  - Revenue characteristics

4.14 / GOVERNMENTAL GAAP GUIDE

EXHIBIT II
ILLUSTRATIVE NOTE DESCRIBING THE REPORTING ENTITY

Note 1: Reporting Entity

The City of Centerville was created in 1919 and operates under an elected Mayor/Council form of government. The city's major operations include health services, public safety, fire protection, recreation and parks, and general administrative services. In addition, the City of Centerville exercises sufficient control over other governmental agencies and authorities that are included as part of the city's reporting entity. Agencies and authorities which were evaluated for possible inclusion in the reporting entity and the criteria used as the basis for evaluation are summarized below.

	MANIFESTATION OF OVERSIGHT RESPONSIBILITY					OTHER CRITERIA		
	Financial Interde-pendency	Governing Authority Selection	Designation of Management	Influence on Operations	Accountability for Fiscal Matters	Scope of Public Service	Special Financing Relationship	Included in Reporting Entity
Centerville School District	yes	no	no	no	yes	yes	n/a	YES
Public Housing Corporation of Centerville	yes	yes	no	yes	yes	yes	n/a	YES
Centerville Museum	no	no	no	no	no	no	yes	NO
Centerville Urban Renewal Corporation	yes	yes	yes	no	yes	yes	yes	YES
Industrial Development Corporation of Centerville	no	no	no	no	no	yes	n/a	NO
Centerville Flood Control District	yes	yes	yes	yes	yes	yes	n/a	YES
Centerville Transit Authority	yes	no	yes	no	yes	yes	yes	YES

EXHIBIT III

Illustrative Note Describing Basis for Excluding Units from the Reporting Entity

NOTE 2: Financial Statements not Included in Reporting Entity

As discussed in Note 1, the City of Centerville's financial statements do not include the Centerville Museum or the Industrial Development Corporation of Centerville. A description of these entities and the reasons for their exclusion from the reporting entity are summarized below.

Centerville Museum

The Centerville Museum was organized in 1951 and construction of its facilities began the following year on land owned by the city. Currently, the city leases the land to the museum, and this relationship suggests that the museum should be part of the reporting entity. However, the following factors suggest that the museum should not be included in the reporting entity:

- Contributors to the museum elect all the members of the governing board.
- The governing board is solely responsible for the employment of museum personnel.
- The museum's management is solely responsible for the day-to-day operations of the museum.
- The city is neither entitled to operating surpluses nor responsible for operating deficits of the museum.
- The museum is exclusively responsible for administration of its fiscal affairs.
- The museum is open to the public-at-large and not exclusively for the enjoyment of residents of Centerville.

Based on these factors, it has been concluded that the City of Centerville has no oversight responsibility for the museum, and therefore the financial statements of the museum are excluded from the reporting entity.

Industrial Development Corporation of Centerville

The Industrial Development Corporation of Centerville was organized in 1972 to promote and develop commercial and industrial properties, and encourage employment within the city. The following factors strongly suggest that the unit be excluded from the reporting entity's financial statements:

- The corporation's governing board is approved by the mayor, but there is no continuing relationship between the corporation and the city.
- The management of the corporation is selected by the governing board.
- The operation of the corporation is the exclusive responsibility of the corporation's management and the city has no authority to interfere with these operations.
- The corporation is responsible for its financial affairs, including the funding of deficits and the disposition of surpluses.
- The city does not guarantee the corporation's outstanding debt.

Although the city must approve the corporation's issuance of debt and the corporation operates within the geographical boundaries of the city, these factors were not considered significant enough to warrant inclusion of the corporation in the financial statements of the City of Centerville.

GASB Research Project

The GASB has established Research Project 3-3 (Reexamination of NCGA-3 and NCGA-7) to reconsider the definition of a governmental reporting entity, including the reporting of discrete activities and joint ventures.

LITERATURE REFERENCES

Material in this chapter is based on the following authoritative pronouncements which are grouped according to the major headings used within the chapter. A dual reference (both paragraph and page number) is used for NCGA-1 and NCGA-2 because the original pronouncements do not use paragraph numbers.

The Governmental Reporting Entity

Introduction
NCGA-3   *Defining the Governmental Reporting Entity,* ¶¶ 5 and 7.

The Reporting Entity
NCGA-3   *Defining the Governmental Reporting Entity,* ¶¶ 4 and 8.
NCGA-1   *Governmental Accounting and Financial Reporting Principles,* pp. 21-22/ ¶ 139.
NCGA-7   *Financial Reporting for Component Units Within the Governmental Reporting Entity,* ¶ 5.

Basic Criteria
NCGA-3   *Defining the Governmental Reporting Entity,* ¶¶ 3, 9, 10, 13, 14, 16 and 17 and the appendix.
NCGA INTERPRETATION-7   *Clarification as to the Application of the Criteria in NCGA Statement 3 Defining the Governmental Reporting Entity,* ¶ 5 and Appendix B.

Other Criteria
NCGA-3   *Defining the Governmental Reporting Entity,* ¶ 11.
NCGA INTERPRETATION-7   *Clarification as to the Application of the Criteria in NCGA Statement 3 Defining the Governmental Reporting Entity,* Appendix A.

Evaluation of Criteria
NCGA-3   *Defining The Governmental Reporting Entity,* ¶¶ 12 and 16.
NCGA INTERPRETATION-7   *Clarification as to the Application of the Criteria in NCGA Statement 3 Defining the Governmental Reporting Entity,* ¶¶ 3, 10, 11 and 12.

Disclosures
NCGA-3   *Defining the Governmental Reporting Entity,* ¶ 15.
NCGA-7   *Financial Reporting for Component Units Within the Governmental Reporting Entity,* ¶¶ 9 and 23.

APPENDIX
THE FINANCIAL REPORTING ENTITY
(DISCUSSION MEMORANDUM)

In June 1988, the GASB issued a Discussion Memorandum entitled "The Financial Reporting Entity" to gather comments concerning current practices and possible alternative criteria used to determine the scope of the governmental financial reporting entity. Currently, the criteria for determining the governmental financial reporting entity are addressed in NCGA-3 (Defining the Governmental Reporting Entity), NCGA-7 (Financial Reporting for Component Units Within the Governmental Reporting Entity), and NCGA Interpretation-7 (Clarification as to the Application of the Criteria in NCGA Statement-3 Defining the Governmental Reporting Entity). There is, however, uncertainty in how to the apply these criteria. There is also disagreement as to which financial reporting method should be used to present the combined financial statements of the primary governmental unit and component units.

Currently, the criteria for defining the reporting entity are based on two concepts. First, criteria should reflect the concept that the reporting entity is defined in a broad manner. Opponents of the current criteria argue that such a broad definition results in the inclusion of some component units that should not be considered a part of the reporting entity. Second, criteria should reflect the assumption that all functions of government are ultimately the responsibility of elected officials. This concept suggests that all functions should eventually be included in the financial statements of the primary governmental unit, which is directed by elected officials. Opponents of the second concept note that certain governmental functions are independent of city, county, or state governmental units and should not be considered a part of another reporting entity.

The Discussion Memorandum also notes that there is concern with the methods used to integrate the financial statements of component units into the overall financial report. Current practice encourages the use of the *blending* method, where a component unit's accounts and transactions are merged with the primary governmental unit as if the activities of the component unit were originally accounted for directly in the records of the primary governmental unit. Opponents argue that other methods, such as discrete presentation and disclosures in notes, should be used.

In general, the Discussion Memorandum raises the issues of what components should be included in the governmental financial reporting entity and how component information should be included in the financial report. These issues are discussed below.

Criteria for Evaluating a Potential Component Unit

As discussed earlier in this chapter, the criteria used to determine whether a potential component unit should be included in a governmental reporting entity are (1) ability to exercise oversight responsibility, (2) scope of public service, and (3) special financing relationship. The evaluation of the ability to exercise oversight responsibility is determined by considering (1) financial interdependency, (2) selection of governing authority, (3) designation of management, (4) ability to significantly influence operations, and (5) accountability for fiscal matters.

Some argue that the current guidance for determining the ability to exercise oversight responsibility is not well defined: Although it is clear that there are a number of factors that must be considered, there is no indication of which factors, if any, are the dominant ones. The result is an inconsistent application of the criteria, which results in governmental reporting entities similar from an operational perspective but not comparable from a reporting perspective. To correct this perceived deficiency, the Discussion Memorandum notes that some suggest that either a conceptual or quantitative benchmark be established. Once the benchmark is achieved, the potential component unit will be included in the reporting entity.

If a conceptual benchmark is established, professional judgment becomes the basis for determining which potential component units should be included in the reporting entity. In this case, however, there is a potential for preparers of governmental financial reports to apply the conceptual benchmark in an inconsistent manner. On the other hand, if a quantitative benchmark is established, a certain degree of arbitrariness is inherent in the evaluation process.

The GASB is faced with the difficult task of establishing criteria that can be applied with consistent results, yet allowing for a degree of professional judgment to reasonably ensure that governmental financial reporting entities will be meaningfully defined.

Integrating Component Unit Information into the Financial Report

Once it is determined that a potential component unit should be part of the financial reporting entity, consideration must be given to the method selected to include the component unit's financial information with the primary governmental unit's financial report.

The use of various methods of inclusion suggests that there are different relationships between a primary governmental unit and its component units. With respect to this suggestion, the Discussion Memorandum raises the following question.

> Should financial reporting convey the totality of the primary government and its component units as if the totality was an entity in itself, or should financial reporting attempt to show the nuances of the relationships between the primary government and its component units so that it portrays the financial effect of the components on the primary government?

The Discussion Memorandum notes that the following methods may be used to include the financial statements of a component unit in the reporting entity:

- Full integration
- Partial integration
- Nonintegration (note disclosure)
- Combination of the above methods

Full integration Under the full integration method, the financial information of the primary governmental unit and the component unit are presented as if the activities of the component unit were an integral part of the primary governmental unit's activities. Those opposed to the full integration method suggest that the resulting financial report may convey a false impression that the assets of the component unit are available to, and the liabilities of the component unit are obligations of, the primary governmental unit. Also, it is argued that the mixing of the financial information makes it difficult to identify information applicable only to the primary government.

Partial integration Under the partial integration method, it is argued that the financial information of the component unit is presented on the face of the reporting entity's financial statements, with the manner of presentation allowing for the identification of financial information applicable to the primary governmental unit. Two examples of partial integration techniques include discrete presentation and the equity method.

The discrete presentation technique displays the component unit's financial information in a separate column. This technique can be applied in various ways. For example, there could be a separate column for each component unit, a single column for all component units, or multiple columns of component units based on functional activities or fund type.

The equity method presentation displays the net equity (assets minus liabilities) of the component unit in the reporting entity's balance sheet. Likewise, the component unit's results of operations are presented as a single item in the reporting entity's activity statement.

Nonintegration Nonintegration of the component unit's financial information is achieved through note disclosure. It is argued that nonintegration does not distort the financial information applicable to the primary government, although interested parties can integrate relevant information contained in the note with the primary governmental unit if they desire.

Combination of methods Some argue that no single inclusion method should be used exclusively to incorporate the financial information of a component unit. Rather, the relationship between the primary government and the component unit should be evaluated and an appropriate inclusion technique should be selected as a result of the evaluation. For example, in some relationships, full integration may be appropriate while in others note disclosure would be applicable.

The selection of the appropriate inclusion method would be based on a *degree of involvement* criterion. As noted in the Discussion Memorandum, "each component unit would be reported by the method that most appropriately demonstrates the primary government's involvement with, responsibility for, and control over the component unit."

Joint Ventures

A special reporting problem arises when a governmental entity has two or more oversight units. The Discussion Memorandum states that "a joint venture encompasses all organizations that are owned, operated, or controlled by two or more participants as a separate and specific activity in which the participants retain an ongoing financial interest or responsibility." The scope of the Discussion Memorandum is limited to reporting a joint venture's resources and activities in the financial report of a participating government. It does not discuss separate financial reporting by a joint venture. The basic problem addressed by the Discussion Memorandum is the appropriate method for reporting financial information of a jointly controlled entity. Some argue that the existence of joint control precludes a joint venture from being classified as a component unit.

The issue of presentation of a joint venture is generally complicated by the lack of an equity interest in the joint venture; that is, the joint venture may not issue capital stock, or a significant amount of resources may be provided through debt instruments issued by the joint venture. Also, it may be unclear as to whether the oversight units are entitled to dividends or are responsible for operating deficits. Thus, a public-entity joint venture is different from a commercial joint venture.

The Discussion Memorandum lists the following as possible methods that could be used to present the joint venture's financial information in the primary governmental unit's financial report:

- Single-line and pro rata methods
- Equity method
- Modified equity methods
- Cost method
- Disclosure method

Single-line and pro rata methods Because of the joint control characteristic of a joint venture, some argue that only a portion of the resources and results of operations should be reflected in the oversight unit's financial report. This may be accomplished by reporting a portion of net assets and net earnings as single-line items in the overall financial statements. Alternatively, pro rata amounts of specific assets, liabilities, revenues, and expenditures/expenses could be presented.

Equity method The equity method, as described in paragraph 6b of APB-18 (The Equity Method of Accounting for Investments in Common Stock), is summarized as follows.

> An investor initially records an investment in the stock of an investee at cost, and adjusts the carrying amount of the investment to recognize the investor's share of the earnings or losses of the investee after the date of acquisition. The amount of the adjustment is included in the determination of net income by the investor, and such amount reflects adjustments similar to those made in preparing consolidated statements including adjustments to eliminate intercompany gains and losses, and to amortize, if appropriate, any difference between investor cost and underlying equity in net assets of the investee at the date of investment. The in-

vestment of an investor is also adjusted to reflect the investor's share of changes in the investee's capital. Dividends received from an investee reduce the carrying amount of the investment. A series of operating losses of an investee or other factors may indicate that a decrease in value of the investment has occurred which is other than temporary and which should be recognized even though the decrease in value is in excess of what would otherwise be recognized by application of the equity method.

Many argue that the equity method is appropriate for reporting an enterprise fund's investment in a joint venture, yet they also argue that the equity method is not appropriate to account for a governmental fund's investment in a joint venture. Others would argue that the net interest in a joint venture by a governmental fund should be presented in the governmental entity's General Fixed Assets Account Group (GFAAG).

Modified equity methods The equity method is often referred to as a one-line consolidation in that the interest in the net assets and net earnings of the joint venture are shown as single-line items in the balance sheet and activity statement, respectively. Some argue that the equity method should be expanded so that more financial information would be presented separately in the oversight unit's financial statements. For example, the proportional interest in the assets and liabilities could be presented separately in the oversight unit's balance sheet, or the proportional share of each account of the joint venture could be presented.

Those opposed to an expanded equity method approach suggest that the presentation is misleading because no single entity controls the joint venture or has a right to a portion of its net assets.

Cost method The cost method, as described in paragraph 61 of APB-18, is summarized below.

> An investor records an investment in the stock of an investee at cost, and recognizes as income dividends received that are distributed from net accumulated earnings of the investee since the date of acquisition by the investor. The net accumulated earnings of an investee subsequent to the date of investment are recognized by the investor only to the extent distributed by the investee as dividends. Dividends received in excess of earnings subsequent to the date of investment are considered a return of investment and are recorded as re-

ductions of cost of the investment. A series of operating losses of an investee or other factors may indicate that a decrease in value of the investment has occurred which is other than temporary and should accordingly be recognized.

Opponents of the cost method note that often there is no cost basis to the oversight unit because the joint venture may raise all of its capital through debt issuances. Also, the cost method can result in an inconsistency between the joint venture's activity and the effects of that activity on the oversight government's financial statements. For example, the joint venture may have earnings in one period and cash distributions related to the earnings in a subsequent period.

Disclosure method In order to avoid the artificial pro ration of net assets and net earnings of a joint venture, some would suggest that adequate presentation could be achieved through the preparation of a note to the financial statements. Furthermore, it is argued that the disclosure method is more appropriate to public-entity joint ventures, in which case the oversight unit functions more as a sponsor rather than as a participant in joint venture affairs.

GOVERNMENTAL FINANCIAL REPORTING

A governmental reporting entity should prepare a Comprehensive Annual Financial Report (CAFR) that includes all of its funds and account groups. The presentation should summarize the activities and operations performed by all units that constitute the reporting entity. The combined financial position and results of operations are presented as if there were a single operating unit (reporting entity).

CAFR—An Overview

A governmental financial report is broader than the simple presentation of the reporting entity's financial statements. A financial report includes the entity's financial statements as well as schedules and statistical tables. Specifically, the CAFR includes the following financial sections (referred to as the *financial reporting pyramid*):

- General purpose financial statements (combined financial statements—overview)
- Combining financial statements (by fund type)
- Individual fund and account group statements (optional)
- Schedules

General purpose financial statements General purpose financial statements (GPFS) present a financial overview of the *reporting* entity. The GPFS are presented in a columnar format and include combined financial statements for all governmental fund types, proprietary fund types, fiduciary fund types, and account groups. An optional *total* column (labeled *memorandum only*) may be included in the GPFS. The GPFS are referred to as *liftable* because under some circumstances it may be preferable to present the GPFS rather than the CAFR. For example, the GPFS may be part of a governmental document describing the potential issuance of debt securities. When the GPFS are presented separately, an accompanying transmittal letter should inform the user that the GPFS are part of the CAFR, and that the CAFR is available for those who need more details concerning the reporting entity. The auditor's report should precede the GPFS when these overview financial statements are presented separately.

There is a difference in the reporting focus of the CAFR and the GPFS. The CAFR's reporting focus is the individual fund and is more detailed in nature. The GPFS's reporting focus is the fund type and therefore takes a broader financial reporting perspective. Specifically, the GPFS include the following basic financial statements:

- Combined Balance Sheet—All Fund Types and Account Groups
- Combined Statement of Revenues, Expenditures, and Changes in Fund Balances—All Governmental Fund Types
- Combined Statement of Revenues, Expenditures, and Changes in Fund Balances—Budget and Actual (for all fund types for which there is a legally adopted annual budget including the General Fund and Special Revenue Funds)
- Combined Statement of Revenues, Expenses, and Changes in Retained Earnings (or Equity)—All Proprietary Fund Types
- Combined Statement of Changes in Financial Position—All Proprietary Fund Types

As suggested by the above titles, the GPFS include combined information about fund types rather than specific details about a particular fund. In addition to the five combined statements listed here, the GPFS must include appropriate notes.

Combining financial statements The next level of the CAFR includes financial information to support the general purpose financial statements (combined financial statements). This level of detail is referred to as *combining financial statements* and must be presented when a reporting entity has more than one fund in any fund type. Each fund of a fund type is presented in a separate column in the combining financial statements. A total column is also presented and includes the sums of each line entry for all funds of the fund type. Each line entry amount in the total column of the combining financial statement should agree with that line entry amount shown in that fund type's single column presentation in the combined financial statements. For example, if a reporting entity has five Special Revenue Funds, each of the five funds would be presented in a separate column in the combined financial statements. The total column presented would sum each line entry for all five Special Revenue Funds. Each line entry amount in the total column of the combining financial statements should agree with that line entry amount shown in that fund type's single column presentation (Special Revenue

Funds column) in the combined financial statements. Combining financial statements are presented for all governmental fund types, proprietary fund types, and fiduciary fund types.

Individual fund and account group statements The next level of reporting detail in the CAFR is not required but may be necessary under some circumstances in order to achieve the standard of adequate disclosure. NCGA-1 (Governmental Accounting and Financial Reporting Principles) describes these circumstances as follows:

- A government unit has only one fund of a specific type.
- Detail to assure disclosure sufficient to meet CAFR reporting objectives is not presented in the combining statements.

Also, this section of the CAFR may be used to present financial information on a comparative basis with the prior year(s) or present budgetary information regarding those funds for which a budget is legally adopted.

Schedules Information presented in this section of the CAFR is not necessary for the fair presentation in accordance with generally accepted accounting principles unless the information was referred to in notes to the financial statements. This section may include various types of information, including additional analysis of data presented in the combined or combining financial statements, or disclosures required by specific contractual agreements. The characteristics and complexity of the reporting entity determines whether one, two, three, or four levels of reporting are necessary to achieve fair presentation of the financial information.

The interrelationships of the CAFR sections are illustrated in Exhibit I.

Content and Format of Financial Statements

A variety of financial statements are included in the CAFR. The level of detail in any financial statement is dependent upon the level of presentation (combined, combining, etc.) within the CAFR. For example, individual fund or detailed budgetary information and comparative data from previous periods usually should be presented in individual fund statements or schedules, and not in the

Governmental Financial Reporting

EXHIBIT I
INTERRELATIONSHIPS OF CAFR SECTIONS

	Governmental Fund Types					Fiduciary Fund Type	Totals (memorandum only)
	General	Special Revenue	Debt Service	Capital Projects		Expendable Trust	
• Combined Financial Statements—Overview (General Purpose Financial Statements):	$	$	$	$		$	$
Excess of revenues over expenditures		$100					

SPECIAL REVENUE FUNDS

	Parks	Gasoline tax	Parking meters
• Combining Financial Statements by Fund Type:	$	$	$
	$	$	$
	$	$	$
Excess of revenues over expenditures	$ 60	$ 30	$ 10

SPECIAL REVENUE FUND FOR PARKS

	Comparative Financial Statements		Comparison of Budget & Actual		
	19X5	19X4	Budget	Actual	Variance
• Individual Fund and Account Group Statements:	$	$	$	$	$
	$ 60	$ 55	$ 58	$ 60	$ 2

	19X4
	Actual
	$ ...
	$ 55

Excess of revenues over expenditures

← INCREASED LEVEL OF DETAIL

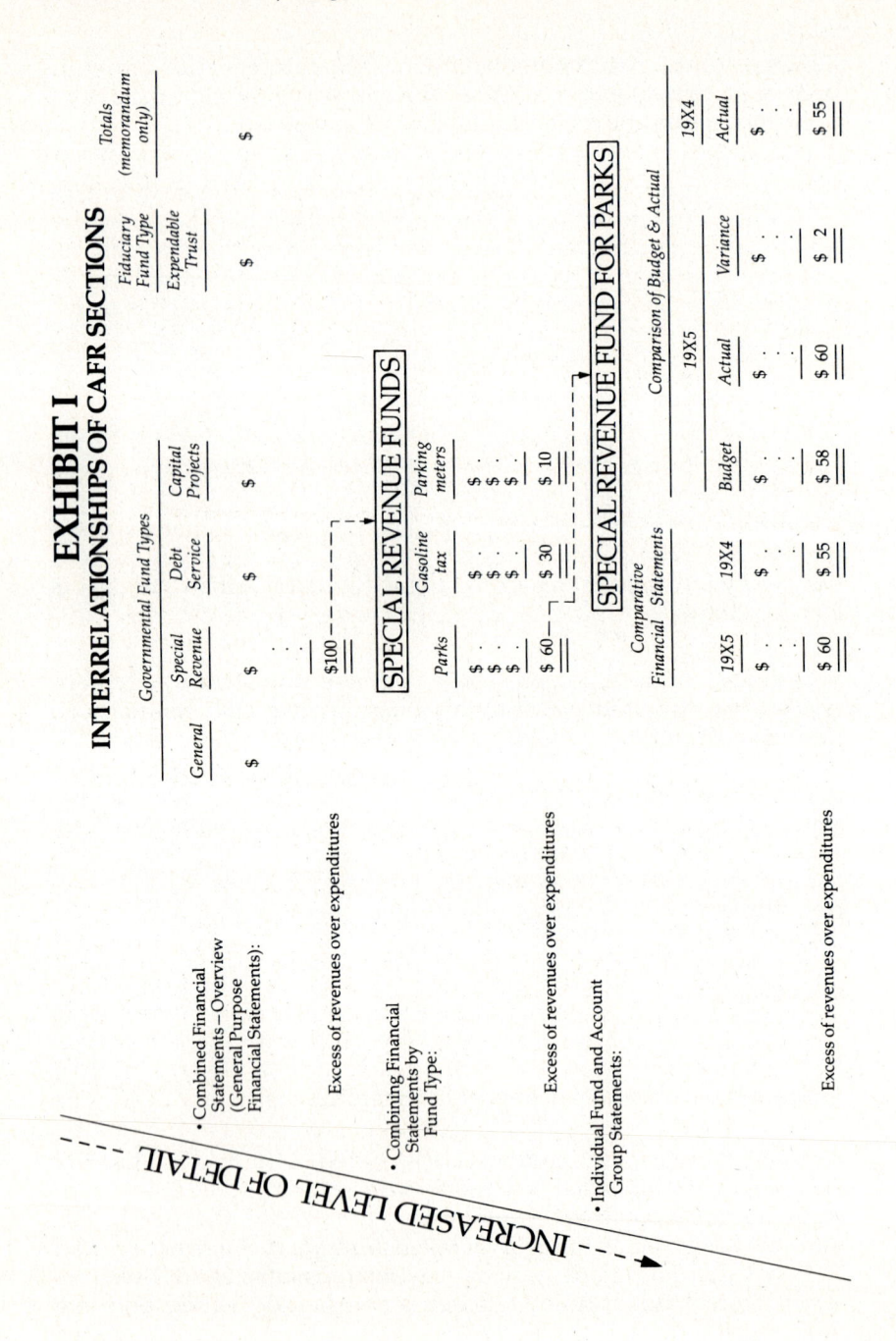

GPFS or the combining financial statements. In general, a financial statement should not exceed two pages. Financial statements should include appropriate notes to achieve fair presentation in accordance with generally accepted accounting principles. When combined financial statements are presented, an optional total column may be used but the column should be labeled *memorandum only*. The total column represents combined financial information rather than consolidated information because interfund transactions are generally not eliminated. A note to the financial statements should disclose the nature of the total column, including an indication whether interfund eliminations have been made.

An example of such a note is presented below:

▶ Total columns on the Combined Statements—Overview are captioned *memorandum only* to indicate that they are presented only to facilitate analysis. The total amounts do not present financial position, results of operations, or changes in financial position in conformity with generally accepted accounting principles. Interfund eliminations are not made in the aggregation of this information. The information is not comparable to consolidated information. ◀

The total column for combining financial statements need not be labeled *memorandum only*.

The specific content and format of governmental financial statements are briefly described below:

Balance sheet A balance sheet summarizes the financial position of (1) an individual fund, (2) several funds of the same type (combining balance sheet), or (3) each fund type and account group (combined balance sheet). A combined balance sheet, which includes governmental fund types, proprietary fund types, fiduciary fund types, and account groups may include a total column. The total column may reflect the elimination of interfund balances. If eliminations are reflected in the total column in the combined balance sheet or the combining balance sheet, the nature of the eliminations should be disclosed in the financial statements.

Operating statement Activity for each fund should be summarized in a common format for all governmental funds (Statement of Revenues, Expenditures, and Changes in Fund Balance) and all proprietary funds

(Statement of Revenues, Expenses, and Changes in Retained Earnings/Fund Balance).

The presentation of the results of operations is influenced by the measurement focus. For a governmental fund, the measurement focus is generally the flow of current financial resources, and the operating statement summarizes changes in the financial condition (expendable resources) of the fund. Expenditures represent decreases in financial resources, and revenues reflect increases in financial resources. Thus, activity for a governmental fund is summarized to measure the excess (deficit) of revenues over expenditures.

The results of operations for a proprietary fund are similar to those of a commercial enterprise in that the measurement focus is the flow of all economic resources, and the operating statement measures revenues and expenses of the fund. Unless a relevant GASB pronouncement or a pronouncement sanctioned by the GASB exists, accounting principles applicable to commercial enterprises should be followed in the preparation of the operating statement of the proprietary fund. Expenses represent the outflow or consumption of assets or incurrences of liabilities, while revenues reflect inflows or enhancements of assets or settlements of liabilities. For a proprietary fund, revenues and expenses are matched in order to determine net income (loss) for the accounting period.

The operating statements for both governmental funds and proprietary funds are presented on an all-inclusive basis. That is, the only items that would not be used to compute the excess of revenues and other sources over expenditures and other uses for a governmental fund or net income for a proprietary fund would be prior period adjustments and residual equity transfers.

An analysis of changes in the fund balance or retained earnings for the period is usually included with the operating statement accounts. The analysis should reconcile the beginning balance of the fund balance for a governmental fund and the beginning balance of retained earnings for a proprietary fund, with their respective ending balances. Thus, the results of operations and the analysis of the changes in fund balance or retained earnings are usually presented in a single financial statement. There is no single format that must be observed in the preparation of the statement; however, to facilitate the preparation of a CAFR with different reporting levels, a consistent format should be used by the reporting entity. Three examples of financial statement formats for governmental funds as illustrated in NCGA-1 are presented below:

Example #1

Revenues	$100,000
Expenditures	80,000
Excess of revenues over (under) expenditures	20,000
Other financing sources (uses)	5,000
Excess of revenues and other sources over (under) expenditures and other uses	25,000
Fund balance—beginning of period	60,000
Fund balance—end of period	$ 85,000

Example #2

Revenues	$100,000
Other financing sources	15,000
Total revenues and other sources	115,000
Expenditures	80,000
Other uses	10,000
Total expenditures and other uses	90,000
Excess of revenues and other sources over (under) expenditures and other uses	25,000
Fund balance—beginning of period	60,000
Fund balance—end of period	$ 85,000

Example #3

Fund balance—beginning of period	$ 60,000
Revenues	100,000
Other financing sources	15,000
Total revenues and other sources	115,000
Expenditures	80,000
Other uses	10,000
Total expenditures and other uses	90,000
Excess of revenues and other sources over (under) total expenditures and other uses	25,000
Fund balance—end of period	$ 85,000

Operating statements of proprietary funds must be consistent with reporting standards applicable to commercial enterprises.

When there has been a restatement of the beginning balance of the fund balance or retained earnings, the effects of the restatement should appear immediately after the previous beginning balance as illustrated below:

Fund balance—beginning of period— as previously reported	$ 60,000
Restatement (explanation or reference to a note)	50,000
Fund balance—beginning of period— as restated	$110,000

In addition, any residual equity transfers must appear after the excess of revenues and other sources over (under) expenditures and other uses.

Activities of Trust Funds may be presented in a separate financial statement, or they may be combined with the appropriate governmental fund or proprietary fund. An Agency Fund, due to its nature, does not have results of operations; however, a Combining Statement of Changes in Assets and Liabilities—All Agency Funds should be presented.

Statement of changes in financial position Proprietary funds presented on an individual, combining, or combined basis must include a statement of changes in financial position. When a total column is presented in the combined statements, the column may be with or without interfund eliminations. If interfund eliminations are made, they must be adequately described in the financial statements or the accompanying notes. In addition to the interfund elimination disclosure, the accounting standards applicable to the preparation of a statement of changes in financial position for a commercial enterprise must be followed.

COMPREHENSIVE ANNUAL FINANCIAL REPORT

The previous discussion presented an overview of the basic reporting concepts that form the foundation for the preparation of the CAFR. The following discussion presents a more detailed analysis of the sections that are part of the CAFR. NCGA-1 states the general outline and minimum content of the CAFR as follows:

- Introductory Section
- Financial Section
  — Auditor's Report
- General Purpose Financial Statements (Combined Statements—Overview)

- Combined Balance Sheet—All Fund Types and Account Groups
- Combined Statement of Revenues, Expenditures, and Changes in Fund Balances—All Governmental Fund Types
- Combined Statement of Revenues, Expenditures, and Changes in Fund Balances—Budget and Actual—General and Special Revenue Fund Types (and similar governmental fund types for which annual budgets are legally adopted)
- Combined Statement of Revenues, Expenses, and Changes in Retained Earnings (or Equity)—All Proprietary Fund Types
- Combined Statement of Changes in Financial Position—All Proprietary Fund Types
- Notes to the financial statements
• Combining and Individual Fund and Account Group Statements and Schedules
  - Combining Statements—By Fund Type (where a governmental unit has more than one fund of a given fund type)
  - Individual fund and account group statements
  - Schedules
• Statistical Tables Section

An illustration of a CAFR is presented in the Appendix of the *Governmental GAAP Guide*.

Introductory Section

Generally, the introductory section of the CAFR contains such items as a title page, table of contents, letter of transmittal, and Certificate of Achievement, if appropriate. A letter of transmittal is a cover letter that summarizes the basis for the financial report, highlights financial activity for the period, and may refer to other significant events that have occurred during the period. The letter is usually addressed to the chief executive of the governmental unit and/or the legislative body and is generally signed by the chief financial officer of the state or local government. The Certificate of Achievement Program is a voluntary quality control program and is administered by a special committee of the Government Finance Officers Association. The review process of governmental financial statements is performed annually by the special committee but is not performed concurrently with the audit of the statements. Thus, the Certificate of Achievement is applicable only to the previous CAFR and not the current CAFR in which it is contained.

Financial Section

The financial section of the CAFR consists of the auditor's report, the general purpose financial statements, and the combining and individual fund and account group statements and schedules.

Auditor's Report

Generally accepted auditing standards are applicable to audits of governmental entities examined by an independent auditor. The independent auditor may report on the CAFR as a whole (Combined Financial Statements Presented with Combining, Individual Fund, and Account Group Financial Statements and Supporting Schedules), the general purpose financial statements (Combined Financial Statements), or components of the reporting unit.

An example of an auditor's report on Combined Financial Statements Presented with Combining, Individual Fund, and Account Group Financial Statements and Supporting Schedules is presented below.

▶ We have audited the accompanying general purpose financial statements of the City of Centerville, N.J., and the combining, individual fund, and account group financial statements of the City of Centerville as of and for the year ended June 30, 19X5, as listed in the table of contents. These financial statements are the responsibility of the entity's management. Our responsibility is to express an opinion on these financial statements based on our audit.

We conducted our audit in accordance with generally accepted auditing standards. Those standards require that we plan and perform the audit to obtain reasonable assurance about whether the financial statements are free of material misstatement. An audit includes examining, on a test basis, evidence supporting the amounts and disclosures in the financial statements. An audit also includes assessing the accounting principles used and significant estimates made by management, as well as evaluating the overall financial statement presentation. We believe that our audit provides a reasonable basis for our opinion.

In our opinion, the general purpose financial statements referred to above present fairly, in all material respects, the financial position of the City of Centerville, N.J., as of June 30, 19X5, and the results of its operations and the changes in financial position of its proprietary fund types for the year then ended in conformity with generally accepted accounting principles. Also, in our opinion, the combining, individual fund, and account group financial statements referred to above present fairly, in all material respects, the financial position of each of the individual funds and account groups of the City of Centerville, N.J., as of June 30, 19X5, and the results of operations of such funds and the changes in financial position of individual proprietary funds for the year then ended in conformity with generally accepted accounting principles.

Our audit was made for the purpose of forming an opinion on the general purpose financial statements taken as a whole and on the combining, individual fund, and individual account group financial statements. The accompanying financial information listed as supporting schedules in the table of contents is presented for purposes of additional analysis and is not a required part of the financial statements of the City of Centerville, N.J. Such information has been subjected to the auditing procedures applied in the audit of the general purpose, combining individual fund, and individual account group financial statements and, in our opinion, is fairly stated in all material respects in relation to the financial statements of each of the respective individual funds and account groups, taken as a whole. ◄

An example of an auditor's report on the general purpose financial statements is presented below.

► We have audited the accompanying general purpose financial statements of the City of Centerville, N.J., as of and for the year ended June 30, 19X5, as listed in the table of contents. These financial statements are the responsibility of the entity's management. Our responsibility is to express an opinion on these financial statements based on our audit.

We conducted our audit in accordance with generally accepted auditing standards. Those standards require that we plan and perform the audit to obtain reasonable assurance about whether the financial statements are free of material misstatement. An audit includes examining, on a test basis, evidence supporting the amounts and disclosures in the financial statements. An audit also includes assessing the accounting principles used and significant estimates made by management, as well as evaluating the overall financial statement presentations. We believe that our audit provides a reasonable basis for our opinion.

In our opinion, the general purpose financial statements referred to above present fairly, in all material respects, the financial position of the City of Centerville, N.J., as of June 30, 19X5, and the results of its operations and the changes in financial position of its proprietary fund types for the year then ended in conformity with generally accepted accounting principles. ◄

General Purpose Financial Statements

The general purpose financial statements provide a combined financial overview of the various funds of the reporting entity and consist of the following:

Governmental Financial Reporting

- Combined Balance Sheet—All Fund Types and Account Groups
- Combined Statement of Revenues, Expenditures, and Changes in Fund Balances—All Governmental Fund Types
- Combined Statement of Revenues, Expenditures, and Changes in Fund Balances—Budget and Actual—General and Special Revenue Fund Types
- Combined Statement of Revenues, Expenses, and Changes in Retained Earnings (or Equity)—All Proprietary Fund Types
- Combined Statement of Changes in Financial Position—All Proprietary Fund Types
- Notes

The financial statements discussed below are illustrated in the Appendix.

Combined Balance Sheet The Combined Balance Sheet shows the financial position for all governmental fund types, proprietary fund types, and fiduciary funds, as well as all account groups. The presentation is usually in a columnar format with each column representing the combined financial positions of a fund type. The amounts shown in the single column presentation for each fund type in the Combined Balance Sheet should agree with the amounts in the total column presented for each fund of each fund type in the combining balance sheet. A total column may be presented in the Combined Balance Sheet, but it is not a requirement. When a total column is presented, and interfund transactions and balances have been eliminated in the preparation of the Combined Balance Sheet, the statement or notes to the statement should clearly describe the eliminations.

Combined Statement of Revenues, Expenditures, and Changes in Fund Balances—All Governmental Fund Types All operating results for governmental funds that have the flow of current financial resources as their measurement basis are combined in this statement. Included in this group are the five governmental fund types (General Fund, Special Revenue Funds, Debt Service Funds, Capital Projects Funds), and fiduciary fund types (Expendable Trust Funds). Alternatively, operating statements of fiduciary funds may be presented separately. A total column may be presented but is not required. The main portions of the combined operating statement are the revenue section, expenditure section, other financing sources (uses) section, and the fund balance section.

Combined Statement of Revenues, Expenditures, and Changes in Fund Balances—Budget and Actual For comparison purposes, certain operating results of governmental fund types must be presented on a budget and actual basis. The funds included in this combined statement are only those funds that adopt annual budgets. The budget may be adopted by the legislature or the unit's governing board. Generally, this statement includes information from the General Fund and Special Revenue Funds, but other funds may be included as well. Only the budgeted and actual combined results of all funds of a fund type need to be presented. The budgeted and actual results of the individual funds of a fund type need not be presented. At the minimum, the presentation must include the budgeted amounts and the actual amounts reported on the budget basis, although many reporting entities include a column for variances.

Combined Statement of Revenues, Expenses, and Changes in Retained Earnings (or Equity) Results of operations from funds that have the flow of total economic resources as their measurement focus are combined in this statement. The basis for presentation is generally accepted accounting principles used by commercial enterprises. Included in this combined presentation are the operating results of proprietary funds (Enterprise Funds and Internal Service Funds) and certain fiduciary funds (Nonexpendable Trust Funds). Major portions of the operating statement include operating revenues, operating expenses, nonoperating revenues and expenses, and retained earnings or fund balances. Since the statement is based on accrual concepts and cost allocation (including depreciation), a net income amount is identified.

Combined Statement of Changes in Financial Position A Combined Statement of Changes in Financial Position must be presented for proprietary funds, Nonexpendable Trust Funds, and Pension Trust Funds. The general format of the combined financial statement should be consistent with the standards established in APB-19 (Reporting Changes in Financial Position). For example, a schedule summarizing the changes in the elements that make up the definition of funds, such as working capital, should be presented as a supplement to the basic financial statement. The combined totals for the Enterprise Funds column and the Internal Service Funds column should agree with the total columns in the Combined Statement of Changes in Financial Position for all Enterprise Funds and Internal Service Funds, respectively. A total column may be used in the combined financial statement but is not mandatory.

Disclosures There are three types of disclosures that should accompany the Comprehensive Annual Financial Report, namely notes to the financial statements, narrative explanations, and required supplementary information.

Notes to the financial statements General purpose financial statements must be accompanied by appropriate notes. These notes are an integral part of the financial statements and are necessary for fair financial statement presentation. Each page of the financial statements should be referenced to the notes. The specific content of each note is determined by the preparer and based on the governmental unit's circumstances, unless a pronouncement mandates minimum disclosure requirements in a particular area. Care should be exercised to avoid the inclusion of material that is unnecessary.

A summary of significant accounting policies should appear as the initial note. Alternatively, the summarization may be presented as a *stand-alone item* and not part of the notes, in which case there must be a reference on each page of the financial statements to the summary. The summary of significant accounting policies note would include disclosures such as the criteria used in defining the reporting entity, revenue recognition methods, and the accounting treatment of infrastructure assets.

NCGA-1 concluded that the following notes to a governmental unit's financial statements at the general purpose financial statement level are essential to fair presentation:

- A. Summary of significant accounting policies
    1. Criteria used to determine the scope of the reporting entity and component units combined to form the reporting entity, including key criteria considered
    2. Revenue recognition policies
    3. Method of encumbrance accounting and reporting
    4. Policy with regard to reporting infrastructure assets
    5. Policy with regard to capitalization of interest costs on fixed assets
- B. Significant contingent liabilities
- C. Encumbrances outstanding
- D. Significant effects of subsequent events
- E. Pension plan obligations
- F. Material violations of finance-related legal and contractual provisions
- G. Debt service requirements to maturity
- H. Commitments under noncapitalized (operating) leases
- I. Construction and other significant commitments
- J. Changes in general fixed assets
- K. Changes in general long-term debt
- L. Any excess of expenditures over appropriations in individual funds
- M. Deficit fund balance or retained earnings of individual funds

N. Interfund receivables and payables
O. Cash deposits with financial institutions
P. Investments

After NCGA-1 was issued, governmental units tended to make only those disclosures established by the Statement, and in many instances virtually reproduced word for word the illustrative notes contained in the 1980 GAAFR. Subsequently, NCGA Interpretation-6 (Notes to the Financial Statements Disclosure) was issued to emphasize that notes should not be limited only to those illustrated in NCGA-1 and suggested that additional disclosures may include the following:

A. Claims and judgements (NCGA-4)
B. Property taxes (NCGA Interpretation-3)
C. Segment information for enterprise funds (NCGA Interpretation-2)
D. Budget basis of accounting and budget/GAAP reporting differences not otherwise reconciled in the general purpose financial statements (NCGA Interpretation-10)
E. Short-term debt instruments and liquidity
F. Related-party transactions
G. Capital leases (NCGA-5)
H. Contingencies (NCGA-1, p. 9/para. 46)
I. Joint ventures (NCGA-7)
J. Special termination benefits (NCGA Interpretation-8)
K. Extinguishment of debt (NCGA Interpretation-9)
L. Grants, entitlements, and shared revenues (NCGA-2 and AICPA Statement of Position 75-3)
M. Nature of total column use in combined financial statements (AICPA Statement of Position 80-2)
N. Methods of estimation of fixed asset costs (NCGA-1, p. 10/para. 49)
O. Fund balance designation (NCGA-1, p. 17/para. 120)
P. Interfund eliminations in combined financial statements not apparent from headings (NCGA-1, p. 22/paras. 145-148)
Q. Pension plans—in both separately issued plan financial statements and employer statements (NCGA-6)
R. Bond, tax, or revenue anticipation notes excluded from fund or current liabilities (NCGA Interpretation-9)
S. Nature and amount of inconsistencies in financial statements caused by transactions between component units having different fiscal year-ends (NCGA-7)

T. Separate summary of significant accounting policies for discrete presentations (NCGA-9)
U. Relationship of component unit to oversight unit in separately-issued Component Unit Financial Report or Component Unit Financial Statements (NCGA-7)
V. Deferred compensation plans (GASB-2)
W. Reverse repurchase and dollar reverse repurchase agreements (GASB-3)
X. Demand bonds (GASB Interpretation-1)

> **OBSERVATION:** *The original listing contained in NCGA Interpretation-6 has been expanded to include those disclosures required by subsequent pronouncements issued by the NCGA and the GASB.*

The list of disclosures presented above is illustrative of the typical notes that may be part of the general purpose financial statements. The list should not be considered all-inclusive since the reporting environment and the characteristics of the reporting entity determine the appropriate level and type of disclosures.

Illustrative notes that should be included in this section of the CAFR are shown at the end of this chapter.

Narrative explanations Information or comments not required to be included in the financial statements and related notes or schedules should be presented as narrative explanations. Narrative explanations may be presented in a separate section of the CAFR, directly on the financial statements or schedules, or on divider pages. These explanations are made to facilitate an understanding of combining financial statements, statements of individual funds, and account groups and schedules. In addition, they may be used to demonstrate compliance with finance-related legal and contractual requirements.

An example of a narrative description which could appear on a divider page as an introduction to the combining financial statements of the governmental fund appears below:

> This Section contains Statements of the Governmental Fund Types through which transactions with General Governmental Functions are recorded. The primary accounting focus of these funds is determination of and changes in financial position and stewardship of resources.

Required Supplementary Information GASB-5 identified a third type of disclosure, namely required supplementary information. Required supplementary information consists of statements, schedules, statistical data, and other information that the GASB believes is necessary to supplement a governmental entity's basic financial statements. Required supplementary information may be reported (1) as part of the general purpose financial statements (immediately after the notes to the financial statements) or (2) with statistical tables. Under either reporting format, required supplementary information should be clearly identified as such.

Combining Statements—by Fund Type

The general purpose financial statements include combined financial statements for each fund type. For example, in the combined statements there will be a column for cumulative information for all Special Revenue Funds, Capital Projects Funds, and so on. Since there may be several individual funds in each fund type, combining financial statements for each fund type must be included in the CAFR. For instance, a governmental unit may have five Special Revenue Funds. The combining financial statements of the Special Revenue Funds would contain a column for each individual fund and a total column that sums each of the line entries for all five funds. The information in the total column of the combining financial statements must agree with the information in the fund type's single column presentation in the combined financial statements. Similar information from other combined fund types will also be included in the combined financial statement. Although more detailed data may be presented in the combining financial statements, the total for Special Revenue Funds will be the same in both the combining and combined financial statements. The overall format and terminology used in the combining and combined financial statements should be similar in order to provide a basis for easy cross-reference between the two sets of financial statements.

Individual Fund and Account Group Statements

It may be unnecessary to present individual fund and account group statements in the CAFR if adequate disclosure is achieved through the presentations in the combining and combined financial statements.

However, financial statements of an individual fund and account groups may be presented for the following reasons:

- There is only one fund of a fund type; therefore, no combining financial statements for that fund type are prepared.
- Information for a particular fund as presented in the combining financial statements is not sufficient to achieve adequate disclosure.
- Information concerning budgetary data and prior year comparative information is presented.

The presentation of individual fund statements provides a basis for disclosing more detailed information than could be presented in combining or combined financial statements; however, the format and terminology used in the individual fund statements should be consistent with those used in the combined and combining financial statements.

Schedules

Additional disclosures may be made in schedules that accompany the CAFR. Such disclosures are not considered necessary to the fair presentation of the financial statements unless there is a cross-reference from the financial statements to the schedule. NCGA-1 states that schedules are used for the following purposes:

- To demonstrate finance-related legal and contractual compliance (for example, additional disclosures required by a debt instrument)
- To present other information considered useful
- To provide details of information otherwise summarized in the financial statements

Some examples of information that may appear in a schedule are presented below:

- Budget information for a fund that is not legally bound to adopt an annual budget
- Detailed presentation of expenditures or expenses by activity, object, class, or other basis
- Detailed list of bonded debt outstanding

- Detailed list of investments on both a cost and market basis
- Combined or combining schedules that include more than one fund or account group
- Detailed schedule of interfund transfers

Statistical Tables Section

Information included in the statistical tables section is not part of the governmental unit's financial statements even though the material is part of the CAFR. Statistical tables may include nonaccounting information and often cover more than two fiscal years. In general, the purpose of presenting statistical tables is to give the user a historical perspective that will enhance the analysis of the governmental unit's financial condition.

The following statistical tables must be included in the CAFR unless circumstances clearly demonstrate that the requirement (that is, the required table) is not applicable to a particular entity.

- General Governmental Expenditures by Function—Last Ten Fiscal Years
- General Revenues by Source—Last Ten Fiscal Years
- Property Tax Levies and Collections—Last Ten Fiscal Years
- Assessed and Estimated Actual Value of Taxable Property—Last Ten Fiscal Years
- Property Tax Rates—All Overlapping Governments—Last Ten Fiscal Years
- Special Assessment Billings and Collections—Last Ten Fiscal Years (if the government is obligated in some manner for related special assessment debt)
- Ratio of Net General Bonded Debt to Assessed Value and Net Bonded Debt per Capita—Last Ten Fiscal Years
- Computation of Legal Debt Margin (if not presented in the General Purpose Financial Statements)
- Computation of Overlapping Debt (if not presented in the General Purpose Financial Statements)
- Ratio of Annual Debt Service for General Bonded Debt to Total General Expenditures—Last Ten Fiscal Years
- Revenue Bond Coverage—Last Ten Fiscal Years
- Demographic Statistics
- Property Value, Construction, Bank Deposits—Last Ten Years

- Principal Taxpayers
- Miscellaneous Statistics

Professional judgment should be used to determine whether statistical tables other than the ones listed above should be presented in the CAFR.

REPORTING BY COMPONENT UNITS

When a separate governmental unit (component unit) is subject to the oversight responsibility of another governmental unit (oversight unit), the financial results of the two units are combined to form the reporting entity. A reporting entity may be comprised of several component units in addition to the oversight unit. There is some flexibility as to how a component unit's financial statements are presented in the reporting unit's CAFR.

Including the Component Unit in the Reporting Entity

If the component unit is accounted for financially in a single fund, such as a Special Revenue Fund or Enterprise Fund, its financial statements may be reflected in the combining financial statements of the reporting entity just as for any other governmental fund. Because they are separate governmental units, some component units may account for their activities in several types of funds and account groups. For example, a school district may maintain a General Fund, Special Revenue Funds, Capital Projects Funds, and a General Fixed Assets Account Group, as well as other funds and account groups. When multiple funds and account groups are used by the component unit, each fund or account group should be included in the appropriate combining financial statements of the reporting entity with one exception: the component unit's General Fund should not be combined with the oversight unit's General Fund. NCGA-7 (Financial Reporting for Component Units Within the Governmental Reporting Entity) concludes that the component unit's General Fund should be reported as a separate Special Revenue Fund.

Rather than merging all of the component units' funds and account groups into the reporting entity's combining financial statements, funds of a particular type may be grouped together based on their common function or activity. This may be a preferred presentation when a complex reporting unit, such as a state, is composed of numerous funds or component units. For instance, rather than present a single combining and/or combined statement format for all Enterprise Funds, similar Enterprise Funds may be grouped into categories such as transportation or economic development funds. An important criterion for determining whether to present a functional grouping of similar funds is the materiality of the individual fund in relationship to the total fund type as presented in the reporting entity's CAFR.

The reporting entity's fiscal year must be the same as the oversight unit's fiscal year, and NCGA-7 concludes that a component unit's fiscal year should be the same as the oversight unit's fiscal year (reporting unit's fiscal year), if practicable. When the component unit's fiscal year is different from the oversight unit's fiscal year, the component unit's financial statements for the year ending during the oversight unit's fiscal year should be included in the financial statements of the reporting entity. However, there is an exception to this rule. If the component unit's current fiscal year ends within one quarter after the date of the oversight unit's fiscal year, the component unit's financial statements (that is, those financial statements that end within one quarter after the oversight unit's fiscal year) may be incorporated in the reporting entity's financial statements. However, once the fiscal year of the component unit is determined, the same fiscal year should be used consistently from year to year in the preparation of the reporting entity's financial statements.

There may be inconsistencies among the balances in interfund accounts (due to/due from; transfers in/transfers out) when the oversight unit and component unit have different year-end dates. If considered significant, these inconsistencies of balances should be explained in a note to the financial statements.

Transactions between separate governmental units that are considered part of the same reporting entity may create intergovernmental receivables and payables between the two units. Because these units are part of a single reporting entity, the account names for financial reporting purposes should be changed to due to/due from other funds.

> **OBSERVATION:** *Governmental units may enter into a lease agreement that should be treated as a capital lease by the lessee unit and a direct financing lease by the lessor unit as a result of applying the criteria included in FASB-13 (Accounting for Leases). When the governmental units are determined to be component units of the same reporting entity, the agreement should be treated as an operating lease,*

thereby eliminating the intergovernmental payable on the lessee's books and the intergovernmental receivable on the lessor's books.

NCGA-7 notes that operating transfers among component units and between a component unit and the oversight unit have been variously classified as intergovernmental revenues, operating revenue/expenditures/expenses, and/or operating transfers. In determining the proper classification of transfers among units of the same reporting entity, the following guidelines, as stated in NCGA-1 (Principle 10), should be observed:

Quasi-external transactions Transactions that would be treated as revenues, expenditures, or expenses if they involved organizations external to the governmental unit—e.g., payments in lieu of taxes from an Enterprise Fund to the General Fund; Internal Service Fund billings to departments; routine employer contributions from the General Fund to a Pension Trust Fund; and routine service charges for inspection, engineering, utilities, or similar services provided by a department financed from one fund to a department financed from another fund—should be accounted for as revenues, expenditures, or expenses in the funds involved.

Reimbursements Transactions which constitute reimbursements of a fund for expenditures or expenses initially made from it which are properly applicable to another fund—e.g., an expenditure properly chargeable to a Special Revenue Fund was initially made from the General Fund, which is subsequently reimbursed—should be recorded as expenditures or expenses (as appropriate) in the reimbursing fund and as reductions of the expenditure or expense in the fund that is reimbursed.

Therefore, all interfund transactions are considered transfers (operating transfers or residual equity transfers) except for (1) quasi-external transactions and reimbursements as described above, and (2) loans or advances among the governmental units that make up the reporting entity.

NCGA-1 requires that a combined statement based on budgeted and actual operating results be presented for the General Fund and Special Revenues Fund and other governmental fund types where an annual budget is legally adopted. For component units, this presentation requirement must also be observed. The adoption of a budget for the component unit may result from action taken by the legislature, the oversight unit's governing board, or the component unit's governing board.

Although each component unit's individual fund statements and account groups must be included in the combining financial statements of the reporting entity, the CAFR may be expanded to allow additional financial presentations for the component unit. Immediately after the statistical section of the CAFR, a separate section may include the financial statements of the component unit or a more expanded disclosure referred to as the Component Unit Financial Report (CUFR).

Discrete Presentation by the Component Unit

A component unit may adopt accounting principles that are not in conformity with governmental accounting and reporting standards. The component unit's financial statements may be presented in a separate column of the reporting entity's financial statements (1) if the accounting principles used by the component unit are generally accepted but not in conformity with governmental accounting and reporting standards and (2) if the inclusion of the component unit with other funds would distort the overall presentation. When a discrete presentation format is adopted for the component unit, a note should clearly describe the accounting policies used by the component unit and the relationship of the oversight unit and the component unit.

> **OBSERVATION:** *The above paragraph, which is based on paragraph 9 of NCGA-7, should be interpreted with a bit of caution. Based on an AICPA Auditing Interpretation (December 1984), it is clear that pronouncements of the GASB (and its predecessor) are the highest level of authoritative support in the governmental accounting area and pronouncements of the FASB are to be followed only if the issue has not been addressed by the GASB. Therefore, the above paragraph would apply to those situations where governmental generally accepted accounting principles have not been established by a GASB pronouncement but an alternative accounting principle is acceptable for commercial enterprises and the latter principle is being used by the component unit.*

Governmental Financial Reporting

Separate Presentation by the Component Unit

Although a component unit's financial statements must be included in the overall reporting unit's CAFR and general purpose financial statements, there may be circumstances in which the component unit may issue a separate financial report. When the component unit issues a separate financial report, a note to the separate report should clearly indicate that the component unit is also included in the reporting entity's financial report.

The component unit's separate financial report may be in the form of a Component Unit Financial Report (CUFR) or Component Unit Financial Statements (CUFS).

CUFR   The Component Unit Financial Report is similar to the reporting entity's CAFR. The CUFR would include all the component unit's funds and account groups. Sections of the report should include the following where appropriate:

- Introductory Section
- Combined Financial Statements
- Combining Financial Statements
- Individual Fund Statements
- Notes to the Financial Statements
- Schedules
- Narrative Explanations
- Statistical Tables

CUFS   The Component Unit Financial Statements are similar to the reporting entity's *liftable* general purpose financial statements. The CUFS should include the component units' basic financial statements and accompanying notes that are necessary for achieving fair presentation.

The decision to issue separate financial information (CUFR or CUFS) is made by the component unit.

> **OBSERVATION:** *An oversight unit may also decide to issue separate financial statements in addition to the CAFR or general purpose financial statements of the reporting unit. The issuance of separate financial statements by the oversight unit is not a substitute for the financial reporting by the reporting entity. When the oversight unit*

issues separate financial statements, there should be adequate disclosure that the oversight unit is an integral part of the reporting entity. (Technically, an oversight unit is a component unit which exercises oversight responsibility over other component units.)

JOINT VENTURES

NCGA-7 defines a joint venture as follows:

> A legal entity or other contractual arrangement participated in by a government as a separate and specific activity for the benefit of the public or service recipients in which the government retains an ongoing financial interest (e.g., an equity interest in either assets or liabilities) and/or responsibility.

Criteria established in NCGA-3 (Defining the Governmental Reporting Entity) are used to determine whether a joint venture's financial statements should be included in the reporting entity's CAFR and general purpose financial statements. The joint venture must be accounted for in a manner consistent with governmental accounting principles.

If it is determined that a joint venture is not part of the reporting entity, the joint venture must nonetheless use accounting principles consistent with GASB (and its predecessor) pronouncements. When the investment in the joint venture is made by a proprietary or similar Trust Fund, the investment must be accounted for in accordance with APB-18 (The Equity Method of Accounting for Investments in Common Stock). The equity method can be used to account for governmental joint ventures even though common stock is not issued by the entity. The equity method requires that the investor entity (governmental unit) increase its investment by its share of the joint venture's net income and reduce its investment by distribution made by the joint venture.

When the investment in the joint venture is made by a governmental fund or similar Trust Fund and the joint venture is not part of the reporting entity, the joint venture investment should be disclosed in a note to the financial statements if the equity method is not used.

> **OBSERVATION:** *There is a potential reporting dilemma that may be encountered when the joint venture is not part of the reporting*

entity (criteria in NCGA-3 are not met) and the investment is made by a governmental fund or similar Trust Fund. The measurement basis for a governmental fund (current financial resources measurement basis) is different from a joint venture that uses accounting principles applicable to a commercial enterprise (total economic resources measurement basis). Thus, in applying the equity method in this situation, the governmental fund would be incorporating a measurement basis not considered acceptable for its financial reporting purposes.

NCGA-7 requires that the following disclosures must be made for joint ventures accounted for either as a proprietary joint venture or a governmental fund joint venture:

- A general description of each joint venture, including:
  — Identification of the participants and their percentage shares
  — Description of the arrangements for selecting the governing body or management
  — Disclosure of the degree of control the participants have over budgeting and financing
- Condensed or summary financial information on each joint venture, including:
  — Balance sheet date
  — Total assets, liabilities, and equity
  — Reporting entity's share of assets, liabilities, equity, and changes therein during the year, if known
- Joint venture debt, both current and long-term, and the security for the debt. (Security for the debt is defined as the resources that are expected to be used to repay the debt and/or may be legally or otherwise obligated to such debt.)

INTERIM FINANCIAL REPORTING

Interim financial reports may be prepared on a monthly, quarterly, year-to-date, or some other basis. These reports are usually prepared for internal rather than external purposes and may contain budgetary as well as actual financial results. The preparation of budgetary financial reports on an interim basis may serve as an effective technique for management control and legislative review of governmental operations. Because interim financial reporting has a managerial emphasis, NCGA-1 concludes that it is inappropriate to promulgate rules to define accounting and reporting standards in the area. Professional judgment rather than reference to specific pronouncements must be the basis for effective interim financial reporting.

MINIMUM REPORTING STANDARDS

Pronouncements by the GASB and the NCGA provide minimum, not maximum, reporting standards. The observance of these standards, such as the preparation of a CAFR or general purpose financial statements, does not suggest that other presentations or disclosures are not necessary or desirable for a fair financial presentation.

The governmental unit's finance officer should consider whether it is useful to prepare supplemental information or special reports in addition to those prescribed. For example, a governmental unit may present condensed financial information or other reports that summarize the unit's financial position and activity. Although governmental units are encouraged to experiment with the current financial reporting model, NCGA-1 makes it clear that condensed financial statements and information are supplements to and not substitutes for the CAFR and general purpose financial statements. In fact, when condensed financial information is presented, there should be a reference in the condensed information to the CAFR or general purpose financial statements and the information should be *reconcilable* with the combined, combining, and individual fund and account group statements.

LITERATURE REFERENCES

Material in this chapter is based on the following authoritative pronouncements and publications which are grouped according to the major headings used within the chapter. A dual reference (both paragraph and page number) is used for NCGA-1 and NCGA-2 because the original pronouncements do not use paragraph numbers.

CAFR — An Overview
NCGA-1 *Governmental Accounting and Financial Reporting Principles*, pp. 18, 19, 20, and 25/¶¶ 129, 135, 136, 141, 142, 164, 166, and 167.
NCGA-7 *Financial Reporting For Component Units Within The Governmental Reporting Entity*, ¶¶6 and 7.

Content and Format of Financial Statements
NCGA-1   *Governmental Accounting and Financial Reporting Principles,* pp. 16 and 22-24/¶¶109, 110, 144-146, 148, 150-152, and 156.
SOP 80-2   *Accounting and Financial Reporting by Governmental Units,* ¶14.
FASB:CS-6   *Elements of Financial Statement,* ¶¶78 and 80.

Comprehensive Annual Financial Report
NCGA-1   *Governmental Accounting and Financial Reporting Principles,* pp. 19 and 20/¶139.

Introductory Section
NCGA-1   *Governmental Accounting and Financial Reporting Principles,* p. 19/ ¶139.

Financial Section
NCGA-1   *Governmental Accounting and Financial Reporting Principles,* p. 19/ ¶139.

Auditor's Report
AICPA AUDIT GUIDE   *Audits of State and Local Governmental Units (1986),* pp. 200-202.
SOP 80-2   *Accounting and Financial Reporting by Governmental Units,* ¶¶17 and 18.

General Purpose Financial Statements
NCGA-1   *Governmental Accounting and Financial Reporting Principles,* pp. 22-24/¶¶144, 153, 157, and 159.
NCGA-7   *Financial Reporting for Component Units Within the Governmental Reporting Entity,* ¶17.
NCGA INTERPRETATION-6   *Notes to the Financial Statements Disclosure,* ¶¶3, 6-8, and Appendix.
GASB-5   *Disclosure of Pension Information by Public Employee Retirement Systems and State and Local Governmental Employers,* ¶ 7.

Combining Statements—by Fund Type
NCGA-1   *Governmental Accounting and Financial Reporting Principles,* pp. 20 and 21/¶141.

Individual Fund and Account Group Statements
NCGA-1   *Governmental Accounting and Financial Reporting Principles,* p. 121/ ¶141.

Schedules
NCGA-1   *Governmental Accounting and Financial Reporting Principles,* p. 21/ ¶141.

Statistical Tables Section
NCGA-1   *Governmental Accounting and Financial Reporting Principles,* pp. 24 and 25/¶¶160 and 161.

Reporting by Component Units
NCGA-7   *Financial Reporting for Component Units Within the Governmental Reporting Entity,* ¶5.

Including the Component Unit in the Reporting Entity
NCGA-7   *Financial Reporting for Component Units Within the Governmental Reporting Entity,* ¶¶10-13 and 15-21.
NCGA-5   *Accounting and Financial Reporting Principles for Lease Agreements of State and Local Governments,* ¶24.
NCGA-1   *Governmental Accounting and Financial Reporting Principles,* p. 15/ ¶¶103-106.

Discrete Presentation by the Component Unit
NCGA-7   *Financial Reporting for Component Units Within the Governmental Reporting Entity,* ¶9.

Separate Presentation by the Component Unit
NCGA-7   *Financial Reporting for Component Units Within the Governmental Reporting Entity,* ¶¶5, 15, and 26.

Joint Ventures
NCGA-7   *Financial Reporting for Component Units Within the Governmental Reporting Entity,* ¶¶5 and 27-29.
APB-18   *Equity Method for Investments in Common Stock,* ¶19.

Interim Financial Reporting
NCGA-1   *Governmental Accounting and Financial Reporting Principles,* pp. 18 and 19/¶¶ 133 and 134.

Minimum Reporting Standards
NCGA-1   *Governmental Accounting and Financial Reporting Principles,* p. 26/ ¶¶172, 173, and 175.

ILLUSTRATIVE NOTES

NCGA Interpretation-6 (Notes to the Financial Statements Disclosure) concludes that notes to financial statements are most useful when they are presented in a logical sequence. Although professional judgment must ultimately determine the best sequence of the notes, NCGA Interpretation-6 recommended the following sequence:

I. *Summary of Significant Accounting Policies (including departures from GAAP, if any)*
   A. Principles used in determining the scope of entity for financial reporting purposes (see NCGA-3)
   B. Basis of presentation—fund accounting
      i) Fund categories/generic fund types
      ii) Account groups
   C. Basis of accounting
      i) Modified accrual—governmental, Expendable Trust, and Agency Funds
      ii) Accrual—proprietary, Nonexpendable Trust, and Pension Trust Funds
   D. Budgetary data
      i) General budget policies
      ii) Encumbrances
      iii) Budget basis of accounting
   E. Assets, liabilities, and fund equity
      Disclosure of valuation bases and significant or unusual accounting treatment for material account balances or transactions. These should be described in the order of appearance in the balance sheet.
   F. Revenues, expenditures, and expenses
      i) Unusual or significant accounting policy for material revenue, expenditures, and expenses
      ii) Property tax revenue recognition (see NCGA Interpretation-3)
      iii) Vacation, sick leave, and other compensated absences (see NCGA-4)

II. *Stewardship, Compliance, and Accountability*
   A. Material violations of finance-related legal and contractual provisions
   B. Deficit fund balance or retained earnings of individual funds
   C. Any excess of expenditures over appropriations in individual funds, if any, and explanations therefore, including remedial action planned by or required of the issuer

Governmental Financial Reporting

III. Detail Notes on All Funds and Account Groups
  A. Assets
     i) Pooling of cash and investments
     ii) Investments
     iii) Property taxes
     iv) Due from other governments—grants receivables
     v) Changes in general fixed assets
     vi) Summary of proprietary fund fixed assets (including construction in progress)
  B. Liabilities
     i) Pension plan obligations (GASB-5)
     ii) Other employee benefits
     iii) Construction and other significant commitments
     iv) Claims and judgments (see NCGA-4)
     v) Lease obligations (capital and operating)
     vi) Long-term debt
        a) Description of individual bonds issues and leases outstanding
        b) Changes in general long-term debt
        c) Summary of debt service requirements to maturity
        d) Disclosure of legal debt margin
        e) Bonds authorized but unissued
        f) Synopsis of revenue bond covenants
     vii) Short-term debt and liquidity
  C. Interfund receivables and payables
  D. Fund equity
     i) Reservation of retained earnings
     ii) Reservation of fund balance
     iii) Unreserved fund balance—designations
IV. Segment Information—Enterprise Funds (see NCGA Interpretation-2)
V. Related-Party Transactions
VI. Summary Disclosure of Significant Contingencies
  A. Litigation
  B. Federally assisted programs—compliance audits
VII. Significant Effects of Subsequent Events

The following section presents in the sequence recommended in NCGA Interpretation-6 examples of notes as they might appear in a financial statement. Be aware that the notes presented below are for illustrative purposes only. They do not include all disclosure situations and each note, if applicable to a particular governmental unit, should be modified to reflect the unique reporting circumstances of

GOVERNMENTAL GAAP GUIDE / 5.31

the specific reporting entity. Each note is an independent example and is not internally consistent with other notes presented.

I. Summary of Significant Accounting Policies
   A. Principles used in determining the scope of entity for financial reporting purposes

Reporting Entity   The City of Centerville was created in 1919 and operates under an elected Mayor/Council form of government. The City's major operations include health services, public safety, fire protection, recreation and parks, and general administrative services. In addition, the City exercises sufficient control over other governmental agencies and authorities that are included as part of the City's reporting entity.

The National Council on Governmental Accounting (NCGA), in order to clarify which organizations, functions, and activities of government should be included in general purpose financial statements, issued NCGA-3 (Defining the Governmental Reporting Entity), in December 1981. The NCGA has been replaced by the Governmental Accounting Standards Board (GASB), but the latter organization has endorsed NCGA-3. In issuing NCGA-3, the NCGA's intention was to provide a basis for making comparisons among units of government or between time periods for a given government, to reduce the possibility of arbitrary exclusion or inclusion of organizations in financial reports, and to enable financial statement users to identify the operations for which governmental entities are responsible. The NCGA concluded that the basic criterion for including an agency, institution, authority, or other organization in a governmental unit's reporting entity is the exercise of oversight responsibility over such agencies by the governmental units' elected officials. Oversight responsibility is defined to include, but is not limited to:

Financial interdependency   When a separate agency produces a financial benefit for or imposes a financial burden on a unit of government, that agency is part of the reporting entity. Manifestations of financial interdependency include responsibility for financing deficits, entitlements to surpluses, and guarantees of, or "moral responsibility" for, debt.

Selection of governing authority   An authoritative appointment is one where the entity's chief elected official maintains a significant continuing relationship with the appointed officials with respect to carrying out important public functions.

Designation of management When management is appointed by and held accountable to a governing authority that is included in the entity, the activity being managed falls within the entity.

Ability to significantly influence operations This ability includes, but is not limited to, the authority to review and approve budgetary requests, adjustments, and amendments.

Accountability for fiscal matters Fiscal authority normally includes the authority for final approval over budgetary appropriations, responsibility for funding deficits and operating deficiencies, disposal of surplus funds, control over the collection and disbursement of funds, and maintenance of title to assets.

There may be, however, factors other than oversight that are so significant that exclusion of a particular agency from a reporting entity's financial statements would be misleading. These other factors include:

(a) *Scope of Public Service*—Aspects to be considered include who the activity benefits and whether it is conducted within the entity's geographic boundaries and generally available to its citizens.

(b) *Special Financial Relationship*—Such a relationship may have been created to benefit the entity by providing for the issuance of debt on behalf of the entity.

Based on the criteria established by NCGA-3, as supplemented by NCGA Interpretation-7 (Clarification as to the Application of the Criteria in NCGA-3—Defining the Governmental Reporting Entity), the reporting entity includes the Centerville School District, the Public Housing Corporation of Centerville, Centerville Urban Renewal Corporation, the Centerville Flood Control District, and the Centerville Transit Authority.

The City of Centerville's financial statements do not include the Centerville Museum or the Industrial Development Corporation of Centerville. A description of these entities and the reasons for their exclusion from the reporting entity are summarized below.

Centerville Museum

The Centerville Museum was organized in 19X1, and construction of its facilities began the following year on land owned by the city. Currently, the city leases the land to the museum, and this relationship suggests that the museum should be part of the reporting entity. The following factors suggest that the museum should not be included in the reporting entity:

- Contributors to the museum elect all the members of the governing board.
- The governing board is solely responsible for the employment of museum personnel.
- The museum's management is solely responsible for the day-to-day operations of the museum.
- The city is neither entitled to operating surplus nor responsible for operating deficits of the museum.
- The museum is exclusively responsible for administration of its fiscal affairs.
- The museum is open to the public-at-large and not exclusively for enjoyment of residents of Centerville.

Based on these factors it has been concluded that the City of Centerville has no oversight responsibility for the museum, and therefore the financial statements of the museum are excluded from the reporting entity.

Industrial Development Corporation of Centerville

The Industrial Development Corporation of Centerville was organized in 19X2 to promote and develop commercial and industrial properties, and to encourage employment within the city. The following factors strongly suggest that the unit be excluded from the reporting entity's financial statements:

- The corporation's governing board is approved by the mayor, but there is no continuing relationship between the corporation and the city.
- The management of the corporation is selected by the governing board.

Governmental Financial Reporting

- The operation of the corporation is the exclusive responsibility of the corporation's management, and the city has no authority to interfere with these operations.
- The corporation is responsible for its financial affairs including the funding of deficits and the disposition of surpluses.
- The city does not guarantee the corporation's outstanding debt.

Although the city must approve the corporation's issuance of debt and the corporation operates within the geographical boundaries of the city, these factors are not considered significant enough to warrant inclusion of the corporation in the financial statements of the City of Centerville.

    B. *Basis of presentation—fund accounting*
        i) *Fund categories/generic fund types*
        ii) *Account groups*

Fund Accounting   The accounts of the City of Centerville are organized on the basis of funds and account groups, each of which is considered a separate accounting entity. The City has created several types of funds and a number of discrete funds within each fund type. Each fund is accounted for by a separate set of self-balancing accounts that comprises its assets, liabilities, fund balance, revenues, and expenditures/expenses. The individual funds account for the governmental resources allocated to them for the purpose of carrying on specific activities in accordance with laws, regulations, or other restrictions.

The funds are grouped into three fund types and eight generic funds as described below:

Governmental Fund Types   These are the funds through which most governmental functions typically are financed. The funds included in this category are as follows:

General Fund   This fund is established to account for resources devoted to financing the general services that the City performs for its citizens. General tax revenues and other sources of revenue used to finance the fundamental operations of the City are included in this fund. This fund is charged with all costs of operating the government for which a separate fund has not been established.

Governmental Financial Reporting

Special Revenue Funds These funds are established to account for the proceeds of specific revenue sources other than special assessments, expendable trusts, or major capital projects that are legally restricted to expenditures for specified purposes.

Debt Service Funds These funds are established for the purpose of accumulating resources for the payment of interest and principal on long-term general obligation debt other than those payable from Enterprise Funds.

Proprietary Fund Types These funds account for operations that are self-supporting through user charges. The funds included in this category are Enterprise Funds and Internal Service Funds.

Enterprise Funds These funds are established to account for operations that are financed and operated in a manner similar to private business enterprises, where the intent is that the costs of providing goods or services to the general public on a continuing basis be financed or recovered primarily through user charges.

Internal Service Funds These funds are established to account for the financing of goods or services provided by one department to other departments of the City on a mostly cost-reimbursement basis.

Fiduciary Fund Types These funds account for assets held by the City as a trustee or agent for individuals, private organizations, and other units of governments. These funds are as follows:

Pension Trust Fund This fund was established to provide pensions for City employees and employees of certain other governmental units. The principal revenue source for this fund is employer and employee contributions.

Nonexpendable Trust Fund This fund is used to account for funds that are to be used for emergency loans to City employees.

Expendable Trust Fund These funds are used to account for funds that are to be used for educational expenditures incurred by City employees and for funds held in escrow for other parties.

In addition to the three broad types of governmental funds, the City also maintains two account groups as described below:

General Fixed Assets Account Group This is not a fund but rather an account group that is used to account for general fixed assets acquired principally for general purposes and excludes fixed assets in the Enterprise Funds and the Internal Service Funds.

General Long-Term Debt Account Group This is not a fund but rather an account group that is used to account for the outstanding principal balances of general obligation bonds and other long-term debt not reported in proprietary funds.

C. *Basis of accounting*
  i) *Modified accrual—governmental, Expendable Trust, and Agency Funds*
  ii) *Accrual—proprietary, Nonexpendable Trust, and Pension Trust Funds*

Basis of Accounting Governmental funds, Expendable Trust Funds, and Agency Funds utilize the modified accrual basis of accounting. Under this method, revenues are recognized in the accounting period in which they become both available and measurable. Licenses and permits, charges for services, fines and forfeits, and miscellaneous revenues are recorded as revenues when received in cash. General property taxes, self-assessed taxes, and investment earnings are recorded when earned (when they are both measurable and available). Expenditures are recognized in the accounting period in which the fund liability is incurred, if measurable, except expenditures for debt service, prepaid expenses, and other long-term obligations which are recognized when paid.

All proprietary funds, Nonexpendable Trust Funds, and Pension Trust Funds are accounted for using the accrual basis of accounting. Their revenues are recognized when they are earned, and their expenses are recognized when they are incurred. Interest on revenue bonds, proceeds of which are used in financing the construction of certain assets, is capitalized during the construction period net of interest on the investment of unexpended bond proceeds.

Agency Fund assets and liabilities are accounted for on the modified accrual basis.

D. Budgetary data
   i) General budget policies
   ii) Encumbrances
   iii) Budget basis of accounting

Budgetary Accounting Formal budgetary accounting is employed as a management control for all funds of the City. Annual operating budgets are adopted each fiscal year through passage of an annual budget ordinance and amended as required for the General Fund, Special Revenues Funds, Debt Service Funds, and proprietary funds and the same basis of accounting is used to reflect actual revenues and expenditures/expenses recognized on a generally accepted accounting principles basis. Budgets for certain Special Revenue Funds and Capital Projects Funds are made on a project basis, spanning more than one fiscal year. Budgetary control is exercised at the departmental level or by projects.

All unencumbered budget appropriations, except project budgets, lapse at the end of each fiscal year.

E. Assets, liabilities, and fund equity
   Disclosure of valuation bases and significant or unusual accounting treatment for material account balances or transactions should be described in the order of appearance in the balance sheet.

Cash To facilitate better management of the City's cash resources, excess cash is combined in pooled operating accounts. Each fund's portion of total cash is based on its equity in the pooled cash amount. Cash in excess of current operating needs is invested on a pooled investment basis and earnings thereon are distributed to the appropriate fund based on the average daily balance of cash and temporary investments included in the combined pool of cash and temporary investments. Temporary investments are reported at cost.

Receivables Receivables are reported at their gross value and are reduced by the estimated portion that is expected to be uncollectible.

Investments Debt securities are valued at amortized cost since it is the general policy of the City to hold such investments until they mature. Equity securities are valued at cost or market, whichever is lower. Writedowns from cost to market are recognized when there has been a decline that appears to be other than temporary.

Due to and due from other funds Interfund receivables and payables arise from interfund transactions and are recorded by all funds affected in the period in which transactions are executed.

Interest receivable Interest on investments and certain receivables are recorded as revenue in the year they are earned and available to pay liabilities of the current period.

Inventories Inventories for all governmental funds are valued at average cost. The purchase method is used to account for inventories. Under the purchase method, inventories are recorded as expenditures when purchased; however, material amounts of inventories are reported as assets of the respective fund. Reported inventories in these funds are equally offset by a fund balance reserve, which indicates that they are unavailable for appropriation even though they are a component of reported assets.

Inventories of the proprietary funds are valued at the lower of cost (first-in, first-out) or market.

Restricted assets Enterprise Funds, based on certain bond covenants, are required to establish and maintain a prescribed amount of resources (consisting of cash and temporary investments) that can be used only to service outstanding debt.

Property, plant, and equipment Fixed assets used in governmental fund type operations are accounted for in the General Fixed Assets Account Group. Public domain (infrastructure) fixed assets consisting of certain improvements other than buildings, such as roads, sidewalks, and bridges, are not capitalized. Property, plant, and equipment acquired or constructed for general governmental operations are recorded as expenditures in the fund making the expenditure and capitalized at cost in the General Fixed Assets Account Group.

Property, plant, and equipment acquired for proprietary funds is capitalized in the respective funds to which it applies.

Property, plant, and equipment is stated at cost. Where cost could not be determined from the available records, estimated historical cost was used to record the estimated value of the assets. Assets acquired by gift or bequest are recorded at their fair market value at the date of transfer.

Depreciation of exhaustible fixed assets used by proprietary funds is charged as an expense against operations, and accumulated depreciation is reported on proprietary funds' balance sheets. Depreciation has been provided over the estimated useful lives using the straight-line method of depreciation.

Advances Advances to and advances from governmental funds represent noncurrent portions of interfund receivables and payables. The governmental fund making the advance establishes a fund balance reserve equal to the amount of the advance.

Long-term debt Long-term obligations of the City are reported in the General Long-Term Debt Account Group. Long-term liabilities for certain general obligation bonds, revenue bonds, and mortgage bonds are reported in the appropriate Enterprise Fund.

Pensions The provision for pension cost is recorded on an accrual basis, and the City's policy is to fund pension costs as they accrue.

Fund equity The unreserved fund balance for governmental funds represents the amount available for budgeting future operations. The reserved fund balance for governmental funds represents the amount that has been legally identified for specific purposes.

Unreserved retained earnings for proprietary funds represent the net assets available for future operations or distribution. Reserved retained earnings for proprietary funds represent the net assets that have been legally identified for specific purposes.

F. *Revenues, expenditures, and expenses*
  i) *Unusual or significant accounting policy for material revenue, expenditures, and expenses*
  ii) *Property tax revenue recognition*
  iii) *Vacation, sick leave, and other compensated absences*

Revenues Revenues for governmental funds are recorded when they are determined to be both measurable and available. Generally, tax revenues, fees, and nontax revenues are recognized when received. Grants from other governments are recognized when qualifying expenditures are incurred. Expenditures for governmental funds are recorded when the related liability is incurred.

Revenues and expenses of proprietary funds are recognized in essentially the same manner as in commercial accounting.

Property tax revenue Property taxes are levied on July 1 based on the assessed value of property as listed on the previous January 1. Assessed values are an approximation of market value. A revaluation of all real property must be made every seven years. The last revaluation date was January 1, 19X2.

Property rates are recognized as revenue when they are levied because they are considered to be both measurable and available. Proper allowances are made for estimated uncollectible accounts and delinquent accounts.

Vacation, sick leave, and other compensated absences Compensated vacation absences are recorded as expenditures in governmental funds when they are paid. Unpaid vacation leave at year-end is recorded in the General Long-Term Debt Account Group. These unpaid amounts will be paid from expendable available resources provided for in the budget of future years.

For proprietary funds, vacation leave is accrued as an expense when earned by employees.

Sick leave benefits and other compensated absences for governmental funds and proprietary funds are not accrued in the financial statements because they do not vest or accumulate.

II. *Stewardship, Compliance, and Accountability*
   A. *Material violations of finance-related legal and contractual provisions*

Compliance with bond covenants Certain bond covenants require that the City's total debt, both current and noncurrent, not exceed $2 billion. During the fiscal year, the limit was exceeded on two occasions for less than thirty days.

Deposits with financial institutions State statutes require that the City's deposits be collateralized by securities held in the name of the City by the trust department of a bank that does not hold the collateralized deposits. During the year, the City on one occasion permitted a bank to hold securities that collateralized deposits that were held by the same bank.

   B. *Deficit fund balance or retained earnings of individual funds*

C. *Any excess of expenditures over appropriations in individual funds, if any, and explanations thereof, including remedial action planned by or required of the issuer*

Excess of expenditures over appropriations for Special Revenue Fund During the fiscal year, expenditures of the Parks and Recreation Special Revenue Fund exceeded appropriations. The excess occurred because of unexpected expenditures that were incurred by the City to satisfy recently mandated public safety measures passed by the state legislature. State grants are expected to be received over the next eighteen months that will substantially reimburse the City for expenditures incurred to comply with the state statute.

III. *Detail Notes on All Funds and Account Groups*
    A. *Assets*
        i) *Pooling of cash and investments*
        ii) *Investments*
        iii) *Property taxes*
        iv) *Due from other governments—grants receivables*
        v) *Changes in general fixed assets*
        vi) *Summary of proprietary fund fixed assets (including construction in progress)*

Pooling of cash and investments To facilitate better management of the City's resources, substantially all cash is combined in pooled operating accounts. The amounts reflected as cash in the balance sheet represent the individual fund's equity in pooled cash balances. Cash in excess of current needs is invested on a pooled investment basis and earnings therefrom are allocated to each fund on the basis of its cash balance at the end of each month. The carrying amount of the City's deposits with financial institutions was $3,400,000 and the bank balance was $3,650,000. The bank balance is categorized as follows:

Amount insured by the FDIC and FSLIC, or collateralized with securities held by the City in its name	$1,850,000
Amount collateralized with securities held by the pledging financial institution's trust department in the City's name	1,550,000

Uncollateralized (including $140,000 bank balance that is collateralized with securities held by the pledging financial institution's trust department but not in the name of the Centerville Parking Authority)   250,000

Total bank balance $3,650,000

The portion of the total bank balance categorized as "Uncollateralized" is the property of the Centerville Parking Authority, an Enterprise Fund.

Investments Investments, including repurchase agreements, made by the City and information concerning reverse repurchase agreements are summarized below. The investments that are represented by specific identifiable investment securities are classified as to credit risk by the three categories described below:

Category 1   Insured or registered, or securities held by the City or its agent in the City's name

Category 2   Uninsured and unregistered, with securities held by the counterparty's trust department or agent in the City's name

Category 3   Uninsured and unregistered, with securities held by the counterparty, or by its trust department or agent but not in the City's name

	Category 1	Category 2	Category 3	Carrying amount	Market value
U.S. government securities	$120,000			$120,000	$124,000
Commercial paper	20,000			20,000	20,000
Repurchase agreements	40,000	$60,000	$20,000	120,000	130,200
	$180,000	$60,000	$20,000	$260,000	$274,200
Investment in state investment pool				28,000	29,000
				288,000	303,200
Investments held by brokers-dealers under reverse repurchase agreements					
U.S. government securities				24,000	25,200
U.S. instrumentality securities				20,000	22,000
				44,000	47,200
Total investments				$332,000	$350,400

Governmental Financial Reporting

Property taxes The City is responsible for assessing, collecting, and distributing property taxes in accordance with enabling state legislation. Property taxes become a lien on the first day of the levy year and may be paid in two equal installments. The first installment is due on or before April 30 and the second installment, which bears interest at the rate of 6%, is due on or before October 31.

All property taxes are recognized in compliance with NCGA Interpretation-3 (Revenue Recognition—Property Taxes) which states that such revenue is recorded when it becomes measurable and available. Available means due, or past due and receivable within the current period and collected no longer than 60 days after the close of the current period.

Property taxes receivable as of June 30, 19X5, are comprised of the following:

Year of levy	General Fund	Special Revenue Fund
19X5	$1,100,000	$250,000
19X4	300,000	40,000
19X3	250,000	10,000
19X2	120,000	5,000
Before 19X2	20,000	2,000
Total property taxes receivable	1,790,000	307,000
Less allowance for uncollectibles	320,000	70,000
	$1,470,000	$237,000

Due from other governments—grants receivables The City participates in a variety of federal, state, and local programs that enables it to receive grants to partially or fully finance activities of the City. Amounts due from other governments as of June 30, 19X5, are summarized below:

Fund	Federal grants	State grants	County grants	Total
General	$300,000	$140,000	$ 50,000	$ 490,000
Special Revenue	100,000	100,000	120,000	320,000
Capital Projects	40,000	400,000	10,000	450,000
	$440,000	$640,000	$180,000	$1,260,000

The amounts listed above are based on expenditures incurred by the City and, under terms of the grant agreement or legislation, are expected to be received within sixty days of the close of the current period.

Changes in general fixed assets
A summary of changes in general fixed assets is as follows:

	Balance, July 1, 19X4	Additions	Deletions	Balance, June 30, 19X5
Land	$1,500,000	$ 120,000	$ 150,000	$ 1,470,000
Buildings	4,700,000	350,000	100,000	4,950,000
Improvements (other than buildings	800,000	120,000	40,000	880,000
Equipment	1,350,000	400,000	250,000	1,500,000
Construction in progress	750,000	1,780,000	980,000	1,550,000
Total	$9,100,000	$2,770,000	$1,520,000	$10,350,000

Construction in progress is composed of the following:

	Project authorization	Expended to June 30, 19X5	Committed	Required future financing
Senior citizens center	$3,000,000	$1,100,000	$400,000	None
2nd street underpass	750,000	200,000	150,000	None
Vine street storm system	320,000	250,000	30,000	None
Total	$4,070,000	$1,550,000	$580,000	

Summary of proprietary fund fixed assets (including construction in progress)
A summary of a proprietary fund plant, property, and equipment as of June 30, 19X5, is as follows:

	Water and sewer	Transportation	Total
Land	$ 700,000	$ 4,500,000	$ 5,200,000
Buildings	2,400,000	6,000,000	8,400,000
Equipment	1,850,000	22,700,000	24,550,000
Capitalized leases	320,000	3,550,000	3,870,000
Construction in progress	870,000	125,000	995,000
Total	$6,140,000	$36,875,000	$43,015,000

B. Liabilities
    i) Pension plan obligations
    ii) Other employee benefits
    iii) Construction and other significant commitments

- iv) Claims and judgments
- v) Lease obligations (capital and operating)
- vi) Long-term debt
  - a) Description of individual bond issues and leases outstanding
  - b) Changes in general long-term debt
  - c) Summary of debt service requirements to maturity
  - d) Disclosure of legal debt margin
  - e) Bonds authorized but unissued
  - f) Synopsis of revenue bond covenants
- vii) Short-term debt and liquidity

Pension plan obligations All full-time employees of the City of Centerville are covered by the State Public Employee Retirement System, which is a cost-sharing multiple-employer PERS.

All full-time employees are eligible and must participate in the State PERS. The pension plan provides pension benefits, deferred allowances, and death and disability benefits. A member may retire after reaching the age of 55 or accumulating 25 years of service with the City or another entity covered by the State PERS. Benefits vest after 12 years of service. Employees who retire at or after age 55 with 12 or more years of service are entitled to pension payments for the remainder of their lives equal to 2% of their final, five-year average salary times the number of years for which they were employed by a participant in the State PERS. The final, five-year average salary is the average salary of the employee during the final five years of full-time employment exclusive of overtime.

Pension provisions include deferred allowances whereby an employee may terminate his or her employment with the City after accumulating 25 years of service but before reaching the age of 55. If the employee does not withdraw his or her accumulated contributions, the employee is entitled to all pension benefits upon reaching age 55.

Pension provisions include death and disability benefits, whereby the disabled employee or surviving spouse is entitled to receive annually an amount equal to 45% of the employee's final, five-year average salary exclusive of overtime payments. The disabled employee is entitled to receive disability payments for life, while the surviving spouse may receive death benefits for life or as long as he or she does not remarry. Benefits are determined by state statute.

Both the City's current-year covered payroll and its total current-year payroll for all employees amount to $5,000,000.

Employees of the City are required to pay 4% of their gross earnings to the pension plan. The City makes annual contributions to the pension plan equal to the amount required by state statutes. During 19X5, the City was required to contribute 9% of its gross payroll to the plan.

Total contributions made during fiscal year 19X5 amounted to $650,000, of which $450,000 was made by the City and $200,000 was made by employees. These contributions represented 9% (City) and 4% (employees) of covered payroll.

The amount of the total pension benefit obligation is based on a standardized measurement established by GASB-5 that, with some exceptions, must be used by a PERS. The standardized measurement is the actuarial present value of credited projected benefits. This pension valuation method reflects the present value of estimated pension benefits that will be paid in future years as a result of employee services performed to date, and is adjusted for the effects of projected salary increases. A standardized measure of the pension benefit obligation was adopted by the GASB to enable readers of PERS financial statements to (a) assess the PERS funding status on a going-concern basis, (b) assess progress made in accumulating sufficient assets to pay benefits when due, and (c) make comparisons among other PERS and among other employers.

Total unfunded pension benefit obligation of the State PERS as of June 30, 19X5, was as follows:

	(in millions)
Total pension benefit obligations	$265
Net assets available for pension benefits, at market	201
Unfunded pension benefit obligation	$ 64

The measurement of the total pension benefit obligation is based on an actuarial valuation as of June 30, 19X5. Net assets available to pay pension benefits were valued as of the same date.

The City's 19X5 required contribution to the State PERS represents 3.5% of the total current-year actuarially determined contribution requirements for all employers covered by the pension plan.

Ten-year historical trend information is presented in the 19X5 State PERS Comprehensive Annual Financial Report. This information is useful in assessing the pension plan's accumulation of sufficient assets to pay pension benefits as they become due.

During 19X5 and as of June 30, 19X5, the State PERS held no securities issued by the City or other related parties.

Other employee benefits City employees receive vested rights to two-weeks' paid vacation at the end of their first year of full-time em-

Governmental Financial Reporting

ployment with no pro rata payment if employment is terminated before the completion of a full year of service. An expenditure/expense for vacation pay is recognized each month on a pro rata basis, after taking into consideration the expected termination rate during the period.

Construction and other significant commitments As of June 30, 19X5, the City had the following commitments with respect to unfinished capital projects:

Capital project	Remaining financial commitment	Expected date of completion
#104-Intersection improvements	$ 750,000	April 30, 19X6
#109-Fire station	220,000	May 1, 19X6
#124-Recreation facility	130,000	September 1, 19X6
Total	$1,100,000	

Claims and judgments The City participates in a number of federal, state, and county programs that are fully or partially funded by grants received from other governmental units. Expenditures financed by grants are subject to audit by the appropriate grantor government. If expenditures are disallowed due to noncompliance with grant program regulations, the City may be required to reimburse the grantor government. As of June 20, 19X5, significant amounts of grant expenditures have not been audited but the City believes that disallowed expenditures, if any, based on subsequent audits will not have a material effect on any of the individual governmental funds or the overall financial position of the City.

Lease obligations The City is obligated under certain leases accounted for as capital leases. The leased assets and related obligations are accounted for in the General Fixed Assets Account Group and the General Long-Term Debt Account Group, respectively. Assets under capital leases totaled $10,000,000 as of June 30, 19X5, and accumulated amortization on those assets totaled $3,500,000. The following is a schedule of future minimum lease payments under capital leases, together with the net present value of the minimum lease payments as of June 30, 19X5:

Year ending June 30	General long-term obligation account group
19X6	$100,000
19X7	95,000
19X8	95,000
19X9	80,000
19Y0	60,000
Later years	170,000
Minimum lease payments for all capital leases	600,000
Less: Amount representing interest at the City's incremental borrowing rate of interest	90,000
Present value of minimum lease payments	$510,000

In addition, the City is obligated under certain leases accounted for as operating leases. Operating leases do not give rise to property rights or lease obligations, and therefore the results of the lease agreements are not reflected in the City's account groups. The following is a schedule by years of future minimum rental payments required under operating leases that have initial or remaining noncancelable lease terms in excess of one year as of June 30, 19X5:

Year ending June 30	Amounts
19X6	$20,000
19X7	18,000
19X8	18,000
19X9	15,000
19Y0	10,000
Later years	45,000
Total minimum payments required	$126,000

The following schedule shows the composition of total rental expenditures for all operating leases except those with terms of a month or less that were not renewed:

	Year ending June 30, 19X5	Year ending June 30, 19X4
Minimum rentals	$15,000	$22,000
Contingent rentals	17,000	12,000
Less: Sublease rentals	(4,000)	(2,000)
	$28,000	$32,000

Governmental Financial Reporting

Long-term debt The following is a summary of the City's long-term debt transactions for the year ended June 30, 19X5:

	General obligation bonds	Revenue bonds	Capitalized leases	Total
Debt outstanding, July 1, 19X4	$13,000,000	$11,000,000	$750,000	$24,750,000
Additions:				
New bonds issued	4,000,000	2,000,000		6,000,000
Leases capitalized			200,000	200,000
Reductions:				
Principal repayments	(2,000,000)	(1,000,000)	(50,000)	(3,050,000)
Debt outstanding, June 30, 19X5	$15,000,000	$12,000,000	$900,000	$27,900,000

Debt outstanding as of June 30, 19X5, is composed of the following:

	Interest rate	Maturity date	Amount issued	Amount outstanding
General obligations bonds:				
19X1 Public parks	6%	9/1/Z1	$ 5,000,000	$ 3,000,000
19X3 Public libraries	6%	6/1/Y8	9,000,000	6,000,000
19X4 Traffic improvement	8%	3/1/Z4	2,000,000	2,000,000
19X5 Fire stations	7%	7/1/Y6	4,000,000	4,000,000
				15,000,000
Revenue bonds:				
19X3 Water and sewer	5%	5/1/Z3	15,000,000	10,000,000
19X5 Water and sewer	6%	2/1/Z5	2,000,000	2,000,000
				12,000,000
Capitalized leases:				
19X3 Vehicles	8%	*	1,900,000	700,000
19X5 Vehicles	9%	*	200,000	200,000
				900,000
Total debt outstanding, June 30, 19X5				$27,900,000

*monthly installments

Presented below is a summarization of debt service requirements to maturity by year:

Year	General obligation bonds	Revenue bonds	Capitalized leases	Total
19X6	$ 1,880,000	$ 870,000	$ 450,000	$ 3,200,000
19X7	1,880,000	870,000	400,000	3,150,000
19X8	1,880,000	870,000	350,000	3,100,000
19X9	1,880,000	870,000	200,000	2,950,000
19Y0	1,880,000	870,000		2,750,000
19Y1	1,880,000	870,000		2,750,000
19Y2	1,880,000	870,000		2,750,000
19Y3	1,880,000	870,000		2,750,000
19Y4	1,880,000	870,000		2,750,000
19Y5	1,880,000	870,000		2,750,000
19Y6	1,880,000	870,000		2,750,000
19Y7	5,600,000	870,000		6,470,000
19Y8	10,395,000	870,000		11,265,000
19Y9	1,060,000	870,000		1,930,000
19Z0	1,060,000	870,000		1,930,000
19Z1	1,060,000	870,000		1,930,000
19Z2	5,310,000	870,000		6,180,000
19Z3	160,000	15,745,000		15,905,000
19Z4	2,106,667	120,000		2,226,667
19Z5		2,120,000		2,120,000
	$47,431,667	$32,775,000	$1,400,000	$81,606,667

The amount of long-term debt that can be incurred by the City is limited by State statute. Total outstanding long-term obligations during a year can be no greater than 12.5% of the assessed value of taxable property as of the beginning of the fiscal year. As of June 30, 19X5, the amount of outstanding long-term debt was equal to 7.3% of property assessments as of July 1, 19X4.

On May 1, 19X5, the City was authorized by voter approval to issue the following long-term debt:

General obligation bonds:	
Street and curbing improvements	$2,000,000
Landfill acquisition sites	4,000,000
Revenue bonds:	
Airport development	1,500,000
	$7,500,000

Governmental Financial Reporting

As of June 30, 19X5, none of the authorized bonds listed above had been issued.

All outstanding revenue bonds are secured by a first lien on net revenues earned by Enterprise Funds. Net revenues are defined in the revenue bond agreements. The Enterprise Funds are required to establish user fees and rates that will yield net revenues equal to at least 1.3 times the debt service that will become due in the following fiscal year.

Short-term debt and liquidity The City has statutory authorization to negotiate temporary debts that will not mature beyond the close of its fiscal year. During January 19X5, the City issued $1,000,000 of tax and revenue anticipation notes in order to alleviate a temporary operating cash flow deficiency. On April 1, 19X5, approximately 40% of the tax and revenue anticipation notes were liquidated and the balance of the debt was liquidated during the month of May. No tax and revenue anticipation notes were outstanding as of June 30, 19X5.

During 19X5, the City negotiated a line of credit with a consortium of banks in order to meet future operating cash deficiencies that may arise. As of June 30, 19X5, the City has not drawn against this line of credit.

C. *Interfund receivables and payables*

Interfund transactions between various governmental and proprietary fund types occur during the fiscal year. Principally, these transactions arise from operating subsidies, debt service requirements, construction of capital assets, and quasi-external transactions. Transactions that have not resulted in the actual transfer of cash as of the end of the fiscal year are recorded as amounts due from (fund receivable) and due to (fund liability) other funds. For financial reporting purposes, current amounts due from and due to the same fund are offset and the net amounts are shown in the respective fund balance sheet. At the end of each fiscal year, the amount of interfund receivables is equal to the amount of interfund payables. The amounts of interfund receivables and payables were $3,450,000 and consisted of the following interfund amounts:

Governmental Financial Reporting

	Amounts due to other funds	*Amounts due from other funds*
General fund	$3,450,000	
Special revenue funds		$ 275,000
Capital projects funds		2,800,000
Enterprise funds		375,000
Total	$3,450,000	$3,450,000

D. Fund equity
    i) Reservation of retained earnings
    ii) Reservation of fund balance
    iii) Unreserved fund balance—designations

Reservations of retained earnings of proprietary funds are created by increases in assets restricted for debt service, and renewals and replacements. These increases result from earnings on restricted assets and other interfund transfers to restricted accounts. Earnings on restricted assets are included in the net income of proprietary funds. When reserved retained earnings are increased, there is an equal reduction in the portion of retained earnings that is unreserved. Specific reservations of retained earnings are summarized below:

Reserve for debt service This reserve was created to segregate a portion of the fund balance account for debt service, including both principal payments and interest payments. The reservation was established to satisfy legal restrictions imposed by various bond agreements.

Reserve for encumbrances This reserve represents encumbrances outstanding at the end of the year based on purchase orders and contracts signed by the City but not completed.

Reserve for inventories This reserve is created to represent the portion of the fund balance that is not available for expenditures because the City expects to use these resources within the next budgetary period.

Reserve for land held for resale This reserve identifies a portion of the fund balance that is equal to the book value of land that is held for resale but is not expected to be available to finance expenditures of the next budgetary period.

Designations of fund balances of governmental funds are created to indicate tentative plans for financial resource utilization in a future period. Because designations reflect tentative managerial plans or intent, the City is not bound by such designations. Designations are reported as part of the unreserved portion of the fund balance accounts, although they are separately identified as designated for a particular purpose. Specific designations of the fund balance accounts are summarized below:

Designation for contingencies This designation is created for possible losses that arise from contingencies that are unasserted as of the date of the balance sheet.

Designation for capital projects This designation is created to identify tentative capital projects that are being considered for funding by the City.

IV. Segment Information—Enterprise Funds

The following Enterprise Funds have been created to provide various services to the general public:

Airport Fund Established to account for the operation of the City of Centerville Airport.

Water System Fund Established to account for the operation of the City's water system.

Landfill Fund Established to account for the operation of the City's garbage disposal activities.

Segment information of these Enterprise Funds is summarized below for the year ended June 30, 19X5:

	Airport	Water system	Landfill
Operating revenues	$2,000,000	$3,500,000	$1,700,000
Depreciation	140,000	265,000	120,000
Operating income (loss)	104,000	75,000	(140,000)
Operating grants	—	—	95,000
Operating interfund transfers	—	—	100,000
Tax revenues	—	—	205,000

Governmental Financial Reporting

Net income (loss)	70,000	25,000	(126,000)
Current capital contributions	200,000	350,000	150,000
Property, plant, and equipment			
Additions	350,000	120,000	50,000
Dispositions	101,000	17,000	—
Net working capital	720,000	305,000	18,000
Total assets	3,450,000	7,800,000	450,000
Bonds and other long-term liabilities payable from operating revenues	1,200,000	4,500,000	—
Total equity	1,870,000	2,800,000	78,000

V. Related-Party Transactions

The City provides certain legal, engineering, and printing services to the Industrial Development Corporation of Centerville (IDCC). Although the IDCC was created by the City and its governing board is approved by the mayor, it is not part of the City's financial reporting entity. Services provided by the City to the IDCC are billed at an amount that will approximately recover the City's full cost of providing such services. This basis of billing has been used by the City consistently over the years to determine the amount of revenues and expenditures/expenses arising from quasi-external transactions.

Total billings for the period amounted to $37,000, and this amount was reported as revenue by the General Fund ($31,000) and the Internal Service Fund ($6,000) and an expense by the IDCC. As of the end of the year, an intergovernmental receivable of $6,000 arising from the services provided to the IDCC was reported by the General Fund ($4,000) and the Internal Service Fund ($2,000).

VI. Summary Disclosure of Significant Contingencies
A. Litigation

The City is a defendant in a number of lawsuits arising principally from claims against the City for alleged improper actions by City employees, including alleged improper police action, negligence, and discrimination. Total damages claimed are substantial; however, it has been the City's experience that such actions are settled for amounts substantially less than the claimed amounts. The City Attorney estimates that the potential claims against the City not co-

Governmental Financial Reporting

vered by various insurance policies would not materially affect the financial condition of the City.

B. Federally assisted programs—compliance audits

The City receives substantial grants from the federal, state, and county governments, all of which are subject to audit by the respective governments. Subsequent audits may disallow expenditures financed by governmental grant programs, although past audits have resulted in minor violations of grant regulations and no requests for reimbursement. Grants approximating $12,000,000 have not been subject to audit as of June 30, 19X5. It is the opinion of management that requests for reimbursement, if any, by either the federal, state, or local governments based on subsequent audits will not be material in relation to the City's financial statements as of June 30, 19X5.

VII. Significant Effects of Subsequent Events

On July 15, 19X5, the City issued tax revenue and anticipation notes in the amount of $10,000,000. The interest rate of this debt is 7.03%. The notes will be repaid in fiscal year 19X6 from Unrestricted Funds, primarily sales and property tax revenues. The note resolution requires that the City set aside in a Restricted Fund one quarter of the principal and interest due in the months of September, December, March, and June of fiscal year 19X6. Repayment of the notes is scheduled for June 20, 19X6.

APPENDIX
STATEMENT OF CASH FLOWS FOR CERTAIN GOVERNMENTAL FUNDS (EXPOSURE DRAFT)

OBSERVATION: *In September 1989, the GASB issued GASB-9 (Reporting Cash Flows of Proprietary and Nonexpendable Trust Funds and Governmental Entities That Use Proprietary Fund*

Accounting). The standards established by this Statement are essentially the same as those discussed in this Appendix. This Statement is effective for annual financial statements for fiscal years beginning after December 15, 1989.

In November, 1987, the Financial Accounting Standards Board (FASB) issued FASB-95 (Statement of Cash Flows), superseding APB-19 (Reporting Changes in Financial Position). The issuance of FASB-95 raised the question of whether governmental entities using proprietary fund accounting would have to prepare a statement of cash flows rather than a statement of changes in financial position.

In November 1988, the Governmental Accounting Standards Board (GASB) issued an Exposure Draft entitled "Reporting Cash Flows of Proprietary and Nonexpendable Trust Funds and Governmental Entities That Use Proprietary Fund Accounting." The Exposure Draft addresses the need for and the format of a statement of cash flows for certain governmental funds. This Appendix summarizes the concepts proposed in the GASB Exposure Draft, describing the Exposure Draft's deviations from FASB-95.

Fundamental Approach

The Exposure Draft essentially adopts the fundamental concepts expressed in FASB-95, proposing that a governmental fund using proprietary fund accounting should prepare a statement of cash flows identifying the major flows of cash during an accounting period instead of preparing a statement of changes in financial position. In this case, the focus of the analysis would be cash, or cash and cash equivalents, as they are defined in FASB-95. The Exposure Draft suggests that the statement of cash flows may be prepared using either the direct method or the indirect method. Under the direct method, cash flows from operating activities would be presented by major categories. Under the indirect method, cash flows from operating activities would be determined by adjusting net operating income.

The standards proposed in the Exposure Draft deviate from the standards established in FASB-95 only to a limited extent. Apparently, the GASB does not wish to create a comparability issue by having two separate sets of reporting standards with respect to the preparation of the statement of cash flows: A set of standards for commercial enterprises and a set of standards for governmental entities using proprietary fund accounting. The GASB's philosophy in this regard is expressed in the following statement reproduced from the Exposure Draft.

> To reduce the potential for other departures from FASB Statement 95, which might result from interpretation, the Board decided that, generally, the language in FASB Statement 95 should be repeated, where appropriate, in this Statement (Exposure Draft). As a result, the requirements and language in this Statement (Exposure Draft) closely follows, and sometimes are identical to, the requirements and language in FASB Statement 95 (paragraph 54).

The balance of this Appendix describes the proposed deviations from FASB-95.

Classifications of Cash Flows

FASB-95 identifies three broad categories to be used in summarizing cash flows for a period. These categories are cash flows from (1) operating activities, (2) investing activities, and (3) financing activities. The GASB Exposure Draft, however, proposes that *four* categories be used to summarize cash flows, as follows:

- Cash flows from operating activities
- Cash flows from noncapital financing activities
- Cash flows from capital and related financing activities
- Cash flows from investing activities

As illustrated in the above listing, the Exposure Draft suggests that cash flows related to financing activities (the FASB's position) be further divided into noncapital activities and capital activities.

The rationale for using two categories of financing activities is based on the possibility that in the future all governmental funds may be able to use a single cash flow format. Under present arrangements, funds that use proprietary fund accounting would present a cash flow statement, but governmental funds that use the governmental accounting model would not present a cash flow statement. Furthermore, in the future, if a cash flow statement is adopted as part of the governmental accounting model, some of the activities would be classified differently depending upon whether proprietary fund accounting or the governmental fund accounting model is followed. For example, under the governmental accounting model, a capital expenditure is considered an operating activity, but under the commercial accounting model, a capital expenditure is considered an investing activity. By adopting a four-category scheme rather than a three-category scheme, the GASB believes it would be easier to resolve conflicts between the two models if the current governmental accounting model is changed.

> **OBSERVATION:** *The GASB has several ongoing research projects that may significantly change the current governmental accounting model to one that more closely resembles a commercial model.*

The Exposure Draft notes in paragraph 51 that the use of two categories for capital and financing activities will necessitate the following modifications to FASB-95:

a. Construction and acquisition of capital assets are not classified as investing as specified in FASB Statement 95; instead, they are major elements in the capital and related financing category.
b. The financing category in FASB Statement 95 includes cash inflows and outflows related to *both* capital and noncapital borrowing. Capital borrowing activity is another major element of the capital and related financing category.
c. To show the complete picture of *all* cash inflows and outflows from financing, acquiring, and disposing of capital assets, it is necessary to include interest expenditures in this category rather than in the operating category.
d. Similarly, interest on noncapital debt is classified as noncapital financing so that it is treated consistently with capital interest and gives a more complete picture of *all* inflows and outflows arising from noncapital debt transactions.
e. The nature of investing activity in the governmental environment is focused on the acquisition and disposition of debt and equity instruments of other entities rather than on the investment of ownership capital in capital assets. Therefore, it is more useful to reclassify investment earnings (interest and dividends) as inflows from investing rather than from operating activities.

Cash Flows from Operating Activities

The GASB Exposure Draft proposes that cash flows from operating activities focus on operating income (loss) rather than on net income (loss) for the period.

Certain governmental entities, for example municipal utilities, that follow proprietary fund accounting exclude some activities when computing their net operating income or loss for the period. These exclusions generally consist of interest income and expense, operating grants, and gains and losses from the disposition of assets. These excluded components of income would be included in other sections of the statement of cash flows depending upon their character. For example, interest paid on construction bonds would be categorized as part of cash flows from capital and related financing activities. Thus, cash flows from operating activities would be restricted to revenues and expenses that are specifically related to the delivery of the governmental service or the production of the good by the governmental entity.

Restricted Assets

Some governmental entities' assets cannot be used for current operations. These restricted assets may include cash and cash equivalents. In its Exposure Draft, the GASB takes the position that restricted assets meeting the definition of cash or cash equivalents should be considered cash or cash equivalents in the preparation of a statement of cash flows. For example, to determine the net amount of cash flows for the period, the difference between the beginning and ending balances of cash and restricted cash would need to be determined.

Public Employee Retirement Systems (PERS)

Financial reporting by PERS is an unsettled area. Accounting and reporting standards established by either (1) NCGA-1 (Governmental Accounting and Financial Reporting Principles), (2) NCGA-6 (Pension Accounting and Financial Reporting: Public Employee Retirement Systems and State and Local Governmental Employers), or (3) FASB-35 (Accounting and Reporting by Defined Benefit Pension Plans) can be used by a governmental entity. The requirements for a statement of cash flows (formerly a statement of changes in financial position) are not the same under the three pronouncements.

Currently, the GASB has a research project that is concerned with pension accounting, including reporting by PERS. A future GASB pronouncement is expected to address the issue of which financial statements should be presented by a PERS.

Because of the inconsistent requirements of existing authoritative pronouncements and the likelihood of a future pronouncement that will address the issue directly, the GASB proposes in its Exposure Draft that PERS and pension trust funds not be required to include a statement of cash flows or the previous statement of changes in financial position.

BUDGETARY ACCOUNTING AND REPORTING

The Budgetary Process

A budget is a plan of financial operations which provides a basis for the planning, controlling, and evaluating of governmental activities. The budget process is a political process that usually begins with the chief executive of a governmental unit submitting a budget to the unit's legislative branch for consideration. Ultimately the legal authority for governmental expenditures is reflected in an appropriations bill(s).

The budgetary process for governmental units is far more significant than the same process for commercial enterprises due to the public nature of the process and fiduciary responsibility of public officials. The importance of the budgetary process is emphasized by the fact that NCGA-1 (Governmental Accounting and Financial Reporting Principles) concluded that every governmental unit (governmental fund types, proprietary fund types, and fiduciary fund types) should prepare an annual comprehensive budget. It further recommended that the annual budget be prepared and serve as a basis for control and evaluation of a fund even if the fund was not legally required to adopt a budget.

While the NCGA recommended that all funds adopt a budget for control purposes, there is a recognition that the nature of budgeting is different among the three types of funds.

Budgeting for Proprietary Funds Generally a proprietary fund should prepare a flexible budget, which changes as the activity level changes. In a proprietary fund, overall activity is measured in terms of revenues and expenses and will fluctuate, in part, depending upon the demand for goods and services by the public (Enterprise Fund) or by other governmental agencies (Internal Service Fund). The flexible budget is generally not considered as appropriations, but rather serves as an approved plan that can facilitate budgetary control and operational evaluations. It allows the governmental unit to prepare several budgets at different activity levels in order to establish an acceptable comparative basis for planned activity and actual results.

> **OBSERVATION:** NCGA-1 *discusses the preparation of several budgets based on anticipated activity levels. Even if several budgets are prepared, the budget ultimately used as a comparison with actual results should be based on the actual, not the anticipated activity level. The preparation of the budget based on actual activity is feasible since the flexible budgeting approach can be expressed in terms of a formula (Total Expenses = Fixed Expenses + Variable Expenses) and should be applicable at any activity level.*

The basis of accounting used to prepare a budget for a proprietary fund should be the same as the basis used to record the results of actual transactions. It is not appropriate to integrate the budgetary system into the proprietary fund's accounting system when a flexible budget system is used; however, if a fixed budget is used, perhaps due to a legal requirement or preference, it may be useful to integrate the budgetary system into the fund's accounting system.

Budgeting for Fiduciary Funds Fiduciary funds include Agency Funds, Nonexpendable Trust Funds, Pension Trust Funds, and Expendable Trust Funds. Budgets are usually not appropriate for Agency Funds because, in the capacity of an agent, the governmental unit performs only a custodial function. Nonexpendable Trust Funds and Pension Trust Funds are similar to proprietary funds and may use budgetary controls as described in the above paragraphs. Expendable Trust Funds are similar to governmental fund types and, where appropriate, should follow the guidelines described in the following paragraphs. Budgetary controls that are applicable to Special Revenue Funds are also applicable to the Expendable Trust Funds that are similar to Special Revenue Funds.

Budgeting for Governmental Funds Governmental funds (General Fund, Special Revenue Funds, Capital Projects Funds, and Debt Service Funds) generally use a fixed budget that reflects a specific estimate for revenues and expenditures. A flexible budget is inappropriate for a governmental fund type because overall estimates of revenues and expenditures do not have a significant relationship to the demand for governmental services. Once expenditures and revenues are incorporated into the budget, the total estimated expenditure appropriation amount becomes a limit for current expenditures, and the estimated revenue amount becomes the basis for comparison to actual revenues.

Because the appropriated budget is used as the basis for control and comparison of budgeted and actual amounts, the basis for preparing the budget should be the same as the governmental fund's basis of accounting. The modified accrual basis is the recommended basis of accounting for governmental fund types, and, ideally, the budget should reflect a similar basis for establishing expenditures and estimating revenues. When the budget basis and basis of accounting are different, a governmental unit usually maintains its records on the budget basis (legal basis) and uses supplementary information to convert the budget-based information to a modified accrual basis (generally accepted accounting principles) for financial reporting purposes. Also, to facilitate the comparison of budgeted amounts and actual expenditures and revenues, similar terms and classifications should be used in the preparation of the budget and the presentation of the financial report.

> **OBSERVATION:** *From an accounting perspective, it is preferable that the budgetary system be on the same basis as the financial accounting system, namely the modified accrual basis. However, some would strongly argue that a budget should be based on the cash basis because it is more consistent with the operations and financing of a governmental unit and is better understood by legislators.*

Budgetary Accounting System

Budgetary control is enhanced when the legally adopted budget is integrated into the governmental unit's formal accounting system. The integration of the budget and accounting system is referred to as the budgetary accounting system. Budgetary accounts are used in a budgetary accounting system.

A budgetary accounting system should be used by certain governmental fund types. NCGA-1 concludes that budgetary accounts should be used in the General Fund and Special Revenue Funds. Other governmental funds that should employ a budgetary accounting system are those subject to the controls of an annually adopted budget, and those processing numerous revenue, expenditure, and transfer transactions through the fund. The following example illustrates when it may be appropriate to use budgetary accounts, to some degree, in other governmental funds:

- *Capital Projects Fund*—Various construction projects are being currently financed through the fund.

Conversely, the following illustrations would suggest that the budgetary accounts are unnecessary:

Budgetary Accounting and Reporting

- *Debt Service Fund*—Receipts and expenditures for a period are established by sinking fund provisions of a debt agreement, and few transactions are processed each period.
- *Capital Projects Fund*—Various construction projects are under contract with independent contractors that are exclusively responsible for the progress of the project (turnkey projects).

Ultimately, professional judgment must be used to determine if a budgetary accounting system is necessary to provide adequate control over revenues and expenditures of a particular governmental fund.

Budgetary accounts are used exclusively for control; therefore, they do not affect the actual results of operations for the accounting period. Two important aspects of a budgetary accounting system are (1) accounting for the budget and (2) accounting for encumbrances.

Accounting for the Budget NCGA Interpretation-10 (State and Local Government Budgetary Reporting) defines the appropriated budget as follows:

> The expenditure authority created by the appropriation bills or ordinances that are signed into law and related estimated revenues . . . (including) all reserves, transfers, allocations, supplemental appropriations, and other legally authorized legislative and executive changes.

The appropriated budget for the current fiscal year may be recorded in the following manner:

Estimated Revenues (Control)	400,000,000	
Appropriations (Control)		390,000,000
Fund Balance (Budgetary)		10,000,000
To record operating budget.		

The estimated revenues account is a budgetary account and represents the total anticipated revenues on a budgetary basis that are expected to be available during the fiscal year. The estimated revenues account functions as an overall control account, and the specific revenue sources, such as property taxes, fines, and intergovernmental revenues, would be recorded in revenue subsidiary ledgers. Actual revenues are recorded in nonbudgetary accounts as they are recognized throughout the accounting period. Also, as actual revenues are recorded, similar postings are made to the subsidiary ledgers. The overall control account and the subsidiary ledgers provide a

Budgetary Accounting and Reporting

basis for the subsequent comparison of the estimated revenues with the actual revenues for the period. Thus, the estimated revenues account (a budgetary account) is used to compare estimated revenues with actual revenues for the period, but it does not function as a control account for revenues.

Appropriations is a budgetary account which represents the total authorized expenditures for a current fiscal period. The appropriations account is a control account with the details of the approved expenditures being recorded in appropriations subsidiary ledgers. During the year, expenditures are recorded in both (1) nonbudgetary accounts such as public safety and health and welfare expenditures and (2) appropriations subsidiary ledger accounts. Throughout the fiscal year, the appropriations account and its subsidiary ledger accounts can be used to control the level of expenditures to avoid exceeding appropriated amounts. Thus, the appropriations account (a budgetary account) is used both for control and comparative purposes.

The difference between estimated revenues and appropriations as authorized in the budget is debited or credited to the fund's fund balance account (budgetary). The entry in the fund balance account reflects either an anticipated operating surplus (credit) or deficit (debit) for the current budgetary period.

As suggested earlier, the use of budgetary accounts does not affect the actual revenues and expenditures recognized during the accounting period. This is accomplished by simply reversing, at the end of the period, the budgetary accounts created when the budget was initially recorded. For example, the earlier entry used to illustrate the recording of the budget would be reversed as follows:

Fund Balance (Budgetary)	10,000,000	
Appropriations	390,000,000	
Estimated Revenues		400,000,000
To close budgetary accounts.		

The discussion of recording the budget illustrated only budgetary accounts related to anticipated revenues and expenditures. When the fund has other financial sources (uses) that are part of the adopted budget, appropriate budgetary accounts, as illustrated below, should be used.

Budgetary Account	*Proprietary Account*
Estimated Operating Transfers In	Transfers In
Authorized Operating Transfers Out	Transfers Out
Estimated Bond Proceeds	Bond Proceeds

Budgetary Accounting and Reporting

When the additional budgetary and proprietary accounts are used, the budgetary accounts are closed by simply reversing the original entry that recorded the budget.

Alternatively, the budgetary accounts can be grouped with related (proprietary) accounts as part of the closing to emphasize the comparative purpose of using the budgetary accounting system. This type of closing, along with the use of other budgetary accounts, is illustrated below:

Revenues	397,500,000	
Operating Transfers In	3,500,000	
Bond Proceeds	2,000,000	
Fund Balance	3,000,000	
Estimated Revenues		400,000,000
Estimated Operating Transfers In		4,000,000
Estimated Bond Proceeds		2,000,000

To close all revenue related budgetary and proprietary accounts.

Appropriations	390,000,000	
Authorized Operating Transfers Out	6,000,000	
Expenditures		385,000,000
Operating Transfers Out		5,000,000
Fund Balance		6,000,000

To close all expenditure related budgetary and proprietary accounts.

Accounting for Encumbrances Encumbrances represent commitments related to contracts not yet performed (executory contracts), and are used to control expenditures for the year and to enhance cash management. A governmental unit often issues purchase orders or signs contracts for the purchase of goods and services to be received in the future. At the time these commitments are made, the following budgetary entry should be made for control purposes:

Encumbrances	100,000	
Reserve For Encumbrances		100,000

To record the issuance of a purchase order for supplies.

The encumbrances account does not represent an expenditure for the period, only a commitment to expend resources. Likewise, the account reserve for encumbrances is not synonymous with a liability account since the liability is recognized only when the goods are received or the services are performed.

When an executory contract is completed (or virtually completed),

Budgetary Accounting and Reporting

the budgetary accounts are eliminated and the actual expenditure and related liability are recorded, as illustrated below:

Reserve For Encumbrances   100,000
    Encumbrances   100,000
To record the receipts of supplies and cancellation of the outstanding encumbrance.

Expenditure   97,000
    Vouchers Payable   97,000
To record the expenditure for supplies.

The original encumbrance entry is based on the estimated cost of goods and services and may, as illustrated above, differ from the eventual cost of the item.

During the budgetary period, the governmental unit can determine the remaining amount of the new commitments that can be signed by comparing the amount of appropriations to the sum of expenditures recognized and encumbrances outstanding.

At the end of the fiscal year, some encumbrances may be outstanding. NCGA-1 concludes that encumbrances outstanding at the end of the year are not expenditures for the year, and the reserve for encumbrances account is not to be treated as a liability. The treatment of the two budgetary accounts at the end of the year depends upon whether appropriations, even if encumbered at the year-end, are allowed to lapse.

Lapsing appropriations When there are outstanding encumbrances at the end of the fiscal year, it is highly likely that the governmental unit will honor the open purchase orders or contracts that support the encumbrances. For reporting purposes, as noted earlier, outstanding encumbrances are not considered expenditures for the fiscal year. If the governmental unit allows encumbrances to lapse, even though it plans to honor the encumbrances, the appropriations authority expires and the items represented by the encumbrances are usually reappropriated in the following year's budget.

NCGA-1 concludes that when outstanding encumbrances are allowed to lapse at year end but the state or local government intends to honor the commitment, the encumbrances should be disclosed either as a reservation of the fund balance or in a note to the financial statements, and authorization for the eventual expenditure should be included in the following year's budget appropriations.

To illustrate the accounting that is necessary to observe the NCGA-1 requirements, assume that encumbrances of $100,000 are outstand-

Budgetary Accounting and Reporting

ing at December 31, 19X5, but the governmental unit intends to honor the encumbrances and reappropriate funds to pay for the commitments in the 19X6 fiscal year. At the end of 19X5, the following entries should be made:

Reserve For Encumbrances	100,000	
Encumbrances		100,000

To close encumbrances outstanding at the end of the fiscal year.

Fund Balance	100,000	
Fund Balance—Reserve For		
Encumbrances		100,000

To reserve the fund balance by the estimated amount that will be reappropriated in 19X6 for outstanding encumbrances.

The first entry simply closes the encumbrances accounts because they are strictly budgetary accounts. The second entry meets the requirement of NCGA-1 in that the fund balance is reserved by the amount of the outstanding encumbrances.

At the beginning of the next fiscal year (January 1, 19X6), the following entries are made:

Encumbrances	100,000	
Reserve For Encumbrances		100,000

To recognize outstanding encumbrances from the prior year.

Fund Balance—Reserve For		
Encumbrances	100,000	
Fund Balance		100,000

To remove the restriction on the current fund balance based on outstanding encumbrances from the prior year.

The first entry re-establishes budgetary control over the outstanding encumbrances, while the next entry removes the fund balance restriction which is no longer needed with the re-establishment of budgetary control. That is, the appropriations control account created in the January 1, 19X6, budget will include the $100,000 since an expenditure for this amount is anticipated during 19X6.

From this point the normal entries for encumbrances and expenditures are followed. For example, if the goods or services are received on January 28, 19X6, the following entries would be made:

Expenditures	99,000	
Vouchers Payable		99,000

To record the receipts of goods or services.

Budgetary Accounting and Reporting

Reserve For Encumbrances	100,000	
Encumbrances		100,000
To remove encumbrances on vouchered commitments.		

It should be noted that the expenditures are reflected in the 19X6 financial statements as required by NCGA-1.

When encumbrances that have lapsed are reappropriated and treated in the manner described above, there are no differences between the budgetary accounting basis and the GAAP basis. That is, the budgetary expenditures represented by the encumbrances are reflected in the budget in the same year that the expenditures are shown in the (GAAP) statement of operations.

Nonlapsing appropriations Encumbrances that are outstanding at year-end and are nonlapsing do not require reappropriation the following year since the appropriation authority does not expire. NCGA-1 requires that outstanding encumbrances that are nonlapsing be reported as a fund balance reserve. To illustrate, assume that encumbrances of $100,000 are outstanding as of December 31, 19X5. At the end of 19X5, the following entries would be made:

Fund Balance	100,000	
Encumbrances		100,000
To close encumbrances outstanding at the end of the fiscal year.		

Reserve For Encumbrances	100,000	
Fund Balance—Reserve For		
Encumbrances		100,000
To reserve the fund balance by the estimated amount that represents outstanding encumbrances at the end of the fiscal year.		

The two entries close the encumbrances accounts to avoid reporting budgetary accounts in the financial statements. The first entry closes the encumbrances account directly to the fund balance so that they are not shown as expenditures in the current fiscal year as required by GAAP. The second entry establishes a fund balance reserve as required by NCGA-1.

At the beginning of the next fiscal year (January 1, 19X6), the following entry would be made:

Fund Balance—Reserve For		
Encumbrances	100,000	
Reserve For Encumbrances—19X5		100,000
To recognize outstanding encumbrances from the prior year.		

Budgetary Accounting and Reporting

This entry re-establishes the reserve for encumbrances account (a budgetary account), but indicates that the reserve is applicable to amounts appropriated in the previous year's budget.

When goods or services are received, the following entry would be made during 19X6:

Expenditures—19X5	99,000	
Vouchers Payable		99,000
To record the receipt of goods or services.		

At the end of 19X6, the following closing entry would be made:

Reserve For Encumbrances—19X5	100,000	
Expenditures—19X5		99,000
Fund Balance		1,000
To close expenditures encumbered during the prior year.		

This closing entry enables 19X5 encumbered expenditures to be reported as an expenditure in 19X6 as required by GAAP.

When nonlapsing encumbrances are treated in the manner illustrated, there are differences between the budgetary accounting amounts and the GAAP basis amounts. The budget-based information reflects expenditures based on liabilities incurred and encumbrances outstanding, whereas the actual (GAAP basis) financial statement does not include amounts encumbered at the end of the fiscal year. As explained in the following section of this chapter, there must be a reconciliation between budgeted financial statements not prepared on a GAAP basis and the actual financial statements, which must be presented on a GAAP basis.

Once a method of accounting for encumbrances is established, it should be used on a consistent basis and described in the Summary of Significant Accounting Policies. An example of this type of disclosure is presented below:

▶ As required by the Laws of the State, the encumbrances method of accounting is used for all funds. Under this method, commitments, such as purchase orders and other contracts, in addition to expenditures made or accrued, are recorded. In accordance with generally accepted accounting principles, outstanding encumbrances at year-end for which goods or services are received are reclassified as expenditures and accounts payable. All other encumbrances in the annual budgeted funds are reversed at year-end and are either cancelled or are included as reappropriations of fund balance for the subsequent year. Encumbrances at year end in funds which are budgeted on a project basis automatically carry forward along with their related appropriations and are not subject to an annual cancellation and reappropriation. ◀

Budgetary Reporting

General Purpose Financial Statements A Combined Statement of Revenues, Expenditures, and Changes in Fund Balances—Budget and Actual, General and Special Revenue Fund Types must be presented as part of the general purpose financial statements. If the reporting entity consists of other funds that adopt an annual budget, these funds must be included, along with the General Fund and the Special Revenue Funds, on a budget and actual basis in general purpose financial statements. The combined statement includes only funds that have appropriated budgets that were adopted by the oversight unit's legislature or governing board or by a component unit's governing board.

If the reporting entity's budget basis is the same as its accounting basis (modified accrual basis), the amounts in the columns of its Combined Statement of Revenues, Expenditures, and Changes in Fund Balances, All Governmental Fund Types will be the same as the "actual" amounts in the columns of the Combined Statement of Revenues, Expenditures, and Changes in Fund Balances—Budget and Actual, General and Special Revenue Fund Types. At a minimum, the latter financial statement should present budgeted and actual columns for each combined fund presented. An example of the combined budget/actual financial statement is presented in Exhibit I.

The financial statement format illustrated in Exhibit I presents the minimum disclosures as required by NCGA-1. The presentation may be expanded to include columns for variances for each fund type and a "totals" column with columns for combined budgeted, actual, and variance amounts. If total columns are used, they should be marked "memorandum only."

The reporting entity's basis for accounting may differ from the required reporting accounting basis. For example, the financial report must be presented on a modified accrual basis (GAAP basis), but the cash basis may be the legally mandated basis for budgetary purposes. When this occurs, the budgeted amounts are presented as adopted by the legislature or governing board; however, the actual amounts (accounting basis) must be converted to the basis used for budgeting. Thus, the amounts in the columns of the Combined

EXHIBIT I

Combined Statement of Revenues, Expenditures, and Changes in Fund Balances—Budget and Actual (GAAP Basis) General and Special Revenue Fund Types

City of Centerville
Combined Statement of Revenues, Expenditures, and Changes in Fund Balances—Budget (GAAP Basis) and Actual
General and Special Revenue Fund Types
Year Ended June 30, 19X5

	General Fund Budget	General Fund Actual	Special Revenue Funds Budget	Special Revenue Funds Actual
Revenues				
Taxes	$600,000	$590,000	$345,000	$360,000
Other	100,000	105,000	120,000	115,000
Total revenues	700,000	695,000	465,000	475,000
Expenditures				
General government	200,000	205,000	120,000	135,000
Public safety	150,000	160,000	100,000	95,000
Health and welfare	100,000	95,000	80,000	80,000
Total expenditures	450,000	460,000	300,000	310,000
Excess of revenues over (under) expenditures	250,000	235,000	165,000	165,000
Other financing sources (uses)				
Proceeds from bond sales	50,000	50,000	—	—
Transfers from other funds	—	—	10,000	5,000
Transfers to other funds	(90,000)	(120,000)	—	—
Total other financing sources (uses)	(40,000)	(70,000)	10,000	5,000
Excess of revenues and other sources over (under) expenditures and other uses	$210,000	165,000	$175,000	170,000
(Increase) decrease in reserve for encumbrances		(20,000)		10,000
Net change in unreserved fund balance for year		145,000		180,000
Fund balance-unreserved July 1, 19X4		(125,000)		10,000
Fund balance-unreserved June 30, 19X5		$ 20,000		$190,000

Statement of Revenues, Expenditures, and Changes in Fund Balances, All Governmental Fund Types will not be the same as the "actual" amounts in the columns of the Combined Statement of Revenues, Expenditures, and Changes in Fund Balances—Budget and Actual, General and Special Revenue Fund Types. As explained later, these differences must be disclosed in a note to the financial statements.

> **OBSERVATION:** *There may be a fund that does not have a legally adopted annual budget, but the fund may be categorized in a fund type that presents its financial statements on an actual and budgeted basis. A method of handling this reporting problem is to exclude the fund from the fund type's combined financial statements on an actual and budgeted basis and disclose the reason for exclusion in a note to the financial statements.*

In the general purpose financial statements, only combined statements for budget and actual results should be presented. Individual fund financial statements on a budgeted and actual basis should not be presented, except for the General Fund.

> **OBSERVATION:** *Individual fund financial statements on a budgeted and actual basis may be presented in the combining statements section of the Comprehensive Annual Financial Report (see Appendix, Illustration of Comprehensive Annual Financial Report).*

Comprehensive Annual Financial Report For individual fund types that adopt an annual budget, the comparison of budgeted and actual amounts should be presented as part of the Comprehensive Annual Financial Report. When the individual fund type's budgetary basis is the same as its accounting basis, the budgeted information may simply be presented on a comparative basis with actual results in the fund type's Statement of Revenues, Expenditures, and Changes in Fund Balance. Of course, when the dual presentation is made, the name of the financial statement must be changed to the Statement of Revenues, Expenditures, and Changes in Fund Balance—Budget and Actual (Name of Fund). An example of this financial statement format prepared on a GAAP basis is presented in Exhibit II.

When the individual fund's budgetary basis is different from its accounting basis, the budget-to-actual comparison cannot be made in

Budgetary Accounting and Reporting

EXHIBIT II

Statement of Revenues, Expenditures, and Changes in Fund Balances—Budget (GAAP Basis) and Actual

City of Centerville
Statement of Revenues, Expenditures, and Changes
in Fund Balances—Budget (GAAP Basis) and Actual
Special Revenue Funds
Year Ended June 30, 19X5

	Parks Fund Budget	Parks Fund Actual	Parking Meters Fund Budget	Parking Meters Fund Actual
Revenues				
Taxes	$120,000	$117,000	$75,000	$80,000
Charges and fees	70,000	75,000	22,000	19,000
Total revenues	190,000	192,000	97,000	99,000
Expenditures				
Public safety	—	—	94,000	97,000
Recreation and parks	185,000	197,000	—	—
Total expenditures	185,000	197,000	94,000	97,000
Excess of revenues over (under) expenditures	5,000	(5,000)	3,000	2,000
Other financing sources (uses)				
Transfers from other funds	6,000	9,000	4,000	5,000
Transfers to other funds	(5,000)	(7,000)	—	—
Total other financing sources (uses)	1,000	2,000	4,000	5,000
Excess of revenues and other sources over (under) expenditures and other uses	$ 6,000	(3,000)	$ 7,000	7,000
(Increase) decrease in reserve for encumbrances		2,000		(4,000)
Net change in unreserved fund balance for year		(1,000)		3,000
Fund balance—unreserved July 1, 19X4		8,000		2,000
Fund balance—unreserved June 30, 19X5		$ 7,000		$ 5,000

6.14 / GOVERNMENTAL GAAP GUIDE

the Statement of Revenues, Expenditures, and Changes in Fund Balance. Under this circumstance, the budgeted information and the actual results (on the same basis as the budget) should be presented in a schedule rather than a financial statement.

Minimum Reporting Standards The prior discussion has been concerned exclusively with budgetary reporting on a comparative basis with actual results for funds that adopt an annual *appropriated budget* (see prior definition). NCGA-1 recognizes that governmental units may be subject to control through the implementation of other types of budgets. For example, NCGA-1 defines a nonappropriated budget as follows:

> A financial plan for an organization, program, activity, or function approved in a manner authorized by constitution, charter, statute, or ordinance but not subject to appropriation and therefore outside the boundaries of the definition of "appropriated budget."

The NCGA takes the position that "more comprehensive budget presentations are generally to be preferred over the minimum standards." Thus, the existence of the minimum disclosure requirement (annual appropriated budgets) should not inhibit a reporting entity from presenting additional budgeting information. Even if additional budgetary disclosures are not made, there should be a disclosure in notes to the financial statements describing budgetary controls, including appropriated budgets and other budget or financial control plans used by the reporting entity.

Reconciling Budget and GAAP Information When there are differences between the reporting entity's budgetary basis and its basis of accounting, the results of operations as shown in the Combined Statement of Revenues, Expenditures, and Changes in Fund Balances—Budget and Actual, General and Special Revenue Fund Types will differ from the related amounts shown in the Combined Statement of Revenues, Expenditures, and Changes in Fund Balances, All Governmental Fund Types. These differences may arise because of (1) entity differences, (2) perspective differences, (3) basis differences, or (4) timing differences.

Entity differences The reporting entity may include component units whose activities are not part of the appropriated budget. For example, a component unit may be subject to a legal nonappropriated budget, and thus be excluded from the appropriated budget;

Budgetary Accounting and Reporting

but, based on the criteria established in NCGA-3 (Defining the Governmental Reporting Entity), the component may be part of the overall reporting entity.

Perspective differences   The structure of the budget itself determines its perspective. The financial information contained in the budget may be constructed to reflect various points of view including the governmental unit's organizational structure, fund structure, or program structure. For example, budgetary information may be prepared on a program basis whereby all expenditures associated with a particular objective may be grouped irrespective of which organizational unit or fund makes the expenditure.

> *OBSERVATION: When there is a difference between the perspective for budgeting purposes and financial reporting purposes, it is often difficult, if not impractical, to reconcile the two sets of financial information. For example, if the budgetary system uses a program basis and the financial reporting system uses the fund basis, it is unlikely that a meaningful reconciliation can be prepared. In this case, the reconciliation between the GAAP basis financial statements and the budgeted financial statements would be limited to entity, basis, and timing differences.*

Basis differences   The budgeting basis may differ from the accounting basis. For example, the governmental unit may be required by law to use the cash basis for budgeting purposes, but may be required by financial reporting purposes to use the modified accrual basis (GAAP basis).

Timing differences   There may be differences between the budgetary amounts and the GAAP-basis amounts due to the different treatment of such items as continuing appropriations and biennial budgeting. For example, a governmental unit may treat encumbrances that are outstanding at the end of the year as expenditures of the current period for budgetary purposes, but, for reporting purposes, they cannot be classified as expenditures of the current period.

In the notes to the general purpose financial statements, differences between the budgetary-based financial statements and the GAAP-based financial statements must be reconciled. An example of a reconciliation is presented in Exhibit III. Alternatively, the reconciliation may take the form of a separate financial statement or schedule. Exhibit IV is an example of a reconciliation of the actual-accounting basis and the budgetary-accounting basis, using the financial statement format.

EXHIBIT III
Budgetary/GAAP Reporting Reconciliation

NOTE 12: Budgetary Reporting Basis

Financial statements in this report are based on the legally enacted basis (modified accrual basis with certain exceptions) and the generally accepted accounting principles (GAAP) basis. The financial statements prepared on the legally enacted basis differ from the GAAP basis statements in that both expenditures and encumbrances are applied against the current budget, while adjustments affecting activity budgeted in prior years are accounted for through a fund balance or as a reduction of expenditures. Certain interfund transfers and reimbursements are budgeted as revenues and expenditures.

The following schedule reconciles the differences between the legally enacted basis and the GAAP basis. The Special Revenue Funds' legally enacted basis revenues column includes (1) the expenditures, and encumbrances that are the respective combined totals of the City of Centerville and its school district, for which separate budgets have been adopted, and (2) the GAAP basis revenues and expenditures for the Municipal Authority Fund, for which annual budgets are not adopted.

	General Fund	Special Revenue Funds
Revenue on GAAP basis	$10,000,000	$2,000,000
Prior year revenue refunded	400,000	250,000
Prior year revenue adjustments	50,000	30,000
Interfund transfers and reimbursements	(25,000)	20,000
Adjustment for advances	—	(40,000)
Revenue on legal basis	$10,425,000	$2,260,000

EXHIBIT IV
Budgetary/GAAP Reporting Reconciliation

City of Centerville
General Fund
Statement of Revenues, Expenditures, Changes in Fund Balances—
Budget and Actual (Budgeting Basis Variance with GAAP)
Year Ended June 30, 19X5
(expressed in thousands)

	Actual on GAAP basis	Adjustment to budgetary basis	Actual on budgetary basis	Budget	Variance favorable (unfavorable)
Revenues					
Taxes	$ 590	—	$590	$600	$ (10)
Other	105	$10	115	100	15
Total revenue	695	10	705	700	5
Expenditures					
General government	205	(7)	198	200	2
Public safety	160	(20)	140	150	10
Health and welfare	95	15	110	100	(10)
Total expenditures	460	(12)	448	450	2
Excess of revenues over (under) expenditures	235	22	257	250	7
Other financing sources (uses)					
Proceeds from bond sale	50		50	50	—
Transfers to other funds	(120)	—	(120)	(90)	(30)
Total other financing sources and uses	(70)	—	(70)	(40)	(30)
Excess of revenues and other sources over (under) expenditures and other uses	165	22	187	$210	$(23)
(Increase) decrease in reserve for encumbrances	(20)	20	—		
Net change in unreserved fund balance for year	145	42	187		
Fund balance—unreserved July 1, 19X4	(125)	—	(125)		
Fund balance—unreserved June 30, 19X5	$ 20	$ 42	$ 62		

LITERATURE REFERENCES

Material in this chapter is based on the following authoritative pronouncements which are grouped according to the major heading used within the chapter. A dual reference (both paragraph and page number) is used for NCGA-1 and NCGA-2 because the original pronouncements do not use paragraph numbers.

The Budgetary Process
NCGA-1 *Governmental Accounting and Financial Reporting Principles*, p. 13/¶¶ 77, 79 and 80.

Budgeting For Proprietary Funds
NCGA-1 *Governmental Accounting and Financial Reporting Principles*, pp. 13 and 14/¶¶ 78, 82 and 94-97.

Budgeting For Fiduciary Funds
NCGA-1 *Governmental Accounting and Financial Reporting Principles*, p. 14/¶ 98.

Budgets For Governmental Funds
NCGA-1 *Governmental Accounting and Financial Reporting Principles*, pp. 13, 14, 17, and 18/¶¶ 78, 84, 85, 88, 89, and 124-126.

Budgetary Accounting System
NCGA-1 *Governmental Accounting and Financial Reporting Principles*, pp. 13 and 14/¶¶ 89-92.

NCGA Interpretation-10 *State and Local Government Budgetary Reporting*, ¶ 11.

SOP 80-2 *Accounting and Financial Reporting by Governmental Units*, ¶ 5.

Budgetary Reporting
NCGA-1 *Governmental Accounting and Financial Reporting Principles*, pp. 19, 23 and 24/¶¶ 139 and 153-155.

NCGA-7 *Financial Reporting for Component Units Within the Governmental Reporting Entity*, ¶ 17.

NCGA Interpretation-10 *State and Local Government Budgetary Reporting*, ¶¶ 11, 13 and 16-25.

FINANCIAL STATEMENT TERMINOLOGY AND CLASSIFICATION

A governmental reporting entity should use consistent terminology and classifications in its accounting system. From an internal perspective, the use of a common language and classification scheme enhances management's ability to evaluate and control operations. For financial reporting purposes, the consistent use of terms and classifications in the budgeting, accounting, and reporting systems facilitates the preparation of financial statements and makes those financial statements more understandable to user groups.

The consistent use of common terms and the implementation of a single classification scheme should be reflected in the preparation of a governmental fund's Statement of Operations, Statement of Changes in Fund Balance, and Balance Sheet. For illustrative purposes, the Statement of Operations and Statement of Changes in Fund Balance are discussed separately in this chapter, but, for financial reporting purposes, they must be combined and presented as a single financial statement.

STATEMENT OF OPERATIONS

A governmental fund's results of operations are presented in a Statement of Revenues and Expenditures. This statement should reflect the all-inclusive concept in that all financial transactions and events that affect the fund's operations for the period should be presented in the activity statement. A governmental fund's activity statement is not referred to as an income statement because the accounting basis for its preparation is the modified accrual, not the accrual. Similarly, net income is not an element that is presented in a governmental fund's activity statement for the above stated reason, and also because the statement does not reflect allocations of various economic resources such as the depreciation of property, plant, and equipment.

An example of a Statement of Operations (combined with an analysis of changes in fund balance) that illustrates the major classifications that appear in a governmental fund's activity statement is presented in Exhibit I, which is used as a focal point for the following discussion.

Financial Statement Terminology and Classification

EXHIBIT I
Statement of Revenues, Expenditures, and Changes in Fund Balance
Governmental Fund Type

City of Centerville
Statement of Revenues, Expenditures,
and Changes in Fund Balance
General Fund
Year ended June 30, 19X5

		(000)
Revenues		
Property taxes		$ 75,000
Intergovernmental revenue		35,000
Charges for services		20,000
Investment and interest income		15,000
Fines and forfeitures		10,000
Miscellaneous revenues		5,000
Total revenues		160,000
Expenditures		
General government		50,000
Public safety		30,000
Public services		25,000
Highways and streets		20,000
Other		15,000
Debt service		
Principal retirement		20,000
Interest and fiscal charges		5,000
Total expenditures		165,000
Excess of revenues over (under) expenditures		(5,000)
Other financing sources (uses)		
Proceeds from bond sales		10,000
Transfers from other funds		20,000
Transfers to other funds		(15,000)
Total other financing sources (uses)		15,000
Excess of revenues and other sources over (under) expenditures and other uses		10,000
Fund balance, July 1, 19X4		
(as previously stated)		500,000
Prior period adjustment (see Note X)		(165,000)
Fund balance, July 1, 19X4 (as restated)		335,000
Less: Increase in fund balance reserved		
for inventories and encumbrances	$20,000	
Residual equity transfer to		
enterprise fund	10,000	(30,000)
Fund balance, June 30, 19X5		$305,000

Revenues

NCGA-1 (Governmental Accounting and Financial Reporting Principles) defines revenues as "increase in (sources of) fund financial resources other than from interfund transfers and debt issue proceeds." Revenues should be classified by fund and source. Revenues that are applicable to a particular fund should be reflected in that fund's activity statement and not attributed to another fund. Sources of revenues include taxes arising from intergovernmental revenues, fines, charges for services, interest, and special assessments.

As a supplement to the accumulation of revenues by fund and source, revenues may be classified in various ways to facilitate management evaluation and preparation of special reports or analyses, or to aid in the audit or review of accounts. For example, revenues may be classified by the operating division or branch responsible for their actual collection.

Expenditures

Governmental expenditures represent decreases in or uses of fund financial resources except for those transactions that result in transfers to other funds. Initially, expenditures should be classified according to the fund that is accountable for the disbursement. To facilitate both internal and external analysis and reporting, expenditures may be classified further by (1) function (or program), (2) organization unit, (3) activity, (4) character, and (5) object class.

Function (or program) classification Functions refer to major services provided by the governmental unit or responsibilities established by specific laws or regulations. Classifications included as functions are public safety, highways and streets, general governmental services, education, and health and welfare. Rather than use a functional classification, a governmental unit that employs program budgeting may group its expenditures by program classifications and subclassifications. A program classification scheme groups activities that are related to the achievement of a specific purpose or objective. Program groupings would include activities such as programs for the elderly, drug addiction, and adult education.

Organization unit classification An accounting system should incorporate the concept of responsibility accounting so that information

Financial Statement Terminology and Classification

reflecting a unit's responsibility for activities and expenditures will be present in the system. When an organization is responsible for certain expenditures, but the expenditures are not coded so the disbursements can be associated with the organization, it becomes difficult to hold the organizational unit responsible for the activity. As implied by the name, organization unit classification generally groups expenditures based on the operational structure (department, agencies, etc.) of the governmental unit. Often, functions or programs are administered by two or more organizational units. For example, the public safety function is partially the responsibility of both the police department and the fire department.

Activity classification Function or program classifications are broad in nature and often do not provide a basis for adequately analyzing governmental operations. For this reason, expenditures may be associated with specific activities, thus allowing measurement standards to be established. These standards can be used (1) as a basis for evaluating the economy and efficiency of operations and (2) as a basis for budget preparation. Also, grouping expenditures by activity is an important part of management accounting in which decisions may require the development of accounting data different from the information presented in the external financial reports. For example, in a make-or-buy decision, it may be necessary to consider a depreciation factor in computing a per unit cost figure (for external reporting purposes, depreciation is not generally presented).

Character classification Categorizing expenditures by character refers to the fiscal year that will benefit from the expenditure. Character classifications include the following.

Character	Period(s) Benefited
Current expenditures	Current period
Capital outlays	Current and future periods
Debt service	Current, future, and prior periods
Intergovernmental	(Depends on the nature of the programs financed by the revenue transfer)

As discussed below, object classes are subdivisions of grouping expenditures by character.

Object class classification Object classes represent the specific items purchased or services acquired within the overall character classifications. For example, debt service expenditures can be further classified as payments for principal and interest, while current expenditures by object class may include the purchase of supplies and disbursements for payroll.

NCGA-1 recognizes that classifying expenditures by object class should be restrained because the user, on an internal as well as an external basis, could be overwhelmed by voluminous information that does not enhance the decision making process.

Operating Transfers

Operating transfers represent transfers of funds from one governmental fund to another governmental fund when both governmental funds are part of the same reporting entity. Transfers are not considered revenues by the receiving fund or expenditures or expenses by the disbursing fund. An operating transfer is a legally authorized transfer between funds in which one fund is responsible for the initial receipt of funds (tax collection, receipt of grants, etc.), and another fund is authorized to use the resources to finance its operating expenditures or expenses.

An operating transfer may be recorded in the following manner:

Receiving Fund			Disbursing Fund		
Cash	10,000		Transfers Out	10,000	
Transfers In		10,000	Cash		10,000

It is also acceptable to record an operating transfer in the following way when one fund is legally required to receive the initial revenue, and another fund is legally required to expend the fund received:

Receiving Fund			Disbursing Fund		
Cash	10,000		Revenues	10,000	
Revenues (by source, such as property taxes, etc.)		10,100	Cash		10,100

For financial reporting purposes, transfers affecting governmental funds should be classified on the activity statement as "Other Financing Sources (Uses)." Transfers that involve a proprietary fund should be presented under the caption "Operating Transfers."

Examples of transfers include the following transactions:

- Transfer of property taxes collected by the General Fund to a school district accounted for as a Special Revenue Fund
- Transfer of funds from the General Fund to an Enterprise Fund as part of an operating subsidy
- Transfer of funds from a Special Revenue Fund to a Debt Service Fund to support principal and interest payments
- Transfer of funds from an Enterprise Fund to the General Fund to finance general governmental expenditures

Quasi-External Transactions

Not all transfers between governmental funds of the same reporting entity are treated as operating transfers. The basic philosophy concerning operating transfers is that operating transfers represent intragovernmental transactions and, therefore, cannot be considered as revenue, expenditures, or expenses of the related parties (funds) for financial reporting purposes. There is an exception, namely quasi-external transactions.

A quasi-external transaction is a transaction between governmental funds whereby the transaction would have been classified as a revenue, expenditure, or expense transaction had it been consummated with an external party. NCGA-1 lists the following as examples of quasi-external transactions:

- Payments in lieu of taxes from an Enterprise Fund to the General Fund
- Internal Service Fund billings to governmental departments that use its services
- Routine employer contributions from the General Fund to a Pension Trust Fund
- Routine service charges for inspection, engineering, utilities, or similar services provided by a department financed from one fund to a department financed from another fund

The above transactions and similar transactions give rise to the recording of revenues, expenditures, and expenses by the funds involved in the transaction. For example, a payment from an Enterprise Fund to the General Fund in lieu of property taxes would be recorded as follows:

	General Fund			Enterprise Fund	
Cash	10,000		Expenses	10,000	
Revenues		10,000	Cash		10,000

Reimbursements

A fund may incur an expenditure or expense that will be reimbursed by another fund. A reimbursement is considered an expenditure or expense of the fund that is legally responsible for the transaction as determined by the appropriation authority. The expenditure or expense is initially recognized in the fund that expects to be reimbursed (reimbursed fund). For example, the following entry would be made when an expenditure is made by the General Fund that will eventually be reimbursed by a Special Revenue Fund:

General Fund (reimbursed fund)			Special Revenue Fund (reimbursing fund)
Expenditure	10,000		None
Cash		10,000	

When the Special Revenue Fund reimburses the General Fund for the expenditure, the transaction is recorded as follows:

	General Fund			Special Revenue Fund	
Cash	10,000		Expenditure	10,000	
Expenditure		10,000	Cash		10,000

When there are reimbursement transactions, the basic objectives are to record the expenditure or expense only once and to reflect the expenditure or expense in the fund that was legally given the authority to make the disbursement. Also, reimbursements do not represent interfund transfers, loans, or advances, and, therefore, an interfund receivable or payable should not be used to account for the transaction. (An interfund transfer, loan, or advance may be established only when it is properly authorized as described above.)

NCGA-1 lists the following situations as circumstances that would create a reimbursement between funds:

- One fund inadvertently pays expenditures or expenses of another fund.

- As a matter of convenience one fund pays expenditures or expenses of another fund.

- One fund makes a single payment for two or more funds because the amount attributable to each fund is uncertain or is to be determined at a later date.
- The reimbursing fund does not have the resources to finance the initial payment.

Proceeds from Issuance of Debt

Proceeds from the issuance of debt are sources of fund financial resources, but they are not classified as revenues. When short-term debt is issued, the transaction should be recorded as a liability by the fund incurring or responsible for the payment of the debt. If the debt is long-term and is issued by either an Enterprise Fund or Trust Fund, the liability is reflected in the respective fund's balance sheet.

Proceeds from the issuance of long-term debt, except for the ones described in the previous paragraph, are presented as other financing sources on the activity statement of the fund that receives the proceeds. The liability itself is not presented in that fund's balance sheet but is recorded in the General Long-Term Debt Account Group. For example, if long-term bonds are sold and the proceeds are available to the General Fund, the transaction is recorded as follows:

General Fund			General Long-Term Debt Account Group		
Cash	10,000		Amounts to Be Provided for Payment of Bonds	10,000	
Proceeds From Bond Sale		10,000	Bonds Payable		10,000

STATEMENT OF CHANGES IN FUND BALANCE

As noted earlier, the Statement of Changes in Fund Balance must be combined with the governmental unit's Statement of Operations. NCGA-1 refers to this combined-statement presentation as an all-inclusive approach to financial reporting, and presents the following justification for such an approach:

> (the all-inclusive approach clarifies) questions as to whether certain changes in fund balance or other equity should be reported directly in a statement of changes in equity while

other changes are shown in the operating statement (for example, transfers). The all-inclusive format eliminates the need for separate statements of changes in fund balance and retained earnings or equity in most cases, since such changes usually are set forth clearly under this approach.

An example of the analysis of changes in a governmental unit's fund balance account is presented in the lower portion of Exhibit I.

> **OBSERVATION:** *The NCGA's adoption of the all-inclusive approach does not entirely resolve the reporting difficulties that may arise in trying to determine whether a transaction is an operating transaction or an equity (fund balance) transaction. While the transaction must appear on the combined financial statement, a decision must be made on whether it should be used to compute the excess of revenues over (under) expenditures. Thus, there is still room for disagreement on where an item should be placed on the combined financial statement.*

Three transactions that would not be used to compute the excess of revenues and other sources of financing over (under) expenditures and other uses of financing would be (1) prior period adjustments, (2) changes in amount of the fund balance that is reserved, and (3) residual equity transfers.

Prior-Period Adjustments

FASB-16 (Prior Period Adjustments) concludes that the following operating transactions should be excluded from the current period's activity statement:

- Correction of an error in the financial statements of a prior period
- Adjustments that result from realization of income tax benefits of pre-acquisition operating loss carryforwards of purchased subsidiaries

For obvious reasons, the second item listed above is not applicable to governmental financial reporting.

A correction of an error should be presented as an adjustment to the beginning balance in the fund balance, and all previous financial statements affected by the error and presented in the financial report must be restated. When only a single year's financial statement is presented in the financial report, the effects of the error on the beginning year's fund balance and the previous year's "excess of revenues and other sources over (under) expenditures and other uses" should be disclosed. When comparative financial statements are presented in the financial report, the effects on the "excess of revenues and other sources over (under) expenditures and other uses" and the beginning balance of the fund balances for each year presented should be disclosed. Generally, there is no need to disclose information concerning the effects of prior-period adjustments for financial statements presented in the financial report that is issued after the year of initial disclosure of the prior-period adjustment.

> **OBSERVATION:** *Although there is no promulgation that requires the disclosure of information concerning the effects of prior-period adjustments for financial statements presented in the financial report that is issued after the year of initial disclosure, in practice the disclosure is generally repeated in subsequent periods in an abbreviated form.*

APB-20 (Accounting Changes) states that errors in financial statements may result from the following:

- Mathematical mistakes
- Mistakes in the application of accounting principles
- Oversight of facts that existed at the time the financial statements were prepared
- Misuse of facts that existed at the time the financial statements were prepared
- A change from an accounting principle that is not generally accepted to one that is generally accepted

> **OBSERVATION:** *A GASB pronouncement has not addressed the issue of prior-period adjustments (although there is an example of a prior-period adjustment is NCGA-1, paragraph 152 (page 23)). For this reason, pronouncements issued by the FASB (and its predecessors) must be followed and interpreted in the context of the governmental reporting environment.*

Fund Balance Reserve

The term "reserve" should be used in governmental financial reporting only to identify the portion of the fund balance (1) segregated for some future purpose (for example, reserve for encumbrances) or (2) not available for expenditures to be appropriated in the following period (for example, reserve for inventories). If a portion of the fund balance is designated as reserved, the balance should be reported as unreserved fund balance.

Residual Equity Transfers

A residual equity transfer is presented on the Statement of Changes in fund balance because the transfer generally represents nonrecurring or nonroutine transfers of equity between funds. A residual equity transfer may represent the creation of a new fund or the expansion of an existing fund. On the other hand, a residual equity transfer may occur when a fund is being liquidated or contracted.

For a governmental fund, equity transfers should be shown as an increase or decrease to the beginning balance of the fund balance. For a proprietary fund, the residual equity transfer should be presented as an increase or decrease to the fund's contributed capital or retained earnings based on the circumstances of the transfer. For example, a transfer of a capital contribution from the General Fund to an Enterprise Fund would be accounted for as follows:

General Fund			Enterprise Fund	
Residual Equity Transfer	1,000		Cash	1,000
Cash		1,000	Contributed Capital General Fund	1,000

BALANCE SHEET

Items that appear on the balance sheet for a governmental fund are not classified as current or noncurrent. Because the measurement focus is generally the flow of current financial resources, only those resources that are available to finance expenditures are presented as assets. For example, fixed assets are not shown in the General Fund because these assets do not represent resources available to finance expenditures. Likewise, liabilities are presented in a governmental fund's balance sheet only when such liabilities require the use of expendable resources available during the subsequent accounting period. For this reason, long-term debt is not shown as a liability in a governmental fund's statement of position.

Financial Statement Terminology and Classification

An example of a balance sheet for the governmental fund is presented in Exhibit II.

EXHIBIT II

Governmental Fund Type Balance Sheet

City of Centerville
Balance Sheet
General Fund
June 30, 19X5

		(000)
ASSETS		
Cash on deposit		$110,000
Taxes receivable		120,000
Allowance for uncollectible accounts		(10,000)
Interest and dividends receivable		25,000
Interfund receivables		
Special revenue funds		23,000
Capital projects funds		12,000
Inventories		30,000
Other assets		30,000
Total assets		$340,000
LIABILITIES AND FUND BALANCE		
Liabilities		
Accounts payable		3,000
Vouchers payable		6,000
Interfund payables		
Debt service funds		8,000
Enterprise funds		1,000
Accrued expenses		4,000
Other liabilities		3,000
Total liabilities		25,000
Fund balance		
Reserved fund balance		
Reserved for inventories	$30,000	
Reserved for encumbrances	10,000	
Total fund balance reserved		40,000
Unreserved fund balance		
Designated for debt service	40,000	
Designated for self-insurance	50,000	
Undesignated fund balance	185,000	
Total fund balance unreserved		275,000
Total fund balance		315,000
Total liabilities and fund balance		$340,000

Interfund Receivables and Payables

Each fund is a distinct fiscal and accounting entity, and interfund transactions should be appropriately recorded in each fund affected by a transaction. NCGA-1 notes that interfund receivables and payables may arise from (1) interfund loans (that generally must be legally approved) or (2) quasi-external transactions. For example, if an Enterprise Fund bills the General Fund for services the former fund has rendered, the following entries would be made:

General Fund			Enterprise Fund		
Expenditures	1,000		Interfund Receivable—		
Interfund Payable–			General Fund	1,000	
Enterprise Fund		1,000	Revenues		1,000

When a fund has both an interfund receivable from and an interfund payable to the same fund, the amounts should be recorded in separate accounts. For financial reporting purposes, however, it is permissible to present a net interfund receivable or payable. Interfund receivables and payables not due from or to the same fund should not be netted on the fund's balance sheet.

Reserves and Designations

As suggested earlier, the term reserve should be used only to identify that portion of the fund balance segregated for future purposes or not available to finance expenditures of the subsequent accounting period. Valuation accounts, such as the allowance for uncollectible property taxes, should not be referred to in the financial statements as a reserve. Likewise, estimated liabilities or deferred revenues should not be classified as reserves. Amounts that are properly classified as fund balance reserves should be reported as part of the fund balance section of the balance sheet and not placed somewhere between the liability section and the fund balance section.

Portions of the fund balance may be identified by management to reflect tentative plans or commitments of governmental resources. The tentative plans or commitments may be related to items such as debt retirement. Designated amounts are not the same as fund balance reserves since they represent planned actions, not actual commitments. A fund balance reserve arises from statutory requirements or actions already taken by the governmental unit. For this reason designated amounts should not be classified with fund balance reserves but rather should be reported as part of the unreserved fund balance. The amount and nature of the designated amount should be explained in (1) a separate line in the balance sheet, (2) a parenthetical comment, or (3) a note to the financial statements.

PROPRIETARY FUNDS

A Balance Sheet, Statement of Revenues and Expenses, Statement of Changes in Retained Earnings (or Equity), and Statement of Changes in Financial Position must be prepared for all proprietary funds. Terminology and classification schemes used in the preparation of similar financial statements of a commercial enterprise must be observed in the preparation of a proprietary fund's financial statements.

In November 1987, the FASB issued FASB-95 (Statement of Cash Flows), which superseded APB-19 (Reporting Changes in Financial Position). As an interim solution to the conflicting reporting formats between the two pronouncements, the GASB has informally concluded that governmental entities are not required to follow the reporting standards established by FASB-95. Thus, governmental entities may continue to present a statement of changes in financial position rather than a statement of cash flows for proprietary and similar funds. The GASB has placed the topic on its agenda and intends to resolve the matter expeditiously.

LITERATURE REFERENCES

Material in this chapter is based on the following authoritative pronouncements, which are grouped according to the major headings used within the chapter. A dual reference (both paragraph and page number) is used for NCGA-1 and NCGA-2 because the original pronouncements do not use paragraph numbers.

Introduction
NCGA-1 *Governmental Accounting and Financial Reporting Principles,* pp. 15, 17, and 18/¶¶ 100, 124, and 126.

Statement of Operations
NCGA-1 *Governmental Accounting and Financial Reporting Principles,* p. 10/¶ 57.

Revenues
NCGA-1 *Governmental Accounting and Financial Reporting Principles*, p. 16/¶¶ 109 and 110.

Expenditures
NCGA-1 *Governmental Accounting and Financial Reporting Principles*, pp. 16 and 17/¶¶ 109 and 111-116.

Operating Transfers
NCGA-1 *Governmental Accounting and Financial Reporting Principles*, pp. 16 and 17/¶¶ 105-106.
SOP 77-2 *Accounting for Interfund Transfers of State and Local Governmental Units*, ¶ 4.

Quasi-External Transactions
NCGA-1 *Governmental Accounting and Financial Reporting Principles*, p. 15/¶¶ 101-103.

Reimbursements
NCGA-1 *Governmental Accounting and Financial Reporting Principles*, p. 15/¶¶ 101, 102, and 104.

Proceeds from Issuance of Debt
NCGA-1 *Governmental Accounting and Financial Reporting Principles*, p. 16/¶¶ 107 and 108.

Statement of Changes in Fund Balance
NCGA-1 *Governmental Accounting and Financial Reporting Principles*, p. 16/¶ 106.

Prior-Period Adjustments
FASB-16 *Prior Period Adjustments*, ¶ 11.
APB-9 *Reporting the Results of Operations*, ¶ 26.
APB-20 *Accounting Changes*, ¶ 13.

Fund Balance Reserve
NCGA-1 *Governmental Accounting and Financial Reporting Principles*, p. 17/¶¶ 118-119.

Residual Equity Transfers
NCGA-1 *Governmental Accounting and Financial Reporting Principles*, pp. 15-16/¶¶ 105-106.

Financial Statement Terminology and Classification

Balance Sheet
NCGA-1   *Governmental Accounting and Financial Reporting Principles*, pp. 6 and 9/¶¶ 19 and 44.

NCGA-4   *Accounting and Financial Reporting Principles for Claims and Judgments and Compensated Absences*, ¶ 7.

Interfund Receivables and Payables
NCGA-1   *Governmental Accounting and Financial Reporting Principles*, p. 7/ ¶ 22.

Reserves and Designations
NCGA-1   *Governmental Accounting and Financial Reporting Principles*, p. 17/ ¶¶ 118-121.

Proprietary Funds
NCGA-1   *Governmental Accounting and Financial Reporting Principles*, p. 17/ ¶¶ 117 and 122.

Governmental
Accounts and Transactions

REVENUES

The measurement focus for a governmental fund is the flow of current financial resources. Revenues are defined as an increase in the governmental unit's current financial resources. NCGA-1 (Governmental Accounting and Financial Reporting Principles) notes that revenues are recognized when they are susceptible to accrual, which means they must be both measurable and available. Revenues are measurable when the amount of the revenue is subject to reasonable estimation. In order to be available, revenues must be subject to collection within the current period, or after the end of the period but in time to pay liabilities outstanding at the end of the current period.

Governmental units must account for a variety of revenues, including property taxes, sales taxes, user charges, and grants and fines, to name but a few. These various revenues may be accounted for by using the accrual basis, modified accrual basis, or cash basis. Professional judgment must be exercised to determine which basis of accounting should be used to account for a specific revenue source.

Property Taxes

Property taxes are assessed for a fiscal year and are expected to finance expenditures of the year of assessment. Usually on the assessment date or levy date, the property taxes become a lien against the assessed property, but the actual amounts paid to the governmental unit may be made on a quarterly or monthly basis during the year covered by the assessment. Property taxes should be recorded as revenue on a modified accrual basis and, therefore, are recorded when they are both measurable and available.

Measurable The amount of the property taxes receivable is based on the assessed value of the property and the current property tax rate used by the governmental unit. Nonetheless, all property taxes assessed will not be collected, and the measurability criterion can be satisfied only if the governmental unit can make a reasonable estimate of the amount of uncollectible property taxes.

When reasonable estimates can be made, the property tax levy may be recorded as follows:

GOVERNMENTAL GAAP GUIDE / **10.01**

Revenues

Property Taxes Receivable—Current	400,000	
Revenues—Property Taxes		370,000
Allowance For Uncollectible Property		
Taxes—Current		30,000

The property tax levy is recorded net of the estimated amount of uncollectible property taxes. No bad debts expense account is used because only expenditures, not expenses, are recorded by governmental funds.

> *OBSERVATION: For financial reporting purposes, bad debts expense should not be reported in a governmental fund type's operating statement because the measurement focus is the flow of current financial resources. The revenue is reported as a net amount because only the net amount is expected to be available during the fiscal period. Since revenues are reported net, it is not appropriate to record a bad debts expense because the "expense" does not represent an actual expenditure of current financial resources during the period. Reporting revenues on a net basis does not mean that a governmental unit cannot budget for bad debts expense and monitor the "expense" through its financial accounting system. When this is done, however, the bad debts expense account used for budgeting or internal purposes must be netted against the related gross revenue account and reported as net revenue for financial reporting purposes. In the following illustration, bad debts expense is not recorded, but the example journal entries could easily be modified to accommodate the use of a bad debts expense account for internal reporting purposes.*

During the fiscal year, the routine transactions (such as writeoffs of accounts and collections on account) affecting the receivables and allowance accounts may be recorded as follows:

Allowance For Uncollectible Property		
Taxes—Current	20,000	
Property Taxes Receivable—Current		20,000
Cash	350,000	
Property Taxes Receivable—Current		350,000

It may be determined during the fiscal year that the allowance for uncollectible accounts was either over-provided for or under-provided for. When this conclusion is reached, the allowance account and the revenue account are appropriately adjusted to reflect the change in the accounting estimate. For example, in the current illustration, if it is decided that the allowance provision for the year should have been $27,000 and not $30,000, the following entry would be made:

Allowance For Uncollectible Property Taxes—Current	3,000	
Revenues—Property Taxes		3,000

Again, it should be noted that the adjustment is made directly through the revenue account, thus avoiding the use of a bad debts expense account.

At the end of the year, it may be decided to transfer the balance in the current receivables account to a delinquent account for internal control and analysis. The transfer does not substitute for the writeoff of an account when a specific account has been identified as uncollectible. In fact, for reporting purposes, the current and delinquent balances are usually combined since they both represent specific accounts that are expected to be ultimately collected. To continue with the illustration, assume that all of the remaining net receivables are considered collectible, but they are technically delinquent at the end of the fiscal year. In this case, the following entry would be made:

Property Taxes Receivable—Delinquent	30,000	
Allowance For Uncollectible Property Taxes—Current	7,000	
Property Taxes Receivable—Current		30,000
Allowance For Uncollectible Property Taxes—Delinquent		7,000

Available As noted earlier, revenues are considered available when they can be used for expenditures incurred during the current year, or are expected to be collected after the end of the year but in time to pay liabilities outstanding at the end of the current year. With this general guideline, the question arises as to how soon after the year-end must the property tax receivable be collected. NCGA Interpretation-3 (Revenue Recognition—Property Taxes) specifically states that the property tax must be collected within sixty days after the end of the period in which the property tax revenue was recognized. In unusual circumstances, NCGA Interpretation-3 allows the use of a period greater than sixty days; but, if a greater period is used, there must be disclosures in the financial statement to identify the length of the period used and the facts that justify the use of a period greater than sixty days.

Revenues

When it is concluded that assessed property tax revenue will not be available, the revenue cannot be recognized in the current assessment period. Continuing with the current illustration, if it is concluded that $4,000 of the property taxes receivable at the end of the fiscal year will not be collected until more than sixty days after the close of the period, the following entry would be made:

Revenues—Property Taxes	4,000	
Deferred Revenues—Property Taxes		4,000

Deferred revenues When property taxes are received in advance of the actual levy or assessment date, the receipt should be recorded as deferred revenue. Subsequently, the revenue is recognized in the period that the tax is levied, assuming the measurable and available criteria are met.

When property taxes are delinquent but are expected to be collected, they should be reported as deferred revenue if it is estimated that the taxes will not be available to pay current obligations of the governmental fund. Generally, this would mean that the delinquent property taxes are not expected to be collected within sixty days of the close of the fiscal year. For example, if it is assumed that the previously illustrated $7,000 of delinquent property taxes are not expected to be collected within sixty days of the close of the fiscal year, the following entry would be made:

Revenues—Property Taxes (30,000–7,000)	23,000	
Deferred Revenues—Property Taxes		23,000

Disclosures The governmental unit must disclose the important dates associated with assessed property taxes. These dates may include the lien dates, due dates, and collection dates. In addition, some units may be prohibited from recognizing property tax revenues based on the measurable and available criteria. When this circumstance exists, the nature of the prohibition should be disclosed in a note to the financial statements. Moreover, the fund balance should be reserved by the amount of the property tax revenue that is recognized under generally accepted accounting principles but is not consistent with the legal requirement that must be observed by the governmental unit.

> **OBSERVATION:** *NCGA-1 concludes that property taxes, as well as other taxes, may be subject to accrual. This conclusion should not be interpreted as meaning that property taxes are accounted for on a*

full accrual basis. Property taxes are accrued when they satisfy the measurable and available criteria; however, this is a very narrow application of the accrual concept. For example, delinquent property taxes may be collected several months after the close of the fiscal year in which they are due and, therefore, would not be considered revenue in that fiscal year. Although under the accrual concept, delinquent property taxes (assuming they are collectible) would be considered revenue in the period they are due. The accounting basis applicable to property taxes is more accurately described as the modified accrual basis, not the accrual basis.

Taxpayer-Assessed Revenues

Generally, taxpayer-assessed revenues such as income taxes and gross receipts taxes are accounted for on a cash basis. However, known refunds, based on tax returns received, should be recorded on an accrual basis, with a liability being established on the day the return is received. For example, if at the close of the fiscal year (June 30, 19X5), a municipality has received returns for gross receipts taxes with refund claims totaling $450,000, the following entry would be made:

Revenues—Gross Receipts Taxes	450,000	
Tax Refunds Payable		450,000

The accrual basis can be used to account for taxpayer-assessed revenues when both the liability and the collectibility of the tax have been established. An example of the latter may include a situation in which a taxpayer has actually filed a tax return with an amount due, and, although the payment is delayed, it is nonetheless assured.

> **OBSERVATION:** *The AICPA Audit Guide entitled* Audits of State and Local Governmental Units *(1986) notes that some states are using historical experience, including advanced mathematical and statistical techniques, to estimate the amount of receivable or payable (refunds) that should be accrued for income taxes at the end of a fiscal period.*

Sales Taxes

Like other taxpayer-assessed revenues, sales taxes generally are accounted for on a cash basis. However, if the liability and collectibility

Revenues

of the sales taxes have been established (usually through the filing of a tax return), the sales taxes are accounted for on the accrual basis. For example, sales taxes that have been collected by retailers but are not payable to the governmental unit until after the close of the fiscal year should not be accrued. There are exceptions to the accounting standard that sales taxes should be recorded on a cash basis. These general exceptions and examples of the exceptions are presented below:

General Exception to Cash Basis	*Example of General Exception*
Taxes collected by one governmental unit that will be remitted to another governmental unit in time to pay outstanding obligations at the end of the current year should be accrued.	Sales taxes collected by the state, but due to be paid to various municipalities within 60 days of the municipalities' fiscal year-end.
Taxes due but not collected by the due date should be accrued.	Sales taxes that are due by the close of the fiscal year, but receipt is delayed until after the close of the fiscal year.

OBSERVATION: *The generalizations concerning exceptions described above are discussed in the pronouncements in the context of sales taxes. However, these guidelines could be applied to other sources of revenues accounted for on a cash basis.*

Sales taxes that are received before they are due should be recorded as deferred revenue.

Grants, Entitlements, and Shared Revenues

State and local programs may be financed by grants, entitlements, and shared revenues provided by another governmental unit. For example, a state government may provide grants directly to local police departments specifically in order to increase the number of police officers available for patrol duty. NCGA-2 (Grant, Entitlement, and Shared Revenue Accounting and Reporting by State and Local Governments) provides the following definitions for these sources of revenue:

- *Grant*—A contribution or gift of cash or other assets from another government to be used or expended for a specified purpose, activity, or facility.
- *Operating grant*—Grants that are intended to finance operations or that may be used for either operations or for capital outlays at the discretion of the grantee.
- *Capital grant*—A contribution or gift of cash or other assets restricted by the grantor for the acquisition or construction of fixed (capital) assets.
- *Entitlement*—The amount of payment to which a state or local government is entitled as determined by the federal or other government (for example, the Director of the Office of Revenue Sharing) pursuant to an allocation formula contained in applicable statutes.
- *Shared revenue*—A revenue levied by one government but shared on a predetermined basis, often in proportion to the amount collected at the local level, with another government or class of government.

Grants, entitlements, and shared revenues are recognized as revenues based on the method of accounting used by the particular fund that receives the resources. That is, receipts by governmental fund types (General, Special Revenue, Capital Projects, and Debt Service) and Expendable Trust Funds would be recorded on the modified accrual basis. Receipts by proprietary fund types (Enterprise, Internal Service), Nonexpendable Trust Funds, and Pension Trust Funds would be recorded on an accrual basis. Each grant, entitlement, or shared revenue should be carefully evaluated to determine which specific fund should be held accountable for the resources received.

Governmental Fund Types Grants, entitlements, and shared revenues should be recorded as revenues when they meet the measurable and available criteria. These sources of financial resources are often subject to various restrictions imposed by the governmental unit providing the funds. Such restrictions must be carefully evaluated in the context of the revenue recognition criteria to determine when the resources become measurable and available.

In general, governmental units receiving grants are entitled to the resources when appropriate expenditures under the grant program are made. Thus, the critical event is the point at which an expenditure is incurred. At that point, grant revenue should be simultaneously recognized along with the expenditure. The receipt of a grant and subsequent expenditure of the grant may be recorded in the following manner:

Revenues

Grant is received from another governmental unit.

Cash	10,000	
Deferred Revenue		10,000

Expenditures that qualify under the grant program are incurred.

Expenditures—Current	6,000	
Vouchers Payable		6,000
Deferred Revenue	6,000	
Grant Revenues		6,000

Entitlements and shared revenues generally are subject to forfeiture only if prescribed regulations are not observed by the governmental unit. Thus, entitlements and shared revenues may be recognized before they are actually received if they (1) can be reasonably estimated and (2) are available to finance expenditures of the current period.

When grants, entitlements, or shared revenues have not met the measurable and available criteria and no resources have been received from the disbursing governmental unit, the recipient governmental unit may disclose the nature and amount of the item in a note to the financial statements, but receivable and deferred revenue accounts should not be established. On the other hand, when the revenue criteria are not met but the grant, entitlement, or shared revenue has been received, the amount should be recorded as deferred revenue.

General governmental expenditures financed by grants, entitlements, and shared revenues should be recorded in the General Fund and not in a Special Revenue Fund unless specifically required. Other governmental expenditures should be recorded in the most appropriate governmental fund, based on the nature of the expenditures. Examples of other governmental expenditures and the fund in which they should be recorded are listed below:

Nature of Expenditure	Recording Fund
Capital expenditures financed by a capital grant or through shared revenues	Capital Projects Fund (except for expenditures related to proprietary funds)
Expenditures for general obligation bonds financed by a grant	Debt Service Fund

Grants, entitlements, and shared revenues that are used to finance a governmental fund's operating or capital expenditures are presented in the Statement of Revenues and Expenditures as revenues. Expenditures financed by these revenues are recorded as expenditures and classified by character (current expenditures, debt service expenditures, or capital outlays) on the governmental fund's operating statement. When capital expenditures are made, the fixed assets acquired or constructed should be recorded in the General Fixed Assets Account Group.

Proprietary Fund Types Enterprise Funds and Internal Service Funds should use the accrual basis of accounting to determine when grants, entitlements, and shared revenues should be recorded. In determining whether (1) the earnings process is complete or virtually complete and (2) an exchange has taken place, due consideration should be given to the qualifying restrictions that may be imposed by the terms of the grant, entitlement, or shared revenue.

The specific account used to record a grant, entitlement, or shared revenue depends upon its purpose. The receipt of the resources should be recorded as nonoperating revenue if (1) the resources were made available to finance current operations or (2) the revenue may be used to finance current operations or capital expenditures based on the discretion of the recipient governmental unit. On the other hand, if the resources were provided to finance only capital expenditures, the grant, entitlement, or shared revenue is recorded as contributed capital and not as nonoperating revenue. For example, if a governmental unit received a $400,000 operating grant and $100,000 capital grant, the following entry would be made:

Cash	500,000	
Revenues From Operating Grants		
(Nonoperating)		400,000
Contributed Capital—Capital Grants		100,000

The contributed capital account is shown in the equity section of the proprietary fund's balance sheet.

All depreciable property of a proprietary fund (irrespective of the source of the property) must be depreciated in accordance with generally accepted accounting principles as applied by a commercial enterprise.

However, depreciable fixed assets financed by resources restricted for capital expenditures may be accounted for by either of the following alternatives.

Revenues

Alternative 1—depreciation is closed to retained earnings When depreciable property is acquired through grants, entitlements, or shared revenues restricted for capital expenditures, it will be accounted for in a manner similar to all other depreciable property. Depreciation expense and accumulated depreciation will be recorded, and the depreciation expense will be presented as an operating expense and closed along with other operating expenses directly to retained earnings (through an income summary account).

Alternative 2—depreciation is closed to contributed capital When depreciable property is acquired through grants, entitlements, or shared revenues restricted for capital expenditures, a contributed capital account is established when the resources are received. Depreciation expense and accumulated depreciation will be recorded, but the depreciation expense at the end of the year will be closed directly to the contributed capital account. On the Statement of Revenues, Expenses, and Changes in Retained Earnings, the depreciation expense will be presented as an operating expense and will be used to compute net income. Then, the depreciation expense will be added to the net income figure to identify the net increase (decrease) in retained earnings for the year, and the net increase (decrease) will be added to (subtracted from) the beginning balance of retained earnings.

The effects of the two alternatives on the proprietary fund's operating statement are contrasted in the following table.

	Alternative 1 (Depreciation is closed to retained earnings)	*Alternative 2* (Depreciation is closed to contributed capital)
Operating revenues	$100,000	$100,000
Operating expenses (including depreciation expense of $20,000 on depreciable property financed by capital grants)	90,000	90,000
Operating income	10,000	10,000
Nonoperating revenues (expenses)	5,000	5,000
Operating income before transfers	15,000	15,000
Operating transfers	6,000	6,000
Net income	21,000	21,000

Add depreciation on fixed assets acquired by capital grants that reduces contributed capital from capital grants	—	20,000
Net increase (decrease) in retained earnings	21,000	41,000
Retained earnings—beginning of year	120,000*	120,000*
Retained earnings—end of year	$141,000	$161,000

---

*It is assumed that the capital grant was made during the current year. Otherwise the beginning balances of retained earnings under the two assumptions would also be different because of depreciation expense being added back in prior years.

The difference between the retained earnings balances under the two alternatives is reflected in the contributed capital from capital grants account. Thus, the total equity of the fund is the same for both alternatives.

Fiduciary Fund Types Grants, entitlements, and shared revenues received by Expendable Trust Funds should be accounted for on a modified accrual basis, while similar receipts by Nonexpendable Trust Funds and Pension Funds should be accounted for on an accrual basis.

Agency Funds do not use operating accounts such as revenues or expenditures because they serve only a custodial function, not an operations function. However, an Agency Fund (primary recipient fund) may initially account for the receipt of grants, entitlements, and shared revenues that eventually will be expended by another governmental fund (secondary recipient fund). This "pass through" transaction requires that the secondary recipient fund use its normal recognition criteria to determine when revenues, contributed capital, expenditures, and expenses should be recognized. The Agency Fund's custodial role precludes the recognition of operating transactions associated with the pass through transaction. For example, the following entries would be made in an Agency Fund and an Enterprise Fund when a capital grant available to the Enterprise Fund is initially recorded in an Agency Fund:

Agency Fund			*Enterprise Fund*		
Cash	400,000		Due from Agency Fund	400,000	
Due to Enterprise Fund		400,000	Contributed Capital— Capital Grant		400,000

Revenues

The Enterprise Fund should record the amount due from the Agency Fund and the related contributed capital only if the accrual recognition criteria have been met.

> **OBSERVATION:** *A transaction should be accounted for initially as a "pass through" transaction in an Agency Fund only (1) when the appropriate fund cannot be determined when resources are initially received, or (2) due to legal or contractual provisions of the grant.*

The example assumes that a cash transfer will be made to the (secondary) recipient fund, and actual expenditures or expenses will be made from this fund. Under some circumstances, actual expenditures for operating transactions applicable to the recipient fund may be made by the Agency Fund. As noted in NCGA-2, it may be necessary to record the operating transaction in the Agency Fund in order to (1) provide an adequate audit trail or (2) facilitate the preparation of special purpose reports or financial statements required under the provisions of the grant, entitlement, or shared revenue program.

If the operating transactions are recorded in the Agency Fund, memoranda revenue, expenditure, and expense accounts should be used. The memoranda entries are recorded as they occur in the Agency Fund but the same transactions are subsequently recorded by the recipient fund based on the recognition criteria (basis of accounting) used by the recipient fund. To illustrate, assume that an Agency Fund is utilized to account for the receipt of an operating grant available to finance expenses of an Enterprise Fund. The following transactions and entries demonstrate the "dual" recording approach necessary when memoranda entries are employed:

Transaction: An Agency Fund receives a $100,000 operating grant that is to benefit an Enterprise Fund, but the grant is to be accounted for in the Agency Fund.

Journal Entry			*Memorandum Entry*	
Cash	100,000		Cash	100,000
Due to Enterprise Fund		100,000	Grant Revenue	100,000

Transaction: Expenses applicable to the Enterprise Fund as authorized under grant are made by the Agency Fund.

Revenues

Journal Entry		Memorandum Entry	
Due to Enterprise		Expenses 30,000	
Fund	30,000	Cash	30,000
Cash	30,000		

For financial reporting purposes, the Agency Fund's assets and liabilities must be combined with the recipient fund's (Enterprise Fund in this example) financial statements.

NCGA-2 concludes that the dual recording approach illustrated above should be used only when it serves a purpose, such as in the following situations:

- Grant accounting period is different from the recipient fund's accounting period.
- Grant is utilized by multiple funds (as explained below).

An Agency Fund should be used to account for grants, entitlements, or shared revenues that, at the discretion of the recipient governmental unit, may be used to finance expenditures of various funds. When the recipient fund is identified, the resources are transferred to the identified fund and operating accounts are recorded in the latter fund, not the Agency Fund. For financial reporting purposes, assets that remain in the Agency Fund at the close of the fiscal year should be disclosed in a note to the financial statements.

Disclosures Accounting and reporting requirements established by the grant, entitlement, or shared revenue program may not be consistent with generally accepted accounting principles. The recipient governmental unit's financial accounting system should be designed to meet both requirements, perhaps through the utilization of supplemental accounting records, if necessary. When GAAP-based financial statements do not demonstrate compliance with the special reporting requirements imposed by the grantor governmental unit, it may be necessary to demonstrate compliance through the presentation of schedules or narrative explanations in the Comprehensive Annual Financial Report or the preparation of special purpose reports.

> **OBSERVATION:** *Guidelines established in NCGA-2 (Grant, Entitlement, and Shared Revenue Accounting by State and Local Governments) do not apply to interfund transactions, unrestricted resources received from other governments, or resources received from private contributors. For example, a governmental unit's Enterprise Fund may receive resources from a real estate developer in much the*

Revenues

> same way that a grant is received. The receipt should be reported by the Enterprise Fund as contributed capital, but the question arises as to whether depreciation on contributed fixed assets can be accounted for under the second alternative method described previously. Neither NCGA-2 nor any other governmental promulgation establishes authoritative support for the alternative treatment of depreciation in this circumstance (Alternative 2).

Miscellaneous Revenues

Miscellaneous revenues received by governmental fund types should be recorded on a cash basis. NCGA-1 lists fines and forfeits, golf and swimming fees, inspection charges, parking fees, and parking meter receipts as examples of miscellaneous revenue.

Quasi-External Transactions

Generally, a transfer of resources from one governmental fund to another governmental fund when both funds are part of the same reporting entity is not recorded as an expenditure or expense by the disbursing fund or as revenue by the receiving fund. The exception to this rule is a quasi-external transaction.

A quasi-external transaction is a transaction between governmental funds whereby the transaction would have been classified as a revenue, expenditure, or expense transaction had the transaction been consummated with an external party. NCGA-1 lists the following as examples of quasi-external transactions:

- Payments in lieu of taxes from an Enterprise Fund to the General Fund
- Internal Service Fund billings to governmental departments that use its services
- Routine employer contributions from the General Fund to a Pension Trust Fund
- Routine service charges for inspection, engineering, utilities, or similar services provided by a department financed from one fund to a department financed from another fund

The above transactions and similar transactions give rise to the recording of revenues, expenditures, and expenses by the funds involved in the quasi-external transaction. For example, a payment by a Special Revenue Fund to an Enterprise Fund for services rendered by the Enterprise Fund would be recorded as follows:

Special Revenue Fund			Enterprise Fund		
Expenditure	10,000		Cash	10,000	
Cash		10,000	Revenue		10,000

Other Financing Resources

Operating transfers received from a fund that is a component of the same reporting entity should not be classified as operating revenue. For governmental fund types, operating transfers are presented as "Other Financing Sources" on the Statement of Revenues, Expenditures, and Changes in Fund Balance. Operating transfers received by proprietary fund types should be presented in the "Operating Transfers" section of the Statement of Revenues, Expenses, and Changes in Retained Earnings (or Equity). Also, for governmental fund types, proceeds from the issuance of long-term debt should be recorded as other financing sources, not as operating revenue.

Financial Reporting Disclosures

Revenues should be presented in the financial statements of the governmental unit by fund and by source. In addition, revenue recognition methods should be disclosed in the Summary of Significant Accounting Policies. An example of a disclosure of revenue recognition methods is presented below.

▶ **Revenue:** Generally, revenues of governmental fund types and Expendable Trust Funds are recognized when measurable and available except for certain revenue sources which are not susceptible to accrual. Material revenues in the following categories are considered susceptible to accrual because they are both measurable and available to finance expenditures of the current period:

- Property Taxes
- Intergovernmental Revenues and Grants

Revenues

- Rents and Concessions
- Payments in Lieu of Property Taxes
- Sanitation Service

Grant revenues are considered measurable and available and are recorded simultaneously with the grant expenditure unless such recognition is prohibited by the grant requirements.

The following revenues are not considered susceptible to accrual because they are not both measurable and available to finance expenditures of the current period:

- Utilities Service Taxes
- Licenses and Permits
- Franchise Revenue
- Charges for Services (except the above named)

The accrual basis of accounting is followed for proprietary funds, Nonexpendable Trust Funds, and Pension Trust Funds.

In the Water and Sewer Utility System, operating revenues are recorded on the accrual basis when billed; however, the accompanying financial statements do not include an estimate for unbilled customer service receivables as the change in such estimate from the prior period to the current fiscal period is not considered to be material. ◄

LITERATURE REFERENCES

Material in this chapter is based on the following authoritative pronouncements, which are grouped according to the major headings used within the chapter. A dual reference (both paragraph and page number) is used for NCGA-1 and NCGA-2 because the original pronouncements do not use paragraph numbers.

Introduction
NCGA-1 *Governmental Accounting and Financial Reporting Principles*, pp. 11 and 16/¶¶ 62, 63, and 109.

Property Taxes
NCGA-1 *Governmental Accounting and Financial Reporting Principles*, pp. 11 and 12/¶¶ 62 and 65.

NCGA Interpretation-3 *Revenue Recognition—Property Taxes*, ¶¶ 7, 8, 9, and 11.

Revenues

Taxpayer-Assessed Revenues
NCGA-1   *Governmental Accounting and Financial Reporting Principles*, p. 12/¶ 67.
AICPA Audit Guide   *Audits of State and Local Governmental Units (1978)*, pp. 14 and 15.

Sales Taxes
NCGA-1   *Governmental Accounting and Financial Reporting Principles*, p. 12/¶ 67.
SOP 75-3   *Accrual of Revenues and Expenditures by State and Local Governmental Units*, ¶ 4.
AICPA Audit Guide   *Audits of State and Local Governmental Units (1978)*, p. 16.

Grants, Entitlements, and Shared Revenues
NCGA-2   *Grant, Entitlement, and Shared Revenue Accounting and Reporting by State and Local Governments*, pp. 1-3/¶¶ 2-18.
SOP 75-3   *Accrual of Revenues and Expenditures by State and Local Governmental Units*, ¶ 4.
APB Statement-4   *Basic Concepts and Accounting Principles Underlying Financial Statements of Business Enterprises*, ¶¶ 148-153.
NCGA-1   *Governmental Accounting and Financial Reporting Principles*, pp. 5, 13, and 22/¶¶ 12, 13, 88, and 148.

Miscellaneous Revenues
NCGA-1   *Governmental Accounting and Financial Reporting Principles*, p. 12/¶ 67.

Quasi-External Transactions
NCGA-1   *Governmental Accounting and Financial Reporting Principles*, p. 15/¶¶ 102 and 103.

Other Financing Resources
NCGA-1   *Governmental Accounting and Financial Reporting Principles*, p. 16/¶¶ 106-108.

Financial Reporting Disclosures
NCGA-1   *Governmental Accounting and Financial Reporting Principles*, pp. 12 and 16/¶¶ 69 and 110.

SPECIAL ASSESSMENTS

Prior to issuance of GASB-6, a Special Assessment Fund was used to account for resources that were raised by assessing only the properties of taxpayers who would directly benefit from either the construction or improvement of a capital asset or the provision for special services. Generally, the use of a Special Assessment Fund to account for special assessments resulted in a deficit fund balance. Although capital outlays were recorded as expenditures, the special assessment debt was recorded as a liability of the Special Assessment Fund (rather than as an other source of financing). In addition, the special assessment levied against property owners was not recorded as revenue until the measurable and available criteria were satisfied.

With the issuance of GASB-6, the likelihood that a fund balance deficit will result from special assessments is significantly reduced. This is accomplished by treating the special assessment debt like all other debt issued by a governmental unit. The proceeds of the special assessment debt should be recorded as an other source of financing, and the debt should be reported as part of the governmental unit's General Long-Term Debt Account Group (GLTDAG) if the unit is directly liable or in some manner liable for the special assessment debt.

Another significant aspect of accounting standards established by GASB-6 is the prohibition of the use of a Special Assessment Fund for governmental financial reporting. The rationale for the prohibition was that special assessment transactions and balances are no more unique than capital expenditures, debt service expenditures, and special levies that are accounted for in the other four governmental funds (General Fund, Capital Projects Funds, Debt Service Funds, and Special Revenue Funds) or in Enterprise Funds. Special assessment transactions and balances will generally be accounted for in a number of different funds. If legal requirements are not satisfied because a separate Special Assessment Fund cannot be used for financial reporting purposes, it may be necessary to make additional disclosures in notes, schedules, and explanations, or perhaps by the preparation of separate special reports.

GASB-6 did not address the issue of recognizing revenue from special assessments before the revenue is measurable and available.

Special Assessments

The GASB decided not to establish unique revenue recognition criteria for special assessment transactions. The GASB plans to address this issue when it promulgates standards related to its measurement focus/basis of accounting research project.

Services Financed by Special Assessments

Special assessments that are used to finance special types of service or special levels of service should be accounted for in either the General Fund, a Special Revenue Fund, or an Enterprise Fund. The number of separate funds established should be kept to the minimum level that will satisfy legal and administrative requirements. Therefore, in some cases, services financed by special assessments may be accounted for in the General Fund.

If it is necessary to establish a separate fund, special assessment transactions related to services should be accounted for in a Special Revenue Fund or an Enterprise Fund. One characteristic that distinguishes a Special Revenue Fund from an Enterprise Fund is that services accounted for in a Special Revenue Fund are financed indirectly by the user because the user does not pay for the service based on actual use. On the other hand, an Enterprise Fund generally obtains most of its financial resources from direct charges levied against the user based on the amount of services consumed by the user. For example, a special assessment levy for snow removal from streets and sidewalks in a business district that is based on the property valuation of each business should be accounted for in a Special Revenue Fund rather than in an Enterprise Fund.

The recording of revenues and expenditures/expenses related to services financed by special assessments should be consistent with the basis of accounting applicable to the governmental fund or proprietary fund used to account for the special assessment transactions. When the General Fund or a Special Revenue Fund is used, the modified accrual basis should be used to account for revenues and expenditures. Thus, revenues should be recorded when they are both measurable and available, and expenditures should be recognized when current expendable financial resources are expected to be used to pay for the expenditures. When an Enterprise Fund is used to account for the transactions, the accrual basis of accounting should be used. Thus, revenues should be recognized when earned and realizable, and expenses should be recorded when consumed or subject to amortization.

Capital Improvements Financed by Special Assessment—Related Debt

Capital improvements financed by special assessments have two distinct phases, namely the construction phase and the debt service phase. When a governmental unit is directly liable or obligated in some manner (as defined in the section entitled Governmental Liability for Debt) for the special assessment debt, the capital construction and related debt service transactions should be accounted for in a manner similar to other governmental capital outlays and debt service payments. For this reason, special assessment transactions related to capital improvements may be accounted for in a Capital Projects Fund, Debt Service Fund, General Long-Term Debt Account Group (GLTDAG), and General Fixed Assets Account Group (GFAAG). (If there are no legal or administrative requirements that necessitate the use of a separate Capital Projects Fund or Debt Service Fund, the General Fund could be used in place of these two funds.)

> OBSERVATION: *A Debt Service Fund must be used when resources are accumulated for the payment of principal and interest due in future years.*

Capital Projects Fund A Capital Projects Fund would be used to account for the proceeds from the issuance of the special assessment debt. The special assessment debt may be bonds, notes, or some other long-term debt instrument. The receipt of the debt proceeds would be recognized as an other source of financing for the Capital Projects Fund. In addition, the Capital Projects Fund would record expenditures related to the construction or acquisition of the capital improvement.

Debt Service Fund A Debt Service Fund would be used to account for the accumulation of resources to finance the servicing of the special assessment debt. If a special levy is assessed, the levy would be recorded in the Debt Service Fund. Revenue related to the special assessment levy would be recognized when the revenue is both measurable and available. The portion of the levy that is not considered to be available and measurable would be reported as deferred revenue in the Debt Service Fund.

Debt service payments (principal repayments and interest payments) related to the special assessment debt would be accounted

Special Assessments

for in the Debt Service Fund. As with other debt service payments, they should be recognized as expenditures when due, and they should not be accrued. In addition, interest related to the special assessments receivable should be recognized as revenue when the measurable and available criteria are satisfied. However, GASB-6 notes that interest revenue on special assessments receivable may be recorded when due since the interest revenue will approximately offset the interest expenditures related to the special assessment debt.

GLTDAG When special assessment debt is issued and the governmental unit is directly liable or obligated in some manner for its repayment, the special assessment debt should be recorded in the GLTDAG. The special assessment debt would be recorded as a liability in the GLTDAG and reduced as the debt is repaid. (The classification of special assessment debt in the GLTDAG is discussed in the section entitled Classification of Special Assessment Debt.)

GFAAG Expenditures for capital improvements are recognized in the GFAAG unless a capital improvement is related to an Enterprise Fund (see section entitled Enterprise Funds). Many special assessments for capital improvements are related to infrastructure assets, which do not have to be capitalized.

To illustrate capital improvements financed by special assessment debt, assume that a governmental unit agrees to construct special street lighting in its business district at a cost of $1,000,000. The contract to install the special lighting is signed on February 15, 19X1, and the project is completed by an independent contractor on June 30, 19X1. In order to pay the contractor, three-year, 6% special assessment installment notes are issued on June 30, 19X1. The notes are to be repaid in three equal installments beginning on June 30, 19X2. A special assessment of $1,000,000 is levied against enterprises in the business district on June 30, 19X1, and three equal assessment payments that carry an interest rate of 10% will be paid over the next three years beginning on June 30, 19X2. The special assessment transactions would be accounted for as described below.

Transaction: The special lighting contract is signed on February 15, 19X1.

CAPITAL PROJECTS FUND
Encumbrances	1,000,000	
Reserve For Encumbrances		1,000,000

Special Assessments

Transaction: The three-year special assessment notes are issued on June 30, 19X1.

CAPITAL PROJECTS FUND
Cash   1,000,000
    Proceeds From Issuance Of Notes   1,000,000

GLTDAG
Amount To Be Provided For Repayment
  of Notes   1,000,000
    Special Assessment Debt With
      Governmental Commitment   1,000,000

The governmental unit will make three equal annual debt service payments of $374,111 ($1,000,000 divided by 2.673, where 2.673 is the present value factor for an annuity at an interest rate of 6% for three periods) to the holders of the notes beginning on June 30, 19X2.

> **OBSERVATION:** *In this example, it is assumed that the governmental entity is obligated in some manner for the special assessment debt. The extent of a governmental entity's obligation for special assessment debt is addressed in the section entitled Governmental Liability for Debt.*

Transaction: The independent contractor is paid on June 30, 19X1.

CAPITAL PROJECTS FUND
Reserve For Encumbrances   1,000,000
    Encumbrances   1,000,000

Expenditures—Capital Outlays   1,000,000
    Vouchers Payable/Cash   1,000,000

GFAAG
Infrastructure Assets—Lighting   1,000,000
    Investment In Infrastructure Assets—
      Special Assessments   1,000,000

Note: Because the asset is infrastructure, capitalization is optional.

Transaction: A special assessment is levied against enterprises in the business district on June 30, 19X1.

Special Assessments

DEBT SERVICE FUND
  Special Assessments Receivable—
    Noncurrent   930,414
      Deferred Revenue   930,414

The amount of the special assessments receivable is $930,414 ($374,111 × 2.487, where 2.487 is the present value factor for an annuity at an interest rate of 10% for three periods). The present value of the receivable ($930,414) differs from the present value of the special assessment debt ($1,000,000) because the interest rates (risk) related to each debtor (individual property owners versus the governmental unit) are different.

> **OBSERVATION:** *If the interest rates related to the special assessment debt and the special assessment levy are the same, the present value of the special assessment debt and the present value of the special assessments receivable would be the same. In most cases, this is unlikely since the governmental unit will generally have an incremental borrowing rate (lower risk and special tax treatment) that is lower than the composite incremental borrowing rate for the property owners being assessed.*

Transaction: The first special assessment levy installment is received on June 30, 19X2.

DEBT SERVICE FUND
  Cash   374,111
    Interest Income   93,041
    Special Assessments Receivable—
      Noncurrent   281,070

  Deferred Revenue   281,070
    Revenue—Special Assessments   281,070

GLTDAG
  Amount Available In Debt Service Fund   314,111
    Amount To Be Provided For
      Repayment Of Notes   314,111

The amounts of special assessment revenue and interest income recognized are based on the following amortization table:

Special Assessments

Date	Cash	Interest income @10%	Reduction of special assessments receivable	Carrying value of special assessments receivable
6/30/X1				$930,414
6/30/X2	$374,111	$93,041	$281,070	649,344
6/30/X3	374,111	64,934	309,177	340,167
6/30/X4	374,111	33,944 [R]	340,167	-0-

[R] Rounded

Transaction: The first debt service payment on the special assessment notes is made on June 30, 19X2.

DEBT SERVICE FUND
Expenditures—Principal Repayments   314,111
Expenditures—Interest Payments   60,000
    Vouchers Payable/Cash   374,111

GLTDAG
Special Assessment Debt With Governmental Commitment   314,111
    Amount Available In Debt Service Fund   314,111

The amount of the payments made to reduce the special assessment notes is based on the following amortization table:

Date	Cash	Interest income @6%	Reduction of special assessment notes	Carrying value of special assessment notes
6/30/X1				$1,000,000
6/30/X2	$374,111	$60,000	$314,111	685,889
6/30/X3	374,111	41,153	332,958	352,931
6/30/X4	374,111	21,180 [R]	352,931	-0-

[R] Rounded

Entries for 19X3 and 19X4 would be similar to the entries recorded in 19X2. The results of the entries for the three-year period in the Debt Service Fund are summarized below.

	Receipts from special assessments			Expenditures for special assessment debt		
Year	Receivable	Income	Total	Principal	Interest	Total
19X2	$281,070	$ 93,041	$ 374,111	$ 314,111	$ 60,000	$ 374,111
19X3	309,177	64,934	374,111	332,958	41,153	374,111
19X4	340,167	33,944	374,111	352,931	21,180	374,111
	$930,414	$191,919	$1,122,333	$1,000,000	$122,333	$1,122,333

Special Assessments

In this example, the amount of the total receipts from the special assessments and the amount of the expenditures for the debt servicing were the same. This occurred because it was assumed that the beneficiaries of the special assessment capital outlays were responsible for the funding of the capital improvement.

Governmental Liability for Debt

Because property owners are generally obligated to finance all or part of the repayment of special assessment debt, a question arises whether the special assessment debt should be reported in a governmental unit's GLTDAG. When the governmental unit is primarily liable for the special assessment debt, the debt should be reported as part of its GLTDAG. In addition, special assessment debt should be reported in the GLTDAG when the governmental unit is "obligated in some manner" to repay the debt in cases where property owners default. GASB-6 concludes that a governmental unit is obligated in some manner to pay the special assessment debt if one of the following two circumstances exists:

- The governmental unit is legally obligated to assume all or part of the special assessment debt if property owners default.
- The governmental unit, although not required to do so, may assume secondary responsibility for all or part of the special assessment debt, and the governmental unit has either taken such action in the past or has indicated that it will take such action.

The following specific conditions would indicate that a governmental unit is obligated in some manner to repay the special assessment debt:

a. When lien foreclosure proceeds are inadequate and the governmental unit is required to fund the deficiencies
b. When reserves, guarantees, or sinking funds must be established by a governmental unit
c. When delinquencies occur and the governmental unit is required to fund such delinquencies until proceeds are received from foreclosures
d. When properties put up for sale because of delinquencies are not sold at public auction and must be acquired by the governmental unit
e. When the governmental unit is authorized and in fact estab-

lishes reserves, guarantees, or sinking funds (even if an authorized fund has not yet been established, the governmental unit may still be obligated in some manner with respect to the special assessment debt based on the conditions described in (g) and (h) below)
f. When the governmental unit is authorized and in fact establishes a separate fund to be used to purchase or redeem special assessment debt (even if an authorized fund has not yet been established, the governmental unit may still be obligated in some manner with respect to the special assessment debt based on the conditions described in (g) and (h) below)
g. When it is explicitly indicated by contract that the governmental unit may finance delinquencies, although there is no legal duty to do so
h. When it is probable that the governmental unit will accept responsibility for defaults based on either legal decisions within the state or on action previously taken by the governmental unit with respect to special assessment defaults

As the above conditions suggest, the GASB takes a very broad approach in identifying special assessment debt that should be reported by a governmental unit in its GLTDAG. This broad approach to debt classification is further endorsed in GASB-6 when the phrase *obligated in some manner* is described as including all situations *except for the following:*

- The governmental unit is prohibited from assuming responsibility for the special assessment debt in case of default
- The governmental unit is not legally liable to assume the special assessment debt in case of default and has in no way indicated that it will or may assume the debt.

Classification of Special Assessment Debt

When property owners are responsible for paying all or a portion of special assessment debt issued to finance capital improvements, the accounting for the special assessment is dependent upon whether (a) the debt is general obligation debt, (b) the governmental unit is obligated in some manner to repay the debt, or (c) the governmental unit is in no way obligated to repay the debt.

Special Assessments

General Obligation Debt General obligation debt is backed by the full faith and credit of a governmental unit. When special assessment debt is backed by a governmental unit, the debt is to be recorded in the GLTDAG in a manner similar to the accounting used to record all other general obligation debt. For example, if special assessment bonds of $900,000 are issued and the bonds are backed by the full faith and credit of a state or local government, the following entry would be made in the GLTDAG:

Amount To Be Provided For Repayment Of Special Assessment Bonds	900,000	
Special Assessment Bonds Payable		900,000

(The proceeds from the sale of the special assessment debt would be recorded in a Capital Projects Fund, or in the General Fund if there were no legal or administrative reason to establish a separate Capital Projects Fund.)

Obligated in Some Manner A governmental unit is obligated in some manner to pay special assessment debt when (a) the governmental unit is legally obligated to assume all or part of the special assessment debt if property owners default or (b) the governmental unit may assume secondary responsibility for all or part of the debt and the unit has either taken such action in the past or has indicated that it will take such action. Special assessment debt that a governmental unit is obligated for in some manner should be recorded in its GLTDAG, but the debt should be referred to as "Special Assessment Debt With Governmental Commitment." For example, if $500,000 of special assessment notes are issued and the debt is not backed by the full faith and credit of a governmental unit but the unit is obligated for the debt in some manner, the following entry would be made in the GLTDAG to record the special assessment debt:

Amount To Be Provided For Repayment Of Special Assessment Notes	500,000	
Special Assessment Debt With Governmental Commitment		500,000

Special assessment debt may be issued when the governmental unit is both (a) obligated in some manner for the debt and (b) obligated to pay part of the special assessment based on the public benefit portion of the capital improvement, or because the governmental unit owns property that is subject to the special assessment.

Under this circumstance, the portion of the special assessment debt represented by the special assessment obligation of the governmental unit should be recorded in the GLTDAG as a general obligation debt and the balance of the special assessment debt should be recorded as "Special Assessment Debt With Governmental Commitment." In the previous illustration, for example, if it were assumed that the $500,000 special assessment debt was to be financed in part ($50,000) by special assessments levied directly against property owned by the governmental unit, the following entry would be made in the GLTDAG:

Amount To Be Provided For Repayment Of Special Assessment Notes	450,000	
Amount To Be Provided For Payment Of Special Assessment Levy	50,000	
Special Assessment Debt With Governmental Commitment		450,000
Special Assessments Payable		50,000

> **OBSERVATION:** *When a portion of the special assessment debt is classified as general obligation debt, a question arises of how the payment of the special assessment should be accounted for in the General Fund and in a Debt Service Fund. If the general obligation debt is based on special assessments levied directly against property owned by the governmental unit, the eventual payment of the special assessment by the General Fund to the Debt Service Fund should be treated as an expenditure (General Fund) and as revenue (Debt Service Fund) because the payment represents a quasi-external transaction. On the other hand, if the general obligation debt is based on a public benefit portion of the capital improvement (quasi-external transaction criteria are not met), the payment of the special assessment by the General Fund to the Debt Service Fund should be treated as an interfund transfer rather than as a quasi-external transaction.*

The portion of special assessment debt (for which a governmental unit is somewhat obligated) that is a direct obligation of an Enterprise Fund or is to be repaid from operating revenues of an Enterprise Fund should be recorded as a liability of the Enterprise Fund and not reported as a liability in the governmental unit's GLTDAG.

No Obligation to Pay Debt In some cases, special assessment debt may be issued with the governmental unit having no obligation to

Special Assessments

repay the debt. Under this circumstance, the special assessment debt would not be reported as part of the unit's GLTDAG. However, if a portion of the special assessment is to be paid by the governmental unit based on the public benefit portion of the capital improvement or because the governmental unit owns property that is subject to the special assessment, this portion of the special assessment debt would be recorded as a general obligation debt in the governmental unit's GLTDAG. For example, assume that special assessment bonds of $850,000 are issued, but the governmental unit is in no way responsible for the payment of the special assessment debt. If the governmental unit owns property that is subject to the special assessment and must pay assessments of $70,000 in order to finance the capital improvement, the following entry would be made in the GLTDAG:

Amount To Be Provided For Payment Of Special Assessment Levy	70,000	
Special Assessments Payable		70,000

When the special assessment bonds are issued, the proceeds of $850,000 would be recorded as an other financing source in the General Fund or a Capital Projects Fund, but the special assessment debt of $850,000 (except for the amount of the assessment that must be paid by the governmental unit—$70,000) would not be recorded in any governmental fund.

Special Assessment Reserve, Guarantee, or Sinking Fund

A governmental unit may be required or authorized to establish a reserve, guarantee, or sinking fund to accumulate resources in case property owners default on their special assessments. A Debt Service Fund must be used when resources are accumulated for principal and interest payments due in future years. For example, if a governmental unit is required under the special assessment debt agreement to make payments of $20,000 per year in order to finance a sinking fund for possible special assessment defaults, the following entries would be made, assuming that the total payment is applicable to the payment of special assessment principal defaults:

GENERAL FUND

Transfers Out—Debt Service Fund	20,000	
Cash		20,000

DEBT SERVICE FUND
Cash   20,000
    Transfers In—General Fund   20,000

GLTDAG
Amount Available In Debt Service Fund   20,000
    Amount Available To Be Provided For
    Repayment Of Special Assessment
    Bonds Payable   20,000

No Governmental Obligation for Debt

When a governmental unit is in no way obligated for the special assessment debt, the debt is not reported in the unit's financial statements. Nonetheless, it is necessary to account for the two distinct phases (construction phase and debt service phase) in the governmental unit's financial statements. Special assessment transactions related to capital improvements may be accounted for in a Capital Projects Fund, Agency Fund, and GFAAG. Because the special assessment debt is not the responsibility of the governmental unit, the GLTDAG is not utilized.

Capital Projects Fund A Capital Projects Fund would be used to account for the proceeds from the issuance of the special assessment debt. The receipt of debt proceeds should not be referred to as proceeds from issuance of special assessment debt. GASB-6 suggests that a title such as "Contribution From Property Owners" be used to identify the receipt as an other source of financing. Payments for the capital improvement would be recorded as expenditures in the Capital Projects Fund.

Agency Fund An Agency Fund (rather than a Debt Service Fund) should be used to account for debt service transactions. Because the governmental unit is in no way responsible for the special assessment debt, it functions in an agency role with respect to the collections of special assessments from property owners and the payment of principal and interest to the special assessment debt-holders.

When the special assessment is levied, a receivable is recorded in the Agency Fund along with a liability to be paid to the debt-holders. As payments are received from property owners, the receivable is reduced, but no portion of the receipts should be recorded as interest income because an Agency Fund, in its fiduciary role, does not prepare an operating statement. Likewise, payments to the special as-

Special Assessments

sessment debt-holders should not be designated as principal expenditures and interest expenditures but rather as a reduction to the liability related to the debt-holders.

GFAAG Expenditures for capital improvements are recognized in the GFAAG unless a capital improvement is related to an Enterprise Fund. Even though the governmental unit is not responsible for the special assessment debt, a capital improvement has been made, and accountability for the fixed asset should be established in the governmental unit's GFAAG.

To illustrate the accounting for capital improvements financed by special assessment debt for which the governmental unit is not obligated in any manner, the example used earlier (see section entitled Capital Improvements Financed by Special Assessment—Related Debt) will be used again. The special assessment transactions, assuming the governmental unit is not obligated in any manner for the debt, would be accounted for as described below.

Transaction: The special lighting contract is signed on February 15, 19X1.

CAPITAL PROJECTS FUND
Encumbrances   1,000,000
    Reserve For Encumbrances   1,000,000

Transaction: The three-year special assessment notes are issued on June 30, 19X1.

CAPITAL PROJECTS FUND
Cash   1,000,000
    Contribution From Property Owners   1,000,000

GLTDAG
No entry

Transaction: The independent contractor is paid on June 30, 19X1.

CAPITAL PROJECTS FUND
Reserve For Encumbrances   1,000,000
    Encumbrances   1,000,000

Expenditures—Capital Outlays   1,000,000
    Vouchers Payable/Cash   1,000,000

GFAAG
    Infrastructure Assets—Lighting   1,000,000
        Investment In Infrastructure Assets—
           Special Assessments   1,000,000

Transaction: A special assessment is levied against enterprises in the business district on June 30, 19X1.

AGENCY FUND
    Special Assessments Receivable—
      Noncurrent   930,414
        Due To Holders Of Special Assessment
            Notes   930,414

Transaction: The first special assessment levy installment is received on June 30, 19X2.

AGENCY FUND
    Cash   374,111
      Special Assessments Receivable—
        Noncurrent   281,070
      Due To Holders Of Special Assessment
        Notes   93,041

GLTDAG
    No entry

Transaction: The first debt service payment on the special assessment notes is made on June 30, 19X2.

AGENCY FUND
    Due To Holders Of Special Assessment
        Notes   374,111
        Vouchers Payable/Cash   374,111

GLTDAG
    No entry

Financing Special Assessments with Current Resources

A capital improvement may be initially financed with currently available resources of the governmental unit rather than with proceeds from the issuance of special assessment debt. Payments that are made directly from a governmental fund (usually the General Fund) for capital improvements should be recorded as capital expenditures in the fund making the payments. Resources that are transferred from a governmental fund to a Capital Projects Fund should be recorded as interfund transfers, and capital outlays eventually made by the Capital Projects Fund should be recorded as capital expenditures.

The levy of the special assessment against property owners should be recorded in the governmental fund that initially provided the resources used to finance the capital improvement. The portion of the special assessment that should be recorded as revenue is the amount that is both measurable and available. The balance of the special assessment should be recorded as deferred revenue.

Enterprise Funds

In most circumstances, capital assets constructed for an Enterprise Fund and financed by special assessments should be accounted for in a manner similar to other capital improvements financed by special assessments. However, the capital asset should be recorded by the Enterprise Fund rather than reported as part of the governmental unit's GFAAG. The cost of the capital asset, net of resources provided by the Enterprise Fund, should be recorded as contributed capital by the Enterprise Fund. The special assessment debt related to the construction of the capital asset should be recorded as a liability of the Enterprise Fund only if one of the following conditions exists:

- Enterprise Fund is directly liable for the special assessment debt
- Enterprise Fund is not directly liable for the special assessment debt, but the debt is expected to be repaid from revenues of the Enterprise Fund

Debt expected to be repaid by an Enterprise Fund should be reported as debt of the Enterprise Fund even though the debt may be backed by the full faith and credit of the governmental unit.

Although GASB-6 concludes that most capital assets constructed for an Enterprise Fund and financed by special assessments will be accounted for as described in the previous paragraph, it is acceptable to record all special assessment transactions solely in the Enterprise Fund. Under this approach, the special assessment levy would be recorded as a receivable and contributed capital. Special assessment debt for which the Enterprise Fund is directly liable or expected to

Special Assessments

repay from its revenues would be accounted for in the Enterprise Fund. The accrual basis of accounting should be used to account for special assessments receivable and the related interest income, and special assessment debt and the related interest expense.

To illustrate the accounting for special assessment capital improvements related to an Enterprise Fund and solely accounted for in an Enterprise Fund, the example used earlier (see section entitled Capital Improvements Financed by Special Assessment—Related Debt) will be used. It is assumed that the Enterprise Fund is directly liable for the special assessment note issued to initially finance the construction of the capital asset. (All entries are recorded in the Enterprise Fund, whose fiscal year ends June 30.)

Transaction: The special lighting contract is signed on February 15, 19X1.

    No entry

Transaction: The three-year special assessment notes are issued on June 30, 19X1.

Cash	1,000,000	
Special Assessment Notes Payable—Noncurrent		685,889
Special Assessment Notes Payable—Current		314,111

Transaction: The independent contractor is paid on June 30, 19X1.

Fixed Assets	1,000,000	
Vouchers Payable/Cash		1,000,000

Transaction: A special assessment is levied against enterprises in the business district on June 30, 19X1.

Special Assessments Receivable—Noncurrent	649,344	
Special Assessments Receivable—Current	281,070	
Contributed Capital—Special Assessments		930,414

Special Assessments

Transaction: The first special assessment levy installment is received on June 30, 19X2.

Cash	374,111	
Interest Income		93,041
Special Assessments Receivable— Current		281,070
Special Assessments Receivable—Current	309,177	
Special Assessments Receivable— Noncurrent		309,177

Transaction: The first debt service payment on the special assessment notes is made on June 30, 19X2.

Special Assessment Notes Payable— Current	314,111	
Interest Expense	60,000	
Cash		374,111
Special Assessment Notes Payable— Noncurrent	332,958	
Special Assessment Notes Payable— Current		332,958

Transaction: Depreciation based on the straight-line method and an assumed economic life of 10 years is recorded.

Depreciation Expense	100,000	
Accumulated Depreciation		100,000

> **OBSERVATION:** *Although the GASB accepted two methods of accounting for special assessment capital projects that benefit Enterprise Funds, it did not suggest that one method was preferable to the other. The GASB did conclude that generally the guidance provided by paragraph 15 of GASB-6 should be followed (see section entitled Capital Improvements Financed by Special Assessment—Related Debt). The GASB concluded in an appendix to GASB-6 that "reporting all transactions and balances in an Enterprise Fund is not appropriate in many instances (paragraph 42)." The basic concern by the GASB is that project cash and receivables, and the special assessment debt, often do not meet the definitions of assets and liabilities. Thus, even though it is not suggested in the accounting standards paragraphs of GASB-6, the governmental financial statement pre-*

parer must carefully review the facts related to the special assessment to determine whether there is any justification for reporting all special assessment transactions and balances in an Enterprise Fund.

Special Assessment Districts as Component Units

A component unit applies the criteria established by GASB-6 to determine how special assessment transactions and accounts should be reported. When the component unit's financial statements are combined with the oversight unit's financial statements to form the reporting entity, the component unit's special assessment debt should be reported as a liability in the reporting entity's financial statements based on GASB-6 criteria even though the oversight unit may not be responsible in any way for the component unit's special assessment debt.

Disclosures

The disclosures in the governmental unit's financial statements with respect to special assessment debt depend upon whether the unit is responsible for the debt.

Governmental Unit Obligated for Debt When the governmental unit is primarily obligated or obligated in some manner for the repayment of special assessment debt, the following disclosures that are applicable to all general obligation debt should be made in the unit's financial statements:

- Nature of governmental unit's obligation for special assessment debt
- Description of individual special assessment debt issues
- Description of requirements or authorizations for the establishment of guarantees, reserves, or sinking funds if defaults occur
- Changes in general long-term debt (special assessment debt for which the unit is primarily responsible) and special assessment debt with governmental commitment (special assessment debt for which the unit is obligated in some manner)
- Summary of debt service requirements to maturity
- Special assessment debt authorized but unissued

In addition, the amount of the special assessments receivable that is delinquent should be disclosed on the face of the balance sheet or in a note to the statements.

Governmental Unit Not Obligated for Debt When the governmental unit is not obligated in any manner for repayment of the special assessment debt, the following disclosures should be made in the unit's financial statements:

- State the present amount of special assessment debt
- State that the governmental unit is in no manner obligated to repay the special assessment debt
- State that the governmental unit functions as an agent for the property owners by collecting assessments, forwarding collections to special assessment debt-holders and, if appropriate, beginning foreclosures

Statistical Tables

NCGA-1 (page 24/paragraph 161) requires that a variety of information be disclosed in statistical tables when a statistical section of a Comprehensive Annual Financial Report is prepared. GASB-6 revises paragraph 161(f) to read as follows:

- Special Assessment Billings and Collections: Last Ten Fiscal Years (if the government is obligated in some manner for related special assessment debt)

Effective Date and Transition

The accounting and reporting standards established by GASB-6 are applicable to financial statements for periods beginning after June 15, 1987; however, earlier application is encouraged.

When GASB-6 is applied, prior-period financial statements presented should be restated, if practical. For the most part, this means that special assessment transactions and balances previously presented in Special Assessment Funds must be presented in various other governmental funds, such as the General Fund, Special Revenue Funds, Capital Projects Funds, Debt Service Funds, and Enterprise Funds. For the first year in which GASB-6 standards are

Special Assessments

applied, the nature of any restatements made to prior-period financial statements and the effects of the restatements should be disclosed. If it is not practical to restate one or more prior-period financial statements, the reason for not restating the financial statements should be disclosed.

LITERATURE REFERENCES

Material in this chapter is based on the following authoritative pronouncements, which are grouped according to the major headings used within the chapter. A dual reference (both paragraph and page number) is used for NCGA-1 and NCGA-2 because the original pronouncements do not use paragraph numbers.

Introduction
GASB-6   *Accounting and Financial Reporting for Special Assessments,* ¶ 13.
NCGA-1   *Governmental Accounting and Financial Reporting Principles,* p. 5/
   ¶¶ 11-13.

Services Financed by Special Assessments
GASB-6   *Accounting and Financial Reporting for Special Assessments,* ¶ 14.
NCGA-1   *Governmental Accounting and Financial Reporting Principles,* pp. 6-8/
   ¶¶ 19, 20, 26, and 31.

Capital Improvements Financed by Special Assessment—Related Debt
GASB-6   *Accounting and Financial Reporting for Special Assessments,* ¶ 15.
NCGA-1   *Governmental Accounting and Financial Reporting Principles,* pp. 8,
   9, 11, and 12/¶¶ 30, 31, 40, 62, and 72.

Governmental Liability for Debt
GASB-6   *Accounting and Financial Reporting for Special Assessments,* ¶ 16.

Classification of Special Assessment Debt
GASB-6   *Accounting and Financial Reporting for Special Assessments,* ¶ 17.

Special Assessment Reserve, Guarantee, or Sinking Fund
GASB-6   *Accounting and Financial Reporting for Special Assessments,* ¶ 18.
NCGA-1   *Governmental Accounting and Financial Reporting Principles,* p. 8/
   ¶ 20.

No Governmental Obligation for Debt
GASB-6   *Accounting and Financial Reporting for Special Assessments,* ¶ 19.

Special Assessments

Financing Special Assessments with Current Resources
GASB-6   *Accounting and Financial Reporting for Special Assessments,* ¶ 22.

Enterprise Funds
GASB-6   *Accounting and Financial Reporting for Special Assessments,* ¶ 23.
NCGA-1   *Governmental Accounting and Financial Reporting Principles,* p. 9/ ¶ 42.

Special Assessment Districts as Component Units
GASB-6   *Accounting and Financial Reporting for Special Assessments,* ¶ 24.

Disclosures
GASB-6   *Accounting and Financial Reporting for Special Assessments,* ¶¶ 20 and 21.

Statistical Tables
GASB-6   *Accounting and Financial Reporting for Special Assessments,* ¶ 25.
NCGA-1   *Governmental Accounting and Financial Reporting Principles,* p. 25/ ¶ 161.

Effective Date and Transition
GASB-6   *Accounting and Financial Reporting for Special Assessments,* ¶ 27.

EXPENDITURES

There are significant differences between the recognition of expenditures by governmental units and the recognition of expenses by commercial enterprises. *Expenditures* are defined in NCGA-1 (Governmental Accounting and Financial Reporting Principles) as "decreases in (use of) fund financial resources other than through interfund transfers." On the other hand, FASB:CS-6 (Elements of Financial Statements) defines *expenses* as "outflows or other using up of assets or incurrences of liabilities during a period from delivering or producing goods, rendering services, or carrying out other activities that constitute the entity's ongoing major or central operations." The unique nature of expenditures of a governmental entity is described in this chapter.

The Governmental Accounting Model

The measurement of expenditures during an accounting period is significantly influenced by two interrelated characteristics of the governmental accounting model, the *measurement focus* and the *basis of accounting*.

Measurement Focus The measurement focus of an accounting model determines *what* should be measured. In governmental accounting, the measurement focus is concerned with the flow of expendable financial resources for a period. Only those events or transactions that represent the outflow of expendable financial resources are designated as governmental expenditures. An expenditure for a particular period represents a reduction in expendable financial resources or a claim (liability) at the end of the period that will be paid by using current expendable financial resources.

Governmental expenditures do not include amortizations that may arise from the purchase of assets in prior periods because the amortization process does not affect expendable financial resources. For example, the depreciation of a fixed asset that was acquired in a previous period is not recognized as a governmental expenditure; however, an expenditure for the fixed asset is recognized in the year that the fixed asset was acquired. Thus, the emphasis is on the measurement of the outflow of expendable resources for a particular accounting period.

Expenditures

Basis of Accounting The basis of an accounting system is concerned with *when* to measure transactions and events and *when* to reflect them in the governmental entity's financial statements. In governmental accounting, the modified accrual method serves as the basis of accounting. Expenditures are recognized when the related liability is incurred. Furthermore, when a transaction or event has occurred that will eventually lead to the reduction of a governmental fund's financial resources, the item is not recorded as an expenditure if current financial resources are not reduced. For example, if it is probable that a legal claim will result in the eventual payment to a plaintiff and the amount is subject to reasonable estimation, no expenditure is recognized if the actual payment is expected to be made a few years after it has been concluded that the governmental unit has incurred a liability. The estimated liability would be reported as part of the governmental entity's General Long-Term Debt Account Group. The legal claim will reduce the fund's financial resources, but the modified accrual basis as applied in the governmental accounting model would not consider the event to be an expenditure. The expenditure for the claim would be recognized when the actual claim is paid, or when a year-end liability (claim) will be paid using current expendable financial resources.

The remainder of this chapter discusses specific governmental expenditures and reporting concepts. Additional discussion of governmental expenditure issues can be found in the chapters concerning governmental liabilities (Chapters 40-43).

Interest and Principal Payments

NCGA-1 notes that most expenditures are measurable and should be recorded when the related fund liability is incurred. An exception to this generalization is the treatment of interest and principal payments for long-term debt. Interest and principal on long-term debt are not recorded as expenditures as they accrue, but when they become due and payable.

The rationale for the treatment of interest and principal payments on a cash basis is based on the nature of the Debt Service Fund. It is argued that the interest that accrues during the accounting period will not use current expendable financial resources of the Debt Service Fund. For example, assume that $100,000 of 6% bonds were issued on June 30, 19X1, and that the bonds pay interest on July 1 of each year beginning in 19X2. During the fiscal year ending June 30, 19X2, no interest expenditure is recognized because the actual interest is due and payable on July 1, 19X2. On July 1, 19X2, the following entries would be made, assuming that the cash required to pay the interest is transferred from the General Fund to the Debt Service Fund:

GENERAL FUND
Transfers Out—Debt Service Fund   6,000
     Cash   6,000

DEBT SERVICE FUND
Cash   6,000
     Transfers In—General Fund   6,000

Expenditures—Interest   6,000
     Cash   6,000

NCGA-1 concludes that it is appropriate to disclose debt service requirements for the following year, but the interest and principal payments should be recorded as expenditures in the year of payment. If the interest were accrued, the expenditures and liabilities of the Debt Service Fund would be overstated.

> **OBSERVATION:** *While it is true that the Debt Service Fund expenditures and liabilities would be overstated, it can be strongly argued that the transferring fund's transfers-out and liability accounts are understated when interest is not accrued. The nonaccrual of interest allows a governmental unit to manipulate, at least to some degree, the recognition of expenditures by carefully timing the due dates for interest as well as maturing debt (especially for serial bonds).*

When funds have been transferred to the Debt Service Fund during the fiscal year in anticipation of making debt service payments shortly after the end of the period, it is acceptable to accrue interest and maturing debt in the Debt Service Fund in the year the transfer is made. Also, if the transfer includes an amount for a principal payment, that amount should be removed from the General Long-Term Debt Account Group. To continue with the example, assume that the $6,000 interest transfer is made by the General Fund to the Debt Service Fund on June 30, 19X2. The following entries would be made on June 30:

GENERAL FUND
Transfers Out—Debt Service Fund   6,000
     Cash   6,000

Expenditures

DEBT SERVICE FUND
Cash	6,000	
Transfers In—General Fund		6,000
Expenditures—Interest	6,000	
Interest Payable		6,000

When interest is paid on July 1, 19X2, the payment is recorded as follows:

DEBT SERVICE FUND
Interest Payable	6,000	
Cash		6,000

There are additional exceptions to the general rule that an expenditure should be recorded when the related liability is incurred. These exceptions include claims, judgments, and special termination benefits (see Chapter 41), compensated absences (see Chapter 42), and pensions (see Chapter 66).

Interfund Transactions

Interfund transactions represent reductions in the expendable financial resources of the transferring fund, but the transaction may or may not be accounted for as an expenditure of the transferring fund. Transactions between funds may be classified as (1) loans and advances, (2) quasi-external transactions, (3) reimbursements, (4) residual equity transfers, and (5) operating transfers.

Loans and Advances Loans and advances between units of the same governmental reporting unit do not affect the operating statements of either governmental fund involved in the transaction. For example, assume a $100,000 loan is made by an Enterprise Fund to the General Fund. The transaction would be accounted for in the following manner:

ENTERPRISE FUND
Due From Other Funds—General Fund	100,000	
Cash		100,000

GENERAL FUND
Cash	100,000	
Due To Other Funds—Enterprise Fund		100,000

There is no requirement to eliminate the interfund loans and advances when the reporting entity's combined balance sheet is prepared. If the amounts are eliminated, the nature of the eliminations must be disclosed in the financial statements.

Quasi-External Transactions In general, transfers between funds do not give rise to operating expenditures and revenues because the transfer does not represent an arm's-length transaction. An exception to this philosophy is the treatment of quasi-external transactions.

A quasi-external transaction is a transaction between funds that are part of the same reporting entity, but the nature of the exchange suggests the existence of a more-or-less normal buyer/seller relationship. Furthermore, it is argued that had the governmental fund dealt with an external party, the transaction would have given rise to the recognition of an expenditure (or expense). In essence, the "purchasing" governmental fund has acquired a good or service that in most instances could have been purchased from an unrelated business enterprise. The following are examples of quasi-external transactions:

- Internal Service Fund billings to governmental departments that use its services
- Payments in lieu of taxes from an Enterprise Fund to the General Fund
- Routine service charges for inspection, engineering, utilities, or similar services provided by a department financed from one fund to a department financed from another fund

To illustrate the accounting for a quasi-external transaction, assume that an engineering department of an Internal Service Fund bills the General Fund $50,000 for engineering services rendered. The quasi-external transaction would be recorded as follows:

GENERAL FUND
Expenditures—Engineering	50,000	
Due To Other Funds—Internal Service Fund		50,000

INTERNAL SERVICE FUND
Due From Other Funds—General Fund	50,000	
Revenues—Engineering Services		50,000

Expenditures

Reimbursements Some expenditures (or expenses) that are the legal responsibility of one fund may be paid for by another fund, with the understanding that the latter fund will be reimbursed by the former fund. The fund that makes the initial payment should recognize the disbursement as an expenditure. To illustrate, assume that a $20,000 expenditure of a Capital Projects Fund is paid for by the General Fund, with the understanding that the General Fund will be reimbursed for the payment at a later date. The initial payment is recorded in the following manner:

GENERAL FUND (REIMBURSED FUND)
 Expenditures   20,000
  Cash   20,000

CAPITAL PROJECTS FUND (REIMBURSING FUND)
 No entry

When the reimbursing fund (Capital Projects Fund) repays the reimbursed fund (General Fund), the expenditures account of the reimbursed fund is credited and the expenditures account of the reimbursing fund is debited. To continue with the example, the repayment by the Capital Projects Fund to the General Fund would be recorded as follows:

GENERAL FUND
 Cash   20,000
  Expenditures   20,000

CAPITAL PROJECTS FUND
 Expenditures   20,000
  Cash   20,000

This entry reverses the initial entry that was made by the reimbursed fund (General Fund). Therefore, the net effect of these journal entries is to record the expenditure in only one fund, the reimbursing fund.

NCGA-1 lists the following situations as circumstances that would create a reimbursement between funds:

- One fund makes a single payment for two or more funds because the amount attributable to each fund is uncertain or is to be determined at a subsequent date.
- The reimbursing fund has insufficient funds to finance the initial payment.

- One fund inadvertently pays expenditures (expenses) of another fund.
- As a matter of convenience, one fund pays expenditures (expenses) of another fund with the understanding that there will be a reimbursement at a later date.

Reimbursements do not represent interfund transfers, loans, or advances, and, therefore, an interfund receivable or payable should not be used to account for such transactions.

> **OBSERVATION:** *Some accountants would argue that the initial payment made by the reimbursed fund should be recorded as an interfund receivable, and the expenditure should be recorded in the reimbursing fund. Such an approach classifies the expenditure in the fund that is legally or contractually responsible for the item from the very beginning of the transaction. However, an interfund receivable/payable should not be established unless the transaction is a properly approved interfund loan and not a reimbursement transaction as described above. The characteristics of the interfund transaction determines how the transaction should be recorded. This philosophy is endorsed by NCGA-1, which states that "interfund reimbursement accounting methods should not be used to disguise improper interfund loans, nor should reimbursements be confused with interfund transfers . . ."*

Residual Equity Transfers NCGA-1 defines residual equity transfers as "nonrecurring or nonroutine transfers of equity between funds." Residual equity transfers do not represent expenditures of the transferring fund and, therefore, should be presented as part of the analysis of the change in the fund's fund balance. A transfer of equity may represent the creation or expansion of a fund, or the liquidation or contraction of a fund.

For governmental fund types, residual equity transfers should be shown as an increase or decrease in the beginning balance of the fund balance. For a proprietary fund, the residual equity transfer should be presented as an increase or decrease in the fund's contributed capital or retained earnings, based on the circumstances of the transfer. For example, a transfer of a capital contribution of $100,000 by the General Fund to an Internal Service Fund would be accounted for in the following manner:

Expenditures

GENERAL FUND
    Residual Equity Transfer (Fund Balance)   100,000
        Cash   100,000

INTERNAL SERVICE FUND
    Cash   100,000
        Contributed Capital—General Fund   100,000

Operating Transfers Operating transfers result in the reduction of a fund's expendable resources, but they are not classified as expenditures. An operating transfer is a legally authorized transfer between funds in which one fund is responsible for the initial receipt of funds (property taxes, etc.), and another fund is responsible for the actual disbursement. In an operating transfer, the disbursing fund records the transaction as "Other Financing Uses" of resources and not as an operating expenditure. In a similar manner, the fund receiving the transfer does not record the receipts as revenue but rather as "Other Financing Sources" of funds. For example, a $100,000 operating transfer from the General Fund to a Special Revenue Fund would be recorded as follows:

GENERAL FUND
    Transfers Out—Special Revenue Fund   100,000
        Cash   100,000

SPECIAL REVENUE FUND
    Cash   100,000
        Transfers In—General Fund   100,000

It is also acceptable to record an operating transfer in the following manner when one fund (disbursing fund) is legally required to receive the initial revenue, and another fund (receiving fund) is legally required to expend the funds received (assumes disbursing fund initially recorded the receipt of resources as revenue):

DISBURSING FUND
    Revenues (by source)   100,000
        Cash   100,000

RECEIVING FUND
    Cash   100,000
        Revenues (by source)   100,000

Again, the transfer does not give rise to an expenditure.

Expenditures

The following are examples of operating transfers:

- Transfer of property taxes collected by the General Fund to a school district accounted for as a Special Revenue Fund
- Transfer of funds by the General Fund to an Enterprise Fund as part of an operating subsidy
- Transfer of funds from a Special Revenue Fund or the General Fund to a Debt Service Fund to support principal interest payments
- Transfer from an Enterprise Fund to the General Fund in order to finance general governmental expenditures

Operating transfers must be treated consistently by all funds involved in the transfers. At the end of the period, the total amount of transfers out should equal the amount of transfers in for the governmental reporting entity.

Encumbrances

An encumbrance represents a commitment related to unperformed contracts for goods and services. At the time the commitment is made, the following budgetary entry is made:

Encumbrances	10,000	
Reserve For Encumbrances		10,000

The issuance of a purchase order or the signing of a contract would create an encumbrance. The encumbrances account does not represent an expenditure for the period, only a commitment to expend resources. Likewise, the account reserve for encumbrances is not synonymous with a liability account, since the liability is recognized only when the goods are received or the services are performed. When an executory contract is completed, the budgetary accounts are eliminated, and the actual expenditure and related liability are recorded as illustrated below:

Reserve For Encumbrances	10,000	
Encumbrances		10,000
Expenditure	10,000	
Vouchers Payable		10,000

GOVERNMENTAL GAAP GUIDE / **20.09**

Expenditures

Proprietary Funds

Enterprise Funds and Internal Service Funds should recognize and classify their expenses in a manner similar to commercial enterprises.

LITERATURE REFERENCES

Material in this chapter is based on the following authoritative pronouncements, which are grouped according to the major headings used within the chapter. A dual reference (both paragraph and page number) is used for NCGA-1 and NCGA-2 because the original pronouncements do not use paragraph numbers.

Introduction
NCGA-1 *Governmental Accounting and Financial Reporting Principles*, p. 16/ ¶ 109.
FASB:CS-6 *Elements of Financial Statements*, ¶ 80.

The Governmental Accounting Model
NCGA-1 *Governmental Accounting and Financial Reporting Principles*, p. 12/ ¶ 70.
NCGA-4 *Accounting and Financial Reporting Principles for Claims and Judgments and Compensated Absences*, ¶ 16.

Interest and Principal Payments
NCGA-1 *Governmental Accounting and Financial Reporting Principles*, p. 12/ ¶ 72.

Interfund Transactions
NCGA-1 *Governmental Accounting and Financial Reporting Principles*, pp. 15, 16, and 22/¶¶ 101-106 and 145.

Encumbrances
NCGA-1 *Governmental Accounting and Financial Reporting Principles*, p. 14/ ¶ 91.

Proprietary Funds
NCGA-1 *Governmental Accounting and Financial Reporting Principles*, p. 17/ ¶ 117.

ASSETS

On the balance sheet of a governmental fund, assets are not classified as current or noncurrent. However, when assets are presented on a governmental fund's balance sheet, it is implied that they are current. The 1980 GAAFR defines current assets as follows:

> Those assets which are available or can be made readily available to finance current operations or to pay current liabilities. Those assets which will be used up or converted into cash within one year.

Thus, in governmental accounting, current assets represent expendable financial resources that are available for appropriation and expenditure. Assets that are not expendable financial resources (non-current assets) are presented in the General Fixed Assets Account Group.

CURRENT ASSETS (EXPENDABLE FINANCIAL RESOURCES)

Financial resources are considered expendable when they are available for subsequent appropriation and expenditure. Examples of expendable financial resources include cash, various receivables, and short-term investments. Other items that may be reported as fund assets are discussed below.

Materials and Supplies

Inventory items, such as materials and supplies, are current assets of a governmental fund, but they are not current financial resources. As discussed in Chapter 3, governmental funds, for the most part, measure the flow of current financial resources; however, one of the exceptions to this generalization is the accounting for inventories. Inventories may be accounted for by using either the consumption method (flow of economic resources) or the purchase method (flow of current financial resources). NCGA-1 (Governmental Accounting

Assets

and Financial Reporting Principles) concludes that when the inventory amount is significant, that amount must be reported in the governmental fund's balance sheet.

Consumption method The consumption method of accounting for inventories is not consistent with the fundamental governmental concept that only expendable financial resources should be presented in a fund's balance sheet. Under the consumption method, a governmental expenditure is recognized only when the inventory items are used. For example, if a governmental unit purchased $100,000 of supplies, the following entry would be made:

Supplies	100,000	
Vouchers Payable		100,000

At the end of the period, an inventory of supplies would be made, and the amount of inventory consumed would be recognized as a current expenditure. To continue with the example, assume that supplies worth $25,000 remain at the end of the accounting period. The current period's expenditure for supplies would be recorded in the following manner:

Expenditures—Supplies	75,000	
Supplies		75,000

Because inventories are reported as an asset (even though they do not represent expendable financial resources), it is necessary to reserve the fund balance by an amount equal to the carrying value of the inventories. Thus, in the above example, the following entry would be made at the end of the accounting period:

Fund Balance	25,000	
Fund Balance—Reserved For Supplies		25,000

The reserved fund balance changes from period to period as the level of inventories changes. For example, if the level of supplies declines to $10,000 at the end of the next period, the following journal entry would be made:

Fund Balance—Reserved For Supplies	15,000	
Fund Balance		15,000

Assets

Purchase method The purchase method of accounting for inventories is consistent with the governmental concept of reporting only expendable financial resources. Under the purchase method, purchases of inventories are recognized as expenditures when the goods are received and the transaction is vouchered. To illustrate, assume the same facts as those used in the consumption method example presented above. When the supplies are acquired, the transaction would be recorded as follows:

Expenditures—Supplies	100,000	
Vouchers Payable		100,000

At the end of the period, no adjustment is made to the expenditures account even though only $75,000 of goods were consumed. However, as noted above, NCGA-1 requires that an inventory item must be presented on the balance sheet if the amount of inventory is considered significant. If it were concluded that the ending inventory of supplies was significant, the following entry would be made at the end of the accounting period:

Supplies	25,000	
Fund Balance—Reserved For		
Supplies		25,000

Again, the reserved fund balance would change from period to period as the level of inventories changed. For example, if the inventory of supplies decreased to $10,000 at the end of the next period, the effect of the decline would be recorded as follows:

Fund Balance—Reserved For Supplies	15,000	
Supplies		15,000

Under both the consumption method and the purchase method, the reserved fund balance would be presented under the broad caption of fund balance in a manner similar to the following illustration:

Fund Balance	
Fund Balance—Reserved For Supplies	$ 25,000
Fund Balance—Unreserved	400,000
Total	$425,000

Prepayments and Deferrals

Prepaid items and deferrals may include such items as prepaid expenses, deposits, and deferred charges. Like inventory items, prepayments and deferrals do not represent expendable financial resources; however, NCGA-1 concludes that these items may be accounted for by using either the allocation method or the nonallocation method.

> **OBSERVATION:** *NCGA-1 does not specifically refer to an allocation method and a nonallocation method, but rather describes the process of allocation.*

Allocation method When the allocation method is used to account for prepayments and deferrals, an asset is established at the date of payment and subsequently amortized over the accounting periods that are expected to benefit from the initial payment. For example, if a state or local government purchased a three-year insurance policy for $45,000, the transaction would be recorded as follows under the allocation method:

Prepaid Insurance	45,000	
Vouchers Payable		45,000

At the end of each year, the partial expiration of the insurance coverage would be recorded as follows:

Expenditures—Insurance	15,000	
Prepaid Insurance		15,000

Prepayments and deferrals are reported as assets of the specific governmental fund that will derive future benefits from the expenditure. In the above example, the governmental fund would report prepaid insurance as an asset of $30,000 at the end of the first year of the insurance coverage.

Because prepayments and deferrals are not current financial resources, the governmental fund's fund balance should be reserved by the amount presented in the asset balance. Thus, at the end of the first year in the current example, the following entry would be made:

Fund Balance	30,000	
Fund Balance—Reserved For Prepaid Insurance		30,000

Assets

The balance in the reserved fund balance would fluctuate each year as a result of changes in the carrying value of the prepayment and deferral accounts.

The allocation method is not consistent with the basic governmental concept that only current financial resources should be presented in the fund's balance sheet.

Nonallocation method   The nonallocation method of accounting for prepayments and deferrals is consistent with the basic governmental concept that only expendable financial resources are reported by a specific governmental fund. Payments for the prepaid items or deferrals are fully recognized as an expenditure in the year of payment. Under the nonallocation method no asset for the prepayment or deferral is created, and no expenditure allocation to future accounting periods is required. To continue with the previous example, the only entry that will be made if the nonallocation method is used is to recognize the expenditure in the year of payment as shown below:

Expenditures—Insurance	45,000	
Vouchers Payable		45,000

> *OBSERVATION: As noted earlier, NCGA-1 requires that significant amounts of inventories must be recorded in the balance sheet no matter which accounting method is used. Surprisingly, however, no similar requirement is extended to significant amounts of prepayments and deferrals. Apparently, it can be assumed that significant amounts of prepayments and deferrals must be reported in a governmental fund's balance sheet.*

Since the expenditure account is closed to the fund balance account and no asset is recognized, there is no need to establish a fund balance reserve for prepaid insurance when the nonallocation method is used.

Escheat Property

Property which escheats to a state or local government should be accounted for in either an Expendable Trust Fund or the governmental fund that is eventually entitled to the property. If escheat property

Assets

represents expendable financial resources, it should be recognized as other sources of financial resources when the property becomes measurable and available. For example, assume that certain marketable equity securities worth $5,000 escheat to a local government, and, based on state law, the assets are available to pay general governmental expenditures. To record the legal passage of title to the government, the following entry would be made in the General Fund:

Investments—Marketable Equity Securities	5,000	
Other Sources Of Financial Resources—Escheat Property		5,000

When the state or local government is required to hold the escheat property in perpetuity for its owners, a fund balance reserve must be established. To illustrate, assume that in the example above the investment is not available to the governmental unit but, instead, must be held until claimed by the property owner. The following entry would be made in an Expendable Trust Fund:

Investments—Marketable Equity Securities	5,000	
Fund Balance—Reserved For Escheat Property		5,000

When escheat property is held for another government, the property should be accounted for in an Agency Fund.

Interfund Receivables/Payables

Each governmental fund is a distinct fiscal and accounting entity. Therefore, interfund transactions should be recorded in each fund that is a party to the interfund transaction. Interfund receivables and payables may arise from (1) interfund loans that generally must be legally approved, (2) quasi-external transactions, or (3) interfund transfers. To illustrate the recording of an interfund transaction, assume that $100,000 is transferred from the General Fund to a Special Revenue Fund as part of a legally approved advancement that must eventually be repaid. The advancement would be recorded as follows:

GENERAL FUND
   Advances To Other Funds—Special
      Revenue Fund   100,000
         Cash   100,000

SPECIAL REVENUE FUND
   Cash   100,000
      Advances From Other Funds—
         General Fund   100,000

If an advance is considered noncurrent, the fund that made the advance (General Fund) should reserve its fund balance account to indicate that the advancement is not currently available to finance operations.

When a fund has both an interfund receivable from and an interfund payable to the same fund, the amounts should be recorded in separate accounts; but for financial reporting purposes, it is permissible to present a net (current) interfund receivable or payable. Interfund receivables and payables that are not due from or due to the same fund should *not* be netted on the fund's balance sheet.

When the governmental reporting entity's combined balance sheet is prepared, interfund receivables and payables of funds that make up the reporting entity may either be presented or eliminated. If the interfund receivables and payables are eliminated, that fact must be disclosed in the reporting entity's financial statements.

FIXED ASSETS

Governmental fixed assets include such items as land, land improvements, buildings, fixtures, and equipment, as well as property under construction, and should be recorded at cost. At the acquisition date of the property, cost is measured by the amount of consideration given or received. In addition to the capitalization of the cost to purchase or construct the property, ancillary costs should be capitalized. Ancillary costs include such charges as freight costs and related professional expenditures. In addition, NCGA-1 requires that a governmental unit disclose its accounting policy with respect to the capitalization of interest costs associated with constructed assets.

In some instances, the acquired cost of property may not be available, and some alternative basis must be used to record the fixed asset. For instance, some governmental units may not have documented the original cost of acquired or constructed property,

Assets

and it may be impossible or time consuming to reconstruct the actual cost of the property. In this situation, the original cost of the property may be estimated and used as the basis for capitalization. When estimates are used, the financial statements should disclose the estimation methods employed and the extent to which estimates were used.

There is, of course, no cost basis when property is donated to the governmental unit. When property is acquired through donation, the fixed asset should be recorded at its estimated fair market value at the date of gift.

Fixed Assets of Governmental Funds

The balance sheet of a governmental fund presents only those assets that represent financial resources available for current appropriation and expenditure. General fixed assets represent past expenditures, not financial resources available to finance current governmental activities. For this reason, general fixed assets of a governmental unit are not presented in a specific fund but, rather, are accounted for in the General Fixed Assets Account Group. For example, the acquisition of equipment financed by the General Fund would be recorded as follows:

GENERAL FUND
    Expenditures—Equipment   10,000
        Cash   10,000

GENERAL FIXED ASSETS ACCOUNT GROUP
    Equipment   10,000
        Investment In General Fixed Assets—
            General Fund   10,000

The General Fixed Assets Account Group is not a fund, but it does provide a basis for the accountability and control of fixed assets not appropriately recorded in an Enterprise Fund, Internal Service Fund, or a Nonexpendable Trust Fund.

Infrastructure or public domain fixed assets are immovable assets that are generally of value only to the state or local government. Included in this fixed asset type are highways, bridges, sidewalks, drainage systems, and lighting systems. Since these assets are not portable, reporting infrastructure as part of the General Fixed Assets Account Group is optional; however, the accounting policy used to account for infrastructure fixed assets must be disclosed in the governmental unit's financial statements.

Fixed Assets of Expendable Trust Funds

All fixed assets of an Expendable Trust Fund should be accounted for in that fund based on the terms of the trust agreement. Depreciation of fixed assets of an Expendable Trust Fund should not be recorded in the fund's operating statement.

Fixed Assets of Proprietary Funds or Nonexpendable Trust Funds

Fixed assets of Enterprise Funds and Internal Service Funds are recorded in each of the respective funds, not in the General Fixed Assets Account Group. NCGA-1 concludes that these funds should reflect their fixed assets for the following reasons:

- Fixed assets are used in the production of the fund's service or product.
- Depreciation on the fixed assets is an essential element in determining the fund's total expenses, net income, and changes in fund equity.
- Fixed assets may serve as security for the issuance of debt by the fund.

A proprietary fund must account for fixed assets and related depreciation charges in a fashion that complies with the accounting and reporting standards applicable to commercial enterprises.

Similarly, Nonexpendable Trust Funds must account directly in their financial statements for their specific fixed assets. NCGA-1 points out that this manner of accounting for fixed assets by Nonexpendable Trust Funds results in the following benefits:

- Enhances the likelihood of compliance with trust agreement terms
- Discourages mismanagement of trust assets
- Facilitates the computation of depreciation when the trust corpus must not be spent.

Leased Property

NCGA-5 (Accounting and Financial Reporting Principles for Lease Agreements of State and Local Governments) requires that a lease

Assets

agreement that satisfies the criteria established by FASB-13 (Accounting for Leases) should be capitalized. FASB-13 states that noncancelable leases that meet any one of the following criteria must be capitalized:

- The lease transfers ownership of the property to the lessee by the end of the lease term.
- The lease contains a bargain purchase option.
- The lease term is equal to 75 percent or more of the estimated economic life of the leased property.
- The present value at the beginning of the lease term of the minimum lease payments, excluding that portion of the payments representing executory costs, to be paid by the lessor, including any profit thereon, equals or exceeds 90 percent of the excess of the fair value of the leased property to the lessor at the inception of the lease over any related investment tax credit retained by the lessor and expected to be realized by him.

When lease agreements are capitalized, the property rights acquired under the lease are reported in the General Fixed Assets Account Group (unless the property is acquired by an Enterprise Fund, Internal Service Fund, or Nonexpendable Trust Fund). Assume, for example, that the present value of minimum lease payments is $750,000. To record the property rights, and the related lease obligation, the following entries are made:

GENERAL FIXED ASSETS ACCOUNT GROUP
  Assets Under Capital Leases   750,000
    Investment In General Fixed Assets—
      Capital Leases   750,000

GENERAL LONG-TERM DEBT ACCOUNT GROUP
  Amount To Be Provided For Lease
    Payments   750,000
    Obligations Under Capital Lease
      Agreement   750,000

A more detailed discussion of accounting for lease agreements can be found in Chapter 43.

Depreciation

A governmental fund's activity statement reports the sources and uses of financial resources. Depreciation is the allocation of the cost of property over its economic life, and therefore does not affect a fund's financial resources. For this reason, depreciation is not recorded in a fund's activity statement. The actual purchase of a fixed asset results in a reduction of a fund's financial resources (expenditure) when current financial resources are used to finance the acquisition. For example, if equipment is purchased for $100,000 and the payment is made from the General Fund, an expenditure of $100,000 is reflected in the General Fund's Statement of Revenues and Expenditures. Even though the economic life of the equipment is, say, five years, no depreciation expense is recognized during the five-year period.

NCGA-1 concludes that depreciation may be (but does not have to be) recorded in the General Fixed Assets Account Group. The entry to record depreciation in the General Fixed Assets Account Group is as follows:

Investment In General Fixed Assets	X	
Accumulated Depreciation		X

Although depreciation is not recorded in a specific fund, this does not preclude the governmental unit from considering depreciation calculations in evaluating various governmental activities and programs. For example, depreciation calculations may be an important cost element to be considered in the following situations:

- Establishing total cost of such activities as garbage collection, fire protection, etc.
- Evaluating make-or-buy decisions
- Establishing reimbursable cost under a particular intergovernmental program
- Establishing fee schedules

Depreciation expense should be recorded in the financial statements of Enterprise Funds, Internal Service Funds, and Nonexpendable Trust Funds, using depreciation accounting and reporting standards applicable to commercial enterprises. Depreciable fixed assets of a proprietary fund financed through grants, entitlements, or shared revenues restricted for capital expenditures may be accounted for by either of the following alternatives.

Assets

Alternative 1—depreciation is closed to retained earnings Depreciation expense and accumulated depreciation will be recorded, and the depreciation expense will be presented as an operating expense and closed along with other operating expenses directly to retained earnings in a manner similar to the procedures used by commercial enterprises.

Alternative 2—depreciation is closed to contributed capital Depreciation expense and accumulated depreciation will be recorded, but the depreciation expense will be closed directly to the contributed captial account that was created when the restricted grant, entitlement, or shared revenue was received. On the Statement of Revenues, Expenses, and Changes in Retained Earnings, the depreciation expense will be presented as an operating expense. Then, the depreciation expense will be added to net income to determine the net increase (decrease) in retained earnings for the period, and the net increase (decrease) will be added to (subtracted from) the beginning balance of retained earnings.

The effects of the two methods of accounting for depreciation on fixed assets financed by restricted grants, entitlements, or shared revenues are contrasted below:

	Alternative 1 (Depreciation is closed to retained earnings)	*Alternative 2* (Depreciation is closed to contributed capital)
Operating revenues	$450,000	$450,000
Operating expenses (including depreciation of $50,000 on depreciable property financed by a capital grant)	430,000	430,000
Operating income	20,000	20,000
Nonoperating revenues (expenses)	5,000	5,000
Operating income before transfers	25,000	25,000
Operating transfers	10,000	10,000
Net income	35,000	35,000
Add depreciation on fixed assets acquired by capital grants that reduces contributed capital from capital grants	—	50,000

Net increase (decrease) in retained earnings	35,000	85,000
Retained earnings—beginning of year	200,000*	200,000*
Retained earnings-end of year	$235,000	$285,000

*It is assumed that the capital grant was made during the current year. Otherwise the beginning balances of retained earnings under the two assumptions would also be different. The differences between the retained earnings balances under the two alternatives are reflected in the contributed capital (from capital grants) account.

Disclosures

NCGA-1 requires that the governmental unit's financial statements contain a Statement of Changes in General Fixed Assets unless similar information is adequately disclosed in notes to the financial statements. An example of the financial statement is presented below:

City of Centerville
Statement of Changes in General Fixed Assets
For Year Ended June 30, 19X5

	Balance July 1, 19X4	Additions	Deletions	Balance July 30, 19X5
Land	$200,000	$100,000	$ 50,000	$250,000
Building	550,000	200,000	100,000	650,000
Improvements	60,000	5,000	10,000	55,000
Equipment	30,000	10,000	20,000	20,000
Work in progress	25,000	40,000	45,000	20,000
Totals	$865,000	$355,000	$225,000	$995,000

In addition to disclosures concerning changes in general fixed assets, NCGA-1 requires that the following should be disclosed in a state or local government's financial statements:

- Accounting policy used to account for infrastructure fixed assets
- Accounting policy used to account for the capitalization of interest costs during construction of fixed assets
- Methods and amounts used to estimate the cost of governmental fixed assets
- Disclosures required by FASB-13 with respect to noncapitalized lease commitments

Assets

An example of a note disclosing certain information related to a governmental unit's general fixed assets is presented below:

▶ Fixed assets (including public domain) are valued at historical cost, estimated historical cost if actual historical cost is not available, estimated fair value on the date donated, or at the lower of cost or fair market value if transferred from the General Fixed Assets Account Group to the Enterprise Fund or Internal Service Fund.

Fixed assets used in governmental fund type operations (general fixed assets) are accounted for in the General Fixed Assets Account Group. Public domain (infrastructure) general fixed assets consisting of certain improvements other than buildings, including drainage and sewerage systems, are capitalized along with other general fixed assets. No depreciation has been provided on general fixed assets. ◀

LITERATURE REFERENCES

Material in this chapter is based on the following authoritative pronouncements, which are grouped according to the major headings used within the chapter. A dual reference (both paragraph and page number) is used for NCGA-1 and NCGA-2 because the original pronouncements do not use paragraph numbers.

Introduction
NCGA-1   *Governmental Accounting and Financial Reporting Principles,* p. 9/
    ¶¶ 38 and 49.
1980 GAAFR   *Governmental Accounting, Auditing, And Financial Reporting,* p. 12.

Current Assets (Expendable Financial Resources)
NCGA-1   *Governmental Accounting and Financial Reporting Principles,* p. 9/
    ¶ 39.

Materials and Supplies
NCGA-1   *Governmental Accounting and Financial Reporting Principles,* p. 12/
    ¶ 73.

Prepayments and Deferrals
NCGA-1   *Governmental Accounting and Financial Reporting Principles,* p. 12/
    ¶ 73

Assets

Escheat Property
NCGA INTERPRETATION-9 *Certain Fund Classifications and Balance Sheet Accounts,* ¶ 11.

Interfund Receivables/Payables
NCGA-1 *Governmental Accounting and Financial Reporting Principles,* pp. 7 and 22/¶¶ 22 and 145.

Fixed Assets
NCGA-1 *Governmental Accounting and Financial Reporting Principles,* pp. 9 and 10/¶¶ 48-50.

Fixed Assets of Governmental Funds
NCGA-1 *Governmental Accounting and Financial Reporting Principles ,* p. 9/ ¶¶ 39-41.

Fixed Assets of Expendable Trust Funds
NCGA-1 *Governmental Accounting and Financial Reporting Principles,* p. 9/ ¶ 38.

Fixed Assets of Proprietary Funds or Nonexpendable Trust Funds
NCGA-1 *Governmental Accounting and Financial Reporting Principles,* p. 8/ ¶¶ 34-37.

Leased Property
NCGA-1 *Governmental Accounting and Financial Reporting Principles,* p. 9/ ¶ 40.
FASB-13 *Accounting for Leases,* ¶ 7.
NCGA-5 *Accounting and Financial Reporting Principles for Lease Agreements of State and Local Governments,* ¶ 12.

Depreciation
NCGA-1 *Governmental Accounting and Financial Reporting Principles,* p. 10/ ¶¶ 52-56.
NCGA-2 *Grant, Entitlement, and Shared Revenue Accounting and Reporting by State and Local Governments,* p. 3/¶ 18.

Disclosures
NCGA-1 *Governmental Accounting and Financial Reporting Principles,* pp. 9, 10, and 21/¶¶ 40, 41, 48, and 143.
NCGA-5 *Accounting and Financial Reporting Principles for Lease Agreements of State and Local Governments,* ¶ 27.

APPENDIX
CAPITAL ASSETS OF GOVERNMENTAL ENTITIES (DISCUSSION MEMORANDUM)

In August 1987, the GASB issued a Discussion Memorandum entitled "Accounting and Financial Reporting for Capital Assets of Governmental Entities" to gather comments concerning current practices and possible alternative practices for the accounting and reporting of capital assets. The Discussion Memorandum is part of the GASB's overall evaluation of the governmental accounting model. It is also viewed as an integral part of the current debate over the country's infrastructure and the possible need for significant increases in capital expenditures by state and local governments.

GASB Concepts Statement-1 (Objectives of Financial Reporting) identifies the following as the objective of financial reporting by governmental entities.

> Financial reporting should assist users in assessing the level of services that can be provided by the governmental entity and its ability to meet its obligations as they become due.

In addition to the broad objective reproduced above, GASB Concepts Statement-1 also identifies the following supporting objective.

> Financial reporting should provide information about a governmental entity's physical and other nonfinancial resources having useful lives that extend beyond the current year, including information that can be used to assess the service potential of those resources. This information should be presented to help users assess long- and short-term capital needs.

Current accounting for capital assets is very narrow—largely an attempt to provide physical accountability of capital assets. The GASB has taken a much broader view of accounting and reporting standards for capital assets in its Discussion Memorandum. This broad perspective is reflected in the major topics addressed in the Discussion Memorandum, including:

- Reporting infrastructure and general capital assets
- Valuing capital assets
- Computing and reporting depreciation
- Reporting accumulated depreciation

- Computing and reporting cost of deferred maintenance
- Reporting budgeted data for capital projects
- Reporting capital projects plans
- Reporting age, condition, and capacity of capital assets

Reporting Infrastructure and General Capital Assets

Capital assets are "long-lived tangible assets obtained or controlled as a result of past transactions, events, or circumstances." Capital assets include land, buildings, equipment and infrastructure. Public domain assets such as roads, bridges, and sidewalks are examples of infrastructure. Capital assets can be classified as general capital assets (related to governmental-type activities) and fund capital assets (related to business-type activities). For the most part, the Discussion Memorandum addresses the accounting and reporting of general capital assets, including infrastructure.

Currently, general capital assets are reported in the governmental entity's General Fixed Assets Account Group (GFAAG); however, the reporting of infrastructure in the GFAAG is optional.

The optional reporting of infrastructure is based on the concept of physical accountability. It is argued that infrastructure is immovable and therefore the risk of loss or misuse is remote. Although a discussion memorandum is only supposed to raise issues rather than recommend solutions, it is somewhat obvious that the GASB views current accounting and reporting of infrastructure as deficient. The tone of the GASB with respect to infrastructure in particular and capital assets in general is best described in the following paragraph taken from chapter 4, paragraph 2 of the Discussion Memorandum.

> Experts believe that to reverse the decline in public capital investments, governments will need to develop sound capital investment monitoring, planning, and budgeting procedures. Many believe that a key component of sound capital planning is maintaining a comprehensive inventory of capital assets, including infrastructure, together with information on the current condition, maintenance requirements, and value of those assets.

The arguments supporting the presentation of infrastructure are briefly summarized below. It is argued that the presentation of infrastructure would:

Assets

- Provide a basis for effective management of all capital assets
- Provide a basis for measuring and evaluating existing infrastructure
- Establish an essential element for effective capital planning
- Contribute to a more accurate measurement of both fund equity and interperiod equity
- Provide a consistent basis for comparing the financial position of governmental entities

Those opposed to the reporting of infrastructure offer the following arguments:

- The costs related to the mandatory requirement of reporting infrastructure are greater than the benefits.
- The presentation of infrastructure on a historical cost basis does not create a useful basis for decision making.
- Infrastructure does not meet the definition of an asset and in fact represents a liability because additional future resources must be provided in order to operate, maintain, and replace infrastructure.

If it is concluded that infrastructure should be reported, there is still the issue of *where* the information should be reported. The options include presentation on the face of the financial statements, in the GFAAG, in a note to the financial statements, in a schedule in the general purpose financial statements, or in a schedule in the statistical section of the CAFR. The issue of presentation of general capital assets is also raised in the Discussion Memorandum.

Valuing Capital Assets

If it is concluded that general capital assets should be reported, there is a question as to which valuation base should be used in the presentation. In current practice, historical cost is used to present general capital assets in the governmental entity's GFAAG. The Discussion Memorandum identifies and defines the following possible alternatives to the historical cost basis.

Constant dollar accounting—A method of reporting all financial statement elements (including capital assets) in dollars, each of which has the same general purchasing power. This method of reporting is often described as reporting in units of general purchasing power or as reporting in units of current purchasing power.

Current cost accounting—A method of reporting based on the amount of cash (or its equivalent) that would have to be paid if the same asset—either an identical asset or an asset with equivalent service capacity—was acquired or constructed currently.

The strength of the historical cost basis is its verifiability. In most cases, historical cost is relatively easy to substantiate. Also, because accountability is the overriding objective of governmental financial reporting, historical cost provides an acceptable basis for satisfying this objective. Of course, the historical cost basis is not very effective in generating relevant information for decision making during a period of rising prices.

In order to reflect the effects of changing prices, the constant dollar basis could be adopted. The constant dollar basis incorporates the effects of changing prices without sacrificing verifiability; however, only general price changes are taken into consideration and all capital assets are therefore treated in the same manner.

To overcome the nondiscriminating adjustments for inflation under the constant dollar basis, the current cost basis could be used to value general capital assets. Under this method, the current cost of individual assets is determined. The Discussion Memorandum defines replacement cost (a technique for estimating current cost) as "the current cost of replacing an existing asset with one of equivalent service capacity." The Discussion Memorandum also notes that the term is used in a more general sense as the current price of that asset. The difficulty with the current cost basis is that a significant amount of subjectivity can be introduced into the financial reporting process.

As with all valuation methods, there is an inverse relationship between objectivity and relevance. The GASB faces the difficult problem of identifying a basis that provides an adequate measure of each, while satisfying the financial reporting objectives of governmental financial reporting.

Computing and Reporting Depreciation

One of the distinguishing features of governmental financial reporting is the lack of recognizing depreciation in the entity's statement of operations. The Discussion Memorandum defines depreciation as "an accounting procedure that distributes the cost or other recorded value of capital assets, less salvage value (if any), over the estimated useful life of the asset in a systematic and rational manner."

In current practice, depreciation may be recognized in the governmental entity's GFAAG as a reduction of the carrying value of a general capital asset. Based on the GASB's proposed measurement focus (flow of financial resources), depreciation does not represent a reduction in the financial resources of a governmental entity and, therefore, is not part of the measurement of activity (excess of revenue over (under) expenditures) for the accounting period.

Proponents of recognizing depreciation in a governmental entity's statement of operations suggest that almost all general capital assets are subject to the phenomenon of depreciation. Thus, in each accounting period the full cost of producing services to its taxpayers should include the recognition of depreciation. Furthermore, due to the lack of periodic depreciation recognition, it is difficult to effectively use the financial report to assess interperiod equity.

Also, the lack of recognizing depreciation does not enhance the comparability of financial statements among governmental entities. The Discussion Memorandum cites the following two circumstances where a governmental entity reflects depreciation or an amount that approximates depreciation in its statement of operations:

- A governmental entity acquires property rights for general capital assets through a capital lease where the lease payments are made over the approximate economic life of the capital asset.
- A governmental entity establishes an Internal Service Fund to manage its general capital assets. The basis for charging operating departments includes a provision for depreciation.

The Discussion Memorandum notes that there are several "middle ground" positions between the extremes of either recognizing depreciation in the statement of operations or not. The Discussion Memorandum provides the following example of a depreciation strategy that could be implemented by the GASB.

- Long-lived capital assets (most infrastructure, building, monuments, and parks) that require little ongoing maintenance and rehabilitation or for which maintenance and rehabilitation will indefinitely maintain the serviceability of the asset should not be depreciated.
- Intermediate- and long-lived capital assets (some buildings, water purification, and sewage treatment plants) that will be

used up over a projectable period of time, even if maintenance and rehabilitation are performed regularly, should be depreciated with the charge disclosed in other than governmental fund operating statements.
- Short-term capital assets (autos, trucks, buses, computer equipment) that are used up relatively quickly and that have some of the characteristics of a prepaid expenditure/expense should be depreciated, perhaps in operating statements.

Reporting Accumulated Depreciation

As noted earlier, governmental generally accepted accounting principles call for optional presentation of accumulated depreciation in the GFAAG. Those who support the optional presentation believe that a reporting entity should have some flexibility in reporting accumulated depreciation in order to meet the perceived needs of various user groups based on the specific circumstances of the entity. For example, a governmental entity may report accumulated depreciation to demonstrate the relationship between the undepreciated cost of a capital asset and the balance in the long-term liability (as reported in the General Long-Term Debt Account Group) that was incurred to finance the purchase of the capital asset. Also, those who support the optional presentation argue that the benefits would not exceed the cost of requiring all entities to report accumulated depreciation.

On the other hand, others argue that the optional presentation of accumulated depreciation does not provide a basis for comparing the financial statements of one governmental entity with those of another entity. Furthermore, the presentation of accumulated depreciation may provide some indication of the age or remaining service life of general capital assets. Finally, the requirement to report accumulated depreciation may encourage governmental entities to evaluate and utilize general capital assets more effectively. Those benefits may accrue because an entity would have to develop information about (1) the estimated economic life and salvage value of a particular asset and (2) the possible need for changing the depreciation rate to a higher or lower level due to changing conditions.

Computing and Reporting Cost of Deferred Maintenance

The full use of a capital asset over the entire life of the asset usually depends upon an effective maintenance program. In most cir-

Assets

cumstances, the delay or omission of maintenance costs will reduce the economic life of the capital asset or reduce the efficiency of the asset. The Discussion Memorandum provides the following definitions related to maintenance and the consequences of deviating from a maintenance program.

Maintenance—The act of keeping capital assets in a state of good repair. Maintenance includes preventive maintenance, normal periodic repairs, replacement of parts, structural components, and so forth, and other activities needed to maintain the asset so that it continues to provide normal services and achieve its optimum life.

Deferred maintenance—The difference between the estimated outlays that would have been required to keep a capital asset in its normal operating condition and the amount of actual outlay. Deferred maintenance may result in accelerated impairment of an asset or higher cost to restore it to normal operating condition.

Cost of deferred maintenance—The cost of returning a capital asset to its normal operating condition, considering age and use, that has resulted from normal and periodic maintenance not being performed or being performed sporadically. The cost of deferred maintenance may be the same as or more or less than the sum of each year's deferred maintenance amounts.

Some argue that users of the financial statements are interested in a governmental entity's adherence to a capital maintenance program. The possible results of deviating from the capital maintenance program, it is argued, should be quantified and presented in the governmental entity's financial report. This information could be presented in a number of formats:

- Compute the cost of deferred maintenance. Report that cost as an operating expenditure/expense and fund liability.
- Compute the effects of deferred maintenance on the estimated economic life of a capital asset. Change the computation of annual depreciation for governmental funds (as presented in the GFAAG) and proprietary funds (as presented in the statement of operations).
- Compute the cost of deferred maintenance (on a current and cumulative basis). Report the information in a note to the financial statements in a supplemental schedule, a schedule in the statistical section of the CAFR, or a separate periodic report.

Opponents to computing and reporting the effects of deferred maintenance argue that the information is highly subjective and does not increase the utility of the financial statements, especially when the cost of developing the information is considered.

Reporting Budgeted Data for Capital Projects

Some argue that governmental financial reports should include information on capital projects so that actual expenditures can be compared with budgeted expenditures. Current practice requires that budgeted versus actual data be presented only for (1) General Fund, (2) Special Revenue Funds, and (3) other funds for which an annual budget is adopted.

It is suggested that presenting budgeted data for capital projects would enable a user to more effectively evaluate management's performance of the construction of capital assets that takes place over more than one budgetary period. In addition, users would be likely to identify capital projects that are experiencing significant cost overruns or delays, which may have a detrimental effect on the future financial position of the governmental entity. Budgeted data could be presented so that actual expenditures could be compared to the original budget, and, if applicable, revised budgets. Also, some argue that the budgeted data should include an estimate of the cost to complete the capital project.

Opponents of the presentation of budgeted data for capital projects question the usefulness of such data—especially since it is likely to be presented at a high level of aggregation. Solving this problem would, it is argued, require a significant expansion of the presentation of budgeted data on a disaggregated basis, increasing the complexity of governmental financial reports.

Reporting Capital Projects Plans

Conventional governmental accounting principles do not require reporting of capital projects plans unless the reporting entity has entered into binding commitments. Proponents of reporting argue that the presentation of future capital projects is important because such a presentation provides insight into how the governmental entity expects to meet the needs of its citizens and to what extent future operating budgets may be affected by the expansion of the capital asset base.

Assets

The Discussion Memorandum suggests that disclosures relative to capital projects plans could include the following:

- Narrative descriptions of major capital projects
- General descriptions of smaller projects by function
- Current appropriations and projected appropriations for each year of the plan by major capital project, and summaries by function for smaller projects
- Estimates of capital expenditures for each year covered by the plan
- Projections for each year of increases in operating and maintenance costs associated with the projects
- A statement about the extent to which required legislative approvals have been obtained for each major project by function
- A statement or schedule of the proposed method of financing planned capital projects
- A statement about the extent to which required legislative or voter approvals for the issuance of debt securities for specific projects has already been obtained
- Projected start and completion dates for major projects
- Discussion of long-range capital needs (expressed in dollars over a period of time), capital spending priorities, and ways in which the current plans are intended to fulfill long-range needs

Those opposed to presenting capital projects plans question whether it is proper to report expected rather than past events. In addition, opponents argue that future capital plans should not be given a higher level of visibility than future operating plans.

Reporting Age, Condition, and Capacity of Capital Assets

As noted earlier, one objective of governmental financial reporting is to provide information to assess the service potential of resources, including long-term capital (asset) needs. At present, little information is included in the typical governmental financial report that satisfies this reporting objective. The Discussion Memorandum identifies the following three factors that could provide a basis for assessing capital asset needs:

Age of capital assets—The expected life of an asset, the time it has already been in service, and its expected remaining useful life.

Condition of capital assets—Evaluation of the physical condition of an asset, its ability to perform as planned, and its continued usefulness.

Capacity of capital assets—Measure of the level of activity, units of service, and so forth, that can reasonably be expected to be provided by an asset.

Age of Capital Assets The Discussion Memoradum raises the issue of how to assess the need to replace general capital assets. In part, this may be accomplished by preparing schedules that identify both the age and expected useful life of the assets. Information in these schedules should reflect the following concepts:

- Maintenance and other factors may have an effect on the life of a capital asset.
- Climate and other conditions under which the asset is operated may have an effect on the life of a capital asset.
- Technology may change the original estimate of the life of a capital asset.

Opponents argue that an attempt to portray a meaningful profile of the age of a governmental entity's capital assets would be very subjective and, in the final analysis, provide little useful information.

Condition of Capital Assets In order to assess the condition of a capital asset, the Discussion Memorandum notes that it is necessary to (1) acquire an understanding of the asset, (2) identify its performance capacity, (3) determine its actual ability to perform, and (4) identify expectations for its continued performance. All of these factors are indeed beyond the conventional scope of the accounting process, and thus would require the expertise of other professionals. Nonetheless, the Discussion Memorandum notes that some asset evaluation methods have been developed. For example, the American Association of State Highway Transportation Officials has developed a system for evaluating the condition of streets and highways.

Those who argue against presenting information about the condition of capital assets assert that the information is very subjective and costly to produce.

Capacity of Capital Assets A variety of measurement bases must be used to determine the capacity of a governmental entity's capital

Assets

assets. These measurement bases could include the square footage of buildings, number of classrooms, and miles of road. While information concerning the capacity of capital assets can be an important element in determining capital needs, the use of various bases generates subjective data that are very difficult to aggregate.

Broad Scope of Discussion Memorandum

The GASB has raised a number of important reporting issues with respect to capital assets; although it is unlikely that the GASB will issue a Statement that encompasses all of the concepts discussed in the Discussion Memorandum, it is likely that governmental generally accepted accounting principles applicable to capital assets will significantly change within the next few years.

DEPOSIT AND INVESTMENT PORTFOLIO DISCLOSURES AND REVERSE REPURCHASE AGREEMENTS

Excess funds held by state and local governmental entities may be used to make various investments or may be deposited with financial institutions. There is a risk that the governmental unit will not fully realize its investment or collect all of its deposits. Based on the fiduciary responsibility assumed by a governmental unit with respect to its constituents, the GASB has taken the position that a governmental reporting entity should disclose information concerning its investments and deposits that will enable constituents to better assess the risks associated with investments and deposits. GASB-3 (Deposits with Financial Institutions, Investments (including Repurchase Agreements), and Reverse Repurchase Agreements) addressed these disclosure requirements, and also discussed accounting standards and disclosure requirements related to repurchase agreements and reverse repurchase agreements.

> **OBSERVATION:** *The origin of GASB-3 was the highly publicized ESM Government Securities, Inc., scandal which involved repurchase agreements and reverse repurchase agreements entered into by state and local governmental units. The GASB recognized that the risks associated with repurchase agreements and reverse repurchase agreements are similar to the risks related to investments and deposits with financial institutions. The scope of the project which eventually led to the issuance of GASB-3 was expanded to include the disclosure of information about investments and deposits, as well as repurchase agreements and reverse repurchase agreements.*

Many legislatures and local governing bodies attempt to control the risk associated with investment and deposit activity by restricting the type of transactions a governmental unit may execute. Restrictions on the types of investments and deposits that can legally be made and collateral requirements for deposits with financial institutions are two control features that minimize the possibility of losses arising from investment and deposit activity. Also, the management of the state or local government may adopt an investment strategy that considers the possible loss that could occur from each investment and deposit decision.

Once a governmental unit executes its investment strategy, the actual risk associated with investments and deposits with financial institutions varies depending upon the characteristics surrounding each investment or deposit. GASB-3 identified credit risk and market risk as two major types of risks that governmental units accept when they make investments and deposits.

Credit Risk   There is a chance that a governmental unit will (1) not recover its investments from the issuers of securities, (2) not be able to withdraw its deposits from financial institutions, or (3) not recover securities or collateral held by another party. The level of credit risk is based upon both the characteristics of the other party to the investment or deposit transaction (counterparty), and the characteristics of the specific contract that represents the investments or deposit.

Market Risk   In addition to credit risk, a governmental unit faces the risk that there will be a market decline in an investment, in the collateral for a deposit, or in securities related to a repurchase agreement. The level of market risk is determined by the following factors:

- The length of time before an investment matures
- The likelihood of an investment being sold before its maturity in order to meet operational requirements
- The value of collateral in relationship to the amount of the investment
- The frequency of collateral being adjusted to reflect market value changes

Investments

A governmental unit may acquire a variety of investments including federal governmental securities, bankers' acceptances, and commercial paper issued by business enterprises. Rather than directly acquire securities, a governmental unit may indirectly acquire investments by purchasing shares in a mutual fund, or by investing funds where the resources of several governmental entities are pooled and managed by a party determined by statute or regulation.

The level of risk related to investments made by governmental entities can be affected by several factors as described in the following paragraphs.

Custodial responsibility The level of credit risk depends in part upon the party that has custody of the securities. The lowest level of risk occurs when the governmental entity or its independent third-party agent holds the securities in the name of the governmental entity. Somewhat greater risk is incurred when the securities are held by a financial institution's trust department or agent in the governmental entity's name. Even more credit risk exists when the securities are in the custody of another party and not held in the governmental entity's name.

Registration of ownership The risk of loss can be reduced by registering securities only in the name of the governmental entity.

Insurance When a broker-dealer has custody of securities owned by a governmental entity, credit risk can be reduced through insurance coverage. SEC-registered brokers-dealers may be insured by the Securities Investor Protection Corporation, which provides limited coverage for losses. Insurance to cover losses in excess of those covered under the federal program may also be obtained by a broker-dealer.

Credit-worthiness Governmental entities may assess credit risk of a particular investment by evaluating the credit-worthiness of the issuer through direct analysis of financial statements and other information, or the governmental entity may use credit rating services.

Deposits

Excess funds of a governmental entity may be deposited with a financial institution. The level of risk related to such deposits is affected by the following factors.

Insurance Depository insurance provides reimbursement to a governmental unit for its deposits, subject to a maximum payout, when the financial institution that holds the deposits encounters financial difficulties. GASB-3 describes the following as depository insurance:

- Federal depository insurance funds, such as those maintained by the Federal Deposit Insurance Corporation and Federal Savings and Loan Insurance Corporation

- State depository insurance funds
- Multiple financial institution collateral pools that insure public deposits

In a multiple financial institution collateral pool, all financial institutions that hold public funds provide collateral to a common pool. If one of the financial institutions fails, the entire pledged collateral for all financial institutions can be used to pay off the deposits made by governmental entities. If the total collateral is insufficient to cover all governmental deposits, the agreement may require that the other financial institution members of the pool pay an assessment to cover any deficiency. When an additional assessment agreement exists, the deposits are considered insured. When there is no additional assessment agreement, the deposits are considered collateralized, and the percentage of the collateralization coverage is determined by dividing the total fair value of the collateral by the total uninsured governmental deposits.

Collateral Credit risk can be reduced by requiring, either through legislation or separate agreement, financial institutions to pledge collateral as security for deposits. The collateral agreement may allow for the periodic review of the market value of collateral to determine whether the financial institution must provide additional collateral for the deposit. Also, the level of credit risk is affected by the party that holds the collateral. The least risk occurs when the governmental entity or its independent third-party agent has custody of the collateral.

Credit-worthiness The governmental entity may evaluate the credit-worthiness of the financial institution that may be used as a depository, and the party that may hold collateral that secures a deposit. The evaluation may include the review of audited financial statements or regulatory reports filed by financial institutions.

Repurchase Agreements

GASB-3 defines a repurchase agreement in the following manner:

> An agreement in which a governmental entity (buyer-lender) transfers cash to a broker-dealer or financial institution (seller-borrower); the broker-dealer or financial institution transfers securities to the entity and promises to repay the cash plus interest in exchange for the same securities.

In a dollar repurchase agreement, the parties agree that the securities eventually returned to the broker-dealer or financial institution will usually be of the same issuer, although the same certificates will not be returned. Two types of dollar repurchase agreements are fixed coupon agreement and yield maintenance agreements. In a *fixed coupon agreement* the governmental entity agrees to return securities with the same maturities and interest rates as the original securities transferred. In a *yield maintenance agreement,* the governmental unit agrees to return securities that yield a rate of return specified in the agreement. Repurchase agreements may mature (1) in one day (overnight agreement), (2) in more than one day but at a specified date (term agreement), or (3) on demand by either party to the agreement (open agreement).

There is disagreement as to whether a repurchase agreement is in substance a collateralized loan (borrower/lender transaction) or two separate transactions involving the purchase and sale of an investment (buyer/seller transaction). To illustrate the accounting for each approach, assume that a governmental unit (buyer/seller) enters into a repurchase agreement with a financial institution (seller/borrower) whereby securities with a fair value of $500,000 are exchanged as part of an overnight repurchase agreement. The financial institution agrees to repurchase the securities for $500,000 plus $100 interest. If the repurchase agreement is accounted for as a borrower/lender transaction, the following entries would be made by the governmental entity:

ENTRY AT LENDING DATE
Loans Receivable—Repurchase Agreements	500,000	
Cash		500,000

ENTRY AT REPAYMENT DATE
Cash	500,100	
Loans Receivable—Repurchase Agreements		500,000
Interest Income		100

If the repurchase agreement is accounted for as a buyer/seller transaction, the following entries would be made by the governmental entity:

ENTRY AT PURCHASE DATE
Investment In Securities	500,000	
Cash		500,000

ENTRY AT SALES DATE

Cash	500,100	
Investment In Securities		500,000
Interest Income		100

Some governmental units prefer to treat a repurchase agreement as a buyer/seller transaction because by statute they may not be permitted to lend money to private borrowers through repurchase agreements. The AICPA's SOP 85-2 (Accounting for Dollar Repurchase—Dollar Reverse Repurchase Agreements by Sellers-Borrowers) states that yield maintenance repurchase agreements should be treated as buyer/seller transactions by the parties involved.

The credit risk associated with repurchase agreements is due in part to the lack of adequate regulation in some areas of the governmental securities market. While some dealers in governmental securities are subject to regulation, other dealers are unregulated. The level of risk related to repurchase agreements is affected by the following factors.

Credit-worthiness A governmental entity may evaluate the credit-worthiness of the broker-dealer or financial institution involved in the repurchase agreement. Because the repurchase agreement requires the broker-dealer or financial institution to repurchase securities from the governmental entity at a later date, there is a risk that the other party will not be in a financial position to repurchase the securities. To determine the credit-worthiness of the other party, the governmental entity may review its audited financial statements, the scope of its activities, and the adequacy of its management.

Written agreements In order to clearly identify the rights and responsibilities of each party to the repurchase agreement, there should be a written contract between the governmental unit and the broker-dealer or financial institution, and the governmental unit and the custodian that will hold the securities involved in the repurchase agreement. Items that may be part of the agreement with the broker-dealer or financial institution include the following:

- Governmental unit's right to sell securities if the other party defaults
- Designation of the party that will act as custodian of the securities
- Action to be taken if the market value of securities fall below a stated amount

- Type of collateral to be pledged

Items that may be part of the agreement with the custodian may include the following:

- Description of circumstances under which the custodian is to disburse cash under the repurchase agreement
- Authority to obtain additional securities if margin requirement is not maintained
- Segregation of securities under the repurchase agreement from other assets held by the custodian
- Periodic reports on the market value of securities

In addition, the written contract should be structured so that under the provisions of the Federal Bankruptcy Code, the securities in the repurchase agreement can be quickly liquidated.

Custodial responsibility In order to evaluate the credit risk associated with repurchase agreements, a governmental unit should consider which party should be responsible for the custody of the securities and in which party's name the securities should be held. The lowest level of risk occurs when the governmental entity or its independent third-party agent holds the securities in the name of the governmental entity.

Collateral The securities in a repurchase agreement serve as the collateral for the provision that the broker-dealer or financial institution will repurchase the securities at a later date. The level of credit risk is affected by the difference between the repurchase price and the fair value of the securities (margin).

Yield maintenance agreements As noted earlier, under a yield maintenance repurchase agreement, the governmental entity guarantees that the securities returned to the broker-dealer or financial institution will yield a specified rate of return. In this type of agreement, the governmental unit is exposed to a market risk. If interest rates rise between the dates the securities are *purchased* and *resold*, the governmental unit will suffer a loss.

Reverse Repurchase Agreements

GASB-3 defines a reverse repurchase agreement in the following manner:

> An agreement in which a broker-dealer or financial institution (buyer/lender) transfers cash to a governmental entity (seller/borrower); the entity transfers securities to the broker-dealer or financial institution and promises to repay the cash plus interest in exchange for the same securities.

> **OBSERVATION:** *Governmental units rarely use reverse repurchase agreements. When used, they are generally employed to cover a temporary cash deficit (for example, fund payroll) or to obtain a higher yield that is being earned on the underlying collateral.*

Reverse repurchase agreements have the same basic characteristics as a repurchase agreement, except the governmental unit is in the position of the seller/borrower rather than the buyer/lender. Thus, there is a disagreement as to whether the governmental entity should treat a reverse repurchase agreement as a borrower/lender transaction or as a buyer/seller transaction (see discussion under Repurchase Agreements/credit-worthiness). To illustrate the accounting for each approach, assume that a governmental unit (seller/borrower) enters into a reverse repurchase agreement with a financial institution (buyer/lender) whereby securities with a fair market value of $500,000 are exchanged as part of an overnight reverse repurchase agreement. The governmental unit agrees to repurchase the securities for $500,000 plus $100 interest. If the reverse repurchase agreement is accounted for as a borrower/lender transaction, the following entries would be made by the governmental unit:

ENTRY AT BORROWING DATE
Cash	500,000	
Loans Payable—Reverse Repurchase Agreements		500,000

ENTRY AT REPAYMENT DATE
Loans Payable—Reverse Repurchase Agreements	500,000	
Expenditures—Interest	100	
Cash		500,100

The governmental unit would also recognize interest income on the securities that were used as collateral in the reverse repurchase agreement.

If the reverse repurchase agreement is accounted for as a buyer/seller transaction, the following entries would be made by the governmental entity:

ENTRY AT SALES DATE
Cash	500,000	
Investment In Securities		500,000

ENTRY AT PURCHASE DATE
Investment In Securities	500,000	
Accrued Interest Receivable	100	
Cash		500,100

At the time of the assumed sale of the investment, the governmental unit would recognize a gain or loss on the sale when the carrying value of the investment is different from the market value of the investment. In the example, it is assumed that the carrying value and market value are the same as of the date of the sale and the date of the repurchase of the securities.

In a reverse repurchase agreement, a credit risk exists in that the broker-dealer or financial institution may not return the securities to the governmental entity at the conclusion of the agreement. The credit risk is based on the difference between the market value of the underlying securities (including accrued interest) and the amount of the obligation under the reverse repurchase agreement (including accrued interest). This difference is referred to as the *margin*. Factors that affect this type of credit risk include the credit-worthiness of the other party and the designation of which party will have custodial responsibility over the securities.

A governmental unit may be exposed to a market risk when the proceeds from the reverse repurchase agreement are used to invest in other securities. If the maturity date of the newly acquired securities is different from the date of the reverse repurchase agreement, there is a possibility that because interest rates are rising, the newly acquired securities will be sold at an amount insufficient to meet the obligation under the reverse repurchase agreement.

Financial Reporting Standards

The purpose of GASB-3 was to provide users of financial statements with information to assess the risk related to a governmental entity's investments, including repurchase agreements, deposits with financial institutions, and reverse repurchase agreements. The following disclosures related to investment risk must be made in notes to the governmental entity's financial statements:

- Legal or contractual provisions for deposits and investments, including repurchase agreements
- Deposits and investments, including repurchase agreements, as of the balance sheet date and during the period
- Legal or contractual provisions for reverse repurchase agreements
- Reverse repurchase agreements as of the balance sheet date

These disclosures, except as described in subsequent paragraphs, should be made for the reporting entity as a whole rather than on a fund or fund type basis; however, GASB-3 does not prohibit the disclosure of additional information or a separate presentation of information by fund or fund type.

Legal or Contractual Provisions for Deposits and Investments The governmental entity should disclose the types of investments that can be acquired by the oversight entity based on legal and contractual restrictions. There may be significantly different restrictions for component units, or the restrictions may vary significantly among funds or fund types. Under both of these circumstances, the different investment restrictions should be disclosed when investment activities for the component unit's individual funds or individual fund types are material in relationship to the reporting entity's investment activities. Violation of these and other investment restrictions should be disclosed in notes to the financial statements.

An example of a note that describes legal or contractual provisions for deposits and investments, including repurchase agreements, is presented below.

▶ The City follows the practice of pooling cash and investments of all funds with the City Treasurer except for restricted funds generally neld by outside custodians on behalf of Enterprise Funds, investments of the Employees' Retirement Fund held by trustees, and Imprest Funds. Each fund's portion of total cash and investments is summarized by fund type in the combined balance sheet as equity in pooled cash and investments.

Various restrictions on deposits and investments, including repurchase agreements, are imposed by statutes. These restrictions are summarized below.

Deposits All deposits with financial institutions must be collateralized in an amount equal to 110% of uninsured deposits. The collateral must be held by the pledging financial institution's trust department. Briefly during the year, the value of the collateralized property fell to 103% of uninsured deposits.

Investments The City is authorized to make direct investments in U.S. government, federal agency, and instrumentality obligations. In addition, the City may invest in investment-grade bonds, commercial paper rated A-1 by Standard and Poor's Corporation or P-1 by Moody's Commercial Paper Record, repurchase agreements, and the state treasurer's investment pool. When repurchase agreements are executed, the market value of the securities must be equal to 105% of the cost of the repurchase agreement. On two occasions during the year, which represented 13% of all repurchase agreement transactions, the market value of securities were equal to 103% and 104% of the cost of the repurchase agreement. ◀

Deposits and Investments (Including Repurchase Agreements) Factors affecting the credit risk associated with deposits and investments, including repurchase agreements, are disclosed in notes to the financial statements.

Deposit disclosures When deposits with financial institutions are fully insured, or collateralized by securities held by the governmental entity or its agent in the governmental entity's name, the only disclosure that is necessary is a statement that deposits with financial institutions are fully insured or collateralized. On the other hand, when deposits are not fully insured or collateralized, the credit risk associated with deposits must be described by making the following disclosures:

- Carrying amount of total deposits, if not separately displayed on the balance sheet
- Amount of total bank balance classified in these three categories of risk:
  — Insured or collateralized with securities held by the entity or by its agent in the entity's name
  — Collateralized with securities held by the pledging financial institution's trust department or agent in the entity's name

Deposit and Investment Portfolio Disclosures and Reverse Repurchase Agreements

— Uncollateralized (this includes any bank balance that is collateralized with securities held by the pledging financial institution, or by its trust department or agent but not in the entity's name)

If the amount of uncollateralized bank deposits during the year significantly exceeded the amount of uncollateralized bank deposits as of the balance sheet date, the reason for this situation should be briefly described in the note.

Presented below is an example of a disclosure note for deposits held by financial institutions.

▶ The carrying amount of the City's deposits with financial institutions was $3,400,000 and the bank balance was $3,650,000. The bank balance is categorized as follows:

Amount insured by the FDIC and FSLIC, or collateralized with securities held by the City in its name	$1,850,000
Amount collateralized with securities held by the pledging financial institution's trust department in the City's name	1,550,000
Uncollateralized (including $140,000 bank balance that is collateralized with securities held by the pledging financial institution's trust department but not in the name of the Centerville Parking Authority)	250,000
Total bank balance	$3,650,000

The portion of the total bank balance categorized as Uncollateralized is the property of the Centerville Parking Authority, an Enterprise Fund. ◀

Investment disclosures Investment information, including repurchase agreements, that should be disclosed include the carrying value and market value of the investments and the types of investments held by the governmental entity. The credit risk associated with investments is described by classifying investments in the following categories (the term *securities* used in the following descriptions includes securities underlying repurchase agreements as well as investments):

- Securities insured (Securities Investor Protection Corporation or additional insurance coverage) or registered in the name of the governmental entity or held by the entity or by its agent in the entity's name
- Securities uninsured and unregistered and held by the counterparty's trust department or by its agent in the entity's name
- Securities uninsured and unregistered and held by the counterparty, its trust department, or its agent, but not held in the entity's name (this includes the portion of the carrying amount of any repurchase agreement that exceeds the market value of the underlying securities)

The carrying value and market value of the following items related to investment securities should be disclosed but should not be classified in one of the three categories described above:

- Securities related to reverse repurchase agreements
- Investments in pools managed by another government (the investments should be categorized if the reporting entity owns specific identifiable investment securities of the pool)
- Investments in mutual funds
- Other investments which are not evidenced by securities that exist in physical or book entry form

When the amount of uninsured and unregistered securities held during the year by the counterparty, its trust department, or its agent, but not held in the governmental entity's name (the third category of credit risk) significantly exceeded the amount of the securities held as of the balance sheet date, the reason for this situation should be briefly described in a note to the financial statements.

Presented below is an example of a note disclosure for investments, including those related to repurchase agreements and reverse repurchase agreements, as required by GASB-3.

▶ Investments made by the City, including repurchase agreements, and information concerning reverse repurchase agreements are summarized below. The investments that are represented by specific identifiable investment securities are classified as to credit risk by the three categories described below:

Deposit and Investment Portfolio Disclosures and Reverse Repurchase Agreements

Category 1— Insured or registered, or securities held by the City or its agent in the City's name

Category 2— Uninsured and unregistered, with securities held by the counterparty's trust department or agent in the City's name

Category 3— Uninsured and unregistered, with securities held by the counterparty, or by its trust department or agent but not in the City's name

	Category 1	Category 2	Category 3	Carrying amount	Market value
U.S. government securities	$300,000			$300,000	$310,000
Commercial paper	50,000			50,000	51,000
Repurchase agreements	100,000	$150,000	$50,000	300,000	325,000
	$450,000	$150,000	$50,000	650,000	686,000
Investment in state investment pool				70,000	72,000
				720,000	758,000
Investments held by brokers-dealers under reverse repurchase agreements:					
U.S. government securities				60,000	63,000
U.S. instrumentality securities				50,000	55,000
				110,000	118,000
Total investments				$830,000	$876,000

◄

Because this disclosure is for the combined reporting entity as a whole, it is possible that unrealized investment losses may be offset by unrealized investment gains for different funds or component units. When a fund or component unit has unrealized investment losses, the carrying value and market value of the total investments of the fund or component unit should be disclosed.

In addition, the following disclosures should be made by the state or local governmental unit with respect to investments:

- Disclosure of types of investments held during the period but not held as of the balance sheet date.
- The carrying amount, if applicable, and market value of securities to be resold based on commitments as of the balance sheet

date under yield maintenance repurchase agreements. Also, the terms of the agreement should be disclosed.

Deposit and investment disclosures The disclosure of information related to deposits, investments, and reverse repurchase agreements is presented for the reporting entity as a whole. When the credit risk implied by the disclosures of the reporting entity is different from the credit risk of the oversight unit, additional or separate disclosures should be made to adequately describe the credit risk associated with deposits, investments, and reverse repurchase agreements of the oversight unit.

Losses from deposit and investment transactions that are the results of defaults by counterparties and subsequent recovery of such losses should be disclosed either in the governmental entity's operating statement or in notes to the financial statements.

Financial Institutions and Brokers-Dealers as Counterparties

GASB Technical Bulletin 87-1 (GASB:TB 87-1)(Applying Paragraph 68 of GASB Statement 3) addressed the question of whether a financial institution or broker-dealer that purchases securities on behalf of a governmental entity is considered a counterparty to the transaction. Classifying a financial institution or broker-dealer (that purchases securities for a governmental entity) as a counterparty is important in determining how investments are categorized under paragraph 68 of GASB-3. Uninsured or unregistered securities (including repurchase agreements) may be classified in one of the following three categories:

Category A Uninsured and unregistered investments held by the governmental entity or held by the governmental entity's agent in the name of the governmental entity.

Category B Uninsured or unregistered investments held in the name of the governmental entity but held by the counterparty's trust department or the counterparty's agent.

Category C   Uninsured and unregistered investments held by the counterparty, the counterparty's trust department or the counterparty's agent, but the investments are not held in the governmental entity's name.

A financial institution or broker-dealer may act as the governmental entity's custodial agent, in which case the investment would be classified in Category A. On the other hand, a financial institution or broker may be a counterparty to an investment transaction, in which case the investment would be classified in either Category B or Category C. When the financial institution or broker-dealer fills both roles (custodial agent and counterparty), the role of the counterparty must prevail with respect to classifying the investment; therefore, the investment would be classified in Category B or Category C but not in Category A.

GASB:TB 87-1 also addresses the definition of a trust department with respect to the dual role (custodial agent and counterparty) of a broker-dealer. A trust department is authorized and registered under state or federal laws and is part of a financial institution such as a commercial bank or savings and loan association. An important characteristic of a trust department is that in its fiduciary role it holds assets for other parties and those assets are legally separate from the assets of the financial institution of which it is a part.

Based on this description, GASB:TB 87-1 concludes that nonfinancial institution broker-dealers cannot have a trust department. A nonfinancial institution broker-dealer could, through its so-called "trust department," be the governmental entity's custodial agent. However, if the broker-dealer is also a counterparty to the investment transaction, the investment could not be classified in either Category B (because GASB:TB 87-1 does not consider the broker-dealer's "trust department" to be a legal trust department) or Category A (because the broker-dealer would be considered both the custodial agent and the counterparty, and as noted earlier, the role as the counterparty would prevail in categorizing the investment as required by GASB-3).

GASB:TB 87-1 presents two examples to illustrate the classification of investments whereby a financial institution or broker-dealer is a counterparty to an investment transaction.

Example 1   A governmental entity instructs a broker to purchase $800,000 of U.S. government securities, and the broker holds the investment but identifies the securities as owned by the governmental entity in its internal records. Since the broker is a member of the Securities Investor Protection Corporation (SIPC), its customer's account is insured to $500,000. Part of the investment ($500,000) should be classified as insured (Category A) and the balance ($300,000) should be classified as uninsured or unregistered and held by a counterparty (Category C).

Example 2 A governmental entity instructs a financial institution to purchase $800,000 of U.S. government securities. The financial institution's trade department executes the transaction and the securities are held by the financial institution's trust department. The financial institution is not a member of the SIPC. The trust department identifies the securities as owned by the governmental entity in its internal records. The entire investment should be classified as uninsured and unregistered and held by the counterparty's trust department (Category B).

In Example 2, if it were assumed that the trade department of the financial institution held the securities, then the investment would be classified as uninsured and unregistered and held by the counterparty (Category C).

Book Entry Systems

GASB:TB 87-1 provided guidance in determining how the use of a book entry system affects the credit risk of securities that are owned by a governmental entity or securities that are related to a repurchase agreement entered into by a governmental entity. For the most part, only financial institutions and broker-dealers can be members of the Federal Reserve or participants in the Depository Trust Company (DTC). Governmental entities may have accounts in the Federal Reserve book entry system, but those accounts are not similar to Federal Reserve member accounts because of their lack of flexibility. Additionally, governmental entities may have access to the Federal Reserve or DTC book entry system through a Federal Reserve member or a DTC participant, but this is not equivalent to having an account directly with those organizations.

More importantly, the Federal Reserve or DTC book entry system is not a critical issue in determining how investments should be categorized under GASB-3. The Federal Reserve or DTC generally should not be considered an agent of the governmental entity, a counterparty's trust department or agent, or acounterparty. As described below, the characteristics of the investment transactions must be evaluated to identify which party "holds" the governmental entity's securities.

Entity's Agent In order for securities to be classified in Category A, there must be an agency relationship between the governmental entity and the party holding the securities. The agency relationship should have the following characteristics:

- There is a contractual relationship between the governmental entity and the custodial agent.
- The contract names the custodial agent as the governmental entity's agent.
- The securities held by the custodial agent are held in the name of the governmental entity.

In order to satisfy the condition that a custodial agent holds securities in the name of a governmental entity, the governmental entity must have unconditional rights and claims to the securities held by the agent. For securities that are part of a repurchase agreement, the governmental entity must have unconditional rights and claims to the securities if the counterparty defaults on the repurchase agreement. For securities to be considered held in the name of a governmental entity in the Federal Reserve or DTC book entry system, the following conditions must be satisfied:

- Securities must be held in a separate custodial or fiduciary account (a custodial or fiduciary account is an account that is separate from the account in which the custodian's own securities are held).
- The custodian's internal control records must identify the securities as being owned by or pledged to the governmental entity.

The custodial or fiduciary account does not have to specifically identify the governmental entity as the party that owns the securities or the entity to which the securities are pledged.

Counterparty's Trust Department or Agent When the governmental entity's uninsured and unregistered securities are held by a counterparty's trust department or counterparty's agent, the classification of the securities into Category B or Category C depends upon whether the securities are held in the name of the governmental entity. The following factors suggest that the securities are held in the name of the governmental entity:

- The counterparty's trust department or agent uses a separate custodial or fiduciary Federal Reserve or DTC account.
- The counterparty's trust department or agent in its internal accounting records identifies the securities as belonging to the governmental entity.
- The counterparty's trust department or agent recognizes the governmental entity's rights to the securities.

If it is concluded that the counterparty's trust department or agent holds the securities in the name of the governmental entity, the securities should be classified in Category B. Category C should be used to classify the securities if it is concluded that the securities are not held in the name of the governmental entity.

Counterparty In the following circumstances, uninsured and unregistered securities should be classified in Category C even though the securities are held by a custodian:

- The custodian of the securities keeps the securities in its Federal Reserve account and the custodian is a counterparty to the sale or the pledging of the securities.
- The custodian of the securities keeps the securities in its DTC account and the custodian is a counterparty to the sale.

The circumstances surrounding an investment transaction must be evaluated to determine how uninsured and unregistered securities should be classified when the securities are pledged through the DTC. There must be a written agreement between a pledgee and the DTC in order to pledge securities through the DTC book entry system. A pledgee must be a DTC participant and for this reason, a governmental entity must have a participant act as a pledgee for the entity. Securities should be considered under the control of the pledgee if the DTC procedures and the written agreement give the pledgee the following rights:

- The pledgee has the right to have the securities moved from the pledger's account to the pledgee's account.
- The pledgee has the right to approve any release of the pledge on the securities.

When these conditions are satisfied, the securities are classified in either Category A, B, or C depending upon (a) who fills the role of the pledgee (the governmental entity's agent, the counterparty's trust department, or the counterparty's agent) and (b) in whose name the securities are held (the governmental entity or some other party).

Legal or Contractual Provisions for Reverse Repurchase Agreements If reverse repurchase agreements were used during the period, the governmental entity should disclose the source of legal or contractual authorization for such transactions. Also, significant violations of restrictions related to reverse repurchase agreements should be disclosed.

An example of a note that describes the legal or contractual provisions for reverse repurchase agreements is presented below.

▶ The City, under state statute, is allowed to enter into reverse repurchase agreements. A reverse repurchase agreement is a transaction in which a broker-dealer or financial institution transfers cash to the City and the City transfers securities to the broker-dealer or financial institution and promises to repay the cash plus interest in exchange for the same or similar securities. By state statute, proceeds from reverse repurchase agreements are to be used only for investment purposes; however, on several occasions during the period, the City used the proceeds to temporarily finance current operations. ◀

Reverse Repurchase Agreements Disclosures for reverse repurchase agreements as of the balance sheet date depend upon whether the transaction is based on a yield maintenance agreement.

Yield maintenance agreement In a yield maintenance agreement, the securities that are to be returned to the governmental entity provide a yield specified in the agreement. The following disclosures should be made for commitments to repurchase securities based on yield maintenance reverse repurchase agreements as of the balance sheet date:

- The market value of securities to be repurchased at the balance sheet date
- A description of the terms of the agreement

Other agreements For all reverse repurchase agreements outstanding as of the balance sheet date, other than yield maintenance agreements, the total amounts of the obligation under the agreements (including accrued interest) and the total market value of the securities related to the agreements should be disclosed. The difference between the two amounts is a measure of the credit risk exposure for the governmental entity in reverse repurchase agreements.

Losses from reverse repurchase agreements because of defaults by counterparties, and subsequent recovery of such losses, should be disclosed either in the governmental entity's operating statement or in notes to the financial statements.

An example of a note that illustrates disclosure requirements for reverse repurchase agreements is presented below.

▶ The City was obligated under certain reverse repurchase agreements as of the balance sheet date. Credit risk exposure for the City arises when a broker-dealer or financial institution does not return the securities or their value at the conclusion of the reverse repurchase agreement. The amount of the potential economic loss is the difference between the market value of the securities related to the reverse repurchase agreements, including accrued interest, and the amount of the obligation, including accrued interest, under the reverse repurchase agreement. As of the balance sheet date, the City is exposed to potential economic losses of $5,000. ◀

Accounting and Reporting for Repurchase/Reverse Repurchase Agreements

In addition to requiring certain disclosures for investments, deposits with financial institutions, repurchase agreements, and reverse repurchase agreements, GASB-3 established accounting and reporting guidelines for repurchase and reverse repurchase agreements. Descriptions of the accounting and reporting standards follow for each specific type of agreement.

Repurchase agreements The governmental entity should report income from repurchase agreements as interest income.

Reverse repurchase agreements The governmental entity should report assets and liabilities arising from a reverse repurchase agreement as separate line items in its balance sheet. The liability account should be reported as a debt of a governmental fund and identified as obligations under reverse repurchase agreements. The asset should be reported as an investment.

Dollar fixed coupon repurchase agreements The governmental entity should report income from dollar fixed coupon repurchase agreements as interest income.

Dollar yield maintenance repurchase agreements When a governmental entity enters into a dollar yield maintenance repurchase agreement, the transaction should be accounted for as a purchase and sale of securities with an appropriate recognition of a gain or loss at the time of the sale of the securities.

Dollar fixed coupon reverse repurchase agreements The governmental entity should report assets and liabilities arising from a dollar fixed coupon reverse repurchase agreement as separate line items in its balance sheet. The liability account should be reported as a debt of a governmental fund and identified as obligation under reverse repurchase agreements. The asset should be reported as an investment.

Dollar yield maintenance reverse repurchase agreements When a governmental entity enters into a dollar yield maintenance reverse repurchase agreement, the transaction should be accounted for as a sale and purchase of securities with an appropriate recognition of a gain or loss at the time of the sale of the securities.

LITERATURE REFERENCES

Material in this chapter is based on the following authoritative pronouncements and publications, which are grouped according to the major headings used within the chapter. A dual reference (both paragraph and page number) is used for NCGA-1 and NCGA-2 because the original pronouncements do not use paragraph numbers.

Introduction
GASB-3 *Deposits with Financial Institutions, Investments (including Repurchase Agreements), and Reverse Repurchase Agreements,* ¶¶ 1, 2, and 4.

Deposit and Investment Portfolio Disclosures and Reverse Repurchase Agreements

Credit Risk
GASB-3 *Deposits with Financial Institutions, Investments (including Repurchase Agreements), and Reverse Repurchase Agreements*, ¶ 14.

Market Risk
GASB-3 *Deposits with Financial Institutions, Investments (including Repurchase Agreements), and Reverse Repurchase Agreements*, ¶ 15.

Investments
GASB-3 *Deposits with Financial Institutions, Investments (including Repurchase Agreements), and Reverse Repurchase Agreements*, ¶¶ 20 and 22-31.

Deposits
GASB-3 *Deposits with Financial Institutions, Investments (including Repurchase Agreements), and Reverse Repurchase Agreements*, ¶¶ 8-11 and 16-21.

Repurchase Agreements
GASB-3 *Deposits with Financial Institutions, Investments (including Repurchase Agreements), and Reverse Repurchase Agreements*, ¶¶ 20, 32, 34-54, and 59.
AICPA SOP 85-2 *Accounting for Dollar Repurchase-Dollar Reverse Repurchase Agreements by Sellers-Borrowers*, ¶¶ 33 and 34.

Reverse Repurchase Agreements
GASB-3 *Deposits with Financial Institutions, Investments (including Repurchase Agreements), and Reverse Repurchase Agreements*, ¶¶ 33 and 60-62.

Financial Reporting Standards
GASB-3 *Deposits with Financial Institutions, Investments (including Repurchase Agreements), and Reverse Repurchase Agreements*, ¶¶ 63 and 64.

Legal or Contractual Provisions for Deposits and Investments
GASB-3 *Deposits with Financial Institutions, Investments (including Repurchase Agreements), and Reverse Repurchase Agreements*, ¶¶ 65 and 66.

Deposits and Investments Including Repurchase Agreements
GASB-3 *Deposits with Financial Institutions, Investments (including Repurchase Agreements), and Reverse Repurchase Agreements*, ¶¶ 67-75.

Financial Institutions and Broker-Dealers as Counterparties
GASB:TB 87-1 *Applying Paragraph 68 of GASB Statement 3*, ¶¶ 1-7.

Book Entry Systems
GASB:TB 87-1 *Applying Paragraph 68 of GASB Statement 3*, ¶¶ 8-13.

Deposit and Investment Portfolio Disclosures and Reverse Repurchase Agreements

Legal or Contractual Provisions for Reverse Repurchase Agreements
GASB-3   *Deposits with Financial Institutions, Investments (including Repurchase Agreements), and Reverse Repurchase Agreements,* ¶¶ 76 and 77.

Accounting and Reporting For Repurchase/Reverse Repurchase Agreements
GASB-3   *Deposits with Financial Institutions, Investments (including Repurchase Agreements), and Reverse Repurchase Agreements,* ¶¶ 78-83.

LIABILITIES

The accounting and financial statement presentation of liabilities of governmental funds depends upon the characteristics of the specific debt. Based on these characteristics, the debt may be designated as a current liability or a long-term liability.

CURRENT LIABILITIES

The measurement focus for governmental funds, is generally the flow of current financial resources. Liabilities that will consume expendable financial resources of the fund responsible for payment during the fiscal period are presented in that fund's balance sheet. There is no explicit current liability classification on a governmental fund's balance sheet (the financial statement is unclassified). However, the mere presentation of the liability in the balance sheet of the governmental fund implies that the debt is current and will require the use of expendable financial resources.

> *OBSERVATION: The definition of current liabilities differs significantly between a governmental fund and a commercial enterprise. ARB-43 (Restatement and Revision of Accounting Research Bulletins) describes current liabilities as those items that will be liquidated through the use of current assets; current assets are defined as resources expected to be realized or consumed within the entity's operating cycle. Thus, the term to maturity of a current liability of a commercial enterprise could be a year or longer, depending on the entity's operating cycle.*
>
> *A liability of a governmental fund is classified as current when it is expected to be liquidated with expendable available financial resources. The term to maturity for a current liability of a governmental fund is much shorter than that of a commercial enterprise and, in many instances, the liability must be payable within a maximum of 60 days of the balance sheet date (because of the restrictive definition of expendable available financial resources).*

LONG-TERM LIABILITIES

Noncurrent obligations of a governmental reporting entity may be presented in one of two ways, depending upon the nature of the liability.

Long-term liabilities directly associated with and expected to be paid from a specific fund are accounted for in that specific fund. All other long-term liabilities are accounted for in the General Long-Term Debt Account Group.

Specific Fund Liabilities

NCGA-1 (Governmental Accounting and Financial Reporting Principles) concludes that long-term liabilities related to and expected to be paid from proprietary funds and certain trust funds should be recorded directly in those particular funds. These liabilities are classified as debt of the specific fund even though the debt may be backed by the full faith and credit of the governmental unit.

Proprietary funds In the classification and presentation of long-term liabilities of Enterprise Funds and Internal Service Funds, generally accepted accounting principles applicable to commercial enterprises must be observed except when the GASB has specifically addressed the issue. A current area of conflict is the accounting and reporting of long-term liabilities with respect to pensions. At the present time, a governmental unit may follow any one of the following authoritative pronouncements:

- NCGA-1 (The related material contained in the 1968 GAAFR may be considered as illustrative of the principles of NCGA-1 to the extent such material is consistent with NCGA-1.)
- NCGA-6 (Pension Accounting and Financial Reporting: Public Employee Retirement Systems and State and Local Government Employers)
- FASB-35 (Accounting and Reporting by Defined Benefit Plans)

Nonexpendable Trust Funds The measurement focus of and the basis of accounting for Nonexpendable Trust Funds are the same as those used by proprietary funds. Thus, any debt issued by and subject to retirement through a Nonexpendable Trust Fund must be presented in the trust fund's balance sheet.

General Long-Term Debt Account Group

All long-term liabilities that are not accounted for in a proprietary fund or Nonexpendable Trust Fund must be presented in the General Long-Term Debt Account Group. NCGA-1 emphasizes the point that general long-term debt includes more than liabilities that are created through a loan arrangement or agreement. Liabilities related to certain lease agreements, pension plans, compensated absences, and other liabilities that are long-term in nature may be included in the General Long-Term Debt Account Group.

Long-term debt represents obligations that will be met by expending resources that are not considered expendable available resources as of the current balance sheet date. The segregation of general long-term debt in a separate account group maintains the fundamental concept of governmental accounting, whereby a specific governmental fund presents in the balance sheet only available expendable resources and the liabilities that will use those resources.

The proceeds from the issuance of long-term debt are recorded in the governmental fund that is authorized to receive the funds. As suggested earlier, the proceeds are not recorded as a liability in the fund but rather as a source of (nonoperating) financing on the fund's statement of operations. The debt itself is recorded in the General Long-Term Debt Account Group and properly identified as term bonds, serial bonds, or by some other appropriate designation. The actual resources that will be used to service the long-term debt may be accumulated in a Debt Service Fund if legally mandated. When interest payments and principal repayments are required to be made from a Debt Service Fund, these expenditures are recorded in that fund. Otherwise, the payments are recorded as expenditures of the General Fund.

Transactions related to long-term debt may affect more than a single fund and/or the account group. The typical entries for recording long-term debt transactions are summarized below.

Transaction: General long-term debt (serial bonds) are issued and the proceeds, as authorized in the bond issuance, are made available to the General Fund.

Liabilities

GENERAL FUND
Cash	100,000	
Proceeds From Issuance Of Debt		100,000

GENERAL LONG-TERM DEBT ACCOUNT GROUP
Amount To Be Provided For Repayment Of Serial Bonds	100,000	
Serial Bonds Payable		100,000

Transaction: Funds are transferred from the General Fund to the Debt Service Fund to pay debt principal.

GENERAL FUND
Transfers Out	20,000	
Cash		20,000

DEBT SERVICE
Cash	20,000	
Transfers In		20,000

GENERAL LONG-TERM DEBT ACCOUNT GROUP
Amount Available In Debt Service Fund	20,000	
Amount To Be Provided For Repayment Of Serial Bonds		20,000

Transaction: Principal ($5,000) and interest ($10,000) payments are made by the Debt Service Fund.

DEBT SERVICE FUND
Expenditures—Principal	5,000	
Expenditures—Interest	10,000	
Cash		15,000

GENERAL LONG-TERM DEBT ACCOUNT GROUP
Serial Bonds Payable	5,000	
Amount Available In Debt Service Fund		5,000

Bond, Tax, and Revenue Anticipation Notes

NCGA Interpretation-9 (Certain Fund Classifications and Balance Sheet Accounts) addresses the issue of accounting for bond, tax, and revenue anticipation notes. Anticipation notes are issued with the expectation that the governmental fund will receive specific resources in the near future and that these resources will be used to retire the liability. Tax anticipation notes are often issued as part of a cash management strategy that recognizes that certain taxes (such as property taxes), will not be collected evenly over the fiscal year. Bond anticipation notes may be issued with the understanding that as soon as the proceeds from the issuance of specific long-term bonds are received, the bond anticipation notes will be extinguished.

Tax and revenue anticipation notes For governmental funds, notes issued in anticipation of the receipt of taxes or revenues should be presented as a liability of the fund that will actually receive the proceeds from the issuance of the notes. The tax or revenue anticipation note represents a liability that will be extinguished by the use of expendable available resources of the fund.

Bond anticipation notes Notes issued in anticipation of proceeds from the subsequent sale of bonds may be classified as part of the General Long-Term Debt Account Group when the conditions surrounding the notes satisfy the requirements established in FASB-6 (Classification of Short-Term Obligations Expected to be Refinanced). FASB-6 concludes that what is typically considered a current liability may be treated as a long-term liability when (1) the intention is to refinance the debt on a long-term basis and (2) the intention can be substantiated through a post balance-sheet issuance of the long-term debt or by an acceptable financing agreement.

The actual issuance of the bonds must occur after the balance sheet date but before the balance sheet is issued in order to satisfy the post balance-sheet condition for a governmental unit. The amount of the bond anticipation notes that is included in the General Long-Term Debt Account Group cannot be greater than the proceeds of the actual bond sale. In addition, the maturity date of the newly issued bonds (or serial bonds) must be sufficiently later than the balance sheet date so as not to require the use of a fund's available expendable resources to retire the maturing bonds.

When the governmental unit's intention to refinance the bond anticipation notes is substantiated through a financing agreement, FASB-6 requires that the following guidelines be applied to the agreement:

- The agreement must not expire within one year (or operating cycle) from the date of the enterprise's balance sheet and during that period the agreement is not cancelable by the lender or the prospective lender or investor (and obligations incurred under

Liabilities

the agreement are not callable during that period), except for violation of a provision with which compliance is objectively determinable.
- No violation of any provision in the financing agreement exists at the balance sheet date and no available information indicates that a violation has occurred thereafter but prior to the issuance of the balance sheet, or, if one exists at the balance sheet date or has occurred thereafter, a waiver has been obtained.
- The lender or the prospective lender or investor with which the enterprise has entered into the financing agreement is expected to be financially capable of honoring the agreement.

> **OBSERVATION:** *NCGA Interpretation-9 simply states that the criteria set forth in FASB-6 should be applied to bond anticipation notes in determining appropriate presentation. No attempt was made to tailor the language of FASB-6 to the unique nature of governmental accounting. As reproduced above, FASB-6 refers to the entity's operating cycle, and obviously a governmental unit does not have an operating cycle. Presumably the term operating cycle should be interpreted as the period after the year-end in which resources are considered available to pay liabilities outstanding as of the balance sheet date. In most circumstances, this period is probably no greater than sixty days beyond the end of the year.*

A violation of the financing agreement, as referred to above, means "failure to meet a condition set forth in the agreement, or breach or violation of a provision such as a restrictive covenant, representation, or warranty, whether or not a grace period is allowed or the lender is required to give notice." The conditions of an agreement or provision that constitutes a violation should be determinable or measurable and should not be subject to various interpretations by the parties involved in the transaction. For example, if a condition for a violation of a financing agreement refers to a material adverse change in the financial condition of the governmental unit, then the agreement is not a viable financing agreement because the condition is not objectively determinable or measurable when stated in such general terms.

When the intent to refinance the bond anticipation notes is substantiated by a financing agreement, the maximum amount of the notes that can be presented in the General Long-Term Debt Account Group is the amount of the estimated bond proceeds expected to be realized under the agreement. If a portion of the actual bond proceeds are restricted for purposes other than the extinguishment of the bond anticipation notes, the restricted portion must be classified as a current liability. For example, if the bond anticipation notes total $10,000,000 and the actual bonds when sold under the financing agreement are expected to yield $12,000,000, but $4,000,000 of the proceeds are restricted for other purposes, only $8,000,000 of the $10,000,000 bond anticipation notes can be classified as part of the General Long-Term Debt Account Group. If the amount available under the financing agreement fluctuates depending on some measurable factor, the amount of the notes to be classified as long-term is based on a *reasonable estimate* of the minimum amount that will be available under the agreement. When a reasonable estimate cannot be made, none of the bond anticipation notes can be classified as long-term debt.

When a liability for bond anticipation notes meets the criteria for classification as part of the General Long-Term Debt Account Group, a note to the financial statements must contain (1) a general description of the financing agreement and (2) the terms of any new debt incurred or expected to be incurred as a result of the agreement. If the criteria established by FASB-6 have not been satisfied, bond anticipation notes must be presented as a liability in the financial statements of the fund that recorded the proceeds from the issuance of the notes.

To illustrate the accounting for bond anticipation notes, assume that $10,000,000 of bond anticipation notes are issued and the proceeds are recorded in the Capital Projects Fund. If the criteria established in FASB-6 are met, the following entries would be made:

CAPITAL PROJECTS FUND
   Cash   10,000,000
      Proceeds From Issuance Of Bond
         Anticipation Notes   10,000,000

GENERAL LONG-TERM DEBT ACCOUNT GROUP
   Amount To Be Provided For Repayment
     Of Bond Anticipation Notes   10,000,000
      Bond Anticipation Notes Payable   10,000,000

If the criteria of FASB-6 are not satisfied, the following entry would be made:

CAPITAL PROJECTS FUND
   Cash   10,000,000
     Bond Anticipation Notes Payable   10,000,000

GENERAL LONG-TERM DEBT ACCOUNT GROUP
   No Entry

Liabilities

A proprietary fund must apply FASB-6 to determine whether bond anticipation notes should be presented on the proprietary fund's balance sheet as a current or long-term liability.

Demand Bonds

Governmental units may raise funds by issuing long-term bonds that give the right to redeem the bonds. For example, the bond agreement may allow an investor in 30-year bonds to redeem the bonds anytime after the debt has been outstanding for five years. The call provision allows the bondholder to reduce the risk of incurring a capital loss if long-term interest rates rise, and the governmental unit is able to issue long-term debt at interest rates that approximate lower short-term interest rates.

When demand bonds are issued, the question arises of whether the governmental unit should treat the debt as current or long-term. That is, (1) should a governmental fund account for the demand bonds in a specific fund, or classify the debt as part of the General Long-Term Debt Account Group, or (2) should a proprietary fund classify the debt as a current liability or long-term liability? GASB Interpretation-1 (Demand Bonds Issued by State and Local Governmental Entities) addressed the issue.

When demand bonds are redeemed, the funds needed to retire the debt may come from the governmental unit's available cash, proceeds from the resale of the redeemed bonds by remarketing agents, short-term credit arrangements, or long-term credit arrangements. A short-term credit agreement may be based on standby liquidity agreements or other arrangements entered into by the governmental unit. In instances where the redeemed bonds are not readily resold, there may be a *take out agreement* whereby a financial institution agrees to convert the bond to long-term debt, such as installment notes. A key factor in determining the appropriate accounting for demand bonds is the existence of a take out agreement.

GASB Interpretation-1 concludes that the issues surrounding the accounting for demand bonds are similar to the issues associated with bond anticipation notes as discussed in NCGA Interpretation-9. NCGA Interpretation-9 concludes that bond anticipation notes should be classified as general long-term debt "if all legal steps have been taken to refinance the bond anticipation notes and the intent is supported by an ability to consummate refinancing the short-term note on a long-term basis in accordance with the criteria set forth in the Statement of Financial Accounting Standards (SFAS) No. 6."

Liabilities

GASB Interpretation-1 is applicable to demand bonds that have an exercisable provision for redemption at or within one year of the governmental unit's balance sheet date. Such bonds may be reported as general long-term debt of a governmental fund or long-term debt of a proprietary fund when all of the following criteria are met:

- Before the financial statements are issued, the issuer has entered into an arm's-length financing (take out) agreement to convert bonds "put" but not resold into some other form of long-term obligation.
- The take out agreement does not expire within one year from the date of the issuer's balance sheet.
- The take out agreement is not cancelable by the lender or the prospective lender during that year, and obligations incurred under the take out agreement are not callable by the lender during that year.
- The lender or the prospective lender or investor is expected to be financially capable of honoring the take out agreement.

> **OBSERVATION:** *GASB Interpretation-1 tailors the criteria established in FASB-6 to governmental accounting. As noted earlier, FASB-6 refers to an entity's operating cycle; however, GASB Interpretation-1 substitutes a period of one year for the operating cycle period. It should be noted that the use of the one year period is inconsistent with the governmental accounting model in that a liability is considered long-term when it will not require the use of a fund's available expendable resources. Thus, Interpretation-1 extends the period for determining a fund liability to a considerably longer period than conventionally accepted.*

Even when a take out agreement is cancelable or the obligation created by the take out agreement is callable during the year, the demand bonds may be considered long-term debt if (1) violations can be objectively determined and (2) no violations have occurred prior to the issuance of the financial statements. However, if violations have occurred and a waiver from the take out agreement lender has been obtained, the debt should be considered long-term for financial reporting purposes.

When the conditions of GASB Interpretation-1 have not been met, demand bonds must be presented as a liability of the fund that received the proceeds from the sale of the bonds, or a current liability if the proceeds were received by a proprietary fund. If demand

Liabilities

bonds are issued and no take out agreement has been executed at their *issuance date* or at the balance sheet date, the bonds cannot be considered a long-term liability.

To illustrate the accounting for demand bonds, assume that $4,000,000 of demand bonds are issued and the proceeds are to be used by a Capital Projects Fund. When the criteria established by GASB Interpretation-1 are met (long-term liability exists), the following entries are made:

CAPITAL PROJECTS FUND
Cash	4,000,000	
Proceeds From Issuance Of Demand Bonds		4,000,000

GENERAL LONG-TERM DEBT ACCOUNT GROUP
Amount To Be Provided For Repayment Of Demand Bonds	4,000,000	
Bonds Payable		4,000,000

When the demand bonds are issued and the criteria established in GASB Interpretation-1 are not met, the following entry would be made:

CAPITAL PROJECTS FUND
Cash	4,000,000	
Bonds Payable On Demand		4,000,000

GENERAL LONG-TERM DEBT ACCOUNT GROUP
No Entry

If the demand bonds are presented for redemption, the redemption should be recorded as an expenditure of the fund from which debt service is normally paid. To illustrate, assume that the $4,000,000 demand bonds are redeemed and paid out of the Debt Service Fund from funds transferred from the General Fund. The following entries would be made if the demand bonds were originally classified as general long-term debt, and the debt is converted to long-term installment notes as determined under the terms of a take out agreement.

GENERAL FUND
Cash	4,000,000	
Proceeds From Issuance Of Long-Term Installment Notes To Finance Redemption Of Demand Bonds		4,000,000

Liabilities

Transfers Out (To Debt Service Fund)	4,000,000	
Cash		4,000,000

DEBT SERVICE FUND

Cash	4,000,000	
Transfers In (From General Fund)		4,000,000
Expenditures (For Redemption Of Demand Bonds)	4,000,000	
Cash		4,000,000

GENERAL LONG-TERM DEBT ACCOUNT GROUP

Amount Available In Debt Service Fund (For Redemption Of Demand Bonds)	4,000,000	
Amount To Be Provided For Repayment Of Demand Bonds		4,000,000
Bonds Payable (On Demand)	4,000,000	
Amount Available In Debt Service Fund (For Redemption Of Demand Bonds)		4,000,000
Amount To Be Provided For Repayment Of Long-Term Installment Notes	4,000,000	
Long-Term Installment Notes Payable		4,000,000

If the demand bonds redeemed were originally recorded as a liability of the Capital Projects Fund (no take out agreement), the following entries would be made to redeem the demand bonds:

GENERAL FUND

Transfers Out (To Debt Service Fund)	4,000,000	
Cash		4,000,000

DEBT SERVICE FUND

Cash	4,000,000	
Transfers In (From General Fund)		4,000,000
Expenditures (For Redemption Of Demand Bonds)	4,000,000	
Cash		4,000,000

CAPITAL PROJECTS FUND

Bonds Payable On Demand	4,000,000	
Other Financing Sources (Retirement Of Fund Liabilities By Payments Made By Other Funds)		4,000,000

Liabilities

It should be noted that the liability of the Capital Projects Fund is reduced by simultaneously crediting other financing sources. The latter account would appear on the Capital Projects Fund's Statement of Revenues and Expenditures.

Demand bonds that were originally classified as general long-term debt because a take out agreement existed at the issuance date of the bonds would have to be reclassified if the original take out agreement expires. Under this circumstance, it would be necessary to establish a liability in the fund that originally recorded the demand bond proceeds. For example, if the $4,000,000 demand bonds illustrated earlier were originally recorded as part of the General Long-Term Debt Account Group, the following entries would be made if the take out agreement expires:

CAPITAL PROJECTS FUND
Other Financing Uses (Reclassification
Of General Long-Term Debt As A
Fund Liability)   4,000,000
  Bonds Payable On Demand   4,000,000

GENERAL LONG-TERM DEBT ACCOUNT GROUP
Bonds Payable (On Demand)   4,000,000
  Amount To Be Provided For Repayment Of Demand Bonds   4,000,000

Again, any actual bond redemption, occurring after the debt is reclassified as the liability of a specific governmental fund should be recorded as an expenditure of the fund which accounts for the servicing of the debt.

> **OBSERVATION:** *The date of reclassification is not the date the take out agreement expires. If the take out agreement expires within one year of the date of the balance sheet, the debt must be reclassified as the liability of a specific governmental fund.*

When a governmental unit has demand bonds outstanding, irrespective of the exercisable date of the demand provision, GASB Interpretation-1 requires that the following information be disclosed:

- General description of the demand bond program
- Terms of any letters of credit or other standby liquidity agreements outstanding
- Commitment fees to obtain the letters of credit

Liabilities

- Any amounts drawn on the letters of credit as of the balance sheet date
- A description of the take out agreement (expiration date, commitment fees to obtain the agreement, and terms of any new obligation under the take out agreement)
- Debt service requirements if the take out agreement is exercised

The above disclosure requirements were effective as of the release date of GASB Interpretation-1 (December 1984). If installment notes arise from the exercise of the take out agreement, the amount of the installment loan should be part of the schedule of debt service requirements.

The disclosures discussed above are in addition to the general long-term debt disclosures as required by NCGA-1 and NCGA Interpretation-6 (Notes to the Financial Statements Disclosure). These general disclosure requirements are discussed later in this chapter.

The demand bond accounting standards established by GASB Interpretation-1 (except for the disclosure requirements that became effective with the release of the Interpretation) are applicable to financial statements for fiscal years ended after June 15, 1985. However, after the effective date demand bonds that were initially treated as long-term debt but do not meet the standards established by GASB Interpretation-1, must be reclassified as a fund liability or a current liability of a proprietary fund. The reclassification in governmental funds is treated as a prior period adjustment, and prior years' financial statements that are presented on a comparative basis must be restated. For example, if proceeds from the issuance of $4,000,000 demand bonds were initially recorded in the Capital Projects Fund, and the liability was presented as part of the General Long-Term Debt Account Group, the following entries would be made to adhere to the accounting standards established by GASB Interpretation-1 with respect to reclassifying the demand bonds as a liability of the Capital Projects Fund:

CAPITAL PROJECTS FUND
Fund Balance (Prior Period Adjustment)   4,000,000
   Bonds Payable On Demand   4,000,000

GENERAL LONG-TERM DEBT ACCOUNT GROUP
Bonds Payable (On Demand)   4,000,000
   Amount To Be Provided For
     Repayment Of Demand Bonds   4,000,000

Liabilities

EXTINGUISHMENT OF DEBT

A governmental unit may extinguish debt in a manner whereby the unit (1) has no further legal responsibilities under the original debt agreement, or (2) continues to be legally responsible for the debt but the extinguishment is considered an in-substance defeasance (retirement). NCGA Interpretation-9 (Certain Fund Classifications and Balance Sheet Accounts) concludes that early extinguishments, including advance refundings, should be accounted for in accordance with FASB-76 (Extinguishment of Debt).

FASB-76 concludes that debt is considered to be extinguished under the following circumstances:

- The debtor pays the creditor and is relieved of all its obligations with respect to the debt. This concludes the debtor's reacquisition of its outstanding debt securities in the public securities market, regardless of whether the securities are cancelled or held as so-called treasury bonds.
- The debtor is legally released from being the primary obligor under the debt either judicially or by the creditor and it is probable (as defined in FASB-5—Accounting for Contingencies) that the debtor will not be required to make future payments with respect to the debt under any guarantees.
- The debtor irrevocably places cash or other assets in a trust to be used solely for satisfying scheduled payments of both interest and principal of a specific obligation and the possibility that the debtor will be required to make future payments with respect to that debt is remote. In this circumstance, debt is extinguished even though the debtor is not legally released from being the primary obligor under the debt obligation (in-substance defeasance).

When debt is extinguished as an in-substance defeasance transaction, only monetary assets can be contributed to the irrevocable trust. The monetary assets must be (1) denominated in the same currency in which the debt is payable, and (2) essentially risk free with respect to the timing, amount, and collection of principal and interest. FASB-76 lists the following as examples of essentially risk free assets denominated in U.S. dollars:

- Direct obligations of the U.S. government
- Obligations guaranteed by the U.S. government

Liabilities

- Securities that are backed by U.S. government obligations as collateral under an arrangement by which the interest and principal payments on the collateral generally flow immediately through to the holder of security

The monetary assets must generate cash flows that approximate the debt service requirements of the original debt. That is, cash must be available from the trust to pay interest and make principal repayments as they become due. The cash flows must be sufficient to meet trustee fees and similar administrative expenditures if these expenditures are expected to be made from the assets of the trust. If the administrative expenditures are to be paid directly by the governmental unit, a liability for the total expected administrative expenditures should be recognized in the period in which the debt is considered extinguished.

> **OBSERVATION:** *The liability recognized based on the expected administrative expenditures financed by the governmental unit may be classified as part of the General Long-Term Debt Account Group if the expenditures do not require current appropriation and expenditure of governmental fund financial resources.*

The amount of the debt considered to be retired based on an in-substance defeasance transaction must be disclosed as long as the debt remains legally outstanding. In addition, disclosures should include a general description of the in-substance defeasance transaction.

ADVANCE REFUNDINGS AND DEFEASED DEBT

GASB-7 (Advance Refundings Resulting in Defeasance of Debt) establishes both accounting standards and disclosure standards for advance refundings of debt. The accounting standards apply to governmental funds whose measurement focus is the flow of current financial resources. Funds included in this category would be the General Fund, Special Revenue Funds, Debt Service Funds, and Capital Projects Funds. An advance refunding of debt would be recorded in one of these funds and the related debt (both the new debt and the old debt) would be accounted for in the governmental unit's General Long-Term Debt Account Group (GLTDAG).

Liabilities

The disclosure standards established by GASB-7 apply to all governmental entities, and include state and local governments as well as public benefit corporations, public authorities, Public Employee Retirement Systems, governmental utilities, governmental hospitals, and public colleges and universities.

> **OBSERVATION:** *Accounting standards for advance refundings of debt for funds and entities that have a measurement focus similar to that of a commercial enterprise (flow of economic resources) are established by APB-26 (Early Extinguishment of Debt). For example, funds such as an Enterprise Fund or Internal Service Fund would account for defeased debt based on criteria established by APB-26, but would also have to make note disclosures required by GASB-7.*

Accounting Standards

When debt reported in a governmental unit's GLTDAG is defeased through an advance refunding (including an in-substance defeasance), the proceeds from the issuance of the new debt should be recorded as "Other Financing Source—Proceeds Of Refunding Debt" in the governmental fund that receives the proceeds from the issuance of the new debt. The newly issued debt should also be recorded as a liability in the governmental unit's GLTDAG. When payments to the escrow agent to defease the old debt are made from the proceeds of the newly issued debt, the payments should be recorded as "Other Financing Use—Payment To Refunded Debt Escrow Agent." The defeased debt should be removed from the governmental unit's GLTDAG.

> **OBSERVATION:** *GASB-7 uses the term "bond" instead of the more general term "debt" in its account titles when referring to advance refundings resulting in defeasance of debt. The defeasance of the old debt could be accomplished through refinancing other than by issuing bonds. Therefore, the general term "debt" is used for the term "bond" throughout this analysis and explanation.*

For example, if a governmental unit defeased $500,000 of long-term notes by issuing $500,000 of long-term bonds, the following entries would be made assuming that the proceeds from the issuance of the new debt were recorded in the General Fund:

Liabilities

GENERAL FUND
Cash   500,000
     Other Financing Source— Proceeds
         Of Refunding Debt   500,000
To record the issuance of long-term bonds.

Other Financing Use—Payment To
    Refunded Debt Escrow Agent   500,000
      Cash   500,000
To record the payment to the escrow agent for debt defeasance.

GLTDAG
Amount To Be Provided For Repayment
    Of Bonds   500,000
      Bonds Payable   500,000

Notes Payable   500,000
    Amount To Be Provided For Repay-
      ment Of Notes   500,000

When payments made to the escrow agent to defease the debt are made from the governmental unit's resources and not from proceeds generated from the issuance of new debt, the payments should be recorded as a debt service expenditure and not as an other financing use. For example, if it is assumed in the previous illustration that the debt was defeased by issuing $400,000 of bonds and using $100,000 from the Debt Service Fund, the following entries would be made:

GENERAL FUND
Cash   400,000
    Other Financing Source—Proceeds
      Of Refunding Debt   400,000

Other Financing Use—Payment To
    Refunded Debt Escrow Agent   400,000
      Cash   400,000

DEBT SERVICE FUND
Expenditures—Principal   100,000
    Cash   100,000

GLTDAG
Amount To Be Provided For Repayment
    Of Bonds   400,000
      Bonds Payable   400,000

Notes Payable   500,000
    Amounts Available In Debt Service
      Fund (For Payment Of Notes)   500,000

Liabilities

Payments made to the escrow agent from current governmental resources that represent accrued interest on the defeased debt should be recorded as a debt service expenditure (interest) and not as an other financing use.

A governmental unit may issue a single debt that will be used to defease a number of smaller liabilities outstanding. In addition, part of the defeased debts, rather than being reported in the governmental unit's GLTDAG, may be reported as liabilities in Enterprise Funds, Internal Service Funds, or other funds that have a measurement focus similar to that of a commercial enterprise. Under these circumstances, the accounting standards established by GASB-7 must be observed for the portion of the defeased debt reported in the GLTDAG, and accounting standards established by APB-26 must be observed for the portion of the defeased debt applicable to proprietary and similar funds.

To illustrate the accounting for the issuance of a single debt used to defease various liabilities reported in the GLTDAG and proprietary funds, assume that new bonds are issued for $500,000. The proceeds from the new debt issuance are used to defease $300,000 of debt reported in the GLTDAG and $190,000 of debt reported in an Enterprise Fund. (It is assumed that the book value of the debt in the Enterprise Fund is $190,000; however, the debt will require a $200,000 payment to be defeased.) The following entries would be made to account for the advance debt refunding, assuming that the proceeds from the sale of the bonds are recorded in the General Fund:

GENERAL FUND

Cash	500,000	
Other Financing Source—Proceeds Of Refunding Debt		500,000
Other Financing Use—Payment To Refunded Debt Escrow Agent	300,000	
Residual Equity Transfer (Fund Balance)	200,000	
Cash		500,000

GLTDAG

Amount To Be Provided For Repayment Of Bonds	500,000	
Bonds Payable		500,000
Notes Payable	300,000	
Amount To Be Provided For Repayment Of Notes		300,000

Liabilities

ENTERPRISE FUND
Notes Payable	190,000	
Extraordinary Loss—Early Extinguishment Of Debt	10,000	
Contributed Capital—General Fund		200,000

> **OBSERVATION:** *In the illustration above, it was assumed that the transaction represents a residual equity transfer because the transaction is nonrecurring or nonroutine. Also, it was assumed that the Enterprise Fund had no responsibility to repay the General Fund. If this had not been assumed, the General Fund would have recorded an amount due from the Enterprise Fund and the Enterprise Fund would have recorded an amount due to the General Fund.*

> **OBSERVATION:** *The provisions of GASB-7 are applicable to defeased debt with a fixed interest rate. Debt with a variable interest rate cannot be defeased in a manner that will satisfy the criteria for an in-substance defeasance as defined by GASB-7. For this reason, the provisions of GASB-7 are not applicable to defeased debt that has a variable interest rate. On the other hand, the provisions of GASB-7 are applicable to defeased old debt with a fixed interest rate when the debt is defeased by issuing new debt with a variable interest rate. However, when new debt with a variable interest rate is issued, the note disclosure should describe the effects of possible changes of interest rates on the difference in cash flows and the economic gain or loss computations.*

Disclosure Standards

GASB-7 establishes disclosure standards for advance refundings by all governmental entities. The disclosure standards are applicable to all advance refundings resulting in the defeasance of debt irrespective of whether the defeased debt is presented in the GLTDAG or as a liability of a specific fund.

A note to the financial statements should provide a general description of an advance refunding that results in debt defeasance. *At a minimum,* the note should contain the following disclosures:

1. The difference between (a) the cash flow requirements necessary to service the old debt over its life and (b) the cash flow requirements necessary to service the new debt and other payments necessary to complete the advance refunding

Liabilities

2. The economic gain or loss that arises because of the advance refunding

The life of the old debt is based on its stated maturity date and not on its call date, if any.

> **OBSERVATION:** *The two disclosures described above are the only disclosure requirements for advance refunding mandated by GASB-7; however, in Appendix A (paragraph 22) of GASB-7, it is noted that the GASB believes that, generally, disclosures should include (1) amounts of the old and new debt, (2) additional amounts paid to the escrow agent, and (3) management's explanation for an advance refunding that results in an economic loss. The GASB also concluded that ultimately the specific disclosures by a particular governmental entity are dependent upon "such things as the number and relative size of the entity's advance refunding transactions, the fund structure of the reporting entity, and the number and type of refundings of its component units."*

Difference in Cash Flow Requirements The cash flow requirements of the old debt are simply the sum of all future interest and principal payments that would have to be paid by the governmental entity if the debt remained outstanding until its maturity date. The cash flow requirements of the new debt are the sum of all future interest and principal payments that will have to be paid to service the debt in the future, and other payments that are made from the governmental entity's current resources rather than from proceeds from the issuance of the new debt. Any proceeds from the issuance of the new debt that represent accrued interest (when the bonds are sold between interest payment dates) should not be included as cash flow requirements related to the new debt.

When new debt is issued in an amount that exceeds the amount needed to defease the old debt, only the portion of the new debt needed to defease the old debt should be included as cash flow requirements related to the new debt.

Economic Gain or Loss The economic gain or loss is computed by determining the difference between the present value of cash flow requirements of the old debt and the present value of cash flow requirements of the new debt. The interest or discount rate used to determine the present value of the cash flows is a rate that generally must be computed through trial and error (either manually or by

Liabilities

using a computer software package). The objective is to identify an interest rate that, when applied to the cash flow requirements for the new debt, produces an amount equal to the sum of the (1) proceeds of the new debt (net of premium or discount) and (2) accrued interest, less the (a) underwriting spread and (b) nonrecoverable issuance costs.

Issuance costs related to the advance refunding may include such transaction costs as insurance, legal, administrative, and trustee costs. These costs may be either recoverable (through the yield in the escrow fund) or nonrecoverable. Treasury Department regulations establish the maximum allowable yield of the escrow fund and certain issuance costs (allowable costs) may be used to reduce the amount defined as proceeds from the issuance of the new debt. The effect of the Treasury Department regulations is to increase the allowable amount that can be legally earned in the escrow fund. Although issuance costs may be allowable under the Treasury Department regulations, they may not be recoverable through the escrow fund because (1) the interest rate on U.S. securities purchased by the escrow fund may be less than the legal maximum rate allowed by the Treasury Department or (2) the escrow fund may be used to liquidate the old debt on a call date and the investment period may be too short to allow for the full recovery of the allowable costs through escrow earnings. When issuance costs are considered allowable costs by the Treasury Department and they are recovered through the escrow fund, the result is that such costs are not an actual cost to the governmental entity. These are referred to as recoverable costs and are not used to compute the interest or discount rate used to determine the present value of the cash flow requirements related to the old debt and new debt.

> ***OBSERVATION:*** *Although GASB-7 addressed the question of how issuance costs should be used to compute the economic gain or loss on the advance refunding, it did not establish accounting standards for the issuance costs. Under current generally accepted accounting principles, issuance costs may be recorded as a separate expenditure or may be netted against the proceeds of the new debt.*

Computing the Required Disclosures

In order to clarify the computation of the differences in cash flow requirements and the economic gain or loss arising from an advance refunding, GASB-7 presented three examples in an appendix. Pre-

Liabilities

sented below are the steps that may be followed to compute the required disclosures. After a general description of the steps, Example II from GASB-7 is used to demonstrate how the suggested steps can be applied to a specific set of circumstances.

Step 1: Compute the amount of resources that will be required to (1) make a payment to the escrow agent in order to defease the debt and (2) pay issuance costs.

The resources may be generated entirely from the issuance of new debt, or the refunding may be partially financed by using other resources of the governmental unit.

> **OBSERVATION:** *If the old debt is defeased entirely by using other resources of the governmental unit (no new debt is issued), the transaction is not subject to the accounting and disclosure standards established by GASB-7 because it does not satisfy the definition of an advance refunding. Although this method of financing the defeasance is not discussed in GASB-7, it would appear that the accounting standards established by GASB-7 would be appropriate—that is, funding of the irrevocable trust would be treated as a debt service expenditure. The disclosure standards established by GASB-7 would not be appropriate because there would, of course, be no new debt service requirements. On the other hand, if a governmental entity accumulates sufficient funds internally to pay off all or part of a debt, the debt would not be considered defeased because an irrevocable trust, as described in GASB-7, would not be established.*

The payment to the escrow agent must be large enough to make all interest payments and the principal payment based on either the call date or maturity date of the old debt. Either the call date or the maturity date is used, depending on which one is specified as the retirement date in the escrow fund agreement. The amount of the required payment to the escrow agent is also dependent upon the rate of return that can be earned in the escrow fund. The escrow rate of return is determined by the market investment conditions and the allowable yield on the escrow investment as determined by Treasury Department regulations.

The amount of the issuance costs must be added to the amount that is paid to the escrow agent in order to determine the total amount of resources required to defease the debt.

Step 2: Compute the effective interest rate target amount.

The effective interest rate target amount is computed by subtracting the amount of nonrecoverable issuance costs from the amount of the resources required to defease the old debt and to pay issuance costs (computed in Step 1). By reducing the amount required to defease the old debt (and to pay issuance costs) by the nonrecoverable issuance costs, the effective interest rate (to be computed in Step 3) will be decreased. If all issuance costs are recoverable and the new debt is sold at par, the coupon rate on the new debt will be the same as the effective interest rate.

Step 3: Compute the effective interest rate.

The effective interest rate is the interest rate used to discount the debt service requirements on the new debt so that it is exactly equal to the effective interest rate target amount (computed in Step 2). The computation of the effective interest rate is relatively easy if you have access to a microcomputer and a software program. If you do not have access to a microcomputer, the computation of the effective interest rate is tedious because it must be determined through trial and error and by using interpolation.

Step 4: Compute (1) the difference between the cash flow required to service the old debt and the cash flow required to service the new debt and (2) the economic gain or loss resulting from the advance refunding.

The difference between the cash flow requirements can be computed as shown below:

Cash Flow Requirements

Total interest payments on old debt (using the maturity date of the old debt)	$X	
Principal payment to retire old debt	X	
Total cash flow requirements to service old debt		$X
Total interest payments on new debt	$X	
Principal payment to retire new debt	X	
Other resources used to defease old debt	X	
Less: Accrued interest on new debt at date of issuance	−X	
Total cash flow requirements to service new debt		−X
Difference in cash flow requirements		$X

Liabilities

The economic gain or loss on the advance refunding can be computed as follows:

Present value of cash flow requirements to service old debt		$X
Present value of cash flow requirements to service new debt	$X	
Other resources used to defease old debt	X	
Less: Accrued interest on new debt at date of issuance	−X	−X
Economic gain (loss) on advance refunding		$X

Comprehensive Illustration

On December 31, 19X1, term bonds of $100 with a 20% interest rate (paid annually on December 31) and a call date of December 31, 19X2, and a maturity date of December 31, 19X3, are defeased. The escrow fund yield is 12.74% and issuance costs are $5, of which $2.65 are recoverable costs. The escrow agreement requires that the old debt be retired on its call date (December 31, 19X2). The refunding of the old debt is financed entirely through the issuance of new debt that has an interest rate of 10% and matures on December 31, 19X3.

Step 1: Compute the amount of resources that will be required to (1) make a payment to the escrow agent and (2) pay issuance costs.

Debt service requirements on old debt (to call date)		
Interest on 12/31/X2	$ 20.00	
Principal on 12/31/X2	100.00	
Total debt service requirements	120.00	
Present value factor	x .887*	
Required payment to escrow agent		$106.44
Issuance costs		5.00
Amount of new debt		$111.44

* Present value factor for escrow fund assuming a yield (i) of 12.74% for 1 year (n), where the present value factor =

$$\frac{1}{(1+i)^n} = \frac{1}{(1+.1274)^1} = .887$$

Step 2: Compute the effective interest rate target amount.

Resources required to defease the old debt	$106.44
Issuance costs	5.00
Less: Nonrecoverable issuance costs ($5.00 − $2.65)	− 2.35
Effective interest rate target amount	$109.09

Step 3: Compute the effective interest rate.

Initially, you must make a reasonable estimate of what the effective interest rate will be. Since the escrow fund yield rate is 12.74% and the effective interest rate target amount ($109.09) is less than the amount of the new debt ($111.44), the effective interest rate must be less than 12.74%. Therefore, you may estimate that the rate is 12% and then compute the present value of the new debt service cash flow requirements as follows:

Present Value of New Debt Service Cash Flow Requirements at 12%

Interest payment made on new debt on 12/31/X2 ($111.14 × 10%)	$ 11.14	
Present value factor for an amount at an interest rate of 12% for 1 period	× .89286	$ 9.95
Interest payment made on new debt on 12/31/X3 ($111.14 × 10%)	$11.14	
Present value factor for an amount at an interest rate of 12% for 2 periods	× .79719	8.88
Principal payment made to retire new debt on 12/31/X2	$111.44	
Present value factor for an amount at an interest rate of 12% for 2 periods	× .79719	88.84
Present value of debt service on new debt		$107.67

Because the present value of the debt service payments ($107.67) is less than the effective interest rate target amount ($109.09), the effective interest rate must be less than 12%. Therefore, you may estimate that the rate is 11% and then compute the present value of the new debt service cash flow requirements as follows:

Liabilities

*Present Value of New Debt Service Cash
Flow Requirements at 11%*

Interest payment made on new debt on 12/31/X2 ($111.14 × 10%)	$ 11.14	
Present value factor for an amount at an interest rate of 11% for 1 period	x .90090	$ 10.03
Interest payment made on new debt on 12/31/X3 ($111.14 × 10%)	$11.14	
Present value factor for an amount at an interest rate of 11% for 2 periods	x .81162	9.04
Principal payment made to retire new debt on 12/31/X2	$111.44	
Present value factor for an amount at an interest rate of 11% for 2 periods	x .81162	90.45
Present value of debt service on new debt		$109.52

Because the present value of debt service payments ($109.52) is greater than the effective interest rate target amount ($109.09), the effective interest rate must be greater than 11%.

At this point, it is known that the approximate effective interest rate is between 11% and 12%. Interpolation must be used to compute the approximate effective interest rate, using the following equation:

$$\text{Effective interest rate} = \frac{\text{Present value of debt service payments on new debt at 11\%} - \text{Effective interest rate target amount}}{\text{Present value of debt service payments on new debt at 11\%} - \text{Present value of debt service payments on new debt at 12\%}}$$

$$= \frac{\$109.52 - \$109.09}{\$109.52 - \$107.67}$$

$$= \frac{.43}{1.85}$$

$$= .23 \text{ of } 1\%$$

$$= .23\%$$

Thus, the effective interest rate is approximately 11.23% (11% + .23%) and the present value factors can be computed as follows:

Liabilities

$$\text{Present value factor for an amount at an interest rate of 11.23\% for 1 period} = \frac{1}{(1 + .1123)^1}$$
$$= .89905$$

$$\text{Present value factor for an amount at an interest rate of 11.23\% for 2 periods} = \frac{1}{(1.1123)^2}$$
$$= .80830$$

Step 4: Compute difference in cash flow requirements and the economic gain or loss on the refunding.

Cash Flow Requirements

Total interest payment on old debt ($20 + $20)	$40.00	
Principal payment to retire old debt	100.00	
Total cash flow requirements to service old debt		$140.00
Total interest payments on new debt ($11.14 + $11.14)	22.28	
Principal payment to retire new debt	111.44	
Other resources used to defease old debt	—	
Less: Accrued interest on new debt at date of issuance	—	
Total cash flow requirements to service new debt		133.72
Difference in cash flow requirements		$ 6.28

Computation of Economic Gain or Loss

Present value of cash flow requirements to service old debt:		
Interest payment 12/31/X2 ($20 x .89905)	$17.98	
Interest payment 12/31/X3 ($20 x .80830)	16.17	
Principal payment 12/31/X3 ($100 x .80830)	80.83	$114.98
Present value of cash flow requirements to service new debt:		
Interest payment 12/31/X2 ($11.14 x .89905)	10.01	
Interest payment 12/31/X3 ($11.14 x .80830)	9.00	
Principal payment 12/31/X3 ($111.44 x .80830)	90.08	
Other resources used to defease old debt	—	
Less: Accrued interest on new debt at date of issuance	—	109.09
Economic gain on advance refunding		$ 5.89

Liabilities

Thus, the difference between the cash flow requirements is $6.28, and the economic gain is $5.89.

Generally, the disclosures concerning advance refundings required by paragraph 11 of GASB-7 should be made by major fund type (General Fund, Special Revenue Fund, Capital Projects Fund, Debt Service Fund, Internal Service Fund, Enterprise Fund, and Trust and Agency Funds) and account group. An alternative disclosure format may be necessary in order to avoid presenting misleading information. For example, it may be more informative to provide disclosure for individual funds of a fund type when the gains and losses in the combined fund type approximately offset one another.

For periods after an in-substance debt defeasance has occurred, the amount of the defeased debt outstanding should be disclosed by fund type and account group.

> **OBSERVATION:** *It should be noted that the required disclosures for defeased debt outstanding are applicable only to in-substance defeased debt and not to legally defeased debt.*

Presented below are examples of notes to a financial statement that provide disclosures for (1) an advance refunding resulting in defeased debt and (2) prior-year defeasance of debt outstanding.

▶ **NOTE X—Defeased Debt**

On December 31, 19X1, the City of Centerville issued general obligation bonds of $111.44 (par value) with an interest rate of 10% to advance refund term bonds with an interest rate of 20% and a par value of $100. The term bonds mature on December 31, 19X3, and are callable on December 31, 19X2. The general obligation bonds were issued at par and, after paying issuance costs of $5.00, the net proceeds were $106.44. The net proceeds from the issuance of the general obligation bonds were used to purchase U.S. government securities and those securities were deposited in an irrevocable trust with an escrow agent to provide debt service payments until the term bonds are called on December 31, 19X2. The advance refunding met the requirements of an in-substance debt defeasance and the term bonds were removed from the City's General Long-Term Debt Account Group.

As a result of the advance refunding, the City reduced its total debt service requirements by $6.28, which resulted in an economic gain (difference between the present value of the debt service payments on the old and new debt) of $5.89.

NOTE Y—Prior Years' Debt Defeasance

In prior years, the City has defeased various bond issues by creating separate irrevocable trust funds. New debt has been issued and the proceeds have been used to purchase U.S. government securities that were placed in the trust funds. The investments and fixed earnings from the investments are sufficient to fully service the defeased debt until the debt is called or matures. For financial reporting purposes, the debt has been considered defeased and therefore removed as a liability from the City's General Long-Term Debt Account Group. As of December 31, 19X1, the amount of defeased debt outstanding but removed from the General Long-Term Debt Account Group amounted to $795.◄

Effective Date

The provisions of GASB-7 are applicable to financial periods beginning after December 15, 1986; however, earlier application is encouraged. For financial statements that have been issued prior to the publication of GASB-7, a governmental entity may restate the previously issued financial statements in order to reflect the provisions of GASB-7. Restatement of the previously issued financial statements is allowed, but it is not required.

LIABILITY DISCLOSURES

NCGA-1 requires that the following disclosures with respect to liabilities and related transactions be presented in the general purpose financial statements:

- Significant contingent liabilities (See Chapter 41)
- Encumbrances outstanding
- Pension plan obligations (See Chapter 66)
- Accumulated unpaid employee benefits, such as vacation and sick leave (See Chapter 42)
- Debt service requirements to maturity
- Commitments under noncapitalized leases (See Chapter 43)
- Construction and other significant commitments
- Changes in general long-term debt (See Chapter 67)

Liabilities

In addition, NCGA Interpretation-6 (Notes to the Financial Statements Disclosure) requires that the following liability related disclosures be made:

- Claims and judgments (See Chapter 41)
- Short-term debt instruments and liquidity
- Capital leases (See Chapter 43)
- Contingencies (See Chapter 41)

Accounting standards and reporting requirements applicable to liabilities not illustrated in this chapter are explained in the following chapters in this section of the *Governmental GAAP Guide*.

LITERATURE REFERENCES

Material in this chapter is based on the following authoritative pronouncements, which are grouped according to the major headings used within the chapter. A dual reference (both paragraph and page number) is used for NCGA-1 and NCGA-2 because the original pronouncements do not use paragraph numbers.

Current Liabilities
NCGA-1   *Governmental Accounting and Financial Reporting Principles*, p. 6/ ¶ 18.
APB-43   *Restatement and Revision of Accounting and Research Bulletins*, Chapter 3A, pp. 20-21.

Long-Term Liabilities
NCGA-1   *Governmental Accounting and Financial Reporting Principles*, p. 8/ ¶¶ 32-33.

Specific Fund Liabilities
NCGA-1   *Governmental Accounting and Financial Reporting Principles*, pp. 6 and 9/¶¶ 18 and 42.
GASB Interpretation-1   *Authoritative Status of NCGA Pronouncements and AICPA Industry Audit Guide*, ¶ 9.

General Long-Term Debt Account Group
NCGA-1   *Governmental Accounting and Financial Reporting Principles*, pp. 7-9 and 16/¶¶ 26, 33, 42-45, and 107-108.

Liabilities

Bond, Tax, and Revenue Anticipation Notes
NCGA INTERPRETATION-9   *Certain Fund Classifications and Balance Sheet Accounts,* ¶ 12.
FASB-6   *Classification of Short-Term Obligations Expected to be Refinanced,* ¶¶ 10-12 and 15.

Demand Bonds
GASB INTERPRETATION-1   *Demand Bonds Issued by State and Local Governmental Entities,* ¶¶ 1-5 and 10-14.
NCGA INTERPRETATION-9   *Certain Fund Classifications and Balance Sheet Accounts,* ¶ 12.

Extinguishment of Debt
NCGA INTERPRETATION-9   *Certain Fund Classifications and Balance Sheet Accounts,* ¶¶ 13-14.
FASB-76   *Extinguishment of Debt,* ¶¶ 3-6.

Advance Refundings and Defeased Debt
GASB-7   *Advance Refundings Resulting in Defeasance of Debt,* ¶¶ 7-15.

Liability Disclosures
NCGA-1   *Governmental Accounting and Financial Reporting Principles,* p. 24/ ¶ 158.
NCGA INTERPRETATION-6   *Notes to the Financial Statements Disclosure,* ¶ 5.

APPENDIX
ACCOUNTING FOR DEBT USING THE TOTAL FINANCIAL RESOURCE MEASUREMENT FOCUS (EXPOSURE DRAFT)

As noted earlier in this chapter, the accounting and reporting of debt of a governmental entity is based on the flow of current financial resources measurement focus and the modified accrual basis of accounting. In August 1989, the GASB issued a revised Exposure Draft entitled "Measurement Focus and Basis of Accounting—Governmental Fund Operating Statements." The Exposure Draft proposes that a governmental entity use the flow of financial resources measurement focus and the accrual basis to prepare financial statements. If the proposals contained in the Exposure Draft are adopted by the GASB, there will be significant changes in governmental accounting. The purpose of this Appendix is to discuss how debt would be accounted for and reported under the proposed changes.

Liabilities

Long-Term Debt

Although the Exposure Draft proposes the adoption of the financial resources measurement focus, debt of a governmental entity would continue to be classified as either part of the entity's GLTDAG or debt of a particular fund (operating debt) based on the characteristics of the debt. The criteria for presenting debt as either part of the GLTDAG or as governmental fund debt would be different from previously established criteria. Specifically, it is proposed that debt be classified as either general long-term debt or operating debt.

General Long-Term Capital Debt   Debt that is issued to acquire capital assets or for certain nonrecurring projects or activities that have long-term benefit and that is expected to be retired by use of financial resources of governmental funds is referred to as general long-term capital debt. Capital assets are defined in the Exposure Draft as "long-lived, tangible assets (for example, equipment, buildings, land, and infrastructure) obtained or controlled as a result of past transactions or events." Proceeds from the issuance of long-term debt used to finance the acquisition of capital assets should be reported as an other financing source, and the debt should be reported as part of GLTDAG. For example, if $10,000,000 of long-term bonds were issued to finance the construction of a governmental building, the issuance of the bonds would be recorded as follows:

CAPITAL PROJECTS FUND
  Cash   10,000,000
    Proceeds From Issuance Of
      Long-Term Capital Debt   10,000,000

GLTDAG
  Amount To Be Provided For Repayment
    Of Long-Term Capital Debt   10,000,000
    Bonds Payable   10,000,000

Although the GLTDAG includes, for the most part, long-term debt instruments, it may also include debt that matures within one year or less if all of the following conditions are satisfied:

- At least part of the short-term debt is expected to be replaced by other debt

- The time period covered by all of the debt (the debt originally issued and the replacement debt) extends beyond one year

Expenditures for servicing debt reported in the governmental entity's GLTDAG should be recognized when due (maturity date). Thus, the accrual basis would not be applicable to interest expenditures on general long-term capital debt. When funds have been transferred to the Debt Service Fund during the fiscal year in anticipation of making debt service payments shortly after the end of the period, it would be acceptable to accrue interest in the Debt Service Fund in the year that the transfer is made.

In addition to debt issued to acquire capital assets, or for certain nonrecurring projects or activities that have long-term benefit, the GLTDAG may include long-term vendor financing, such as capital leases and installment purchases. Debt related to a lease should be reported as a liability in the GLTDAG when the criteria established by FASB-13 (Accounting for Leases, as amended) are satisfied. For example, if equipment is leased for five years with a capitalized value of $200,000 based on the guidelines established by FASB-13, the following entries would be made:

GENERAL FUND

Expenditures—Capitalized Leases	200,000	
Other Financing Sources— Capitalized Leases		200,000

GLTDAG

Amount To Be Provided For Capitalized Lease Payments	200,000	
Obligations Under Capital Lease Agreements		200,000

GENERAL FIXED ASSETS ACCOUNT GROUP

Assets Under Capital Leases	200,000	
Investment In General Fixed Assets—Capital Leases		200,000

Debt related to the installment purchase of capital assets should be measured as a liability based on many of the concepts discussed in APB-21 (Interest on Receivables and Payables). That is, the transaction should be based on the fair value of the exchange, which is presumed to be the face (principal) value of the installment notes, assuming the stated interest rate is reasonable. When no interest rate is stated or the rate is unreasonable, a reasonable interest rate must be imputed based on the characteristics of the exchange.

Deep discount debt (where the stated interest rate is less than seventy-five percent of the effective interest rate) should be reported net of the discount in the GLTDAG. The discount should be amor-

Liabilities

tized using the effective interest method; however, the effect of the amortization should be shown only in the GLTDAG and should not be used to compute annual interest expenditures. For example, assume that long-term capital debt with a face value of $10,000,000 and no interest rate matures in five years. The debt is issued for $6,210,000 at an effective interest rate of 10%. The following entries would be made to record the issuance of the deep discount debt:

GLTDAG
Amount To Be Provided For Repayment Of Long-Term Capital Debt	6,210,000	
Discount On Bonds Payable	3,790,000	
Bonds Payable		10,000,000

CAPITAL PROJECTS FUND
Cash	6,210,000	
Proceeds From Issuance Of Long-Term Capital Debt		6,210,000

At the end of the first year after the initial issuance of the debt, the following entry would be made to reflect the amortization of the discount:

GLTDAG
Amount To Be Provided For Repayment Of Long-Term Capital Debt	621,000	
Discount On Bonds Payable (10% of $6,210,000)		621,000

Again, it should be emphasized that the amortization of the bonds' discount does not appear on the entity's statement of operations.

The following information related to deep discount debt should be disclosed in a note to the financial statements:

- Stated interest rate
- Effective interest rate
- Face amount of debt (if not reported on the balance sheet)

Operating Debt Debt that is issued for purposes other than the financing of capital assets or for certain nonrecurring projects or activities that have long-term benefit is referred to as governmental fund debt and is reported in a specific governmental fund rather than in the governmental entity's GLTDAG. Governmental fund debt includes revenue anticipation notes, tax anticipation notes, and debt that is issued to finance operations.

Governmental fund debt should be reported in the specific governmental fund (the fund that received the proceeds) as a liability, net of discount or premium, if any. For example, if $10,000,000 of long-term bonds were issued for purposes other than financing the acquisition of capital assets or for certain nonrecurring projects or activities that have long-term benefit, the issuance of the bonds would be recorded as follows, assuming they were issued at a two percent discount:

GENERAL FUND
Cash	9,800,000	
Discount On Bonds Payable	200,000	
Bonds Payable		10,000,000

Expenditure for servicing debt reported in a specific governmental fund is subject to accrual and should be recognized as an expenditure based on the passage of time. In addition, any discount or premium related to the operating debt should be amortized using the effective interest method. For example, if it is assumed in the previous illustration that the debt carried an 8% interest rate but the effective interest rate was 9%, the following entry would be made at the end of the first year of the life of the debt (assuming a Debt Service Fund is not used to account for servicing the debt):

GENERAL FUND
Expenditure—Interest (9% of $9,800,000)	882,000	
Discount on Bonds Payable		82,000
Cash (8% of $10,000,000)		800,000

In addition to debt related to noncapital asset financing, similar-purpose debt related to long-term vendor financing should be accounted for as an operating debt.

CLAIMS, JUDGMENTS, AND SPECIAL TERMINATION BENEFITS

The general long-term debt of a governmental unit includes more than specific debt instruments such as bonds and notes payable. NCGA-4 (Accounting and Financial Reporting Principles for Claims and Judgments and Compensated Absences) concludes that general long-term debt may include amounts that represent potential claims and judgments that may have to be paid by the governmental unit. NCGA-4 establishes the criteria for determining whether to classify claims and judgments as (1) part of general long-term debt, (2) a specific liability of a governmental fund type, or (3) a disclosure in the financial statements.

Claims and Judgments as Governmental Liabilities

A state or local government may be subject to a variety of claims and judgments. These potential liabilities can arise from various sources such as grievances concerning employees' back pay, disputes concerning taxing authority, refunds due to noncompliance with grant agreements, and personal and property damages resulting from actions taken by governmental employees.

A loss contingency arises when there *appears* to be an impairment of an asset or an incurrence of a liability. Governmental claims and judgments are examples of loss contingencies (incurrence of a liability), in that there is a degree of uncertainty whether the governmental unit will actually suffer an economic loss from the actions taken by external parties. A governmental loss contingency generally has the following claim cycle:

- The actual occurrence of the loss contingency
- The date the loss contingency can be estimated
- The settlement date of the loss contingency
- The actual payment date of the judgment

The governmental unit may have had considerable experience with some types of claims, and the loss contingency may be subject to reasonable estimation soon after the occurrence of the event that created the loss contingency. The claims experience of the governmental unit may be used to estimate a specific claim or the outcome of similar claims as a group. On the other hand, NCGA-4 notes that the following conditions may make it difficult to estimate the outcome of a governmental claim:

- Certain types of claims may be filed in amounts far greater than those that can reasonably be expected to be agreed upon by the government and the claimant, or awarded by a court.
- The time permitted between the occurrence of an event causing a claim and the actual filing of the claim may be lengthy.
- The time that may elapse between filing and ultimate settlement and payment of a claim may be extremely lengthy.
- The adjudicated loss may be paid over a period of years after settlement.

> **OBSERVATION:** *The conditions listed above are not unique to the governmental environment and, therefore, cannot be used as the basis for arguing that loss contingencies for governmental units are different from loss contingencies of commercial enterprises when determining whether an accrual should be made.*

The completion of the claim cycle (from date of occurrence to date of payment) may extend over a period of several months or years. Under this circumstance, the loss contingency arising from the claim assumes the characteristics of general long-term debt and should be classified as part of the General Long-Term Debt Account Group. However, if the claim when accrued will require the use of expendable available financial resources, the claim should be recognized as a liability of the governmental fund that is expected to pay the claim.

Accounting for a Loss Contingency

NCGA-4 concludes that FASB-5 (Accounting for Contingencies) should be followed to determine the appropriate accounting for loss contingencies arising from claims. A critical first step in determining how to account for a loss contingency is to assess the probability that an actual economic loss will eventually occur. FASB-5 identifies the following three possible outcomes of a loss contingency:

- *Probable* The future event or events are likely to occur.
- *Reasonably possible* The chance of the future event or events occurring is more than remote but less than likely.
- *Remote* The chance of the future event or events occurring is slight.

These three subjective probabilities are used to determine whether a loss contingency arising from a claim should be (1) accrued or (2) disclosed in the governmental unit's financial statements.

Loss Contingency Accrued A loss contingency arising from a claim is accrued as of the balance sheet date when both of the following conditions exist:

- Information available prior to issuance of the financial statements indicates that it is *probable* that an asset has been impaired or liability has been incurred at the date of the most recent accounting period for which financial statements are being presented. (It is implicit in this condition that it must be probable that one or more future events will occur confirming the fact of the loss.)
- The amount of the loss can be reasonably estimated.

If these conditions exist, the loss contingency is recorded as a liability of a governmental fund when the claim liability will be discharged through the use of expendable available financial resources. If expendable available financial resources will not be used to meet the claim, the liability is classified as part of the General Long-Term Debt Account Group. For example, assume a $100,000 claim has arisen from property damages caused by a governmental emergency vehicle. If it is concluded that the claim will be settled for approximately $40,000, but it will take about 18 months to settle the claim, the following entry is made:

GENERAL LONG-TERM DEBT ACCOUNT GROUP
Amount To Be Provided For Payment Of
  Certain Claims And Judgments   40,000
    Estimated Liabilities For Claims and
      Judgments   40,000

If it is assumed that $5,000 of the personal property claim will be paid from expendable available financial resources of the General Fund

Claims, Judgments, and Special Termination Benefits

and the balance ($35,000) will be paid in approximately 18 months, the following entries would be made:

GENERAL FUND
Expenditures—Personal Property Claims   5,000
    Estimated Liabilities For Claims And
        Judgments   5,000

GENERAL LONG-TERM DEBT ACCOUNT GROUP
Amount To Be Provided For Payment Of
    Certain Claims And Judgments   35,000
    Estimated Liabilities For Claims And
        Judgments   35,000

> **OBSERVATION:** *A separate Debt Service Fund may be established only if legally mandated or when resources are being accumulated for payment of the claims and judgments.*

NCGA-4 requires that the event be disclosed on the face of the Statement of Revenues and Expenditures or in a note to the financial statement. Presented below is the presentation on the face of the financial statement:

Expenditures:
    Claims and judgments ($40,000 [total amount
    determined for the year under FASB-5] less
    $35,000 [recorded as long-term obligations]) $5,000

> **OBSERVATION:** *It is unclear how soon after the balance sheet date the amount must be paid in order for the loss contingency to be part of a specific fund's liability. NCGA-4 simply states: "liabilities due on demand—such as from adjudicated or settled claims—should be recorded as an expenditure in the governmental fund. The amount recorded in the General Long-Term Debt Account Group would be the amount estimable under FASB Statement No. 5 as a contingent liability, or where the established liability has a fixed due date other than the balance sheet date—for instance, a portion of a court judgment is payable from future resources" (paragraph 41). It may be appropriate to consider loss contingencies that will be paid within 60 days of the balance sheet date as current. The 60-day criterion is based on the suggested revenue recognition guidelines established in NCGA Interpretation-3 (Revenue Recognition—Property Taxes).*

Claims, Judgments, and Special Termination Benefits

The estimation of claims may be based on (1) a case by case analysis, (2) an application of a historical experience factor to outstanding claims on an aggregate basis, or (3) a combination of the two. When a historical experience factor is applied to aggregate claims outstanding, there should be an appropriate stratification of the claims by their nature and amount in order to enhance the likelihood that a reasonable estimate can be made.

The estimate may be in the form of a range rather than a single point estimate. FASB Interpretation-14 (Reasonable Estimation of the Amount of a Loss) concludes that the existence of more than one reasonable estimate of a loss contingency does not preclude the accrual of the contingency. If point estimates within the range have differing probabilities, the one with the greatest probability should be accrued and the balance should be disclosed in a note to the financial statements. When all point estimates within the range have the same probability, the lowest amount within the range should be accrued and the difference between the highest and lowest amount within the range should be disclosed in a note to the financial statements.

To illustrate the above guidelines, assume that personal liability claims aggregating $20,000,000 exist at the balance sheet date and that it is probable that the claims, at least to some extent, will be paid. Further, the following reasonable estimates of the eventual payments have been developed:

Reasonable estimate of the loss	Probability of payment
$2,000,000	40%
$4,000,000	45%
$5,000,000	15%

In this situation, an accrual of $4,000,000 would be made (either as a specific fund liability, as part of the General Long-Term Debt Account Group, or split between the two), and disclosure of the nature of the contingency and the exposure to an additional loss of possibly $1,000,000 would be made in a note to the financial statements. On the other hand, if a reasonable estimate of the loss is between $2,000,000 and $5,000,000 and the probability of each loss ($2,000,000, $4,000,000, and $5,000,000) is 33 1/3%, an accrual of $2,000,000 would be made and the balance ($3,000,000) disclosed in a note.

The accrual of a loss contingency is not dependent upon an actual claim existing as of the balance sheet date. All that is needed is the occurrence of an event on or before the balance sheet date that may lead to a loss contingency. If the governmental unit becomes aware of the claim after the balance sheet date but before the issuance of the financial statements, the claim must be evaluated for possible accrual. FASB-5 lists the following factors to consider in determining whether a claim is the basis for a loss contingency accrual:

- Nature of the claim
- Progress of the case (including progress after the date of the financial statements but before those statements are issued)
- Opinions or views of legal counsel and other advisers
- Experience of governments in similar cases
- Decisions by the governmental unit as to how to respond to the claim

If legal counsel is unable to express an opinion that the claim will be dismissed without liability, this does not automatically imply that the claim should be accrued. Likewise, the filing of a lawsuit or a claim does not automatically require that a loss contingency be accrued. On the other hand, a loss contingency may have to be accrued even if a claim has not been asserted as of the date of the financial statements or the date when the financial statements are issued. Unasserted claims must be accrued when (1) it is probable that the claim will eventually be asserted, (2) it is probable that the unasserted claim will lead to an actual incurrence of a liability, and (3) a reasonable estimate of the loss can be made. For example, a preliminary investigation by a federal agency may indicate that some part of a grant must be returned by a local government because certain regulations associated with the grant were not observed. If it is both probable that the federal government will assert a claim and that the claim will be successful, a liability should be accrued assuming the claim is subject to reasonable estimation.

Loss Contingencies Disclosed When a loss contingency arising from a claim is either not probable or not subject to reasonable estimation, the contingency must be disclosed in the financial statements when it is *reasonably possible* that a loss will eventually be incurred. The financial statement disclosure should describe the nature of the loss contingency and an estimate of the possible loss or range of loss. If an estimate of the loss cannot be made based on the available information, the disclosure should state that no estimate can be made.

An example of a note describing a loss contingency is presented below:

▶ Auditors of the U.S. Department of Education have examined certain student financial aid programs administered by the Centerville Community College in fiscal years 19X1 through 19X4. While the auditors' final report has not been issued, their preliminary findings assert that the college should reimburse the federal government an aggregate of approximately $3,000,000. The college disagrees with the auditors' findings and is actively defending its position. Should the college be required to make such a refund, a substantial portion may be reimbursed by the college's insurance coverage. While the ultimate outcome of the above matter cannot be predicted at this time, it is the opinion of management that the disposition of this matter will not have a material adverse effect on the financial position of the college ◀

Events may occur subsequent to the balance sheet date but before the financial statements are issued that should be evaluated in the context of FASB-5. These events may suggest that (1) it is probable that a liability was incurred after the balance sheet date, or (2) it is reasonably possible that a liability was incurred after the balance sheet date. In neither case should a loss contingency be accrued because the liability did not exist as of the balance sheet date; however, it may be necessary to disclose the subsequent event to avoid issuing misleading financial statements. If the subsequent event is disclosed, the nature of the claim and the estimate of the loss or range of loss resulting from the claim should be described in the financial statements. If an estimate of the loss cannot be made, this fact should be part of the disclosure.

The disclosure of a subsequent event that did not result in a liability as of the balance sheet date may be presented in the form of pro forma financial data. If a reasonable estimate of the loss arising from the claim can be made, the financial statements as of the balance sheet date can be modified, on a pro forma basis only, to reflect the subsequent event. The pro forma financial statements serve as a supplement to and not a substitute for the historical cost financial statements, and may be presented in columnar form on the face of the governmental unit's historical cost financial statements.

FASB-5 does not require the disclosure of unasserted claims if "there has been no manifestation by a potential claimant of an awareness of a possible claim or assessment unless it is considered probable that a claim will be asserted and there is a reasonable possibility that the outcome will be unfavorable."

Claims, Judgments, and Special Termination Benefits

Disclosure of Loss Contingencies Accrued Even though a claim has been accrued as a loss contingency, it may nonetheless be necessary to disclose the nature of the loss and the amount of the loss in order to avoid the issuance of misleading financial statements.

Proprietary Funds

NCGA-4 concludes that Enterprise Funds and Internal Service Funds should follow FASB-5 without modification to account for claims and judgments.

Trust Funds

The basis of accounting for Expendable Trust Funds is similar to the accounting basis used by governmental fund types. However, Nonexpendable Trust Funds and proprietary funds use a similar accounting basis. Expendable Trust Funds should account for claims and judgments in a manner consistent with FASB-5 as modified by NCGA-4 and explained in this chapter. Nonexpendable Trust Funds and Pension Trust Funds should apply FASB-5 without modification to account for claims and judgments.

> *OBSERVATION: NCGA-4 concludes that Expendable Trust Funds should follow the accounting and reporting standards that apply to governmental fund types (paragraph 19). This would mean that the noncurrent portion of the Expendable Trust Fund's claims and judgments would be reported in the governmental unit's General Long-Term Debt Account Group. However, an Expendable Trust Fund, while using the governmental accounting model, accounts for all of its assets (including fixed assets). Likewise, it would seem that the fund must also account for all of its liabilities, including noncurrent liabilities. It should also be noted that NCGA-1 states that "long-term liabilities of proprietary funds and Trust Funds should be accounted for through those funds" (paragraph 32).*

Self-Insurance Funds

Claims and judgments of all governmental funds may be paid from a single self-insurance fund, such as an Internal Service Fund, rather than from several different governmental funds. When a self-insurance fund is established to pay all claims and judgments, the creation of such a fund does not transfer the legal responsibility for payment to the single fund, since the governmental unit's full faith and credit must support the claim or judgment.

A complete discussion of a self-insurance Internal Service Fund is found in Chapter 64 (Proprietary Funds).

Fund Balance Designation for Loss Contingencies

Some governmental units may reserve a portion of their fund balance for loss contingencies instead of establishing a separate self-insurance fund for claims and judgments. For financial reporting purposes the reserve for loss contingencies is presented as a fund balance designation. Unlike a fund balance reserve, which represents (1) a portion of the fund balance not appropriable for expenditures, or (2) a legal restriction, a designation is based on the governmental unit's discretion. If it wishes, the governmental unit can rescind the loss contingency designation. Designations are reported as part of the unreserved fund balance and identified as a designation on the face of the financial statements, in a note, or as a parenthetical comment.

When a portion of the fund balance is designated for possible loss contingencies, actual expenditures for claims and judgments or accruals cannot be charged against the designated amount. Also, no portion of the designation can be transferred to income for the period.

Identifying a portion of a fund balance as a reserve for loss contingencies does not substitute for the recognition of a loss contingency as required by FASB-5. In other words, if it is probable that a loss contingency has occurred, and the amount is subject to reasonable estimation, an actual liability (either within a specific fund or as part of the General Long-Term Debt Account Group) must be established.

Termination Benefits

A state or local government may, for a short period of time, offer employees special inducements to retire, usually at an early age. The inducements may include a lump sum payment as well as future periodic payments. If a special termination plan is offered, NCGA Interpretation-8 (Certain Pension Matters) requires that governmental units follow the accounting and reporting standards established by FASB-74 (Accounting for Special Termination Benefits Paid to Employees).

> **OBSERVATION:** *In 1985, FASB-74 was superseded by the issuance of FASB-88 (Employers' Accounting for Settlements and Curtailments of Defined Benefit Pension Plans and for Termination Benefits). Although FASB-74 should no longer be followed by commercial enterprises, governmental units must continue to observe the accounting and reporting standards established by FASB-74 as required by NCGA Interpretation-8.*

When a special termination plan is offered for a short period of time, the governmental unit should recognize a liability equal to the lump sum payments plus the present value of future periodic payments to be made under the plan. The estimate of the total cost of the plan should be based on an acceptable actuarial cost method. The amount of the liability accrued that will be liquidated with expendable available financial resources should be recognized as a liability of a specific governmental fund. The balance of the total liability (present value) should be reported as part of the General Long-Term Debt Account Group. To illustrate, assume that a governmental unit offers for a short period of time a special early retirement plan and the actuarially estimated cost of the benefits to be paid to those employees accepting early retirement under the plan are as follows:

Lump sum payments (payable immediately)	$ 400,000
Present value of periodic payments (first payments are to begin one year after termination date)	1,600,000
Total benefits to be paid (present value)	$2,000,000

The special termination benefits would be recorded as follows:

GENERAL FUND
Expenditures—Special Termination	400,000	
Liability Under Special Termination Benefits Plan		400,000

GENERAL LONG-TERM DEBT ACCOUNT GROUP
Amount To Be Provided For Payment Of Special Termination Benefits	1,600,000	
Special Termination Benefits Payable		1,600,000

NCGA Interpretation-8 requires that the following information with respect to the special termination plan be presented either on the face of the financial statements or in notes to the financial statements:

Expenditures:
Special termination benefits ($2,000,000 [total amount determined for the year by an acceptable actuarial cost method] less $1,600,000 [recorded as long-term obligations]) $400,000

Because the deferred portion of the special termination benefits is initially recorded at present value, at the end of each subsequent period it is necessary to adjust the long-term liability to reflect the present value of the obligation as of the reporting date. For example, in the previous illustration, if at the end of the following year the present value of the deferred termination benefits were $1,710,000, the following entry would be made:

GENERAL LONG-TERM DEBT ACCOUNT GROUP
Amount To Be Provided For Payment
Of Special Termination Benefits
($1,710,000 − $1,600,000)   110,000
    Liability Under Special
    Termination Benefits Plan   110,000

No expenditure is recognized for the increased present value. An expenditure will be recognized in a governmental fund when the benefits become a current liability.

LITERATURE REFERENCES

Material in this chapter is based on the following authoritative pronouncements, which are grouped according to the major headings used within the chapter. A dual reference (both paragraph and page number) is used for NCGA-1 and NCGA-2 because the original pronouncements do not use paragraph numbers.

Introduction
NCGA-4 *Accounting and Financial Reporting Principles for Claims and Judgments and Compensated Absences,* ¶¶ 5, 7, and 14.

Claims and Judgments as Governmental Liabilities
NCGA-4 *Accounting and Financial Reporting Principles for Claims and Judgments and Compensated Absences,* ¶¶ 9-14.

FASB-5 *Accounting for Contingencies,* ¶ 8.

Accounting for a Loss Contingency
NCGA-4 *Accounting and Financial Reporting Principles for Claims and Judgments and Compensated Absences,* ¶¶ 12, 15, and 16.

FASB-5 *Accounting for Contingencies,* ¶¶ 3, 8-11, and 35-38.

FASB INTERPRETATION-14 *Reasonable Estimation of the Amount of a Loss,* ¶¶ 2 and 3.

Proprietary Funds
NCGA-4 *Accounting and Financial Reporting Principles for Claims and Judgments and Compensated Absences,* ¶ 18.

Trust Funds
NCGA-4 *Accounting and Financial Reporting Principles for Claims and Judgments and Compensated Absences,* ¶ 19.

Self-Insurance Funds
NCGA-4 *Accounting and Financial Reporting Principles for Claims and Judgments and Compensated Absences,* ¶ 20.

NCGA INTERPRETATION-11 *Claim and Judgment Transactions for Governmental Funds,* ¶¶ 5 and 6.

NCGA-1 *Governmental Accounting and Financial Reporting Principles,* p. 16/ ¶ 106.

Fund Balance Designations for Loss Contingencies
NCGA-4 *Accounting and Financial Reporting Principles for Claims and Judgments and Compensated Absences,* ¶ 21.

NCGA-1 *Governmental Accounting and Financial Reporting Principles,* p. 17/ ¶¶ 118 and 120.

Termination Benefits
NCGA INTERPRETATION-8 *Certain Pension Matters,* ¶¶ 10 and 12.

FASB-74 *Accounting for Special Termination Benefits Paid to Employees,* ¶¶ 1 and 2.

APPENDIX
ACCOUNTING AND FINANCIAL REPORTING FOR RISK MANAGEMENT ACTIVITIES (DISCUSSION MEMORANDUM)

In September 1987, the GASB issued a Discussion Memorandum entitled "Accounting and Financial Reporting for Risk Management Activities" to gather comments concerning current practices and possible alternative practices for the accounting and reporting of risk management activities and losses related to property and liability insurance contracts.

The two major elements of risk management are risk control and risk financing. *Risk control* strategies attempt to minimize the likelihood of accidental losses. For example, to reduce losses arising from vehicular accidents, a city may choose to expend more funds to keep its fleet of vehicles well maintained. *Risk financing* strategies attempt to help restore the economic damages of these accidental losses.

Risk retention and risk transfer are the two elements of risk financing. In risk retention, the governmental entity assumes the risk of accidental losses, while in risk transfer, the financial risk of losses is transferred to an insurer.

In practice, there are hybrid strategies that involve both a degree of risk retention and risk transfer. For example, obtaining an insurance contract with a deductible clause involves both risk retention (the deductible amount) and risk transfer (amount in excess of the deductible). Another hybrid strategy is the creation of *pools* whereby two or more governmental entities attempt to share the financial risk of accidental losses. The Discussion Memorandum defines the following as pools:

- A *captive insurance company* is a wholly owned subsidiary created for the purpose of providing insurance coverage to the parent company or its affiliates.
- A *joint powers authority* is a separate governmental agency or entity created by two or more individual governmental entities to accomplish a specific purpose or exercise a specific power.
- A *risk retention group* is a multiple-owner captive insurer formed under the provisions of the Liability Risk Retention Act of 1986 and chartered and licensed as a liability insurance company under the laws of a state of its choice. Its primary activity consists of assuming and spreading all, or any portion, of the liability exposure of its members. Members must be (1) engaged in similar businesses or activities or (2) related in the risk of loss to

which they are exposed by virtue of any related, similar, or common business, trade, product, services, premises, or operations.

With respect to risk management and risk financing, the Discussion Memorandum raises the following fundamental questions:

- What is the most appropriate method of accounting for retained risk of loss and for risk of loss that is transferred to a public entity risk pool?
- What is the most appropriate method for recognizing and measuring claim liabilities and expenditures/expenses?
- Should the criteria of FASB-5 be supplemented or replaced for governmental entities with measurement and recognition criteria based on a concept of systematic and rational funding?
- Should the requirements of FASB-60 be applicable to public entity risk pools?
- Should the requirements of FASB-60 be applicable to individual governments that retain their risks of loss?

These issues are discussed as they apply to governmental risk pools and governmental entities other than risk pools.

Governmental Risk Pools

Governmental entities may create governmental risk pools that have many of the characteristics of a commercial insurer; that is, excess resources are invested by the pool to generate investment income that will be used to cover administrative costs and reduce premiums. Future premiums charged to participants are adjusted based on past experience, and participants benefit or suffer accordingly depending upon whether an operating surplus or deficit is incurred.

For analytical purposes, the Discussion Memorandum distinguishes between governmental risk pools in which pool participants have either transferred the risk of loss to the pool or not.

Risk of Loss Transferred by Pool Participant When a governmental entity transfers the risk of loss to a pool, the pool in some respects resembles a commercial insurer. Commercial insurers must observe the accounting and reporting standards mandated by FASB-60 (Accounting and Reporting by Insurance Enterprises). The Discussion

Memorandum raises the question of whether governmental risk pools should be required to follow (1) FASB-60, (2) some of the requirements of FASB-60, or (3) accounting and reporting standards established through a GASB statement. The accounting and reporting standards of FASB-60 are summarized below.

Investments Based on the requirements established by FASB-60, investments held by an insurance company should be reported as follows:

- Investments in common and nonredeemable preferred stocks are reported at cost.
- Investments in bonds and redeemable preferred stock expected to be held to maturity are reported at amortized cost.
- Investments in bonds and redeemable preferred stock expected to be sold before maturity are reported at market.
- Investments in mortgage loans are reported at amortized cost less an allowance for uncollectible amounts.
- Investments in real estate are reported at depreciated cost.

Those who favor the adoption of FASB-60 standards for governmental risk pools argue that the basic objective of financial reporting by risk pools and commercial insurers is the same: Financial statements should assist users in determining the present and future ability of the entity to pay liabilities as they become due.

Opponents to the adoption of FASB-60 standards argue that the basic financial reporting objective could be better satisfied if all investments were valued at market. Market valuations would, it is argued, provide a more relevant representation of the resources held by the governmental risk pool.

Unrealized investment gains and losses FASB-60 requires that unrealized gains and losses on investments measured on a market basis be reported as part of equity rather than reported on the statement of operations. Supporters argue that the statement of operations should reflect only actual transactions rather than unrealized gains and losses that arise from using a (judgmental) market valuation technique. It is also argued that this rationale is a fundamental tenet of commercial accounting and that there is no unique characteristic of a governmental risk pool that would justify a deviation from the well-established position.

Some, on the other hand, argue that unrealized gains and losses are a valid component of measuring operations for a period of time.

Decisions have been made to retain an investment and those decisions should result in rewards (unrealized gains) or punishments (unrealized losses) that are reflected on the statement of operations.

The question of presentation of unrealized gains and losses becomes even more important if the GASB decides to require that all investments be measured at market value.

Premiums related to catastrophe and shock losses Generally, property and liability insurance contracts are short-duration contracts; that is, at the end of the contract, premiums can be adjusted or coverage can be cancelled and these actions can take place after a fixed period of short duration. In addition, insurers are exposed to catastrophe and shock losses during the period of the contract. The Discussion Memorandum provides the following definitions of these losses:

- Catastrophe—A conflagration, earthquake, windstorm, explosion, or similar event resulting in substantial losses.
- Shock loss—A much larger loss than anticipated. (Usually a loss large enough to have an effect on an insurer's underwriting results.)

Catastrophe and shock losses are impossible to predict because they occur in a random fashion.

If an insurer establishes a premium schedule that provides an amount for *normal* losses and an amount for catastrophe and shock losses, a question arises as to when the premium related to the catastrophe and shock losses should be recognized as revenue. FASB-60 requires that the total premium be recognized as revenue over the life of the short-duration contract. Also, insurers recognize claims based on FASB-5 (Accounting for Contingencies). Thus, insured loss and related liability are recognized by an insurer when it is probable that the liability has been incurred and a reasonable estimate of the liability can be made.

Some argue that by observing FASB-60 for revenue recognition and FASB-5 for expense recognition, revenues and expenses are not properly matched. The revenue related to the catastrophe or shock premium is recognized in one period(s) and the loss related to the occurrence of the insured event is likely to occur in a subsequent period. An alternative would be to report the amount related to the catastrophe or shock loss premium as a deferred revenue. When the catastrophe or shock loss occurs, the related deferred revenue would be reported as revenue and there would be a proper matching with the loss recognized in the same period.

The adoption of the alternative described above, or a variation of the alternative, would introduce a significant amount of judgment into the revenue recognition process for insurers. Those opposed to this alternative raise the following question: If catastrophe and shock losses are random events not subject to prediction, how can an *unarbitrary* amount of the total premium that should be reported as unearned revenue be determined? In addition, the adoption of the alternative would introduce the concept of *income smoothing*. It is argued that variations in reported net earnings from period to period would be reduced (suggesting a reduction of risk associated with the operations of an insurer), although the fundamental nature of the business would continue to expose the insurer to significant losses from random events.

Discounting claim liabilities FASB-60 and other related pronouncements do not specifically address whether insurers' liabilities should be discounted, but FASB-60 does require disclosure if discounting is used to measure claim liabilities. Those who favor discounting note that a claim liability is often settled several years after the liability is initially recorded in the financial statements. Conceptually, this results in an overstatement of an insurer's claim liabilities. However, it is recognized that while an insurer may not explicitly use discounting to value its claim liabilities, it may implicitly discount these liabilities. For example, some suggest that insurers deliberately understate claim liabilities so that the liabilities will be reported at amounts that approximate their present value.

Those who oppose the use of discounting to value claim liabilities argue that introducing discounting adds an additional level of complexity and subjectivity to an accounting area already difficult to understand and already demands a significant amount of judgment.

If it is concluded that claim liabilities should be presented at their present value, an additional controversial question arises as to which discount rate should be used by the insurer. Possible discount rates that could be used include a settlement rate, an investment rate, or a borrowing rate. A settlement rate is the rate that could be used to settle a monetary liability with uncertain terms. The investment rate could either be an opportunity rate (possible return on invested funds) or actual rate (return on existing assets). Also, the borrowing rate could either be an opportunity rate (possible rate for borrowed funds) or actual rate (rate on existing liabilities).

Claims, Judgments, and Special Termination Benefits

Disclosure requirements The Discussion Memorandum summarizes disclosure requirements by FASB-60 as they apply to short-duration contracts as follows:

- The basis for estimating liabilities for claim adjustment expenses and unpaid claims
- The carrying amount of liabilities for unpaid claims and claim adjustment expenses on short-duration contracts that are reported at present value and the range of interest rates used to discount those liabilities
- Whether the insurance enterprise considers an anticipated investment income in determining if a premium deficiency on short-duration contracts exists
- The nature and significance of reinsurance transactions to the insurance enterprise's operations, including reinsurance premiums assumed and ceded, and estimated amounts that are recoverable from reinsurers that will be used to reduce liabilities for unpaid claims and claim adjustment expenses

Some argue that the disclosure requirements established by FASB-60 should apply to governmental risk pools so that there will be comparability with similar commercial enterprises. On the other hand, others argue that specific disclosure requirements should not be established and that the governmental risk pools themselves should determine which disclosures are most useful under the circumstances.

In addition, some question the appropriateness of certain disclosures established by SEC Industry Guide 6 (Disclosures Concerning Unpaid Claims and Claim Adjustment Expenses of Property-Casualty Insurance Underwriters).

Risk of Loss Not Transferred by Pool Participant Some governmental risk pools are formed with the risk of loss being retained by pool participants. For example, a periodic premium for each participant may be based on the actual loss experienced by each participant. In this case, some would argue that governmental risk pools should use governmental agency fund accounting to reflect the agency relationship between a participant and the pool.

Others argue that the same accounting and reporting standards should be applied to all governmental risk pools irrespective of whether the risk of loss has been transferred to the pool. If there is a difference of accounting and reporting, it is argued, that difference should be reflected by the participants and not by the pool.

Governmental Entities Other Than Pools

Some governmental entities do not form pools and therefore retain the risk of loss related to property and liability casualties. Currently, FASB-5 applies to the measurement of liabilities arising from uninsured or partially insured claims. Thus, a liability is recognized when it is probable that a claim liability has been incurred and a reasonable estimate of the claim can be made.

> **OBSERVATION:** Based on current governmental generally accepted accounting principles, only the portion of the claim liability that will consume current expendable resources is presented as a fund expenditure. The balance is presented as part of the entity's General Long-Term Debt Account Group. However, if the outstanding Exposure Draft entitled "Measurement Focus and Basis of Accounting—Governmental Funds" is adopted, the full amount of the claim liability would be reported as a fund liability and expenditure.

Those who support the continued use of FASB-5 to measure claim liabilities argue that only liabilities arising from events that have occurred should be reflected in the financial statements. Future losses (catastrophe or shock losses) should not be anticipated or presented in the financial statements.

On the other hand, others argue that FASB-5 is not appropriate in that some provision for future losses should be provided on a current basis in order to absorb future losses. Establishing a reserve of this nature would also help achieve the goal of interperiod equity in that citizens of a community suffering a catastrophe or shock loss should not be exclusively responsible for funding the unexpected loss.

The Discussion Memorandum summarizes the following approaches as possible alternatives to using FASB-5:

- Use FASB Statement 5 as the basic recognition criteria and add a provision for future catastrophe or shock losses.
- Do not use FASB Statement 5 but, instead, record an amount that is computed based on an actuarial funding method.

Both methods are more conservative than using FASB-5.

Other accounting and reporting issues related to governmental entities other than pools are summarized below.

Selection of Fund Type Currently, risk management activities are reported in a variety of funds, including the General Fund, Special Revenue Funds, Internal Service Funds, and Trust Funds. The Discussion Memorandum raises the issue of which governmental fund should be used to account for risk management activities.

Those opposed to using the General Fund argue that it is difficult to assess the funding status of the programs related to risk management activities; therefore, by using a separate governmental fund, the activities could be summarized in a single fund, providing a basis for comparing risk management activities of all governmental entities. The concept of accounting and reporting risk management activities in a single fund is further enhanced if assets are being held in trust (restricted resources) for the purpose of paying claim liabilities.

On the other hand, others raise the question of whether restricted assets are actually owned by a separate fund, since there is no agreement between the governmental entity and the claimant.

Investments The accounting issues discussed earlier with respect to investments held by governmental risk pools are also applicable to investments held by governmental entities other than risk pools that segregate resources for the purpose of paying claim liabilities.

Discounting Claim Liabilities The accounting issues discussed earlier with respect to discounting claim liabilities for governmental risk pools are also applicable to governmental entities other than risk pools.

Interfund Transactions If an Internal Service Fund is used to account for risk management activities, a question arises of how transactions between the Internal Service Fund and the other (benefited) funds should be accounted for and reported. Specifically, the Discussion Memorandum raises the following questions:

- If an Internal Service (or other) Fund recognizes claim liabilities and expenses in accordance with FASB Statement 5 but the individual funds reimburse the Internal Service (or other) Fund on an actuarial basis, should the individual funds recognize expenditures in accordance with FASB Statement 5, or may an actuarial basis be used?

- If an Internal Service (or other) Fund charges for an anticipated catastrophe or shock loss, should the individual funds recognize expenditures based on FASB Statement 5 and show the additional amount as a deferred charge, or should they report the entire amount as an expenditure? Should the Internal Service (or other) Fund report the additional amount as revenue or as deferred revenue?

The accounting issues related to these questions were discussed earlier as they affect governmental risk pools.

Also, there is disagreement as to whether the Internal Service Fund's charge to other funds is a revenue/expenditure transaction or an interfund transaction. The resolution of this issue depends, to an extent, on whether it is assumed that risk of loss has been transferred from the governmental entity to the Internal Service Fund or whether the risk of loss is retained by the governmental entity.

Other Issues

In addition to addressing accounting and reporting issues related to governmental risk pools and governmental entities other than pools discussed earlier, the Discussion Memorandum raises the following questions:

- How should expenditures be measured when payments are made to a risk pool but risk of loss has not been transferred?
- Should an expenditure and a liability be accrued in accordance with FASB Statement 5 when a claims-made insurance policy has not been renewed and tail coverage has not been purchased?
- Should an accrual, based on the criteria of FASB Statement 5, be made for possible additional premium charges in retrospectively rated insurance policies?
- How should entities account for policyholder dividends?
- What financial statement disclosure requirements are appropriate for an entity's risk management activities?
- What fund type should be used to account for activities of a governmental entity (other than a pool) providing insurance coverage to individuals or organizations that are not a part of the governmental entity?

- Should Enterprise Funds, entities accounted for in a similar manner (such as public benefit corporations and authorities, governmental utilities, and hospitals), and colleges and universities that have not transferred risk of loss to another legal entity continue to use FASB Statement 5 to recognize and measure their claim liabilities and related expenses, or should some other criteria be used?

COMPENSATED ABSENCES

NCGA-1 (Governmental Accounting and Financial Reporting Principles) notes that general long-term debt may include items that are not debt issuances *per se*. An item that can either be reported (1) as a liability of a specific governmental fund, or (2) as part of the General Long-Term Debt Account Group is an obligation that arises from compensated absences policies adopted by state and local governments. NCGA-4 (Accounting and Financial Reporting Principles for Claims and Judgments and Compensated Absences) addressed the issue by requiring that accounting and reporting standards established by FASB-43 (Accounting for Compensated Absences) be followed by state and local governments.

> ***OBSERVATION:*** *FASB-43 explicitly exempted state and local governments from the accounting and reporting standards established by the Statement. Thus, prior to the issuance of NCGA-4, governmental units could account for compensated absences in a number of ways, including the cash basis.*

Compensated Absences as Governmental Liabilities

Employee benefits may include compensation for absences that arise from situations such as vacations, holidays, and illnesses. These benefits are referred to as compensated absences and are the subject of FASB-43. FASB-43 does not apply to other employee benefit payments, such as severance or termination pay, postretirement benefits, deferred compensation, or long-term disability pay, made by state and local governments.

FASB:CS-6 (Elements of Financial Statements) defines a liability as "probable future sacrifices of economic benefits arising from a present obligation of a particular entity to transfer assets or provide services to other entities in the future as a result of past transactions or events." Compensated absences may give rise to liabilities that should be reflected in a governmental entity's financial statements. The liability may be recorded as a liability of a specific governmental fund (in essence, a current liability) when the obligation will be liquidated by the use of expendable available financial resources of the governmental fund. Alternatively, payments associated with compensated absences policies may extend over several months or years and, therefore, should be presented as part of the General Long-Term Debt Account Group.

> **OBSERVATION:** *Prior to the issuance of NCGA-4, the accounting for accumulated unused vacation and sick pay leave benefits was established by SOP 75-3 (Accrual of Revenues and Expenditures by State and Local Governmental Units). SOP 75-3 did not require an accrual for accumulated unused vacation and sick leave benefits. The nature and estimated amount of the benefits were to be disclosed in a note to the financial statements; however, no disclosure was required when the estimated amount at the end of the fiscal year did not exceed a normal year's accumulation. NCGA-4 supersedes that portion of SOP 75-3 which applies to accumulated unused vacation and sick pay leave benefits.*

Accounting for Compensated Absences

The recognition of a liability, as defined above, for compensated absences is dependent upon whether employee rights vest or accumulate. FASB-43 defines these two terms as follows:

- *Vested rights*—represent rights which the employer has an obligation to make payment even if an employee terminates; thus, they are not contingent on an employee's future service.
- *Accumulated rights*—represent rights that are earned but unused rights to compensated absences that may be carried forward to one or more periods subsequent to that in which they are earned, even though there may be a limit to the amount that can be carried forward.

Based on the characteristics of the compensated absences plan, the governmental unit must either make an accrual for the benefits or make certain disclosures with respect to the benefit plan.

Accrual of compensated absences When all of the following four conditions exist, a governmental unit must accrue a liability for employees' compensation for future absences:

- The employer's obligation relating to employees' rights to receive compensation for future absences is attributable to employees' services already rendered.

- The obligation relates to rights that vest or accumulate.
- Payment of the compensation is probable.
- The amount can be reasonably estimated.

The first of the four criteria recognizes the need to record a liability in the period in which the benefit was earned by the employee. For example, if an employee has a vested right to a three-week vacation during the second year of employment, the actual benefit is earned and should be accrued during the first year of employment subject to reductions due to expected turnover rates.

> **OBSERVATION:** *NCGA-4 and FASB-43 both use the vested or accumulated rights criterion as a basis for accrual. It should be recognized that compensated absences that do not vest or accumulate may nonetheless require accrual if they represent a liability. FASB-43 recognized this possibility when it was concluded in an appendix that "individual facts and circumstances must be considered in determining when nonvesting rights to compensated absences are earned by services rendered" (paragraph 12).*

In order for the compensated absences to be accrued the payments must be probable. FASB-5 (Accounting for Contingencies) defines probable as the "future event or events that are likely to occur."

The final criterion for accrual states that the future payments under the benefits plan must be subject to reasonable estimation. Guidance in estimating the amount of the compensated absences to be accrued can be found in FASB Interpretation-14 (Reasonable Estimation of the Amount of a Loss). This Interpretation concludes that when a range (rather than a single point estimate) for an accrual is estimated, the amount within the range with the greatest probability of occurrence should be the basis for accrual. For example, assume that the following range for possible accrual of compensated absences has been developed:

Reasonable estimate of future benefits earned under compensated absences plan	Probability of payment
$1,000,000	20%
$1,400,000	40%
$1,600,000	25%
$1,900,000	15%

Compensated Absences

The amount of accrual (either as a specific fund liability or as part of the General Long-Term Debt Account Group) should be $1,400,000. If all point estimates within the range have the same probability of occurrence, the minimum amount of the range should be accrued. In the above example, if all four point estimates had a 25% probability of occurrence, the accrual would be $1,000,000, with the disclosure of possible additional losses of $900,000.

NCGA-4 requires that the governmental unit *inventory* liabilities for compensated absences at the end of each accounting period and prepare an adjustment based on current salary costs. Thus, accruals made in prior years would have to be increased to reflect increases in the annual compensation base of employees.

When the amount of the accrual for compensated absences has been determined, the actual accrual will be reflected either as a liability of a specific governmental fund or as part of the General Long-Term Debt Account Group. The amount to be reflected as a specific governmental fund liability is the portion of the accrual that will be liquidated with expendable available financial resources. To illustrate the accounting for compensated absences, assume that the estimated accrual at the end of the period is $300,000, of which $50,000 is expected to be paid from expendable available financial resources of the General Fund. The following entries would be made to record the accrual:

GENERAL FUND
Expenditures—Compensated Absences   50,000
    Estimated Liability For Compensated
      Absences   50,000

GENERAL LONG-TERM DEBT ACCOUNT GROUP
Amount To Be Provided For Payment
    Of Compensated Absences   250,000
    Estimated Liability For Compensated
      Absences   250,000

The accrual for compensated absences may be disclosed on the face of the financial statements or in notes to the financial statements in the following manner:

Expenditures:
    Compensated absences ($300,000 [total amount determined for the year under NCGA-4] less $250,000 [recorded as long-term obligations]) $50,000

> **OBSERVATION:** *The above disclosure is not mandated by NCGA-4; however, the disclosure is similar to the disclosure requirements established for claims and judgments by the very same Statement.*

An example of a note to the financial statements describing the nature and amount of the accrual of compensated absences is presented below:

▶ Accumulated unpaid vacation and sick pay are accrued when incurred in the proprietary funds. Only the current portion of the unpaid sick pay benefits is accrued in the governmental funds. The long-term portion of the unpaid sick pay and all the unpaid vacation pay are reported in the General Long-Term Debt Account Group. The current portion of the unpaid sick pay is the accumulation, as described below, for those employees who have reached retirement age. The methods of accrual are in accordance with NCGA-4.

Employees may accumulate sick leave without limitation as to the number of hours of accumulation. However, the maximum accumulation of vacation leave is limited to the number of hours accruable during two years. Employees are paid 100% of their accumulated vacation pay when they terminate their employment for any reason. Accumulated sick pay is paid only under the following conditions: (a) 50% to 55% (depending on employee's classification) of the total accumulation is paid upon retirement or death; (b) 50% of the accumulation in excess of 120 days is paid for full-time employees terminated for any other reason after 10 full years of continuous service.

The amount of the accrued sick pay and vacation pay is as follows:

	Current portion	Long-term portion
Governmental funds	$1,750,000	$8,785,000
Proprietary funds	$ 125,000	$ 910,000

◀

> **OBSERVATION:** *FASB-43 did not address the issue of whether the gross amount or the present value of the estimated liability for compensated absences should be accrued. Presumably both approaches are acceptable.*

Nonaccrual of compensated absences When all of the criteria for accrual, as listed earlier, do not exist, there is no accrual for compensated absences. If all of the criteria exist, except for the fourth criterion (subject to reasonable estimation), that fact must be disclosed in the financial statements. Examples of nonvesting rights to compensated absences that often do not accumulate and therefore are not accrued include benefits for jury duty and military leave.

Accumulated Sick Pay Benefits

There is one exception to the general rule of accrual for compensated absences. Even if the four criteria exist, FASB-43 states that an entity is not required to accrue a liability for "nonvesting accumulating rights to receive sick pay benefits" (compensation for absences due to illness). Thus, a governmental entity is free to either accrue or ignore the estimated liability that arises from nonvesting accumulating sick pay benefits. Once a specific method of accounting is adopted, it must be applied consistently from period to period.

> **OBSERVATION:** *It should be noted that because there are acceptable alternative accounting methods for accounting for nonvesting accumulating sick pay benefits, the method selected must be disclosed as part of the "Summary of Significant Accounting Policies" as required by APB-22 (Disclosure of Accounting Policies).*

The stated reason that FASB-43 does not require (but does not prohibit) the accrual of nonvesting accumulating sick pay benefits is to "minimize the estimating burden" that is needed to implement the Statement.

> **OBSERVATION:** *Apparently, there was another reason for the exception. Two members of the FASB dissented to the exception because they believed sick pay benefits are part of compensation when, and only when, the employee becomes sick, not when the employee accumulated the sick pay benefits.*

Sick pay benefits must be the result of actual illness in order for the exception to apply. In some circumstances, sick pay benefits may be routinely allowed by the employer when the employee is not ill, or the employee may be allowed to take compensated *terminal leave* prior to retirement. Benefits of this nature are subject to accrual if the four criteria discussed earlier exist.

Proprietary Funds

NCGA-4 requires that Enterprise Funds and Internal Service Funds follow FASB-43 without modification in accounting for compensated absences.

Trust Funds

Expendable Trust Funds use the same accounting basis (modified accrual) that apply to governmental fund types, while Nonexpendable Trust Funds and proprietary funds use a similar accounting basis (accrual basis). As discussed in this chapter, Expendable Trust Funds should account for compensated absences in a manner consistent with FASB-43 as modified by NCGA-4. Nonexpendable Trust Funds and Pension Trust Funds should apply FASB-43 without modification to account for compensated absences.

LITERATURE REFERENCES

Material in this chapter is based on the following authoritative pronouncements, which are grouped according to the major headings used within the chapter. A dual reference (both paragraph and page number) is used for NCGA-1 and NCGA-2 because the original pronouncements do not use paragraph numbers.

Introduction
NCGA-1 *Governmental Accounting and Financial Reporting Principles,* p. 9/ ¶ 43.
NCGA-4 *Accounting and Financial Reporting Principles for Claims and Judgments and Compensated Absences,* ¶ 23.

Compensated Absences as Governmental Liabilities
FASB-43 *Accounting for Compensated Absences,* ¶¶ 1 and 2.
FASB:CS-6 *Elements of Financial Statements,* ¶ 35.
NCGA-4 *Accounting and Financial Reporting Principles for Claims and Judgments and Compensated Absences,* ¶ 7.

Accounting for Compensated Absences
FASB-43 *Accounting for Compensated Absences,* ¶ 6.
NCGA-4 *Accounting and Financial Reporting Principles for Claims and Judgments and Compensated Absences,* ¶¶ 16, 22, and 24-26.
FASB-5 *Accounting for Contingencies,* ¶ 3.

Compensated Absences

FASB INTERPRETATION-14   *Reasonable Estimation of the Amount of a Loss,* ¶ 3.

Accumulated Sick Pay Benefits
FASB-43   *Accounting for Compensated Absences,* ¶¶ 7 and 17.
APB-22   *Disclosure of Accounting Policies,* ¶ 12.

Proprietary Funds
NCGA-4   *Accounting and Financial Reporting Principles for Claims and Judgments and Compensated Absences,* ¶ 27.

Trust Funds
NCGA-4   *Accounting and Financial Reporting Principles for Claims and Judgments and Compensated Absences,* ¶ 28.

LEASES

Liabilities and assets of a long-term nature that are not specifically related to proprietary funds or certain trust funds are recorded in a governmental reporting entity's General Long-Term Debt Account Group and General Fixed Assets Account Group. These two account groups may include long-term debt that does not arise from the issuance of actual debt instruments and long-term assets that are not legally owned by the governmental unit.

As discussed in this chapter, certain leases may be, in part, accounted for in the governmental unit's account groups. NCGA-5 (Accounting and Financial Reporting Principles for Lease Agreements of State and Local Governments) requires that governmental funds follow the accounting and reporting standards established by FASB-13 (Accounting for Leases, as amended), with appropriate modifications to reflect the distinguishing characteristics of governmental accounting.

A governmental unit may enter into a lease agreement either as a lessee or lessor. The first part of this chapter addresses the accounting issues of the lessee.

LESSEE ACCOUNTING

A lease agreement conveys property rights to the lessee for a specific period of time. Although actual title to the property is not transferred to the lessee, a lease agreement must be evaluated to determine whether the transaction should be treated as an *in-substance purchase*. From the lessee's perspective, the lease may be classified as a capital lease or an operating lease.

Capital Leases

A lease agreement is classified as a capital lease (in-substance purchase) when substantially all of the risks and benefits of ownership are assumed by the lessee. A capital lease is, for the most part, viewed as an installment purchase of property rather than the rental of property.

FASB-13 requires that a lease be capitalized if any one of the following four criteria is a characteristic of the lease transaction:

Criterion #

I   The lease transfers ownership of the property to the lessee by the end of the lease term.

II   The lease contains a bargain purchase option.

III   The lease term is equal to 75 percent or more of the estimated economic life of the leased property. However, if the beginning of the lease term falls within the last 25 percent of the total estimated economic life of the leased property, including earlier years of use, this criterion shall not be used for purposes of classifying the lease.

IV   The present value at the beginning of the lease term of the minimum lease payments, excluding that portion of the payments representing executory costs, to be paid by the lessor, including any profit thereon, equals or exceeds 90 percent of the excess of the fair value of the leased property to the lessor at the inception of the lease over any related investment tax credit retained by the lessor and expected to be realized by him. However, if the beginning of the lease term falls within the last 25 percent of the total estimated economic life of the leased property, including earlier years of use, this criterion shall not be used for purposes of classifying the lease.

A bargain purchase option exists when the lessee can exercise a provision in the lease and buy the property sometime during the term of the lease at an amount substantially less than the estimated fair value of the property. Judgment must be used in determining whether the purchase option price will be a bargain price at the option date. If there is reasonable assurance at the inception of the lease that the purchase option will be exercised, the option is considered a bargain purchase option.

Lease payments include the minimum rental payments based on the term of the lease, exclusive of executory costs, such as payments for insurance and property taxes. Contingent rental payments are not included as part of the lease payments unless they are based on an existing index or rate, such as the prime interest rate. The lease payments include any residual value guaranteed by the lessee (or related party) at the end of the term of the lease. Also, any penalty payment that must be made because of a failure to renew or extend the lease is considered a lease payment.

> **OBSERVATION:** *When the lease contains a bargain purchase option, the minimum lease payments include only (1) the minimum rental payments over the term of the lease and (2) the bargain purchase option.*

FASB-13 defines the lease term as the fixed noncancelable term of the lease plus the following periods, if applicable:

- Periods for which failure to renew the lease imposes a penalty on the lessee in an amount such that at the inception of the lease renewal appears to be reasonably assured
- Periods covered by a bargain renewal option
- Periods covered by ordinary renewal options during which a guarantee by the lessee of the lessor's debt related to the leased property is expected to be in effect
- Periods covered by ordinary renewal options preceding the date as of which a bargain purchase is exercisable
- Periods that represent renewals or extensions of the lease at the lessor's option (however, the lease term cannot extend beyond the date of a bargain purchase option)

In determining the present value of the lease payments, the lessee should use its incremental borrowing rate. However, the lessee should use the lessor's implicit interest rate to determine the present value of the lease payments if:

1. The lessee can determine the lessor's implicit interest rate and
2. The lessor's implicit interest rate is less than the lessee's incremental borrowing rate.

The lessee incremental borrowing rate is the estimated interest rate the lessee would have had to pay if the leased property had been purchased by the lessee and financed over the period covered by the lease.

Recording a Capital Lease A state or local government should record a capital lease at an amount equal to the present value of the

Leases

minimum lease payments; however, the amount recorded cannot exceed the fair value of the leased property. Because general fixed assets do not represent current financial resources available for appropriation and expenditure, the property rights capitalized should be reported as part of the governmental unit's General Fixed Assets Account Group. Likewise, the long-term obligation created by the capitalized lease does not require the use of current financial resources, and therefore should be reported as part of the General Long-Term Debt Account Group. In addition, NCGA-5 concludes that when the capitalized lease represents the purchase or construction of general fixed assets, the transaction should be shown as an expenditure and other financing sources in a governmental fund. There is no need to account for the capital lease in a separately created Debt Service Fund or Capital Projects Fund unless these funds are legally mandated. A Debt Service Fund would be used when resources are being accumulated for payment of the lease payments in future periods.

To illustrate the accounting for a capital lease, assume that equipment is leased for a five-year period, which is the economic life of the equipment. The lease is signed on June 30, 19X1, and beginning on this date, five annual payments of $50,000 will be made. The governmental unit's incremental borrowing rate (and the lessor's implicit interest rate) is 10%, and the fair value of the property is $208,493 at the inception of the lease. The present value of the minimum lease payments is also $208,493, as shown below:

Annual lease payments	$ 50,000
Present value of an annuity due, interest rate is 10% and the number of periods is 5	× 4.16986
Present value of minimum lease payments	$208,493

The capitalized lease would be recorded as follows in the account groups and the General Fund, assuming no separate Debt Service Fund or Capital Projects Fund is used to account for the transaction:

GENERAL FIXED ASSETS ACCOUNT GROUP
Assets Under Capital Leases	208,493	
Investment In General Fixed Assets—		
Capital Leases—General Fund		208,493

GENERAL LONG-TERM DEBT ACCOUNT GROUP

Amount To Be Provided For Lease Payments	208,493	
Obligations Under Capital Lease Agreements		208,493
Obligations Under Capital Lease Agreements	50,000	
Amount To Be Provided For Lease Payment		50,000

GENERAL FUND

Expenditures—Capitalized Leases	208,493	
Other Financing Sources— Capitalized Leases		208,493
Expenditures—Capital Lease Principal Payment	50,000	
Cash (Vouchers Payable)		50,000

In subsequent periods, the lease payments are recorded as expenditures of the fund from which the lease payment is made. If the expenditure is recorded by object classes (as described in NCGA-1, page 17/paragraph 116), an amortization schedule must be prepared to distinguish the principal and interest portions of the lease payment. An amortization schedule based on the example discussed above is presented below:

Amortization Schedule

Date	Lease payment	Interest expenditure @ 10%	Principal expenditure	Amount of general long-term debt
6/30/X1				$208,493
6/30/X1	$50,000		$50,000	158,493
6/30/X2	50,000	$15,849	34,151	124,342
6/30/X3	50,000	12,434	37,566	86,776
6/30/X4	50,000	8,678	41,322	45,454
6/30/X5	50,000	4,546	45,454	-0-

The second lease payment (6/30/X2) would be recorded in the following manner:

Leases

GENERAL LONG-TERM DEBT ACCOUNT GROUP
Obligations Under Capital Lease
　Agreements　　　　　　　　　　　　　　34,151
　　Amount To Be Provided For Lease
　　　Payments　　　　　　　　　　　　　　　　　　　34,151

GENERAL FUND
Expenditures—Capital Lease Principal
　Payments　　　　　　　　　　　　　　34,151
Expenditures—Capital Lease Interest
　Payments　　　　　　　　　　　　　　15,849
　　Cash (Vouchers Payable)　　　　　　　　　　　50,000

If the lease payments are to be paid from a Debt Service Fund, any transfers from the General Fund to the Debt Service Fund are treated as operating transfers and not as expenditures of the General Fund.

Depreciation NCGA-1 precludes the recognition of depreciation as an expense in a governmental fund, because depreciation is neither a source nor a use of financial resources of the governmental unit. Accumulated depreciation may be recognized in the General Fixed Assets Account Group, but the recognition of depreciation is strictly optional.

If depreciation is recorded in the General Fixed Assets Account Group, and either Criterion I or Criterion II (as discussed earlier) of the lease capitalization criteria is met, the governmental unit's normal depreciation policies for owned assets should be followed. When Criterion I and Criterion II are not met, the normal depreciation policies should be followed, but the amortization period should be the lease term and not the economic life of the leased property.

To return to the original example, assume that the governmental unit does account for accumulated depreciation in its General Fixed Assets Account Group and uses the straight-line depreciation method. Since the lease does not contain a clause that either transfers ownership of the property (Criterion I) or allows for the purchase of the asset at a bargain purchase price (Criterion II), the equipment must be depreciated over the five-year period covered by the lease (in the example, the life of the lease is the same as the economic life of the property). Depreciation would be recorded by making the following entry:

GENERAL FIXED ASSETS ACCOUNT GROUP
Investment In General Fixed Assets—
  Capital Leases—General Fund   41,699
    Accumulated Depreciation—Assets
      Under Capital Leases
      ($208,493/5 years)   41,699

Contingent rentals In general, contingent rental amounts are not used to determine minimum lease payments that are to be capitalized. For example, the following amounts are not part of minimum lease payments:

- Escalation of minimum lease payments due to increases in construction or acquisition cost of leased property
- Escalation of minimum lease payments due to increases in some measure of cost or value during the construction or preconstruction period
- Lease payments that are based on future use of the property (such as number of machine hours)

When the lease payments are based on an existing index or rate (such as the consumer price index), the estimated future lease payments should be included in the minimum lease payments using the position of the index or rate at the inception of the lease. Subsequent changes in the rental payments are contingent rentals and should be accrued as the index or rate changes.

Increases or decreases in lease payments due to the mere passage of time are not contingent rental payments and must be included as part of the minimum lease payments.

To illustrate the accounting for contingent rentals, assume a governmental unit signs a 10-year lease agreement for which annual payments are to be $300,000 plus or minus $5,000 for each percentage point that the average prime interest rate exceeds or is less than 6%. If the prime interest rate is 7% at the inception of the lease, the minimum lease payments to be capitalized are $305,000 ($300,000 + $5,000). If the actual prime interest rate is 10% during the second year of the lease, the additional $15,000 is treated as an expenditure of the second period (assuming the payment will be made from current available financial resources).

Fiscal Funding Clauses Noncancellation is a precondition to the capitalization of a lease. In general, a lease subject to cancellation cannot be capitalized; however, if the lease is subject to cancellation

Leases

based on the occurrence of a *remote* event, the lease may be capitalized if one of the four capitalization criteria is met.

A lease with a governmental unit may contain a clause stating that the lease is cancelable if the governmental unit does not appropriate the funds necessary to make the required lease payments during the budgeting period. FASB:TB 79-10 (Fiscal Funding Clauses in Lease Agreements) draws the following conclusion with respect to the existence of fiscal funding clauses in lease agreements:

> The existence of a fiscal funding clause in a lease agreement would necessitate an assessment of the likelihood of lease cancellation through exercise of the fiscal funding clause. If the likelihood of exercise of the fiscal funding clause is assessed as being remote, a lease agreement containing such a clause would be considered a noncancelable lease; otherwise, the lease would be considered cancelable and thus classified as an operating lease.

Disclosures—Capital Leases NCGA-5 requires that the disclosure standards established by FASB-13 must be observed with respect to lease agreements. Accordingly, the following information for capital leases must be disclosed in a state or local government's financial statements:

- The gross amount of assets recorded under capital leases as of the date of each balance sheet presented by major classes according to nature or function. This information may be combined with the comparable information for owned assets.
- Future minimum lease payments as of the date of the latest balance sheet presented, in the aggregate and for each of the five succeeding fiscal years, with separate deductions from the total for the amount representing executory costs, including any profit thereon, included in the minimum lease payments and for the amount of the imputed interest necessary to reduce the net minimum lease payments to present value.
- The total of minimum sublease rentals to be received in the future under noncancelable subleases as of the date of the latest balance sheet presented.
- Total contingent rentals actually incurred for each period for which an operating statement is presented.
- Assets recorded under capital leases and the accumulated amortization (if the governmental unit decides to amortize the capital lease) thereon shall be separately identified in the General Fixed Assets Account Group as obligations under capital leases.

In addition to the above disclosures, there should be a general description of the lease agreement including such items as the existence of renewal or purchase options, and restrictions imposed by the lease agreement.

Presented below is an example of a note to the financial statements describing capitalized lease agreements:

▶ The City is obligated under certain leases accounted for as capital leases. The leased assets and related obligations are accounted for in the General Fixed Assets Account Group and the General Long-Term Debt Account Group, respectively. Assets under capital leases totaled $10,000,000 at June 30, 19X1, and accumulated amortization on those assets totaled $3,500,000. The following is a schedule of future minimum lease payments under capital leases, together with the net present value of the minimum lease payments as of June 30, 19X1.

Year ending June 30	General long-term debt account group
19X2	$100,000
19X3	95,000
19X4	95,000
19X5	80,000
19X6	60,000
Later years	170,000
Minimum lease payments for all capital leases	600,000
Less: Amount representing interest at the City's incremental borrowing rate of interest	90,000
Present value of minimum lease payments	$510,000

◀

Operating Leases

When a lease does not satisfy any one of the four capitalization criteria, the agreement gives rise to an operating lease. An operating lease does not require that the minimum lease payments be capitalized. Thus, neither an asset nor a liability is recorded at the inception of the lease in the governmental unit's account groups. The rental expenditures are recognized as they become payable.

Leases

To illustrate the accounting for an operating lease, assume that in the earlier example the lease agreement was classified as an operating lease. At the inception of the lease (June 30, 19X1), the lease would be recorded as follows:

GENERAL FUND
Expenditures—Rent 50,000
    Cash (Vouchers Payable) 50,000

FASB-13 requires that the following information be disclosed for operating leases:

Noncancelable operating leases (remaining lease term exceeds 1 year)

- Future minimum rental payments required as of the date of the latest balance sheet presented, in the aggregate and for each of the five succeeding fiscal years
- The total of minimum rentals to be received in the future under noncancelable subleases as of the date of the latest balance sheet presented

All other operating leases (remaining lease term exceeds 1 month)

- Amount of rental expenditure for each operating statement presented
- Separate identification of minimum rentals, contingent rentals, and sublease rentals.

Presented below is an example of a note to the financial statements describing a governmental unit's operating leases:

▶ The City is obligated under certain leases accounted for as operating leases. Operating leases do not give rise to property rights or lease obligations, and therefore the results of the lease agreements are not reflected in the City's account groups.
The following is a schedule by years of future minimum rental payments required under operating leases that have initial or remaining noncancelable lease terms in excess of one year as of June 30, 19X1:

Year ending June 30	Amounts
19X2	$ 20,000
19X3	18,000
19X4	18,000
19X5	15,000
19X6	10,000
Later years	45,000
Total minimum payments required	$126,000

The following schedule shows the composition of total rental expenditures for all operating leases except those with terms of a month or less that were not renewed:

	Year ending June 30	
	19X1	19X0
Minimum rentals	$15,000	$22,000
Contingent rentals	17,000	12,000
Less: Sublease rentals	(4,000)	(2,000)
	$28,000	$32,000

LESSOR ACCOUNTING

When a governmental unit is the lessor in a lease agreement, the agreement must be reviewed to determine whether the transaction should be treated as an *in-substance* sale of the property. From the lessor's perspective, the lease may be classified as a direct financing lease or an operating lease.

Direct Financing Lease

A direct financing lease transfers substantially all of the risks and benefits of ownership from the lessor to the lessee. In a direct financing lease, the lessor simply finances the *in-substance* purchase of the property by the lessee.

FASB-13 requires that a lease be classified as a direct financing lease when (1) any one of the four capitalization criteria (as discussed earlier) used to define a capital lease for the lessee is met, and (2) both of the following criteria are satisfied:

- Collectibility of the minimum lease payments is reasonably predictable.
- No important uncertainties surround the amount of the unreimbursable costs yet to be incurred by the lessor under the lease.

Minimum lease payments are considered collectible even though it may be necessary to estimate them based on past experience with uncollectible amounts from specific groupings of similar receivables.

An important uncertainty with respect to unreimbursed future costs is an indication that the risks of ownership have not been transferred to the lessee. For example, if the lessor guarantees to replace obsolete property, the lease should not be treated as a direct financing lease. On the other hand, if the lessor is responsible for executory costs that may vary in future periods, this uncertainty alone does not preclude classifying the lease as a direct financing lease.

The lessor's minimum lease payments are the same as the lessee's minimum lease payments plus any (1) residual values, or (2) rental payments guaranteed by a third party not related to the lessor or lessee. In determining the present value of the minimum lease payments, the lessor should use its implicit interest rate. FASB-13 defines implicit interest as follows:

> The discount rate that, when applied to (a) the minimum lease payments, excluding that portion of the payments representing executory costs to be paid by the lessor, together with any profit thereon, and (b) the unguaranteed residual value accruing to the benefit of the lessor causes the aggregate present value of the beginning of the lease term to be equal to the fair value of the leased property to the lessor at the inception of the lease, minus any investment tax credit retained by the lessor and expected to be realized by him.

Recording a Direct Financing Lease   A governmental unit should record as a lease receivable (or gross investment) the total minimum lease payments plus the unguaranteed residual value of the leased property. NCGA-5 concludes that "only the portion of the lease receivable that represents revenue/other financing sources that are measurable and available" is to be reflected in the current Statement of Revenues and Expenditures as revenue/other financing sources. Measurable refers to the ability to estimate the amount of the lease payment that will actually be collected from the lessee. Available means that the cash flow must be collected during the current accounting period or shortly after the end of the period but in time to pay liabilities of the current period.

> **OBSERVATION:** *The measurability criterion should have been met when the decision was made to treat the lease as a direct financing lease, since one of the conditions established by FASB-13 refers to collectibility (see earlier discussion). The availability criterion is not specifically addressed by NCGA-5 but, perhaps, a useful guide can be found in NCGA Interpretation-3 (Revenue Recognition—Property Taxes), which concludes that property taxes can be accrued when they are expected to be realized within sixty days after the close of the fiscal year.*

The carrying value of the leased property should be removed from the General Fixed Assets Account Group because in the direct financing lease assumption the transaction is treated as an in-substance sale of the property. In a direct financing lease, the difference between the total lease receivable and the carrying value of the leased property represents unearned interest income. The unearned interest income is amortized over the term of the lease using the effective interest method. The earned interest income is recognized only when the measurable and available criteria are satisfied.

Accounting for a direct financing lease can be illustrated by referring to the earlier example used to demonstrate the accounting for a lessee's capital lease. The total amount of the lease receivable is recorded as follows, assuming the payments under the lease will be available to the General Fund:

GENERAL FUND
Lease Payments Receivable		
($50,000 × 4 years)	200,000	
Cash	50,000	
Deferred Revenue—Lease Principal		
Payments		158,493
Deferred Revenue—Lease Interest		
Payments		41,507
Other Financing Sources—Lease		
Principal Payments		50,000

> **OBSERVATION:** *The deferred revenue—lease principal payments amount is reported as a liability amount. The deferred revenue—lease interest payments is a contra asset amount to be offset against the lease payments receivable amount.*

The amount of the last four lease payments ($200,000) is deferred because they are not available financial resources. They are divided be-

Leases

tween other financing sources (principal repayments), and interest revenue based on the amortization schedule presented earlier. The four remaining payments, based on the original amortization schedule, are summarized below:

	Lease payments applicable to		
Date	Interest	Principal	Total
6/30/X2	$15,849	$ 34,151	$ 50,000
6/30/X3	12,434	37,566	50,000
6/30/X4	8,678	41,322	50,000
6/30/X5	4,546	45,454	50,000
	$41,507	$158,493	$200,000

In addition, assuming the leased property had a carrying value of $208,493, the following entry would be made in the General Fixed Assets Account Group:

GENERAL FIXED ASSETS ACCOUNT GROUP
Investment In General Fixed Assets   208,493
     Equipment   208,493

As payments are collected, the receivable account is reduced and the appropriate revenue and other financing sources amounts are recognized. For example, the following entries would be made to record the second lease payment on June 30, 19X2:

GENERAL FUND
Cash   50,000
     Lease Payments Receivable   50,000

Deferred Revenue—Lease Principal
   Payments   34,151
Deferred Revenue—Lease Interest
   Payments   15,849
     Other Financing Sources—
       Lease Principal Payments   34,151
     Interest Revenue   15,849

Bad debts If a state or local government executes several leases that are accounted for as direct financing leases, it may be necessary to provide an estimate for uncollectible payments. Because the governmental accounting model is based on the modified accrual basis, the use of a bad debts expense account is inappropriate; however, an allowance account is established by reducing the amount of deferred revenue initially recognized when the direct financing lease was recorded. (If a portion of the lease receivable has been recognized as earned at the end of the period based on the measurable and available criteria, revenue would be debited instead of deferred revenue.) To return to the original illustration, assume that it is estimated that 5% of the total lease payments receivable will not be paid. To implicitly recognize the bad debts element of the transaction, the following entry would be made:

GENERAL FUND

Deferred Revenue—Lease Principal Payments	10,000	
Allowance For Doubtful Accounts— Lease Payment Receivable ($200,000 × 5%)		10,000

The allowance amount is a contra asset amount that is presented as a reduction to the lease payments receivable amount.

Initial direct costs Costs that are directly related to the negotiation and consumation of the lease are referred to as initial direct costs and include such expenditures as legal fees, cost of credit investigation, and commissions. A provision for bad debts related to lease payments is not considered an initial direct cost. Initial direct costs should be recognized as expenditures when incurred, and an equal amount of unearned revenue should be recognized in the same period. For example, in the previous illustration if the initial direct costs were $6,500, the following entries would be made:

GENERAL FUND

Expenditures—Initial Direct Cost Of Leases	6,500	
Cash (Vouchers Payable)		6,500
Deferred Revenue—Lease Interest Payments	6,500	
Other Financing Sources—Lease Payments		6,500

The implicit interest rate used by the lessor should be computed after deducting the amount of initial direct costs. (Thus, in the current example, the implicit interest rate would be less than 10%.)

Leases

Contingent rentals As noted earlier, contingent rentals are generally not included in the lessee's minimum lease payments. Contingent rentals are recognized by the lessor as other financing sources when they become measurable and available.

Disclosures—Direct Financing Leases State and local governments should make the following disclosures in their financial statements with respect to direct financing leases:

- The components of the net investment in direct financing leases as of the date of each balance sheet presented:
  — Future minimum lease payments to be received, with separate deductions for (1) amounts representing executory costs, including any profit thereon, included in the minimum lease payments, and (2) the accumulated allowance for uncollectible minimum lease payments receivable.
  — The unguaranteed residual values accruing to the benefit of the lessor.
  — Unearned income.
- Future minimum lease payments to be received for each of the five succeeding fiscal years as of the date of the latest balance sheet presented.
- The amount of unearned income included in the activity statement to offset initial direct costs charged against revenue for each period for which an activity statement is presented.
- Total contingent rentals included in revenue for each period for which an activity statement is presented.

In addition, there should be a general description of the direct financing lease agreements.

Presented below is an example of a note to the financial statements describing a governmental unit's direct financing lease operations.

▶ The City's leasing operations consist exclusively of leasing various computer units and support equipment that were purchased in previous years but are no longer used. These leases are classified as direct financing leases and expire at various intervals over the next seven years.

The following lists the components of the net investment in direct financing leases as of June 30:

	19X2	19X1
Total minimum lease payments to be received	$450,000	$520,000
Less: Amounts representing estimated executory costs	(5,000)	(7,000)
Minimum lease payments receivable	445,000	513,000
Less: Allowance for uncollectibles	(40,000)	(43,000)
Net minimum lease payments receivable	405,000	470,000
Estimated residual values of leased property	15,000	20,000
	420,000	490,000
Less: Unearned income	(105,000)	(125,000)
Net investment in direct financing leases	$315,000	$365,000

Minimum lease payments do not include contingent rentals which may be received as stipulated in the lease contracts. These contingent rental payments occur only if the use of the equipment exceeds a certain level of activity each year. Contingent rentals amounted to $12,000 in 19X2 and $18,000 in 19X1. At June 30, 19X2, minimum lease payments for each of the five succeeding fiscal years are as follows:

Year	Amount
19X3	$80,000
19X4	$80,000
19X5	$75,000
19X6	$70,000
19X7	$65,000

◀

OBSERVATION: *In most in-substance sale lease agreements, a governmental unit would account for the transaction as a direct financing lease since the governmental unit is seldom involved in a lease agreement that gives rise to a manufacturer's or dealer's profit. However, a sales-type lease may occur even when the lessor is not a manufacturer or dealer. FASB-13 notes that a sales-type lease arises when the lessor realizes a profit or loss on the lease transaction. This would occur when the fair value of the lease property (at the inception of the lease) is greater or less than the carrying value of the property. For a governmental unit, the accounting for a sales-type lease is essentially the same as the accounting for a direct financing lease since no profit or loss is recognized when the lease is recorded.*

Operating Leases

When a lease agreement does not satisfy at least one of the four common criteria (common to both lessee and lessor accounting), or both of the unique criteria for a lessor (collectibility and no uncertain reimbursable costs), the lease is classified as an operating lease. In an operating lease there is no simulated sale and the lessor simply records rent revenues as they become measurable and available. In addition, the leased property is not removed from the General Fixed Assets Account Group.

To illustrate the accounting for an operating lease by a lessor, assume that in the earlier example the lease agreement was classified as an operating lease. At the inception of the lease (June 30, 19X1), the first lease payment would be recorded as follows:

GENERAL FUND
Cash	50,000	
Revenue—Rent		50,000

FASB-13 concludes that rent revenue receipts that vary in amount over the life of the lease should be recognized on a straight line basis, unless "another systematic and rational basis is more representative of the time pattern in which use benefit from the leased property is diminished." If the rent payments are greater in the earlier life of the lease, part of the payment must be deferred. To illustrate, assume that a three-year lease agreement provides for rent payments of $15,000, $13,000, and $8,000 over the three-year period. The operating lease would be accounted for in the following manner:

Year 1:
Cash	15,000	
Revenue—Rent		12,000
Deferred Revenue—Rent		3,000

Year 2:
Cash	13,000	
Revenue—Rent		12,000
Deferred Revenue—Rent		1,000

Year 3:
Cash	8,000	
Deferred Revenue—Rent	4,000	
Revenue—Rent		12,000

OBSERVATION: *In most instances uneven lease payments will be characterized by higher payments in the early part of the lease. However, if the payments in the early part of the lease are not smaller, the straight line revenue recognition method cannot be used because the accrued rent does not meet the availability criterion.*

For operating leases, initial direct costs should be recognized as an expenditure when incurred. Unlike similar costs for commercial enterprises, these costs cannot be capitalized and amortized over the life of the lease.

When a governmental unit has operating leases, there must be a disclosure in the financial statements describing the general characteristics of the lease agreements. In addition, the following disclosures must be made:

- The cost and carrying amount, if different, of property on lease or held for leasing by major classes of property according to nature or function; and the amount of accumulated depreciation in total as of the date of the latest balance sheet presented (the recognition of accumulated depreciation is optional for governmental entities).
- Minimum future rentals on noncancelable leases as of the date of the latest balance sheet presented, in the aggregate and for each of the five succeeding fiscal years.
- Total contingent rentals included in income for each period for which an activity statement is presented.

Presented below is an example of a note to the financial statements of a governmental unit in which operating leases are described.

▶ The following schedule provides an analysis of the City's investment in property on operating leases and property held for lease by major classes as of June 30, 19X1:

Microcomputers	$127,000
Peripheral computer equipment	15,000
Other	3,000
	145,000
Less: Accumulated depreciation as reflected in the General Fixed Assets Account Group	(22,000)
	$123,000

The following is a schedule by years of minimum future rentals on noncancelable operating leases as of June 30, 19X1:

Year ending June 30	
19X2	$12,000
19X3	11,000
19X4	8,000
19X5	5,000
19X6	4,000
Later years	15,000
Total minimum future rentals	$55,000

Minimum future rentals do not include contingent rentals which may be received as stipulated in the lease contracts. These contingent rental payments occur only if the use of the equipment exceeds a certain level of activity each year. Contingent rentals amounted to $2,000 in 19X2 and $3,000 in 19X1. ◄

RELATED PARTIES

FASB-13 concludes that leases between related parties should be evaluated in the same manner as leases between unrelated parties. Specifically, the common criteria (for lessees and lessors) and the unique criteria (for lessor only) should be used to determine whether a lease transaction should be treated as an in-substance purchase or sale of the leased property. However, if it is obvious that the relationship of the parties has significantly affected the terms of the agreement, the accounting treatment must be modified to reflect the substance, rather than the form, of the agreement.

A governmental related-party transaction may arise between a state or local government and a public authority. A public authority is created to raise funds through the issuance of debt, the proceeds of which will be used to purchase or construct fixed assets. These assets may be leased by the public authority to the state or local government with title passing to the governmental unit at the end of the lease term.

The accounting treatment of a lease between a state or local government and a public authority is dependent upon whether the public authority is part of the overall governmental reporting entity. NCGA-7 (Financial Reporting for Component Units Within the Governmental Reporting Entity) defines the reporting entity as the oversight unit and all related component units that are combined to constitute the governmental reporting entity. When the state or local government's elected officials can exercise oversight responsibility over the public authority, the public authority is considered to be part of the reporting entity.

If the public authority is considered to be part of the reporting entity, the lease classification criteria established by FASB-13 are not applied. The financial statement of the public authority appropriately reflects its fixed assets and long-term debt related to the leased property, and these financial statements are simply combined with the state or local government's financial statements.

On the other hand, when the public authority is not considered to be part of the overall reporting entity, FASB-13 must be used to classify the lease. Specifically, the criteria are applied to determine whether the state or local government should capitalize the lease, and whether the public authority should treat the lease as a direct financing lease.

Finally (as required in general by FASB-13), the nature and extent of the leasing agreement between a state or local government and a public authority should be disclosed in the financial statements of the parties involved in the lease.

SALE-LEASEBACK TRANSACTION

In a sale-leaseback transaction, the party selling the property immediately leases the property from the purchaser of the property. The parties involved in a sale-leaseback agreement are referred to as the seller-lessee and purchaser-lessor.

Seller-Lessee Accounting

A state or local government that is the seller-lessee in a sale-leaseback transaction must apply the common criteria established by FASB-13 to classify the lease part of the transaction as either a capital or operating lease. Thus, the accounting and reporting standards discussed earlier in this chapter with respect to a lessee are applicable to the seller-lessee.

There is often an additional complication that must be considered when accounting for the seller-lessee side of the transaction. When the leased property is sold at an amount in excess of the carrying value of the property, the effects of the gain must not be recognized, since there is some question as to whether an arm's-length transaction, at least with respect to the gain, has occurred. In commercial accounting the gain must be deferred and amortized (1) in proportion to the amortization of the leased assets if a capital lease exists, or (2) in proportion to the rental expense recognized if an operating lease exists.

> **OBSERVATION:** *If the property leased is land and a capital lease exists, the gain is amortized on a straight-line basis over the lease term.*

In governmental accounting no gain is recognized when an asset is sold, but when a lease is capitalized a portion of the other financing source that represents the gain element must be deferred and amortized as described above.

To illustrate seller-lessee accounting, assume that a governmental unit sells equipment that has a fair value and carrying value (in the General Fixed Assets Account Group) of $80,000. The sales price is $100,000. Immediately, the same equipment is leased back for four years at an annual payment of $31,547 and payments are to begin one year after the lease is signed. The implicit interest rate, which is known by the governmental unit, is 10%, and the economic life of the equipment is four years.

The initial sale of the equipment is recorded by making the following entries, assuming the General Fund is to receive the proceeds of the sale:

GENERAL FUND
Cash	100,000	
Proceeds From Sale Of Fixed Assets		100,000

GENERAL FIXED ASSETS ACCOUNT GROUP
Investment In General Fixed Assets	80,000	
Equipment		80,000

The leaseback portion of the transaction is recorded in the following manner:

GENERAL LONG-TERM DEBT ACCOUNT GROUP
Amount To Be Provided For Lease Payments	100,000	
Obligations Under Capital Lease Agreements		100,000

GENERAL FIXED ASSETS ACCOUNT GROUP
  Assets Under Capital Leases　　　　　　　100,000
    Investment In General Fixed
      Assets—Capital Leases　　　　　　　　　　　　　　100,000

GENERAL FUND
  Expenditures—Capitalized Leases　　　　100,000
    Other Financing Sources—
      Capitalized Leases　　　　　　　　　　　　　　　　80,000
    Deferred Revenue—Sale-
      Leaseback Transaction　　　　　　　　　　　　　　20,000

The amount recorded in the General Long-Term Debt Account Group represents the present value of the total lease payments using a discount rate of 10% ($100,000 = $31,547 × 3.16986). The amount of the deferred revenue is the difference between the fair value and book value of the equipment and the sales price of the equipment ($100,000 - $80,000 = $20,000). The deferred revenue would be recognized as revenue over either the life of the lease or the life of the asset based on the amortization standards established by FASB-13. Because amortization is often not recorded in the General Fixed Assets Account Group, the deferred revenue would be recognized as revenue over the life of the asset if Criterion I or Criterion II is met, or over the life of the lease in all other situations. In the current example, because the life of the asset and the life of the lease are the same (4 years), $5,000 of revenue would be recognized in each of the next four years. Entries one year after the lease is signed would appear as follows, assuming debt principal and interest are paid by the General Fund:

GENERAL FUND
  Expenditures—Interest (100,000 × 10%)　　10,000
  Expenditures—Debt Principal　　　　　　　　21,547
    Cash　　　　　　　　　　　　　　　　　　　　　　　　31,547

  Deferred Revenue—Sale-
    Leaseback Transactions　　　　　　　　　　5,000
      Revenue—Sale-Leaseback
        Transactions　　　　　　　　　　　　　　　　　　5,000

GENERAL LONG-TERM DEBT ACCOUNT GROUP
  Obligations Under Capital Lease
    Agreements　　　　　　　　　　　　　　　　21,547
      Amount To Be Provided For Lease
        Payments　　　　　　　　　　　　　　　　　　　　21,547

OBSERVATION: *NCGA-5 does not address the complications that arise when the sale-leaseback standards established by FASB-13 are applied to the governmental accounting model. In the above example, it was assumed that the fair value and book value of the equipment were the same. In most situations this would not be true. In addition, it is likely that the book value of the equipment would be its original cost since depreciation of governmental fixed assets is optional. In this situation, it would probably be prudent to estimate the fair value of the equipment and use that basis to determine the amount of the deferred gain. If this is not done, the governmental unit is somewhat free to inflate the price of the property sold and increase the amount of the periodic lease payments accordingly. This action would distort the amount of proceeds from the sale of the property recognized as other financing sources.*

Also, since fixed assets are not generally depreciated, the basis for amortizing the deferred revenue is unclear. Presumably, the deferred revenue can be amortized on a variety of "rational and systematic" approaches such as straight-line, double declining balance, and so on.

Purchaser-Lessor Accounting

A state or local government that is the purchaser-lessor in a sale-leaseback agreement uses the criteria established in FASB-13 to classify the lease as either a direct financing lease or operating lease.

PROPRIETARY FUNDS

NCGA-5 requires that Enterprise Funds and Internal Service Funds follow accounting and reporting standards established by FASB-13 (as amended) without modification in accounting for lease transactions.

TRUST FUNDS

Expendable Trust Funds use the same accounting basis (modified accrual) that applies to governmental funds, while Nonexpendable Trust Funds and proprietary funds use a similar accounting basis (accrual basis). As discussed in this chapter, Expendable Trust Funds should account for leases in a manner consistent with FASB-13 as modified by NCGA-5. Nonexpendable Trust Funds and Pension

Leases

Trust Funds should apply FASB-13 without modification to account for lease transactions.

LITERATURE REFERENCES

Material in this chapter is based on the following authoritative pronouncements, which are grouped according to the major headings used within the chapter. A dual reference (both paragraph and page number) is used for NCGA-1 and NCGA-2 because the original pronouncements do not use paragraph numbers.

Introduction
NCGA-1   *Governmental Accounting and Financial Reporting Principles*, p. 9/ ¶¶ 38 and 43.
NCGA-5   *Accounting and Financial Reporting Principles for Lease Agreements of State and Local Governments*, ¶ 11.

Capital Leases
FASB-13   *Accounting for Leases*, ¶¶ 5 and 7.
FASB-29   *Determining Contingent Rentals*, ¶ 11.
NCGA-5   *Accounting and Financial Reporting Principles for Lease Agreements of State and Local Governments*, ¶ 12.

Recording a Capital Lease
FASB-13   *Accounting for Leases*, ¶ 10.
NCGA-5   *Accounting and Financial Reporting Principles for Lease Agreements of State and Local Governments*, ¶¶ 13 and 14.
NCGA-1   *Governmental Accounting and Financial Reporting Principles*, pp. 16 and 17/¶¶ 115 and 116.

Depreciation
NCGA-1   *Governmental Accounting and Financial Reporting Principles*, p. 10/¶¶ 54 and 56.
FASB-13   *Accounting for Leases*, ¶ 11.

Contingent Rentals
FASB-29   *Determining Contingent Rentals*, ¶ 11.
FASB-13   *Accounting for Leases*, ¶ 5.

Fiscal Funding Clauses
NCGA-5   *Accounting and Financial Reporting Principles for Lease Agreements of State and Local Governments,* ¶¶ 18 and 21.
FASB Technical Bulletin 79-10   *Fiscal Funding Clauses in Lease Agreements,* ¶ 3.

Disclosures—Capital Leases
FASB-13   *Accounting for Leases,* ¶¶ 13 and 16.
NCGA-5   *Accounting and Financial Reporting Principles for Lease Agreements of State and Local Governments,* ¶ 27.

Operating Leases
FASB-13   *Accounting for Leases,* ¶¶ 15 and 16.
NCGA-5   *Accounting and Financial Reporting Principles for Lease Agreements of State and Local Governments,* ¶ 27.

Direct Financing Lease
FASB-13   *Accounting for Leases,* ¶¶ 5 and 8.

Recording a Direct Financing Lease
NCGA-5   *Accounting and Financial Reporting Principles for Lease Agreements of State and Local Governments,* ¶ 15.
NCGA-1   *Governmental Accounting and Financial Reporting Principles,* p. 11/¶ 62.
NCGA Interpretation-3   *Revenue Recognition—Property Taxes,* ¶¶ 6 and 8.
FASB-29   *Determining Contingent Rentals,* ¶ 13.

Bad Debts
FASB-13   *Accounting for Leases,* ¶ 8.

Initial Direct Costs
FASB-17   *Accounting for Leases—Initial Direct Costs,* ¶ 6.
FASB-13   *Accounting for Leases,* ¶ 18.

Contingent Rentals
FASB-29   *Determining Contingent Rentals,* ¶ 13.

Disclosures—Direct Financing Leases
FASB-13   *Accounting for Leases,* ¶ 23.

Operating Leases
FASB-13   *Accounting for Leases,* ¶¶ 19 and 23.
NCGA-5   *Accounting and Financial Reporting Principles for Lease Agreements of State and Local Governments,* ¶ 27.

Leases

Related Parties
FASB-13   *Accounting for Leases,* ¶ 29.
NCGA-5   *Accounting and Financial Reporting Principles for Lease Agreements of State and Local Governments,* ¶¶ 22-26.
NCGA-7   *Financial Reporting for Component Units Within the Governmental Reporting Entity,* ¶ 5.
NCGA-3   *Defining the Governmental Reporting Entity,* ¶ 9.

Sale-Leaseback Transactions
FASB-28   *Accounting for Sales with Leasebacks,* ¶ 2.

Seller-Lessee Accounting
FASB-28   *Accounting for Sales with Leasebacks,* ¶ 3.
FASB-13   *Accounting for Leases,* ¶ 33.

Purchaser-Lessor Accounting
FASB-13   *Accounting for Leases,* ¶ 34.

Proprietary Funds
NCGA-5   *Accounting and Financial Reporting Principles for Lease Agreements of State and Local Governments,* ¶ 16.

Trust Funds
NCGA-5   *Accounting and Financial Reporting Principles for Lease Agreements of State and Local Governments,* ¶ 17.

PENSION DISCLOSURES

GASB-5 establishes pension disclosure requirements that should be presented as financial statement notes and required supplementary information in statements prepared by public employee retirement systems (PERS) and governmental employers. GASB-5 discusses many of its disclosure requirements in the context of a PERS but for this Statement the term PERS also includes *pension plans that are administered directly by a governmental employer.*

A governmental reporting entity can account for pension activity by observing standards established by either (a) NCGA-1 (Governmental Accounting and Financial Reporting Principles), (b) NCGA-6 (Pension Accounting and Financial Reporting: Public Employee Retirement Systems and State and Local Government Employers), or (c) FASB-35 (Accounting and Reporting by Defined Benefit Pension Plans). The issuance of GASB-5 did not affect the standards established by these three pronouncements. It did, however, establish a common set of disclosures that must be presented as notes or as required supplementary information.

There are a number of actuarial cost methods that can be used to estimate an entity's pension obligation. GASB-5 recognizes only one method, namely the actuarial present value of credited projected benefits, which is referred to in the Statement as *the standardized pension obligation measure.* Thus, with some exceptions, a governmental unit must use the standardized pension obligation measure. It should be noted, however, that the requirements cover only notes and required supplementary information disclosures. GASB-5 does not require that the pension obligation that appears in the balance sheet be measured in this manner.

GASB-5 describes the actuarial present value of credited projected benefits as follows:

> It is the present value of benefits estimated to be payable in the future as a result of employee service to date, computed by attributing an equal benefit amount (including the effects of both projected salary increases and any step-rate benefits) to each year of credited and expected future employee service, using assumptions that reflect the best judgment of future events affecting the actuarial present value.

Pension Disclosures

Attribution refers to allocating pension costs or benefits to periods of employee service. The standardized pension obligation measure attributes equal benefit amounts to each year of credited and expected future employee service, except for prospective-only benefits amendments. In the latter case, benefit amounts are attributed only to years subsequent to the effective date of the amendment.

DEFINED BENEFIT PENSION PLAN INFORMATION

A defined benefit pension plan is "a pension plan that defines an amount of pension benefit to be provided, usually as a function of one or more factors such as age, years of service, or compensation." Specific disclosure requirements for defined benefit pension plans vary depending upon a number of factors including the financial reporting unit, the type of defined benefit pension plan, and the manner by which the plan is funded. For discussion purposes, defined benefit pension plan disclosures may be grouped as follows:

- Pension Disclosures in Separately Issued PERS Financial Reports
- Pension Disclosures in Employer Financial Reports
  - Single-Employer/Agent Multiple-Employer PERS
  - Single-Employer PERS Included as a Pension Trust Fund in the Employer Reporting Entity
  - Multiple-Employer PERS Included as a Pension Trust Fund in the Employer Reporting Entity
  - Employers Contributing to Cost-Sharing Multiple-Employer PERS
  - Component Units' Pension Information in the Reporting Entity's Financial Reports
- Noncontributing Employers
- Unfunded Pension Arrangements
- Reporting by Nonemployer Contributors

PENSION DISCLOSURES IN SEPARATELY ISSUED PERS FINANCIAL REPORTS

A defined benefit pension plan which is administered through a PERS that reports *separately* from a state or local governmental unit should make a variety of disclosures in notes to its separately issued financial statements. These notes should disclose (1) a description of the pension plan, (2) significant accounting policies and plan asset matters, (3) the funding status and progress, (4) contributions required and contributions made, and (5) the location of 10-year historical trend information.

Plan Description

The note to the financial statements that describes the plan should identify the type of PERS, employee coverage, plan provisions and eligibility, and contribution obligations.

Type of PERS   The PERS should be identified as the administrator of (a) a single-employer plan, (b) an agent multiple-employer plan, or (c) a cost-sharing multiple-employer plan. A single-employer plan is a pension plan to which only one employer contributes. A multiple-employer plan is a pension plan to which two or more employers contribute and may be classified as an agent PERS or a cost-sharing PERS, which are defined as follows:

- Agent Multiple-Employer PERS: An aggregation of single-employer PERS, with pooled administrative and investment functions; that is, the PERS acts as a common investment and administrative agent for each employer. Each entity participating in an agent PERS receives a separate actuarial valuation to determine its periodic contribution rate. (FASB-87 uses the term "multiple-employer plan" for similar situations involving nongovernmental entities.)
- Cost-Sharing PERS: A multiple-employer PERS that is essentially one large pension plan with cost-sharing arrangements. All risks and costs, including benefit costs, are shared proportionately by the participating entities. One actuarial valuation is performed for the PERS as a whole, and the same contribution rate applies to each participating entity. (FASB-87 uses the term "multiple-employer plan" for similar situations involving nongovernmental entities.)

Even though the PERS reports as a separate entity, the note to its financial statements should disclose whether the PERS is a component unit of a reporting entity and, if so, the reporting entity should be identified.

The number as well as the type of (a) contributing employers and (b) nonemployer contributors should be identified.

Employee Coverage The plan description should disclose the type of employees covered by the plan and the current plan membership. In addition, there should be separate disclosures of the following:

- The number of retirees and beneficiaries currently receiving benefits and the number of terminated employees who are entitled to receive benefits but not currently receiving benefits
- The number of current employees (a) fully vested, (b) partially vested, and (c) nonvested

Plan Provisions and Eligibility The note disclosure should describe the benefits provided to employees by the plan, and the authority under which the plan was established. Also, there should be a description of the eligibility requirements that must be met before an employee is covered by the plan. The requirements for vesting should also be disclosed.

Contribution Obligations The basis for requiring contributions to the plan should be disclosed. In addition, the specific contributions that must be made by the employer and employees should be described in the note.

Significant Accounting Policies and Plan Asset Matters

In notes to the financial statements of the PERS, there should be adequate disclosures of significant accounting policies used by the PERS and plan asset matters. The disclosure of significant accounting policies should be consistent with reporting requirements established by APB-22 (Disclosure of Accounting Policies). Disclosures of plan asset matters include the identification of significant investments in a single organization and financial interest in related parties.

Significant Accounting Policies The basis of accounting used by the PERS should be disclosed. Generally, the basis of accounting will be the accrual basis for Pension Trust Funds (as required by NCGA-1, paragraph 57). The valuation methods used to report plan assets in the financial statements of the PERS should be disclosed.

When the cost basis is used to value securities held by the plan, the disclosures in the financial statements should include a description of the accounting method used to record exchanges or swaps of securities.

If there has been a change in accounting policies used during the accounting period that affects the valuation of net assets available for pension benefits, the dollar value of the effects should be disclosed.

Significant Investments The concentration of investments in a single organization should be disclosed. When investments in a single organization are equal to or greater than 5 percent of the pension plan's net assets available for pension benefits, the amount and identification of the investment must be disclosed. Disclosure is not necessary when the securities held by the pension plan represent investments in U.S. government securities or investments guaranteed by the U.S. government.

> **OBSERVATION:** *Although GASB-5 does not require a PERS to disclose investments in securities issued or guaranteed by the U.S. government, disclosure requirements established by GASB-3 (Deposits with Financial Institutions, Investments [including Repurchase Agreements], and Reverse Repurchase Agreements) must be observed.*

Related Parties There should be disclosures of assets held by the pension plan that represent a financial interest in a related party. The financial interest may include investments, loans, or lease agreements whereby the PERS is the lessor. A related party may include the following:

- A PERS official
- A governmental employer official
- A party related to a PERS official
- A party related to a governmental employer official
- A nonemployer contributor to the pension plan
- A component unit or other governmental agency that is included in the reporting entity of an employer or other governmental agency that participates in the pension plan

When a PERS allows an employee to borrow from amounts contributed by the employee, there is no need to disclose the resulting loan held by the PERS as a related party loan.

OBSERVATION: Because the above relationships represent related-party transactions, the accounting and reporting standards established by FASB-57 (Related Party Disclosures) should also be considered. Based on FASB-57, the disclosures include (a) the nature of the relationship involved; (b) a description of the transactions, including transactions to which no amounts or nominal amounts were ascribed for each of the periods for which income statements are presented, and such other information deemed necessary to an understanding of the effects of the transactions on the financial statements; (c) the dollar amounts of transactions for each of the periods for which income statements are presented and the effects of any change in the method of establishing the terms from that used in the preceding period; and (d) amounts due from or to related parties as of the date of each balance sheet presented and, if not otherwise apparent, the terms and manner of settlement.

Funding Status and Progress

GASB-5 concludes that a fundamental purpose of pension disclosures made by a PERS is to provide users with information so that the funding status of a PERS can be assessed. Such disclosures should enable users to determine whether pension benefits earned by employees are being funded on a current basis or deferred and funded in future periods.

Pension Benefit Obligation Measurement There are a number of actuarial methods that can be used to measure the estimated pension obligation of a PERS. For example, the pension obligation could be determined by using the credited projected benefits actuarial cost method, the entry age actuarial cost method, or the attained age actuarial cost method. The application of these three actuarial cost methods (as well as other actuarial cost methods) to similar pension plans using the same actuarial assumptions will create different measurements of the pension benefit obligation.

In order to provide a consistent measurement of the pension benefit obligation for all governmental pension plans, GASB-5 identified a single standardized disclosure measure. The standardized disclosure measure used is the *actuarial present value (APV) of credited projected benefits, prorated on service, and discounted at a rate equal to the expected return on present and future plan assets.*

Pension Disclosures

OBSERVATION: *Although GASB-5 adopted a standardized measure of the pension benefit obligation, this does not mean that there will be absolute comparability among the measurement of pension obligations by all governmental pension plans. Each pension fund must individually establish an interest rate to be used to discount future pension payments and adopt a variety of actuarial assumptions. The use of different interest rates and actuarial assumptions will of course result in different measurements of the pension benefit obligation.*

The credited projected benefits represent *that portion of an individual's projected benefit allocated to service to date, determined in accordance with the terms of a pension plan and based on future compensation as projected to retirement.* This actuarial method considers the pension amounts to be paid at various times in the future based on a variety of actuarial assumptions, and takes into account *the effect of advancement in age, and past and anticipated future compensation and service credits.*

OBSERVATION: *The APV of credited projected benefits disclosures by GASB-5 is different from the APV of accumulated plan benefits disclosures established by FASB-35 (Accounting and Reporting by Defined Benefit Pension Plans). GASB-5 disclosures take into consideration the salary upon which benefits will eventually be paid and therefore incorporate the effects of future salary increases and step-rate benefits. FASB-35 disclosures are based on salary levels earned through the actuarial valuation date and ignore estimated future salary adjustments.*

A note to the PERS financial statements should state that the pension benefit obligation is quantified by using the standardized disclosure measure of the present value of pension benefits that is adjusted for changes in future salary levels and any step-rate benefits. The note should also state that the standardized measured amount is the actuarial present value of credited projected benefits and should help the reader of the financial statements (a) assess the PERS funding status on a going-concern basis, (b) assess progress made in accumulating assets to pay benefits as they become due, and (c) make comparisons with the funding status and progress of other PERS. It should be stated in the note that the standardized measure is independent of any actuarial funding method that may have been used to determine the periodic contributions to be made to the PERS.

OBSERVATION: *The disclosure requirements established by GASB-5 are applicable to PERS and pension plans administered directly by a governmental unit. The selection of a standardized measure for the pension benefit obligation by GASB-5 does not mean that the standardized measure must also be used to determine how a pension plan should be funded, the measurement of the pension expenditure on the governmental unit's financial statements, or the presentation of a pension liability in a Pension Trust Fund or in a governmental unit's General Long-Term Debt Account Group. The GASB has an ongoing research project that will eventually result in the establishment of pension accounting and reporting standards for state and local governments.*

It is possible, if not likely, that conformance with the disclosure requirements established by GASB-5 will require that more than one actuarial computation be made. That is, one or more actuarial cost methods may be used to determine the fund requirements for the pension plan and the amount of pension expenditure/expense for the period; and the standardized measure method will be used to compute the information necessary to satisfy the disclosure requirements mandated by GASB-5.

Recognizing that two or more actuarial computations may be excessively costly for some PERS and the related employer, GASB-5 provides an exemption for certain PERS. A single-employer PERS does not have to use the standardized measure approach (APV of credited projected benefits) to quantify the pension benefit obligation if the following conditions are satisfied:

- The plan covers fewer than 100 current employees.
- The governmental employer covered by the plan has fewer than 200 total current employees.
- Actuarially determined pension contributions are based on one of the following funding methods:
  — *Projected unit credit* — A method under which the benefits of each individual included in an actuarial valuation are allocated by a consistent formula to valuation years. The actuarial present value of benefits allocated to a valuation year is called the normal cost. The actuarial present value of benefits allocated to all periods prior to a valuation year is called the actuarial accrued liability.
  — *Entry age normal* — A method under which the actuarial present value of the projected benefits of each individual in-

cluded in an actuarial valuation is allocated on a level basis over the earnings or service of the individual between entry age(s) and assumed exit age(s). The portion of this actuarial present value allocated to a valuation year is called the normal cost. The portion of this actuarial present value not provided for at a valuation date by the actuarial present value of future normal costs is called the actuarial accrued liability.
— *Attained age*—A method under which the excess of the actuarial present value of projected benefits over the actuarial accrued liability with respect to each individual in an actuarial valuation is allocated on a level basis over the earnings or service of the individual between the valuation date and assumed exit. The portion of this actuarial present value allocated to a valuation year is called the normal cost. The actuarial accrued liability is determined using the unit credit actuarial cost method.

If a "small" PERS uses either of the three actuarial cost methods described above to determine its pension funding requirements, the actuarially computed liability created as a by-product of using one of the three actuarial methods may be used in place of the standardized measure required by GASB-5. When the disclosures are based on one of these three actuarial cost methods, the note to the PERS financial statements should state that the method used is a substitute for the required standardized measure of the pension benefit obligation. In addition, the note should include a description of the procedures used to implement the actuarial cost method. The description would include the following, depending upon which of the three actuarial cost methods is used by the PERS:

- Projected unit credit
  - Description of how benefits are allocated to specific time periods
  - Identification of procedures used to project benefits (if applicable)
  - Description of any other method used to value a portion of the pension plan's benefits
- Entry age normal
  - Statement of whether the allocation is based on earnings or service
  - Identification of where aggregation is used in the calculation process

Pension Disclosures

- Explanation of how entry age is established
- Description of procedures used when different benefit formulas apply to various periods of service
- Description of any other method used to value a portion of the pension plan's benefits
• Attained age
  - Statement of whether the allocation is based on earnings or on service
  - Identification of where aggregation is used in the calculation process
  - Description of any other method used to value a portion of the pension plan's benefits

Actuarial Valuation Date Notes to the PERS financial statements should disclose the valuation date used to compute the pension benefit obligation. GASB-5 requires an actuarial valuation of the obligation at least biennially (every two years). For the year in which there is no actuarial valuation, there must be an actuarial update of the pension benefit obligation. An actuarial update is not as comprehensive an analysis as an actuarial valuation. An actuarial update is an "estimate or projection of the pension obligation developed by using techniques and procedures considered necessary by the actuary." The specific procedures to be used by the actuary to adequately update the pension benefit obligation depends upon the significance of changes in factors that provide the basis for actuarial assumptions used to measure the obligation. If significant changes have occurred for benefit provisions since the last actuarial valuation, an actuarial valuation (not an actuarial update) must be performed.

It is suggested that the dates of the actuarial valuations and actuarial updates coincide with the balance sheet date.

> **OBSERVATION:** *In its Exposure Draft on pension disclosures, the GASB proposed that when the actuarial valuation date differs from the balance sheet date, the pension benefit obligation would have to be updated to the balance sheet date. Because the additional cost required for such an update did not justify the expected benefits, the GASB omitted the balance sheet update requirement.*

Once an actuarial valuation date is selected, the actuarial update date must be exactly one year later. For example, if the actuarial valuation date is August 1, 19X5, the actuarial update date must be August 1, 19X6.

Certain small single-employer PERS and the related employer (as defined earlier) are encouraged, but not required, to perform an actuarial update; however, they must perform an actuarial valuation of the pension benefit obligation at least every two years.

Significant Actuarial Assumptions The measurement of the pension benefit obligation is dependent upon the establishment of a number of actuarial assumptions. GASB-5 requires that significant actuarial assumptions be disclosed in notes to the PERS financial statements. Significant actuarial assumptions include the following:

- Discount rate used to determine the present value of the pension benefit obligation
- Projected salary increases due to inflation
- Projected salary increases due to merit or seniority
- Postretirement benefit increases

The discount rate used to determine the present value of future pension payments should be equal to the *estimated long-term rate of return on current and future investments of the pension plan*. Thus, the present value of future pension payments is in part determined by the expected returns on investments made and investments to be made by the pension plan. The discount rate used should not be selected in a manner that unduly reflects actual investments, but should take into consideration long-term future investment returns.

> **OBSERVATION:** *Since the discount rate is a composite rate based on current and expected investments, the rate is subjective. Allowing pension plans to individually select a discount rate somewhat defeats the purpose of the GASB's endorsement of a standardized measure of the pension obligation (APV of credited projected benefits). In its Exposure Draft on pension disclosures, the GASB emphasized the subjective nature of actuarial assumptions by proposing a disclosure that would explain the effects of 1% changes in the interest rate used to measure the obligation. This disclosure requirement was omitted from GASB-5.*

Pension Benefit Obligation The amount of the pension benefit obligation based on the APV of credited projected benefits must be disclosed in a note to the financial statements. In addition, the total amount of the obligation should be apportioned to the following components:

Pension Disclosures

- Obligation applicable to retirees and beneficiaries who are receiving pension payments and former employees who are entitled to receive pension payments in the future but who are not currently receiving payments
- Obligation applicable to current employees based on accumulated employee contributions including allocated investment income
- Obligation applicable to current employees based on employer-financed vested benefits
- Obligation applicable to current employees based on employer-financed nonvested benefits

Pension Fund's Net Assets The amount of net assets available to pay pension benefits should be disclosed. The measurement date for the net assets should be the same date that was used to determine the actuarial present value of the pension benefit obligation. The basis for determining the value of assets should be the same basis that was used to value the assets for presentation in the PERS balance sheet. When the basis of the assets of the pension plan is other than the market basis, the market value of the assets available for pension benefits must also be disclosed in the note to the PERS financial statements.

Underfunded/Overfunded Obligation The disclosure should identify the difference between the total pension benefit obligation and the net assets available for benefits. When the obligation is greater than the net assets, the difference should be labeled "Unfunded Pension Benefit Obligation." When the net assets are greater than the obligation, the difference should be labeled "Assets In Excess Of Pension Benefit Obligation."

Changes in Assumptions or Benefits Significant changes in actuarial assumptions or employee pension benefit provisions should be explained in the note disclosure. The explanation should describe how the change affected the dollar valuation of the pension benefit obligation.

Contribution Required and Contribution Made

One of the primary objectives of GASB-5 is to provide information to users in order for them to determine whether employers are making actuarially determined contributions to the PERS.

Funding Policy GASB-5 defines funding policy as "the policy for the amounts and timing of contributions to be made by employer(s), participants, and any other sources to provide the benefits a pension plan specifies." The PERS should describe the funding policy in a note to its financial statements. The description should specifically state how the actuarial computations of funding requirements affect the actual funding policy. As explained below, additional disclosures to be made are dependent upon whether pension fund contributions are actuarially determined.

Actuarially Determined Contributions Actuarially determined pension contribution requirements refer to "amounts required to be paid annually to a pension fund, based on an actuarial cost method or funding method." An actuarial cost method or funding method is "a procedure for determining the actuarial present value of pension plan benefits and expenses and for developing an actuarially equivalent allocation of such value to time periods, usually in the form of a normal cost and an actuarial accrued liability." Normal cost refers to the actuarial present value of pension benefits that are allocated to a particular year based on the use of a specific actuarial cost method. A variety of actuarial cost methods exist. Listed below are the actuarial cost methods described in Appendix E of GASB-5:

- Unit credit actuarial cost method
- Entry age actuarial cost method or entry age normal actuarial cost method
- Attained age actuarial cost method
- Aggregate actuarial cost method
- Frozen entry age actuarial cost method
- Frozen attained age actuarial cost method
- Individual level actuarial cost method or individual level premium actuarial cost method
- Individual spread gain actuarial cost method or individual aggregate actuarial cost method
- Projected actuarial cost method or forecast actuarial cost method

> **OBSERVATION:** *It should be emphasized that the actuarial cost method used to determine the funding for a pension plan or the expenditure/expense recognition is a separate computation from the standardized measure of the pension benefit obligation disclosure required by GASB-5.*

Pension Disclosures

When the pension contribution requirements are actuarially computed, the note should contain the following disclosures:

- Identify the funding method used and the period and method used to amortize any unfunded actuarially accrued liability (the actuarially accrued liability is "that portion, as determined by a particular actuarial cost method, of the actuarial present value of pension plan benefits and expenses which is not provided for by future normal costs")
- Comment that the same actuarial assumptions were used to compute both the pension contribution requirements and the pension benefit obligation measured on the standardized basis (if different actuarial assumptions were used, the differences should be explained in the note)
- Disclose the amount of the pension contribution requirements and disclose the amounts that are intended to (a) cover normal cost and (b) amortize the unfunded actuarially accrued liability, if any
- Disclose contributions made by employer(s) and employees
- For single-employer PERS and cost-sharing multiple-employer PERS, disclose the contributions made by employer(s) and employees as a percentage of the current-year covered payroll (covered payroll or covered compensation is defined as "all compensation paid to active employees covered by the PERS on which contributions are based")
- Explain how changes during the current year due to (a) actuarial assumptions, (b) benefit provisions, (c) actuarial funding method, or (d) other significant factors affected the computation of the pension contribution requirements (the explanation should include the dollar impact of each of the four categories)

Nonactuarially Determined Contributions When the pension fund contribution requirements are not actuarially computed, the following disclosures should be made in the note:

- Comment that the pension contribution requirements were not actuarially determined
- Explain how the pension contributions were determined
- Comment whether an actuary was used to determine the actuarial implications of using a nonactuarial method and, if applicable, describe the implications identified by the actuary
- Disclose contributions made by employer(s) and employees

- For single-employer PERS and cost-sharing multiple-employer PERS, disclose the contributions made by employer(s) and employees as a percentage of the current-year covered payroll
- Explain how changes during the year in the method used to compute the pension contribution requirements affected the computation of the amounts (the explanation should include the dollar impact of each change)

Location of 10-Year Historical Trend Information

The note to the PERS financial statements should specifically refer to 10-year historical trend information. Also, it should be explained in the note that the information is presented to enable the reader to assess the progress made by the PERS in accumulating sufficient assets to pay pension benefits as they become due.

Disclosure of 10-Year Historical Trend Information

GASB-5 concludes that the primary objective of pension disclosures by PERS and governmental employers is to supply users with information in order to assess the following:

- Funding status of a PERS on a going-concern basis
- Progress made in accumulating sufficient assets to pay benefits when due
- Contributions made by employers were actuarially determined

In order to achieve the objectives listed above, 10-year historical trend information should be presented as required supplementary information immediately following the presentation of notes to the PERS financial statements. Required supplementary information is not part of a reporting entity's general purpose financial statements; however, the GASB considers required supplementary information as a necessary supplement to the general purpose financial statements that may consist of statements, schedules, statistical presentations, or other information.

> **OBSERVATION:** *From an audit perspective (Statement on Auditing Standards-27 [Supplementary Information Required by the Financial Accounting Standards Board]), an auditor need apply only*

Pension Disclosures

> *limited procedures on the supplementary information since supplementary information is not part of the basic financial statements. If a PERS omits the supplementary information or departs from the disclosure requirements, or if an auditor does not perform the required limited procedures on the supplementary information, the PERS could still receive an unqualified opinion on the basic financial statements. However, the auditor would add a paragraph to explain the deficiency.*

Ten-year historical trend information for the pension plan should provide an analysis of the plan's (a) net assets and pension obligation and (b) revenues and expenditures.

Net Assets and Pension Obligation For a 10-year period the supplementary information concerning net assets and pension obligation should include the following:

- Net assets available for pension benefits using (a) the same valuation date as the valuation date used to determine the pension benefit obligation and (b) the same valuation method used to value the assets for presentation in the PERS balance sheet
- Pension benefit obligation based on the standardized measure of the liability (for qualifying small single-employer PERS, an alternative measure of the pension benefit obligation may be presented as described in the section entitled Pension Benefit Obligation Measurement)
- Net assets as a percentage of the pension benefit obligation
- Dollar value difference between net assets and the pension benefit obligation
- Annual covered payroll
- Dollar value difference between net assets and the pension benefit obligation as a percentage of annual covered payroll

Revenues and Expenditures For a 10-year period the supplementary information related to pension revenues and expenditures should include the following:

- Total revenue and individual sources of revenue, such as employer and employee contributions, investment income, and other income
- Total expenditures and types of expenditures, such as pay-

ments for benefits, administration of the plan, refunds to employees, and other items
- Employer contributions as a percentage of annual covered payroll (not required for agent multiple-employer PERS)
- Comments on whether contributions were made in accordance with actuarially determined amounts (if the actual contributions are different from the actuarial or legal requirements, the presentation should disclose both the actual contributions made and the required contributions)

When the 10-year historical trend information has been significantly affected by changes in (a) actuarial assumptions, (b) pension benefit provisions, (c) actuarial funding methods, (d) accounting policies, or (e) other factors, the timing, nature, and dollar effect of the changes should be disclosed for each year in which a significant change occurred.

Information related to the standardized measure of the pension benefit obligation as required by GASB-5 may not be available for all years during the 10-year period. Information should be presented for a particular year only when the standardized measure information is available. (Eventually, with the passage of time, this transition rule will be unnecessary.)

The supplementary information should contain commentaries that will facilitate the understanding of the 10-year historical trend information by financial statement users. GASB-5 lists the following comments (modified where appropriate based on the unique reporting characteristics of a particular PERS) as being helpful in explaining the relationship of the 10-year historical trend information and the objectives of reporting pension information:

- Changes in (a) actuarial assumptions, (b) pension benefit provisions, (c) actuarial funding methods, (d) accounting policies, and (e) other changes that will affect the comparability of the information from year to year.
- Changes listed above may affect trends in pension contribution requirements and ratios based on the pension benefit obligation.
- An isolated analysis of the pension benefit obligation or the unfunded portion (or assets in excess) of the pension benefit obligation can be misleading.
- Adequate funding of the PERS is in part indicated by expressing net assets available for pension benefits as a percentage of the pension benefit obligation. A high percentage would indicate adequate funding for the PERS and an increase or decrease in

Pension Disclosures

the percentage over time would suggest that adequate funding of the PERS is improving (increasing percentages) or deteriorating (decreasing percentages).

- The analysis of funding progress for the PERS can be enhanced by expressing the unfunded pension benefit obligation (or assets in excess of the pension benefit obligation) as a percentage of the annual covered payroll since the analysis approximately adjusts for the effects of inflation.

Note Illustration

Following is an example of notes to a separately issued PERS financial report. Presented immediately following the note is the 10-year historical trend information (see Exhibit I).

▶ A. Plan Description

Substantially all full-time employees of the City of Centerville and its related agencies are covered by the City of Centerville PERS. The PERS is the administrator of a single-employer pension plan that was established by the City in accordance with the City charter and state statutes. Although the PERS presents separate financial statements, it is also a component unit (reporting as a Pension Trust Fund) of the City's financial reporting entity.

As of June 30, 19X5, employee membership data related to the pension plan were as follows:

Retirees and beneficiaries currently receiving benefits and terminated employees entitled to benefits but not yet receiving them	6,853
Active plan participants:	
Vested	5,675
Nonvested	32,500
Total	38,175

The pension plan provides pension benefits, deferred allowances, and death and disability benefits. A member may retire after reaching the age of 55 or accumulating 25 years of service in one of the departments or agencies of the city. Benefits vest after 12 years of service. Employees who retire at or after age 55 with 12 or more years of service are entitled to pension payments for the remainder of their lives equal to 2% of their final, five-year average salary times the number of years for which they were employed by the City. The final, five-year average salary is the average salary of the employee during the final five years of full-time employment with the City exclusive of payments for overtime.

Pension provisions include deferred allowances whereby an employee may terminate his or her employment with the City after accumulating 25 years of service but before reaching the age of 55. If the employee does not withdraw his or her accumulated contributions, the employee is entitled to all pension benefits upon reaching the age of 55.

Pension provisions include death and disability benefits whereby the disabled employee or surviving spouse is entitled to receive annually an amount equal to 45% of the employee's final, five-year average salary exclusive of overtime payments. The disabled employee is entitled to receive disability payments for life, while the surviving spouse may receive death benefits for life or as long as the spouse does not remarry.

Employees of the City are required to pay 4.3% of their gross earnings to the pension plan. The payments are deducted from the employee's wages or salary and remitted by the City to the PERS on a monthly basis. If an employee leaves the employment of the City before 12 years of service, the accumulated contributions plus earned interest are refunded to the employee or the employee's designated beneficiary.

The City makes annual contributions to the pension plan equal to the amount required by state statutes.

B. Summary of Significant Accounting Policies and Plan Asset Matters

The City of Centerville PERS financial statements are prepared on the accrual basis of accounting. Contributions from the City and the City's employees are recognized as revenue in the period in which employees provide services to the City. Investment income is recognized as earned by the pension plan. The net appreciation (depreciation) in the fair value of investments held by the pension plan is recorded as an increase (decrease) to investment income based on the valuation of investments as of the date of the balance sheet.

Investments in securities are valued at current market prices. Corporate bond securities are assigned a value based on yields currently available on securities of issuers with credit ratings similar to the securities held by the pension plan. Unrestricted capital stock securities are assigned a value based on quoted market prices. The estimated value assigned to restricted capital stock securities is based on a multiple of current earnings less an appropriate discount. The earnings multiple is based on current multiples and earnings for companies similar to the securities held by the pension plan.

No investment in any one organization represents 5% or more of the net assets available for pension benefits.

There are no investments in, loans to, or leases with parties related to the pension plan.

C. Funding Status and Progress

Presented below is the total pension benefit obligation of the City of Centerville PERS. The amount of the total pension benefit obligation is based on a standardized measurement established by GASB-5 that, with some exceptions, must be used by a PERS. The standardized measurement is the actuarial present value of credited projected benefits. This pension valuation method reflects the present value of estimated pension benefits that will be paid in future years as a result of employee services performed to date and is adjusted for the effects of projected salary increases and any step-rate benefits. A standardized measure of the pension benefit obligation was adopted by the GASB to enable readers of the PERS financial statements to (a) assess the City of Centerville PERS funding status on a going-concern basis, (b) assess progress made in accumulating sufficient assets to pay benefits when due, and (c) make comparisons among PERS.

Because the standardized measure is used only for disclosure purposes by the City of Centerville PERS, the measurement is independent of the actuarial computation made to determine contributions to the PERS. The actuarial funding method used to determine contributions to the PERS is explained in Part D of this note.

A variety of significant actuarial assumptions are used to determine the standardized measure of the pension benefit obligation and these assumptions are summarized below:

- The present value of future pension payments was computed by using a discount rate of 7%. The discount rate is equal to the estimated long-term rate of return on current and future investments of the pension plan.
- Future pension payments reflect an assumption of a 5% (compounded annually) salary increase as a result of inflation.
- Future pension payments reflect an assumption of a 2% (compounded annually) salary increase as a result of seniority and/or merit adjustments.
- Future pension payments reflect no postretirement benefit increases, which is consistent with the terms of the pension agreement.

The standardized measure of the unfunded pension benefit obligation as of June 30, 19X5, is as follows:

Pension benefit obligation:	(in millions)
Retirees and beneficiaries currently receiving benefits and terminated employees not yet receiving benefits	$90.2
Current employees—	
Accumulated employee contributions including allocated investment income	97.4
Employer-financed vested	93.8
Employer-financed nonvested	138.7
Total pension benefit obligation	420.1
Net assets available for benefits, at market	365.8
Unfunded pension benefit obligation	$ 54.3

No changes in actuarial assumptions or benefit provisions that would significantly affect the valuation of the pension benefit obligation occurred during 19X5.

D. Contributions Required and Contributions Made

Periodic employer contributions to the pension plan are determined on an actuarial basis using the entry age normal actuarial cost method. Normal cost is funded on a current basis. The unfunded actuarial accrued liability is funded over a 30-year period. Periodic contributions for both normal cost and the amortization of the unfunded actuarial accrued liability are based on the level percentage of payroll method. The funding strategy for normal cost and the unfunded actuarial accrued liability should provide sufficient resources to pay employee pension benefits on a timely basis.

Total contributions to the pension plan in 19X5 amounted to $56,250,000, of which $35,500,000 and $20,750,000 were made by the City of Centerville and its employees, respectively. The contributed amounts were actuarially determined as described above and were based on an actuarial valuation as of June 30, 19X5. The pension contributions represent funding for normal cost ($45,800,000) and the amortization of the unfunded actuarial accrued liability ($10,450,000). Contributions made by the City of Centerville and its employees represent 7.4% and 4.3%, respectively, of covered payroll for the year.

Significant actuarial assumptions used to compute pension contribution requirements are the same as those used to determine the standardized measure of the pension obligation.

The computation of the pension contribution requirements for 19X5 was based on the same actuarial assumptions, benefit provisions, actuarial funding method, and other significant factors used to determine pension contribution requirements in previous years.

E. Location of Ten-Year Historical Trend Information

Ten-year historical trend information related to the pension plan is presented on pages XX-XX. The information is presented to enable the reader to assess the progress made by the City of Centerville PERS in accumulating sufficient assets to pay pension benefits as they become due. ◄

EXHIBIT I
City of Centerville PERS
Required Supplementary Information
Analysis of Funding Progress
(in millions)

Fiscal year	(1) Net assets available for benefits*	(2) Pension benefit obligation	(3) Percentage funded (1)/(2)	(4) Unfunded pension benefit obligation (2)−(1)	(5) Annual covered payroll	(6) Unfunded pension benefit obligation as a percentage of covered payroll (4)/(5)
19W6	$ 36.4	$85.8	42.4%	$49.4	$121.4	40.7%
19W7	55.0	107.4	51.2	52.4	145.2	36.1
19W8	77.3	145.6	53.1	68.3	166.9	40.9
19W9	104.3	182.0	57.3	77.7	204.1	38.1
19X0	133.1	204.3	65.1	71.2	243.6	29.2
19X1	144.6	214.5	67.4	69.9	267.9	26.1
19X2	180.3	258.0	69.9	77.7	308.2	25.2
19X3	226.7	301.9	75.1	75.2	348.1	21.6
19X4	293.8	360.9	81.4	67.1	417.6	16.1
19X5	365.8	420.1	87.1	54.3	480.1	11.3

Isolated analysis of the dollar amounts of net assets available for benefits, pension benefit obligation, and unfunded pension benefit obligation can be misleading. Expressing the net assets available for benefits as a percentage of the pension benefit obligation provides one indication of the City of Centerville PERS funding status on a going-concern basis. Analysis of this percentage over time indicates whether the system is becoming financially stronger or weaker. Generally, the greater this percentage, the stronger the PERS. Trends in unfunded pension benefit obligation and annual covered payroll are both affected by inflation. Expressing the unfunded pension benefit obligation as a percentage of annual covered payroll approximately adjusts for the effects of inflation and aids analysis of the progress made in accumulating sufficient assets to pay benefits when due. Generally, the smaller this percentage, the stronger the PERS.

*Net assets are presented at market values as explained in an earlier part of the note.

EXHIBIT I
(continued)

City of Centerville PERS
Required Supplementary Information
Revenues by Source and Expenses by Type

Revenues by Source

Employer Contributions

Fiscal year	Employee contributions	Dollar amount	Percentage of annual covered payroll	Investment income	Total
19W6	$4,950,000	$8,750,000	7.2%	$1,250,000	$14,950,000
19W7	6,100,000	10,500,000	7.2	1,975,000	18,575,000
19W8	7,200,000	12,250,000	7.3	3,900,000	23,350,000
19W9	8,200,000	13,750,000	6.7	5,350,000	27,300,000
19X0	9,850,000	15,950,000	6.5	6,250,000	32,050,000
19X1	11,225,000	18,270,000	6.8	9,050,000	38,545,000
19X2	12,875,000	21,905,000	7.1	10,670,000	45,450,000
19X3	14,850,000	26,505,000	7.6	16,105,000	57,460,000
19X4	17,440,000	31,108,000	7.4	23,251,000	71,799,000
19X5	20,750,000	35,500,000	7.4	35,590,000	91,840,000

Expenses by Type

Fiscal year	Benefits	Administrative expenses	Refunds	Total
19W6	$983,000	$293,000	$675,000	$1,951,000
19W7	1,485,000	381,000	1,093,000	2,959,000
19W8	2,130,000	473,000	1,960,000	4,563,000
19W9	2,764,000	517,000	1,465,000	4,746,000
19X0	3,437,000	707,000	1,597,000	5,741,000
19X1	4,095,000	840,000	2,738,000	7,673,000
19X2	5,175,000	911,000	3,392,000	9,478,000
19X3	6,217,000	1,032,000	5,295,000	12,544,000
19X4	7,370,000	1,222,000	4,582,000	13,174,000
19X5	8,555,000	1,451,000	5,140,000	15,146,000

Contributions were made in accordance with actuarially determined contribution requirements.

PENSION DISCLOSURES IN EMPLOYER FINANCIAL REPORTS

The previous section discussed pension disclosure requirements when a PERS reports separately from the governmental employer. As noted earlier, PERS may be classified as a single-employer PERS, an agent multiple-employer PERS, or a cost-sharing multiple-employer PERS. The specific disclosures that should be made in an employer's financial report are dependent upon the type of PERS that administers the pension plan. The following five sections of this chapter describe the pension disclosure requirements that must be made in the employer's financial report when an employer contributes to a pension plan administered by the following types of PERS:

- Single-Employer/Agent Multiple-Employer PERS
- Single-Employer PERS Included as a Pension Trust Fund in the Employer Reporting Entity
- Multiple-Employer PERS Included as a Pension Trust Fund in the Employer Reporting Entity
- Employers Contributing to Cost-Sharing Multiple-Employer PERS
- Component Units' Pension Information in the Reporting Entity's Financial Reports

When an employer contributes to more than one PERS, all the applicable reporting disclosures must be observed; however, the disclosures should be made in a manner that does not result in duplicate or repetitious information. In addition, the *total* pension benefit obligation and net assets available to pay pension benefits for all single-employer PERS and agent multiple-employer PERS should be presented in the employer's financial report. The presentation of the obligation and net assets on a total basis is best summarized in a single table.

SINGLE-EMPLOYER/AGENT MULTIPLE-EMPLOYER PERS

The following pension disclosures should be made in an employer's notes to its financial statements for each single-employer PERS and each agent multiple-employer PERS to which an employer contributes.

Description of Plan The note to the employer's financial report should identify the type of PERS, single-employer or agent multiple-employer, and should disclose the name of the PERS. Also, the disclosure should include the employer's (a) current-year covered payroll and (b) total current-year payroll for all employees. There should be a brief description of (a) the type of employees covered by the pension plan benefit provisions, (b) benefit provisions, (c) pension eligibility requirements for employees including vesting requirements, and (d) the authority by which pension benefit provisions have been established. In addition, the note should describe the contribution commitment requirements for both the employer and employees, and the authority by which both parties are obligated to contribute to the pension plan.

Amounts and Types of Securities The notes to the employer's financial statements should disclose the dollar value and nature of securities issued by the employer and held as an investment by the PERS. The securities may include such items as bonds, tax anticipation notes, and other debt instruments issued by the employer.

> **OBSERVATION:** *Because the above relationships represent related party transactions, the accounting and reporting standards established by FASB-57 (Related Party Disclosures) should be considered.*

Funding Status and Progress Although a PERS may be a separate reporting entity, the financial statements of an employer should describe the funding status and funding progress of the PERS that administers its pension plan.

Pension benefit obligation measurement As noted earlier, there are a number of actuarial cost and funding methods that can be used to estimate a PERS pension obligation. GASB-5 identifies a single standardized disclosure measure, namely the APV of credited projected benefits, prorated on service and discounted at a rate equal to the expected return on present and future plan assets.

A note to the employer's financial statements should state that the pension benefit obligation is determined by using the standardized disclosure measure of the present value of pension benefits that is adjusted for changes in future salary levels and any step-rate benefits. The note should also state that the standardized measured amount is the actuarial present value of credited projected benefits

Pension Disclosures

and should help the reader of the employer's financial statements (a) assess the PERS funding status on a going-concern basis, (b) assess progress made in accumulating assets to pay benefits as they become due, and (c) make comparisons with the funding status and progress of other PERS. It should be stated in the note that the standardized measure is independent of any actuarial funding method that may have been used to determine the periodic contributions to the PERS.

A single-employer PERS does not have to use the standardized measure approach (APV of credited projected benefits) to quantify the pension benefit obligation if certain conditions, as described in the section entitled Pension Benefit Obligation Measurement, are satisfied.

Actuarial valuation date The note to the employer's financial statements should disclose the valuation date used to compute the pension benefit obligation. There must be an actuarial valuation of the pension obligation at least biennially. For the year in which there is no actuarial valuation, there must be an actuarial update of the pension benefit obligation. An actuarial update is "an estimate or projection of the pension obligation developed by using techniques and procedures considered necessary by the actuary." If significant changes have occurred for benefit provisions since the last actuarial valuation, an actuarial valuation must be performed.

It is suggested that the dates of actuarial valuations and actuarial updates coincide with the balance sheet date of the PERS. Once an actuarial valuation date is selected, the actuarial update date must be exactly one year later.

Certain small single-employer PERS are encouraged, but not required, to perform an actuarial update; however, they must perform an actuarial valuation of the pension benefit obligation at least every two years. A small single-employer PERS was described in the section entitled Pension Benefit Obligation Measurement.

Significant actuarial assumptions Significant actuarial assumptions used to measure the pension benefit obligation should be disclosed in the note to the employer's financial statements. Significant actuarial assumptions include the following:

- Discount rate used to determine the present value of the pension benefit obligation
- Projected salary increases due to inflation
- Projected salary increases due to merit or seniority
- Postretirement benefit increases

The discount rate used to determine the present value of future pension payments should be equal to the *estimated long-term rate of return on current and future investments of the pension plan.* The discount rate used should not be selected in a manner that unduly reflects actual investments but should take into consideration long-term future investment returns.

Pension benefit obligation The amount of the pension benefit obligation based on the APV of credited projected benefits must be disclosed in a note to the employer's financial statements. In addition, the total amount of the obligation should be apportioned to the following components:

- Obligation applicable to retirees and beneficiaries who are receiving pension payments and former employees who are entitled to receive pension payments in the future but who are not currently receiving payments
- Obligation applicable to current employees based on accumulated employee contributions including allocated investment income
- Obligation applicable to current employees based on employer-financed vested benefits
- Obligation applicable to current employees based on employer-financed non-vested benefits

For some agent multiple-employer PERS, the obligation to pay pension benefits transfers from the individual employer to the PERS as a whole when benefits become payable. In this circumstance, the pension benefit obligation transferred to the PERS and the related net assets available to pay those benefits should not be included as part of the pension obligation or the net assets available for benefits to be disclosed in the employer's financial statements.

Pension fund's net assets The amount of net assets available to pay pension benefits should be disclosed in the employer's financial statements. The measurement date for the assets should be the same date that was used to determine the actuarial present value of the pension benefit obligation. The basis for determining the value of assets should be the same basis that was used to value the assets for presentation in the PERS balance sheet. When the basis of the assets of the pension plan is other than the market basis, the market value of the assets available for pension benefits must also be disclosed in the note to the employer's financial statements. The basis used to measure the assets on the PERS balance sheet should be disclosed.

Underfunded/overfunded obligation The disclosure in the employer's financial statements should identify the difference between the total pension benefit obligation and the net assets available for benefits. When the obligation is greater than the net assets, the difference should be labeled "Unfunded Pension Benefit Obligation." When the net assets are greater than the obligation, the difference should be labeled "Assets in Excess of Pension Benefit Obligation."

Changes in assumptions or benefits Significant changes in actuarial assumptions or employee pension benefit provisions should be explained in the note disclosure. The explanation should describe how the change affected the dollar valuation of the pension benefit obligation.

Contribution Required and Contribution Made One of the primary objectives of GASB-5 is to provide information to help users determine whether employers are making actuarially determined contributions to the single-employer PERS or agent multiple-employer PERS.

Funding policy GASB-5 defines funding policy as "the policy for the amounts and timing of contributions to be made by employer(s), participants, and any other sources to provide the benefits a pension plan specifies." The funding policy of the PERS should be disclosed in the notes to the employer's financial statements. The description should specifically state how the actuarially determined funding requirements affect the actual funding policy. As explained below, additional disclosures to be made are dependent upon whether pension fund contributions are actuarially determined.

Actuarially determined contributions Actuarially determined pension contribution requirements refer to "amounts required to be paid annually to a pension fund, based on an actuarial cost method or funding method." When the pension fund contribution requirements are actuarially computed, the note to the employer's financial statements should contain the following disclosures:

- Identify the funding method used and the period and method used to amortize any unfunded actuarially accrued liability (the actuarially accrued liability is "that portion, as determined by a particular actuarial cost method, of the actuarial present value of pension plan benefits and expenses which is not provided for by future normal costs").

- Comment if the same actuarial assumptions were used to compute both the pension contribution requirements and the pension benefit obligation measured on the standardized basis (if different actuarial assumptions were used, the differences should be explained in the note).
- Disclose the amount of the pension contribution requirements and disclose the amounts that are intended to (a) cover normal cost and (b) amortize the unfunded actuarial accrued liability, if any.
- Disclose the contributions made by employer and employees by amount and as a percentage of the current-year covered payroll (covered payroll or covered compensation is defined as all compensation paid to active employees covered by the PERS on which contributions are based).
- Explain how changes during the current year due to (a) actuarial assumptions, (b) benefit provisions, (c) actuarial funding method, or (d) other significant factors affected the computation of the pension contribution requirements (the explanation should include the dollar impact of each of the four categories).

Nonactuarially determined contributions When the pension fund contribution requirements are not actuarially computed, the following disclosures should be made in the notes to the employer's financial statements:

- Comment that the pension contribution requirements were not actuarially determined.
- Explain how the pension contribution requirements were determined.
- Comment whether an actuary was used to determine the actuarial implications of using a nonactuarial method and, if applicable, describe the implications identified by the actuary.
- Disclose contributions made by the employer and employees by amount and as a percentage of the current-year covered payroll.
- Explain how changes during the year in the method used to compute the pension contribution requirements affected the computation of the amounts (the explanation should include the dollar impact of each change).

Historical Trend Information The pension disclosures in an employer's financial statements should include 3-year historical trend information concerning its related pension plan. The selected 3-year information should include the following:

- Net assets of the pension plan available to pay pension benefits as a percentage of the pension benefit obligation applicable to the employer's employees
- Unfunded (or assets in excess of) pension benefit obligation as a percentage of the employer's annual covered payroll
- Contributions by the employer to the pension plan as a percentage of the employer's annual covered payroll
- Comments on whether the employer's contributions were consistent with the actuarially determined contribution requirements

The GASB recognizes that due to the somewhat unique nature of the 3-year historical trend information, the required information may not be available for years prior to the effective date of GASB-5. For this reason, 3-year information should be presented for only those years for which the information is available. (With the passage of time, this transition rule will become unnecessary.)

The GASB concludes that a requirement to disclose 10-year historical trend information related to a PERS in the employer's financial statements may result in excessive information being presented in the employer's financial statements. It is generally assumed that most interested parties will have access to the financial statements of the employer's PERS and will, therefore, have access to the 10-year historical trend information. There should, however, be a reference in the employer's notes to the 10-year historical trend information (a) available in the PERS separately issued financial report or (b) presented in the employer's financial report. The presentation of the 10-year historical trend information in the employer's financial report is discussed in the following section entitled Disclosure of 10-Year Historical Trend Information. Also, the reference to the 10-year historical trend information should comment that the information provides a basis for determining the progress made by the PERS in accumulating sufficient assets to pay pension benefits as they become due.

Disclosure of 10-Year Historical Trend Information Although selected 3-year historical trend information concerning a PERS must be presented in the employer's financial statements as described above, 10-year historical trend information must be available to users. If the 10-year historical trend information in the PERS separate financial report is publicly available, the information is incorporated into the employer's financial report by reference to the PERS financial report. If the information is not publicly available, it should be included in the employer's Comprehensive Annual Financial Report (CAFR). If the employer does not prepare a CAFR, 10-year historical trend information should be included in the employer's general purpose financial statements immediately after notes to the financial statements.

When 10-year historical trend information is presented as part of the employer's CAFR or as part of its general purpose financial statements, the information should be identified as required supplementary information. Also, the information should include the following disclosures:

- Net assets available for pension benefits using (a) the same valuation date as the valuation date used to determine the pension benefit obligation and (b) the same valuation method used to value the assets for presentation in the PERS balance sheet
- Pension benefit obligation based on the standardized measure of the liability (for qualifying small single-employer PERS, an alternative measure of the pension benefit obligation may be presented as described earlier in the section entitled Pension Benefit Obligation Measurement.
- Net assets as a percentage of the pension benefit obligation
- Dollar value difference between net assets and the pension benefit obligation
- Annual covered payroll
- Dollar value difference between net assets and the pension benefit obligation as a percentage of annual covered payroll

> **OBSERVATION:** *From an audit perspective, Statement on Auditing Standards-52 (Omnibus Statement on Auditing Standards—1987), an auditor need apply only limited procedures on the supplementary information since supplementary information is not a part of the basic financial statements. If an employer omits the supplementary information or departs from the disclosure requirements, or if an auditor does not perform the required limited procedures on the supplementary information, the employer could still receive an unqualified opinion on the basic financial statements. However, the auditor would add a paragraph to explain the deficiency.*

GASB-5 does not require the disclosure of 10-year historical trend information for individual employers in the financial reports of agent multiple-employer PERS. It is assumed that the information will be presented in the employer's CAFR.

Pension Disclosures

> ***OBSERVATION:*** *Paragraph 32(b) of GASB-5 exempts agent multiple-employer PERS from disclosing 10-year historical trend information that expresses employer contributions in dollar amounts and as a percentage of each employer's annual covered payroll.*

For some agent multiple-employer PERS, the obligation to pay pension benefits transfers from the individual employer to the PERS as a whole when pension benefits become payable. In this circumstance, the pension benefit obligation transferred to the PERS and the related net assets available to pay those benefits should not be included as part of the pension obligation or the net assets available for benefits in computing the 10-year historical trend information.

In the earlier discussion of 10-year historical trend information for single-employer/agent multiple-employer PERS, certain comments that help explain the 10-year information were allowed by GASB-5. Similar comments may be used when the 10-year historical trend information is included in the employer's CAFR or general purpose financial statements.

When the 10-year historical trend information has been affected by changes in (a) actuarial assumptions, (b) pension benefit provisions, (c) actuarial funding methods, (d) accounting policies, or (e) other factors, the timing, nature, and total dollar effect should be presented for the year in which the change occurred.

The standardized measure of the pension benefit obligation may not be available for the required 10-year period. Disclosures should be made for those years for which information concerning the pension obligation is available. (Eventually, this transition rule will be unnecessary.)

Note Illustration

Following are examples of notes to an employer's financial statements related to a single-employer PERS.

▶ A. Plan Description

The City of Centerville contributes to the Centerville Pension Employees Retirement System, which is a single-employer pension employees retirement system (PERS). It is the responsibility of the Centerville PERS to function as an investment and administrative agent for the City of Centerville with respect to the pension plan.

For the year ended June 30, 19X5, the City's total payroll for all employees and the City's total covered payroll amounted to $98,750,000. *Covered payroll* refers to all compensation paid by the City to active employees covered by the Centerville PERS on which contributions to the pension are based.

Based on state statutes, all full-time employees must participate in city or municipality pension plans. Under the provisions of the City's pension plan, pension benefits vest after ten years of full-time employment. An employee may retire at age 60 and receive annual pension benefits equal to 2% of the employee's salary earned during the last five years of employment, multiplied by the number of full-time years of employment with the City. The five-year salary base does not include overtime. Also, the pension plan provides for death benefits (after two years of full-time employment) and disability benefits (after five years of full-time employment). All pension, death, and disability benefits are determined by state statutes.

Under provisions of state statutes, all full-time employees must contribute 7% of their gross earnings to the pension plan. In addition, the City must provide annual contributions sufficient to satisfy the actuarially determined contribution requirements as mandated by state statutes.

B. Related-Party Investments

As of June 30, 19X5, the Centerville PERS held bond anticipation notes of $500,000 issued by the City. The bond anticipation notes carry a 6% interest rate, which is a competitive interest rate. The notes were acquired on June 1, 19X5. On July 21, 19X5, the bond anticipation notes were retired when the City issued the related long-term bonds to various nonrelated investors. No other debt instruments issued by the City were held by the Centerville PERS during the fiscal year ended June 30, 19X5.

C. Funding Status and Progress

Presented below is the total pension benefit obligation of the City of Centerville PERS. The amount of the total pension benefit obligation is based on a standardized measurement established by GASB-5 that, with some exceptions, must be used by a PERS. The standardized measurement is the actuarial present value of credited projected benefits. This pension valuation method reflects the present value of estimated pension benefits that will be paid in future years as a result of employee services performed to date and is adjusted for the effects of projected salary increases. A standardized measure of the pension benefit obligation was adopted by the GASB to enable readers of PERS financial statements to (a) assess the City of Centerville PERS funding status on a going-concern basis, (b) assess progress made in accumulating sufficient assets to pay benefits when due, and (c) make comparisons among PERS.

Because the standardized measure is used only for disclosure purposes by the City of Centerville PERS, the measurement is independent of the actuarial computation made to determine contributions to the PERS. The actuarial funding method used to determine contributions to the PERS is explained in Part D of this note.

Pension Disclosures

A variety of significant actuarial assumptions are used to determine the standardized measure of the pension benefit obligation and these assumptions are summarized below:

- The present value of future pension payments was computed by using a discount rate of 7%. The discount rate is equal to the estimated long-term rate of return on current and future investments of the pension plan
- Future pension payments reflect an assumption of a 5% (compounded annually) salary increase as a result of inflation
- Future pension payments reflect an assumption of a 2% (compounded annually) salary increase as a result of seniority and/or merit adjustments
- Future pension payments reflect no postretirement benefit increases, which is consistent with the terms of the pension agreement

The standardized measure of the unfunded pension benefit obligation as of June 30, 19X5, is as follows:

	(in millions)
Pension benefit obligation:	
Retirees and beneficiaries currently receiving benefits and terminated employees not yet receiving benefits	$13.5
Current employees—	
Accumulated employee contributions including allocated investment income	2.3
Employer-financed vested	7.1
Employer-financed nonvested	8.4
Total pension benefit obligation	31.3
Net assets available for benefits, at market	20.1
Unfunded pension benefit obligation	$11.2

No changes in actuarial assumptions or benefit provisions that would significantly affect the valuation of the pension benefit obligation occurred during 19X5.

D. Contributions Required and Contributions Made

Periodic employer contributions to the pension plan are determined on an actuarial basis using the entry age normal actuarial cost method. Normal cost is funded on a current basis. The unfunded actuarial accrued liability is funded over a 30-year period. Periodic contributions for both normal cost and the amortization of the unfunded actuarial accrued liability are based on the level percentage of payroll method. The funding strategy for normal cost and the unfunded actuarial accrued liability should provide sufficient resources to pay employee pension benefits on a timely basis.

Total contributions to the pension plan in 19X5 amounted to $2,885,000 of which $1,825,000 and $1,060,000 were made by the City of Centerville and its employees, respectively. The contributed amounts were actuarially determined as described above and were based on an actuarial valuation as of June 30, 19X5. The pension contributions represent funding for normal cost ($2,452,250) and the amortization of the unfunded actuarial accrued liability ($432,750). Contributions made by the City of Centerville and its employees represent 7.4% and 4.3%, respectively, of covered payroll for the year.

Significant actuarial assumptions used to compute pension contribution requirements are the same as those used to determine the standardized measure of the pension obligation.

The computation of the pension contribution requirements for 19X5 was based on the same (a) actuarial assumptions, (b) benefit provisions, (c) actuarial funding method, and (d) other significant factors as used to determine pension contribution requirements in the previous year.

E. Trend Information

Historical trend information for the City of Centerville PERS is presented below:

	Fiscal year		
	19X5	19X4	19X3
• Net assets available for benefits as a percentage of the pension benefit obligation applicable to the City's employees	62.4%	61.9%	61.3%
• Unfunded pension benefit obligation as a percentage of the City's annual covered payroll*	131.9%	138.3%	140.1%
• City's contributions to the pension plan as a percentage of annual covered payroll	7.4%	7.3%	7.3%

*Showing the unfunded pension benefit obligation as a percentage of the City's annual covered payroll approximately adjusts for the effects of inflation for analytical purposes.

Ten-year historical trend information is disclosed on pages XX-XX of the City of Centerville PERS separate financial report.

Historical trend information is presented in order for a reader to assess the progress made in accumulating sufficient assets to pay pension benefits as they become payable. ◄

SINGLE-EMPLOYER PERS INCLUDED AS A PENSION TRUST FUND IN THE EMPLOYER REPORTING ENTITY

GASB-5 establishes pension reporting disclosures for both a single-employer PERS that prepares a separate financial report and the employer that contributes to the single-employer PERS. When the single-employer PERS is reported as a Pension Trust Fund in the employer reporting entity, pension information must be disclosed in a manner to avoid making duplicate disclosures. A single set of disclosures should be made in the employer reporting entity by incorporating the following disclosure requirements that have been described in earlier sections of this chapter:

- Pension disclosure requirements for separately issued PERS financial reports (see section entitled Pension Disclosures in Separately Issued PERS Financial Reports)
- Pension disclosure requirements for employer financial reports (see section entitled Single-Employer/Agent Multiple-Employer PERS)
- Ten-year historical trend information (incorporated by reference or reproduced in the employer CAFR or general purpose financial statements)

The disclosure requirements described above should be modified to avoid disclosing the same information more than once in the employer reporting entity when a single-employer PERS is included in the reporting entity as a Pension Trust Fund.

> **OBSERVATION:** *Paragraph 35(f) of GASB-5 requires that there be a reference in the employer financial report to the 10-year historical trend information either (a) in the separately issued PERS financial report or (b) reproduced in the employer CAFR or general purpose financial statements. When the single-employer PERS is included as a Pension Trust Fund in the employer reporting entity, the employer may incorporate the 10-year historical trend information into its financial statements by making reference to the separately issued PERS financial report, if publicly available, or to the employer CAFR when the 10-year historical trend information is reproduced in the latter report.*

MULTIPLE-EMPLOYER PERS INCLUDED AS A PENSION TRUST FUND IN THE EMPLOYER REPORTING ENTITY

GASB-5 establishes pension reporting disclosures for both a multiple-employer PERS that prepares a separate financial report and the employer that contributes to the multiple-employer PERS. When the multiple-employer PERS is reported as a Pension Trust Fund in the employer reporting entity, pension information must be disclosed in a manner to avoid making duplicate disclosures. The presentation in the employer financial report should incorporate the following disclosure requirements, which are discussed in other sections of this chapter:

- Pension disclosure requirements for separately issued PERS financial reports (see section entitled Pension Disclosures in Separately Issued PERS Financial Reports)
- Pension disclosure requirements for employer financial reports (see section entitled Single-Employer/Agent Multiple-Employer PERS)
- Ten-year historical trend information (incorporated by reference or reproduced in the employer CAFR or general purpose financial statements)
- Pension disclosure requirements for employers contributing to cost-sharing multiple-employer PERS (see section entitled Employers Contributing to Cost-Sharing Multiple-Employer PERS)

When the above disclosure requirements are combined to present a single set of disclosures in the employer financial report, the disclosure requirements related to the employer should be emphasized. In addition, there should be a reference to the separate PERS financial report for those interested in obtaining pension information related to the PERS.

> **OBSERVATION:** *Disclosures that describe the funding status of a pension plan are required by the following paragraphs of GASB-5:*
> - **30(c):** *Funding status in separately issued PERS financial reports*
> - **35(c):** *Funding status in employer financial reports (for single-employer PERS and agent multiple-employer PERS)*
> - **39(g):** *Total PERS pension benefit obligation and total PERS net assets available for benefits (for cost-sharing multiple-employer PERS)*

Pension Disclosures

- **Footnote 17 (paragraph 39):** *Allocated share of pension benefit obligation and allocated share of net assets available for benefits (for cost-sharing multiple-employer PERS whose contributions to the PERS exceed 50% of the total required contribution)*

GASB-5 notes that the disclosure requirements established by the above paragraphs may best be achieved by preparing a "side by side" presentation.

> **OBSERVATION:** *Paragraph 35(f) of GASB-5 requires that there be a reference in the employer financial report to the 10-year historical trend information either (a) in the separately issued PERS financial report or (b) reproduced in the employer CAFR or general purpose financial statements. When the multiple-employer PERS is included as a Pension Trust Fund in the employer reporting entity, the employer may incorporate the 10-year historical trend information into its financial statements by making reference to the separately issued PERS financial report, if publicly available, or to the employer CAFR when the 10-year historical trend information is reproduced in the latter report.*

EMPLOYERS CONTRIBUTING TO COST-SHARING MULTIPLE-EMPLOYER PERS

In a cost-sharing multiple-employer PERS, all risks and costs are shared proportionately among the participating employers. In addition, a single actuarial valuation is computed for the PERS as a whole and all participating employers make payments to the PERS based on the same contribution rate. Employers that contribute to a cost-sharing multiple-employer PERS must make disclosures in their financial statements concerning (a) description of the plan, (b) contributions required and made, (c) funding status and progress, and (d) related party investments.

Description of Plan The PERS to which the employer contributes should be identified as a cost-sharing multiple-employer PERS. The plan description should disclose the type of employees covered by the plan, benefits provided to employees by the plan, and the authority under which the pension plan was established. Also, there should be a description of the eligibility requirements that must be met before an employee is covered by the plan. The description of the eligibility requirements should include vesting requirements.

Included in the description of the pension plan should be an identification of the authority that was used to establish contribution requirements. Also, the contribution requirements by both the employer and employees should be disclosed. The amount of the employer's current-year covered payroll and total current-year payroll for all employees should be included in the note.

Contributions Required and Made The note to the employer's financial statements should disclose the following concerning contributions to the cost-sharing multiple-employer PERS:

- Amount of actuarially determined employer contribution requirements
- Amount of contributions made by employers
- Amount of contributions made by employees
- Amount of contributions made by employer as a percentage of the employer's current-year covered payroll
- Amount of contributions made by employees as a percentage of the employer's current-year covered payroll

The effects of changes during the current year resulting from modification of (a) actuarial assumptions, (b) pension benefit provisions, (c) actuarial fund method, or (d) other significant factors should be disclosed. The impact of the changes should be determined based on the effect on the employer's contribution rate and shown as a percentage of the employer's current-year covered payroll.

Fund Status and Progress The disclosure in the employer's financial statements should state that the pension benefit obligation is determined by using the standardized disclosure measure of the present value of pension benefits, adjusted for changes in future salary levels, and any step-rate benefits. The note should also state that the standardized measured amount is the actuarial present value of credited projected benefits and should help the reader of the employer's financial statements (a) assess the PERS funding status on a going-concern basis, (b) assess progress made in accumulating assets to pay benefits as they become due, and (c) make comparisons with the funding status and progress of other PERS and other employers.

The note to the employer's financial statements should also identify the total pension benefit obligation (standardized disclosure measure) and the total net assets available to pay pension benefits. The net assets should be valued as of the same date that was used to value the pension obligation of the PERS. It should be noted that the disclosure refers to the total obligation and net assets of the cost-sharing multiple-employer PERS, which of course is made up of more than one employer. Rather than disclose the total obligation and net assets of the PERS, an employer that contributes more than 50% of the actuarially determined contribution requirements for all employers may disclose only its allocated share of the pension benefit obligation and net assets. The method of allocating the pension benefit obligation and net assets (employer's actuarially determined contribution requirement as a percentage of total current-year actuarially determined contribution requirements for all employers) should be disclosed.

Irrespective of whether an employer discloses the PERS total pension benefit obligation and net assets or the employer's allocated share, the note to the employer's financial statements should identify the employer's actuarially determined contribution requirement as a percentage of the total current-year actuarially determined contribution requirements for all employers.

Finally, the disclosure should contain a reference to the 10-year historical trend information presented as part of the PERS separately issued financial report. The statement should be made that the 10-year historical trend information can be used to evaluate the PERS progress in acquiring assets to pay pension benefits as they become due.

Related-Party Investments When the PERS assets include loans to the employer or related parties, the note should disclose the amount of the loan and the type of loan (such as notes, bond anticipation notes, and similar securities).

> **OBSERVATION:** *Because the above relationships represent related-party transactions, the accounting and reporting standards established by FASB-57 (Related Party Disclosures) should be considered.*

Note Illustration

Following is an example of a note to an employer's financial statements that describes a pension plan administered by a cost-sharing multiple-employer PERS.

Pension Disclosures

▶ A. Plan Description

All full-time employees of the City of Centerville are covered by the State Public Employee Retirement System, which is a cost-sharing multiple-employer PERS.

All full-time employees are eligible and must participate in the State PERS. The pension plan provides pension benefits, deferred allowances, and death and disability benefits. A member may retire after reaching the age of 55 or accumulating 25 years of service with the City or another entity covered by the State PERS. Benefits vest after 12 years of service. Employees who retire at or after age 55 with 12 or more years of service are entitled to pension payments for the remainder of their lives equal to 2% of their final, five-year average salary times the number of years for which they were employed by a participant in the State PERS. The final, five-year average salary is the average salary of the employee during the final five years of full-time employment exclusive of overtime.

Pension provisions include deferred allowances whereby an employee may terminate his or her employment with the City after accumulating 25 years of service but before reaching the age of 55. If the employee does not withdraw his or her accumulated contributions, the employee is entitled to all pension benefits upon reaching the age of 55.

Pension provisions include death and disability benefits, whereby the disabled employee or surviving spouse is entitled to receive annually an amount equal to 45% of the employee's final, five-year average salary exclusive of overtime payments. The disabled employee is entitled to receive disability payments for life, while the surviving spouse may receive death benefits for life or as long as he or she does not remarry. Benefits are determined by state statute.

Both the City's current-year covered payroll and its total current-year payroll for all employees amount to $5,000,000.

B. Contributions Required and Made

Employees of the City are required to pay 4% of their gross earnings to the pension plan. The City makes annual contributions to the pension plan equal to the amount required by state statutes. During 19X5, the City was required to contribute 9% of its gross payroll to the plan.

Total contributions made during fiscal year 19X5 amounted to $650,000, of which $450,000 was made by the City and $200,000 was made by employees. These contributions represented 9% (City) and 4% (employees) of covered payroll.

C. Funding Status and Progress

The amount of the total pension benefit obligation is based on a standardized measurement established by GASB-5 that, with some exceptions, must be used by a PERS. The standardized measurement is the actuarial present

Pension Disclosures

value of credited projected benefits. This pension valuation method reflects the present value of estimated pension benefits that will be paid in future years as a result of employee services performed to date, and is adjusted for the effects of projected salary increases. A standardized measure of the pension benefit obligation was adopted by the GASB to enable readers of PERS financial statements to (a) assess the PERS funding status on a going-concern basis, (b) assess progress made in accumulating sufficient assets to pay benefits when due, and (c) make comparisons among other PERS and among other employers.

Total unfunded pension benefit obligation of the State PERS as of June 30, 19X5, was as follows:

	(in millions)
Total pension benefit obligations	$265
Net assets available for pension benefits, at market	201
Unfunded pension benefit obligation	$ 64

The measurement of the total pension benefit obligation is based on an actuarial valuation as of June 30, 19X5. Net assets available to pay pension benefits were valued as of the same date.

The City's 19X5 required contribution to the State PERS represents 3.5% of the total current-year actuarially determined contribution requirements for all employers covered by the pension plan.

Ten-year historical trend information is presented in the 19X5 State PERS Comprehensive Annual Financial Report. This information is useful in assessing the pension plan's accumulation of sufficient assets to pay pension benefits as they become due.

D. Related-Party Investments

During 19X5 and as of June 30, 19X5, the State PERS held no securities issued by the City or other related parties. ◄

COMPONENT UNITS' PENSION INFORMATION IN THE REPORTING ENTITY'S FINANCIAL REPORTS

A component unit is a separate governmental unit whose financial statements are combined with those of its oversight unit to form a single financial reporting entity. Information related to the component unit's pension plan must be disclosed in the reporting entity's financial statements to satisfy the disclosure requirements mandated by GASB-5.

The extent of pension disclosures for the component unit's pension information in the reporting entity's financial statements is dependent upon whether the component unit's separate financial report is publicly available and whether the disclosures in the report satisfy the disclosure standards established by GASB-5. If the financial report is not publicly available (or the pension information requirements by GASB-5 are not met), the reporting entity's financial statements must contain pension disclosure information that satisfies disclosure requirements related to single-employer or agent multiple-employer PERS or related to cost-sharing multiple-employer PERS.

If the component unit's financial report is publicly available (and contains sufficient pension disclosures), the disclosures in the reporting entity's financial statements can be abbreviated by referring to the component unit's financial report and presenting condensed pension information. The condensed pension information can be limited to the following disclosures, depending upon what type of PERS administers the component unit's pension plan:

- Single-employer or agent multiple-employer PERS
  — Amount of pension benefit obligations (standardized measure)
  — Amount of net assets available for pension benefits
  — Comments on whether actuarially determined contributions were paid by the component unit to the PERS
- Cost-sharing multiple-employer PERS
  — Comments on whether actuarially determined contributions were paid by the component unit to the PERS
  — Comments that the component unit made contributions to the same PERS that the oversight unit contributed to, if applicable

Note Illustration

Following is an example of a note to a reporting entity's financial statements that describes condensed information related to a component unit's pension plan.

▶ The Centerville Transit Authority, a component unit of the City's reporting entity, has adopted a pension plan which is administered by the Centerville Transit Authority Public Employee Retirement System (CTAPERS). As of June 30, 19X5, the CTAPERS total pension benefit obligation and net assets available for pension benefits amounted to $16.5 million and $11.4 million, respectively. Contributions made by the CTAPERS were equal to the actuarially determined contribution requirement for the fiscal year ended June 30, 19X5.

Detailed information concerning the Centerville Transit Authority pension plan is presented in its publicly available 19X5 Comprehensive Annual Financial Report. ◀

NONCONTRIBUTING EMPLOYERS

Some governmental employees may be covered by a pension plan, but their employer may not be required to contribute to the retirement system. For example, a state government may have established a pension plan for all municipal law enforcement professionals whereby the pension plan is fully funded by the state and by contributions made by the covered employees.

When employees are covered by a pension plan but their employer is not legally required to contribute to the plan, only the following disclosures should be made in the employer's financial statements:

- Identify the nonemployer that makes pension contributions for the noncontributing employer's employees
- Disclose the amount of the pension contribution made by the nonemployer contributor
- Describe the type of employees covered by the pension plan
- Describe employee eligibility requirements, including vesting requirements
- Disclose the amount of the noncontributing employer's total current-year payroll for all employees
- Disclose the amount of the noncontributing employer's current-year covered payroll
- Describe contribution requirements applicable to the nonemployer contributor and the covered employees
- Identify the authority that mandates the contribution requirements

The limited pension disclosure requirements are appropriate only when the noncontributing employer is not legally required to contribute to the pension plan. If contributions are made by a nonemployer as simply a convenience for the employer, the employer must satisfy the disclosure requirements established for a defined benefit plan or a defined contribution plan.

Note Illustration

Following is an example of a note that describes pension information related to a noncontributing employer.

▶ Teachers and staff of the Centerville School District are covered by the State Education Public Employee Retirement System (SEPERS). The City of Centerville, including its component units, is not legally required to contribute to the SEPERS, which is fully funded by the state and by contributions from covered employees. During 19X5, the state made contributions of $346,000 to the SEPERS on behalf of employees of the school district.

All full-time employees of the school district are covered by and must participate in the SEPERS. Under the pension plan, benefits vest after 12 years of full-time employment. An employee with 30 years of service may retire at age 57 1/2 and receive full retirement benefits.

Based on state statute, employees covered by the pension plan must contribute 5% of their gross earnings to the pension fund. The state is required to make actuarially determined contributions that maintain the financial integrity of the retirement system.

The City of Centerville's total current-year payroll for all of its employees amounted to $14.4 million. The amount of its current-year payroll covered by the pension plan administered by the SEPERS was $3.9 million. ◀

UNFUNDED PENSION ARRANGEMENTS

Some employers may establish a PERS that administers its pension plan on a pay-as-you-go basis. That is, the pension fund is not funded and pension benefits are simply financed by the employer as they become payable to employees or beneficiaries.

When an employer's pension fund is unfunded, the pension disclosure requirements established by GASB-5 must be observed. Thus, disclosure requirements established for a plan administered as a single-employer or agent multiple-employer PERS must be observed, or disclosure requirements established for a plan administered as a cost-sharing multiple-employer PERS must be observed.

> **OBSERVATION:** *It should be reiterated that GASB-5 defines the term PERS as public employee retirement systems and pension plans that are administered directly by the governmental employer.*

REPORTING BY NONEMPLOYER CONTRIBUTORS

Some governmental units may be legally required to contribute to a pension plan that covers individuals who are not employed by the governmental unit. For example, a state government may be required to contribute to a state-wide pension system that covers teachers, even though the teachers are employed by local school districts and not by the state. In this situation the state is referred to as a nonemployer contributor.

When a governmental unit (nonemployer contributor) is legally required to contribute to a pension fund that covers individuals that are not its employees, the governmental unit must satisfy the disclosure requirements established by GASB-5. If the nonemployer contributor contributes to a single-employer or agent multiple-employer PERS, disclosure requirements established for these types of PERS must be satisfied with one modification (see previous discussions, Single-Employer/Agent Multiple-Employer PERS, Single-Employer PERS Included as a Pension Trust Fund in the Employer Reporting Entity, and Multiple-Employer PERS Included as a Pension Trust Fund in the Employer Reporting Entity). The plan description requirement that refers to the amount of the employer's current-year covered payroll and total current-year payroll for all employees should be changed to read "Amount of current-year payroll and number of employees covered by the PERS to which the nonemployer contributor must contribute." If the nonemployer contributor contributes to a cost-sharing multiple-employer PERS, disclosure requirements related to that type of PERS must be satisfied with one modification (see previous discussion, Employers Contributing to Cost-Sharing Multiple-Employer PERS). The plan description requirement that refers to the amount of the employer's current-year covered payroll and total current-year payroll and number of employees should be changed to read "Amount of current-year payroll and number of employees covered by the PERS to which the nonemployer contributor must contribute."

DEFINED CONTRIBUTION PENSION PLAN INFORMATION

There is a significant difference between a defined contribution pension plan and a defined benefit pension plan. In a defined contribution pension plan, *the benefits a participant will receive depend solely on the amount contributed to the participant's account, the returns earned on investments of those contributions, and forfeitures of other participants' benefits that may be allocated to the participant's account.* In a defined benefit pension plan, the benefits are dependent upon such factors as number of years of service, age, compensation, and other factors that are part of the benefit formula. For this reason, the pension disclosure requirements for a defined contribution pension plan are different from those for a defined benefit pension plan.

Some pension plans may have characteristics of both a defined contribution pension plan and a defined benefit pension plan. GASB-5 concludes that such plans must be carefully evaluated to determine whether the disclosure requirements for a defined contribution pension plan or disclosure requirements for a defined benefit pension plan should be observed.

> **OBSERVATION:** *The Exposure Draft that preceded GASB-5 did not propose disclosure requirements for defined contribution pension plans; however, the GASB eventually concluded that disclosure standards should be established for all governmental pension plans.*

The specific disclosure requirements for a defined contribution pension plan are established for separately issued financial statements of a PERS and an employer's financial statements.

Notes to Separately Issued Financial Statements

When a PERS administers a defined contribution pension plan and issues separate financial statements, the financial statements should include a note that (a) describes the pension plan and (b) summarizes significant accounting policies and plan asset matters.

Plan Description   The PERS should be identified as the administrator of a (a) single-employer defined contribution plan or (b) multiple-employer defined contribution plan. Although the PERS reports as a separate entity, the note to its financial statements should disclose whether it is a component unit of a reporting entity. The reporting entity should be identified. The number as well as the type of contributing employers and nonemployer contributors should be included in the plan description. Also, the plan coverage should be described by identifying the type of employees covered by the defined contribution pension plan and the current membership of the plan.

The note disclosure should describe the benefits provided to employees by the plan, and the authority under which those benefits were established. Also, there should be a description of the eligibility requirements that must be met before an employee is covered by the plan. The requirements for vesting should be disclosed in the note. The basis for requiring contributions to the plan should be disclosed. In addition, the specific contributions that must be made by the employer and employees should be described.

Summary of Significant Accounting Policies and Plan Asset Matters The basis of accounting used by the PERS should be disclosed. Generally, the basis of accounting will be the accrual basis. The valuation methods used to report plan assets in the financial statements of the PERS should be disclosed. When the cost basis is used to value assets held by the plan, the disclosures in the financial statements should include a description of the accounting method used to record exchanges or swaps of securities. If the plan's assets are not valued at market in the PERS balance sheet, the market value of the assets should be disclosed.

If there has been a change in accounting policies used during the accounting period that affects the valuation of net assets available for pension benefits, the dollar value of the effects should be disclosed.

The concentration of investments in a single organization should be described. When investments in a single organization are equal to or greater than 5% of the pension plan's net assets available for pension benefits, the amount and identification of the investment must be disclosed. However, disclosure is not necessary when the securities held by the pension plan represent investments in U.S government securities or investments guaranteed by the U.S. government.

> **OBSERVATION:** *Although a PERS does not have to disclose investments in securities issued or guaranteed by the U.S. government under GASB-5, disclosure requirements established by GASB-3 (Deposits with Financial Institutions, Investments (including Repurchase Agreements), and Reverse Repurchase Agreements) must be satisfied.*

There should be disclosures of assets held by the defined contribution pension plan that represent a financial interest in a related party. The financial interest may include investments, loans, or lease agreements whereby the PERS is the lessor. A related party may include the following:

- A PERS official
- A governmental employer official
- A party related to a PERS official
- A party related to a governmental employer official
- A nonemployer contributor to the pension plan
- A component unit or other governmental agency that is included in the reporting entity of an employer that participates in the pension plan

When a PERS allows an employee to borrow from amounts contributed by the employee, there is no need to disclose the resulting loan held by the PERS as a related party loan.

> **OBSERVATION:** *Because the above relationships represent related-party transactions, the accounting and reporting standards established by FASB-57 (Related Party Disclosures) should also be considered.*

Note Illustration

Following is an example of a note that illustrates the disclosure requirements for a defined contribution pension plan administered by a PERS.

▶ A. Plan Description

The Centerville Public Employee Retirement System (CPERS) is a single-employer PERS that administers the City's defined contribution pension plan for its municipal employees. The CPERS prepares and distributes separate financial statements as required by state statute but its financial statements are also included as a component unit of the City of Centerville's reporting entity. The City is the only nonemployee contributor to the pension plan. All employees of the City, including wage earners and salaried supervisory personnel, are covered by the defined contribution pension plan. As of June 30, 19X5 the pension plan's current membership was 2,463 employees.

A defined contribution pension plan provides pension benefits in return for services rendered, provides an individual account for each participant, and specifies how contributions to the individual's account are to be determined instead of specifying the amount of benefits the individual is to receive. Under a defined contribution pension plan, the benefits a participant will receive depend solely on the amount contributed to the participant's account, the returns earned on investments of those contributions, and forfeitures of other participants' benefits that may be allocated to such participant's account. As established by state statute, all full-time municipal employees of the City must participate in the pension plan from the date they are hired. Contributions made by an employee vest immediately and contributions made by the City vest after 5 years of full-time employment. An employee who leaves the employment of the City is entitled to his or her contributions and the City's contributions if vesting requirements are satisfied, plus 3% simple interest. As determined by state statute, each employee must contribute 5% of his or her gross earnings to the pension plan. The City is required to contribute an amount equal to 7% of the employee's gross earnings.

B. Summary of Significant Accounting Policies and Plan Asset Matters

The CPERS financial statements are prepared on the accrual basis of accounting. Contributions from the City and the City's employees are recognized as revenue in the period in which employees provide services to the City. Investment income is recognized as earned by the pension plan. The net appreciation (depreciation) in the fair value of investments held by the pension plan is recorded as an increase (decrease) to investment income based on the valuation of investments as of the date of the balance sheet.

Investments in securities are valued at current market prices. Corporate bond securities are assigned a value based on yields currently available on securities of issuers with credit ratings similar to the securities held by the pension plan. Unrestricted capital stock securities are assigned a value based on quoted market prices. The estimated value assigned to restricted capital stock securities is based on a multiple of current earnings less an appropriate discount. The earnings multiple is based on current multiples and earnings for companies similar to the securities held by the pension plan.

No investment in any one organization represents 5% or more of the net assets available for pension benefits.

There are no investments in, loans to, or leases with parties related to the pension plan. ◄

Employer Disclosures

When an employer contributes to a defined contribution pension plan, the employer's financial statements must include a note that describes certain information related to the pension plan. The employer must make these disclosures whether the pension plan is administered by a PERS, an insurance company, or another organization. GASB-5 requires that the following items be disclosed in the employer's financial statements:

- Plan contributed to by the employer is a defined contribution pension plan
- Amount of the employer's current-year covered payroll
- Amount of the employer's total current-year payroll for all of its employees
- Employer's and employees' obligations to contribute to the plan and the authority that established the obligation
- Plan provisions and eligibility requirements (including types of employees covered by the plan and vesting requirements)
- Amount of employer's contribution requirement and amount actually contributed
- Amount of employees' contribution requirement and amount actually contributed
- Employer's contribution requirement and actual contribution as a percentage of employer's current-year covered payroll
- Employees' contribution requirement and actual contribution as a percentage of employer's current-year covered payroll
- Effects of changes in plan provisions for the current year
- Type and amount of any securities issued by the employer or a related party, and held by the pension plan (includes loans as well as securities)

The disclosure requirements listed above should also be included in a governmental unit's financial statements when the unit is a nonemployer contributor to a defined contribution pension plan. On the other hand, a governmental unit that is a noncontributor employer (another entity is responsible to make contributions to a defined contribution plan that covers its employees) must make disclosures in its financial statements that comply with the disclosure requirements established for noncontributing employers (see section entitled Noncontributing Employers).

Note Illustration

Following is an example of a note to a governmental unit's financial statements when the unit contributes to a defined contribution pension plan.

▶ The City of Centerville contributes to the Centerville Public Employee Retirement System (CPERS), which is a defined contribution pension plan.

A defined contribution pension plan provides pension benefits in return for services rendered, provides an individual account for each participant, and specifies how contributions to the individual's account are to be determined instead of specifying the amount of benefits the individual is to receive. Under a defined contribution pension plan, the benefits a participant will receive depend solely on the amount contributed to the participant's account, the returns earned on investments of those contributions, and forfeitures of other participants' benefits that may be allocated to such participant's account. As established by state statute, all full-time municipal employees of the City must participate in the pension plan from the date they are hired. Contributions made by an employee vest immediately and contributions made by the City vest after 5 years of full-time employment. An employee who leaves the employment of the City is entitled to his or her contributions and the City's contributions if vesting requirements are satisfied, plus 3% simple interest. As determined by state statute, each employee must contribute 5% of his or her gross earnings to the pension plan. The City is required to contribute an amount equal to 7% of the employee's gross earnings.

During the year the City's required and actual contributions amounted to $630,000, which was 7% of its current-year covered payroll. Employees' required and actual contributions amounted to $450,000, which was 5% of the City's current-year covered payroll.

No pension provision changes occurred during the year that affected the required contributions to be made by the City or its employees.

The CPERS held no securities of the City or other related parties during the year or as of the close of the fiscal year. ◀

LITERATURE REFERENCES

Material in this chapter is based on the following authoritative pronouncements, which are grouped according to the major headings used within the chapter. A dual reference (both paragraph and page number) is used for NCGA-1 and NCGA-2 because the original pronouncements do not use paragraph numbers.

Introduction
GASB-5 *Disclosure of Pension Information by Public Employee Retirement Systems and State and Local Governmental Employers,* ¶¶ 1-4, 23-25, and 28-29.
GASB-1 *Authoritative Status of NCGA Pronouncements and AICPA Industry Audit Guide,* ¶ 9.

Pension Disclosures in Separately Issued PERS Financial Reports
GASB-5 *Disclosure of Pension Information by Public Employee Retirement Systems and State and Local Governmental Employers,* ¶¶ 30-34.

Pension Disclosures in Employer Financial Reports
GASB-5 *Disclosure of Pension Information by Public Employee Retirement Systems and State and Local Governmental Employers,* ¶¶ 35 and 36.

Single-Employer/Agent Multiple-Employer PERS
GASB-5 *Disclosure of Pension Information by Public Employee Retirement Systems and State and Local Governmental Employers,* ¶¶ 35 and 36.

Single-Employer PERS Included as a Pension Trust Fund in the Employer Reporting Entity
GASB-5 *Disclosure of Pension Information by Public Employee Retirement Systems and State and Local Governmental Employers,* ¶ 37.

Multiple-Employer PERS Included as a Pension Trust Fund in the Employer Reporting Entity
GASB-5 *Disclosure of Pension Information by Public Employee Retirement Systems and State and Local Governmental Employers,* ¶ 38.

Employers Contributing to Cost-Sharing Multiple-Employer PERS
GASB-5 *Disclosure of Pension Information by Public Employee Retirement Systems and State and Local Governmental Employers,* ¶ 39.

Component Units' Pension Information in the Reporting Entity's Financial Reports
GASB-5 *Disclosure of Pension Information by Public Employee Retirement Systems and State and Local Governmental Employers,* ¶ 40.

Noncontributing Employers
GASB-5 *Disclosure of Pension Information by Public Employee Retirement Systems and State and Local Governmental Employers,* ¶ 41.

Unfunded Pension Arrangements
GASB-5 *Disclosure of Pension Information by Public Employee Retirement Systems and State and Local Governmental Employers,* ¶ 42.

Pension Disclosures

Reporting by Nonemployer Contributors
GASB-5   *Disclosure of Pension Information by Public Employee Retirement Systems and State and Local Governmental Employers,* ¶ 43.

Defined Contribution Pension Plan Information
GASB-5   *Disclosure of Pension Information by Public Employee Retirement Systems and State and Local Governmental Employers,* ¶¶ 45-47.

CERTAIN POSTRETIREMENT BENEFITS

In addition to pension benefits, postretirement benefits may include payments to retirees or their beneficiaries for life insurance benefits and health insurance benefits. The obligation related to these postretirement benefits in many cases is significant and may exceed the amount related to an employer's pension obligation.

When the obligation related to postretirement benefits is long term, the liability should be shown as part of the General Long-Term Debt Account Group. On the other hand, if the obligation or a portion of the obligation is to be extinguished by using current expendable resources, the obligation (or portion of the obligation) should be classified as a liability of the governmental fund responsible for the payment, and a current expenditure should be reflected in the fund's operating statement.

Accounting for Certain Postretirement Benefits

Although the obligation for postretirement benefits other than pensions (hereinafter referred to as postretirement benefits) is often significant, the accounting for these benefits is not standardized. For example, many governmental entities account for postretirement benefits on a pay-as-you-go basis and do not reflect the obligation in their General Long-Term Debt Account Group. Alternatively, postretirement benefits may be accounted for on an accrual basis much the same way as pension costs are recorded.

In 1985, the FASB issued FASB-87 (Employers' Accounting for Pensions), which superseded APB-8 (Accounting for Costs of a Pension Plan). FASB-87 established accounting and reporting standards for pension plans; however, the Statement is not applicable to plans that provide only life insurance or health insurance benefits or both. Also, the standards established by FASB-87 are not applicable to the portion of a pension plan which provides postretirement health care benefits. Although FASB-87 is not applicable to certain life insurance and health insurance benefits, the Statement does not preclude using the accrual basis for accounting for such benefits.

In 1986, the GASB issued GASB-4 (Applicability of FASB Statement-87, "Employers' Accounting for Pensions," to State and Local Governmental Employers) and concluded in that Statement that "state and local governmental employers, including proprietary funds and similar trust funds, should not change their accounting and reporting of pension activities as a result of the issuance of FASB-87." (On the other hand, GASB-4 does not prohibit the observance of the accounting standards established by FASB-87.) The GASB is studying pension accounting issues and it expects to issue perhaps one or more Statements that will provide accounting standards for governmental entities in this area of accounting. Thus, if a governmental entity is accounting for postretirement benefits on a cash basis, there is no need to change its method of accounting in order for its financial statements to be in accordance with generally accepted accounting principles.

> **OBSERVATION:** *The FASB's agenda includes a research project concerned with establishing accounting standards for postretirement benefits. A Statement is expected to be issued in the near future. The GASB is reviewing the FASB's progress in this area and may add the postretirement benefit topic to its agenda sometime in the future.*

Disclosures for Certain Postretirement Benefits

Until the FASB or the GASB issues a pronouncement that addresses the accounting issues related to postretirement benefits, business and governmental entities will continue to account for postretirement costs and the related obligations in a variety of ways. In order to provide some common information for user groups concerning postretirement benefits, the FASB issued FASB-81 (Disclosure of Postretirement Health Care and Life Insurance Benefits). FASB-81 establishes only disclosure requirements and does not promulgate accounting standards for postretirement benefits.

> **OBSERVATION:** *Although the GASB has not specifically stated that disclosure standards established by FASB-81 are applicable to state and local governments, the hierarchy of governmental generally accepted accounting principles identifies FASB pronouncements as a source of generally accepted accounting principles for state and local governments. (See Chapter 1 for discussion of the accounting principles hierarchy.)*

Certain Postretirement Benefits

FASB-81 is applicable to postretirement health care and life insurance benefits provided to employees by an employer. Health care benefits include such benefits as dental, eye and hearing benefits, and all other health care related benefits. The following items are not covered by the disclosure standards identified in FASB-81:

- Death benefits that are accounted for as part of pension cost (such costs are covered by FASB-87)
- Benefits that are part of multiemployer-sponsored plans
- Payments by an employer to a national health plan

The following disclosures should be made by an employer that provides health care and life insurance benefits to its employees or their beneficiaries:

- Nature of postretirement benefits provided
- Employee groups covered by the plan
- Method of accounting used to account for plan benefits
- Method used to fund plan benefits
- Plan benefit expenditures/expenses recognized during the current period (except as explained in the following paragraph)
- Circumstances that affect the comparability of expenditure/expense recognition for all periods presented

Presented below is an example of a note to the financial statements that illustrates the disclosure standards required by FASB-81.

▶ Postretirement benefits, other than pension benefits, are provided to all full-time employees of the City of Centerville. These benefits include certain health care and life insurance benefits. All full-time employees that retire at the normal retirement age are eligible to receive these benefits. Such benefits are accounted for on a cash basis so that payments during the current year represent benefit coverage for currently retired employees or their beneficiaries. During 19X5, these postretirement benefits amounted to $7.5 million. ◀

The disclosures described above may be made on an aggregate basis for all postretirement benefits or they may be made for each major type of benefit. Employers may use reasonable methods to estimate the cost of benefits.

Certain Postretirement Benefits

Under certain conditions, it may be difficult to identify the expenditure/expense for postretirement benefits applicable to currently active employees. If the cost of postretirement benefits for active employees cannot be separately determined as required in the above paragraph, the following disclosures should be made:

- Total cost of benefits for currently active employees and retirees
- Number of active employees covered by the plan
- Number of retirees covered by the plan

Presented below is an example of a note that incorporates the alternative disclosures.

▶Postretirement benefits, other than pension benefits, are provided to all full-time employees of the City of Centerville. These benefits include certain health care and life insurance benefits. All full-time employees who retire at the normal retirement age are eligible to receive these benefits. The cost of the benefits is actuarially determined and recognized as an expenditure/expense over the service lives of those employees who are expected to qualify for the benefits. The actuarially determined cost is funded on a current basis and amounted to $10 million during 19X5. Based on records maintained by the City, it is not possible to separate the cost of providing benefits for active employees from the cost of benefits received by retirees. The plan covers 2,500 active employees and 200 retirees. ◀

FASB-81 emphasizes that the required disclosures are minimum disclosures and encourages employers to provide additional information that may enhance the understanding of the effects of the postretirement benefit plan on the employer's financial statements. Additional disclosures, as discussed in Appendix B of FASB-81, may include the following:

- Information that may facilitate the measurement of future postretirement benefits for active employees and retirees
- Average postretirement benefits per retiree for the most recent year for which the information is available
- Number of retirees covered by the plan
- Number of active employees covered by the plan and their average ages

It should be noted that these disclosures are neither required nor do they constitute an all-inclusive list of additional voluntary disclosures.

> **OBSERVATION:** FASB-81 covers only postretirement health care and life insurance benefits. Other postretirement benefits may be addressed by subsequent FASB or GASB pronouncements.

LITERATURE REFERENCES

Material in this chapter is based on the following authoritative pronouncements, which are grouped according to the major headings used within the chapter. A dual reference (both paragraph and page number) is used for NCGA-1 and NCGA-2 because the original pronouncements do not use paragraph numbers.

Introduction
NCGA-1 *Governmental Accounting and Financial Reporting Principles*, pp. 8 and 9/¶¶ 33 and 42.

Accounting for Certain Postretirement Benefits
GASB-4 *Applicability of FASB Statement No. 87, "Employers' Accounting for Pensions," to State and Local Governmental Employers*, ¶ 10.

FASB-87 *Employers' Accounting for Pensions*, ¶ 8.

Disclosures For Certain Postretirement Benefits
FASB-81 *Disclosure of Postretirement Health Care and Life Insurance Benefits*, ¶¶ 5-7 and 28.

Governmental Funds and Account Groups

GENERAL AND SPECIAL REVENUE FUNDS

BASIC CONCEPTS AND STANDARDS

A fundamental characteristic of governmental accounting is the concept of the fund as the basic unit of financial accountability. NCGA-1 (Governmental Accounting and Financial Reporting Principles) defines a fund as follows:

> A fiscal and accounting entity with a self-balancing set of accounts recording cash and other financial resources, together with all related liabilities and residual equities or balances, and changes therein, which are segregated for the purpose of carrying on specific activities or attaining certain objectives in accordance with special regulations, restrictions, or limitations.

This chapter discusses the nature of the General Fund and Special Revenue Funds. These two funds are described together because they are accounted for in the same manner; however, the funds serve two very distinct purposes in governmental accounting.

General Fund   Every state or local government must have a General Fund that is used to account for all of the unit's financial resources except for those resources that must be accounted for in a special purpose fund.

The General Fund is used to account for the governmental unit's current operations by recording inflows and outflows of financial resources. Current inflows are typically from revenue sources such as property taxes, income taxes, sales taxes, fines, and penalties. Current outflows are generally related to the unit's provision for various governmental services such as health and welfare, streets, public safety, and general governmental administration. In addition to accounting for current operating revenues and expenditures, the General Fund accounts for other sources of financial resources, such as the sale of long-term debt and transfers from other funds, and uses of financial resources such as transfers to other funds.

Although a state or local government can maintain more than one fund in each governmental fund type, it can maintain only one General Fund.

Special Revenue Funds NCGA-1 states that the purpose of a Special Revenue Fund is to account for the proceeds of specific revenue sources (other than special assessments, expendable trusts, or sources for major capital projects) that are legally restricted to expenditures for specified purposes. An example of a Special Revenue Fund is a state gasoline tax for which distributions are made to local governments and expenditures are restricted to the maintenance of the local highway system.

There is a distinguishing characteristic between a Special Revenue Fund and an Enterprise Fund. Services delivered by a Special Revenue Fund are financed indirectly in that the user of the service does not pay for the service based on actual use. An Enterprise Fund generally obtains most of its financial resources based on direct charges levied against the users. For example, property taxes specifically designated as revenue to finance a public school system would be accounted for in a Special Revenue Fund because a citizen is not charged a fee based on the number of his or her children that attend the school system. Conversely, service charges for a local government's water and sewer system are based on the extent to which the service is used by the citizen, and therefore, would be accounted for in an Enterprise Fund. This distinguishing fundamental characteristic illustrates the basic difference between proprietary funds, which generally operate based on direct user charges, and governmental funds, which generally operate based on indirect charges.

NCGA-1 makes the point that a Special Revenue Fund should be used only when it is legally mandated. In many instances, it may be possible to account for restricted resources directly in the General Fund if these restricted resources are used to support expenditures that are usually made from the General Fund.

The remainder of this chapter refers only to the General Fund, but to reiterate, a Special Revenue Fund is accounted for in the exact same manner as a General Fund.

Basis of Accounting

Basis of accounting refers to when revenues, expenditures, and transfers—and the related assets and liabilities—are recognized in the General Fund. Thus, when a transaction or event occurs in the General Fund, the basis of accounting is used to determine when an actual entry should be made. For example, when property taxes are levied, it must be decided whether to record the levy as revenue in the General Fund on the levy date, on the date the tax is due, or on the date the tax is paid.

Three fundamental accounting bases are used, at least to some degree, to account for transactions and events that affect the General Fund. Although these three bases are used, the predominant method is the modified accrual basis.

Cash basis   Under the cash basis of accounting, revenues and expenditures are recorded when cash is received or paid. NCGA-1 recommends that the cash basis not be used to account for transactions and events of the General Fund. Nonetheless, as described later, some transactions that affect the General Fund are accounted for on a cash basis.

Accrual basis   The purpose of accrual accounting is to reflect events that affect an entity in the period in which the transaction or event occurs, and not in the period when a resultant cash flow occurs. In governmental accounting it is accepted that the accrual basis of accounting is the superior accounting basis; however, not all elements of accrual accounting are used to account for transactions and events of the General Fund. For example, there is no attempt to record depreciation and the amortization of deferred cost, or to capitalize the cost of property, plant, and equipment in the General Fund.

Modified accrual basis   The modified accrual basis is used as the basis of accounting for the General Fund. Under the modified accrual basis, elements of both the cash basis and accrual basis are used.

Measurement Focus

In accounting for a General Fund, the measurement focus is used to determine what transactions and events should be recorded. That is, the measurement will identify those resources and obligations that should be reflected in the balance sheet, and those revenues and expenditures that should be presented in the General Fund's Statement of Revenues and Expenditures.

The General Fund's measurement focus is concerned with reflecting those revenues and expenditures, and assets and related liabilities, that properly identify the net financial resources available for subsequent appropriation and expenditures. (This is basically the flow of current financial resources.) Since the measurement focus is to determine the change in net financial resources, accounts such as fixed assets and long-term obligations are not reflected in the

General and Special Revenue Funds

General Fund's balance sheet since these items will neither provide nor use financial resources of the current budgetary period.

In summary, the flow of net financial resources applied on a modified accrual basis determines the appropriate accounting for General Fund activity. This accounting approach is a narrow interpretation of what constitutes assets, liabilities, revenues, and expenditures. Revenues and the related assets are accrued at the end of the period only if the revenue is earned and if the resultant assets are expected to be realized in time to pay for liabilities outstanding at the end of the period. Expenditures and the related liabilities are recognized only when they are expected to use expendable financial resources of the current period (see Chapter 3 for further elaboration).

Budgetary System and Accounts

A budget is a plan of financial operations that establishes a basis for the control and evaluation of activities financed through the General Fund. The budgetary control process is most effective when a budgetary accounting system, including the use of budgetary accounts, is employed.

Budgetary accounts should be used to account for General Fund transactions. Because budgetary accounts are utilized only for control purposes, their use has no effect on the General Fund's actual financial statements. Budgetary accounts are used to record the General Fund's annual budget and certain commitments related to encumbrances.

Recording the budget The adoption of a budget by a legislative body has no effect on the governmental accounting model because, as already suggested, the budget represents various unexecuted transactions and events. Nonetheless, the budget should be recorded in the General Fund as an integral part of the management control process. To illustrate the recording of a budget in a General Fund, assume that a governmental unit adopts a budget with anticipated revenues of $950,000 and estimated expenditures of $900,000. The budget would be recorded in the following manner:

Estimated Revenues (Control)	950,000	
Appropriations (Control)		900,000
Fund Balance		50,000
Subsidiary ledger for estimated revenues:		
Property taxes		$500,000

Sales taxes	300,000
Fines	70,000
Licenses and permits	50,000
Miscellaneous fees and revenues	30,000
Total	$950,000

Subsidiary ledger for appropriations:	
General government	$300,000
Education and adult training	150,000
Street and highway maintenance	130,000
Health and welfare	120,000
Recreation	100,000
Public safety	80,000
Miscellaneous expenditures	20,000
Total	$900,000

The estimated revenues account is a control account that represents the revenues expected to be recorded during the budgetary period. The control account is supported by a subsidiary ledger that provides a basis for the detail analysis of specific revenue sources and for the comparison of actual revenues to estimated revenues. When revenue amounts are actually received, postings are made to nonbudgetary accounts (such as Revenues—Property Taxes) and to the appropriate subsidiary ledger accounts.

Similar to the estimated revenues account, the appropriations account is a budgetary account and is supported by a subsidiary ledger. As actual expenditures are incurred during the budgetary period, expenditure accounts (nonbudgetary accounts) are used to record the transactions with appropriate postings to the appropriations subsidiary ledger. The appropriations account and its subsidiary ledger are used to control the level of expenditures throughout the budgetary period.

When the legislative budget contains nonoperating sources and uses of financial resources, budgetary accounts should also be used to provide a basis of control over these budgetary items. Generally, nonoperating budgetary items will include transfers to and from other funds and expected proceeds from the issuance of long-term debt. To illustrate the recording of this portion of the budget, assume that a governmental unit (through its General Fund) expects to sell long-term debt for $200,000, receive transfers from other funds of $30,000, and make transfers to other funds of $240,000. The nonoperating portion of the General Fund budget would be journalized as follows:

Estimated Bond Proceeds	200,000	
Estimated Operating Transfers In	30,000	
Fund Balance	10,000	
Authorized Operating Transfers Out		240,000
Subsidiary ledger for estimated operating transfers in:		
Gas works fund		$ 15,000
School district food services fund		10,000
Redevelopment authority fund		5,000
Total		$ 30,000
Subsidiary ledger for authorized transfers out:		
Debt service fund		$150,000
Capital projects fund		80,000
Special assessment fund		10,000
Total		$240,000

The accounts estimated bond proceeds, estimated operating transfers in, and authorized operating transfers out are budgetary accounts and are utilized in a manner similar to the previous budgetary accounts discussed.

When budgetary accounts, both operating and nonoperating, are recorded, the difference between the accounts is debited or credited to the fund balance account. Alternatively, a budgetary account entitled estimated fund balance may be used rather than the fund balance account itself. A debit represents an anticipated deficit and a credit arises from an expected surplus for the budgetary period. Because all budgetary accounts are reversed (or closed) at the end of the budgetary period, the debit or credit to the fund balance account does not affect the actual reported balance in the account.

Recording encumbrances General Fund resources are committed for future expenditures by signing executory contracts such as purchase orders and specific contracts for goods and services. An actual expenditure is not recorded until the contract is executed; however, control over executory contracts must be established to make sure disbursement commitments do not exceed legally authorized limits.

Control is established over executory contracts through the use of an encumbrance system. For example, if the governmental unit signs purchase orders of $80,000, the following entry would be made:

Encumbrances (Control)	80,000	
Reserve For Encumbrances		80,000

General and Special Revenue Funds

Subsidiary ledger for encumbrances:	
General government	$50,000
Education and adult training	20,000
Recreation	5,000
Public safety	3,000
Miscellaneous expenditures	2,000
Total	$80,000

The encumbrances account is a budgetary account and does not represent an actual expenditure for financial reporting purposes. Similarly, the account reserve for encumbrances is not a liability but, rather, is a budgetary account. When the actual goods and services are received, the expenditure and related liability account will be recognized. For example, if it is assumed that the previous encumbrances of $80,000 are vouchered for $78,000, the following entries would be made to record the expenditures and reduce the encumbrances:

Expenditures	78,000	
Vouchers Payable		78,000
Subsidiary ledger for expenditures:		
General government		$51,000
Education and adult training		18,000
Recreation		4,000
Public safety		3,000
Miscellaneous expenditures		2,000
Total		$78,000
Reserve For Encumbrances	80,000	
Encumbrances		80,000
Subsidiary ledger for encumbrances:		
General government		$50,000
Education and adult training		20,000
Recreation		5,000
Public safety		3,000
Miscellaneous expenditures		2,000
Total		$80,000

Encumbrances are initially recorded at their expected cost, while expenditures are vouchered based on actual invoices received from vendors. Thus, there may be differences between the amount encumbered and the amount vouchered. Encumbrances that have not been vouchered by the end of the budgetary period are closed. The closing process is discussed later in this chapter.

ACCOUNTS AND TRANSACTIONS

As suggested earlier, numerous expenditures and revenues are accounted for in a governmental unit's General Fund. The basic accounts and transactions that are part of the General Fund are discussed below. These accounts and transactions are classified as those related to revenues, expenditures, assets, liabilities, and interfund transactions.

Revenues and Other Sources of Financing

Revenues represent increases in current financial resources other than increases due to the issuance of long-term debt, or the receipt of transfers from other funds. General Fund revenues are recorded when they are susceptible to accrual, which means that the revenues must be both measurable and available. In order to meet the measurability criterion, revenues must be subject to reasonable estimation. Revenues are considered to be available when they are expected to be collected during the current budgetary period or after the end of the period but in time to pay liabilities outstanding at the close of the budgetary period. If either or both of the criteria are not satisfied, the revenue item is not recorded in the General Fund as revenue. As demonstrated in the following discussion, the application of the measurable and available criteria to the recognition of revenues in the General Fund results in the use of the accrual basis, modified accrual basis, and cash basis.

Property Taxes NCGA Interpretation-3 (Revenue Recognition—Property Taxes) concludes that property taxes should be recorded in the fiscal year in which they are levied, assuming they are also considered available. The availability criterion is satisfied if the property taxes are expected to be collected within the General Fund's current budgetary period or within 60 days after the end of the period. In unusual circumstances the Interpretation allows property taxes to be collected during a period longer than 60 days; however, if a period longer than 60 days is used, the financial statements must disclose both the length of the period used and the reason for using the longer period.

OBSERVATION: *By the very fact that property taxes are levied, NCGA Interpretation-3 assumes that the measurable criterion is satisfied. The amount of the property taxes is simply based on the assessed value of the property and the current property tax rate used by the state or local government. However, all property taxes assessed will not be collected and the measurability criterion can be satisfied only if the governmental unit can make a reasonable estimate of the amount of uncollectible property taxes.*

To illustrate the accounting for property taxes in the General Fund, assume that the property tax of $20,000,000 is levied, of which 5% is estimated to be uncollectible. The following entry would be made to record the levy:

Property Taxes Receivable—Current	20,000,000	
Revenues—Property Taxes		19,000,000
Allowance For Uncollectible		
Property Taxes—Current		1,000,000

The property tax revenue is recorded on a basis net of the estimated amount of uncollectible accounts. Since the General Fund reflects only the flow of current financial resources, it is inappropriate to record an amount for bad debts expense.

Routine transactions that would occur during the period would include the collection of property taxes and the writeoff of specific uncollectible accounts. For example, the following entries would be made if it is assumed that (1) $16,000,000 of the receivables are collected and (2) $750,000 of specific receivables are identified as uncollectible:

Cash	16,000,000	
Property Taxes Receivable—Current		16,000,000
Allowance For Uncollectible Property		
Taxes—Current	750,000	
Property Taxes Receivable—Current		750,000

At the end of the period, receivables that are past due but still expected to be collected should be identified as delinquent, and appropriate steps should be taken to insure prompt collection. To continue with the example, the following entry would be made if it is assumed that the remaining balance in the receivables account is considered delinquent:

General and Special Revenue Funds

Property Taxes Receivable—Delinquent	3,250,000	
Allowance For Uncollectible Property Taxes—Current	250,000	
Property Taxes Receivable—Current		3,250,000
Allowance For Uncollectible Property Taxes—Delinquent		250,000

On a less routine basis, the accounting for property taxes may require (1) a change in estimate or (2) a change in the method of accounting for the property tax.

Change in estimate At the end of the accounting period it may be determined that the allowance for uncollectible accounts for the current period was overstated or understated. To record the revised estimate of uncollectible accounts, the allowance account and revenue account must be adjusted. For example, assume that in the current illustration the amount of the uncollectible account should have been based on a 6%, not 5%, rate.

The revision of the rate would be recorded at the end of the year as follows:

Revenues—Property Taxes	200,000	
Allowance For Uncollectible Property Taxes—Current		200,000

Again, it should be noted that the revised uncollectible account amount is adjusted through the revenue account, and not recorded as a bad debts expense adjustment.

The effects of the revision of the uncollectible accounts rate may not be confined to only the current period's receivables. The rate that had been used over the past few years may have resulted in the consistent understatement or overstatement of uncollectible accounts. If this occurs, the revision is considered a change in estimate. APB-20 (Accounting Changes) concludes that a change in estimate is not accounted for by restating prior financial statements. To illustrate, assume that in the current example the previous two years' uncollectible accounts were understated by $50,000 and $70,000, and that the current year's estimate is understated by $200,000. The change in estimate is recorded as follows in the current budgetary period:

Revenues—Property Taxes	320,000	
Allowance For Uncollectible Property Taxes—Delinquent		120,000

> Allowance For Uncollectible Property
>   Taxes—Current   200,000

Because a change in estimate does not result in a restatement of prior financial statements (a charge through the fund balance account) or a cumulative effects adjustments (a charge through the current Statement of Revenues and Expenditures), the adjustment is made through the current revenue account, with appropriate disclosure in the financial statements if the effects of the change in estimate are considered material.

Change in accounting method When conditions change, the manner in which property taxes are accounted for may change. APB-20 concludes that generally a change in an accounting principle should be accounted for by reporting the cumulative effects of the change on the activity statement for the period in which the change is made. Thus, the cumulative effects of changing to the new revenue recognition method on the fund balance account, as of the beginning of the period, would be shown on the General Fund's Statement of Revenues and Expenditures and Changes in Fund Balance.

To illustrate a change in the method by which revenue is recognized, assume that a state government enacted a personal property tax in 19X1, but because the measurability criterion could not be satisfied, the tax was accounted for on a cash basis. On July 1, 19X4, it is concluded that the state's experience with the personal property tax now enables the state to change from the cash basis to the modified accrual basis. As of July 1, 19X4, it is determined that of the $8,000,000 of personal property tax assessment, $500,000 remains outstanding (all delinquent) and approximately 80% of the outstanding amount will be collected during the fiscal year 19X5 while the balance will be written off as uncollectible. To account for the change to the modified accrual method, the following entry would be made in the General Fund on July 1, 19X4:

> Personal Property Taxes Receivable—
>   Delinquent   500,000
>   Allowance For Uncollectible Personal
>   Property Taxes—Delinquent   100,000
>   Cumulative Effects On Prior Years Of
>   Applying Retroactively The
>   New Method Of Accounting For
>   Personal Property Taxes   400,000

The cumulative effects account would be shown on the Statement of Revenues and Expenditures for the fiscal year ended June 30, 19X5.

General and Special Revenue Funds

Grants, Entitlements, and Shared Revenues Grants, entitlements, and shared revenues are defined in NCGA-2 (Grant, Entitlement, and Shared Revenues Accounting by State and Local Governments) as follows:

- *Grant*—A contribution or gift of cash or other assets from another government to be used or expended for a specified purpose, activity, or facility.
- *Operating grant*—Grants that are intended to finance operations or that may be used for either operations or for capital outlays at the discretion of the grantee.
- *Capital grant*—A contribution or gift of cash or other assets restricted by the grantor for the acquisition or construction of fixed (capital) assets.
- *Entitlement*—The amount of payment to which a state or local government is entitled as determined by the federal or other government (for example, the Director of the Office of Revenue Sharing) pursuant to an allocation formula contained in applicable statutes.
- *Shared revenue*—A revenue levied by one government but shared on a predetermined basis, often in proportion to the amount collected at the local level, with another government or class of government.

The modified accrual basis should be used to account for grants, entitlements, and shared revenues. Because funds received from other governmental units are usually subject to various restrictions and conditions, the circumstances surrounding the grant, entitlement, or shared revenue program must be evaluated to determine whether the measurable and available criteria have been satisfied before revenue is recognized.

A state or local government generally satisfies grant conditions when an appropriate expenditure, as defined by the grant, is incurred. Thus, the receipt of a grant should be initially recorded as deferred revenue, and then revenue should be subsequently recognized in an amount equal to actual expenditures made under the grant program. For example, assume a local government receives a $2,000,000 grant from the state government for certain law enforcement programs. The receipt of the grant would be journalized as follows in the General Fund:

Cash	2,000,000	
Unearned Revenues—Grants		2,000,000

If it is assumed that $500,000 of qualifying grant expenditures are made, the following entries would be made:

Expenditures—Public Safety	500,000	
Vouchers Payable		500,000
Unearned Revenue—Grants	500,000	
Revenues—Grants		500,000

For the most part, entitlements and shared revenues are forfeited only when the state or local government does not follow regulations and guidelines established by the governmental unit that is providing the financial resources. For this reason, entitlements and shared revenues may be accrued before funds are actually received, so long as the measurable and available criteria can be met. For example, if a state government is entitled to $7,000,000 of shared revenue provided by the federal government, the accrual would appear as follows:

Intergovernmental Receivable— Federal Government	7,000,000	
Revenues—Federal Shared Revenues		7,000,000

When funds are received from another governmental unit under a grant, entitlement, or shared revenue program, but the revenue recognition criteria (measurable and available) have not been satisfied, the amount received should be recorded as deferred revenue. If no funds have been received and the measurability and availability criteria have not been met, the nature of the grant, entitlement, or shared revenue may be disclosed in the financial statements, but no accrual should be made.

A Special Revenue Fund should not be used to account for grants, entitlements, or shared revenues unless specifically required by the program.

Sales Taxes Generally the cash basis is used to account for sales tax revenue. For example, tax receipts that are due to be paid shortly after the close of the budgetary period should not be accrued. On the other hand, it is acceptable to establish an accrual for sales tax receipts when the liability and collectibility of the tax have been established. This situation occurs when a sales tax return has been filed by a merchant but the actual receipt of the sales tax, although delayed, is nonetheless assured. Sales taxes collected for one governmental unit by another governmental unit may be accrued if the tax is expected to be received in time to pay outstanding liabilities at the end of the current budgetary year.

Sales tax receipts that are collected before they are due should be accounted for as deferred revenue.

Taxpayer-Assessed Revenues Tax receipts based on a state or city income tax, or a gross receipts tax, are generally not measurable and/or available; therefore, the modified accrual basis is not appropriate. The cash basis should be used to account for taxpayer-assessed revenues. On the other hand, tax refunds based on tax returns filed should be accrued. For example, if a state government at the end of its fiscal year has received income tax returns that represent refund claims of $1,500,000, the following entry would be made:

Revenues—Income Taxes	1,500,000	
Tax Refunds Payable—Income Taxes		1,500,000

It is acceptable to accrue taxpayer-assessed revenue when both the liability and the collectibility of the tax have been established. This circumstance arises when a taxpayer has filed a tax return; although the actual payment (amount due) is delayed, it is nonetheless assured. For example, a large retailer may have filed its gross receipts tax return with an amount due of $750,000, but the check may have been returned by the bank as a *nonsufficient funds check* because the retailer had inadvertently drawn the check on the wrong bank account. Although the actual cash receipts may be delayed for several days, the state government should make the following accrual for the amount due:

Taxes Receivable—Gross Receipts Taxes	750,000	
Revenues—Gross Receipts Taxes		750,000

Miscellaneous Revenues A governmental unit may collect a variety of other revenues such as fines, parking fees, and inspection charges. These miscellaneous sources of revenues should be accounted for on a cash basis unless the measurable and available criteria can be satisfied.

Miscellaneous revenues should be accounted for in the General Fund unless a state or local ordinance mandates the establishment of a separate fund (Special Revenue Fund). If a separate fund is mandated, it may be necessary to account for the revenue source in an Enterprise Fund rather than through a Special Revenue Fund. An Enterprise Fund would be used when a fee is charged to users based on the extent to which the service is utilized. For example, a separate Enterprise Fund, not a Special Revenue Fund, should be established for a city's parking authority.

Quasi-External Revenues   A quasi-external transaction is a transaction between two related governmental funds whereby revenue and an expenditure (or expense) would have been recorded had the other party been an external party. Generally, receipts of cash from related governmental funds are not classified as revenues but rather as interfund transfers. However, if the General Fund receives cash from another fund in a quasi-external transaction, the cash is recognized as revenue. For example, if an Enterprise Fund pays the General Fund $40,000 in lieu of property taxes, the following entry would be made in the General Fund:

Cash	40,000	
Revenues—Property Taxes		40,000

In this example, a $40,000 property tax expense item would be recorded in the Enterprise Fund.

Proceeds from the issuance of long-term debt   When long-term debt is issued and the proceeds are available to the General Fund, the proceeds are recorded as other financial sources. The long-term debt is not recorded as a liability in the General Fund but rather is reported in the General Long-Term Debt Account Group. In the General Fund the proceeds are reported on the Statement of Revenues and Expenditures but classified separately from operating revenues. To illustrate the accounting for the issuance of long-term debt, assume that $10,000,000 of long-term notes are sold and the proceeds are available to the General Fund. The debt transaction would be recorded as follows:

GENERAL FUND
Cash	10,000,000	
Proceeds From Issuance Of		
Long-Term Debt		10,000,000

GENERAL LONG-TERM DEBT ACCOUNT GROUP
Amount To Be Provided For Payment		
Of Notes	10,000,000	
Notes Payable		10,000,000

If short-term debt is issued by the General Fund, the liability is re-

General and Special Revenue Funds

corded in the General Fund because the payment of the debt will require the use of current expendable financial resources.

Classification and Disclosure Revenues should be presented in the General Fund's Statement of Revenues and Expenditures and identified by major source, such as property taxes, income taxes, and so on. The revenue recognition methods used by the General Fund should be explained in the Summary of Significant Accounting Policies.

Expenditures

NCGA-1 describes expenditures as decreases in fund financial resources other than through interfund transfers. Events that represent (1) a reduction of the General Fund's expendable financial resources, or (2) a claim at the end of the period that will be liquidated by using current expendable financial resources, are recorded as expenditures. Expenditures are accrued when incurred if the event or transaction results in a reduction of the General Fund's current financial resources. If there is no reduction in the fund's current financial resources, no expenditure is recorded. For example, a governmental unit may incur an estimated liability for compensated absences, but if the actual payments to employees are expected to be made several months or years beyond the end of the current fiscal year, the expenditure would not be reflected in the General Fund.

Debt Service Payments Unless legally mandated, interest and principal payments may be made from the General Fund rather than from a Debt Service Fund.

An expenditure should generally be accrued when current financial resources will be used to pay the expenditure. An exception to this rule is the accounting for interest and principal payments related to general long-term debt. NCGA-1 concludes that it is not necessary to accrue interest on long-term debt or to recognize the current portion of the debt as a fund liability. Principal and interest payments are recorded as a fund liability when they become due and payable. To illustrate the accounting for interest and principal payments, assume that $1,000,000 of 6% bonds are issued on January 1, 19X1, and pay interest semiannually beginning on July 1, 19X1. The governmental unit's fiscal year ends on June 30. No interest is accrued for the fiscal year ending June 30, 19X1. The expenditure is recorded in the General Fund on July 1, 19X1, as shown here:

Expenditures—Interest	30,000	
Cash		30,000

The expenditure is recognized entirely as a 19X2 fiscal year expenditure; however, debt service requirements for 19X2 should be disclosed in the 19X1 financial statements.

If a Debt Service Fund is used to accumulate and account for debt service payments, and a transfer has been made from the General Fund to the Debt Service Fund before the amounts are due, the accrued interest, and maturing debt if any, may be recorded as a liability of the Debt Service Fund as of the date of the transfer. When the transfer includes a principal portion, there should be an appropriate reduction of the liability in the General Long-Term Debt Account Group. To continue with the current example, assume that the interest payment is transferred to the Debt Service Fund from the General Fund on June 30, 19X1. To record the transfer, the following entries would be made on June 30, 19X1:

GENERAL FUND
Transfers Out—Debt Service Fund	30,000	
Cash		30,000

DEBT SERVICE FUND
Cash	30,000	
Transfers In—General Fund		30,000
Expenditures—Interest	30,000	
Interest Payable		30,000

Quasi-External Expenditures Transactions between funds are not generally recorded as revenue and expenditure items, except when the exchange is based on a quasi-external transaction. Since the quasi-external transaction suggests the existence of a more or less normal buyer-and-seller relationship, the General Fund should recognize an expenditure when it is the *purchasing* party in the transaction. To illustrate, if the General Fund receives a water and sewer bill of $150,000 from the Water Fund (an Enterprise Fund that operates the governmental unit's water and sewage systems), the quasi-external transaction would be recorded in the General Fund as follows:

Expenditures—Utilities	150,000	
Vouchers Payable		150,000

The Water Fund, the other party to the quasi-external transaction, would record the billing as part of its operating revenue.

General and Special Revenue Funds

Reimbursements A reimbursement arises when one fund (the reimbursed fund) pays the expenditures or expenses of another fund (the reimbursing fund) with the understanding that the reimbursing fund will, at a later date, make an appropriate payment to the reimbursed fund. The manner in which the General Fund accounts for a reimbursement transaction depends upon whether it is the reimbursed or reimbursing fund.

General Fund as Reimbursed Fund   When the General Fund is the reimbursed fund, the initial payment of the expenditure or expense is recorded as an expenditure in the General Fund. At this point, no entry is made in the other fund (reimbursing fund). When the other fund reimburses the General Fund, the General Fund reduces its expenditures by the amount received and the other fund recognizes an expenditure or expense.

To illustrate the General Fund as the reimbursed fund, assume that the General Fund pays a utility bill of $50,000 for an Enterprise Fund. The initial payment is recorded as follows in the General Fund:

Expenditures—Utilities	50,000	
Cash		50,000

When the Enterprise Fund reimburses the General Fund at a later date, the General Fund reverses its original entry:

Cash	50,000	
Expenditures—Utilities		50,000

General Fund as Reimbursing Fund   When the General Fund is the reimbursing fund, the initial payment made by the other fund (reimbursed fund) is not recorded in the General Fund. At the later date when the General Fund reimburses the other fund, the expenditure is recorded in the General Fund.

To continue with the current example, assume that the Enterprise Fund made the $50,000 utility bill payment on behalf of the General Fund. At this point no entry would be made in the General Fund. When the General Fund reimburses the Enterprise Fund at a later date, the following entry would be made in the General Fund:

Expenditures—Utilities	50,000	
Cash		50,000

Reimbursements between funds should not be anticipated by recording the initial payment as an interfund transfer, loan, or advance. The initial payment should be recorded as either an expenditure or expense of the reimbursed fund.

Classification and Disclosure The General Fund should include all expenditures of the governmental unit that are not specifically required to be accounted for in another fund. These expenditures may, for internal and external analysis and reporting, be classified by (1) function or program, (2) organizational unit, (3) activity, (4) character, and (5) object class.

Function (or program) classification Expenditure classification by functions relates to the basic activities carried on by the General Fund. These functions may include expenditures for general governmental services, education, public safety, health and welfare, streets and highway maintenance, and recreation. Alternatively, or as an additional classification scheme, expenditures may be classified by major program (and subclassifications), rather than by function, when the governmental unit employs program budgeting. Program budgeting groups expenditures based on the broad programs identified by the governmental unit irrespective of which organizational unit within the government expects to incur the expenditure.

Organizational unit classification Responsibility accounting is the basis for classifying expenditures by the organizational units that form the structure of the state or local government. The various activities that are accounted for through the General Fund are performed by numerous governmental departments, bureaus, divisions, and the like. Expenditures should be classified in a manner that provides a basis for identifying the organizational unit that was responsible for the expenditure.

Activity classification Within the General Fund, expenditures grouped by activity allow for a more detailed analysis of information than expenditures grouped by function or organizational unit. Activities may include specific tasks such as expenditures related to the answering of weather emergency calls, placement of delinquent minors in foster homes, and the maintenance and repair of street signs. Classifying expenditures by activity may provide a basis for the establishment of standards that will eventually be used to evaluate the economy and efficiency of specific activities.

Character classification Expenditures made from the General Fund may be classified by character. Character classification identifies the fiscal period that benefited from the expenditure. The major character classifications for expenditures are summarized below:

- Current expenditures benefit the current period.
- Debt service expenditures benefit prior, current, and future periods.
- Capital outlay expenditures benefit current and future periods.
- Intergovernmental expenditures may benefit prior, current, or future periods depending on the nature of the specific intergovernmental program.

Object class classification Character classification of expenditures made from the General Fund may be further subdivided based on the object class related to each expenditure. For example, capital outlay expenditures may be subdivided as expenditures for land, land improvements, buildings, and equipment. Classifying expenditures by object class can result in numerous classifications and subclassifications, and care must be taken not to create so many categories that the reader of the financial information is overwhelmed by the amount of detail provided.

Assets

Assets of the General Fund include those resources that are considered current expendable financial resources available for subsequent appropriation and expenditure. Assets other than those that are currently expendable, such as fixed assets, are indeed assets, but they are not available to finance future expenditures that will be made from the General Fund.

Current Assets The General Fund's balance sheet is unclassified in that current and noncurrent categories are not presented. However, it is implied that all assets presented in the General Fund are current assets unless otherwise designated. In the governmental accounting model, a current asset is one that is currently available for expenditure. Thus, the General Fund reflects only those assets that can be used to finance expenditures of the current budgetary period.

General and Special Revenue Funds

Current assets of the General Fund may include such items as cash, temporary investments, various receivables, advances and loans, and amounts due from other funds.

Amounts of cash and temporary investments belonging to the General Fund may be pooled with similar assets of other governmental funds in order to maximize the return on invested resources. Adequate records must be maintained to provide a basis for identifying each fund's assets, including interest earned and receivable at the end of the period. The General Fund's portion of the pooled assets may be designated as equity in pooled cash and temporary investments or some other similar designation. The method of allocating interest on pooled resources to each fund should be disclosed in the financial statements. The following is an example of a disclosure of investment practices and accounting policies related to pooled cash:

▶ The City follows the practice of pooling cash and temporary investments of all funds with the City Treasurer, except for funds that are restricted for various reasons. During the current year the net earned interest yield on all funds held by the City Treasurer was 8.4%. The method of allocating interest earned on pooled cash and temporary investments among governmental fund types provides that, unless otherwise restricted, all interest is recorded in the General Fund. During the current year, $150,000 of the total interest of $165,000 was credited to the General Fund. ◀

Temporary investments made by the General Fund should be accounted for at cost, but if market value is significantly less than cost and the decline is other than temporary, the investment should be reported at its market value. To illustrate, assume that on June 15, 19X5, temporary investments of $500,000 were made by the General Fund. The initial investment would be recorded as follows:

Temporary Investments	500,000	
Cash		500,000

At the end of the fiscal year (June 30, 19X5), if the market value of the temporary investment has declined to $350,000 and the decline is other than temporary, the reduction would be reflected in the following entry:

General and Special Revenue Funds

Decline In Market Value Of Temporary Investments	150,000	
Allowance For Decline In Market Value of Temporary Investments		150,000

The temporary investment must be reported at market value in order not to overstate the amount of expendable financial resources that are available to finance future expenditures of the General Fund.

Assets that may appear on the General Fund's balance sheet but are not available to finance future fund expenditures are discussed below.

Materials and supplies Although inventories of materials and supplies are not current financial resources, they must be reported in the General Fund's balance sheet if they are significant in amount. Inventories may be accounted for by using either the consumption method or the purchase method.

When the consumption method is used, inventories are classified as an asset until they are used, at which time an expenditure is recognized. The remaining balance in the inventory account at year end is reported as an asset; however, since inventories are not available to finance current or future General Fund expenditures, a portion of the fund balance equal to the value of the inventory must be reserved.

Alternatively, the purchase method may be used to account for inventory items. Under the purchase method, an expenditure is recognized when the inventory is acquired. At the end of the period, assuming the inventory balance is significant, an inventory account must be established along with a fund balance reserve.

Journal entries for the consumption method and purchase method are contrasted in the following illustration:

Transaction	Consumption method (periodic inventory system)	Purchase method

Supplies of $75,000 are purchased.	Supplies 75,000
	  Cash 75,000
		Expenditures—
		  Supplies 75,000
		    Cash 75,000

Based on a count at the end of the year it is determined that $60,000 of the supplies were used during the year.	Expenditures—
	  Supplies 60,000
	    Supplies 60,000
		No entry

Fund balance reserve is established at the end of the year.	Fund Balance 15,000
	  Fund Balance—
	  Reserved
	  For
	  Supplies 15,000
		Supplies 15,000
		  Fund Balance—
		  Reserved
		  For
		  Supplies 15,000	

Prepayments and deferrals Prepayments and deferrals represent cash disbursements that have occurred, and therefore are not considered current expendable resources. However, similar to inventories, prepayments and deferrals may be reported as assets in the General Fund's balance sheet. The allocation method or the nonallocation method may be used to account for prepayments and deferrals.

Under the allocation method of accounting for prepayments and deferrals, these items are reported as fund assets and their cost is amortized to the periods that benefited from the advance payment. For example, a prepayment for a two-year insurance policy would be prorated and recognized as an expenditure in each of the two years covered by the policy. At the end of the accounting period, because prepayments and deferrals are not available to finance future General Fund expenditures, the fund balance must be reserved by an amount equal to the carrying value of the asset.

When the nonallocation method is used, the entire payment for the prepaid item or deferral is treated as a current expenditure even though future periods benefit from the advance payment.

> **OBSERVATION:** *Although NCGA-1 requires that significant amounts of inventories be presented in the balance sheet when either the consumption method or purchase method is used, there is no similar requirement to report significant amounts of prepayments and deferrals when the nonallocation method is used.*

The following illustrates accounting for prepayments and deferrals when either the allocation or nonallocation method is used:

Transaction	Allocation method	Nonallocation method

Rent of $5,000 covering a two-year period is prepaid.	Prepaid Rent 5,000
	  Cash 5,000
		Expenditures—
		  Rent 5,000
		  Cash 5,000

At the end of the year the prepaid rent is amortized.	Expenditures—
	  Rent 2,500
	  Prepaid Rent 2,500
		No entry

General and Special Revenue Funds

Fund balance is established at the end of the year.	Fund Balance 2,500
	  Fund Balance—
	    Reserved
	    For Prepaid
	    Rent 2,500
		*Prepaid Rent 2,500
		  Fund Balance—
		    Reserved
		    For Prepaid
		    Rent 2,500

*This entry is not explicitly required by NCGA-1—see the preceding observation paragraph.

Noncurrent assets The General Fund does not usually reflect assets that are not available to finance current expenditures. However, assets that are noncurrent, other than fixed assets, may be presented in the General Fund's balance sheet as long as the fund balance is reserved by an equal amount. To illustrate, if a $100,000 advance to a Special Revenue Fund will not be repaid during the subsequent budgetary period, the transaction would be recorded as follows in the General Fund:

```
Advances To Special Revenue Fund      100,000
   Cash                                          100,000

Fund Balance                          100,000
   Fund Balance—Reserved For
      Advances To Special Revenue Fund            100,000
```

A fund balance reserve account is used when a portion of the fund balance is not available for appropriation or is legally segregated for a specific purpose. A fund balance *designation*, rather than a reserve, should be used when the restricted use of funds is tentative and is discretionary in nature. For example, if specific assets were segregated to be used for possible replacement of equipment, the segregated fund balance should be identified as a fund balance designation and not as a fund balance reserve.

Capital Outlays General fixed assets, such as land, buildings, and equipment, purchased by using General Fund resources should be recorded as an expenditure in the General Fund and capitalized in the General Fixed Assets Account Group. For example, if equipment costing $50,000 is purchased by using resources of the General Fund, the following entries would be made to record the transaction:

GENERAL FUND
Expenditures—Capital Outlays   50,000
    Cash   50,000

GENERAL FIXED ASSETS ACCOUNT GROUP
Equipment   50,000
    Investment In General Fixed Assets—
        General Fund   50,000

Escheat Property Property that escheats to a governmental unit should be recorded in the governmental fund that is entitled to the property or in an Expendable Trust Fund. When the escheat property is recorded in the General Fund, it should be recorded as a receipt of an other source of financial resources, assuming that the property is both measurable and available. To illustrate the receipt of escheat property, assume that investments of $10,000 are available to a governmental unit and that the property can be used to finance general expenditures of the government. The passage of the legal title of the property to the governmental unit would be recorded in the General Fund as follows:

Investments   10,000
    Other Sources Of Financial
        Resources—Escheat Property   10,000

In some instances, the property may be received by the governmental unit without clear title, or the property may have to be held in perpetuity for its owner. In this circumstance, since the property is not available for appropriation, the fund balance must be reserved by an amount equal to the recorded value (fair value) of the property.

Classification and Disclosure With respect to General Fund assets, the following disclosures should be made:

- Disclosure of valuation bases and significant or unusual accounting treatment for material account balances or transactions. (Disclosures should be described in the order of appearance in the balance sheet.)
- Detail notes on the following, if appropriate:
  - Pooling of cash and investments
  - Investments

- Property taxes and other receivables
- Due from other governments—grants receivables

The assets that appear on the General Fund's balance sheet are presented in an unclassified format.

Liabilities

General Fund liabilities are debts of the governmental unit that will be met by using current appropriations and expenditures of the General Fund's expendable financial resources. Liabilities that do not require the use of current expendable financial resources but will be retired at a later date by funds made available through the General Fund, are classified as part of the General Long-Term Debt Account Group.

Current Liabilities Although the General Fund's balance sheet is unclassified, a liability presented on the financial statement is considered to be a current liability. Current liabilities of the General Fund include such items as accounts and vouchers payable, notes payable, accrued liabilities, interest payable, and payroll withholdings. These liabilities represent debts that will be paid within a few days or weeks after the close of the state or local government's fiscal year and are generally easy to identify as current rather than noncurrent liabilities. Discussed below are liabilities that must be carefully evaluated to determine whether they are debts of the General Fund or are more appropriately included in the General Long-Term Debt Account Group.

Tax and revenue anticipation notes Governmental units may issue tax and revenue anticipation notes that will be retired when specific taxes or other specified revenues are collected by the unit. For example, a local government may issue property tax anticipation notes a few weeks or months prior to the anticipated receipt of property tax installments to be paid by taxpayers. Notes that are issued in anticipation of taxes and revenues to be collected are classified as debts (current liabilities) of the General Fund if the proceeds from the issuance of the debt are received by the General Fund.

Bond anticipation notes Bond anticipation notes are issued with the understanding that as soon as the proceeds from the issuance of the long-term bonds are received, the bond anticipation notes will be repaid. Unlike tax and revenue anticipation notes, bond anticipation notes may be reported in the General Long-Term Debt Account Group rather than classified as a liability of the General Fund or another governmental fund.

Bond anticipation notes are considered noncurrent when the circumstances related to their issuance satisfy the two classification requirements established by FASB-6 (Classification of Short-Term Obligations Expected to be Refinanced). First, the state or local government must intend to refinance the bond anticipation notes on a long-term basis; and second, the government's intention must be substantiated by a post-balance sheet issuance of the bonds or the existence of an acceptable financing agreement with another party as of the close of the fiscal year.

When the two conditions established by FASB-6 are not satisfied, the bond anticipation notes must be shown as a General Fund liability if the proceeds from the issuance of the anticipation notes were received by the General Fund.

To illustrate the accounting for bond anticipation notes, assume that on June 1, 19X5, a local government issues $5,000,000 of bond anticipation notes and that the proceeds are made available to the General Fund. The local government's fiscal year ends June 30, and the related bonds are issued on July 20, 19X5. Since management's intention to refinance the bond anticipation notes is substantiated by the post-balance sheet issuance of the long-term debt, the bond anticipation notes are classified as part of the General Long-Term Debt Account Group, as illustrated below:

GENERAL FUND
Cash	5,000,000	
Proceeds From Issuance Of Bond Anticipation Notes		5,000,000

GENERAL LONG-TERM DEBT ACCOUNT GROUP
Amount To Be Provided For Repayment Of Bond Anticipation Notes	5,000,000	
Bond Anticipation Notes Payable		5,000,000

The account proceeds from issuance of bond anticipation notes is a nominal account and is reported as an other source of financing on the General Fund's Statement of Revenues and Expenditures.

On July 20, when the long-term bonds are issued, the following entries are made in the General Long-Term Debt Account Group:

Amount To Be Provided For Repayment Of Long-Term Bonds	5,000,000	
Bonds Payable		5,000,000

General and Special Revenue Funds

    Bond Anticipation Notes Payable   5,000,000
        Amount To Be Provided For
            Repayment Of Bond Anticipation
            Notes   5,000,000

On July 20 the bond issuance would result in the following entries in the General Fund (assuming a Debt Service Fund is not used to account for the retirement of the bond anticipation notes) to record the simultaneous issuance and retirement of the two debt instruments:

GENERAL FUND
    Cash   5,000,000
        Proceeds From Issuance Of Bonds   5,000,000

    Expenditures—Repayment Of Bond
        Anticipation Notes   5,000,000
        Cash   5,000,000

The fund affected by the debt extinguishment must record both an expenditure (for the debt retirement) and an other source of financing (for the new debt proceeds).

If the above example is modified by assuming that either of the two conditions required by FASB-6 are not satisfied, the issuance of the bond anticipation notes is recorded as follows:

GENERAL FUND
    Cash   5,000,000
        Bond Anticipation Notes Payable   5,000,000

GENERAL LONG-TERM DEBT ACCOUNT GROUP
    No entry

The account bond anticipation notes payable is shown as a liability on the General Fund's balance sheet.

Demand bonds A bond agreement may contain a clause that allows bondholders to require a governmental unit to redeem the debt during a specified period of time. The demand feature, or *put*, and related circumstances must be evaluated to determine whether the demand bonds should be classified as general long-term debt (General Long-Term Debt Account Group) or short-term debt (a General Fund liability). GASB Interpretation-1 (Demand Bonds Issued by State and Local Governmental Entities) concludes that the accounting issues related to demand bonds are similar to the issues that arise when bond anticipation notes are issued; therefore, the accounting requirements established by FASB-6 (see discussion of bond anticipation notes) are used to determine the appropriate classification of demand bonds.

A critical element in the application of FASB-6 to the accounting for demand bonds is the existence of a *take out agreement*. A take out agreement represents a commitment from a financial institution to convert demand bonds to long-term debt if the demand feature is executed by bondholders.

Demand bonds that have an exercisable provision for redemption at or within one year of the General Fund's balance sheet date may be reported as general long-term debt, rather than as a liability of the General Fund, when the following criteria are satisfied:

- Before the financial statements are issued, the issuer has entered into an arm's-length financing (take out) agreement to convert bonds "put" but not resold into some other form of long-term obligation.
- The take out agreement does not expire within one year from the date of the issuer's balance sheet.
- The take out agreement is not cancelable by the lender or the prospective lender during that year, and obligations incurred under the take out agreement are not callable by the lender during that year.
- The lender or the prospective lender or investor is expected to be financially capable of honoring the take out agreement.

To illustrate the accounting for demand bonds, assume that $10,000,000 of demand bonds are issued and the proceeds are made available to the General Fund. Also, the General Fund will be used to service the debt (no separate Debt Service Fund is mandated). If the GASB Interpretation-1 criteria are satisfied, the debt would be treated as general long-term debt and recorded as follows:

GENERAL FUND
Cash	10,000,000	
Proceeds From Issuance Of		
Demand Bonds		10,000,000

GENERAL LONG-TERM DEBT ACCOUNT GROUP
Amount To Be Provided For		
Repayment Of Demand Bonds	10,000,000	
Bonds Payable (On Demand)		10,000,000

General and Special Revenue Funds

If the demand bonds are presented for redemption, the redemption and the execution of the take out agreement are recorded as follows:

GENERAL FUND
Expenditures—Redemption Of
  Demand Bonds   10,000,000
    Cash   10,000,000

Cash   10,000,000
  Proceeds From Issuance Of Long-
    Term Notes To Finance
    Redemption Of Demand Bonds   10,000,000

GENERAL LONG-TERM DEBT ACCOUNT GROUP
Bonds Payable (On Demand)   10,000,000
  Amount To Be Provided For
    Repayment Of Demand Bonds   10,000,000

Amount To Be Provided For
  Repayment Of Long-Term
  Installment Notes   10,000,000
  Long-Term Installment Notes
    Payable   10,000,000

If the example presented above is modified by assuming that no take out agreement exists, the initial issuance of the demand bonds would be recorded as follows:

GENERAL FUND
Cash   10,000,000
  Bonds Payable On Demand   10,000,000

GENERAL LONG-TERM DEBT ACCOUNT GROUP
No entry

The bonds are shown as a liability of the General Fund even though they may or may not be presented for redemption during the next budgetary year. If the demand bonds are presented for redemption, the redemption would be accounted for in the following manner:

GENERAL FUND
Expenditures—Redemption Of
  Demand Bonds   10,000,000
    Cash   10,000,000

Bonds Payable On Demand   10,000,000
  Other Financing Sources—
    Retirement Of Demand Bonds   10,000,000

General and Special Revenue Funds

The liability of the General Fund is reduced by simultaneously crediting other financing sources. The latter account is presented on the General Fund's Statement of Revenues and Expenditures.

> **OBSERVATION:** *The simultaneous credit to other financing sources is necessary because the original issuance of the bonds did not give rise to a nominal account (Proceeds from issuance of demand bonds); therefore, the retirement of the demand bonds cannot give rise to a net reduction on the Statement of Revenues and Expenditures (the expenditure account and the other financing sources account negate each other on the Statement of Revenues and Expenditures, although each is presented as a separate line item).*

General Long-Term Debt   The proceeds from the issuance of long-term debt not specifically assigned to a particular fund are recorded in the General Fund; however, the liability itself is reflected in the Long-Term Debt Account Group. The proceeds are recorded as a nonoperating source of financing in the General Fund's Statement of Revenues and Expenditures. For example, the issuance of general obligation serial bonds of $6,000,000 would be recorded as follows:

GENERAL FUND
Cash   6,000,000
    Proceeds From Issuance Of Serial
        Bonds   6,000,000

GENERAL LONG-TERM DEBT ACCOUNT GROUP
Amount To Be Provided For
    Repayment Of Serial Bonds   6,000,000
        Serial Bonds Payable   6,000,000

If legally mandated, the actual resources that will be used to service the general long-term debt will be accumulated in a Debt Service Fund; when interest and principal payments are made, an expenditure will be recognized in the Debt Service Fund. If a separate Debt Service Fund is not used to accumulate resources to service the long-term debt, interest and principal payments may be made from the General Fund.

Classification and Disclosure   With respect to General Fund liabilities, the following disclosures should be made:

- Significant contingent liabilities

- Encumbrances outstanding
- Debt service requirements to maturity (for debt serviced from the General Fund)
- Commitments under noncapitalized leases
- Construction and other significant commitments

When demand bonds are outstanding and serviced through the General Fund, the following should be disclosed:

- General description of the demand bond program
- Terms of any letters of credit or other standby liquidity agreements outstanding
- Commitment fees to obtain the letter of credit
- Any amounts drawn on the letters of credit as of the balance sheet date
- A description of the take out agreement (expiration date, commitment fees to obtain the agreement, and terms of any new obligation under the take out agreement)
- Debt service requirements if a take out agreement is exercised

Interfund Transactions

Each governmental fund is a separate and distinct accounting entity. Transactions among governmental funds that are included in the same reporting entity must be appropriately reflected in each fund involved in the interfund transaction. Generally, transactions that take place between two funds of the same reporting entity do not give rise to operating revenues or operating expenditures or expenses. For example, resources transferred from the General Fund to the Capital Projects Fund would usually not be recorded as expenditures in the General Fund or as revenue in the Capital Projects Fund. Exceptions to the basic philosophy of recording interfund transactions were discussed earlier in this chapter under the headings of quasi-external transactions and reimbursements.

Operating Transfers General Fund operating transfers encompass all transfers to or from the General Fund that are not loans or advances, quasi-external transactions, reimbursements, or residual equity transfers. Examples of operating transfers would include an annual operating subsidy transfer from the General Fund to a Special Revenue Fund, and a transfer from the General Fund to the Debt Service Fund to finance debt service requirements during the budgetary period.

When resources are transferred from the General Fund to another fund, a transfers out account is debited. A transfers in account is credited when the General Fund receives resources from another fund. For example, assume that property taxes of $4,000,000 are collected by the General Fund and the law requires 20% of the collection to be transferred to the School District Fund (a Special Revenue Fund). The transfer between the two funds is recorded as follows:

GENERAL FUND
Cash	4,000,000	
Revenues—Property Taxes		4,000,000
Transfers Out—School District Fund	800,000	
Cash		800,000

SCHOOL DISTRICT FUND
Cash	800,000	
Transfers In—General Fund		800,000

There is an acceptable alternative to using interfund transfer accounts when recording a transfer if one fund is legally required to record the initial revenue receipt but another fund is legally responsible for expending the resources. The fund legally required to record the resources credits a revenue account upon receipt; when the transfer is made to the other fund, the revenue account is debited, not a transfers out account. Likewise, the fund legally responsible for expending the resources credits its revenue account when it receives the resources rather than crediting a transfers in account. Using this acceptable alternative, the previous example involving the school district's right to receive a portion of the property taxes would be recorded as follows:

GENERAL FUND
Cash	4,000,000	
Revenues—Property Taxes		4,000,000
Revenues—Property Taxes	800,000	
Cash		800,000

SCHOOL DISTRICT FUND
Cash	800,000	
Revenues—Property Taxes		800,000

General and Special Revenue Funds

Operating transfers out and transfers in are reported on the General Fund's Statement of Revenues and Expenditures as other financing sources (transfers in) and uses (transfers out).

Residual Equity Transfers A residual equity transfer represents a nonrecurring or nonroutine transfer between funds. Residual equity transfers are generally associated with the creation, expansion, liquidation, or contraction of a fund. Because such transfers are not associated with the operations of the General Fund, they are recorded as adjustments to the fund balance of the General Fund. Likewise, the other fund involved in the residual equity transfer records the transfers as either adjustments to its fund balance (Special Revenue Fund, Capital Projects Fund, and Debt Service Fund), or as adjustments to contributed capital (Enterprise Fund and Internal Service Fund).

The accounting for residual equity transfers is illustrated in the following transactions:

Transaction: The General Fund transfers $100,000 to a newly created Enterprise Fund as part of its initial capitalization.

GENERAL FUND
Residual Equity Transfer (Fund Balance)	100,000	
Cash		100,000

ENTERPRISE FUND
Cash	100,000	
Contributed Capital—General Fund		100,000

Transaction: Two years later the General Fund transfers an additional $500,000 to the Enterprise Fund to increase its capitalization.

GENERAL FUND
Residual Equity Transfer (Fund Balance)	500,000	
Cash		500,000

ENTERPRISE FUND
Cash	500,000	
Contributed Capital—General Fund		500,000

Transaction: After five years the Enterprise Fund is liquidated and its net worth of $630,000 is transferred to the General Fund.

GENERAL FUND
  Cash   630,000
    Residual Equity Transfer (Fund
      Balance)   630,000

ENTERPRISE FUND
  Retained Earnings   30,000
  Contributed Capital—General Fund   600,000
    Cash   630,000

Interfund Receivables/Payables Interfund loans or advances and quasi-external transactions may give rise to interfund receivables or payables. For example, if an Enterprise Fund bills the General Fund $5,000 for services rendered, the quasi-external transactions would be recorded as follows:

GENERAL FUND
  Expenditures   5,000
    Due To Other Funds—Enterprise
      Fund   5,000

ENTERPRISE FUND
  Due From Other Funds—General Fund   5,000
    Revenues   5,000

The General Fund may have amounts due to and due from the same governmental fund. For control purposes the amounts should not be netted; however, for financial reporting purposes, the amounts may be combined and presented as a single amount due to, or due from, the other governmental fund, assuming both are current items. Receivables and payables that are not related to the same fund should not be netted for reporting purposes.

Classification and Disclosure When the General Fund's financial statements are presented with other governmental funds to form the reporting entity's combined financial statements, interfund transactions and accounts may be (but do not have to be) eliminated. Interfund eliminations in the combined financial statements that are not apparent from column headings must be adequately disclosed in notes to the financial statements.

FINANCIAL STATEMENTS

Financial statements of the General Fund must be presented as part of the general purpose financial statements and the Comprehensive

Annual Financial Report of the reporting entity. It may be necessary to present schedules to support information contained in the General Fund financial statements. For example, supplementary schedules may present, in detail, sources of revenues and various classifications of expenditures.

Because a governmental unit has only one General Fund, no combining General Fund financial statements are necessary; however, the General Fund's financial statements are grouped with other governmental fund statements to create the combined financial statements for the reporting entity. When a component unit is presented as part of the oversight unit's reporting entity, the component unit's General Fund financial statements should be presented as a Special Revenue Fund and not combined with the oversight's General Fund financial statements.

Combining financial statements must be prepared for Special Revenue Funds when there is more than one fund.

The financial statements of the General Fund usually include the following:

- Statement of Revenues, Expenditures, and Changes in Fund Balance—Budget and Actual
- Statement of Revenues, Expenditures, and Changes in Fund Balance
- Balance Sheet

Statement of Revenues, Expenditures, and Changes in Fund Balance—Budget and Actual

The General Fund (as well as Special Revenue Funds and any other governmental fund type for which an annual budget is adopted) should prepare a statement comparing budgeted results and operating results. As discussed earlier, budgetary accounts are used to record budgetary data and serve as the basis for preparing the operating statement on a budgetary basis. Budgetary information is maintained separately from the actual results and at the end of the budgetary period it is necessary to close the budgetary data as a preliminary step in the preparation of the financial statements.

Closing Budget Related Accounts Budgetary accounts are closed by simply reversing the entries that were made at the beginning of the period to record the budget. The closing of budget-related accounts

General and Special Revenue Funds

is journalized as follows (an entry to open these accounts was made earlier in this chapter):

Fund Balance	50,000	
Appropriations (Control)	900,000	
Estimated Revenues (Control)		950,000
Subsidiary ledger for estimated revenues:		
Property taxes		$500,000
Sales taxes		300,000
Fines		70,000
Licenses and permits		50,000
Miscellaneous fees and revenues		30,000
Total		$950,000
Subsidiary ledger for appropriations:		
General government		$300,000
Education and adult training		150,000
Street and highway maintenance		130,000
Health and welfare		120,000
Recreation		100,000
Public safety		80,000
Miscellaneous expenditures		20,000
Total		$900,000
Authorized Operating Transfers Out	240,000	
Estimated Bond Proceeds		200,000
Estimated Operating Transfers In		30,000
Fund Balance		10,000
Subsidiary ledger for estimated operating transfers in:		
Gas works fund		$ 15,000
School district food services fund		10,000
Redevelopment authority fund		5,000
Total		$ 30,000
Subsidiary ledger for authorized transfers out:		
Debt service fund		$150,000
Capital projects fund		80,000
Special assessment fund		10,000
Total		$240,000

Closing Encumbrances Encumbrances outstanding at the end of the budgetary period do not represent expenditures for the period, and the related reserves for encumbrances cannot be presented as a

General and Special Revenue Funds

General Fund liability. The manner in which the accounts (encumbrances and reserves for encumbrances) are closed depends upon whether the encumbered but unexpended appropriation is allowed to lapse.

Lapsing appropriations When encumbrances of the General Fund lapse at year-end but the state or local government intends to honor the commitment, the fund balance should be reserved by the amount of the encumbrances, or the amount of the encumbrance should be disclosed in the financial statements. In addition, the following year's budget should include authorization for the expenditure. For example, assume that encumbrances of $25,000 are outstanding as of June 30, 19X5. If the encumbrances are allowed to lapse and funds are reappropriated to pay the commitments during the 19X6 fiscal year, the following closing entries would be made as of June 30, 19X5:

Reserve For Encumbrances	25,000	
Encumbrances		25,000
Fund Balance	25,000	
Fund Balance—Reserved For		
Encumbrances		25,000

On July 1, 19X5 (the beginning of the next fiscal year), the following entries would be made assuming that the current period budgetary appropriation amount includes the $25,000:

Encumbrances	25,000	
Reserve For Encumbrances		25,000
Fund Balance	25,000	
Fund Balance—Reserved For		
Encumbrances		25,000

These two entries reestablish budgetary control over the encumbrances and from this point the encumbrances are accounted for like all other encumbrances. Thus, when encumbrances lapse and are re-budgeted for the next year, the expenditure is recognized in the following year and there is no difference between the budgetary accounting basis and the GAAP (actual) basis financial information.

Nonlapsing appropriations When appropriations are nonlapsing, they are not reappropriated in the following fiscal year. Outstanding encumbrances for nonlapsing appropriations must be reported as a reserve of the fund balance. Continuing with the current example but assuming the encumbrances are nonlapsing, the following closing entries would be made as of June 30, 19X5:

Fund Balance	25,000	
Encumbrances		25,000
Reserve For Encumbrances	25,000	
Fund Balance—Reserved For		
Encumbrances		25,000

On July 1, 19X5, the following entry would be made:

Fund Balance—Reserved For		
Encumbrances	25,000	
Reserve For Encumbrances—19X5		25,000

This entry reestablishes budgetary control over the encumbrance but designates it as an encumbrance applicable to the prior fiscal year. During the year when the encumbrances are actually vouchered, the transaction would be recorded as a fiscal year 19X6 expenditure as required by generally accepted accounting principles:

Expenditures—19X5	25,000	
Vouchers Payable		25,000

Finally, at the end of fiscal year 19X6 (June 30, 19X6), the following entry is made:

Reserve For Encumbrances—19X5	25,000	
Expenditures—19X5		25,000

When General Fund appropriations are nonlapsing, there is an inconsistency between the budgeted financial statements and the GAAP (actual) financial statements. The expenditures of the budgeted financial statements include encumbrances outstanding as of the end of the fiscal year, while the GAAP financial statements exclude outstanding encumbrances from recorded expenditures. This inconsistency, along with any other accounting inconsistencies, is disclosed in the financial statements by reconciling the budgeted financial statements to the GAAP financial statements.

Exhibit I illustrates a Statement of Revenues, Expenditures, and Changes in Fund Balance—Budget and Actual for a General Fund.

General and Special Revenue Funds

NCGA-1 recommends, but does not require, that the operating statement and analysis of changes in fund balance be presented as a combined financial statement.

As implied in Exhibit I the budgetary financial statements are prepared on a budgetary basis that differs from generally accepted accounting principles. The differences must be reconciled and disclosed in the financial statements. An example of the required disclosure follows Exhibit I.

EXHIBIT I

Statement of Revenues, Expenditures, and Changes in Fund Balance—Budget and Actual—General Fund

City of Centerville
Statement of Revenues, Expenditures, and Changes in Fund Balance—Budget (Budgetary Basis) and Actual
General Fund
Year Ended June 30, 19X5

	Budget	Actual	Variance
Revenues			
Property taxes	$500,000	$502,000	$2,000
Sales taxes	300,000	301,000	1,000
Fines	70,000	65,000	(5,000)
Licenses and permits	50,000	57,000	7,000
Miscellaneous fees and revenues	30,000	32,000	2,000
Total revenues	950,000	957,000	7,000
Expenditures			
General governments	300,000	297,000	3,000
Education and adult training	150,000	151,000	(1,000)
Street and highway maintenance	130,000	122,000	8,000
Health and welfare	120,000	123,000	(3,000)
Recreation	100,000	95,000	5,000
Public safety	80,000	79,000	1,000
Miscellaneous	20,000	18,000	2,000
Total expenditures	900,000	885,000	15,000
Excess of revenues over (under) expenditures	50,000	72,000	22,000
Other financing sources (uses)			
Proceeds from sale of bonds	200,000	195,000	(5,000)
Transfers from other funds	30,000	27,000	(3,000)
Transfers to other funds	(240,000)	(242,000)	(2,000)
Total other financing sources (uses)	(10,000)	(20,000)	(10,000)

Excess of revenues and other sources over (under) expenditures and other uses	$40,000	52,000	$12,000
(Increase) decrease in reserve for encumbrances		(15,000)	
Net change in unreserved fund balance for year		37,000	
Fund balance—unreserved July 1, 19X4		110,000	
Fund balance—unreserved June 30, 19X5		$147,000	

▶ The City budgets revenues, expenditures, and other sources and uses of funds of the General Fund. Appropriations in the General Fund are charged for encumbrances when commitments are made. Fund balances are reserved for outstanding encumbrances, which serve as authorizations for expenditures in the subsequent year. All budgets are adopted on a modified accrual basis of accounting (GAAP), except that encumbrances are treated as budgeted expenditures in the year of incurrence of the commitment to purchase. Budgetary comparisons in the financial statements are presented in this budgetary basis. Adjustments necessary to reconcile the expenditures at the end of the year on the budgetary basis to the modified accrual basis are as follows:

Budgetary basis expenditures	900,000
Less current year encumbrances outstanding as of June 30, 19X5	(25,000)
Add prior year encumbrances outstanding as of June 30, 19X4	10,000
Modified accrual basis expenditures	$885,000

◂

Statement of Revenues, Expenditures, and Changes in Fund Balance

The prevalent practice is to combine the activity statement and the analysis of the fund balance account into a single financial statement entitled the Statement of Revenues, Expenditures, and Changes in Fund Balance. However, for discussion purposes only, the two financial statements will be examined separately.

General and Special Revenue Funds

Statement of Revenues and Expenditures The current operations of the General Fund are presented in a Statement of Revenues and Expenditures, which must be prepared on a modified accrual basis (generally accepted accounting principles). The Statement of Revenues and Expenditures should be prepared on an all-inclusive basis. Thus, only residual equity transfers and prior period adjustments are excluded from the computation of the excess of revenues and other sources of financing over (under) expenditures and other uses of financing.

Operating revenues and operating expenditures should be segregated from other sources and uses of financial resources in the preparation of the Statement of Revenues and Expenditures. For example, operating transfers out should not be classified as an operating expenditure. However, there is no single acceptable format that must be used in the preparation of the statement. Presented below are three abbreviated formats that are identified as acceptable in NCGA-1. (The following presentations include an analysis of changes in the fund balance; however, the operating statement and the analysis of change in the fund balance may be presented as separate financial statements.)

Format #1

Revenues	$ 957,000
Expenditures	885,000
Excess of revenues over (under) expenditures	72,000
Other financing sources (uses)	(20,000)
Excess of revenues and other sources over (under) expenditures and other uses	52,000
(Increase) decrease in reserve for encumbrances	(15,000)
Net change in unreserved fund balance for year	37,000
Fund balance—unreserved July 1, 19X4	110,000
Fund balance—unreserved June 30, 19X5	$ 147,000

Format #2

Revenues	$ 957,000
Other financing sources	222,000
Total revenues and other financing sources	1,179,000
Expenditures	885,000
Other financing uses	242,000
Total expenditures and other financing uses	1,127,000

General and Special Revenue Funds

Excess of revenues and other sources over (under) expenditures and other uses	52,000
(Increase) decrease in reserve for encumbrances	(15,000)
Net change in unreserved fund balance for year	37,000
Fund balance—unreserved July 1, 19X4	110,000
Fund balance—unreserved June 30, 19X5	$ 147,000

Format #3

Fund balance—reserved July 1, 19X4	$ 110,000
Revenues	957,000
Other financing sources	222,000
Total revenues and other financing sources	1,179,000
Expenditures	885,000
Other financing uses	242,000
Total expenditures and other financing uses	1,127,000
Excess of revenues and other sources over (under) expenditures and other uses	52,000
(Increase) decrease in reserve for encumbrances	(15,000)
Net change in unreserved fund balance for year	37,000
Fund balance—unreserved June 30, 19X5	$ 147,000

Statement of Changes in Fund Balance As stated earlier, the analysis of the changes in the General Fund's fund balance account may be presented as a separate financial statement or preferably combined with the fund's operating statement. The analysis may include prior period adjustments, effects of changes in fund balance reserves, excess of revenues and other sources over (under) expenditures and other uses, and residual equity transfers. Prior period adjustments should appear immediately after the beginning fund balance, and residual equity transfers should appear after the excess of revenues and other sources over (under) expenditures and other uses.

The following is an analysis of the changes in the fund balance of a General Fund:

Fund balance—July 1, 19X4—as previously reported		$110,000
Prior period adjustment for an error correction (see Note X)		(20,000)
Fund balance—July 1, 19X4—as restated		90,000
Excess of revenues and other sources over (under) expenditures and other uses	$52,000	

(Increase) decrease in reserve for encumbrances	(15,000)	37,000
Residual equity transfer to enterprise fund		(12,000)
Fund balance—June 30, 19X5		$115,000

Balance Sheet

The balance sheet for a General Fund is unclassified with respect to assets and liabilities. The major headings include assets, liabilities, and fund balance. Generally, only current expendable assets and current liabilities should be disclosed.

An example of a General Fund balance sheet is presented in Exhibit II.

EXHIBIT II

Balance Sheet

City of Centerville
Balance Sheet
General Fund
June 30, 19X5

Assets	
Cash on deposit	$ 30,000
Equity in consolidated cash account	110,000
Investments	80,000
Taxes receivable	70,000
Accounts receivable	20,000
Allowance for doubtful accounts	(10,000)
Due from other funds	8,000
Inventories	5,000
Other assets	2,000
Total assets	$315,000
Liabilities	
Accounts payable	$120,000
Notes payable	75,000
Accrued expenses	10,000
Due to other funds	20,000
Other liabilities	5,000
Total liabilities	230,000

Fund equity	
Fund balance reserved for inventories	5,000
Fund balance reserved for encumbrances	25,000
Total fund balance reserved	30,000
Fund balance designated for replacement of assets	15,000
Fund balance unreserved	40,000
Total fund balance unreserved	55,000
Total fund balance	85,000
Total liabilities and fund balance	$315,000

Interim Financial Statements

Generally, interim financial statements are prepared only for internal use and may be prepared on a budgetary basis, rather than on a GAAP basis. Also, interim financial statements are seldom as comprehensive as annual financial statements. The fundamental purpose of interim financial statements is to serve as a management control tool, and NCGA-l recognizes that the detail format and content of these statements should be based on perceived management needs rather than on promulgated accounting standards. Thus, there are virtually no governmental promulgations that address accounting and reporting issues related to interim financial reporting for state and local governments.

LITERATURE REFERENCES

Material in this chapter is based on the following authoritative pronouncements and publications, which are grouped according to the major headings used within the chapter. A dual reference (both paragraph and page number) is used for NCGA-1 and NCGA-2 because the original pronouncements do not use paragraph numbers.

Basic Concepts and Standards
NCGA-1 *Governmental Accounting and Financial Reporting Principles*, pp. 6-8/¶¶ 16, 26, and 30.

Basis of Accounting
NCGA-1 *Governmental Accounting and Financial Reporting Principles*, pp. 11 and 12/¶¶ 58, 60, 67, and 71.

FASB:CS-1 *Objectives of Financial Reporting by Business Enterprises,* ¶ 44.
FASB:CS-6 *Elements of Financial Statements,* ¶¶ 139 and 140.

Measurement Focus
NCGA-1 *Governmental Accounting and Financial Reporting Principles,* p. 9/¶ 39.

Budgetary System and Accounts
NCGA-1 *Governmental Accounting and Financial Reporting Principles,* pp. 13 and 14/¶¶ 77 and 89-92.
SOP 80-82 *Accounting and Financial Reporting by Governmental Units,* ¶ 5.

Revenues and Other Sources of Financing
NCGA-1 *Governmental Accounting and Financial Reporting Principles,* pp. 11 and 16/¶¶ 62 and 109.

Property Taxes
NCGA INTERPRETATION-3 *Revenue Recognition—Property Taxes,* ¶¶ 6 and 8.
APB-20 *Accounting Changes,* ¶¶ 18, 19, and 31.

Grants, Entitlements, and Shared Revenues
NCGA-2 *Grant, Entitlement, and Shared Revenues Accounting and Reporting by State and Local Governments,* pp. 1-3/¶¶ 3-18.
SOP 75-3 *Accrual of Revenues and Expenditures by State and Local Governmental Units,* ¶ 4.

Sales Taxes
NCGA-1 *Governmental Accounting and Financial Reporting Principles,* p. 12/¶ 67.
SOP 75-3 *Accrual of Revenues and Expenditures by State and Local Governmental Units,* ¶ 4.

Taxpayer-Assessed Revenues
NCGA-1 *Governmental Accounting and Financial Reporting Principles,* p. 12/¶ 67.

Miscellaneous Revenues
NCGA-1 *Governmental Accounting and Financial Reporting Principles,* p. 12/¶ 67.

Quasi-External Revenues
NCGA-1 *Governmental Accounting and Financial Reporting Principles,* p. 15/¶¶ 102 and 103.

Proceeds from the Issuance of Long-Term Debt
NCGA-1 *Governmental Accounting and Financial Reporting Principles*, p. 16/¶¶ 107-109.

Classification and Disclosure
NCGA-1 *Governmental Accounting and Financial Reporting Principles*, p. 12/¶ 69.

Expenditures
NCGA-1 *Governmental Accounting and Financial Reporting Principles*, pp. 12 and 16/¶¶ 70 and 109.

Debt Service Payments
NCGA-1 *Governmental Accounting and Financial Reporting Principles*, p. 12/¶ 72.

Quasi-External Expenditures
NCGA-1 *Governmental Accounting and Financial Reporting Principles*, p. 15/¶¶ 102-103.

Reimbursements
NCGA-1 *Governmental Accounting and Financial Reporting Principles*, p. 15/¶¶ 102 and 104.

Classification and Disclosure
NCGA-1 *Governmental Accounting and Financial Reporting Principles*, pp. 16 and 17/¶¶ 111-116.

Assets
NCGA-1 *Governmental Accounting and Financial Reporting Principles*, p. 6/¶ 19.

Current Assets
NCGA-1 *Governmental Accounting and Financial Reporting Principles*, pp. 9 and 12/¶¶ 39 and 73.

Materials and Supplies
NCGA-1 *Governmental Accounting and Financial Reporting Principles*, p. 12/¶ 73.

Prepayments and Deferrals
NCGA-1 *Governmental Accounting and Financial Reporting Principles*, p. 12/¶ 73.

General and Special Revenue Funds

Noncurrent Assets
NCGA-1   *Governmental Accounting and Financial Reporting Principles*, p. 17/¶¶ 118 and 120.

Capital Outlays
NCGA-1   *Governmental Accounting and Financial Reporting Principles*, pp. 9 and 10/¶¶ 39-41 and 56.

Escheat Property
NCGA Interpretation-9   *Certain Fund Classifications and Balance Sheet Accounts*, ¶ 11.

Classification and Disclosure
NCGA Interpretation-6   *Notes to Financial Statements Disclosure*, appendix.

Liabilities
NCGA-1   *Governmental Accounting and Financial Reporting Principles*, pp. 6 and 9/¶¶ 19 and 44.

NCGA-4   *Accounting and Financial Reporting Principles for Claims and Judgments*, ¶ 7.

Current Liabilities
NCGA-1   *Governmental Accounting and Financial Reporting Principles*, p. 6/¶ 18.

Tax and Revenue Anticipation Notes
NCGA Interpretation-9   *Certain Fund Classifications and Balance Sheet Accounts*, ¶ 12.

Bond Anticipation Notes
NCGA Interpretation-9   *Certain Fund Classifications and Balance Sheet Accounts*, ¶ 12.

FASB-6   *Classification of Short-Term Obligations Expected to be Refinanced*, ¶¶ 10-12 and 15.

Demand Bonds
GASB Interpretation-1   *Demand Bonds Issued by State and Local Governmental Entities*, ¶¶ 1-5 and 10-14.

NCGA Interpretation-9   *Certain Fund Classifications and Balance Sheet Accounts*, ¶ 12.

General Long-Term Debt
NCGA-1   *Governmental Accounting and Financial Reporting Principles*, p. 8/¶¶ 32 and 33.

General and Special Revenue Funds

Classification and Disclosure
NCGA-1   Governmental Accounting and Financial Reporting Principles, p. 24/¶ 158.
NCGA INTERPRETATION-6   *Notes to the Financial Statements Disclosure*, ¶ 5.
GASB INTERPRETATION-1   *Demand Bonds Issued by State and Local Governmental Entities*, ¶ 11.

Interfund Transactions
NCGA-1   *Governmental Accounting and Financial Reporting Principles*, p. 15/¶¶ 101-104.

Operating Transfers
NCGA-1   *Governmental Accounting and Financial Reporting Principles*, pp. 15 and 16/¶¶ 105 and 106.

Residual Equity Transfers
NCGA-1   *Governmental Accounting and Financial Reporting Principles*, pp. 15 and 16/¶ 105.

Interfund Receivables/Payables
NCGA-1   *Governmental Accounting and Financial Reporting Principles*, pp. 7 and 22/¶¶ 22 and 145.

Classification and Disclosure
NCGA-1   *Governmental Accounting and Financial Reporting Principles*, p. 22/¶¶ 145 and 147.

Financial Statements
NCGA-1   *Governmental Accounting and Financial Reporting Principles*, p. 20/¶ 141.
NCGA-7   *Financial Reporting for Component Units Within the Governmental Reporting Entity*, ¶ 10.

Statement of Revenues, Expenditures, and Changes in Fund Balance—Budget and Actual
NCGA-1   *Governmental Accounting and Financial Reporting Principles*, pp. 14 and 23/¶¶ 91, 92, and 153.

Statement of Revenues and Expenditures
NCGA-1   *Governmental Accounting and Financial Reporting Principles*, pp. 22 and 23/¶¶ 146, 149, and 151.

Statement of Changes in Fund Balance
NCGA-1   *Governmental Accounting and Financial Reporting Principles*, p. 23/¶ 152.

General and Special Revenue Funds

Balance Sheet
NCGA-1   *Governmental Accounting and Financial Reporting Principles*, p. 22/¶ 145.

Interim Financial Statements
NCGA-1   *Governmental Accounting and Financial Reporting Principles*, pp. 18 and 19/¶¶ 133 and 134.

CAPITAL PROJECTS FUND

BASIC CONCEPTS AND STANDARDS

The acquisition or construction of capital projects, other than those financed by Enterprise Funds, Internal Service Funds, or Trust Funds, may be accounted for in a Capital Projects Fund. Usually a Capital Projects Fund is used to account for major capital expenditures such as the construction of civic centers, libraries, and general administrative services buildings. The acquisition of other capital assets such as machinery, furniture, and vehicles is usually accounted for in the governmental fund that is responsible for the financing of the expenditure.

A separate Capital Projects Fund is usually established when the acquisition or construction of the capital project extends beyond a single fiscal year and the financing sources are provided by more than one governmental fund, or the capital asset is financed by specifically designated resources. Specifically designated resources may arise from the sale of general governmental bonds, receipts of grants from other governmental units, designation of a portion of tax receipts, or a combination of these and other financing sources. A Capital Projects Fund must be used when mandated by law or stipulated by regulations or covenants related to the financing source. For control purposes, it may also be advantageous to use a separate Capital Projects Fund even though one is not technically required. As with all governmental funds, the purpose of establishing a specific fund is to establish a basis of accountability for resources provided for a particular purpose. However, the establishment of an excessive number of funds may impede the operations of an efficient financial accounting system.

Basis of Accounting

The basis of accounting for a Capital Projects Fund is the modified accrual basis. Revenues are recognized when they are both measurable and available. Measurability requires that revenues be subject to reasonable estimation, while availability means that revenues are available to finance the Capital Projects Fund's current expenditures. Expenditures are recorded when the related liabilities are incurred.

Measurement Focus

A Capital Projects Fund measures the sources and uses of financial resources and the net financial resources available for subsequent expenditure. For example, proceeds from the issuance of long-term bonds are recorded as available financial resources, but the liability itself is recorded as part of the General Long-Term Debt Account Group because the repayment of the debt will not require the use of financial resources from the Capital Projects Fund. Similarly, the capital asset actually accounted for through the Capital Projects Fund during construction is recorded in the General Fixed Assets Account Group, since the capital asset is not available to finance the Capital Projects Fund's activities.

Budgetary System and Accounts

Control over financial resources and expenditures of the Capital Projects Fund may be accomplished in part through the use of a budget system and the use of related budgetary accounts. Budgetary accounts may be used to record the Capital Projects Fund's budget and commitments accounted for as encumbrances.

Recording the budget Unlike some governmental funds, a Capital Projects Fund is project oriented rather than period oriented, and for this reason it is often not necessary to record the fund's budget for control purposes. For example, the authorization of a bond ordinance by the legislature, or by the public, will identify the specific purpose of the fund as well as the amount of resources that can be used to construct or purchase the capital asset. Subsequent action by the legislature will generally not be necessary, therefore control is established through the original authorization of the general obligation bonds. Also, the recording of a budget may not be necessary when the transactions related to the acquisition of the capital asset are few or relatively simple. For example, it is usually not necessary to have budgetary account integration with the general ledger when the capital project is a *turnkey* job in which contractors are hired to deliver a more or less finished project.

On the other hand, NCGA-1 (Governmental Accounting and Financial Reporting Principles) suggests that it may be necessary to record a budget when numerous sources of financing, various expenditures, and multiple transfers are involved. This general philosophy is also endorsed by the 1980 GAAFR (Governmental Accounting, Auditing, and Financial Reporting) which states that budgetary integration is usually appropriate when more than one project is accounted for in any one Capital Projects Fund. In general, if it is concluded that legal compliance will be facilitated by the integration of budgetary accounts, the Capital Projects Fund's budget should be recorded.

To illustrate the recording of a budget for a Capital Projects Fund, assume that a local governmental unit has decided to construct three strategically located refuse disposal plants over the next four years. The estimated cost of construction is $8,000,000 and will be financed as follows:

Capital grant from the federal government	$2,400,000
Capital grant from the state government	800,000
Issuance of general obligation bonds by the locality	4,000,000
Transfers from the general fund	300,000
Temporary increase in current property taxes dedicated to the construction of the refuse plants (increase will expire after two years)	500,000
Total	$8,000,000

The following journal entry would be made to record the Capital Projects Fund's capital budget:

Estimated Grants—Federal Government	2,400,000	
Estimated Grants—State Government	800,000	
Estimated Bond Proceeds	4,000,000	
Estimated Operating Transfers In—		
General Fund	300,000	
Estimated Revenues—Property Taxes	500,000	
Appropriations		8,000,000

All of the accounts recorded in the above entry are budgetary accounts and are closed at the end of the fiscal year or at the close of the project. Since they are budgetary accounts, they have no effect on the Capital Projects Fund's actual (GAAP-basis) financial statements.

Recording encumbrances Even when budgetary accounts are not used to record the Capital Projects Fund's budget, it is generally useful to employ an encumbrance system to facilitate control over costs incurred in the acquisition or construction of capital assets.

In an encumbrance system, the Capital Projects Fund's resources are restricted when commitments for future expenditures are made

Capital Projects Fund

by signing purchase orders or entering into various contracts. Although the entering into an executory contract is not an acceptable basis for the recognition of an expenditure, the legal commitment is acknowledged by using the encumbrance system. For example, if certain electrical wiring services costing $200,000 in the construction of a building are contracted for, the following entry would be made when the contract is signed:

Encumbrances	200,000	
Reserve For Encumbrances		200,000

The encumbrances and reserve for encumbrances accounts are strictly budgetary accounts and do not represent an expenditure or a liability of the Capital Projects Fund. When the liability associated with the executory contract is established, which is generally based on the delivery of the goods or performance of the service, an expenditure is recognized. In the current example, the following entry would be made when the actual electrical wiring is completed:

Reserve For Encumbrances	200,000	
Encumbrances		200,000
Expenditures—Electrical Wiring	200,000	
Vouchers Payable		200,000

Usually at the end of the fiscal period there will be outstanding encumbrances that will not be vouchered until the following period. Because encumbrances and reserve for encumbrances accounts are budgetary accounts, they must be closed at the end of the period. The closing process will be discussed later in this chapter.

ACCOUNTS AND TRANSACTIONS

A Capital Projects Fund has a limited life in that once the capital asset is acquired or constructed, the Capital Projects Fund is liquidated. The following discussion illustrates accounts and transactions that are typically associated with a Capital Projects Fund.

Revenues and Other Sources of Financing

Under the modified accrual basis for governmental funds, revenues and other sources of financing are recorded when they are considered measurable and available. Thus, Capital Projects Fund revenues and other sources of financing are recognized when they are both subject to reasonable estimation and when they are available to finance the current activities of the fund.

Proceeds from Issuance of Long-Term Debt Financial resources of Capital Projects Funds are often raised by issuing long-term debt instruments, such as bonds and notes. The proceeds from the issuance of long-term debt are recorded in the Capital Projects Fund, but the long-term liability is recorded in the General Long-Term Debt Account Group. For example, if $10,000,000 of long-term bonds are issued to finance the construction of a governmental building, the issuance of the bonds would be recorded as follows:

CAPITAL PROJECTS FUND
  Cash   10,000,000
    Proceeds From Issuance Of Bonds   10,000,000

GENERAL LONG-TERM DEBT ACCOUNT GROUP
  Amount To Be Provided For
    Repayment Of Bonds   10,000,000
    Bonds Payable   10,000,000

NCGA-1 differentiates between revenues and other sources of financing. Proceeds from the issuance of long-term debt are not considered revenue but rather must be classified as other sources of financing on the Capital Projects Fund's Statement of Revenues and Expenditures. Also, because resources are not available until the bonds are actually sold, the proceeds are not recorded when the bond issuance is authorized but rather when the bonds are issued.

> **OBSERVATION:** *Prior to the issuance of NCGA-1, a bond transaction could be recorded at the authorization date by recognizing a* bonds authorized but not issued *account as part of the Capital Projects Fund's liabilities.*

The accounting for the issuance of long-term debt to finance the acquisition or construction of capital assets can be somewhat complicated when the debt is issued between interest payment dates or when the debt is issued at a discount or premium.

Bonds sold between interest payment dates Long-term bonds may be sold on a date that does not coincide with an interest pay-

Capital Projects Fund

ment date. When this occurs, the proceeds from the bond sale include an amount of accrued interest. The accrued interest does not represent other financing sources of the Capital Projects Fund, and it should be recorded as a payable to the governmental fund that is responsible for servicing the long-term debt. For example, assume that $10,000,000 of bonds carrying a 6% interest rate are sold for $10,100,000, including two months of interest ($100,000). The issuance of the bonds between interest payment dates would be recorded as follows, assuming a Debt Service Fund will accumulate resources to make interest and principal payments over the life of the bonds:

CAPITAL PROJECTS FUND
Cash   10,100,000
    Proceeds From Issuance Of Bonds   10,000,000
    Due To Debt Service Fund   100,000

DEBT SERVICE FUND
Due From Capital Projects Fund   100,000
    Accrued Interest Payable   100,000

GENERAL LONG-TERM DEBT ACCOUNT GROUP
Amount To Be Provided For
  Repayment Of Bonds   10,000,000
    Bonds Payable   10,000,000

Alternatively, the portion of the proceeds that represents the accrued interest may be recorded directly in the governmental fund responsible for servicing the debt. If this approach is chosen, the above illustration would be recorded as follows:

CAPITAL PROJECTS FUND
Cash   10,000,000
    Proceeds From Issuance Of Bonds   10,000,000

DEBT SERVICE FUND
Cash   100,000
    Accrued Interest Payable   100,000

GENERAL LONG-TERM DEBT ACCOUNT GROUP
Amount To Be Provided For
  Repayment Of Bonds   10,000,000
    Bonds Payable   10,000,000

Bond premium Unlike the example illustrated above, bonds may be sold at a premium, in which case the question arises of how the premium should be accounted for in the Capital Projects Fund. In some instances legal provisions will dictate how to account for a premium. For example, the bond authorization may require that the bond premium be made available to the Capital Projects Fund, therefore the full amount of the cash received from the sale of the bonds would be recorded as bond proceeds in the Capital Projects Fund.

When there is no legal requirement that mandates how the bond premium is to be treated, it is generally preferable to make the premium available to the governmental fund that is responsible for the servicing of the long-term debt. For example, if bonds with a par value of $10,000,000 are issued for $10,500,000, and it is assumed that a Debt Service Fund will make the interest and principal payments over the life of the debt, the following entries would be made:

CAPITAL PROJECTS FUND
Cash   10,500,000
    Proceeds From Issuance Of Bonds   10,000,000
    Due To Debt Service Fund   500,000

DEBT SERVICE FUND
Due From Capital Projects Fund   500,000
    Proceeds From Issuance Of Bonds—
      Premium   500,000

GENERAL LONG-TERM DEBT ACCOUNT GROUP
Amount To Be Provided For
  Repayment Of Bonds   10,000,000
    Bonds Payable   10,000,000

Alternatively, the cash proceeds that represent the premium may be recorded directly in the Debt Service Fund.

No matter how the premium is accounted for, the par value of the debt is recorded in the General Long-Term Debt Account Group and the premium amount is neither recorded nor amortized in the account group.

Bond discount In some jurisdictions it is illegal to sell governmental bonds at a discount. In those situations where bonds may be sold at a discount the treatment of the discount depends upon the legal provisions associated with bond discounts. In some instances, it may be a legal necessity to transfer funds from the General Fund or some other fund to make up for the reduction in the bond proceeds due to the bond discount. If an interfund transfer must be made, an

Capital Projects Fund

interfund receivable should be recognized at the time the bond proceeds are recorded. For example, if bonds with a par value of $10,000,000 are issued for $9,500,000, and it is assumed that the discount of $500,000 will be made up by a transfer from the General Fund, the following entries would be made:

CAPITAL PROJECTS FUND
Cash	9,500,000	
Due From General Fund	500,000	
Proceeds From Issuance Of Bonds		9,500,000
Transfers In—General Fund		500,000

GENERAL FUND
Transfers Out—Capital Projects Fund	500,000	
Due To Capital Projects Fund		500,000

GENERAL LONG-TERM DEBT ACCOUNT GROUP
Amount To Be Provided For Repayment Of Bonds	10,000,000	
Bonds Payable		10,000,000

When there are no legal provisions that establish guidance for the treatment of the discount, the governmental unit should anticipate whether the discount will be funded by another governmental fund. If it is concluded that the discount will be funded, the discount is treated as shown above. On the other hand, if it appears that the discount will not be funded, the Capital Projects Fund should recognize proceeds equal to the cash receipts from the sale of the bonds and not the par value of the bonds.

Again, no matter how the discount is treated, the par value of the debt is recorded in the General Long-Term Debt Account Group. Also, the discount itself is neither recorded nor amortized in any governmental fund.

Capital Grants Capital assets may be financed entirely or in part from grants made by another governmental unit. A capital grant is a contribution which is restricted to the acquisition or construction of a fixed (capital) asset.

A capital grant should be recognized as revenue by a Capital Projects Fund when the measurable and available criteria are satisfied. Generally, the grantee governmental unit satisfies the requirements of the grantor governmental unit when appropriate expenditures, as defined by the grant program, are incurred. Therefore, the receipts of a capital grant before the incurrence of expenditures by the Capital Projects Fund should be recorded as deferred revenue. Subsequently, as appropriate expenditures are made, there should be simultaneous recognition of the expenditure and the related grant revenue.

To illustrate the accounting for a capital grant, assume that a local government has been awarded a $2,000,000 capital grant to partially finance the construction of an adult education and training center. The awarding of the $2,000,000 capital grant is not recorded by the local government because the financial resources under the capital grant are not available to finance current expenditures. If it is assumed that 40% of the capital grant is released and made available to the locality, the following entry is made:

CAPITAL PROJECTS FUND
Cash   800,000
    Unearned Revenue—Capital Grant   800,000

Subsequently, if $600,000 of expenditures that qualify under the terms of the capital grant are incurred, the following entries are made:

CAPITAL PROJECTS FUND
Expenditures—Capital Outlays   600,000
    Vouchers Payable   600,000

Unearned Revenue—Capital Grant   600,000
    Revenue—Capital Grant   600,000

GENERAL FIXED ASSETS ACCOUNT GROUP
Construction In Progress   600,000
    Investment In General Fixed Assets—
      Capital Projects Fund   600,000

> **OBSERVATION:** NCGA-2 (*Grant, Entitlement, and Shared Revenue Accounting by State and Local Governments*) *concludes that grants, entitlements, and shared revenues that finance expenditures typically made from the General Fund should be accounted for in the General Fund and not a Special Revenue Fund unless legally mandated; however, capital grants (as well as shared revenues to be used to acquire capital assets) should be accounted for in a Capital Projects Fund.*

Shared Revenues NCGA-2 defines shared revenues as revenues levied by one government but shared on a predetermined basis (often in proportion to the amount collected at the local level) with another government or class of government. In some cases, shared revenues may be restricted to the acquisition or construction of capital assets.

Generally, shared revenues restricted to the financing of capital assets are disbursed to the recipient government and are subject to forfeiture only if prescribed expenditure guidelines and regulations are not satisfied. For this reason shared revenues are subject to accrual, assuming the measurable and available criteria can be met. On the other hand, shared revenues that have been received in advance for which revenue recognition criteria have not been satisfied should be recorded as deferred revenue. When shared revenues have not been received and the revenue recognition criteria have not been met, the nature of the shared revenue program and the anticipated amount to be received under the program may be disclosed, but intergovernmental receivable and deferred revenue accounts should not be established.

Dedicated Taxes A Capital Projects Fund may be entitled to a portion of tax receipts collected by a related governmental fund. In this case, the portion of the tax receipts is dedicated or restricted to the acquisition, construction, or improvement of capital assets.

Revenues received from another related governmental fund are subject to accrual if the measurable and available criteria are met, and may be recorded as a transfer from the other governmental fund (other financing source) or as revenue. The receipt of taxes collected by another fund may be recorded as revenue in the Capital Projects Fund only when the Capital Projects Fund is legally required to expend the funds. If the Capital Projects Fund records the dedicated taxes as revenue, the transferring fund must not also recognize the transferred amount as revenue.

To illustrate the accounting for dedicated taxes, assume that a municipality's property tax rate has been increased by 20% for the next three years in order to partially finance the construction of several elementary schools. Based on an ordinance adopted by the municipality, the increase in the property tax must be used exclusively for the construction of elementary schools, and none of the increase can be used for operating expenses. The property tax, for administrative convenience, is accounted for and initially collected in the General Fund but the dedicated portion is transferred to the Capital Projects Fund when collected. At the beginning of the fiscal year, the following entries would be made to record the property tax assessment of $20,000,000, assuming an estimated 5% of the assessment will not be collected:

GENERAL FUND

Property Taxes Receivable	20,000,000	
Revenues — Property Taxes		15,200,000
Allowance For Uncollectible Property Taxes		1,000,000
Due To Capital Projects Fund ($19,000,000 × 20%)		3,800,000

In this example, property taxes are subject to accrual, therefore the Capital Projects Fund can accrue its portion of the tax assessment (net of uncollectibles). If the revenue is accounted for on a cash basis, the fund initially receiving the cash may credit revenues for the full amount and debit revenues when a portion of the tax receipts is transferred to the Capital Projects Fund.

> **OBSERVATION:** Dedicated taxes are different from shared revenues in that shared revenues are received from a nonrelated governmental unit, whereas dedicated taxes are received from another governmental fund that is part of the same governmental reporting entity as the recipient fund.

Investment Income In the early phase of the construction of a capital asset there may be excess resources available in the Capital Projects Fund especially if the construction is at least partially financed by the issuance of long-term debt. Obviously the excess funds will be used to purchase various temporary investments. The types of investments that can be made with the excess funds are usually restricted to low risk investments, and for this reason the income earned from the investments is susceptible to accrual if the *availability* criterion is also satisfied.

Based on state laws or local ordinances, the income earned on the temporary investments may be made available to the Capital Projects Fund or some other governmental fund, such as the Debt Service Fund or the General Fund. When earnings on investments are made available to the Capital Projects Fund, investment income should be recognized as revenue in the Capital Projects Fund. If the Capital Projects Fund is prohibited from spending the investment earnings or it is a common practice of the state or local government to transfer the earnings to another fund, the recipient fund should recognize the investment income. For example, if $400,000 of excess

Capital Projects Fund

cash is invested by the Capital Projects Fund in a 7% certificate of deposit, and three months later the certificate of deposit matures, the following entry is made, assuming the Debt Service Fund is entitled to all investment income generated from temporary investments made by the Capital Projects Fund:

CAPITAL PROJECTS FUND
Cash   407,000
   Investments—Certificates Of Deposit   400,000
   Due To Debt Service Fund   7,000

DEBT SERVICE FUND
Due From Capital Projects Fund   7,000
   Interest Income—Certificates Of
     Deposit   7,000

If the maturity date of the temporary investment falls after the close of the fiscal year, interest income should be accrued in the Debt Service Fund, along with the accrual in the Capital Projects Fund.

Classification and Disclosure Revenues and other financing sources (proceeds from the issuance of long-term debt) must be appropriately identified in the Capital Projects Fund's Statement of Revenues and Expenditures. Revenue recognition methods must be consistently applied and described in the Summary of Significant Accounting Policies.

Expenditures

The purpose of a Capital Projects Fund is to account for resources used to acquire or construct a capital asset; however, once the asset is ready for use by the governmental unit, the accountability for the asset is transferred from the Capital Projects Fund. Resources used in the acquisition or construction of a capital asset are not capitalized in the Capital Projects Fund but rather are considered expenditures of the fund. As the project is constructed, the cumulative expenditures are capitalized in the General Fixed Assets Account Group. When the capital asset is completed and ready for operations, the balance in the construction in progress account is transferred to an appropriate descriptive account title such as building or equipment. The accountability for the newly acquired or constructed asset is maintained through the account group and subsidiary records.

The accounting for expenditures associated with the construction of a capital asset is illustrated by the following transactions:

Capital Projects Fund

Transaction: Purchase orders and contracts of $400,000 related to the construction of an addition to a building are signed.

CAPITAL PROJECTS FUND
Encumbrances				400,000
    Reserve For Encumbrances				400,000

Transaction: Purchase orders and contracts that were encumbered for $150,000 are vouchered for $157,000 and paid.

CAPITAL PROJECTS FUND
Reserve For Encumbrances			150,000
    Encumbrances					150,000

Expenditures—Capital Outlays		157,000
    Vouchers Payable/Cash				157,000

GENERAL FIXED ASSETS ACCOUNT GROUP
Construction In Progress			157,000
    Investment In General Fixed Assets—
    Capital Projects Fund				157,000

Transaction: Construction is completed and the remaining purchase orders and contracts are vouchered for $245,000 and paid.

CAPITAL PROJECTS FUND
Reserve For Encumbrances			250,000
    Encumbrances					250,000

Expenditures—Capital Outlays		245,000
    Vouchers Payable/Cash				245,000

GENERAL FIXED ASSETS ACCOUNT GROUP
Construction In Progress			245,000
    Investment In General Fixed Assets—
    Capital Projects Fund				245,000

Buildings					402,000
    Construction In Progress				402,000

Other transactions that may affect expenditures recognized in the Capital Projects Fund are discussed below.

Capital Projects Fund

Quasi-External Expenditures A quasi-external transaction, unlike an interfund transfer, involves two governmental funds in which the funds perform basically as unrelated parties in the exchange of goods and services. When a Capital Projects Fund acquires goods or services from another fund, the exchange should be classified as an expenditure. For example, if a municipality's Capital Projects Fund uses the municipality's engineering department to prepare blueprints for a capital asset that is to be constructed, the payments made to the engineering department are treated as engineering expenditures and not as transfers out.

Reimbursements A governmental fund may make payments that are the legal responsibility of another fund, with the understanding that the fund making the initial payment will subsequently be reimbursed. When expenditures of the Capital Projects Fund are made by another fund, the initial disbursement should be treated as an expenditure of the other fund. When the Capital Projects Fund reimburses the other fund, an expenditure is recognized in the Capital Projects Fund, and the other fund reduces its expenditures by an equal amount. NCGA-1 concludes that reimbursements do not represent interfund transfers, loans, or advances, and therefore, an interfund receivable and interfund payable should not be established when the initial disbursement is made.

To illustrate the accounting for reimbursed costs, assume that certain construction costs of $70,000 are related to a Capital Projects Fund and are paid by the General Fund because long-term bonds that will finance the construction of the capital asset have not been sold. The payment by the General Fund would be recorded as follows:

GENERAL FUND
Expenditures—Capital Outlays 70,000
    Cash   70,000

CAPITAL PROJECTS FUND
No entry

GENERAL FIXED ASSETS ACCOUNT GROUP
Construction In Progress 70,000
    Investment In General Fixed Assets—
      General Fund   70,000

At a later date when the Capital Projects Fund reimburses the General Fund, the reimbursement is recorded as follows:

Capital Projects Fund

GENERAL FUND
Cash   70,000
    Expenditures—Capital Outlays   70,000

CAPITAL PROJECTS FUND
Expenditures—Capital Outlays   70,000
    Cash   70,000

GENERAL FIXED ASSETS ACCOUNT GROUP
Investment In General Fixed Assets—
    General Fund   70,000
    Investment In General Fixed Assets—
    Capital Projects Fund   70,000

Interest Expenditures   A Capital Projects Fund may incur interest costs when short-term financing is necessary, especially when bond anticipation notes that do not qualify as general long-term debt are issued. Such interest costs are subject to accrual and should be recognized as expenditures of the Capital Projects Fund to the extent they will require the use of available expendable resources. Interest expenditures associated with the construction of a capital asset should be capitalized and reflected as part of the historical cost of the asset in the General Fixed Assets Account Group. FASB-34 (Capitalization of Interest Cost) concludes that the capitalization period begins when the following three conditions are present:

- Expenditures for the capital asset have been made.
- Activities that are necessary to get the capital asset ready for its intended use are in progress.
- Interest cost is being incurred.

The amount of interest cost to be capitalized is equal to the average amount of accumulated expenditures multiplied by the average interest rate on the interest bearing debt of the Capital Projects Fund. The amount of interest cost to be capitalized is limited to the actual amount of interest cost incurred for the period.

As discussed earlier, excess resources may be used to purchase temporary investments, and therefore generate investment income. FASB-62 (Capitalization of Interest Cost in Situations Involving Certain Tax-Exempt Borrowings and Certain Gifts and Grants) concludes that the amount of initial cost to be capitalized on assets acquired with tax-exempt borrowings is equal to the cost of the borrowing less interest earned on related interest-bearing investments acquired with proceeds of the related tax-exempt borrowings. Thus,

Capital Projects Fund

when a Capital Projects Fund has both interest expenditures and interest income, the amount of interest to be capitalized is the net amount of interest expenditures.

> **OBSERVATION:** *NCGA-1 simply states that the accounting policy with respect to the capitalization of interest cost incurred during construction should be disclosed and consistently applied. No other governmental accounting promulgation addresses the accounting issue; however, as discussed above, FASB-34 requires that interest cost associated with the construction of capital assets must be capitalized. The issue is not as critical in governmental accounting as commercial accounting, since the capitalized cost of governmental fixed assets is not subject to depreciation to be reflected in a governmental fund's results of operations.*

When a Capital Projects Fund incurs interest costs, these costs may not have been anticipated and therefore the resources available to acquire or construct the capital asset may be insufficient. Laws or ordinances of the state or local government may dictate how the deficit is to be financed. For example, it may be appropriate to transfer funds from the General Fund to finance the deficit, or a specific appropriation may have to be made by the legislature. In any case, the interest expenditure is recognized by the fund that is responsible for its payment, as provided by law or accepted as past practice of the governmental unit. Resources transferred from one fund in order to finance the interest expenditure (deficit) are treated as transfers out and not as expenditures.

Capital Leases Rather than acquire capital assets by making current payments or issuing bonds or notes to finance the acquisition, a governmental unit may enter into a long-term lease agreement. The accounting for the lease agreement in the Capital Projects Fund depends upon whether the agreement is classified as a capital lease or an operating lease. NCGA-5 (Accounting and Financial Reporting Principles for Lease Agreements of State and Local Governments) requires that governmental units apply the accounting and reporting standards established in FASB-13 (Accounting for Leases, as amended), with appropriate modifications, to reflect the measurement focus of government funds.

Capital Projects Fund

FASB-13 concludes that a lease agreement must be capitalized if any one of the following criteria is satisfied:

- The lease transfers ownership of the property to the lessee by the end of the lease term.
- The lease term contains a bargain purchase option.
- The lease term is equal to 75% or more of the estimated economic life of the leased property.
- The present value at the beginning of the lease term of the minimum lease payments, excluding that portion of the payments representing executory costs, to be paid by the lessor, including any profit thereon, equals or exceeds 90% of the excess of the fair value of the leased property to the lessor at the inception of the lease over any related investment tax credit retained by the lessor and expected to be realized by him.

The third and fourth criteria are not applicable if the beginning of the lease term falls within the last 25% of the economic life of the capital asset.

When a lease is considered a capital lease and the transaction is accounted for in a Capital Projects Fund, journal entries are made to treat the transaction as an *in-substance purchase* of the capital asset financed through the issuance of long-term debt. This means that the property rights associated with the capital asset are recorded in the General Fixed Assets Account Group and the long-term obligation created by the lease becomes part of the General Long-Term Debt Account Group. The capitalized amount is equal to the present value of the minimum lease payments. The present value of the lease payments is shown as an expenditure of the Capital Projects Fund, and there is a simultaneous credit to other financing sources (a nominal account). The subsequent lease payments are recorded as expenditures in the Debt Service Fund (if one is legally mandated) or in the governmental fund (usually the General Fund or a Special Revenue Fund) responsible for the periodic lease payments.

The effects of recording a capital lease are the same as financing the purchase of a capital asset through the issuance of long-term debt. To compare the two financing approaches, assume that on June 30, 19X1, a governmental unit purchases equipment that costs $100,000. The equipment is financed by issuing a four-year 8% note. The acquisition of the equipment, assuming a separate Capital Projects Fund must be used, is recorded as follows:

Capital Projects Fund

CAPITAL PROJECTS FUND
Cash 100,000
  Proceeds From Issuance Of Long-
    Term Note 100,000

Expenditures—Capital Outlays 100,000
  Cash 100,000

GENERAL FIXED ASSETS ACCOUNT GROUP
Equipment 100,000
  Investment In General Fixed Assets—
    Capital Projects Fund 100,000

GENERAL LONG-TERM DEBT ACCOUNT GROUP
Amount To Be Provided For Notes
  Payable 100,000
    Notes Payable 100,000

Alternatively, assume that the equipment is leased over a four-year period which is equal to the equipment's economic life and therefore requires that the lease agreement be capitalized. Four annual lease payments of $30,192 are to be paid beginning on June 30, 19X2. The implicit interest rate is assumed to be 8%. The present value of the minimum lease payments is $100,000, as shown below:

Annual lease payments $ 30,192
Present value of an ordinary annuity, where
  the interest rate is 8% and the number of
  periods is 4 × 3.31213
Present value of minimum lease payments $ 100,000

The leasing of the equipment, assuming a separate Capital Projects Fund must be used, is recorded as follows:

CAPITAL PROJECTS FUND
Expenditures—Capital Outlays 100,000
  Other Financing Sources—Execution
    Of Capital Lease 100,000

GENERAL FIXED ASSETS ACCOUNT GROUP
Assets Under Capital Leases 100,000
  Investment In General Fixed Assets—
    Capital Leases 100,000

Capital Projects Fund

GENERAL LONG-TERM DEBT ACCOUNT GROUP
Amount To Be Provided For Lease
  Payments   100,000
  Obligations Under Capital Lease
    Agreements   100,000

As lease payments are made in subsequent periods, an expenditure is recorded in the Debt Service Fund. Generally, expenditures in the Debt Service Fund are classified by object class, thus an amortization schedule must be prepared to differentiate between the principal repayment and the interest portion of the total lease payment. An amortization schedule for the current example is illustrated below:

Amortization Schedule

Date	Lease payment	Interest expenditure @8%	Principal expenditure	Amount of general long-term debt
6/30/X1				$100,000
6/30/X2	$30,192	$8,000	$22,192	77,808
6/30/X3	30,192	6,225	23,967	53,841
6/30/X4	30,192	4,307	25,885	27,956
6/30/X5	30,192	2,236	27,956	-0-

Using the amortization schedule, the lease payment made on June 30, 19X2, would be recorded as follows, assuming funds are transferred from the General Fund to finance the payments under the lease:

GENERAL FUND
Transfers Out—Debt Service Fund   30,192
  Cash   30,192

GENERAL LONG-TERM DEBT ACCOUNT GROUP
Amount Available In Debt Service Fund
  (For Capital Lease Payments)   22,192
  Amount To Be Provided For Lease
    Payments   22,192

Obligations Under Capital Lease
  Agreements   22,192
  Amount Available In Debt Service
    Fund (For Capital Lease Payments)   22,192

Capital Projects Fund

DEBT SERVICE FUND
Cash	30,192	
Transfers In—General Fund		30,192
Expenditures—Capital Lease Principal Payments	22,192	
Expenditures—Capital Lease Interest Payments	8,000	
Cash		30,192

Once the capital lease is recorded, no subsequent lease payments are recognized as expenditures in the Capital Projects Fund.

Classification and Disclosure Expenditures of a Capital Projects Fund for financial reporting purposes are generally classified as capital outlays (object class). For supplemental reporting or internal analysis, expenditures may be classified by function (or program), organizational unit, activity, or character.

The following information with respect to interest cost should be disclosed:

- For an accounting period in which no interest cost is capitalized, the amount of interest cost incurred and charged as an expenditure during the period
- For an accounting period in which some interest cost is capitalized, the total amount of interest cost incurred during the period and the amount thereof that has been capitalized
- The accounting method used to account for interest costs

Assets

Assets presented in a Capital Projects Fund are implied to be current assets in that they are available to finance current expenditures of the fund. A Capital Projects Fund's current assets may include such items as cash, temporary investments, intergovernmental receivables, supplies, prepayments, and amounts due from other funds.

Temporary investments of cash should be accounted for on a cost basis, although significant declines in the value of the investment that are permanent in nature would require that the investment be reported at market. Permanent declines must be recognized in order to avoid reporting expendable financial resources that are not available to finance future expenditures of the Capital Projects Fund.

Some assets that are not available to finance current expenditures of the fund may appear on the Capital Projects Fund's balance sheet. These assets are briefly described below:

- Materials and supplies accounted for under the consumption method
- Prepayments and deferrals accounted for under the allocation method (capitalized and amortized to subsequent budgetary periods)
- Advances or loans to other funds that are not expected to be repaid during the subsequent budgetary period, but are collectible in some future accounting period

If the above assets are reflected in the balance sheet of the Capital Projects Fund, its fund balance must be reserved or designated by the amount of the reported asset.

Classification and Disclosure The following disclosures, where applicable, should be made with respect to assets that are presented on the balance sheet of the Capital Projects Fund:

- Disclosure of valuation bases and significant or unusual accounting treatment for material account balances or transactions. (Disclosures should be described in the order of appearance in the balance sheet.)
- Detail notes on the following, where appropriate:
  — Pooling of cash and investments
  — Investments
  — Property taxes and other receivables
  — Amounts due from other governments—grants receivables

The assets are presented on the balance sheet in an unclassified format.

Liabilities

Liabilities of a Capital Projects Fund represent obligations that will be retired by using financial resources of the fund. Included as fund liabilities are debts such as accruals for professional fees, freight and transportation charges, and payments due to contractors and vendors.

Capital Projects Fund

To maintain some control over contractors once a project is completed, a portion of the contract may be retained until the governmental unit is satisfied that the project was completed and functions in accordance with contract specifications. While an encumbrance for the full amount of the contract is established when the contract is signed, only a predetermined percentage of the contract will be vouchered once the project is supposedly complete. When the state or local government is satisfied with the work performed, the retained percentage will be vouchered and paid. For example, if a construction contract is signed for $400,000, the typical encumbrance is made as follows in the Capital Projects Fund:

Encumbrances	400,000	
Reserve For Encumbrances		400,000

When the contract is completed, assuming 20% of the contract price is retained until the governmental unit is satisfied with the work, the following entries are made:

Reserve For Encumbrances	400,000	
Encumbrances		400,000
Expenditures—Capital Outlays	400,000	
Vouchers Payable		320,000
Contract Payable—Retained		
Percentage		80,000
Vouchers Payable	320,000	
Cash		320,000

Note: The constructed fixed asset is recognized in the General Fixed Assets Account Group.

Later, after the project has been inspected and approved by appropriate governmental officials, the retained contract percentage is vouchered and paid as shown below:

Contract Payable—Retained Percentage	80,000	
Vouchers Payable/Cash		80,000

As discussed earlier, those liabilities that do not require the use of expendable financial resources of the Capital Projects Fund are classified as part of the General Long-Term Debt Account Group, even though the proceeds from the issuance of long-term debt (for exam-

Capital Projects Fund

ple, bonds or notes) were recorded as other financing sources of the Capital Projects Fund. However, general long-term debt is a broad category and may include more debt items than simply bonds and notes. Other liabilities that may be included in the General Long-Term Debt Account Group related to activities of a Capital Projects Fund include claims and judgments (Chapter 41), compensated absences (Chapter 42), and lease obligations (Chapter 43).

Other liabilities that may be recorded as debt of a Capital Projects Fund are discussed below.

Bond Anticipation Notes Expenditures may be incurred by a Capital Projects Fund before the proceeds from the sale of long-term bonds are available to finance these expenditures. In order to provide short-term financing until the bonds are sold, bond anticipation notes may be sold. When the long-term bonds are issued, the bond anticipation notes will be retired by using part or all of the proceeds from the sale of the bonds.

The recording of bond anticipation notes in a Capital Projects Fund depends upon whether the anticipation notes are considered current (a liability of the fund), or noncurrent (part of the General Long-Term Debt Account Group). NCGA Interpretation-9 (Certain Fund Classifications and Balance Sheet Accounts) concludes that bond anticipation notes may be classified as part of the General Long-Term Debt Account Group when the following conditions are satisfied:

- All legal steps have been taken to refinance the bond anticipation notes.
- The intent is supported by an ability to consummate refinancing the bond anticipation notes on a long-term basis as defined in FASB-6 (Classification of Short-Term Obligations Expected To Be Refinanced).

FASB-6 requires that the intention to refinance be substantiated either through (1) a post-balance sheet issuance of the long-term bonds or (2) the existence of an acceptable financing agreement.

The bond anticipation notes may be classified as noncurrent (part of the General Long-Term Debt Account Group) if the long-term bonds are issued after the date of the Capital Projects Fund's balance sheet but before the fund's financial statements. The maximum amount of the bond anticipation notes to be classified as noncurrent can be no greater than the proceeds from the sale of the long-term bonds. For example, if bond anticipation notes total $10,000,000 and

Capital Projects Fund

long-term bonds of $7,000,000 are issued after the date of the balance sheet, only $7,000,000 of the bond anticipation notes may be classified as part of the General Long-Term Debt Account Group.

If the intent to refinance the bond anticipation notes is substantiated by a financing agreement, the financing agreement must have the following characteristics:

- The agreement does not expire within one year (or operating cycle) from the date of the enterprise's balance sheet, and during that period the agreement is not cancelable by the lender or the prospective lender or investor (and obligations incurred under the agreement are not callable during that period), except for a violation of a provision with which compliance is objectively determinable.
- No violation of any provision in the financing agreement exists at the balance sheet date, and no available information indicates that a violation has occurred thereafter but prior to the issuance of the balance sheet, or, if one exists at the balance sheet date or has occurred thereafter, a waiver has been obtained.
- The lender or the prospective lender or investor with which the enterprise has entered into the financing agreement is expected to be financially capable of honoring the agreement.

When the preconditions for classifying the bond anticipation notes as noncurrent as established by FASB-6 are not satisfied, the bond anticipation notes must be recorded as a liability of the Capital Projects Fund.

To illustrate the accounting for bond anticipation notes, assume that a Capital Projects Fund issues $1,000,000 of bond anticipation notes on June 30, 19X1. If either of the two conditions established by FASB-6 are satisfied, the issuance of the bond anticipation notes is treated as a noncurrent liability as illustrated below:

CAPITAL PROJECTS FUND
Cash	1,000,000	
Proceeds From Issuance Of Bond		
Anticipation Notes		1,000,000

GENERAL LONG-TERM DEBT ACCOUNT GROUP
Amount To Be Provided For Repayment		
Of Bond Anticipation Notes	1,000,000	
Bond Anticipation Notes Payable		1,000,000

Capital Projects Fund

On the other hand, if the requirements of FASB-6 are not satisfied, the issuance of the bond anticipation notes is recorded in the following manner:

CAPITAL PROJECTS FUND
Cash   1,000,000
    Bond Anticipation Notes Payable   1,000,000

GENERAL LONG-TERM DEBT ACCOUNT GROUP
No entry

The account bond anticipation notes payable used in the above example is presented as a liability on the balance sheet of the Capital Projects Fund.

When bond anticipation notes are initially classified as a Capital Projects Fund liability, the treatment of the obligation depends upon whether the long-term bonds are eventually issued. If the bonds are issued, the proceeds from the sale are recorded in the Capital Projects Fund and a liability is recognized in the General Long-Term Debt Account Group. In the current example, if it is assumed that on September 30, 19X1, long-term bonds of $1,000,000 are issued and the bond anticipation notes are retired, the following entries would be made:

CAPITAL PROJECTS FUND
Cash   1,000,000
    Proceeds From Issuance Of Bond
        Anticipation Notes   1,000,000

Bond Anticipation Notes Payable   1,000,000
    Cash   1,000,000

GENERAL LONG-TERM DEBT ACCOUNT GROUP
Amount To Be Provided For Repayment
    Of Long-Term Bonds   1,000,000
        Bonds Payable   1,000,000

If the long-term bonds are not issued, it will be necessary to make transfers from another governmental fund, such as the General Fund or Special Revenue Fund, in order for the Capital Projects Fund to have enough resources to finance the acquisition or construction of the capital asset and repay the bond anticipation notes. As transfers are received from other governmental funds, a *transfers in* account (other financing source) is used. For example, in the current illustration, assume that on September 30, 19X1, because of ad-

Capital Projects Fund

verse market conditions (excessive interest rate is demanded by the market), the governmental unit decides not to issue the long-term bonds and $1,000,000 is transferred from the General Fund to the Capital Projects Fund to be used to retire the bond anticipation notes. The transfer and retirement of the notes would be recorded as follows:

GENERAL FUND
Transfers Out—Capital Projects Fund   1,000,000
    Cash   1,000,000

CAPITAL PROJECTS FUND
Cash   1,000,000
    Transfers In—General Fund   1,000,000

Bond Anticipation Notes Payable   1,000,000
    Cash   1,000,000

Note: In the above examples there would be an interest expenditure on the bond anticipation notes. In these examples, for simplicity it is assumed that another governmental fund is legally responsible for such interest cost. The accounting treatment for interest expenditures of the Capital Projects Fund was discussed earlier in this chapter.

Claims and Judgments During the construction of a capital asset, claims and judgments may arise from property damage or personal injury. NCGA-4 (Accounting and Financial Reporting Principles for Claims and Judgments and Compensated Absences) concludes that claims and judgments should be accounted for in a manner consistent with FASB-5 (Accounting for Contingencies). Thus, a liability for a claim or judgment must be established when (1) the loss is probable (the future event or events are likely to occur) and (2) the amount of the loss can be reasonably estimated.

When it is concluded that a liability should be established for a claim or judgment, the manner in which the liability is recorded depends upon whether the liability is considered current or noncurrent. If available financial resources of the Capital Projects Fund will be used to satisfy the liability, the liability is considered current and must be reflected in the Capital Projects Fund's balance sheet. For example, assume that some houses suffer minor damages during the preparation of a site that is to be used to construct a governmental building. The claims are settled quickly out of court for $10,000, and the actual payments will be made within a few weeks. The claim is considered to be a current liability, and assuming the payment must legally be made from the Capital Projects Fund, the following entry is made:

CAPITAL PROJECTS FUND
   Expenditures—Claims And Judgments   10,000
      Estimated Liability For Claims And
         Judgments   10,000

Expenditures for claims and judgments, unlike other expenditures of the Capital Projects Fund, are not subject to capitalization in the General Fixed Assets Account Group.

When it is concluded that a claim or judgment should be recorded as a liability but the payment of the debt will not require the use of available financial resources of the Capital Projects Fund, the liability would be recorded in the General Long-Term Debt Account Group. For example, if the personal property claims in the previous example were expected to be settled for $10,000 but the actual payments will be made in approximately two years, the following entry would be made:

GENERAL LONG-TERM DEBT ACCOUNT GROUP
   Amount To Be Provided For Payment
      Of Certain Claims And Judgments   10,000
         Estimated Liabilities For Claims
            And Judgments   10,000

Classification and Disclosure   The following disclosures should be made with respect to liabilities of a Capital Projects Fund:

- Significant contingent liabilities
- Encumbrances outstanding
- Construction and other significant commitments

When bond anticipation notes are classified as part of the General Long-Term Debt Account Group, the following must be disclosed:
- A general description of the financing agreement
- The terms of any new debt incurred or expected to be incurred as a result of the agreement

Interfund Transactions

With the exceptions of quasi-external transactions and reimbursements, interfund transactions between the Capital Projects Fund and other governmental funds do not give rise to revenues and expenditures. A Capital Projects Fund may be involved in operating transfers and residual equity transfers when it deals with other governmental funds.

Capital Projects Fund

Operating Transfers Operating transfers include all transfers that do not represent loans or advances, quasi-external transactions, reimbursements, or residual equity transfers. Generally, operating transfers to a Capital Projects Fund may occur depending upon the manner in which the capital asset is to be financed. For example, assume a general services governmental building is expected to cost $3,000,000 and is to be financed by the issuance of $2,500,000 of bonds with the balance transferred from the General Fund. The planned interfund transfer would be recorded as follows:

GENERAL FUND
Transfers Out—Capital Projects Fund   500,000
  Due To Capital Projects Fund   500,000

CAPITAL PROJECTS FUND
Due From General Fund   500,000
  Transfers In—General Fund   500,000

The above accrual is made in the Capital Projects Fund when the funds are determined to be both measurable and available, which generally occurs at the date that appropriations from the General Fund are made.

Subsequent operating transfers may be received by the Capital Projects Fund if unexpected cost of construction or related costs are incurred. Such costs may arise from cost overruns, payments of interest cost, or payments due to claims and judgments. As discussed earlier in this chapter, unexpected costs incurred by a Capital Projects Fund must be financed in accordance with applicable laws or ordinances, or past practices of the governmental unit.

Operating transfers out and transfers in are reported in the Capital Projects Fund's Statement of Revenues and Expenditures as other financing sources (transfers in) and uses (transfers out). Interfund receivables and payables created by operating transfers should be recorded separately for control purposes. Amounts due to and due from the same fund, if they are both current, may be reported on the Capital Projects Fund's Balance Sheet as a single net amount. Receivables and payables that are not related to the same fund should not be netted for financial reporting purposes.

Residual Equity Transfers Transfers of a nonrecurring or nonroutine nature are classified as residual equity transfers and are usually associated with the liquidation of a Capital Projects Fund once the capital asset has been completed and is ready to be placed in operations. Residual equity transfers are shown as adjustments to the fund balance of the Capital Projects Fund because they are nonoperating in nature.

When the capital asset is completed, there may be a surplus or deficit in the Capital Projects Fund because revenues and transfers in were not equal to expenditures and transfers out. The disposition of the fund surplus or deficit is dependent upon a number of factors including past practices, laws and ordinances, and the manner in which the project was financed. For example, a surplus from a Capital Projects Fund that was financed through the issuance of long-term bonds may be transferred to the Debt Service Fund that will service the long-term debt. On the other hand, a surplus financed by a capital grant may have to be returned to the grantor governmental unit. A deficit, especially if it is significant, may require a special appropriation through the General Fund or a supplemental bond approval by the taxpayers.

A residual equity transfer may be illustrated by assuming that a $20,000 surplus remains in a Capital Projects Fund, and by law any surplus must be transferred to the related Debt Service Fund. The transfer from the Capital Projects Fund to the Debt Service Fund would be recorded as follows:

CAPITAL PROJECTS FUND
Fund Balance—Residual Equity
  Transfer To Debt Service Fund   20,000
    Cash   20,000

DEBT SERVICE FUND
Cash   20,000
  Fund Balance—Residual Equity
    Transfer From Capital Projects
      Fund   20,000

GENERAL LONG-TERM DEBT ACCOUNT GROUP
Amount Available In Debt Service Fund
  (For Retirement Of Long-Term Bonds)   20,000
  Amount To Be Provided For
    Repayment Of Long-Term Bonds   20,000

Classification and Disclosure   When financial statements of a Capital Projects Fund are combined with financial statements of other funds and agencies to form the reporting entity's combined financial statements, interfund transactions and accounts may be (but do not have to be) eliminated. Interfund eliminations, if any, in the combined financial statements that are not apparent from columnar headings must be adequately disclosed in notes to the financial statements of the reporting entity.

FINANCIAL STATEMENTS

Financial statements of all Capital Projects Funds must be included in the reporting entity's general purpose financial statements and Comprehensive Annual Financial Report. Supplemental schedules, such as detail classifications of expenditures and presentation of various investments, may support the basic financial statements of the Capital Projects Fund.

There is no requirement that a Capital Projects Fund present a Statement of Revenues, Expenditures, and Changes in Fund Balance on a budget basis and actual basis, unless the fund adopts an annual budget. Generally, only the General Fund and Special Revenue Funds present their results of operations in a comparative budget and actual format. Whether or not such a financial statement is presented for a Capital Projects Fund, if budgetary accounts are used they must be closed at the end of the fiscal year.

Closing Budget Related Accounts When the budget of a Capital Projects Fund is recorded upon its adoption, the budgetary accounts are reversed at the end of the period. Thus, the budgetary accounts have no effect on the actual results of operations for the period. For example, the following closing entry would be made to close the budgetary accounts illustrated earlier in this chapter (see Recording the budget):

Appropriations	8,000,000	
Estimated Grants—Federal Government		2,400,000
Estimated Grants—State Government		800,000
Estimated Bond Proceeds		4,000,000
Estimated Operating Transfers In—General Fund		300,000
Estimated Revenues—Property Taxes		500,000

Closing Encumbrances Encumbrances and the related reserves outstanding at the end of the year do not represent expenditures for the period or liabilities as of the end of the period. For this reason, these two budgetary accounts must be closed. Unlike some other governmental funds, encumbrances for a Capital Projects Fund do not generally lapse, since they are identified with a project rather than with a period. When encumbrances are nonlapsing, there is no need

Capital Projects Fund

to reappropriate the amounts in the following fiscal year. Nonetheless, nonlapsing encumbrances must be reported as a reserve of the fund balance. For example, assume that encumbrances of $400,000 are outstanding as of the end of the fiscal year. The following entries would be made in the Capital Projects Fund to close the encumbrances:

Fund Balance	400,000	
Encumbrances		400,000
Reserve For Encumbrances	400,000	
Fund Balance—Reserved For		
Encumbrances		400,000

On the first day of the next fiscal year, the following entry would be made:

Fund Balance—Reserved For		
Encumbrances	400,000	
Reserve For Encumbrances		400,000

The previous entry reestablishes budgetary control over encumbrances. Thus, the total expenditures to date plus the amount of encumbrances identifies what portion of construction costs for the capital asset has been committed as of any particular date. When encumbrances are vouchered during the next fiscal year, the following entry would be made:

Expenditures—Capital Outlays	400,000	
Vouchers Payable		400,000

The expenditure may be identified as an expenditure resulting from a prior year's commitment, but this is generally not necessary, since a Capital Projects Fund is project-oriented, not period-oriented. At the end of the second fiscal year, the following entry must be made:

Reserve For Encumbrances	400,000	
Expenditures—Capital Outlays		400,000

The previous entry is necessary to remove the reserve established at the beginning of the second fiscal year. Also the expenditure is not closed to the fund balance account because it was, in effect, closed to the fund balance at the end of the prior fiscal year.

As discussed earlier, although budgetary accounts are used to some degree in a Capital Projects Fund, a comparative (budget vs. actual) operating statement is generally not prepared. The financial statements of a Capital Projects Fund usually include the following:

- Statement of Revenues, Expenditures, and Changes in Fund Balance
- Balance Sheet
- Combining Financial Statements

Usually the Statement of Revenues and Expenditures is combined with the Statement of Changes in Fund Balance to form a single financial statement. For discussion purposes, these financial statements are examined as separate statements.

Statement of Revenues, Expenditures, and Changes in Fund Balance

The prevalent practice is to combine the activity statement and the analysis of the fund balance account into a single financial statement for a Capital Projects Fund. The combined financial statement is referred to as the Statement of Revenues, Expenditures, and Changes in Fund Balance. For discussion purposes only, the the two financial statements are examined separately in the following analysis.

Statement of Revenues and Expenditures The modified accrual basis (generally accepted accounting principles) is used to prepare a Capital Projects Fund's Statement of Revenues and Expenditures. If the operating statement does not demonstrate compliance with imposed legal requirements when the modified accrual basis is used, narrative explanations and appropriate schedules should be presented as supplemental information to demonstrate compliance.

The operating statement is all-inclusive in that only residual equity transfers and prior period adjustments are excluded from the computation of the excess of revenues and other sources of financing over (under) expenditures and other uses of financing. The format of the operating statement should segregate operating revenues and expenditures from transfers. An example of a Statement of Revenues and Expenditures combined with the analysis of changes in the fund balance is presented in Exhibit I.

Capital Projects Fund

EXHIBIT I

Statement of Revenues, Expenditures, and Changes in Fund Balance

City of Centerville
Statement of Revenues, Expenditures, and Changes in Fund Balance
Capital Projects Fund
For Year Ended June 30, 19X5

Revenues	
Capital grants—federal government	$2,400,000
Capital grants—state government	800,000
Property taxes	500,000
Total revenues	3,700,000
Expenditures	
Capital outlays	7,950,000
Interest	10,000
Claims and judgments	30,000
Total expenditures	7,990,000
Excess of revenues over (under) expenditures	(4,290,000)
Other financing sources (uses)	
Proceeds from sale of bonds	4,000,000
Transfers from other funds	300,000
Total other financing sources (uses)	4,300,000
Excess of revenues and other sources over (under) expenditures and other uses	10,000
(Increase) decrease in reserve for encumbrances	6,000
Net change in unreserved fund balance for year	16,000
Fund balance—unreserved July 1, 19X4	(12,000)
Fund balance—unreserved June 30, 19X5	$ 4,000

Statement of Changes in Fund Balance The Statement of Changes in Fund Balance reconciles the beginning and ending balances of the Capital Projects Fund's fund balance account. Items that may be included in the analysis are prior period adjustments, effects of changes in fund balance reserves, excess of revenues and other financing sources over (under) expenditures and other financing uses, and residual equity transfers. Prior period adjustments should appear immediately after the beginning fund balance, and residual equity transfers should appear after the excess of revenues and other financing sources over (under) expenditures and other financing uses.

Capital Projects Fund

Balance Sheet

Current expendable assets and current liabilities are presented in the Capital Projects Fund's balance sheet, which is unclassified. The fund balance section may include fund balance reserves, designated amounts, and the balance in the unreserved fund balance account.

An example of a Capital Projects Fund's statement of position is presented in Exhibit II.

EXHIBIT II
Balance Sheet

City of Centerville
Balance Sheet
Capital Projects Fund
June 30, 19X5

Assets	
Cash on deposit	$15,000
Equity in consolidated cash	12,000
Investments	1,000
Taxes receivable	8,000
Allowance for doubtful accounts	(2,000)
Due from other funds	10,000
Other assets	5,000
Total assets	$49,000
Liabilities	
Accounts payable	$10,000
Accrued expenses	5,000
Contracts payable—retained percentage	8,000
Vouchers payable	10,000
Total liabilities	33,000
Fund balance	
Fund balance reserved for encumbrances	12,000
Fund balance unreserved	4,000
Total fund balance	16,000
Total liabilities and fund balance	$49,000

Combining Financial Statements

When there is more than one Capital Projects Fund, combining financial statements for the capital projects governmental fund type must be prepared. All of the Capital Projects Funds are presented in a columnar format with a total column. The amounts shown in the total column must agree with the amounts presented in the combined financial statements of the governmental reporting entity.

Other Financial Statements

NCGA-1 notes that a Capital Projects Fund is project oriented and its life may extend over two or more fiscal years. For this reason it is suggested that results of operations be presented both for the current year and on a cumulative basis since the inception of the project. Thus, the Statement of Revenues, Expenditures, and Changes in Fund Balance should be presented on a dual basis.

> **OBSERVATION:** *Generally, the results of operations on a cumulative basis are not presented as a financial statement in the general purpose financial statements or Comprehensive Annual Financial Report, although the cumulative information may be presented in a schedule to support the financial statements or in a special purpose report.*

LITERATURE REFERENCES

Material in this chapter is based on the following authoritative pronouncements and publications, which are grouped according to the major headings used within the chapter. A dual reference (both paragraph and page number) is used for NCGA-1 and NCGA-2 because the original pronouncements do not use paragraph numbers.

Basic Concepts and Standards
NCGA-1 *Governmental Accounting and Financial Reporting Principles,* pp. 6-8/
¶¶ 16, 26, 30, and 31.

Basis of Accounting
NCGA-1 *Governmental Accounting and Financial Reporting Principles,* pp. 11 and 12/¶¶ 61, 62, and 70.

Measurement Focus
NCGA-1 *Governmental Accounting and Financial Reporting Principles,* p. 9/
¶¶ 39 and 44.

Capital Projects Fund

Budgetary System and Accounts
NCGA-1   *Governmental Accounting and Financial Reporting Principles*, pp. 7, 13, and 14/¶¶ 28, 77, and 89-92.
1980 GAAFR *Governmental Accounting, Auditing, and Financial Reporting*, p. 46.

Revenues and Other Sources of Financing
NCGA-1   *Governmental Accounting and Financial Reporting Principles*, p. 11/ ¶ 62.

Proceeds From Issuance of Long-Term Debt
NCGA-1   *Governmental Accounting and Financial Reporting Principles*, p. 11/¶ 62.

Capital Grants
NCGA-2   *Grant, Entitlement, and Shared Revenue Accounting and Reporting by State and Local Governments*, pp. 1 and 2/¶¶ 3, 7, and 11.

Shared Revenues
NCGA-2   *Grant, Entitlement, and Shared Revenue Accounting and Reporting by State and Local Governments*, pp. 1 and 2/¶¶ 3, 11, and 14.

Dedicated Taxes
NCGA-1   *Governmental Accounting and Financial Reporting Principles*, p. 16/ ¶ 106.

Investment Income
NCGA-1   *Governmental Accounting and Financial Reporting Principles*, pp. 11 and 12/¶¶ 62 and 69.

Classification and Disclosure
NCGA-1   *Governmental Accounting and Financial Reporting Principles*, p. 12/ ¶ 69.

Expenditures
NCGA-1   *Governmental Accounting and Financial Reporting Principles*, pp. 12 and 16/¶¶ 70 and 109.

Quasi-External Expenditures
NCGA-1   *Governmental Accounting and Financial Reporting Principles*, p. 15/ ¶¶ 102 and 103.

Reimbursements
NCGA-1   *Governmental Accounting and Financial Reporting Principles*, p. 15/ ¶¶ 102 and 104.

Interest Expenditures
NCGA-1 *Governmental Accounting and Financial Reporting Principles*, p. 9/ ¶ 48.

FASB-34 *Capitalization of Interest Cost*, ¶¶ 13 and 17.

FASB-62 *Capitalization of Interest Cost In Situations Involving Certain Tax-Exempt Borrowings and Certain Gifts and Grants*, ¶ 4.

Capital Leases
FASB-13 *Accounting for Leases*, ¶¶ 5, 7, and 10.

NCGA-5 *Accounting and Financial Reporting Principles for Lease Agreements of State and Local Governments*, ¶¶ 11, 13, and 14.

Classification and Disclosure
FASB-34 *Capitalization of Interest Cost*, ¶ 21.

NCGA-1 *Governmental Accounting and Financial Reporting Principles*, pp. 16 and 17/¶¶ 111-116.

Assets
NCGA-1 *Governmental Accounting and Financial Reporting Principles*, pp. 6, 9, 12, and 17/¶¶ 19, 39, 73, 118, and 120.

Classification and Disclosure
NCGA Interpretation-6 *Notes to the Financial Statements Disclosure*, appendix.

Liabilities
NCGA-1 *Governmental Accounting and Financial Reporting Principles*, pp. 6 and 9/¶¶ 19 and 44.

Bond Anticipation Notes
NCGA Interpretation-9 *Certain Fund Classifications and Balance Sheet Accounts*, ¶ 12.

FASB-6 *Classification of Short-Term Obligations Expected to Be Refinanced*, ¶¶ 10-12 and 15.

Claims and Judgments
NCGA-4 *Accounting and Financial Reporting Principles for Claims and Judgments and Compensated Absences*, ¶¶ 5, 7, 12, and 14-17.

FASB-5 *Accounting for Contingencies*, ¶¶ 3 and 8-11.

Classification and Disclosure
NCGA-1 *Governmental Accounting and Financial Reporting Principles*, p. 24/ ¶ 158.

NCGA Interpretation-6 *Notes to the Financial Statements Disclosure*, ¶ 5.

FASB-6 *Classification of Short-Term Obligations Expected to Be Refinanced*, ¶ 15.

Capital Projects Fund

Interfund Transactions
NCGA-1 *Governmental Accounting and Financial Reporting Principles*, p. 15/
¶¶ 101-104.

Operating Transfers
NCGA-1 *Governmental Accounting and Financial Reporting Principles*, pp. 15 and 16/¶¶ 105 and 106.

Residual Equity Transfers
NCGA-1 *Governmental Accounting and Financial Reporting Principles*, p. 15/
¶ 105.

Classification and Disclosure
NCGA-1 *Governmental Accounting and Financial Reporting Principles*, p. 22/
¶¶ 145 and 147.

Financial Statements
NCGA-1 *Governmental Accounting and Financial Reporting Principles*, p. 20/
¶ 141.

Statement of Revenues and Expenditures
NCGA-1 *Governmental Accounting and Financial Reporting Principles*, pp. 5, 22, and 23/¶¶ 12, 146, 149, and 151.

Statement of Changes in Fund Balance
NCGA-1 *Governmental Accounting and Financial Reporting Principles*, p. 23/
¶ 152.

Balance Sheet
NCGA-1 *Governmental Accounting and Financial Reporting Principles*, p. 22/
¶ 145.

Combining Financial Statements
NCGA-1 *Governmental Accounting and Financial Reporting Principles*, p. 21/
¶ 141.

Other Financial Statements
NCGA-1 *Governmental Accounting and Financial Reporting Principles*, p. 8/
¶ 28.

APPENDIX
GENERAL CAPITAL ASSETS AND DEBT
(DISCUSSION MEMORANDUM)

In its Exposure Draft entitled "Measurement Focus and Basis of Accounting—Governmental Fund Operating Statements," the GASB proposed to change the measurement focus of governmental entities from the flow of current financial resources to the flow of financial resources. Although this Exposure Draft proposed fundamental changes to governmental accounting, it did not address the accounting for and presentation of general capital assets, general capital debt, and capital debt service expenditures.

In March, 1989, the GASB issued a Discussion Memorandum entitled "Capital Reporting" that reviewed accounting issues relating to the reporting of capital transactions. This Appendix reviews the accounting for capital assets and general capital debt as presented in the Discussion Memorandum. An Appendix at the end of Chapter 62 reviews general capital debt service expenditure issues as described in the Discussion Memorandum.

The discussion of the accounting for and reporting of capital assets and general capital debt can be summarized by comparing the current capital reporting model and two alternatives presented in the Discussion Memorandum, namely, a capital account group model and a capital funds model.

The Capital Account Group Model

Under the capital account group model, the number of account groups would be reduced from two account groups (GLTDAG and GFAAG) to a single capital accounting group that would report capital assets and long-term liabilities issued to finance the acquisition of capital assets. The focus of the Capital Account Group would continue to be the residual effect of the financing activities; that is, capital assets and debt. All other financing activities would continue to be accounted for in other governmental funds. Aside from this change, the current capital reporting model as described in this chapter would be retained in that capital assets and the related long-term debt would not be reported in the entity's balance sheet as part of a specific fund. In this way, expendable financial resources (the current measurement focus) or financial resources (the proposed measurement focus) would not include assets and liabilities that do not affect the net expendable assets or net financial resources of the entity.

Capital Projects Fund

In order to contrast the current capital reporting model with the capital account group model, the following transactions will be illustrated under both of the models.

1. Long-term debt of $90,000 is issued.
2. Capital assets of $70,000 are acquired.
3. Long-term debt of $5,000 is retired.

Under the current capital reporting model, the following entries would be made to record these three transactions:

CURRENT CAPITAL REPORTING MODEL

Transaction 1

CAPITAL PROJECTS FUND
Cash	90,000	
Proceeds From Issuance Of Debt		90,000

GLTDAG
Amount To Be Provided	90,000	
Bonds Payable		90,000

Transaction 2

CAPITAL PROJECTS FUND
Expenditures—Capital Outlays	70,000	
Cash		70,000

GFAAG
General Fixed Assets	70,000	
Investment In General Fixed Assets		70,000

Transaction 3

DEBT SERVICE FUND
Expenditures—Principal Repayments	5,000	
Cash		5,000

GLTDAG
Bonds Payable	5,000	
Amount To Be Provided		5,000

Capital Projects Fund

Under the proposed capital account group model, the following entries would be made to record the three transactions:

PROPOSED CAPITAL ACCOUNT GROUP MODEL

Transaction 1

CAPITAL PROJECTS FUND
Cash 90,000
  Proceeds From Issuance Of Debt 90,000

CAPITAL ACCOUNT GROUP
Bonds Issued 90,000
  Bonds Payable 90,000

Transaction 2

CAPITAL PROJECTS FUND
Expenditures—Capital Outlays 70,000
  Cash 70,000

CAPITAL ACCOUNT GROUP
General Fixed Assets 70,000
  Investment In General Fixed Assets 70,000

Transaction 3

DEBT SERVICE FUND
Expenditures—Principal Repayment 5,000
  Cash 5,000

CAPITAL ACCOUNT GROUP
Bonds Payable 5,000
  Bonds Retired 5,000

Although the accounting for the issuance of debt and the acquisition of capital assets is similar under both models, there are two significant differences. First, under the proposed capital account group model, there is a possibility that a deficit would be reported in the financial statements. To return to the illustration, under the capital account group model, a deficit of $15,000 would be reported in the following manner.

Capital Projects Fund

General Fixed Assets	$ 70,000
Bonds Payable	$ 85,000
Fund Balance (deficit)	(15,000)
Total	$ 70,000

For governmental entities that do not capitalize infrastructure assets, it is likely that a fund balance deficit will arise.

Another difference in using the capital account group model is that an analysis similar to an operating statement can be made for the Capital Account Group, as illustrated below.

Bonds Issued	$(90,000)
Investments In Capital Assets	70,000
Bonds Retired	5,000
Net activity for the year	(15,000)
Fund Balance, beginning of period	-0-
Fund Balance, end of period (deficit)	$(15,000)

The Capital Account Group is *not* a fund; however, the activity analysis presented above provides an opportunity to summarize capital activity for the period and to integrate the results of that activity with the governmental entity's balance sheet through the balance in the fund balance account.

The Capital Funds Model

Under the capital funds model, a new governmental fund would be created by combining the two account groups (GFAAG and GLTDAG) with Capital Projects Funds and the Debt Service Funds. Therefore, this proposed model would now include all of the financing activities rather than just the residual effects, as proposed in the Capital Accounts Group model. (Minor variations of the capital funds model are analyzed in the Discussion Memorandum but are not discussed in this Appendix.)

The Discussion Memorandum suggests that one of the benefits of creating a combined fund is that governmental financial statements would be easier to understand because the number of columns would be reduced. In addition, all of the activities related to the acquisition and financing of capital assets and the servicing of long-term debt would be presented in a single governmental-fund type. Accordingly, this model would not routinely report deficit fund balances, which would be typical in the other model.

To illustrate the accounting and reporting under the capital fund model, the previous three transactions would be journalized as follows:

PROPOSED CAPITAL FUNDS MODEL

Transaction 1

CAPITAL FUND
Cash	90,000	
Bonds Issued	90,000	
Proceeds From Issuance Of Debt		90,000
Bonds Payable		90,000

Transaction 2

CAPITAL FUND
Expenditures—Capital Outlays	70,000	
General Fixed Assets	70,000	
Investment In General Fixed Assets		70,000
Cash		70,000

Transaction 3

CAPITAL FUND
Expenditures—Principal Repayments	5,000	
Bonds Payable	5,000	
Cash		5,000
Bonds Retired		5,000

The balance sheet and the activity statement for the Capital Fund are presented below.

Balance Sheet:
Cash	$15,000
General Fixed Assets	70,000
Total	$85,000
Bonds Payable	$85,000
Fund Balance	-0-
Total	$85,000

Capital Projects Fund

    Activity Statement:
      Financial Resources:

Proceeds From Issuance Of Debt	$90,000
Expenditures—Capital Outlays	70,000
Expenditures—Principal Repayment	5,000
Excess	15,000
Capital Resources:	
Bonds Issued	(90,000)
Investments In Fixed Assets	70,000
Bonds Retired	5,000
Fund Balance, beginning of period	-0-
Fund Balance, end of period	$ -0-

Other Issues

Although the Capital Reporting Discussion Memorandum analyzes alternatives to the current accounting and reporting standards for certain transactions related to the acquisition and reporting of capital assets, a number of related issues are not addressed. Some of these issues include the recognition of depreciation and the reporting of infrastructure assets, which are being addressed in another GASB research project.

Summary

The Discussion Memorandum analyzed in this Appendix represents only one of many GASB projects that, if adopted, will significantly change governmental accounting. It is expected that the GASB Statement that will be derived from the Discussion Memorandum will have the same effective date as several other GASB Statements now being developed. Once adopted, these Statements will affect virtually every aspect of governmental financial reporting.

DEBT SERVICE FUNDS

BASIC CONCEPTS AND STANDARDS

A Debt Service Fund is created to account for resources that will be used to service general long-term debt that is recorded in the governmental unit's General Long-Term Debt Account Group. General long-term debt includes noncurrent bonds and notes, as well as other noncurrent liabilities that might arise from capitalized lease agreements, pension plans, compensated absences, and other long-term liabilities not created by the issuance of a specific debt instrument.

A Debt Service Fund may be used for each obligation; however, the use of multiple funds often complicates a governmental unit's accounting system. In general, Debt Service Funds should be established only if legally required or when resources are being accumulated to meet principal and interest payments that will be made in future periods. When debt service payments are financed through the General Fund on a current basis, the principal and interest payments may be accounted for in the General Fund, and there is no need to create a Debt Service Fund unless legally required. The 1980 GAAFR (Governmental Accounting, Auditing, and Financial Reporting) recommends that a single Debt Service Fund be used to account for a restricted portion of a general property tax that is used to finance principal and interest payments on all general obligation bonds.

A Debt Service Fund is somewhat similar to a sinking fund used by a commercial enterprise in that resources are accumulated for the purpose of eventually retiring long-term obligations. Like other governmental funds, a Debt Service Fund is an accounting entity with a self-balancing set of accounts and separate statements of position and operations. In addition, a Debt Service Fund is project oriented rather than period oriented because once the long-term obligation accounted for in the Debt Service Fund is retired, the fund is terminated.

> *OBSERVATION: Although separate Debt Service Funds can be established for long-term obligations that are not based on an outstanding debt instrument (such as compensated absences and special termination benefits), these obligations are generally accounted for in other funds such as the General Fund or Special Revenue Funds.*

A governmental reporting entity may issue a variety of long-term debt instruments, some of which are not accounted for in a Debt Service Fund and the General Long-Term Debt Account Group. For example, *revenue bonds* represent debt issued by an Enterprise Fund and secured by specific revenues of the fund as well as mortgage liens on certain capital assets of the fund. Revenue bonds are recorded as liabilities of an Enterprise Fund. General long-term debt that is secured by the full faith and credit of the governmental unit is accounted for in the General Long-Term Debt Account Group and may require the establishment of a Debt Service Fund.

> **OBSERVATION:** *An Enterprise Fund may issue a debt that is backed by the full faith and credit of the governmental unit. This type of debt is accounted for in the Enterprise Fund, although it is disclosed as a contingent liability in the General Long-Term Debt Account Group.*

General long-term debt secured by the full faith and credit of the governmental unit includes various types of bond issuances. *Term bonds* mature at a single future date. Generally, periodic actuarially determined payments are made to a Debt Service Fund in order to accumulate a sufficient amount to retire the term bonds. On the other hand, *serial bonds* mature not on a single date, but at various dates over the life of the bond issuance. Serial bonds can be divided into the following four categories:

- *Regular serial bonds*—Periodic principal repayments are made in equal amounts.
- *Irregular serial bonds*—Periodic principal repayments are made in other than equal amounts.
- *Deferred serial bonds*—Periodic principal repayments are made in equal amounts but the first repayment is deferred for more than one year after the initial issuance of the serial bonds.
- *Serial annuity bonds*—Equal periodic principal repayments and interest payments are made over the life of the bond issuance.

Basis of Accounting

The modified accrual basis is used to account for a Debt Service Fund. Revenues and transfers in are recognized when they are both measurable and available. With one exception, expenditures of a Debt Service Fund are recorded when the related liability is incurred. The exception for expenditure recognition relates to the treatment of unmatured principal and interest on general obligation long-term debt as discussed later in this chapter.

Measurement Focus

As with other governmental funds, the measurement focus of a Debt Service Fund is the recording of sources and uses of financial resources and the net financial resources available for subsequent principal repayments and interest payments. Thus, although a Debt Service Fund accounts for principal and interest disbursements related to general long-term debt, the long-term obligation itself is recorded in the General Long-Term Debt Account Group. The general long-term obligation will not use current financial resources of the Debt Service Fund, and therefore, is not recognized as a fund liability until its due date.

Budgetary System and Accounts

Debt Service Fund financial resources and expenditures may be controlled through the use of a budgetary accounting system; however, there is no need to use an encumbrance system.

Recording the budget Unless a Debt Service Fund budget is legally adopted, there is no requirement to record the fund's budget or to prepare financial statements that compare the results of operations for the period on a budget basis and an actual basis. Usually the bond indenture provision that requires the establishment of a Debt Service Fund also controls expenditures to be made from the fund. NCGA-1 (Governmental Accounting and Financial Reporting Principles) concludes that it is unlikely that budgetary accounts should be integrated into the financial accounting system of a Debt Service Fund when the receipts and expenditures (1) are controlled by bond indenture or sinking fund provisions and (2) occur infrequently during the budgetary period.

If the management of the governmental unit concludes that budgetary accounts should be used, the expected revenues and transfers in are recorded along with the anticipated expenditures.

Debt Service Funds

To illustrate the use of budgetary accounts, assume that the following flows of financial resources are expected for the current budgetary period:

Transfers from general fund	$1,000,000
Portion of property tax to be used exclusively to service debt	400,000
Expected premium on new debt issued and to be transferred from a capital projects fund	100,000
Estimated earnings on investments made by the debt service fund	100,000
Expenditures for payment of current interest	600,000
Expenditures of repayment of matured principal	1,000,000

The budgetary items would be recorded as follows:

Estimated Operating Transfers In—		
General Fund	1,000,000	
Estimated Revenue—Property Taxes	400,000	
Estimated Premium Transfer In—		
Capital Projects Fund	100,000	
Estimated Earnings On Investments—		
Debt Service Fund	100,000	
Appropriations		1,600,000

This entry may be recorded and posted like any other journal entry, in which case the entry would be reversed during the closing process at the end of the fiscal year. All the accounts are budgetary accounts; therefore, they have no effect on the Debt Service Fund's results of operations. If it is concluded that the budgetary information is necessary for control purposes, but there is no real need to integrate the accounts into the accounting system, the above entry can be treated simply as a memorandum entry.

Recording encumbrances A Debt Service Fund does not use an encumbrance system because no purchase orders or subsequent contracts are signed. All fund expenditures are determined by the bond indenture agreement.

ACCOUNTS AND TRANSACTIONS

Similar to a Capital Projects Fund, a Debt Service Fund is project oriented in that once the outstanding debt is retired, the Debt

Service Fund is terminated. However, since most governmental units issue debt on a more or less continuous basis, it is likely that the Debt Service Fund, at least the fund used to account for general long-term debt, will not be terminated. Typical accounts and transactions associated with a Debt Service Fund are explained next.

Revenues and Other Sources of Financing

Revenues and other sources of financing are recorded in a Debt Service Fund when they are measurable and available. Although significant amounts of financial resources are made available to a Debt Service Fund from transfers from other funds, activities are also financed from specific revenue sources available to a Debt Service Fund.

Property Taxes When a governmental unit issues long-term bonds, it may increase the property tax rate in order to service the newly issued debt. Property taxes raised for this purpose should be recorded as revenue of the Debt Service Fund if separately levied and should be accounted for like any other property tax assessed by a governmental unit.

Generally, property taxes are recorded as revenue in the fiscal year in which they are levied if the availability criterion can be satisfied. As defined in NCGA-1, *available* means that the tax will be collected during the current period or "soon enough thereafter to be used to pay liabilities of the current period." What constitutes a reasonable period after the end of a current period has been defined in NCGA Interpretation-3 (Revenue Recognition—Property Taxes) as no more than 60 days after the end of the period. The Interpretation does state that in unusual circumstances a period greater than 60 days can be used, but the longer time period and the reason for using it must be disclosed in the financial statements.

> **OBSERVATION:** *By the fact that property taxes are levied, NCGA Interpretation-3 assumes that the measurable criterion is satisfied. The amount of the property taxes is simply based on the assessed value of the property and the current property tax rate used by the state or local government. However, all property taxes assessed will not be collected, and the measurability criterion can be satisfied only if the governmental unit can make a reasonable estimate of the amount of uncollectible property taxes.*

Debt Service Funds

It is unlikely that a Debt Service Fund's portion of the general property tax will be received directly from property owners. Typically, the total property tax will be initially accounted for in another governmental fund (usually the General Fund), and the Debt Service Fund's share will be transferred at a later date. As suggested earlier, the transfer to the Debt Service Fund from the other governmental fund is not an operating transfer but, rather, represents Debt Service Fund revenue. The Debt Service Fund's share of the property tax can be recorded as (1) a liability of the governmental fund that initially receives the property tax or (2) revenue of the governmental fund that initially receives the property tax with a reduction of its revenues when the fund transfers property tax receipts to the Debt Service Fund. For example, assume that the total property tax assessment is $10,000,000, of which $400,000 is legally attributable to the Debt Service Fund. The property tax is initially accounted for in the General Fund and a 5% uncollectibility rate is applicable. If the Debt Service Fund's portion of the property tax is treated as a liability of the General Fund, the following entries would be made to record the property tax assessment:

GENERAL FUND
Property Taxes Receivable—Current   10,000,000
   Revenues—Property Taxes
    ($9,600,000 × 95%)   9,120,000
   Allowance For Uncollectible
    Property Taxes—Current   500,000
   Due To Debt Service Fund   380,000

DEBT SERVICE FUND
Due From General Fund
  ($400,000 × 95%)   380,000
   Revenues—Property Taxes   380,000

GENERAL LONG-TERM DEBT ACCOUNT GROUP
Amount Available In Debt Service
  Fund   380,000
   Amount To Be Provided For
    Repayment Of Bonds   380,000

If $50,000 of property taxes are subsequently transferred to the Debt Service Fund, the transaction would be recorded as follows:

GENERAL FUND
Due To Debt Service Fund   50,000
   Cash   50,000

Debt Service Funds

DEBT SERVICE FUND
Cash   50,000
  Due From General Fund   50,000

When the Debt Service Fund's portion of the property tax is initially treated as revenue of the General Fund, the property tax assessment would be recorded as follows:

GENERAL FUND
Property Taxes Receivable—Current   10,000,000
  Revenues—Property Taxes   9,500,000
  Allowances For Uncollectible
    Property Taxes—Current   500,000

DEBT SERVICE FUND
No entry

To record a $50,000 transfer of property tax receipts to the Debt Service Fund, the following entries would be made:

GENERAL FUND
Revenues—Property Taxes   50,000
  Cash   50,000

DEBT SERVICE FUND
Cash   50,000
  Revenues—Property Taxes   50,000

GENERAL LONG-TERM DEBT ACCOUNT GROUP
Amount Available In Debt Service
  Fund   50,000
  Amount To Be Provided For
    Repayment Of Bonds   50,000

At the end of the fiscal year, if the full amount of the Debt Service Fund's share of the property taxes has not been transferred, the Debt Service Fund would accrue the unreceived portion, assuming that the funds will be made available from the General Fund within 60 days after the end of the fiscal year. In the current example, if at the end of the fiscal year $100,000 of property tax receipts had not been transferred to the Debt Service Fund, the accrual would be made as follows:

GENERAL FUND
Revenues—Property Taxes   100,000
  Due To Debt Service Fund   100,000

Debt Service Funds

DEBT SERVICE FUND
Due From General Fund 100,000
  Revenue—Property Taxes 100,000

GENERAL LONG-TERM DEBT ACCOUNT GROUP
Amount Available In Debt Service Fund 100,000
  Amount To Be Provided For
    Repayment of Bonds 100,000

> **OBSERVATION:** *When a Debt Service Fund is legally entitled to a portion of the levied property tax, it can be argued that the portion of the revenue not collected at the end of the period should be recorded by the Debt Service Fund as a receivable (net of an allowance for uncollectibles), rather than as an amount due from the General Fund. If this approach is used, the General Fund would reduce its net receivable rather than establish an amount due to the Debt Service Fund.*

Shared Revenues NCGA-2 (Grant, Entitlement, and Shared Revenue Accounting and Reporting by State and Local Governments) describes shared revenues as revenues collected by one governmental unit but shared on a predetermined basis with another governmental unit. Generally, shared revenues are subject to forfeiture by the recipient governmental unit only if prescribed regulations are not followed. For this reason, a Debt Service Fund may accrue shared revenues that have been collected by the intermediary governmental unit if (1) the amount of the shared revenues to be received can be reasonably estimated and (2) it is expected that the shared revenues will be available to finance Debt Service Fund expenditures of the current period.

To illustrate the accounting for shared revenues, assume that a local government shares in the revenues generated by a state gasoline tax. A legally predetermined portion of the state gasoline tax is to be used to exclusively service bonded debt issued by local municipalities to finance the construction and improvement of certain highway projects. During a fiscal year, a local government received $300,000 of shared revenues under the program. The receipt of the shared revenues from the state government would be recorded as follows:

DEBT SERVICE FUND
Cash 300,000
  Revenue—Shared State Gasoline Taxes 300,000

GENERAL LONG-TERM DEBT ACCOUNT GROUP
 Amount Available In Debt Service Fund 300,000
  Amount To Be Provided For
   Repayment Of Bonds   300,000

At the end of the fiscal year, if it is assumed that the local government will receive another $70,000 within a few days after the close of its fiscal year, the government would make the following entry to accrue the expected receipt of the shared revenues:

DEBT SERVICE FUND
 Intergovernmental Receivable—
  State Government   70,000
   Revenue—Shared State Gasoline
    Taxes   70,000

GENERAL LONG-TERM DEBT ACCOUNT GROUP
 Amount Available In Debt Service Fund 70,000
  Amount To Be Provided For
   Repayment Of Bonds   70,000

  When shared revenues are made available to a governmental unit with no legal stipulations as to how the revenues are to be spent, the shared revenues would generally be recorded as General Fund or Special Revenue Fund revenue. Portions of the shared revenues subsequently transferred to the Debt Service Fund would be treated as an operating transfer (other sources of financing) and not recorded as revenue of the Debt Service Fund.
  NCGA-2 concludes that shared revenues, as well as grants and entitlements, received for the payment of principal or interest on general long-term debt should be accounted for in a Debt Service Fund.

Investment Income The accounting for regular serial bonds is relatively simple since the periodic principal and interest payments may be financed by current transfers from another fund such as the General Fund or Special Revenue Funds. When term bonds or deferred serial bonds are issued, the accounting becomes somewhat more complicated because resources are typically accumulated in the Debt Service Fund and invested in various short-term and long-term instruments. The income earned from these investments is recorded as investment income of the Debt Service Fund.
  The issuance of term bonds usually requires that funds be transferred periodically to the Debt Service Fund and invested in order to have sufficient resources to retire the term bonds when they mature.

Debt Service Funds

The amount of the periodic transfer is dependent upon the anticipated rate of return that will be earned when the resources are invested. If long-term investments are acquired at an amount other than par value, the discount or premium must be amortized if the management strategy is to hold the investments until maturity.

To illustrate the accounting for term bonds in a Debt Service Fund, assume that general obligation bonds of $2,000,000 are issued on June 30, 19X1. The bonds mature in five years (June 30, 19X6) and the bond indenture agreement requires that a separate Debt Service Fund be established with an annual transfer from the General Fund beginning on June 30, 19X2. Based on consultation with appropriate investment personnel, it is estimated that funds invested by the Debt Service Fund should earn a 6% rate of return. Thus, the annual transfers from the General Fund would be $354,793 ($2,000,000/ 5.63709, where i = 6%, n = 5 for a future amount of an ordinary annuity). On June 30, 19X2, $354,793 is transferred from the General Fund to the Debt Service Fund and recorded as follows:

GENERAL FUND
Transfers Out—Debt Service Fund   354,793
    Cash   354,793

DEBT SERVICE FUND
Cash   354,793
    Transfers In—General Fund   354,793

GENERAL LONG-TERM DEBT ACCOUNT GROUP
Amount Available In Debt Service Fund   354,793
    Amount To Be Provided For
       Repayment Of Bonds   354,793

Immediately on June 30, 19X2, the Debt Service Fund invests in bonds that mature on June 30, 19X6, and carry a zero interest rate. The par value of the bonds is $447,919 but the current acquisition price is $354,793, which results in a yield of 6%. The investment is recorded as follows in the Debt Service Fund:

Investments In Bonds   354,793
    Cash   354,793

At the end of each fiscal period, a portion of the bond discount of $93,126 ($447,919 − $354,793) must be amortized. The "interest" method must be used to amortize the discount, although the straight-line method (or some other method) can be used when the difference between the two methods is immaterial. The following amortization schedule can be used as the basis for recording the periodic interest income:

Date	Interest @ 6%	Amortization of discount	Carrying value of investment
6/30/X2			$354,793
6/30/X3	$21,288	$21,288	376,081
6/30/X4	22,565	22,565	398,646
6/30/X5	23,919	23,919	422,565
6/30/X6	25,354	25,354	447,919

On June 30, 19X3 (end of fiscal year), the following entries would be made:

DEBT SERVICE FUND
Investment In Bonds   21,288
    Interest Income   21,288

GENERAL LONG-TERM DEBT ACCOUNT GROUP
Amount Available In Debt Service Fund   21,288
    Amount To Be Provided For
      Repayment Of Bonds   21,288

The above example follows only the first investment that is made by the Debt Service Fund. At the end of each year, the annual transfer from the General Fund must also be invested. In addition, the expected rate of return on investments will change from year to year, which will require an appropriate increase or decrease in the annual transfer from the General Fund.

> **OBSERVATION:** *Interest income resulting from the amortization of bond discount does not represent resources available to finance current expenditures of the Debt Service Fund. The recognition of income is necessary, even though it violates the basic governmental accounting model, in order not to distort the amount of resources that will eventually be available to the Debt Service Fund when the investment matures. Since the accrued interest income is not available to finance the Debt Service Fund current expenditures, the fund balance should be reserved or designated by an amount equal to the accrued interest income.*

Transfers and Other Sources of Financing   Transfers from other governmental funds to the Debt Service Fund that are to be used to service general long-term debt are treated like all other operating transfers. The governmental fund that transfers the resources debits a transfers out account (other uses of financing), and the Debt Service Fund records a transfers in (other sources of financing).

Bonds of a governmental unit may be issued at a premium. In some instances, the bond authorization may identify which governmental fund is to benefit from the premium. For example, a bond authorized by voters may carry a provision that all amounts in excess of the par value of the bonds will be made available to the General Fund or a Capital Projects Fund. In this case, the bond premium is recorded as an other source of financing in the specified governmental fund. On the other hand, when no specific fund is identified as the fund to receive the bond premium, the bond premium should be made available to the governmental fund that is responsible for servicing the long-term debt. If the debt is being serviced by a Debt Service Fund, the premium should be recognized as an other source of financing of the Debt Service Fund.

To illustrate the accounting for a bond premium that is made available to a Debt Service Fund, assume that $5,000,000 par value bonds are sold for $5,250,000. The proceeds from the sale of the bonds, except for the bond premium, are to be used to construct a capital asset that is being accounted for in a Capital Projects Fund. The issuance of the bonds would be recorded in the following manner:

CAPITAL PROJECTS FUND
Cash	5,250,000	
Proceeds From Issuance Of Bonds		5,000,000
Due To Debt Service Fund		250,000

DEBT SERVICE FUND
Due From Capital Projects Fund	250,000	
Proceeds From Issuance Of Bonds—		
Premium		250,000

GENERAL LONG-TERM DEBT ACCOUNT GROUP
Amount To Be Provided For		
Repayment Of Bonds	5,000,000	
Bonds Payable		5,000,000
Amount Available In Debt Service		
Fund	250,000	
Amount To Be Provided For		
Repayment Of Bonds		250,000

Alternatively, the portion of the bond issuance that represents the bond premium may be recorded directly in the Debt Service Fund, in which case there would be no need to establish interfund accounts.

Classification and Disclosure In the Debt Service Fund's Statement of Revenues and Expenditures, there should be a distinction between revenues and other sources of financing. In addition, major revenue sources should be identified. Revenue recognition methods must be disclosed in the Summary of Significant Accounting Policies.

Expenditures

A Debt Service Fund is created to accumulate resources that will be used to repay long-term obligations as they become due, and to make periodic interest payments associated with the debt. The proceeds from the sale of general long-term debt is not recorded in a Debt Service Fund but, rather, in the fund that is entitled to make expenditures from the proceeds. Also, the long-term obligation is not recorded in a Debt Service Fund but, rather, is part of the General Long-Term Debt Account Group. As principal debt service payments are made over the life of the obligation, an expenditure is recognized in the Debt Service Fund and the amount of the obligation as reflected in the General Long-Term Debt Account Group is reduced.

Basic accounting entries associated with a Debt Service Fund are illustrated by the following transactions:

Transaction: General long-term debt of $5,000,000 (serial bonds) is issued at par and the proceeds are made available to a Capital Projects Fund to finance the construction of a capital asset.

CAPITAL PROJECTS FUND
Cash	5,000,000	
Proceeds From Issuance Of Bonds		5,000,000

GENERAL LONG-TERM DEBT ACCOUNT GROUP
Amount To Be Provided For		
Repayment Of Bonds	5,000,000	
Bonds Payable		5,000,000

Debt Service Funds

DEBT SERVICE FUND
    No entry

Transaction: The General Fund transfers $550,000 to the Debt Service Fund for the repayment of maturing serial bonds ($250,000) and payment of current interest ($300,000).

GENERAL FUND
Transfers Out—Debt Service Fund	550,000	
Cash		550,000

DEBT SERVICE FUND
Cash	550,000	
Transfers In—General Fund		550,000

GENERAL LONG-TERM DEBT ACCOUNT GROUP
Amount Available In Debt Service Fund	250,000	
Amount To Be Provided For Repayment Of Bonds		250,000

Transaction: The Debt Service Fund makes principal repayments of $250,000 for the serial bonds and interest payments of $300,000.

DEBT SERVICE FUND
Expenditures—Principal Repayments	250,000	
Expenditures—Interest Payments	300,000	
Cash		550,000

GENERAL LONG-TERM DEBT ACCOUNT GROUP
Bonds Payable	250,000	
Amount Available In Debt Service Fund		250,000

There is no need to use an encumbrance system to control principal and interest expenditures made from a Debt Service Fund. As discussed earlier, the bond indenture agreement stipulates when expenditures for principal repayments and interest payments must be made.

Unmatured Principal and Interest Under the modified accrual basis, expenditures of a governmental fund are recognized when the related liability is incurred. The one significant exception to this fundamental concept is the accounting treatment for unmatured principal and accrued interest. Unmatured principal and accrued interest are not recognized as a liability of the Debt Service Fund until the amounts are due to be paid. For example, if long-term debt were issued on January 1, 19X5, and the first interest payment were due on July 1, 19X5, there would be no accrual of interest as of June 30, 19X5 (end of fiscal year). Likewise, if a serial bond repayment were due on July 1, 19X5, the liability would not be recorded in the Debt Service Fund's balance sheet as of June 30, 19X5, even though the amount would be due the next day.

The rationale for the nonaccrual of unmatured principal and interest is two-fold. First, the obligation for principal and interest will not be paid with current financial resources of the Debt Service Fund. Generally, the necessary resources needed to pay the principal and interest amounts will be transferred from another fund. In addition, the governmental fund making the transfer to the Debt Service Fund usually budgets transfers in the year that each transfer is made (due date of principal and interest). If the debt service requirements were accrued in the Debt Service Fund, the payments would be shown as expenditures in one period and as transfers during the following period. Thus, principal and interest payments for general long-term debt are accounted for on a cash basis.

When a governmental unit uses a fiscal agent to make principal and interest payments to debt holders, payments to the fiscal agent should be treated as interest expenditures and reduction of debts even if the actual payments to the debt holders will occur shortly after the close of the fiscal year.

Debt Extinguishments Scheduled debt retirements are accounted for as described above. In addition to scheduled retirements, general obligations of a governmental unit may be extinguished by (1) legal defeasance, (2) in-substance defeasance, or (3) debt refunding.

Legal defeasance A state or local government may decide to retire its outstanding debt before maturity for a number of reasons. One reason may be that the interest rate that it is paying may be excessive based on current market conditions. NCGA Interpretation-9 (Certain Fund Classifications and Balance Sheet Accounts) concludes that requirements established by FASB-76 (Extinguishment of Debt) should be followed when debt is retired by legal defeasance. FASB-76 provides the following description of legal defeasance of debt:

- The debtor pays the creditor and is relieved of all its obligations with respect to the debt. This includes the debtor's reacquisition of its outstanding debt securities in the pub-

Debt Service Funds

lic securities market, regardless of whether the securities are cancelled or held as so-called treasury bonds.
- The debtor is legally released from being the primary obligor under the debt either judicially or by the creditor and it is probable that the debtor will not be required to make future payments with respect to the debt under any guarantees.

When a governmental unit extinguishes its debt through legal defeasance, an expenditure is recognized in the Debt Service Fund and the debt is removed from the General Long-Term Debt Account Group. To illustrate, assume that a governmental unit has decided to repurchase a portion of a bond issuance outstanding. The particular bond series outstanding has a par value of $10,000,000, of which $3,000,000 is repurchased in the open market at a price of $3,150,000. The retirement is financed by transferring funds from the General Fund to the Debt Service Fund. The early debt extinguishment would be recorded as follows:

GENERAL FUND
Transfers Out—Debt Service Fund	3,150,000	
Cash		3,150,000

DEBT SERVICE FUND
Cash	3,150,000	
Transfers In—General Fund		3,150,000
Expenditures—Early Extinguishment Of Debt	3,150,000	
Cash		3,150,000

GENERAL LONG-TERM DEBT ACCOUNT GROUP
Amount Available In Debt Service Fund	3,000,000	
Amount To Be Provided For Repayment Of Bonds		3,000,000
Bonds Payable	3,000,000	
Amount Available In Debt Service Fund		3,000,000

OBSERVATION: *If a separate Debt Service Fund is not used to account for the outstanding obligation, the expenditure would be recognized in the General Fund or the governmental fund that financed the early extinguishment of the debt.*

In-substance defeasance Debt of a state or local governmental unit may be retired in an indirect manner referred to as in-substance defeasance. This method of debt extinguishment is described in FASB-76 as follows:

> The debtor irrevocably places cash or other assets in a trust to be used solely for satisfying scheduled payments of both interest and principal of a specific obligation and the possibility that the debtor will be required to make future payments with respect to that debt is remote. In this circumstance, debt is extinguished even though the debtor is not legally released from being the primary obligor under the debt obligation.

The irrevocable trust created by the governmental unit must hold only monetary assets that are (1) denominated in the same currency in which the debt is payable and (2) essentially risk free with respect to the timing, amount, and collection of principal and interest.

To illustrate in-substance defeasance, assume that a state government has $10,000,000 of long-term bonds outstanding that will mature in 17 years. An irrevocable trust is established and $8,400,000 is transferred to the Debt Service Fund where certain investments (monetary assets) are acquired and then transferred to the irrevocable trust. The monetary asset investment of $8,400,000, plus the interest earned at a specified rate will be sufficient to finance all future interest payments and principal retirements as required by the original bond indenture. The in-substance defeasance would be recorded as follows:

GENERAL FUND
Transfers Out—Debt Service Fund	8,400,000	
Cash		8,400,000

DEBT SERVICE FUND
Cash	8,400,000	
Transfers In—General Fund		8,400,000
Investment In Monetary Assets	8,400,000	
Cash		8,400,000
Expenditures—Early Extinguishment Of Debt	8,400,000	
Investment In Monetary Assets		8,400,000

GENERAL LONG-TERM DEBT ACCOUNT GROUP
Bonds Payable   10,000,000
  Amount To Be Provided For
    Repayment Of Bonds   10,000,000

As illustrated, the amount of the debt removed from the General Long-Term Debt Account Group is the par value of the debt.

Debt Refunding

GASB-7 is applicable to advance refundings resulting in defeased debt. An advance refunding occurs when new debt is issued to provide resources to pay debt service requirements (interest and principal) on old debt. The old debt may be defeased legally or in-substance. A legal defeasance occurs when the terms for defeasance as stated in the old debt agreement are satisfied even though the debt may remain outstanding until its call date or maturity date. An in-substance defeasance occurs when the criteria established by GASB-7 are satisfied by creating an irrevocable trust "to be used solely for satisfying scheduled payments of both interest and principal of a specific obligation and the possibility that the debtor will be required to make future payments with respect to that debt is remote." These criteria are verbatim restatements of FASB-76 (Extinguishment of Debt). The following restrictions apply to the nature of the assets placed in the irrevocable trust:

> a. The trust shall be restricted to owning only monetary assets[3] that are *essentially risk free* as to the amount, timing, and collection of interest and principal. The monetary assets shall be denominated in the currency in which the debt is payable. For debt denominated in U.S. dollars, essentially risk-free monetary assets shall be limited to:
>
> (1) Direct obligations of the U.S. government
> (2) Obligations guaranteed by the U.S. government
> (3) Securities that are backed by U.S. government obligations as collateral under an arrangement by which the interest and principal payments on the collateral generally flow immediately through to the holder of the security.
>
> However, some securities described in the previous sentence can be paid prior to scheduled maturity and so are not essentially risk free as to the *timing* of the collection of interest and principal; thus, they do not qualify for ownership by the trust.

b. The monetary assets held by the trust shall provide cash flows (from interest and maturity of those assets) that approximately coincide, as to timing and amount, with the scheduled interest and principal payments on the debt that is being extinguished.

---

[3] A monetary asset is money or a claim to receive a sum of money that is fixed or determinable without reference to future prices of specific goods or services.

A governmental entity may defease debt for a number of reasons, including the desire to take advantage of lower interest rates and the extension of the maturity date of an outstanding debt. When debt is defeased, GASB-7 establishes accounting standards for debt reported in a governmental entity's General Long-Term Debt Account Group; however, GASB-7 does not establish accounting standards for debt reported in a specific fund, such as an Enterprise Fund. However, disclosure requirements are established by GASB-7 for all governmental entities irrespective of the account group or fund in which the defeased debt was reported. The disclosures include the difference between debt service requirements for the old and new debt, and the economic gain or loss resulting from the defeasance.

A more thorough discussion of GASB-7 can be found in chapter 40, Liabilities.

Capital Leases

A Debt Service Fund may be used to account for periodic lease payments that are associated with a capitalized lease. From an accounting perspective, a capitalized lease is treated like the purchase of a capital asset financed by the issuance of long-term debt. Thus, the periodic lease payments are recorded as expenditures of the Debt Service Fund.

NCGA-5 (Accounting and Financial Reporting Principles for Lease Agreements of State and Local Governments) requires that state and local governments apply the accounting and reporting standards established in FASB-13 (Accounting for Leases, as amended). FASB-13 concludes that a lease must be capitalized if any of the following criteria are satisfied:

- The lease transfers ownership of the property to the lessee by the end of the lease term.

- The lease term contains a bargain purchase option.
- The lease term is equal to 75% or more of the estimated economic life of the leased property.
- The present value at the beginning of the lease term of the minimum lease payments, excluding that portion of the payments representing executory costs, to be paid by the lessor, including any profit thereon, equals or exceeds 90% of the excess of the fair value of the leased property to the lessor at the inception of the lease over any related investment tax credit retained by the lessor and expected to be realized by him.

When the beginning of the lease term falls within the last 25% of the economic life of the leased property, the third and fourth criteria are not applicable.

If a lease agreement is classified as a capital lease, the leased property rights are capitalized as part of the General Fixed Assets Account Group and the lease obligation is reported in the General Long-Term Debt Account Group. Both amounts are recorded at the present value of the minimum lease payments. In addition, the governmental fund responsible for the acquisition of the property rights, usually a Capital Projects Fund, simultaneously records the present value of the lease payments as an expenditure and an other source of financing.

Subsequently, when periodic lease payments are made, the expenditure is recognized in the Debt Service Fund. For example, assume that machinery with an economic life of three years is leased on June 30, 19X1. The agreement requires that three annual lease payments of $10,000 be made beginning on June 30, 19X1. The implicit interest rate is assumed to be 10%. The three annual payments would be recorded in the Debt Service Fund and classified as principal expenditures and interest expenditures. The total amount of the capitalized debt is $27,355, which is computed as follows:

Amount of lease payments	$10,000
Present value of an annuity due, when the interest rate is 10% and the number of periods is 3	× 2.73554
Present value of minimum lease payments	$27,355

The following amortization table is prepared to distinguish between the principal portion and the interest portion:

Amortization Schedule

Date	Lease payment	Interest expenditure @ 10%	Principal expenditure	Amount of general long-term debt
6/30/X1				$27,355
6/30/X1	$10,000		$10,000	17,355
6/30/X2	10,000	$1,736	8,264	9,091
6/30/X3	10,000	909	9,091	-0-

Assuming that the annual lease payments are financed by transfers from the General Fund, the lease payment made on June 30, 19X2, would be recorded as follows:

GENERAL FUND
Transfers Out—Debt Service Fund	10,000	
Cash		10,000

DEBT SERVICE FUND
Cash	10,000	
Transfers In—General Fund		10,000
Expenditures—Capital Lease Principal Payments	8,264	
Expenditures—Capital Lease Interest Payments	1,736	
Cash		10,000

GENERAL LONG-TERM DEBT ACCOUNT GROUP
Amount Available In Debt Service Fund (For Capital Lease Payments)	8,264	
Amount To Be Provided For Lease Payments		8,264
Obligations Under Capital Lease Agreements	8,264	
Amount Available In Debt Service Fund (For Capital Lease Payments)		8,264

Capitalized Interest Cost   Various capital assets may be under construction and accounted for in a particular governmental fund, especially a Capital Projects Fund. Interest cost incurred by a Debt Service Fund is subject to capitalization as part of the cost of construction when conditions identified by FASB-34 (Capitalization of Interest Cost) exist. The interest capitalization period begins when the following three conditions are present:

- Expenditures for the capital asset have been made.
- Activities that are necessary to get the capital asset ready for its intended use are in progress.
- Interest cost is being incurred.

To determine the amount of interest cost to be capitalized, the weighted-average amount of accumulated expenditures for the period is multiplied by the governmental unit's average borrowing rate for the period. Rather than use the overall average borrowing rate, however, the following approach can be employed:

- The interest rate for the obligation incurred specifically to finance the construction of the capital asset may be used.
- The overall average borrowing rate would be used for any accumulated expenditures in excess of specific borrowings.

The amount of interest cost to be capitalized is limited to the actual amount of interest expenditures recognized for the period.

To illustrate the capitalization of interest cost, assume that a building is being constructed and accounted for in a Capital Projects Fund. The construction is being partially financed by the issuance of $2,000,000 of serial bonds that carry a 7% interest rate. The weighted-average accumulated expenditures for the period amounted to $3,500,000. General long-term debt of $15,000,000, which is being serviced through a Debt Service Fund, has an overall average interest rate of 6%. Total interest expenditures for the year amounted to $1,040,000 (($2,000,000 x 7%) + ($15,000,000 x 6%)). The amount of interest cost to be capitalized is $230,000 as computed below, assuming that the governmental unit decides to use the interest rate on the specific borrowing in the computation:

	Expenditures	Interest rate	Capitalized cost
Weighted-average accumulated expenditures	$3,500,000		
Specific borrowing	2,000,000	7%	$140,000
Amount of weighted-average expenditures in excess of specific borrowing	$1,500,000	6%	90,000
Total interest to be capitalized			$230,000

The incurrence of the interest cost and capitalization of interest cost on the constructed asset would be recorded in the following manner:

DEBT SERVICE FUND
Expenditures—Interest 1,040,000
    Cash 1,040,000

GENERAL FIXED ASSETS ACCOUNT GROUP
Construction In Progress—Building 230,000
    Investment In General Fixed
    Assets—Debt Service Fund 230,000

Because actual expenditures for interest exceeded interest cost subject to capitalization, the entire $230,000 is capitalized.

> ***OBSERVATION:*** *NCGA-1 simply states that the accounting policy with respect to the capitalization of interest cost incurred during construction should be disclosed and consistently applied. No other governmental accounting promulgation addresses the accounting issue; however, as discussed above, FASB-34 requires that interest cost associated with the construction of capital assets must be capitalized. The issue is not as critical in governmental accounting as in commercial accounting, since the capitalized cost of governmental fixed assets are not subject to depreciation to be reflected in a governmental fund's results of operations.*

As suggested earlier, resources may be accumulated in a Debt Service Fund and invested in various income producing instruments. FASB-62 (Capitalization of Interest Cost in Situations Involving Certain Tax-Exempt Borrowings and Certain Gifts and Grants) concludes that the amount of interest cost to be capitalized on assets acquired with tax-exempt borrowings is equal to the cost of the borrowing less interest earned on related interest-bearing investments acquired with the proceeds of the related tax-exempt borrowings. Thus, when a governmental unit has both interest expenditures and related interest income, the amount of interest to be capitalized with respect to acquired or constructed capital assets is the net amount of interest expenditures. No capitalization of interest could, of course, occur if related interest income equals or exceeds interest expenditures.

Zero Interest-Rate Bonds State or local governments that issue long-term bonds that carry no interest rate are typically accounted

Debt Service Funds

for in a Debt Service Fund where sufficient funds can be accumulated to pay for the bonds at maturity. Zero interest-rate bonds are sold at a deep discount, and the difference between the initial sales price of the bonds and their maturity value represents interest. As discussed earlier, interest is not accrued but, rather, is recognized as an expenditure when due and payable. The interest expenditure for zero interest-rate bonds is recorded when the bonds mature; however, the accrued interest must be recognized as part of the General Long-Term Debt Account group in a manner similar to any other long-term liability.

To illustrate the accounting for zero interest-rate bonds, assume that $3,000,000 (maturity value) of non-interest bearing term bonds are issued to yield a rate of return of 5%. The bonds mature in 10 years and are issued for $1,841,730 ($3,000,000 x 0.61391, where i = 5%, n = 10 for the present value of an amount). The sale of the bonds, assuming the proceeds are made available to the General Fund, is recorded as follows:

GENERAL FUND
Cash	1,841,730	
Proceeds From Issuance Of		
Long-Term Debt		1,841,730

GENERAL LONG-TERM DEBT ACCOUNT GROUP
Amount To Be Provided For Payment		
Of Noninterest-Bearing Term Bonds	1,841,730	
Term Bonds Payable—Noninterest-		
Bearing		1,841,730

Note: General purpose financial statement disclosure of debt service requirements to maturity must be provided.

At the end of the first fiscal year the amount of accrued interest earned by investors on the bonds is $92,087 ($1,841,730 x 5%). Because the interest will not be paid by the Debt Service Fund until the bonds mature, the accrued interest is not recognized as an expenditure. The accrued interest must be included as part of general long-term debt as shown below:

GENERAL LONG-TERM DEBT ACCOUNT GROUP
Amount To Be Provided For Payments		
Of Noninterest-Bearing Term Bonds	92,087	
Term Bonds Payable—Noninterest-		
Bearing		92,087

A separate liability account may be established in the General Long-Term Debt Account Group for the accrued interest, rather than have the accrual included as part of the bonds payable account.

When the bonds mature in 10 years, assuming that sufficient funds have been accumulated in the Debt Service Fund, the following entries are made:

DEBT SERVICE FUND

Expenditures—Principal	1,841,730	
Expenditures—Interest	1,158,270	
Cash		3,000,000

GENERAL LONG-TERM DEBT ACCOUNT GROUP

Term Bonds Payable—Noninterest-Bearing	3,000,000	
Amount Available In Debt Service Fund (For Noninterest-Bearing Term Bonds)		3,000,000

Classification and Disclosure Expenditures of a Debt Service Fund are generally classified as principal and interest expenditures (object class) for financial reporting purposes. For supplemental reporting or internal analysis, expenditures may be classified by function (or program), organizational unit, activity, and character.

The following disclosures as they relate to a Debt Service Fund's activities should be made:

- The amount of debt service requirements for the subsequent fiscal year
- The amount of debt considered to be retired resulting from in-substance defeasance transactions
- For an accounting period in which no interest cost is capitalized, the amount of interest cost incurred and charged as an expenditure during the period
- For an accounting period in which some interest cost is capitalized, the total amount of interest cost incurred during the period and the amount thereof that has been capitalized
- The accounting method used to account for interest costs

Assets

A Debt Service Fund's assets include resources that are considered to be currently available to pay obligations of the fund. Current assets include cash, taxes receivable, interest and dividends receivable, investments, and amounts due from other funds and governmental units.

Some bonds issued by a governmental unit in the past may carry coupons that must be detached and presented to a financial institution for payment. The redeemed coupons are then transferred to the state or local government's fiscal agent (usually a large financial institution) for payment. When the interest payments are due, the state or local government will transfer the necessary cash to the fiscal agent and simultaneously accrue the interest due. For example, if $200,000 of interest is due and cash for this amount is transferred, the following entries would be made in the Debt Service Fund:

Cash—Fiscal Agent	200,000	
Cash		200,000
Expenditures—Interest	200,000	
Interest Payable		200,000

As coupons are presented and the governmental unit is notified of the amounts paid, the cash balance with the fiscal agent is reduced along with the accrued interest payable. At a financial reporting date, it is likely that all coupons will not have been presented for payment, in which case the balance in the fiscal agent cash account is offset against the interest payable account and neither of the accounts is reported in the Debt Service Fund's balance sheet.

> **OBSERVATION:** *Alternatively, the payment of the cash to the fiscal agent can be recorded as an interest expenditure with no recognition of the amount of cash held by the fiscal agent. The use of coupon bonds is becoming more rare since current law requires the registration of all bonds. Thus, the problem of having coupons that have not been presented for payment to the fiscal agent will eventually disappear.*

A Debt Service Fund's assets also include investments that are often long-term in nature. As described earlier, investments that include either a premium or discount must be amortized if it is expected that the investment will be held until maturity. All investments are reported at cost, but they must be reduced to market value if there has been a permanent impairment in the value of the investments. When market values fall below the cost of the investments but the reductions are considered temporary, the market value of the investment portfolio should be disclosed.

Although a Debt Service Fund's assets include noncurrent investments, its fund balance is identified as "designated for future debt service requirements," so there is no suggestion that a surplus exists within the fund.

Classification and Disclosure Assets of a Debt Service Fund are presented in the balance sheet using an unclassified format. Where applicable, the following disclosures should be made with respect to assets of a Debt Service Fund:

- Disclosure of valuation bases and significant or unusual accounting treatment for material account balances or transactions. (Disclosures should be described in the order of appearance in the balance sheet.)
- Detail notes on the following, where appropriate:
  — Pooling of cash and investments
  — Investments
  — Property taxes and other receivables
  — Amounts due from other governments—grants receivable

Liabilities

A Debt Service Fund's liabilities include those obligations that will be paid with available financial resources of the fund. For this reason, a governmental unit's general long-term debt is not included in the Debt Service Fund. Generally the Debt Service Fund would include such liabilities as deferred revenues and accrued fiscal agent charges.

As discussed earlier, the current portion of unmatured debt is not presented as a Debt Service Fund liability but, rather, is included as part of the General Long-Term Debt Account Group. When general long-term debt is due and payable, the liability is reflected in the Debt Service Fund until all the matured bonds have been presented, usually to a fiscal agent, for payment. For example, if $400,000 of serial bonds is due and payable on June 1, 19X5, the following entries are made, assuming the individual payments to bondholders are made by a fiscal agent:

Debt Service Funds

DEBT SERVICE FUND
Expenditures—Principal 400,000
    Serial Bonds Payable   400,000

Cash—Fiscal Agent 400,000
    Cash   400,000

GENERAL LONG-TERM DEBT ACCOUNT GROUP
Serial Bonds Payable 400,000
    Amount Available In Debt Service
    Fund (For Payment Of Serial Bonds)   400,000

As the fiscal agent periodically reports the amount of matured bonds redeemed by bondholders, the serial bond liability is reduced along with the fiscal agent cash account. In the current example, if the fiscal agent reports as of June 30, 19X5, that bonds of $395,000 were redeemed, the following entry would be made in the Debt Service Fund:

Serial Bonds Payable 395,000
    Cash—Fiscal Agent   395,000

For financial reporting purposes, the balances in the fiscal agent cash account and serial bonds payable account are offset, and neither account is reported in the balance sheet.

Unmatured Principal and Interest   Earlier it was noted that while the general rule is that an expenditure is accrued when the related liability is incurred, unmatured principal and accrued interest are not shown as liabilities until they are due and payable. Nonetheless, NCGA-1 does allow for debt service expenditures to be accrued before they are due and payable when resources have been transferred during the current period to finance principal and interest payments due and payable early in the following fiscal year.

To illustrate the accrual of unmatured principal and interest, assume that principal ($700,000) and interest ($200,000) payments are due on July 1, 19X5, for a municipality whose fiscal year ends June 30. On June 30, 19X5, funds of $900,000 are transferred from the General Fund to the Debt Service Fund to finance the debt service payments due on July 1. The following entries would be made on June 30, 19X5, to record the transfer of funds:

General Fund
Transfers Out—Debt Service Fund	900,000	
Cash		900,000

Debt Service Fund
Cash	900,000	
Transfers In—General Fund		900,000
Expenditures—Principal	700,000	
Expenditures—Interest	200,000	
Bonds Payable		700,000
Interest Payable		200,000

General Long-Term Debt Account Group
Amount Available In Debt Service Fund (For Payment Of Serial Bonds)	700,000	
Amount To Be Provided For Repayment Of Bonds		700,000
Bonds Payable	700,000	
Amount Available In Debt Service Fund (For Payment Of Serial Bonds)		700,000

When the actual debt service payments are made on July 1, the accruals for debt service charges are reduced.

Bonds Sold Between Interest Payment Dates When bonds are sold between interest payment dates, the proceeds from the sale of the debt will include accrued interest. The accrued interest is not shown as an other financing source of the fund entitled to the debt proceeds. The portion of the cash proceeds representing the accrued interest should be transferred to the Debt Service Fund. Also, the Debt Service Fund records the accrued interest as a fund liability. For example, assume that bonds are issued for $2,040,000 of which $40,000 represents accrued interest. If the proceeds of the debt issuance are made available to a Capital Projects Fund, the bond sale is recorded in the following manner:

Capital Projects Fund
Cash	2,040,000	
Proceeds From Issuance Of Bonds		2,000,000
Due To Debt Service Fund		40,000

Debt Service Fund
Due From Capital Projects Fund	40,000	
Accrued Interest Payable		40,000

GENERAL LONG-TERM DEBT ACCOUNT GROUP
Amount To Be Provided For
  Repayment Of Bonds   2,000,000
    Bonds Payable   2,000,000

Classification and Disclosure   Liabilities are unclassified in a Debt Service Fund's statement of position. Debt service requirements for the following fiscal year should be disclosed in the financial statements of the fund.

Interfund Transactions

Generally, interfund transactions between a Debt Service Fund and other governmental funds are not recorded as revenue or expenditure transactions. A Debt Service Fund is usually involved with annual operating transfers but also may be associated with residual equity transfers.

Operating Transfers   Loans or advances, quasi-external transactions, reimbursements, and residual equity transfers are not classified as operating transfers. A Debt Service Fund operating transfer usually occurs when another governmental fund is required, legally or through budgetary design, to provide resources for the payment of current debt service requirements or to accumulate resources for the eventual retirement of general long-term debt.

    The amount of the operating transfer received by the Debt Service Fund must be identified as to which portion is for eventual debt retirement and which portion is for current interest payments. The differentiation is necessary so that the accumulation of resources in the Debt Service Fund for debt retirement is properly reflected in the General Long-Term Debt Account Group. For example, assume that a $900,000 operating transfer is made from the General Fund to the Debt Service Fund and that $200,000 is applicable to current interest payments that are due and payable, while the balance is to be accumulated for the retirement of long-term bonds. The operating transfer from the General Fund is recorded in the following manner:

GENERAL FUND
  Transfers Out—Debt Service Fund   900,000
    Cash   900,000

DEBT SERVICE FUND
  Cash   900,000
    Transfers In—General Fund   900,000

Debt Service Funds

GENERAL LONG-TERM DEBT ACCOUNT GROUP
Amount Available In Debt Service
  Fund (For Payment Of Bonds)   700,000
    Amount To Be Provided For
      Repayment Of Bonds   700,000

Some governmental units cannot sell bonds at a discount. In those jurisdictions where bonds may be sold at a discount, the discount may have to be made up by the Debt Service Fund. In this situation the commitment by the Debt Service Fund is treated as an other use of financing and shown on the fund's Statement of Revenues and Expenditures. For example, assume that $3,000,000 of par value bonds are sold for $2,900,000 and that the proceeds are made available to a Capital Projects Fund. The issuance of the bonds at a discount would be recorded as follows, assuming that the Debt Service Fund is legally required to transfer to the Capital Projects Fund an amount equal to the discount:

CAPITAL PROJECTS FUND
Cash   2,900,000
Due From Debt Service Fund   100,000
  Proceeds From Issuance Of Bonds   2,900,000
  Transfers In—Debt Service Fund   100,000

DEBT SERVICE FUND
Transfers Out—Capital Projects Fund   100,000
  Due To Capital Projects Fund   100,000

GENERAL LONG-TERM DEBT ACCOUNT GROUP
Amount To Be Provided For
  Repayment Of Bonds   3,000,000
    Bonds Payable   3,000,000

Residual Equity Transfers A residual equity transfer represents a nonrecurring or nonroutine transfer between governmental funds and generally occurs with the creation, expansion, liquidation, or contraction of a fund. A Debt Service Fund may be affected by a residual equity transfer when a Capital Projects Fund is closed. A Capital Projects Fund is created to account for the acquisition or construction of a capital asset. When revenues and other financing sources exceed expenditures and other financing uses, the surplus may be transferred to the Debt Service Fund that was created to service the long-term debt that was issued to finance the capital project.

To illustrate a residual equity transfer, assume that a capital asset accounted for in a Capital Projects Fund is constructed with a re-

Debt Service Funds

maining surplus after construction of $70,000. The surplus by law must be transferred to the Debt Service Fund. The transfer of the $70,000 from the Capital Projects Fund to the Debt Service Fund would be recorded as follows:

CAPITAL PROJECTS FUND
Fund Balance—Residual Equity Transfer
    To Debt Service Fund   70,000
        Cash   70,000

DEBT SERVICE FUND
Cash   70,000
    Fund Balance—Residual Equity
        Transfer From Capital Projects Fund   70,000

GENERAL LONG-TERM DEBT ACCOUNT GROUP
Amount Available In Debt Service Fund
    (For Retirement Of Long-Term Bonds)   70,000
        Amount To Be Provided For
            Repayment Of Long-Term Bonds   70,000

When a Debt Service Fund is closed because the long-term debt it is servicing is retired, any surplus that remains would be treated as a residual equity transfer.

Classification and Disclosure   Interfund transactions and accounts do not have to be eliminated when the Debt Service Fund's financial statements are combined with other governmental funds' financial statements to form the reporting entity's general purpose financial statements or Comprehensive Annual Financial Report. If the interfund transactions and accounts are eliminated when the financial statements are combined, the nature of the eliminations should be apparent from the columnar headings; otherwise, the eliminations must be disclosed in the financial statements.

FINANCIAL STATEMENTS

A Debt Service Fund's financial statements are included in the reporting entity's general purpose financial statements and its Comprehensive Annual Financial Report. When a Debt Service Fund is used only to make principal and interest payments on a current basis, and resources are not accumulated and invested in long-term instruments, there may be no need to present a balance sheet for the fund. In this case the fund operates as a pass through fund and only a Statement of Revenues, Expenditures, and Changes in Fund Balance need be presented.

If legally mandated, the Debt Service Fund must prepare its activity statement on a budget basis and actual basis. Generally there is no requirement that such a comparative financial statement be prepared. When budgetary accounts are used, irrespective of the requirement to present activity on a budget basis and actual basis, the budgetary accounts must be closed at the end of the period.

Closing Budget Related Accounts When the Debt Service Fund's budget is integrated into the general accounting system, the budgetary accounts are closed at the end of the period in a manner that will have no effect on the financial statements prepared on an actual basis. To illustrate the closing of budgetary accounts, the following entry would be made to close those accounts used in an earlier example in this chapter (see recording the budget):

Appropriations	1,600,000	
Estimated Operating Transfers In—		
General Fund		1,000,000
Estimated Revenue—Property Taxes		400,000
Estimated Premium Transfer In—		
Capital Projects Fund		100,000
Estimated Earnings On		
Investments—Debt Service Fund		100,000

Closing Encumbrances As discussed earlier, there is no need to control commitments of the Debt Service Fund through the use of an encumbrance system.

Once the budgetary accounts as well as the fund nominal accounts are closed, the financial statements of a Debt Service Fund may be prepared. Generally, the following statements are included in a Debt Service Fund's set of financial statements:

- Statement of Revenues and Expenditures
- Statement of Changes in Fund Balance
- Balance Sheet
- Combining Financial Statements

For financial reporting purposes, the Statement of Revenues and Expenditures is combined with the Statement of Changes in Fund Balance to form a single financial statement; however, for discussion purposes the two statements are examined here separately.

Statement of Revenues and Expenditures

A Debt Service Fund's Statement of Revenues and Expenditures is for the most part based on the modified accrual concept in that revenues are recognized when they are susceptible to accrual, and expenditures are recognized when the related liabilities are incurred. The exception to the modified accrual basis is that accrued interest on general long-term debt is not recognized as an expenditure until the amount is due and payable.

The operating statement must be prepared in a manner consistent with generally accepted accounting principles (modified accrual basis); however, it may also be necessary to demonstrate compliance with certain legal or contractual requirements. If the legal or contractual requirements are not met through the presentation of GAAP-basis financial statements, it will be necessary to accept one of the following financial reporting strategies:

- Demonstrate finance-related legal or contractual compliance by presenting additional schedules and narrative explanations in the Comprehensive Annual Financial Report.
- Demonstrate finance-related legal or contractual compliance by presenting a separate legal basis special report.

The Statement of Revenues and Expenditures is presented on an all-inclusive basis. Only residual equity transfers and prior period adjustments are excluded from the computation of the excess of revenues and other sources over (under) expenditures and other uses. The statement should be formatted in a manner that segregates operating revenues and expenditures from other sources and uses of financing. An example of an operating statement combined with an analysis of the changes in fund balance is presented in Exhibit I.

Statement of Changes in Fund Balance

Generally, a Debt Service Fund's fund balance account is either reserved or designated for future debt service requirements. The Statement of Changes in Fund Balance (unreserved, designated, or reserved) may include prior period adjustments, effects of changes in fund balance reserves or designations, excess of revenues and other financing sources over (under) expenditures and other uses of financing, and residual equity transfers. Prior period adjustments should appear immediately after the beginning fund balance, and residual equity transfers should appear after the excess of revenues and other financing sources over (under) expenditures and other financing uses. The analysis of fund balance changes is presented in combination with the entity's activity statements (see Exhibit I).

EXHIBIT I

Statement of Revenues, Expenditures, and Changes in Fund Balance

City of Centerville
Statement of Revenues, Expenditures, and Changes in Fund Balance
Debt Service Fund
For Year Ended June 30, 19X5

Revenues	
Property taxes	$ 410,000
Investment income	120,000
Total revenues	530,000
Expenditures	
Debt service	
Principal	900,000
Interest	680,000
Fiscal agent fees	20,000
Total expenditures	1,600,000
Excess of revenues over (under) expenditures	(1,070,000)
Other financing sources (uses)	
Transfers from other funds	1,000,000
Proceeds from issuance of bonds at a premium	95,000
Total other financing sources (uses)	1,095,000
Excess of revenues and other sources over (under) expenditures and other uses	25,000
Fund balance—reserved for debt service July 1, 19X4	320,000
Fund balance—reserved for debt service June 30, 19X5	$ 345,000

Debt Service Funds

Balance Sheet

The Debt Service Fund's balance sheet includes current assets and current liabilities of the fund, although they are not designated as such. The fund balance section of the balance sheet includes the unreserved portion of the fund balance account as well as reserved and designated amounts. If long-term investments are included on the balance sheet, there should be an equal amount of reserved fund balance, unless the full amount of the fund balance account is captioned as reserved for future debt service requirements.

An example of a Debt Service Fund balance sheet is presented in Exhibit II.

EXHIBIT II
Balance Sheet

City of Centerville
Balance Sheet
Debt Service Fund
June 30, 19X5

Assets	
Cash on deposit	$ 17,000
Equity in consolidated cash account	7,000
Investment (stated at cost which approximates market)	300,000
Due from other funds	24,000
Total assets	$348,000
Liabilities	
Accrued for fiscal agent expenditures	$ 3,000
Fund balance	
Fund balance reserved for future debt service requirements	345,000
Total fund balance	345,000
Total liabilities and fund balance	$348,000

Combining Financial Statements

When a governmental unit's general long-term debt is accounted for in a single Debt Service Fund, and other forms of general long-term debt such as obligations for capitalized leases, compensated ab-

Debt Service Funds

sences, and the like do not require the establishment of separate Debt Service Funds, there is no need to prepare a combining financial statement for the Debt Service Fund. The single Debt Service Fund's financial statements are simply presented in the reporting entity's combined financial statements along with other governmental fund types such as the General Fund, Capital Projects Funds, Enterprise Funds, and so on. On the other hand, when two or more separate Debt Service Funds are used by a state or local government, combining financial statements must be prepared. In this case, all of the Debt Service Funds are presented in a columnar format, including a column for totals. There must be agreement between the amounts shown in the total column of the combined financial statements and the Debt Service Fund column as presented in the governmental reporting entity's combined financial statements.

LITERATURE REFERENCES

Material in this chapter is based on the following authoritative pronouncements and publications which are grouped according to the major headings used within the chapter. A dual reference (both paragraph and page number) is used for NCGA-1 and NCGA-2 because the original pronouncements do not use paragraph numbers.

Basic Concepts and Standards
NCGA-1 *Governmental Accounting and Financial Reporting Principles*, pp. 5 and 7-9/ ¶¶ 16, 26, 30, and 43.
1980 GAAFR *Governmental Accounting, Auditing, and Financial Reporting*, p. 43.

Basis of Accounting
NCGA-1 *Governmental Accounting and Financial Reporting Principles*, pp. 11 and 12/ ¶¶ 61, 62, 70, and 71.

Measurement Focus
NCGA-1 *Governmental Accounting and Financial Reporting Principles*, p. 9/ ¶¶ 39 and 44.

Budgetary System and Accounts
NCGA-1 *Governmental Accounting and Financial Reporting Principles*, p. 14/ ¶ 90.

Revenues and Other Sources of Financing
NCGA-1 *Governmental Accounting and Financial Reporting Principles*, p. 11/ ¶ 62.

Debt Service Funds

Property Taxes
NCGA-1 *Governmental Accounting and Financial Reporting Principles*, pp. 11 and 16/ ¶¶ 62 and 106.
NCGA Interpretation-3 *Revenue Recognition—Property Taxes*, ¶¶ 6 and 8.

Shared Revenues
NCGA-1 *Governmental Accounting and Financial Reporting Principles*, pp. 15 and 16/ ¶ 105.
NCGA-2 *Grant, Entitlement, and Shared Revenue Accounting by State and Local Governments*, pp. 1 and 2/ ¶¶ 4, 7, and 11.

Investment Income
NCGA-1 *Governmental Accounting and Financial Reporting Principles*, pp. 11 and 12/ ¶¶ 62 and 69.
APB-21 *Interest on Receivables and Payables*, ¶ 15.

Transfers and Other Sources of Financing
NCGA-1 *Governmental Accounting and Financial Reporting Principles*, pp. 15 and 16/ ¶¶ 105 and 106.

Classification and Disclosure
NCGA-1 *Governmental Accounting and Financial Reporting Principles*, p. 12/ ¶ 69.

Expenditures
NCGA-1 *Governmental Accounting and Financial Reporting Principles*, pp. 12 and 16/ ¶¶ 70 and 109.

Unmatured Principal and Interest
NCGA-1 *Governmental Accounting and Financial Reporting Principles*, p. 12/ ¶¶ 70 and 72.

Debt Extinguishments
NCGA Interpretation-9 *Certain Fund Classifications and Balance Sheet Accounts*, ¶¶ 13 and 14.
FASB-76 *Extinguishment of Debt*, ¶¶ 3-6.
GASB-7 *Advance Refundings Resulting in Defeasance of Debt*, ¶¶ 2-6.

Capital Leases
FASB-13 *Accounting for Leases*, ¶¶ 5, 7, and 10.
NCGA-5 *Accounting and Financial Reporting Principles for Lease Agreements of State and Local Governments*, ¶¶ 11, 13, and 14.

Debt Service Funds

Capitalized Interest Cost
NCGA-1 *Governmental Accounting and Financial Reporting Principles,* p. 9/ ¶ 48.
FASB-34 *Capitalization of Interest Cost,* ¶¶ 13 and 17.
FASB-62 *Capitalization of Interest Cost in Situations Involving Certain Tax Exempt Borrowings and Certain Gifts and Grants,* ¶ 4.

Zero Interest-Rate Bonds
NCGA-1 *Governmental Accounting and Financial Reporting Principles,* pp. 9 and 13/ ¶¶ 43, 70, and 72.

Classification and Disclosure
NCGA-1 *Governmental Accounting and Financial Reporting Principles,* pp. 16 and 17/ ¶¶ 111-116.
FASB-76 *Extinguishment of Debt,* ¶ 6.
FASB-43 *Capitalization of Interest Cost,* ¶ 21.

Assets
NCGA-1 *Governmental Accounting and Financial Reporting Principles,* pp. 6, 9, and 17/ ¶¶ 19, 39, and 120.

Classification and Disclosure
NCGA INTERPRETATION-6 *Notes to the Financial Statements Disclosure,* appendix.

Liabilities
NCGA-1 *Governmental Accounting and Financial Reporting Principles,* pp. 6 and 9/ ¶¶ 19 and 44.

Unmatured Principal and Interest
NCGA-1 *Governmental Accounting and Financial Reporting Principles,* p. 12/ ¶ 72.

Bonds Sold Between Interest Payment Dates
NCGA-1 *Governmental Accounting and Financial Reporting Principles,* p. 6/ ¶ 18.
NCGA-4 *Accounting and Financial Reporting Principles for Claims and Judgments and Compensated Absences,* ¶ 7.

Classification and Disclosure
NCGA-1 *Governmental Accounting and Financial Reporting Principles,* p. 12/ ¶ 72.

Debt Service Funds

Interfund Transactions
NCGA-1 *Governmental Accounting and Financial Reporting Principles,* pp. 15 and 16/ ¶¶ 101-104.

Operating Transfers
NCGA-1 *Governmental Accounting and Financial Reporting Principles,* pp. 15 and 16/ ¶¶ 105 and 106.

Residual Equity Transfers
NCGA-1 *Governmental Accounting and Financial Reporting Principles,* p. 19/ ¶ 105.

Classification and Disclosure
NCGA-1 *Governmental Accounting and Financial Reporting Principles,* p. 22/ ¶¶ 145 and 147.

Financial Statements
NCGA-1 *Governmental Accounting and Financial Reporting Principles,* p. 20/ ¶ 141.

Statement of Revenues and Expenditures
NCGA-1 *Governmental Accounting and Financial Reporting Principles,* pp. 5, 22, and 23/ ¶¶ 12, 146, 149, and 151.

Statement of Changes in Fund Balance
NCGA-1 *Governmental Accounting and Financial Reporting Principles,* p. 23/ ¶ 152.

Balance Sheet
NCGA-1 *Governmental Accounting and Financial Reporting Principles,* p. 22/ ¶ 145.

Combining Financial Statements
NCGA-1 *Governmental Accounting and Financial Reporting Principles,* p. 21/ ¶ 141.

APPENDIX

GENERAL CAPITAL DEBT SERVICE EXPENDITURES AND RELATED LIABILITIES (DISCUSSION MEMORANDUM)

In March, 1989, the GASB issued a Discussion Memorandum entitled "Capital Reporting" to gather comments concerning accounting issues relating to transactions of governmental funds and related capital debt. In issuing the Discussion Memorandum, the GASB assumed that tentative conclusions reached in its Exposure Draft entitled "Measurement Focus and Basis of Accounting--Governmental Fund Operating Statements" (MFBA Exposure Draft) would be adopted. The Exposure Draft recommended that (1) an accrual basis should be used for accounting for governmental funds and (2) only long-term debt relating to the financing of capital assets or certain nonrecurring projects or activities that have long-term economic benefits should be reported in the governmental entity's General Long-Term Debt Account Group (GLTDAG). Other long-term obligations referred to as operating debt, according to the recommendations, should be presented in specific governmental funds instead.

This Appendix reviews the analysis of general capital debt service expenditures and related liabilities as presented in the Discussion Memorandum. (An Appendix to chapter 61 reviews the discussion of capital assets and general capital debt as presented in the Discussion Memorandum.)

Measurement of Current Debt Expenditures

Governmental generally accepted accounting principles (governmental GAAP) require that current debt expenditures be recognized as such only when they become due, with certain exceptions. Under the measurement focus and basis of accounting proposed in the MFBA Exposure Draft, there would be no change in accounting for current debt expenditures. The Discussion Memorandum raised the issue of whether the accrual concept should be either fully applied to the measurement of service debt expenditures or partially applied. The Discussion Memorandum addressed the applicability of the accrual concept to the measurement of debt service expenditures by discussing the following:

Debt Service Funds

- Stub-period
- Repayment schedule/economic life
- Term bonds
- Deep-discount bonds
- "Level basis" debt
- Premiums/discounts

Stub-Period Essentially, current accounting for debt service expenditures is on a cash basis. Thus accounting periods in which there are no principal or interest payments do not reflect a debt service expenditure. Alternatively, periodic debt service could be measured to reflect (1) interest charges on an accrual basis and principal charges when paid or (2) interest charges on an accrual basis and a proportional amount of principal irrespective of when principal payments are made.

Those who argue for an accrual of interest charges suggest that interest is a period cost and that the actual cash payment for the interest is not the determining factor for recognition on the activity statement. Each accounting period would be charged with an interest cost factor based on the amount of weighted debt outstanding for the period. In this way, the concept of interperiod equity among taxpayers would be achieved in that taxpayers could not push the consequences of borrowing funds from one generation of taxpayers to a subsequent generation.

Another advantage of accruing interest would be the elimination of the current practice of recognizing interest expenditures if sufficient debt service fund resources have been provided in the current year for interest payments due early in the following year. This practice is an exception to current governmental GAAP, which requires that debt service be recognized when due. This exception could provide an entity with the opportunity to manipulate the recognition of debt service expenditures to some degree; that is, an entity could accelerate the accumulation of debt service resources in the Debt Service Fund and recognize a greater amount of interest expenditure in the current period and a lesser amount in the subsequent period.

The concept of accrual accounting can be extended to principal repayments. The total amount of the debt outstanding could be apportioned to each accounting period as an expenditure based on the life of the debt. For example, $1,000,000 of term bonds that mature in ten years would result in a $100,000 debt service expenditure in each of the ten years, even though the debt is not paid until the end of the tenth year. The apportionment of the debt in this manner would be consistent with the interperiod equity concept discussed earlier.

Debt Service Funds

There is also a consistency issue that must be addressed with respect to the accrual of debt service charges. In the GASB's MFBA Exposure Draft, interest on long-term debt that is reported as fund liability (operting debt) must be accrued. It would be difficult to explain why interest on fund liabilities is subject to accrual, while interest on GLTDAG debt is not subject to accrual.

Repayment Schedule/Economic Life Some argue that the important issue to consider when determining interperiod equity is the relationship of the debt repayment schedule and the economic life of the capital asset being financed by the debt.

Ideally, it is argued, the amortization of the debt service should be based on the economic life of the capital asset. For example, use of serial bonds that mature so that the total debt service charges are equal in each year over the life of the asset would achieve the objective of interperiod equity.

Those who support relating the debt service charges to the economic life of the capital asset suggest that the objective could be achieved by recognizing debt service charges (1) as interest is paid and amortizing the principal ratably over the life of the debt or the life of capital asset, or the lesser of the two or (2) amortizing interest and principal ratably over the life of the debt or the life of the capital asset, or the lesser of the two.

Term Bonds The issuance of term bonds presents an interperiod equity problem in that an expenditure for the principal repayment is not recorded until the debt matures. In order to remedy this measurement problem, some would argue that a portion of the bonds should be amortized each year as a debt service expenditure. The allocation could be based on one of the following methods:

- Amortize the debt over the life of the debt
- Amortize the debt over the lesser of the life of the debt or the life of the capital asset financed by the issuance of the debt

Deep-Discount Bonds When a governmental entity issues deep-discount bonds, including zero coupon bonds, the interperiod equity concept becomes very difficult to achieve. The result of issuing deep-discount bonds is that all of the principal portion of the debt and a significant portion of the interest (or all of the interest in the case of zero coupon bonds) is not recognized as an expenditure until the debt matures. For example, if $1,000,000 of zero coupon bonds that mature

Debt Service Funds

in ten years are issued for $550,000, no debt service expenditure is recognized during the first nine years of the life of the debt. During the tenth year, debt service expenditures would be $1,000,000, representing principal expenditures of $550,000 and interest expenditures of $450,000.

A variety of alternative methods could be adopted in order to achieve interperiod equity in the accounting for deep-discount bonds. The Discussion Memorandum lists the following possible solutions:

- Recognize interest annually on an effective-interest basis over the life of the debt. Recognize principal when payment is due.
- Recognize a portion of both principal and interest annually on some rationally determined basis over the life of the debt.
- Recognize interest annually on an effective-interest basis over the life of the debt. Recognize a portion of the principal annually on some rationally determined basis over the life of the assets or the lesser of the life of the assets or the life of the debt.

Each of these alternatives has the effect of spreading debt service expenditures over a longer period of time when compared to current governmental GAAP.

"Level" Basis Debt Some governmental entities issue debt instruments with characteristics that lead to a more or less equal payment for principal and interest in each year. This "leveling" effect is principally accomplished by issuing serial bonds; however, the same effect can be accomplished through the issuance of combination offerings that include serial bonds, and term bonds and/or deep-discount bonds.

The Discussion Memorandum raises the issue of how term bonds and deep-discount bonds should be accounted for in combination offerings. The alternative measurement methods that could be used in combination offerings have been discussed earlier in this Appendix and include (1) the possible amortization of the discount related to deep-discount bonds, and (2) the recognition of a portion of the principal part of the term bonds over the life of the debt or the life of the capital asset acquired through the issuance of the debt.

Premiums/Discounts Generally, debt issued by a governmental entity is issued at a premium or at a discount. Under current governmental GAAP, the face amount of the debt is recorded in the entity's GLTDAG and the discount is recorded as part of the principal expenditure in the year the debt matures.

Alternatively, some would argue that premium or discount is a component of determining the interest expenditure rather than the principal expenditure for a period. Furthermore, an argument can be made that interest should be allocated to each period using the effective interest method or the straight-line method if there is no material difference.

Summary

Because governmental accounting treats the issuance of long-term debt as an inflow of resources on the activity statement, it becomes difficult to properly reflect the results of servicing the debt over the life of the long-term obligation. Various debt characteristics, such as term bonds and deep-discount bonds, distort the measurement of debt service expenditures from period to period. In the Discussion Memorandum, the GASB raised the issue of whether other accounting methods should be adopted so as to "smooth" the effects of debt service charges.

PROPRIETARY FUNDS

BASIC CONCEPTS AND STANDARDS

A proprietary fund is used to account for governmental activities that are similar to activities that may be performed by a commercial enterprise. For example, a hospital may be operated by a governmental unit, such as a municipality, or by a profit-oriented corporation. The accounting and reporting standards used by a proprietary fund and a business enterprise are similar because the activities performed are basically the same. Pronouncements by the Financial Accounting Standards Board and its predecessors must be observed in the preparation of financial statements of a proprietary fund unless a specific accounting issue has been addressed by the Governmental Accounting Standards Board or its predecessor (National Council on Governmental Accounting).

Public benefit corporations and authorities and governmental utilities that conduct business and quasi-business activities should observe commercial accounting principles except in those cases where the GASB or NCGA have addressed a specific accounting issue.

Although a proprietary fund is accounted for in much the same manner as a commercial enterprise, a proprietary fund is nonetheless a governmental fund. NCGA-1 (Governmental Accounting and Financial Reporting Principles) defines a fund as:

> . . . a fiscal and accounting entity with a self-balancing set of accounts recording cash and other financial resources, together with all related liabilities and residual equities or balances, and changes therein, which are segregated for the purpose of carrying on specific activities or attaining certain objectives in accordance with special regulations, restrictions, or limitations.

The basic objective of a proprietary fund as alluded to in the NCGA's definition is different from the fundamental purpose of a commercial enterprise. The purpose of a proprietary fund is not to maximize its return on invested capital. Generally, the purpose of a proprietary fund is to provide a service or product to the public or other governmental units at a reasonable cost. This objective is

Proprietary Funds

achieved through the creation of one of two types of proprietary funds, namely an Internal Service Fund or an Enterprise Fund. These two proprietary funds are accounted for in a similar manner, and for this reason both are discussed in this chapter. Differences in accounting and reporting standards between the two funds are identified and discussed.

Internal Service Fund An Internal Service Fund is created to provide goods or services to other governmental operating units such as departments, bureaus, and agencies. The services provided may include duplicating services, data processing, legal services, motor pools, and centralized maintenance. An Internal Service Fund may also produce goods as a manufacturer does. For example, products may be provided by governmental printing shops, repair facilities, and processing facilities. When a product is provided through an Internal Service Fund, an adequately designed cost accounting system similar to a cost system utilized by a commercial manufacturer should be employed.

The purpose of centralizing certain activities in an Internal Service Fund is to achieve a level of operating efficiency that may not be available if the same activities were performed by multiple units within the governmental organization. For example, a state or local government often centralizes the purchasing function to improve operating efficiency as well as to maintain fiscal control over the activity. Costs associated with the centralized activity are usually recovered from those governmental units that benefit from the goods or services provided through the Internal Service Fund. Thus, the objective of an Internal Service Fund is not to make a profit but rather to recover over a period of time the total cost of providing the goods or services.

A minimum number of funds should be used by a governmental unit. For small reporting entities it may not be necessary to establish any Internal Service Funds. On the other hand, when various services are provided to numerous governmental operating units, in order to determine the cost of each individual service and to restrict the use of specific resources to only authorized uses, it is usually necessary to establish separate Internal Service Funds.

Enterprise Fund Whereas an Internal Service Fund provides a product or service to other related governmental operating units, an Enterprise Fund provides its product or service directly to the public. NCGA-1 concludes that an Enterprise Fund should be established if one of the following conditions exist:

- Operations are financed and operated in a manner similar to private business enterprises—where the intent of the governing body is that the costs (expenses, including depreciation) of providing goods or services to the general public on a continuing basis is financed or recovered primarily through user charges.

- The governing body has decided that periodic determination of revenues earned, expenses incurred, and/or net income is appropriate for capital maintenance, public policy, management control, accountability, or other purposes.

Airports, public transit systems, parking authorities, and port facilities are examples of activities that may be accounted for as an Enterprise Fund.

There is a distinguishing characteristic between an Enterprise Fund and a Special Revenue Fund. Generally, an Enterprise Fund obtains the majority of its resources from fees charged directly to those individuals and institutions that use its service or buy its product. A Special Revenue Fund obtains its resources indirectly because users of the service do not pay for the service based on actual use. For example, service charges for a local government's transportation system are based on the number of times a user enters the transit system. The transit activities would be accounted for in an Enterprise Fund. On the other hand, property taxes specifically designated as revenue to be used to finance a public school system would be accounted for in a Special Revenue Fund, because a citizen is not charged a fee based on the number of his or her children who attend the public school system.

Once it is determined that an activity should be accounted for in an Enterprise Fund, a separate fund should be established for each distinct service provided by the governmental unit. Separate accounting entities facilitate the measurement of the cost incurred to deliver each service. In addition, resources authorized by a state or local government for specific purposes are more easily controlled when separate funds are established. The 1980 GAAFR (Governmental Accounting, Auditing, and Financial Reporting) notes that separate Enterprise Funds should not be established when revenues from closely related services have been cross-pledged as security for a single issue or combined purpose revenue bonds. Combined purpose revenue bonds may be issued, for example, to finance the services provided by separate water and sewer authorities.

The remainder of the discussion in this chapter refers to a proprietary fund and is therefore equally applicable to an Internal Service Fund and an Enterprise Fund unless otherwise stated.

Basis of Accounting

An entity's basis of accounting determines when transactions and economic events are to be recognized. For a proprietary fund, the selection of an accounting basis determines the time period in which revenues, expenses, and transfers are reflected in the fund's financial statements. For example, the purchase of a capital asset could be reported as an expense (1) when the asset is received and placed in production, (2) when the asset is paid for, or (3) as the asset is used in the fund's operations.

The accrual basis of accounting is used by a proprietary fund. NCGA-1 concludes that revenues and expenses of a proprietary fund should be measured in "essentially the same manner as in commercial accounting" in the absence of a specific NCGA or GASB pronouncement. FASB:CS-1 (Objectives of Financial Reporting by Business Enterprises) describes accrual accounting as follows:

> Accrual accounting attempts to record the financial effects on an enterprise of transactions and other events and circumstances that have cash consequences for an enterprise in the periods in which those transactions, events, and circumstances occur rather than only in the periods in which cash is received or paid by the enterprise. Accrual accounting is concerned with the process by which cash expended on resources and activities is returned as more (or perhaps less) cash to the enterprise, not just with the beginning and end of that process.

Accrual accounting encompasses concepts such as the (1) deferral of expenditures and the subsequent amortization of the deferred costs (prepaid expenses, supplies, etc.), (2) deferral of revenues until they are earned (property taxes received in advance), and (3) capitalization of capital expenditures and the subsequent depreciation of these costs (depreciation of cost of equipment).

Measurement Focus

While the basis of accounting determines when transactions and economic events should be reflected in a fund's financial statements, the measurement focus identifies what transactions and economic events should be recognized. The measurement focus is concerned with the inflow and outflow of resources that affect an entity. The balance sheet should reflect those resources that are available to meet current obligations and are to be used in the delivery of goods and services in subsequent periods. The activity statement for the period should summarize those resources received and those consumed during the current period.

A proprietary fund uses the same measurement focus as commercial enterprises, namely the flow of economic resources. The flow of economic resources refers to all of the assets available to the proprietary fund for the purpose of providing goods and services to the public or other governmental units. When the flow of economic resources and the accrual basis of accounting are combined, they provide the foundation for generally accepted accounting principles as applied by commercial enterprises. When the flow of economic resources is applied on an accrual basis for a proprietary fund, all assets and liabilities, both current and long-term, would be presented on the fund's balance sheet. Some of the key differences between the combined accrual method and flow of economic resources used by a proprietary fund, and the accounting model used by other governmental funds (combined modified accrual method and flow of current financial resources) are summarized below:

- Fixed assets would be recorded in a proprietary fund's balance sheet net of accumulated depreciation and not in the General Fixed Assets Account Group.
- Long-term debt would be recorded in a proprietary fund's balance sheet and not in the General Long-Term Debt Account Group.
- The fund balance (including retained earnings) would represent the net assets (total assets minus total liabilities) available to the proprietary fund, and not only those net assets available to pay current expenditures or debts arising from operations.
- Although the NCGA recommends that all funds adopt budgets for control, the proprietary fund's budget, which should generally be a flexible budget to reflect activity levels, results in no formal journal entries.
- An encumbrance system is not used.

The activity statement would include all costs incurred by a proprietary fund associated with providing goods and services during the period. These costs would include depreciation, the cost of inventories consumed during the period, and other operating expenses. On the activity statement, revenues earned during the period would match total costs incurred by the proprietary fund during the period.

As noted earlier, commercial accounting and reporting standards should be followed when preparing a proprietary fund's financial statements. The Financial Accounting Foundation has agreed that the GASB has the authority to issue generally accepted accounting principles for state and local governmental units. Thus, the GASB establishes accounting principles for state and local governments, and the FASB establishes accounting principles for all other reporting entities, including not-for-profit organizations other than state and local governments. Some entities in the public sector, such as hospitals, may be accounted for as an Enterprise Fund and may be subject to accounting standards issued by both the GASB and the FASB. When these entities issue separate general purpose financial statements, they should observe FASB pronouncements unless the GASB has issued a pronouncement applicable to the public sector entity. On the other hand, these entities must observe GASB pronouncements when their financial statements are included in combined general purpose financial statements of the state or local government. If an issue has been addressed by an AICPA Statement of Position (SOP), but neither the GASB nor the FASB has addressed the issue, the SOP standards should be followed. In general, when the GASB has not issued a pronouncement that applies to a particular transaction or economic event, and the FASB has done so, the FASB promulgation is presumed to apply.

Budgetary System and Accounts

While the NCGA recommended that all funds adopt a budget for control purposes, there is a recognition that the nature of budgeting is different between governmental funds and proprietary funds. Generally, a proprietary fund should prepare a flexible budget, which reflects changes in the activity level. A fixed budget is inappropriate for proprietary funds because overall activity is measured in terms of revenues and expenses and will in part fluctuate depending upon the demand for goods and services by the public or governmental agencies. The flexible budget does not provide a basis for appropriations but rather serves as an approved plan that can facilitate budgetary control and operational evaluations. A flexible budget approach allows the governmental unit to prepare several budgets at different activity levels in order to establish an acceptable comparative basis for planned activity and actual results.

The basis of accounting used to prepare a budget for a proprietary fund should be the same as the basis used to record the results of actual transactions. It is not appropriate to integrate the budgetary accounts into the fund's accounting system.

Because a proprietary fund is generally not subject to a legislatively adopted budget, there is no need to use an encumbrance system to control executory contracts and other commitments.

ACCOUNTS AND TRANSACTIONS

A proprietary fund executes transactions that are similar to those executed by a commercial enterprise. As noted earlier, governmental transactions and economic events should be accounted for and reported, for the most part, by observing generally accepted accounting principles applicable to a commercial enterprise. The remainder of this chapter makes no attempt to present a comprehensive description of commercial accounting practices; however, those accounts and transactions that are somewhat unique to the governmental accounting and reporting environment are discussed.

Revenues

FASB:CS-6 (Elements of Financial Statements) defines revenues as "inflows or other enhancements of assets of an entity or settlements of its liabilities (or a combination of both) during a period from delivering or producing goods, rendering services, or other activities that constitute the entity's ongoing major or central operations." For governmental funds (General, Special Revenue, Capital Projects, and Debt Service), revenues are recognized when they are susceptible to accrual (measurable and available), which is a modified accrual concept. On the other hand, a proprietary fund should recognize revenue on an accrual basis, meaning that revenue is considered realized when (1) the earning process is complete or virtually complete and (2) an exchange has taken place. The following observations are made in FASB:CS-5 (Recognition and Measurement in Financial Statements of Business Enterprises) with respect to revenue recognition:

- The two conditions (being realized or realizable and being earned) are usually met by the time product or merchandise is delivered or services are rendered to customers, and revenues from manufacturing and selling activities and gains and losses from sales of other assets are commonly recognized at time of sale (usually meaning delivery).

- If sale or cash receipts (or both) precede production and delivery (for example, magazine subscriptions), revenues may be recognized as earned by production and delivery.
- If product is contracted for before production, revenues may be recognized by a percentage-of-completion method as earned-as production takes place, provided reasonable estimates of results at completion and reliable measures of progress are available.
- If services are rendered or rights to use assets extend continuously over time (for example, interest or rent), reliable measures based on contractual prices established in advance are commonly available, and revenues may be recognized as earned as time passes.
- If products or other assets are readily realizable because they are salable at reliably determinable prices without significant effort (for example, certain agricultural products, precious metals, and marketable securities), revenues and some gains or losses may be recognized at completion of production or when prices of the assets change.
- If products, services, or other assets are exchanged for nonmonetary assets that are not readily convertible into cash or revenues, gains or losses may be recognized on the basis that they have been earned and the transaction is completed. Gains or losses may also be recognized if nonmonetary assets are received or distributed in nonreciprocal transactions. Recognition in both kinds of transactions depends on the provision that the fair values involved can be determined within reasonable limits.

These six broad generalizations are equally applicable to proprietary funds.

Quasi-External Revenues The only transfers between funds of the same reporting entity that are recorded as operating revenues are quasi-external revenue transactions. A quasi-external transaction is a transaction between funds, whereby the exchange would have been classified as revenue had the exchange been consummated with an external party.

Usually all or a significant portion of the operating revenues of an Internal Service Fund arise from quasi-external transactions. The Internal Service Fund bills other governmental funds at amounts that will approximately recover all of the cost of providing the service. The Internal Service Fund records the billing as revenue, while the other governmental fund records an expense or expenditure. For example, if an Internal Service Fund bills the General Fund $1,500 for duplicating services provided, the following entries would be made:

GENERAL FUND
Expenditures—Duplication Charges	1,500	
Due To Internal Service Fund		1,500

INTERNAL SERVICE FUND
Due From General Fund	1,500	
Revenues—Charges For Services		1,500

Although to a much lesser extent than an Internal Service Fund, an Enterprise Fund may also be a party to a quasi-external revenue transaction. This occurs when an Enterprise Fund provides a service to other governmental funds as well as to the public. For example, assume that water and sewer services are billed by an Enterprise Fund to the following funds:

General fund	$18,000
Special revenue fund	2,500
Internal service fund	1,500
Total billings	$22,000

The billings would be recorded in the Enterprise Fund by making the following entry:

Due From General Fund	18,000	
Due From Special Revenue Fund	2,500	
Due From Internal Service Fund	1,500	
Revenues—Water And Sewer Fees		22,000

The General Fund and the Special Revenue Fund would record the billings as an expenditure, while the Internal Service Fund would recognize an expense. Of course, this $22,000 billing would represent a relatively small portion of the Enterprise Fund's total revenues, the bulk of which would be based on charges to the general public.

Grants, Entitlements, and Shared Revenues A proprietary fund's activities may be financed in part by grants, entitlements, or shared revenues. The following terms were defined in NCGA-2 (Grant, Entitlement, and Shared Revenue Accounting and Reporting by State and Local Governments):

Proprietary Funds

Grant—A contribution or gift of cash or other assets from another government to be used or expended for a specified purpose, activity, or facility.

Operating grant—A grant that is intended to finance operations or that may be used for either operations or for capital outlays at the discretion of the grantee.

Capital grant—A contribution or gift of cash or other assets restricted by the grantor for the acquisition or construction of fixed (capital) assets.

Entitlement—The amount of payment to which a state or local government is entitled, as determined by the federal or other government (for example, the Director of the Office of Revenue Sharing) pursuant to an allocation formula contained in applicable statutes.

Shared revenue—A revenue levied by one government but shared on a predetermined basis, often in proportion to the amount collected at the local level, with another government or class of government.

Operating grants, entitlements, and shared revenues received by a proprietary fund should be recorded as nonoperating revenues in the period in which they are both measurable and earned. Measurability is defined by FASB:CS-5 as a quality that can be "quantified in monetary units with sufficient reliability." Generally, for the measurability criterion to be satisfied, the disbursing governmental unit must appropriate resources and identify how the resources are to be distributed to the state or local government.

Grants, entitlements, and shared revenues may be measurable, but they should not be recorded as revenue until the earning process is complete. Due to the nature of these revenue sources, the earning process is not completed by the delivery of goods or services but rather by compliance with regulations associated with the intergovernmental program. Proprietary funds receiving grants are generally entitled to the resources when appropriate expenses under the grant program are made. The revenue recognition event then becomes the point at which an acceptable expense is incurred. For example, if a proprietary fund received an operating grant of $400,000, the following entry would be made in the proprietary fund:

Cash	400,000	
Deferred Revenues—Grants		400,000

If $150,000 of expenses that comply with grant guidelines are incurred, the following entries would be made:

Proprietary Funds

Expenses	150,000	
Accounts Payable		150,000
Unearned Revenues—Grants	150,000	
Nonoperating Revenues—Grants		150,000

Entitlements and shared revenues are generally subject to forfeiture only if prescribed regulations are not observed by the governmental unit. Thus, the critical event is actual receipt of funds, assuming that the governmental unit plans to spend the resources in a manner consistent with prescribed guidelines.

When grants, entitlements, or shared revenues have not met the measurable and earned criteria, and no resources have been received from the disbursing governmental unit, the recipient governmental unit may disclose the nature and amount of the item in a note to the financial statements, but no accrual should be recognized in the proprietary fund. If the proprietary fund has received resources from the disbursing governmental unit, but the revenue recognition criteria have not been satisfied, the amount received under the grant, entitlement, or shared revenue program should be recorded as deferred revenue.

Grants, entitlements, and shared revenues may be recorded as (nonoperating) revenues only if they are available to (1) finance current operations or (2) finance either current operations or capital outlays of the fund (the latter determination must be at the discretion of the governmental unit in order for a grant used for capital outlays to be recorded as revenue). If the resources were provided to finance only capital expenditures of the proprietary fund, the grant, entitlement, or shared revenue is recorded as contributed capital and not as revenue. For example, if a proprietary fund received a $100,000 operating grant and a $150,000 capital grant, the following entry would be made in the fund:

Cash	250,000	
Nonoperating Revenues—Grants		100,000
Contributed Capital—Capital Grants		150,000

The contributed capital account is shown in the equity section of the proprietary fund's balance sheet.

> **OBSERVATION:** *The amount of grants, entitlements, or shared revenues received by a proprietary fund should not, over time, represent the major source of funding. If this were to occur, then the pro-*

prietary fund may no longer be operating primarily by direct user charges and the use of a Special Revenue Fund may be more appropriate.

Classification and Disclosure Revenues of a proprietary fund should be classified and disclosed in a manner consistent with classification guidelines utilized by similar commercial enterprises.

Accounting and reporting requirements established by a grant, entitlement, or shared revenue program may not be consistent with generally accepted accounting principles as applied by commercial enterprises. The proprietary fund's financial accounting system should be designed to meet both the disbursing government's reporting requirements and those mandated through generally accepted accounting principles. Generally this can be accomplished by maintaining supplemental accounting records beyond those that are integrated with the fund's general ledger. When GAAP-based financial statements do not demonstrate compliance with special reporting requirements imposed by the grantor governmental unit, it may be necessary to demonstrate compliance through the presentation of schedules or narrative explanations in the Comprehensive Annual Financial Report or through the preparation of special purpose reports.

Expenses

FASB:CS-6 defines expenses as outflows or other using up of assets or incurrences of liabilities (or a combination of both) during a period from delivering or producing goods, rendering services, or carrying out other activities that constitute the entity's ongoing major or central operations. Governmental funds, other than proprietary funds, recognize an expenditure when the related liability is incurred, and it is expected that the liability will be discharged by expending available financial resources of the fund. For example, a General Fund would record as an expenditure a loss contingency arising from a legal claim only if the claim is to be paid during the current fiscal year or very shortly thereafter. On the other hand, a proprietary fund would record a loss contingency as an expense irrespective of when the related liability is expected to be paid. The recognition of an expense by a proprietary fund, as described in APB Statement-4 and FASB:CS-5, should be consistent with the following guidelines:

- Associating cause and effect—Some expenses (such as cost of goods sold) are recognized upon recognition of revenues that result directly and jointly from the same transactions or other events as the expenses.
- Systematic and rational allocation—Some expenses (such as depreciation and insurance) are allocated by systematic and rational procedures to the periods during which the related assets are expected to provide benefits.
- Immediate recognition—Many expenses (such as selling and administrative salaries) are recognized during the period in which cash is spent or liabilities are incurred for goods and services that are used up either simultaneously with acquisition or soon after.

A proprietary fund's operating statement would include depreciation expense, cost of goods sold (if a manufacturing process is involved), amortization of patents, advertising expenses, and other expense classifications used by a commercial enterprise.

Quasi-External Expenses When a proprietary fund purchases goods or services from a related governmental fund, the exchange is treated as an operating expense and not as an interfund transfer. For example, if an Enterprise Fund pays the General Fund $15,000 in lieu of property taxes, the transaction would be recorded as follows:

GENERAL FUND
Cash   15,000
   Revenues—Receipts In Lieu Of
     Property Taxes   15,000

PROPRIETARY FUND
Expenses—Payments In Lieu Of
   Property Taxes   15,000
     Cash   15,000

Depreciation Expense All depreciable property of a proprietary fund must be depreciated in accordance with generally accepted accounting principles as applied by a commercial enterprise. Unlike depreciation on a governmental unit's general fixed assets, which may be reflected in the General Fixed Assets Account Group, depreciation on fixed assets of a proprietary fund must be shown as an expense on its operating statements with appropriate disclosures in the financial statements. However, a proprietary fund's depreciable assets financed by resources specifically made available for capital expenditures may be accounted for in one of two ways.

In Alternative #1, the depreciable property acquired through grants, entitlements, or shared revenues restricted for capital outlays may be accounted for in a manner similar to all other depreciable property. That is, depreciation expense and accumulated depreciation are recorded, and the depreciation expense is presented as an operating expense and closed along with other operating expenses directly to retained earnings.

In Alternative #2, depreciation expense and accumulated depreciation are recorded but the depreciation expense at the end of the year is closed directly to the proprietary fund's contributed capital account that was created when the restricted grant, entitlement, or shared revenue was received. On the Statement of Revenues, Expenses, and Changes in Retained Earnings, the depreciation expense is presented as an operating expense and is used to compute the fund's net income. Then, the depreciation expense is added to the net income figure to identify the net increase (decrease) in retained earnings for the year, and the latter amount is added to the beginning balance of retained earnings.

To illustrate the two methods of accounting for depreciable property acquired through a restricted grant, entitlement, or shared revenue, assume that a capital grant of $40,000 is received to finance the purchase of equipment. The receipt of the grant and the purchase of the equipment would be recorded as follows:

Cash	40,000	
Contributed Capital—Capital Grants		40,000
Equipment	40,000	
Cash		40,000

If it is assumed that the estimated economic life of the property is four years, its residual value is a nominal amount, and the straight-line method of depreciation is used, depreciation for the year is recorded in the proprietary fund by making the following conventional entry:

Depreciation Expense	10,000	
Accumulated Depreciation		10,000

The manner in which depreciation expense is closed at the end of the year depends upon whether Alternative #1 or Alternative #2, as just described, is used. The following closing entry would be made if the first alternative is used by the proprietary fund:

Revenue And Expense Summary (Retained Earnings)	10,000	
Depreciation Expense		10,000

If Alternative #2 is used, the following closing entry would be made in the proprietary fund:

Contributed Capital—Capital Grants	10,000	
Depreciation Expense		10,000

The effects of the two alternatives on a proprietary fund's operating statement are contrasted below:

	Alternative #1 *Depreciation is closed directly to retained earnings*	*Alternative #2* *Depreciation is closed directly to contributed capital*
Operating revenues	$250,000	$250,000
Operating expenses (including depreciation expense of $10,000 on depreciable property financed by a capital grant)	200,000	200,000
Operating income	50,000	50,000
Nonoperating revenues (expenses)	40,000	40,000
Operating income before transfers	10,000	10,000
Operating transfers in	5,000	5,000
Net income	15,000	15,000
Add depreciation on fixed assets acquired by capital grants that reduces contributed capital from capital grants	—	10,000
Net increase (decrease) in retained earnings	15,000	25,000
Retained earnings— beginning of year	110,000	110,000
Retained earnings— end of year	$125,000	$135,000

Proprietary Funds

The difference between the retained earnings balances under the two alternatives is reflected in contributed capital created from capital grants. The total equity of the proprietary fund is the same for both alternatives.

Classification and Disclosure Expenses of a proprietary fund should be classified and disclosed in a manner consistent with classification guidelines utilized by similar commercial enterprises.

Assets

Assets, as defined in FASB:CS-6, are "probable future economic benefits obtained or controlled by a particular entity as a result of past transactions or events." The Concept Statement also concludes that an asset embodies the following three characteristics:

- A probable future benefit that involves a capacity, singly or in combination with other assets, to contribute directly or indirectly to future net cash inflows.
- A particular enterprise can obtain the benefit and control others' access to it.
- Transactions or other events giving rise to the enterprise's right to or control of the benefit have already occurred.

Governmental funds, other than proprietary funds, report only those assets that are available to finance current operations. For example, a General Fund could not accrue a gain arising from a settled lawsuit, even though the amount is known with certainty, if payments from the other party are to be received over several years. A proprietary fund's financial statements would reflect all assets related to the operations of the fund irrespective of when the asset is expected to be realized.

General fixed assets of a state or local government are recorded in the General Fixed Assets Account Group because these assets do not represent financial resources available to pay current obligations of governmental funds. On the other hand, fixed assets related to a proprietary fund are accounted for directly in that fund and are not reported as part of the General Fixed Assets Account Group.

A proprietary fund's fixed assets include such items as land, buildings, and equipment as well as property under construction. At the acquisition date of the property, cost is measured by the amount of consideration given or received. In addition to the capitalization of the cost to purchase or construct the property, ancillary costs should be capitalized. Ancillary costs include such charges as freight costs and related professional expenditures. In some instances the acquisition cost of property of a proprietary fund may not be available and some alternative basis must be used to record the fixed asset. For instance, some governmental units may not have documented the original cost of acquired or constructed property, and it may be impossible or time consuming to reconstruct the actual cost of the property. Under this condition, the original cost of the property may be estimated and used as the basis for capitalization. When estimations are used, the financial statements should disclose the estimation methods employed and the extent to which estimates were used.

There is, of course, no cost basis when property is donated to the governmental unit. When property is acquired through donation, the fixed asset should be recorded at its estimated fair value at the date of gift. For example, if land that is valued at $3,000,000 is donated to a proprietary fund, the receipt of the land would be recorded as follows:

Land	3,000,000	
Donated Capital		3,000,000

Interest Capitalization Interest cost incurred during the construction of the following assets of a proprietary fund should be capitalized:

- Assets that are constructed or otherwise produced for an enterprise's own use (including assets constructed or produced by others for the enterprise for which deposits or progress payments have been made)
- Assets intended for sale or lease that are constructed or otherwise produced as discrete projects (for example, real estate developments)
- Investments (equity, loans, and advances) accounted for by the equity method while the investee has activities in progress necessary to commence its planned principal operations provided that the investee's activities include the use of funds to acquire qualifying assets for its operations

On the other hand, the construction cost of the following assets related to a proprietary fund should not include an interest cost element:

Proprietary Funds

- Inventories that are routinely manufactured or otherwise produced in large quantities on a repetitive basis
- Assets that are in use or ready for their intended use in the earning activities of the enterprise
- Investments accounted for by the equity method after the planned principal operations of the investee begin
- Investments in regulated investees that are capitalizing both the cost of debt and equity capital
- Assets acquired with gifts and grants that are restricted by the donor or grantor to acquisition of those assets to the extent that funds are available from such gifts and grants (interest earned from temporary investment of those funds that is similarly restricted shall be considered in addition to the gift or grant for this purpose)

Interest costs incurred by a proprietary fund are subject to capitalization based on the guidelines established by FASB-34 (Capitalization of Interest Cost). The interest capitalization period begins when the following conditions are present:

- Expenditures for the capital asset have been made.
- Activities that are necessary to get the capital asset ready for its intended use are in progress.
- Interest cost is being incurred.

To determine the amount of interest cost to be capitalized, the weighted-average amount of accumulated expenditures for the period is multiplied by the proprietary fund's average borrowing rate for the period. Rather than use the overall average borrowing rate, the following approach can be employed:

- The interest rate for the obligation incurred specifically to finance the construction of the capital asset may be used and
- The overall average borrowing rate of the proprietary fund would be used for any accumulated expenditures in excess of specific borrowings.

The amount of interest cost to be capitalized is limited to the actual amount of interest expense recognized for the period.

FASB-62 (Capitalization of Interest Cost in Situations Involving Certain Tax-Exempt Borrowings and Certain Gifts and Grants) concludes that the amount of interest cost to be capitalized for assets constructed with tax-exempt borrowings is equal to the cost of the borrowing, less interest earned on related interest-bearing investments acquired with proceeds of the related tax-exempt borrowings.

> **OBSERVATION:** *It should be noted that FASB-62 is applicable to tax-exempt borrowings. With the restrictions imposed by recent tax legislation, it is likely that governmental units will issue an increased amount of taxable debt.*

Leased Property A proprietary fund may lease property from another party as part of its operations. NCGA-5 (Accounting and Financial Reporting Principles for Lease Agreements of State and Local Governments) concludes that FASB-13 (Accounting for Leases, as amended) should be followed to determine whether lease rights should be capitalized as an asset. FASB-13 requires that a noncancelable lease be capitalized if any one of the following criteria is satisfied:

- The lease transfers ownership of the property to the lessee by the end of the lease term.
- The lease contains a bargain purchase option.
- The lease term is equal to 75% or more of the estimated economic life of the leased property.
- The present value at the beginning of the lease term of the minimum lease payments, excluding that portion of the payments representing executory costs, to be paid by the lessor, including any profit thereon, equals or exceeds 90% of the excess of the fair value of the leased property to the lessor at the inception of the lease over any related investment tax credit retained by the lessor and expected to be realized by him.

In addition, a proprietary fund may lease property to another party. FASB-13 concludes that a lessor should treat the lease transaction as an *in-substance* sale of the property if any one of the previous four criteria is satisfied and if both of the following guidelines exist:

- Collectibility of the minimum lease payments is reasonably predictable.
- No important uncertainties surround the amount of the unreimbursable costs yet to be incurred by the lessor under the lease.

In summary, all provisions of FASB-13, without modification, are applicable to lease agreements entered into by a proprietary fund.

Joint Ventures A state or local government may enter into a joint venture with another party in order to serve the needs of the general public. Although the joint venture is a separate entity, it must be evaluated to determine whether its financial statements should be included as part of the reporting entity's general purpose financial statements. To make this determination, criteria established by NCGA-3 (Defining the Governmental Reporting Entity) and NCGA Interpretation-7 (Clarification as to the Application of the Criteria in NCGA Statement-3 Defining the Governmental Reporting Entity) must be considered. Chapter 5 (Governmental Financial Statements) of this book discusses the application of these criteria.

A proprietary fund may be responsible and accountable for an investment in a joint venture. If it is concluded that the joint venture's financial statements should not be included as part of the reporting entity, the proprietary fund must use the equity method to account for the joint venture investment. The equity method should be applied as described by APB-18 (Equity Method for Investments in Common Stock). APB-18 defines the equity method in the following manner:

> A method of accounting for an investment under which an investor initially records an investment in the stock of an investee at cost, and adjusts the carrying amount of the investment to recognize the investor's share of the earnings or losses of the investee after the date of acquisition. The amount of the adjustment is included in the determination of net income by the investor and such amount reflects adjustments similar to those made in preparing consolidated statements including adjustments to eliminate intercompany gains and losses, and to amortize, if appropriate, any difference between investor cost and underlying equity in net assets of the investee at the date of investment. The investment of an investor also is adjusted to reflect the investor's share of changes in the investee's capital. Dividends received from an investee reduce the carrying amount of the investment. Under the equity method, an investment in common stock is generally shown in the balance sheet of an investor as a single amount. Likewise, an investor's share of earnings or losses from its investment is ordinarily shown in its income statement as a single amount.

NCGA-7 notes that the equity method must be used even when common stock is not issued by a joint venture.

> **OBSERVATION:** *The conclusion that the equity method is applicable to unincorporated joint ventures is supported by AICPA Accounting Interpretation—APB-18 (Investment in Partnerships and Unincorporated Ventures—Question #2). The Interpretation concludes that APB-18 is applicable to investments in partnerships and unincorporated joint ventures with some exceptions. For example, in some industries it is an acceptable practice to report the pro rata portion of each account rather than report a single amount for the investment account and a single amount for the equity in earnings account.*

The initial investment in a joint venture should be recorded based on the fair value of resources contributed to the joint venture by the governmental unit. For example, if an Enterprise Fund invests cash of $500,000 in a joint venture, the investment would be recorded as follows by the Enterprise Fund:

Investment In Joint Venture	500,000	
Cash		500,000

The subsequent accounting for the investment in the joint venture is relatively simple when (1) the Enterprise Fund's share of the joint venture's net assets is equal to the fair value of assets contributed by the Enterprise Fund and (2) the joint venture's net assets are recorded at fair values. When the joint venture determines its income (loss) for the period, the Enterprise Fund increases (decreases) its investment account and recognizes its share of the joint venture's earnings (loss). If, for example, an Enterprise Fund has a one-third interest in a joint venture and the joint venture had earnings of $240,000 for the period, the following entry would be made by the Enterprise Fund:

Investment In Joint Venture ($240,000/3)	80,000	
Equity Interest In Joint Venture		
Earnings		80,000

If the joint venture distributes assets to the Enterprise Fund, the carrying value of the investment in the joint venture should be reduced. In the current example, if it is assumed that the joint venture distributed excess cash of $21,000, the following entry would be made by the Enterprise Fund:

Cash ($21,000/3)	7,000	
Investment In Joint Venture		7,000

Proprietary Funds

If the joint venture incurs substantial losses that reduce the Enterprise Fund's investment to zero, the equity method should not be used to account for subsequent losses sustained by the joint venture unless the Enterprise Fund is responsible for financing deficits or guaranteeing loans held by the joint venture.

Accounting for an investment in a joint venture becomes more complicated when the conditions identified earlier do not exist. ((1) the Enterprise Fund's share of the joint venture's net assets is equal to the fair value of assets contributed by the Enterprise Fund and (2) the joint venture's net assets are recorded at fair values.) The equity method must be applied in a manner that simulates the consolidation of an entity (the so-called one-line consolidation). Thus, the fair values of the joint venture's assets and liabilities must be determined and compared to their book values. The difference between the fair values and the book values must be analyzed to determine whether the Enterprise Fund's equity interest in the joint venture's earnings (loss) for a period should be adjusted. For example, if the fair value of depreciable property held by a joint venture is greater that its book value, the Enterprise Fund must reflect additional depreciation (on the difference) in applying the equity method. To illustrate, if it is assumed that there is a $10,000 difference between the fair value and book value of depreciable property and the property has a remaining life of 5 years, the following entry would be made by the Enterprise Fund to reflect the additional depreciation for a year:

Equity Interest In Joint Venture Earnings ($10,000/5 yrs.)	2,000	
Investment In Joint Venture		2,000

When the difference between the cost of the investment in the joint venture and the Enterprise Fund's interest in the joint venture's net assets is not related to the valuation of specific assets or liabilities, the difference represents the excess of cost over fair value (goodwill) or the excess of fair value over cost. Goodwill must be amortized over a period not to exceed 40 years. Under the equity method, the amortization of goodwill is recorded by reducing both the equity interest in the earnings of the joint venture and the carrying value of the investment account. The amount of the excess of fair value of net assets over cost should be reduced by the Enterprise Fund's share of the joint venture's noncurrent assets (except investments in marketable securities) and the residual amount, if any, should be amortized over a period not to exceed 40 years.

To illustrate an investment in a joint venture where an Enterprise Fund's share of the joint venture's net assets is not equal to the Enter-

Proprietary Funds

prise Fund's contribution, assume that an investment of $500,000 is made for a one-third interest in a joint venture. At the date of the investment, the joint venture's assets were valued as follows:

	Book values	Fair values
Current assets	$200,000	$200,000
Equipment (10-year remaining life)	400,000	600,000
Land	100,000	100,000
	700,000	900,000

(The joint venture has no liabilities.)

The cost of the investment in the joint venture is analyzed below.

Cost of investment in joint venture	$500,000
One-third interest in book value of net assets of joint venture ($700,000 + $500,000)/3	400,000
Excess of cost over book value	100,000
Proportional share of undervaluation of equipment ($200,000/3)	66,667
Excess of cost over fair value (goodwill)	$ 33,333

If it is assumed that at the end of year one, the joint venture had earnings of $240,000 and the goodwill is amortized over 40 years by the Enterprise Fund, the equity interest in the joint venture's earnings for the year would be $72,500 as computed below:

Proportional share of earnings ($240,000/3)	$80,000
Additional depreciation ($66,667/10 yrs.)	6,667
Amortization of goodwill ($33,333/40 yrs.)	833
Equity interest in joint venture earnings	$72,500

To record the earnings for the first year, the following entry would be made by the Enterprise Fund:

Investment In Joint Venture	72,500	
Equity Interest In Joint Venture Earnings		72,500

GOVERNMENTAL GAAP GUIDE / **64.23**

Proprietary Funds

Classification and Disclosure Assets of a proprietary fund should be classified and disclosed in a manner consistent with classification guidelines utilized by similar commercial enterprises. All relevant FASB (and its predecessors') pronouncements and general disclosure requirements should be observed. For example, if a proprietary fund capitalized interest cost during the period, disclosure requirements required by FASB-34 must be made.

If a joint venture is accounted for in the financial statements of a proprietary fund, the following disclosures should be made:

- A general description of each joint venture, including:
  — Identifying the participants and their percentage shares
  — Describing the arrangements for selecting the governing body or management
  — Disclosing the degree of control the participants have over budgeting and financing
- Condensed or summary financial information on each joint venture, including:
  — Balance sheet date
  — Total assets, liabilities, and equity
  — Total revenues, expenses, other financing sources (uses), and net increase (decrease) in retained earnings
  — Reporting entity's share of assets, liabilities, equity, and changes therein during the year, if known
- Joint venture debt, both current and long-term, and the security for the debt (security for the debt is defined as the resources that are expected to be used to repay the debt and/or may be legally or otherwise obligated to such debt)

An illustration of a disclosure requirement for a joint venture is presented below.

▶ The Centerville Water Authority has entered into a joint venture with two other municipalities (Newtown and Milltown). The joint venture was organized to provide water and sewer services to a regional mall and adjacent businesses that are located in all three communities. The joint venture is equally owned by each of the three participating municipalities and is administered by a three-member Board. Each municipality appoints one member to the Board. The joint venture is responsible for adopting a budget and financing its operations subject to approval by each of the three municipalities.

Presented below is a summary of the joint venture's financial position as of June 30, 19X5, and the results of its operations for the year then ended.

	Joint venture	Centerville's 1/3 share
Financial position		
Assets		
Current assets	$ 471,000	$ 157,000
Property, plant, and equipment	1,149,000	383,000
Total assets	$1,620,000	$ 540,000
Liabilities		
Current liabilities	$ 51,000	$ 17,000
Long-term debt	150,000	50,000
Total liabilities	201,000	67,000
Equity		
Contributed capital	984,000	328,000
Retained earnings	435,000	145,000
Total equity	1,419,000	473,000
Total liabilities and equity	$1,620,000	$ 540,000

The long-term debt of the joint venture ($150,000) is secured by the operating assets of the joint venture.

Results of operations		
Operating revenues	$6,390,000	$2,130,000
Operating expenses	6,150,000	2,050,000
Net income	240,000	80,000
Retained earnings 6/30/X4	195,000	65,000
Retained earnings 6/30/X5	$ 435,000	$ 145,000

Liabilities

FASB:CS-6 defines liabilities as "probable future sacrifices of economic benefits arising from present obligations of a particular entity to transfer assets or provide services to other entities in the future as a result of past transactions or events." As noted in FASB:CS-6, a liability embodies the following fundamental characteristics:

Proprietary Funds

- A present duty or responsibility to one or more other entities that entails settlement by probable future transfer or use of assets at a specified or determinable date, on occurrence of a specified event, or on demand.
- The duty or responsibility obligates a particular enterprise, leaving it little or no discretion to avoid the future sacrifice.
- The transaction or other event obligating the enterprise has already happened.

Unlike other governmental funds, a proprietary fund reports both current and noncurrent liabilities that are expected to be paid from the fund. For example, if long-term debt were issued and the proceeds made available to the General Fund, the long-term liability would be reported as part of the governmental unit's General Long-Term Debt Account Group, and the proceeds from the debt issuance would be reported as an other source of financing in the General Fund. When a proprietary fund issues long-term debt, the debt is recorded as a fund liability and is not presented as part of the General Long-Term Debt Account Group.

An Enterprise Fund may receive the proceeds from the issuance of either general obligation bonds or revenue bonds.

General obligation bonds General obligation bonds are full faith and credit bonds, which means that the debt is secured by the general taxing powers of the state or local government. If general obligation bonds are to be repaid (interest and principal) from earnings of the Enterprise Fund, they should be reported as a liability of the fund. On the other hand, general obligation bonds that are to be paid from general taxes and revenues of the governmental unit should be reported as part of the General Long-Term Debt Account Group. In the latter case, the proceeds from the issuance of the bonds that are made available to the Enterprise Fund are treated as a capital contribution.

To illustrate, assume that general obligation bonds of $3,000,000 are issued and that the proceeds are made available to an Enterprise Fund. If the principal and interest on the bonds are to be paid from earnings of the Enterprise Fund, the issuance of the bonds is recorded as follows:

ENTERPRISE FUND
  Cash   3,000,000
    Bonds Payable   3,000,000

Proprietary Funds

GENERAL LONG-TERM DEBT ACCOUNT GROUP
No entry

If it is assumed that the principal interest on the general obligation bonds is to be paid from general revenues and taxes of the governmental unit, the following entries would be made:

GENERAL FUND
Residual Equity Transfer (Fund
  Balance)   3,000,000
    Proceeds From The Issuance Of
      Bonds   3,000,000

ENTERPRISE FUND
Cash   3,000,000
  Contributed Capital—General Fund   3,000,000

GENERAL LONG-TERM DEBT ACCOUNT GROUP
Amount To Be Provided For Repayment
  Of General Obligation Bonds   3,000,000
    Bonds Payable   3,000,000

When general obligation bonds are recorded as liabilities of an Enterprise Fund, the General Long-Term Debt Account Group should report the outstanding debt as a contingent liability.

Revenue bonds Principal and interest on revenue bonds are paid exclusively from the earnings of an Enterprise Fund. If the debt is also secured by specific fixed assets of the Enterprise Fund, they are referred to as mortgage revenue bonds. Revenue bonds are recorded as a liability of the Enterprise Fund. For example, in the previous illustration, if revenue bonds rather than general obligation bonds were issued, the following entry would be made:

ENTERPRISE FUND
Cash   3,000,000
  Revenue Bonds Payable   3,000,000

GENERAL LONG-TERM DEBT ACCOUNT GROUP
No entry

Because revenue bonds are not full faith and credit bonds, they are not shown as a contingent liability in the General Long-Term Debt Account Group.

A proprietary fund's liabilities may include obligations other than those that arise from the issuance of a security debt instrument. These other obligations may be created from capitalized leases, claims and judgments, special employee termination benefits, and pension obligations. These, as well as other liabilities of a proprietary fund, should be accounted for in a manner similar to the accounting and reporting standards applicable to a commercial enterprise.

Self-Insurance Internal Service Fund Like commercial enterprises and other nonprofit organizations, a governmental unit may decide to accept certain risks rather than insure against those risks. These risks may include possible liabilities for workmen's compensation, medical claims, and property damage claims. As part of the self-insurance strategy, a state or local government may establish a separate Internal Service Fund (Self-Insurance Fund) to account for the payment of claims and judgments.

The recognition of a loss contingency in a Self-Insurance Internal Service Fund arising from claims and judgments is governed by accounting and reporting standards established by FASB-5 (Accounting for Contingencies). A loss contingency must be accrued when the following two conditions exist:

- Information available prior to issuance of the financial statements indicates that it is probable that an asset had been impaired, or a liability had been incurred, at the date of the financial statements. (It is implicit in this condition that it must be probable that one or more future events will occur confirming the fact of the loss.)
- The amount of loss can be reasonably estimated.

If these two conditions are met, the loss contingency must be recognized in the Internal Service Fund as an expense and liability. Of course, the resources to eventually pay the claims and judgments will be received from other (insured) governmental funds. The amount transferred by the insured funds is recorded as an operating transfer and not as an expenditure. In addition, the amount of the total transfer that can be recorded as an operating transfer can be no greater than the actuarially determined value of the loss contingency. Any excess must be treated as a residual equity transfer by the insured governmental funds and the Internal Service Fund.

OBSERVATION: *Presumably, the reason that only the amount of the actuarially determined loss contingency can be recognized as an operating transfer is to reduce the possibility of income smoothing. To smooth out the typical irregular payments of claims and judgments, and the resulting erratic effect on the governmental unit's operating statement, an equal transfer could be made each year irrespective of the estimated loss contingencies incurred during the year. FASB-5 prohibits income smoothing (see paragraph 14 of the Statement).*

When a separate Internal Service Fund is established to account for claims and judgments of other governmental funds, loss contingencies are still backed by the full faith and credit of the governmental unit. For this reason, although the liability is recognized in the Internal Service Fund, the loss contingency should be disclosed as a contingent liability in the General Long-Term Debt Account Group.

To illustrate the accounting for a self-insurance fund, assume that all claims and judgments of a governmental unit are accounted for in a separate Internal Service Fund. At the end of the current period, loss contingencies (as determined under FASB-5) that are subject to accrual total $450,000. To record the amount of loss contingencies the following entry would be made in the Internal Service Fund:

Expenses—Claims And Judgments	450,000	
Estimated Liabilities For Claims		
And Judgments		450,000

At the end of the current period the General Fund transfers $450,000 to the Internal Service Fund to fund the estimated loss contingencies. The actuarially determined amount of the loss contingencies is $360,000. The transfer would be recorded as follows:

GENERAL FUND

Transfers Out—Internal Service Fund	360,000	
Residual Equity Transfer (Fund Balance)	90,000	
Cash		450,000

INTERNAL SERVICE FUND

Cash	450,000	
Transfers In—General Fund		360,000
Contributed Capital—General Fund		90,000

Proprietary Funds

If it is assumed that a $50,000 judgment is paid during the following fiscal year, the following entry would be made in the Internal Service Fund:

Estimated Liabilities For Claims And Judgments	50,000	
Cash		50,000

Accounting for a Self-Insurance Internal Service Fund as just illustrated is described in NCGA-4 (Accounting and Financial Reporting Principles for Claims and Judgments); however, the effective date of this approach was extended indefinitely. The reason for the postponement is that there is an inconsistency between the accounting method used by the (self-insured) governmental funds and the Internal Service Fund. The transfer out recorded by the self-insured fund can be no greater than the actuarially determined amount of loss contingencies. On the other hand, the actual expense recognized in the Internal Service Fund is the gross value (not the present value or actuarially determined value) of the loss contingencies as required by FASB-5. NCGA-4 notes that "governmental fund expenditures within function or program classifications and Internal Service Fund revenues may therefore appear understated." In the preceding illustration, the Internal Service Fund recognized an expense of $450,000 but could record a transfer in of only $360,000.

> **OBSERVATION:** *Accounting and reporting standards for insurance companies were established with the issuance of FASB-60 (Accounting and Reporting by Insurance Enterprises). There is disagreement as to whether the standards established by FASB-60 are appropriate for Self-Insurance Internal Service Funds established by a governmental entity. FASB-60 is applicable to separate insurance entities (life insurance enterprises, property and liability insurance enterprises, and title insurance enterprises) where the risk of loss has been transferred from the insured party to the insuring party. When a governmental entity establishes a Self-Insurance Internal Service Fund, the governmental entity retains the risk of loss. Thus, it is apparently inappropriate to apply standards established by FASB-60 to account for a Self-Insurance Internal Service Fund. The GASB is expected to issue an Exposure Draft on state and local government insurance issues in 1988.*

Classification and Disclosure Liabilities of a proprietary fund should be classified and disclosed in a manner consistent with classification guidelines utilized by similar commercial enterprises.

Interfund Transactions

With the exceptions of quasi-external transactions and reimbursements, interfund transactions between a proprietary fund and other governmental funds are not recorded as revenues or expenses/expenditures. A proprietary fund may be affected by annual operating transfers or residual equity transfers.

Operating Transfers A potential problem arises when there are transfers between a governmental fund and a proprietary fund. A governmental fund uses the modified accrual basis to record transactions, while a proprietary fund uses the accrual basis. If these two methods were strictly followed by the types of funds, it is conceivable that an interfund transaction could be recorded in one period by a proprietary fund and in another period by a governmental fund. To avoid this potential inconsistency, operating transfers are recorded neither on the modified accrual basis nor on the accrual basis. NCGA-1 simply mandates that "transfers of financial resources among funds should be recognized in all funds affected in the period in which the interfund receivable(s) and payable(s) arise."

Operating transfers may be made to a proprietary fund to finance current operations. Transfers to a proprietary fund do not represent expenditures of the transferring fund or revenues of the proprietary fund. For example, if the General Fund makes an annual transfer of $25,000 to an Internal Service Fund to subsidize the latter's operations, the following entries would be made to record the operating transfer:

GENERAL FUND
Transfers Out—Internal Service Fund	25,000	
Cash		25,000

PROPRIETARY FUND
Cash	25,000	
Transfers In—General Fund		25,000

Later in the period, if the General Fund is billed $3,000 for services performed by the Internal Service Fund, the exchange represents a quasi-external transaction and would be recorded in the following manner:

Proprietary Funds

GENERAL FUND
Expenditures   3,000
   Due To Internal Service Fund   3,000

INTERNAL SERVICE FUND
Due From General Fund   3,000
   Revenues—Charges For Services   3,000

Residual Equity Transfers   A residual equity transfer between a governmental fund and a proprietary fund represents a nonrecurring or nonroutine transfer. Usually a residual equity transfer arises from the creation, expansion, liquidation, or contraction of a proprietary fund.

A residual equity transfer is charged or credited directly to the governmental fund making or receiving the transfer. Because a proprietary fund does not have a fund balance account, residual equity transfers increase or decrease its contributed capital account. For example, if a governmental unit transfers $400,000 from its General Fund to create an Enterprise Fund, the residual equity transfer is recorded as follows:

GENERAL FUND
Residual Equity Transfer (Fund Balance)   400,000
   Cash   400,000

ENTERPRISE FUND
Cash   400,000
   Contributed Capital—General Fund   400,000

If the Enterprise Fund is liquidated a few years later when its equity balance is $650,000, and this amount is transferred to the General Fund, the transfer is recorded as follows:

GENERAL FUND
Cash   650,000
   Residual Equity Transfer (Fund
     Balance)   650,000

ENTERPRISE FUND
Retained Earnings   250,000
Contributed Capital—General Fund   400,000
   Cash   650,000

Classification and Disclosure Interfund transactions and accounts do not have to be eliminated when a proprietary fund's financial statements are combined with other governmental funds' financial statements to form the reporting entity's general purpose financial statements or the Comprehensive Annual Financial Report. If the interfund transactions and accounts are eliminated when the financial statements are combined, the nature of the eliminations should be apparent from the columnar headings; otherwise, the nature and extent of the eliminations must be disclosed in the financial statements.

FINANCIAL STATEMENTS

A proprietary fund's financial statements are included in the reporting entity's general purpose financial statements and in its Comprehensive Annual Financial Report. Proprietary fund financial statements included in the reporting entity's financial statement must be presented in accordance with GASB (and its predecessors') pronouncements and other generally accepted accounting principles. The hierarchy of authoritative support for generally accepted accounting principles is as follows:

- Pronouncements of the GASB (including NCGA pronouncements identified in GASB-1)
- Pronouncements of the FASB
- Pronouncements of bodies composed of expert accountants that follow a due process procedure, including broad distribution of proposed accounting principles for public comment for the intended purpose of establishing accounting principles or of describing existing practices that are generally accepted
- Practices or pronouncements that are widely recognized as being generally accepted because they represent prevalent practice in a particular industry or the knowledgeable application to specific circumstances or pronouncements
- Other accounting literature

In addition to being included in the reporting entity's financial statements, an Enterprise Fund may issue separate general purpose

Proprietary Funds

financial statements. Public entities accounted for as an Enterprise Fund that may be required to report separately from the reporting entity may include hospitals, universities and colleges, public authorities, and utilities. These separately issued financial statements must be prepared in accordance with FASB (and its predecessors') pronouncements. However, if there is an accounting or reporting conflict between a GASB and FASB pronouncement, the GASB pronouncement would be observed in preparing the public entity's financial statements presented separately.

Generally, the following statements are included in a proprietary fund's set of financial statements:

- Statement of Revenues and Expenses
- Statement of Changes in Retained Earnings
- Balance Sheet
- Statement of Changes in Financial Position
- Combining Financial Statements

In addition, an Enterprise Fund's financial statements may have to include certain disclosures with respect to segment information.

For financial reporting purposes, the Statement of Revenues and Expenses is usually combined with the Statement of Changes in Retained Earnings to form a single financial statement; however, for discussion purposes the two statements are examined separately.

Statement of Revenues and Expenses

A proprietary fund's Statement of Revenues and Expenses is prepared on the accrual basis to reflect the income determination measurement focus; however, NCGA-1 recommends that its format be consistent with those used by other governmental funds included in the reporting entity's financial statements. A common format for all funds facilitates the preparation of combined financial statements and enhances the readability of the financial report. In addition, NCGA-1 notes that a proprietary fund's statement of operations should be prepared in a manner similar to formats used by similar commercial enterprises. As discussed in Chapter 60 of this guide, the operating statements of governmental funds may be presented in various formats. Some of those formats for governmental funds may be inconsistent with the reporting requirements applicable to similar commercial enterprises. While not endorsing a particular format for a proprietary fund, NCGA-1 uses the following general format for purposes of illustration:

Operating revenues	$X
Operating expenses	X
Operating income	X
Nonoperating revenues (expenses)	X
Income before operating transfers	X
Operating transfers from (to) other funds	X
Net income (loss)	X
Retained earnings—beginning of period	X
Retained earnings—end of period	$X

NCGA-1 recommends, but does not require, that the operating statement analysis of retained earnings be presented as a single combined financial statement.

In addition to the main headings illustrated above, a proprietary fund's operating statement may include the following sections:

- Gain or loss on the disposition of a business segment (see APB-30, Reporting the Results of Operations)
- Extraordinary items (see APB-30—Reporting the Results of Operations)
- Cumulative effect of a change in accounting principle (see APB-20—Accounting Changes)

An example of an operating statement combined with an analysis of the changes in retained earnings is presented in Exhibit I.

Proprietary Funds

EXHIBIT I
Statement of Revenues, Expenses, and Changes in Retained Earnings

City of Centerville
Statement of Revenues, Expenses, and Changes
in Retained Earnings
Centerville Airport
June 30, 19X5

Operating revenues	
Charges and fees	$585,000
Rentals and commissions	115,000
Other	35,000
Total operating revenues	735,000
Operating expenses	
Personnel services	225,000
Purchase of services	150,000
Materials and supplies	100,000
Depreciation	35,000
Other	55,000
Total operating expenses	565,000
Operating income (loss)	170,000
Nonoperating revenues (expenses)	
Debt service—interest	(25,000)
Grants	5,000
Other	(40,000)
Total nonoperating revenues (expenses)	(60,000)
Income (loss) before operating transfers	110,000
Operating transfers in (out)	(70,000)
Net income	40,000
(Increase) decrease in retained earnings reserved for debt service	(10,000)
Net change in unreserved retained earnings for year	30,000
Retained earnings—unreserved July 1, 19X4	45,000
Retained earnings—unreserved June 30, 19X5	$ 75,000

Statement of Changes in Retained Earnings

A proprietary fund's Statement of Changes in Retained Earnings reconciles the beginning and ending balances of the retained earnings account. The statement may include prior-period adjustments, effects of changes in appropriations of retained earnings and the net income of the current period.

When a statement of operations and financial position of a proprietary fund is presented, APB-12 (Omnibus Opinion—1967) requires disclosures of changes in the accounts that comprise an entity's equity accounts (generally, retained earnings and contributed capital). The disclosures may be made in a separate financial statement or in notes to the financial statements.

Balance Sheet

A proprietary fund's balance sheet measures all economic resources available to the fund and all obligations of the fund. The classified balance sheet includes categories for current assets, property, plant, and equipment, current liabilities, long-term liabilities, and fund equity.

An Enterprise Fund's balance sheet may include a section that discloses assets that are restricted for a particular purpose. The restricted assets may be accumulated for such reasons as the retirement of debt, future expansion, and current construction of property, or to identify deposits returnable to customers.

Generally, an Enterprise Fund's statement of position follows the conventional format of a commercial enterprise, namely the presentation of current assets followed by noncurrent assets, and current liabilities followed by noncurrent liabilities. In some industries, such as the utilities industry, noncurrent assets and noncurrent liabilities are grouped and presented before current assets and current liabilities. Financial statements that are presented separately from the governmental reporting entity should follow the format prevalent in a particular industry; however, when the financial statements are combined with statements of other governmental funds, a common format should be used by all funds included in the reporting entity.

An example of an Enterprise Fund's Balance Sheet is presented in Exhibit II.

Proprietary Funds

EXHIBIT II
Balance Sheet

City of Centerville
Balance Sheet
June 30, 19X5

ASSETS
Current assets
Cash	$20,000
Accounts receivable	40,000
Allowance for doubtful accounts	(10,000)
Due from other funds	25,000
Inventory	5,000
Other current assets	15,000
Total current assets	95,000

Restricted assets
Cash on deposit	30,000
Investments	60,000
Accounts receivable	10,000
Sinking fund	100,000
Interest receivable	10,000
Total restricted assets	210,000

Property, plant, and equipment
Land	200,000
Buildings	360,000
Equipment	90,000
Under construction	15,000
	665,000
Less accumulated depreciation	140,000
Net property, plant, and equipment	525,000
Total assets	$830,000

LIABILITIES AND FUND EQUITY
Current liabilities
Accounts payable	$10,000
Vouchers payable	5,000
Notes payable	10,000
Due to other funds	30,000
Accrued expenses	20,000
Deferred revenues	5,000
Total current liabilities	80,000

Long-term liabilities
    General obligation bonds   200,000
    Revenue bonds   90,000
    Mortgage notes payable   60,000
        Total long-term liabilities   350,000
Fund equity
    Contributed capital—municipality   200,000
    Contributed capital—others   100,000
        Total contributed capital   300,000
    Retained earnings—reserved for debt service   25,000
    Retained earnings—unreserved   75,000
        Total retained earnings   100,000
            Total equity   400,000
                Total liabilities and fund equity $830,000

Statement of Changes in Financial Position

All proprietary funds should present a Statement of Changes in Financial Position, and the guidelines established by APB-19 (Reporting Changes in Financial Position) should be observed. The statement should summarize the financing and investing activities of the fund and may utilize whatever format is considered to be most informative.

The following items should be disclosed in the Statement of Changes in Financial Position:

- Funds provided from (or used by) operations
- The effects of extraordinary items
- Outlays for purchase of long-term assets (identifying separately such items as investments, property, and intangibles)
- Proceeds from sale (or working capital or cash provided by sale) of long-term assets (identifying separately such items as investments, property, and intangibles) not occurring in the normal course of business, less related expenses involving the current uses of working capital or cash
- Conversion of long-term debt or preferred stock to common stock (or contributed capital)
- Issuance, assumption, redemption, and repayment of long-term debt
- Dividends in cash or in kind or other distributions to shareholders (or capital contributors)

Generally, funds from operations are defined as cash, cash and temporary investments, all quick assets, or working capital. Irrespective of the definition of funds, the net changes in each element of working capital must be disclosed in the Statement of Changes in Financial Position or in a related tabulation.

An example of a Statement of Changes in Financial Position for an Enterprise Fund is presented in Exhibit III.

Combining Financial Statements

When there is more than one Internal Service Fund, combining financial statements for all Internal Service Funds must be prepared. Likewise, when there is more than one Enterprise Fund, combining financial statements for all Enterprise Funds must be prepared. All of the funds' individual statements are presented in a columnar format with a total column. The amounts shown in the total column for all Internal Service Funds and in the total column for all Enterprise Funds must agree, respectively, with the amount presented for each fund in the combined financial statements of the governmental reporting entity.

The combining balance sheet for all Internal Service Funds and the combining balance sheet for all Enterprise Funds will be incorporated into the Combined Balance Sheet—All Fund Types and Account Groups. The combining statements of operations for all Internal Service Funds and the combining statements of operations for all Enterprise Funds will be incorporated into the Combined Statement of Revenues, Expenses, and Changes in Retained Earnings (or Equity)—All Proprietary Fund Types. The combining statements of changes in financial position for all Internal Service Funds and the combining statements of changes in financial position for all Enterprise Funds will be incorporated into the Combined Statement of Changes in Financial Position—All Proprietary Fund Types.

Segment Information—Enterprise Funds

Enterprise Funds are somewhat different from other governmental funds in that they may be evaluated in much the same manner that a commercial enterprise is evaluated. To a certain extent an Enterprise Fund is more likely to be viewed as a separate entity rather than as a component of the overall governmental unit. For this reason, NCGA Interpretation-2 (Segment Information for Enterprise Funds)

Proprietary Funds

EXHIBIT III
Statement of Changes in Financial Position

City of Centerville
Statement of Changes in Financial Position
Centerville Airport
For Year Ended June 30, 19X5

Sources of working capital	
Operations	
Net income (loss)	$ 40,000
Items not requiring working capital	
Depreciation	35,000
Working capital from operations	75,000
Other sources	
Capital contributions	30,000
Proceeds of bond issues	25,000
Other	10,000
Total sources	140,000
Applications of working capital	
Purchase of property, plant, and equipment	45,000
Retirement of debt	25,000
Acquisition of investments	30,000
Other	30,000
Total applications	130,000
Net increase (decrease) in working capital	$ 10,000

Elements of net increase (decrease) in working capital

Cash	$ 5,000
Accounts receivable (net)	10,000
Due from other funds	15,000
Inventory	—
Other current assets	(10,000)
Accounts payable	5,000
Vouchers payable	—
Notes payable	—
Due to other funds	(5,000)
Accrued expenses	(5,000)
Deferred revenues	(5,000)
Net increase (decrease) in working capital	$10,000

GOVERNMENTAL GAAP GUIDE / **64.41**

was issued to identify those Enterprise Funds that must report certain segment information.

> **OBSERVATION:** *NCGA Interpretation-2 is not an interpretation of FASB-14 (Financial Reporting for Segments of a Business Enterprise). The term segment in a governmental reporting context simply means an Enterprise Fund of a state or local government. In effect, the Interpretation mandates a minimum level of disclosure for each Enterprise Fund in a reporting entity's general purpose financial statements.*

Segment information for an Enterprise Fund must be disclosed if one or more of the following conditions exists:

- Outstanding long-term debt
- Adequate disclosure essential (see following discussion)
- Interperiod comparability essential (see following discussion)

These three conditions should be evaluated in the context of materiality. FASB:CS-2 (Qualitative Characteristics of Accounting Information) describes materiality as follows:

> The omission or misstatement of an item in a financial report is material if, in the light of surrounding circumstances, the magnitude of the item is such that it is probable that the judgment of a reasonable person relying upon the report would have been changed or influenced by the inclusion or correction of the item.

Materiality for the purpose of determining segment information disclosure requirements is evaluated by referring to the quantitative and qualitative characteristics of the individual Enterprise Fund and not to Enterprise Fund types taken as a whole.

Outstanding Long-Term Debt An Enterprise Fund may issue debt securities that carry the full faith and credit of the state or local government, or securities that are backed only by the earnings of the fund. In addition, an Enterprise Fund may incur other long-term debts such as liabilities arising from capital leases, claims and judgments, and pension plans. When an Enterprise Fund has material long-term liabilities outstanding, segment information should be disclosed.

Adequate disclosure essential   NCGA Interpretation-2 concludes that a major nonhomogeneous Enterprise Fund must disclose segment information to assure that the general purpose financial statements are not misleading. The more diverse the activities of an Enterprise Fund, the more difficult it is to gain an understanding of an Enterprise Fund through the review of the governmental unit's financial statements. The disclosure of segment information should enhance the analysis of a nonhomogeneous Enterprise Fund.

In a more general vein, segment information disclosures should be made "if such disclosures are necessary to make the general purpose financial statements not misleading." Obviously, this guideline is extremely judgmental, and NCGA Interpretation-2 concludes that this requirement may be satisfied by having governmental officials review the financial statements to determine whether, to the best of their knowledge, any material facts have been omitted. Situations that would require the disclosure of segment information in order to not omit material facts include the following:

- Material intergovernmental operating subsidies to an Enterprise Fund
- Material intragovernmental operating subsidies to or from an Enterprise Fund
- Material Enterprise Fund tax revenues
- Material Enterprise Fund operating income or loss
- Material Enterprise Fund net income or loss

This list is illustrative rather than exhaustive.

Interperiod comparability essential   After applying the criteria described above, it may be concluded that segment information for a particular Enterprise Fund is not necessary. It should be recalled that financial information is more useful when it is presented over a period of time rather than for a single period, or sporadically. Thus, it may be necessary to disclose segment information for an Enterprise Fund because the information has been provided in prior years and/or is likely to be provided in future years.

Minimum Disclosures   When it is concluded that an individual Enterprise Fund should report segment information, at a minimum the following disclosures should be made:

Proprietary Funds

- Types of goods or services provided
- Operating revenues (total revenues from sales of goods or services)(Sales to other funds of the government, if material, should be separately disclosed.)
- Depreciation, depletion, and amortization expense
- Operating income or loss (operating revenues less operating expenses)
- Operating grants, entitlements, and shared revenues
- Interfund operating transfers in and out
- Tax revenues
- Net income or loss (total revenues less total expenses)
- Current capital contributions and transfers
- Property, plant, and equipment additions and deletions
- Net working capital (current assets less current liabilities)
- Total assets
- Bonds and other material long-term liabilities outstanding. (Amounts payable solely from operating revenues should be disclosed separately from amounts also potentially payable from other sources.)
- Total equity

In addition to the above items, the segment information should include any other material facts considered necessary to "make the general purpose financial statements not misleading."

Presentation of Segment Information Segment information is an integral part of the general purpose financial statements, and this assertion must be emphasized by the method of presentation.

Preferably, segment information should be disclosed in a note to the general purpose financial statements. Each financial statement should be marked to acknowledge that accompanying notes to the financial statements are an integral part of the statements. An example of segment information disclosed in a note to the financial statements is presented in Exhibit IV.

An alternative method of presentation is to present some of the disclosures in the following financial statements that compose the set of general purpose financial statements:

- Individual Enterprise Fund statements as columns in the Combined Statement of Revenues, Expenses, and Changes in Retained Earnings (or Equity)—All Proprietary Fund Types, and

Proprietary Funds

EXHIBIT IV

Segment Information Disclosures Made as Part of a Note to the General Purpose Financial Statements

NOTE X: Segment Information for Enterprise Funds

The following Enterprise Funds have been created to provide various services to the general public:

Airport Fund—established to account for the operation of the City of Centerville Airport.

Water System Fund—established to account for the operation of the City's water system.

Landfill Fund—established to account for the operation of the City's waste disposal activities.

Segment information for these Enterprise Funds is summarized below for the year ended, June 30, 19X5:

	Airport	Water system	Landfill
Operating revenues	$2,000,000	$3,500,000	$1,700,000
Depreciation	140,000	265,000	120,000
Operating income (loss)	104,000	75,000	(140,000)
Operating grants	—	—	95,000
Operating interfund transfers	—	—	100,000
Tax revenues	—	—	205,000
Net income (loss)	70,000	25,000	(126,000)
Current capital contributions	200,000	350,000	150,000
Property, plant, and equipment			
Additions	350,000	120,000	50,000
Dispositions	101,000	17,000	—
Net working capital	720,000	305,000	18,000
Total assets	3,450,000	7,800,000	405,000
Bonds and other long-term liabilities payable from operating revenues	1,200,000	4,500,000	—
Total equity	1,870,000	2,800,000	78,000

Proprietary Funds

> Combined Statement of Changes in Financial Position—All Proprietary Fund Types, or
- Combining Enterprise Fund Statement of Revenues, Expenses, and Changes in Retained Earnings (or Equity), and Combining Enterprise Fund Statement of Changes in Financial Position as part of the general purpose financial statements.

Disclosures that cannot be made in these financial statements should be included in a note to the general purpose financial statements.

Quasi-Governmental Enterprises

Public benefit corporations and authorities and governmental utilities that conduct business and quasi-business activities should observe commercial accounting principles except in those cases where the GASB or NCGA have addressed a specific accounting issue.

LITERATURE REFERENCES

Material in this chapter is based on the following authoritative pronouncements and publications which are grouped according to the major headings used within the chapter. A dual reference (both paragraph and page number) is used for NCGA-1 and NCGA-2 because the original pronouncements do not use paragraph numbers.

Basic Concepts and Standards
NCGA-1   *Governmental Accounting and Financial Reporting Principles*, p. 6/ ¶¶ 16 and 18.

Internal Service Fund
NCGA-1   *Governmental Accounting and Financial Reporting Principles*, pp. 7 and 8/¶¶ 26 and 30.
1980 GAAFR   *Governmental Accounting, Auditing, and Financial Reporting*, p. 66.

Enterprise Fund
NCGA-1   *Governmental Accounting and Financial Reporting Principles*, p. 7/ ¶ 26.
1980 GAAFR   *Governmental Accounting, Auditing, and Financial Reporting*, pp. 59-60.

Proprietary Funds

Basis of Accounting
NCGA-1   *Governmental Accounting and Financial Reporting Principles*, pp. 6 and 12/¶¶ 18 and 74.
FASB:CS-1   *Objectives of Financial Reporting by Business Enterprises*, ¶ 44.

Measurement Focus
NCGA-1   *Governmental Accounting and Financial Reporting Principles*, p. 6/ ¶ 18.
GASB Discussion Memorandum   *Measurement Focus and Basis of Accounting—Governmental Funds* (nonauthoritative).
NCGA-4   *Accounting and Financial Reporting Principles for Claims and Judgments and Compensated Absences*, ¶ 7.
AICPA Auditing Interpretation   *An Interpretation of SAS No. 5, The Meaning of "Present Fairly in Conformity with GAAP" in the Independent Auditor's Report*, December 1984.

Budgetary System and Accounts
NCGA-1   *Governmental Accounting and Financial Reporting Principles*, pp. 13 and 14/¶¶ 78, 82, and 94-97.

Revenues
FASB:CS-6   *Elements of Financial Statements*, ¶ 78.
FASB:CS-5   *Recognition and Measurement in Financial Statements of Business Enterprises*, ¶ 84.
APB Statement-4   *Basic Concepts and Accounting Principles Underlying Financial Statements of Business Enterprises*, ¶ 150.

Quasi-External Revenues
NCGA-1   *Governmental Accounting and Financial Reporting Principles*, p. 15/¶¶ 102 and 103.

Grants, Entitlements, and Shared Revenues
NCGA-2   *Grant, Entitlement, and Shared Revenue Accounting and Reporting by State and Local Governments*, pp. 1-3/¶¶ 2-17.
FASB:CS-5   *Recognition and Measurement in Financial Statements of Business Enterprises*, ¶ 65.

Classification and Disclosure
NCGA-1   *Governmental Accounting and Financial Reporting Principles*, pp. 5, 17, and 24/¶¶ 12, 13, 117, and 158.

Expenses
FASB:CS-6   *Elements of Financial Statements*, ¶ 80.

Proprietary Funds

FASB:CS-5 *Recognition and Measurement in Financial Statements of Business Enterprises,* ¶ 86.

APB STATEMENT-4 *Basic Concepts and Accounting Principles Underlying Financial Statements of Business Enterprises,* ¶¶ 157-160 and 181.

Quasi-External Expenses
NCGA-1 *Governmental Accounting and Financial Reporting Principles,* p. 15/¶¶ 102 and 103.

Depreciation Expense
NCGA-1 *Governmental Accounting and Financial Reporting Principles,* pp. 8 and 10/¶¶ 35, 51, and 52.
NCGA-2 *Grant, Entitlement, and Shared Revenue Accounting and Reporting by State and Local Governments,* p. 3/¶ 18.

Classification and Disclosure
NCGA-1 *Governmental Accounting and Financial Reporting Principles,* p. 17/¶ 117.

Assets
NCGA-1 *Governmental Accounting and Financial Reporting Principles,* pp. 8 and 10/¶¶ 32-35 and 49-50.
FASB:CS-6 *Elements of Financial Statements,* ¶¶ 25 and 26.

Interest Capitalization
NCGA-1 *Governmental Accounting and Financial Reporting Principles,* pp. 9 and 10/¶ 48.
FASB-34 *Capitalization of Interest Cost,* ¶¶ 9, 10, and 17.
FASB-42 *Determining Materiality for Capitalization of Interest Cost,* ¶ 4.
FASB-58 *Capitalization of Interest Cost in Financial Statements that Include Investments Accounted for by the Equity Method,* ¶¶ 5 and 6.
FASB-62 *Capitalization of Interest Cost in Situations Involving Certain Tax-Exempt Borrowings and Certain Gifts and Grants,* ¶¶ 4 and 5.

Leased Property
NCGA-5 *Accounting and Financial Reporting Principles for Lease Agreements of State and Local Governments,* ¶ 16.
FASB-13 *Accounting for Leases,* as amended, ¶¶ 7 and 8.

Joint Ventures
NCGA-7 *Financial Reporting for Component Units Within the Governmental Reporting Entity,* ¶¶ 27 and 28.

APB-18   *The Equity Method of Accounting for Investments in Common Stock,* ¶¶ 6b and 11.
APB-18 ACCOUNTING INTERPRETATION   *Investments in Partnerships and Unincorporated Ventures,* Question #2.

Classification and Disclosure
NCGA-1   *Governmental Accounting and Financial Reporting Principles,* p. 6/ ¶ 18.
NCGA-7   *Financial Reporting for Component Units Within the Governmental Reporting Entity,* ¶ 29.

Liabilities
NCGA-1   *Governmental Accounting and Financial Reporting Principles,* pp. 8 and 9/¶¶ 32, 33, 42, and 46.
FASB:CS-6   *Elements of Financial Statements,* ¶¶ 35 and 36.

Self-Insurance Internal Service Fund
NCGA-4   *Accounting and Financial Reporting Principles for Claims and Judgments and Compensated Absences,* ¶¶ 20 and 21.
NCGA INTERPRETATION-11   *Claims and Judgment Transactions for Governmental Funds,* ¶¶ 5 and 6.
FASB-5   *Accounting for Contingencies,* ¶ 8.

Classification and Disclosure
NCGA-1   *Governmental Accounting and Financial Reporting Principles,* p. 6/ ¶ 18.

Interfund Transactions
NCGA-1   *Governmental Accounting and Financial Reporting Principles,* pp. 15 and 16/¶¶ 101-104.

Operating Transfers
NCGA-1   *Governmental Accounting and Financial Reporting Principles,* pp. 12, 15, and 16/¶¶ 75, 102, 105, and 106.

Residual Equity Transfers
NCGA-1   *Governmental Accounting and Financial Reporting Principles,* p. 15/ ¶ 105.

Classification and Disclosure
NCGA-1   *Governmental Accounting and Financial Reporting Principles,* p. 22/ ¶¶ 145 and 147.

Proprietary Funds

Financial Statements
NCGA-1   *Governmental Accounting and Financial Reporting Principles*, p. 20/ ¶ 141.
GASB-1   *Authoritative Status of NCGA Pronouncements and AICPA Industry Audit Guide*, Appendix B, pp. 8 and 9.

Statement of Revenues and Expenses
NCGA-1   *Governmental Accounting and Financial Reporting Principles*, pp. 22 and 23/¶¶ 149 and 151.
APB-20   *Accounting Changes*, ¶¶ 18-30.
APB-30   *Reporting the Results of Operations*, ¶¶ 19-24.

Statement of Changes in Retained Earnings
NCGA-1   *Governmental Accounting and Financial Reporting Principles*, p. 23/ ¶ 152.
APB-12   *Omnibus Opinion—1967*, ¶ 10.

Balance Sheet
NCGA-1   *Governmental Accounting and Financial Reporting Principles*, p. 22/¶ 145.

Statement of Changes in Financial Position
NCGA-1   *Governmental Accounting and Financial Reporting Principles*, p. 24/ ¶ 156.
APB-19   *Reporting Changes in Financial Position*, ¶¶ 10-14.

Combining Financial Statements
NCGA-1   *Governmental Accounting and Financial Reporting Principles*, p. 21/ ¶ 141.

Segment Information—Enterprise Funds
NCGA Interpretation-2   *Segment Information for Enterprise Funds*, ¶¶ 3-8.
FASB:CS-2   *Qualitative Characteristics of Accounting Information*, ¶ 132.

FIDUCIARY FUNDS

Fiduciary Funds are used to account for assets when a governmental unit is functioning either as a trustee or an agent for another party. Because the governmental unit is functioning in a fiduciary capacity, the authority to employ, dispose of, or otherwise use the assets is determined not by a legislative body or oversight board but by the public laws and private agreements that created the trustee or agency relationship.

NCGA-1 (Governmental Accounting and Financial Reporting Principles) classifies Fiduciary Funds in the following manner:

- Expendable Trust Funds
- Nonexpendable Trust Funds
- Agency Funds
- Pension Trust Funds

Accounting and reporting standards for Pension Trust Funds are discussed in Chapter 66. The other three Fiduciary Funds are discussed in this chapter.

Expendable Trust Funds

When the objectives of a Trust Fund can be achieved by spending both the principal and the earnings of the fund, the fund is referred to as an Expendable Trust Fund. An Expendable Trust Fund is accounted for in the same manner as governmental funds, such as the General Fund. The basis of accounting is the modified accrual basis, and the measurement focus is essentially the flow of current financial resources. Generally, there is no need to have budgetary account integration for an Expendable Trust Fund; however, NCGA-1 notes that this may be necessary when the fund is similar to a Special Revenue Fund.

Revenues and Other Sources of Financing The initial creation of an Expendable Trust Fund is treated as an equity transaction, and revenue is not recorded. For example, if $500,000 of securities is given by

Fiduciary Funds

a citizen to pay for educational expenses of needy students, the following entry would be made in the Expendable Trust Fund (Scholarship Fund):

Investments In Securities	500,000	
Fund Balance		500,000

Revenues are recognized in an Expendable Trust Fund when they are both measurable and available. *Measurable* means that the revenue is subject to reasonable estimation. *Available* means that the financial resources related to revenue can be used to finance current expenditures of the fund. Sources of revenues for Expendable Trust Funds may include income from investments, grants, and gifts.

An Expendable Trust Fund may finance its operating expenditures, at least in part, by transfers from other governmental funds. These interfund transfers are not recorded as revenue but as other sources of financing. In the current example, the Scholarship Fund may have been created with the understanding that the governmental unit would annually transfer a certain amount to the Scholarship Fund. If the General Fund makes its annual transfer of $25,000, the transfer would be recorded as follows:

GENERAL FUND
Transfers Out—Scholarship Fund	25,000	
Cash		25,000

SCHOLARSHIP FUND
Cash	25,000	
Transfers In—General Fund		25,000

Expenditures An Expendable Trust Fund's expenditures represent decreases in the fund's financial resources and are recognized when the related liabilities are incurred (modified accrual basis). The trust agreement identifies the types of expenditures that may be incurred. For this reason, the expenditure classification scheme is generally simple for an Expendable Trust Fund. Most of the expenditures are classified by function (or program), although other classification schemes (organization unit, activity, character, and object class) may be employed to facilitate internal and external analysis and reporting.

To control expenditures of an Expendable Trust Fund, an encumbrance system should be employed. An encumbrance represents commitments related to unperformed contracts for goods and services; however, the encumbrance does not represent an expenditure.

for the period. The issuance of a purchase order or the signing of a contract would create an encumbrance. At the end of the period, unvouchered encumbrances must be closed and the Fund Balance reserved by the amount of the outstanding encumbrance.

Assets For the most part, an Expendable Trust Fund's assets include those financial resources that are available to finance current expenditures of the fund. These financial resources may include such items as cash, short-term investments, interfund receivables, and accrued interest income. Fixed assets of an Expendable Trust Fund should be reported as a fund asset rather than in the General Fixed Assets Account Group even though they are not available to finance current expenditures of the fund. Most Expendable Trust Funds would not have fixed assets.

> **OBSERVATION:** *There is an inconsistency in the standards with respect to fixed assets and long-term liabilities of an Expendable Trust Fund. Fixed assets and long-term liabilities are both reported in the Expendable Trust Fund rather than in the governmental entity's Account Groups even though they do not represent expendable resources or claims against current expendable resources.*

Because assets of an Expendable Trust Fund are accounted for in the same manner as other governmental funds (General Fund, Special Revenue Fund, Capital Projects Fund, and Debt Services Fund), there are assets available to the fund that are not currently expendable, but nonetheless are reported on the fund's balance sheet. These assets are briefly described below.

Materials and supplies Inventory items, such as materials and supplies, are not expendable financial resources, but when they are significant they must be reported as a fund asset. Inventories may be accounted for using either the consumption method or the purchase method. Under both methods, the fund balance at the end of the year must be reserved by an amount equal to the reported inventories.

Prepayments and deferrals Prepaid items and deferrals may include such items as prepaid expenses, deposits, and deferred charges. Either the allocation method or the nonallocation method may be used to account for prepayments and deferrals. When the allocation method is used, the balance in the prepayment or deferral account at the end of the period is reported as a fund asset.

Fiduciary Funds

Investments   An Expendable Trust Fund may hold investments that are long-term in nature. Although investments are not expected to be liquidated to finance current expenditures, they are nonetheless listed as assets of the fund. Because the fund balance of an Expendable Trust Fund is usually identified as either reserved or designated for the purpose of the fund, the presentation of a long-term investment as a fund asset is not misleading.

Escheat property   Property that escheats to a state or local government should be accounted for in either an Expendable Trust Fund or the governmental fund that is eventually entitled to the property. If escheat property represents expendable financial resources, it should be recognized as other sources of financial resources when the property becomes measurable and available. On the other hand, if a governmental unit is required to hold the escheat property in perpetuity for its owners, a fund balance reserve must be established.

Liabilities   As noted earlier, the measurement focus of an Expendable Trust Fund is the flow of current financial resources. Liabilities that will consume expendable financial resources during the fiscal period are classified as liabilities of the fund. Due to the nature of an Expendable Trust Fund, its financial statements generally include only current liabilities such as accounts payable, accrued expenses, deferred revenues, and amounts due to other governmental funds.

Financial Statements   The financial statements of an Expendable Trust Fund are included in the governmental unit's general purpose financial statements and Comprehensive Annual Financial Report, and should include the following:

- Statement of Revenues, Expenditures, and Changes in Fund Balance
- Balance Sheet
- Schedules necessary to demonstrate compliance with finance-related legal and contractual provisions

If an Expendable Trust Fund legally adopts an annual budget, a Statement of Revenues, Expenditures, and Changes in Fund Balance—Budget and Actual—should be prepared.

When there is more than one Expendable Trust Fund, combining financial statements for all of the funds must be prepared. All of the Expendable Trust Funds' individual statements are presented in a columnar format with a total column. The amounts shown in the

Fiduciary Funds

total column must agree with the amounts presented in the combined financial statements of the governmental reporting entity.

To illustrate the accounting for an Expendable Trust Fund and the subsequent preparation of fund financial statements, assume that the following transactions occurred and were journalized during the fiscal year ended June 30, 19X5:

Transaction: An Education Trust Fund is established whereby an anonymous citizen and the City of Centerville each agree to contribute $2,000,000 to the fund. In addition, the citizen agrees to give at least $100,000 each year for the next five years and the City agrees to make an annual contribution of $50,000 for the next ten years. The trust agreement is signed and both parties transfer their initial contributions to the fund.

GENERAL FUND
Residual Equity Transfer
  (Fund Balance)   2,000,000
    Cash   2,000,000

EDUCATION TRUST FUND
Cash   4,000,000
  Fund Balance—Reserved For
    Educational Expenditures   4,000,000

Transaction: The City makes its annual operating transfer to the fund.

GENERAL FUND
Transfers Out—Education Trust Fund   50,000
  Cash   50,000

EDUCATION TRUST FUND
Cash   50,000
  Transfers In—General Fund   50,000

Transaction: The anonymous citizen makes her annual transfer of $100,000.

EDUCATION TRUST FUND
Cash   100,000
  Revenues—Donations   100,000

Transaction: Investments of $3,500,000 are made by the Education Trust Fund.

Fiduciary Funds

EDUCATION TRUST FUND
Investments   3,500,000
    Cash   3,500,000

Transaction: During the fiscal year, scholarship payments for $700,000 are awarded to qualifying students.

EDUCATION TRUST FUND
Encumbrances   700,000
    Reserve For Encumbrances   700,000

Transaction: During the fiscal year encumbrances of $680,000 are vouchered as follows (actual cost exceeded encumbrances by $3,000):

Tuition and fees	$380,000
Room and board	260,000
Books and materials	39,000
Other	4,000
Total vouchered	$683,000

EDUCATION TRUST FUND
Reserve For Encumbrances   680,000
    Encumbrances   680,000

Expenditures—Tuition And Fees   380,000
Expenditures—Room And Board   260,000
Expenditures—Books And Materials   39,000
Expenditures—Other   4,000
    Vouchers Payable   683,000

Transaction: During the fiscal year, vouchers of $670,000 are paid.

EDUCATION TRUST FUND
Vouchers Payable   670,000
    Cash   670,000

Transaction: Investment income for the fiscal year was as follows:

Cash received	$275,000
Accrued at year-end (available and measurable)	22,000
Total earned	$297,000

Fiduciary Funds

EDUCATION TRUST FUND
Cash	275,000	
Investment Income Receivable	22,000	
Revenues—Investment Income		297,000

Transaction: On June 30, 19X5, the Education Trust Fund received an interfund bill for $2,000 from the City's Internal Service Fund for computer services utilized during the fiscal year. The fee is due ten days after the close of the period.

EDUCATION TRUST FUND
Expenditures—Administrative	2,000	
Due To Internal Service Fund		2,000

INTERNAL SERVICE FUND
Due From Education Trust Fund	2,000	
Revenues—Charges For Services		2,000

Closing Entry: Outstanding encumbrances are closed (appropriations are considered to be nonlapsing).

EDUCATION TRUST FUND
Fund Balance—Reserved For Educational Expenditures	20,000	
Encumbrances		20,000
Reserve For Encumbrances	20,000	
Fund Balance—Reserved For Encumbrances		20,000

Closing Entry: All nominal accounts are closed.

EDUCATION TRUST FUND
Revenues—Investment Income	297,000	
Revenues—Donations	100,000	
Transfers In—General Fund	50,000	
Fund Balance—Reserved For Educational Expenditures	238,000	
Expenditures—Tuition And Fees		380,000
Expenditures—Room And Board		260,000
Expenditures—Books And Materials		39,000
Expenditures—Other		4,000
Expenditures—Administrative		2,000

The financial statements for the Education Trust Fund are presented in Exhibit I.

Fiduciary Funds

EXHIBIT I

Education Trust Fund Financial Statements

City of Centerville
Statement of Revenues, Expenditures, and Changes in Fund Balance
Education Trust Fund
For Year Ended June 30, 19X5

Revenues	
Investment income	$ 297,000
Donations	100,000
Total revenues	397,000
Expenditures	
Tuitions and fees	380,000
Room and board	260,000
Books and materials	39,000
Administrative	2,000
Other	4,000
Total expenditures	685,000
Excess of revenues over (under) expenditures	(288,000)
Other financing sources (uses)	
Transfers in	50,000
Excess of revenues and other sources over (under) expenditures and other uses	(238,000)
(Increase) decrease in reserve for encumbrances	(20,000)
Net change in fund balance reserved for educational expenditures for year	(258,000)
Fund balance—reserved for educational expenditures, July 1, 19X4	-0-
Residual equity transfers from general fund	2,000,000
Initial contribution by benefactor	2,000,000
Fund balance—reserved for educational expenditures, June 30, 19X5	$3,742,000

City of Centerville
Balance Sheet
Education Trust Fund
June 30, 19X5

Assets	
Cash	$ 255,000
Investment income receivable	22,000
Investments	3,500,000
Total assets	$3,777,000

Liabilities
  Vouchers payable $ 13,000
  Due to internal service fund   2,000
    Total liabilities   15,000
Fund equity
  Fund balance reserved for encumbrances   20,000
  Fund balance reserved for educational expenditures   3,742,000
    Total fund balance   3,762,000
      Total liabilities and fund balance $3,777,000

Nonexpendable Trust Funds

An important objective of accounting for a Nonexpendable Trust Fund is to differentiate between the trust fund's principal and its earnings. The earnings of the trust fund may be used to achieve the objectives of the fund, while the principal must be preserved intact. NCGA-1 concludes that a Nonexpendable Trust Fund should be accounted for in essentially the same manner as a proprietary fund. Thus, the basis of accounting is the accrual basis, and the measurement focus is the flow of all economic resources for a Nonexpendable Trust Fund.

Revenues FASB:CS-6 (Elements of Financial Statements) defines *revenues* as "inflows or other enhancements of assets of an entity or settlements of its liabilities (or a combination of both) during a period from delivering or producing goods, rendering services, or other activities that constitute the entity's ongoing major or central operations." On the accrual basis, revenue should be recognized when (1) the earning process is complete or virtually complete and (2) an exchange has taken place. These broad revenue recognition criteria will be discussed as they apply to the somewhat unique context of a Nonexpendable Trust Fund.

Investment income The principal of a Nonexpendable Trust Fund may be used to acquire various long-term investments. These investments may include the purchase of debt securities and equity securities. Investments in debt securities such as bonds should be accounted for on a cost basis, and amounts representing discount or premium should be amortized to determine periodic interest income. The effective interest method should be used to account for bond discount or premium amortization. The accounting for invest-

Fiduciary Funds

ments in equity securities, such as common stock, depends upon the percentage of ownership held by the Nonexpendable Trust Fund. If the trust fund holds less than 20% of the voting stock, the *cost method* should be used to account for investment income. In addition, when the investment includes marketable equity securities, the lower of aggregate cost or market method as described in FASB-12 (Accounting for Certain Marketable Securities) should be used to measure income for the period. If the ownership percentage is 20% or more of the voting stock, the equity method as described in APB-18 (The Equity Method of Accounting for Investments in Common Stock) should be employed.

Grants, entitlements, and shared revenues NCGA-2 (Grant, Entitlement, and Shared Revenue Accounting by State and Local Governments) concludes that the accrual basis should be used to account for grants, entitlements, and shared revenues that are recorded in a Nonexpendable Trust Fund. The Statement provided the following definitions.

> *Grant*—A contribution or gift of cash or other assets from another government to be used or expended for a specified purpose, activity, or facility.
>
> *Operating grant*—Grants that are intended to finance operations or that may be used for either operations or for capital outlays at the discretion of the grantee.
>
> *Capital grant*—A contribution or gift of cash or other assets restricted by the grantor for the acquisition or construction of fixed (capital) assets.
>
> *Entitlement*—The amount of payment to which a state or local government is entitled as determined by the federal or other government (for example, the Director of the Office of Revenue Sharing) pursuant to an allocation formula contained in applicable statutes.
>
> *Shared revenue*—A revenue levied by one government but shared on a predetermined basis, often in proportion to the amount collected at the local level, with another government or class of government.

Because funds received from other governmental units are usually subject to various restrictions and conditions, the circumstances surrounding the grant, entitlement, or shared revenue must be evaluated to determine whether accrual revenue recognition criteria have been satisfied. Generally, grant conditions are satisfied when the trust fund incurs appropriate expenses as defined by the grant program. Initially, the receipt of the grant may be recorded as deferred revenue until appropriate expenses are incurred. At this point, the expense is recorded along with an equal amount of grant revenue. For the most part, entitlements and shared revenues are forfeited only when the trust fund does not follow regulations established under the program. For this reason, entitlements and shared revenues may be accrued before funds are actually received.

Grants, entitlements, and shared revenues received by a Nonexpendable Trust Fund should be reported as nonoperating revenue. When resources received through a grant, entitlement, or shared revenue are restricted to the acquisition or cost of capital assets, the receipt of the resources should be recorded as contributed equity and not as revenue.

Donations The initial contribution by the creator(s) of a Nonexpendable Trust Fund should be recorded as an addition to fund balance and not as revenue. If the trust fund is established by a transfer from another governmental fund, the donation is accounted for as a residual equity transfer and not as an operating transfer. Donations made in subsequent periods should be treated as operating revenues if received from external parties and as operating transfers if received from other governmental funds.

Expenses FASB:CS-6 defines *expenses* as "outflows or other using up of assets or incurrences of liabilities (or a combination of both) during a period from delivering or producing goods, rendering services, or carrying out other activities that constitute the entity's ongoing major or central operations." Expenses of a Nonexpendable Trust Fund are accounted for in the same manner as those of a proprietary fund. Thus, for the most part, expense recognition criteria and standards applicable to a commercial enterprise are equally applicable to a Nonexpendable Trust Fund.

There is an alternative depreciation presentation that is unique to Nonexpendable Trust Funds (and proprietary funds). All depreciable property of a Nonexpendable Trust Fund must be depreciated in accordance with generally accepted accounting principles, taking into consideration such factors as cost, salvage value, and estimated economic life. When depreciable property of a Nonexpendable Trust Fund has been financed by resources specifically made available for capital expenditures through grants, entitlements, or shared revenues, depreciation may be presented in either of the following ways:

Fiduciary Funds

- Depreciable property may be accounted for in a manner similar to reporting standards used by a commercial enterprise.
- Depreciation may be computed in the conventional manner but then closed directly to the Trust Fund's contributed capital account that was created when the restricted grant, entitlement, or shared revenue was received. On the Statement of Revenues and Expenses the depreciation expense is presented as an operating expense and is used to compute the fund's net income. Then, the depreciation expense is added to the net income figure to identify the net increase or decrease in retained earnings for the year.

Assets FASB:CS-6 defines assets as "probable future economic benefits obtained or controlled by a particular entity as a result of past transactions or events." A Nonexpendable Trust Fund's balance sheet should include all assets that are available to the fund, including fixed assets. The same accounting and reporting principles applicable to a commercial enterprise's assets are used to account for a Nonexpendable Trust Fund's assets.

Liabilities Liabilities are defined by FASB:CS-6 as "probable future sacrifices of economic benefits arising from present obligations of a particular entity to transfer assets or provide services to other entities in the future as a result of past transactions or events." A Nonexpendable Trust Fund should report all liabilities, both current and noncurrent, that are the responsibility of the trust fund.

Financial Statements The financial statements of a Nonexpendable Trust Fund are included in the reporting entity's general purpose financial statements and Comprehensive Annual Financial Report, and include the following:

- Statement of Revenues, Expenses, and Changes in Fund Equity
- Balance Sheet
- Statement of Changes in Financial Position
- Schedules necessary to demonstrate compliance with finance-related legal and contractual provisions

When there is more than one Nonexpendable Trust Fund, combining financial statements for all of the funds must be prepared. All of

Fiduciary Funds

the Nonexpendable Trust Funds' individual statements are presented in a columnar format with a total column. The amounts shown in the total column must agree with the amounts presented in the combined financial statements of the reporting entity.

To illustrate the accounting for a Nonexpendable Trust Fund and the subsequent preparation of fund financial statements, assume that the following transactions occurred and were journalized during the fiscal year ended June 30, 19X5. Because the principal must be preserved in a Nonexpendable Trust Fund, separate Trust Funds are created to account for the principal and the earnings of the fund in the following illustration:

Transaction: An anonymous citizen donates $500,000 to the City of Centerville to finance certain educational expenses of needy students. Based on the terms of the donation, only the earnings from the fund can be used to pay educational expenses. The City receives the $500,000 cash donation and establishes two separate Trust Funds—Educational Endowment Fund and Educational Earnings Fund—to account for fund transactions.

EDUCATIONAL ENDOWMENT FUND
Cash	500,000	
Fund Balance—Reserved For		
Endowments		500,000

Transaction: The following long-term investments are made:

8% bonds, face of $100,000, mature in 5 years	$ 95,000
9% bonds, face of $200,000, mature in 5 years	210,000
Marketable equity securities	180,000
Total investment	$485,000

EDUCATIONAL ENDOWMENT FUND
Investment In Bonds	305,000	
Investment In Marketable Equity		
Securities	180,000	
Cash		485,000

Transaction: During the fiscal year, cash flow from investments amounted to $26,000 for bond interest and $10,000 for dividends.

Fiduciary Funds

EDUCATIONAL ENDOWMENT FUND
Cash   36,000
   Interest Income   26,000
   Dividend Income   10,000

Transaction: On June 30, 19X5, the Educational Endowment Fund received an interfund bill for $1,000 from the City Internal Service Fund for legal and accounting services utilized during the fiscal year.

EDUCATIONAL ENDOWMENT FUND
Expenses—Administrative   1,000
   Due To Internal Service Fund   1,000

INTERNAL SERVICE FUND
Due From Educational Trust Fund   1,000
   Revenues—Charges For Services   1,000

Adjusting Entry: Dividends on investments declared but not received as of the end of the year amounted to $3,000.

EDUCATIONAL ENDOWMENT FUND
Dividends Receivable   3,000
   Dividend Income   3,000

Adjusting Entry: Amortization of bond premium and discount for the year were as follows (straight-line method is used because the results approximate the effective interest method):

   Premium: $10,000/5 years = $2,000
   Discount: $5,000/5 years = $1,000

EDUCATIONAL ENDOWMENT FUND
Interest Income   1,000
   Investment In Bonds   1,000

Adjusting Entry: The market value of the portfolio of marketable equity securities is $178,000.

EDUCATIONAL ENDOWMENT FUND
Unrealized Loss On Valuation Of
  Marketable Equity Securities
  (Fund Equity)   2,000
    Allowance For Valuation Of
      Marketable Equity Securities   2,000

Transaction: Earnings for the fiscal year ($37,000) are transferred from the Educational Endowment Fund to the Educational Earnings Fund.

EDUCATIONAL ENDOWMENT FUND
Transfers Out—Educational Earnings
  Fund   37,000
    Cash   37,000

EDUCATIONAL EARNINGS FUND
Cash   37,000
  Transfers In—Educational
    Endowment Fund   37,000

Transaction: During the fiscal year the following expenses are paid by the Educational Earnings Fund:

Tuition and fees	$18,000
Room and board	12,000
Books and materials	4,000
Other	2,000
Total expenses	$36,000

EDUCATIONAL EARNINGS FUND
Expenses—Tuition And Fees   18,000
Expenses—Room And Board   12,000
Expenses—Books And Material   4,000
Expenses—Other   2,000
  Cash   36,000

Closing Entry: All nominal accounts are closed.

Fiduciary Funds

EDUCATIONAL EARNINGS FUND
Transfers In—Educational Endowment
  Fund   37,000
    Expenses—Tuition And Fees   18,000
    Expenses—Room And Board   12,000
    Expenses—Books And Materials   4,000
    Expenses—Other   2,000
  Fund Balance—Reserved For
    Educational Expenses   1,000

EDUCATIONAL ENDOWMENT FUND
Interest Income   25,000
Dividend Income   13,000
  Expenses—Administrative   1,000
  Transfers Out—Educational Earnings
    Fund   37,000

The financial statements for the Educational Endowment Fund and the Educational Earnings Fund are presented in Exhibit II.

EXHIBIT II

Educational Endowment Fund and Educational Earnings Fund Financial Statements

City of Centerville
Statement of Revenues, Expenses, and Changes in Fund Balance
Educational Endowment Fund
Educational Earnings Fund
For Year Ended June 30, 19X5

	Educational endowment fund	*Educational earnings fund*	*Total*
Revenues			
Interest income	$ 25,000	—	$ 25,000
Dividend income	13,000	—	13,000
Total revenues	38,000	—	38,000
Expenses			
Tuition and fees	—	$ 18,000	18,000
Room and board	—	12,000	12,000
Books and materials	—	4,000	4,000
Other educational expenses	—	2,000	2,000
Administrative	1,000	—	1,000
Total expenses	1,000	36,000	37,000

Operating income before transfers	37,000	(36,000)	1,000
Transfers	(37,000)	37,000	—
Net income	—	1,000	1,000
Fund balance July 1, 19X4	—	—	—
Fund balance contribution during year	500,000	—	500,000
Fund balance—reserved for endowment, June 30, 19X5	500,000	—	
Fund balance—reserved for educational expenses, June 30, 19X5	—	1,000	
Total fund balances, June 30, 19X5	$500,000	$ 1,000	$501,000

Agency Funds

An Agency Fund is created to act as a custodian for other funds, governmental units, or private entities. Assets are recorded by the Agency Fund, held for a period of time as determined by legal contract or circumstances, and then returned to their owners. For example, an Agency Fund may be used to account for taxes collected by one governmental unit for another governmental unit. When the taxes are collected for the other governmental unit, the following entry would be made in the Agency Fund:

Cash	X	
Due To Other Governmental Unit		X

When the taxes are remitted to the other governmental unit as determined by state law or local ordinance, the following entry would be made in the Agency Fund:

Due To Other Governmental Unit	X	
Cash		X

Thus, the basic accounting procedures for an Agency Fund are simple.

The basis of accounting for an Agency Fund is the modified accrual basis. The measurement focus is custodial, since the fund is not involved with the performance of governmental services. An Agency Fund has no revenues or expenditures and therefore there is no fund

Fiduciary Funds

balance or need to measure the results of operations for a period. The custodial nature of an Agency Fund means that there is no need to adopt a budgetary accounting system.

An Agency Fund should be established only when it is legally mandated or when the creation of the fund enhances the operational efficiency or effectiveness of the governmental unit. For example, payroll deductions from gross earnings of governmental employees may be accounted for in an Agency Fund, but unless legally prohibited, the withholdings may be shown as a liability of the governmental fund that incurred the payroll expenditure.

Various custodial relationships may be the basis for the establishment of an Agency Fund. To illustrate the accounting for Agency Funds, the custodial function is discussed as it relates to the following Agency Fund:

- Pass Through Agency Fund
- Discretionary Agency Fund
- Dual Recording Agency Fund

Pass Through Agency Fund Grants, entitlements, or shared revenues may be received and/or spent by one governmental unit or fund on behalf of another governmental unit or fund (secondary recipient). Under this circumstance the receipts of the resources and subsequent accounting for the resources should be made in an Agency Fund. An Agency Fund may simply function as a conduit for the resources, or it may be responsible for the expenditure of resources. In the latter circumstance the Agency Fund's financial statements do not reflect operating accounts. NCGA-2 concludes that "pass through resources should be reported as revenues or contributed capital and as expenditures or expenses, as appropriate, by the secondary recipient."

To illustrate, assume that a $500,000 capital grant is received by a county. Based on the terms of the capital grant, the resources are to be used to partially finance the construction of a capital asset by three municipalities located in the county. The resources, as required by the grant, must be accounted for by the county. The county establishes a Pass Through Agency Fund and records the following transactions during the current fiscal year. The three municipalities account for the construction of the capital asset in a Capital Projects Fund.

Transaction: The county receives the $500,000 capital grant.

Fiduciary Funds

PASS THROUGH AGENCY FUND (COUNTY)
  Cash   500,000
    Due To Municipalities Under Capital
      Grants Program   500,000

Transaction: During the fiscal year, expenditures of $375,000 are paid.

PASS THROUGH AGENCY FUND (COUNTY)
  Expenditures—Capital Outlays   375,000
    Cash   375,000

At the end of the fiscal year, the Pass Through Agency Fund's financial statements cannot reflect operating accounts, therefore, the following entries would be made:

PASS THROUGH AGENCY FUND (COUNTY)
  Due To Municipalities Under Capital
    Grant Program   375,000
      Expenditures—Capital Outlays   375,000

CAPITAL PROJECTS FUND (MUNICIPALITIES COMBINED)
  Expenditures—Capital Outlays   375,000
    Revenues—Capital Grants   375,000

At the end of the period, the Pass Through Agency Fund's financial statement shows only cash of $125,000 and the related liability to the three municipalities, while the three Capital Projects Funds of the municipalities reflect the amount of revenue earned and expenditures incurred during the period.

Discretionary Agency Fund   Resources received through grants, entitlements, or shared revenues may be distributed to two or more funds at the discretion of the governmental unit. The receipt of these discretionary resources should be recorded initially in an Agency Fund. Subsequently, when specific funds are selected for receipt of the resources, appropriate entries should be made in the recipient funds. For example, if a municipality receives a $2,000,000 capital grant from a state government for flood control, but the resources are expected to be used by various funds, the initial receipt of the resources would be recorded as follows:

Fiduciary Funds

DISCRETIONARY AGENCY FUND
Cash   2,000,000
  Due To Undesignated Funds Under
    State Flood Control Program   2,000,000

Later, when it is decided that the resources are to be distributed to a Capital Projects Fund ($1,500,000) and an Enterprise Fund ($500,000), the following entries would be made:

DISCRETIONARY AGENCY FUND
Due To Undesignated Funds Under
  State Flood Control Program   2,000,000
    Cash   2,000,000

CAPITAL PROJECTS FUND
Cash   1,500,000
  Revenues—Capital Grants   1,500,000

ENTERPRISE FUND
Cash   500,000
  Contributed Capital—Capital Grants   500,000

Assets held by a Discretionary Agency Fund at the end of a fiscal year that have not been assigned to a specific fund should be disclosed in notes to the financial statements.

> **OBSERVATION:** *The preceding requirement in NCGA-2 that assets in the Discretionary Agency Fund be disclosed in a note to the financial statements is somewhat confusing. Presumably, the assets should either be reported in the Discretionary Agency Fund's financial statement or in a note to the financial statements, but not both.*

Dual Recording Agency Fund NCGA-2 notes that it may be appropriate to account for operating transactions in an Agency Fund when a governmental unit receives certain grants, entitlements, or special revenues. This approach may be necessary to facilitate the preparation of special reports or to provide an audit trail.

The fundamental rule that operating accounts are not reflected in the financial statements of an Agency Fund is observed by using dual recording procedures. The primary set of entries is booked to discharge the Agency Fund's custodial responsibility, and memorandum entries are made to record the operating transactions. Later, the memorandum entries are used to make appropriate entries in the fund(s) that would have accounted for the resources under normal circumstances.

To illustrate the dual approach, assume that an operating grant of $400,000 is received by a local government and the grant is to be used to finance expenditures of a Capital Projects Fund ($300,000) and a Special Revenue Fund ($100,000). Under the terms of the grant, the resources must be accounted for in a single Agency Fund. The receipt of the operating grant would be recorded as follows (assuming an operating grant is not recorded as revenue until an appropriate expenditure is incurred):

DUAL RECORDING AGENCY FUND
Cash	400,000	
Due To Capital Projects Fund—		
Operating Grant		300,000
Due To Special Revenue Fund—		
Operating Grant		100,000

During the fiscal year, expenditures of $240,000 for the Capital Projects Fund and $80,000 for the Special Revenue Fund (payroll) are made and recorded as follows:

DUAL RECORDING AGENCY FUND
Due To Capital Projects Fund—Operating Grant	240,000	
Due To Special Revenue Fund—		
Operating Grant	80,000	
Cash		320,000

Memorandum Entry For Capital Projects Fund:
Expenditures—Capital Outlays	240,000	
Revenues—Operating Grants		240,000

Memorandum Entry For Special Revenue Fund:
Expenditures—Personnel	80,000	
Revenues—Operating Grants		80,000

Memorandum entries are for informational purposes only and are not reflected in the financial statements of the Agency Fund.

At the end of the fiscal year appropriate reports would be sent to the Capital Projects Fund and Special Revenue Fund, disclosing expenditures paid from the (Dual Recording) Agency Fund. Upon receipt of the report in the current example, the following entries would be made:

Fiduciary Funds

CAPITAL PROJECTS FUND
   Expenditures—Capital Outlays   240,000
      Revenues—Operating Grants   240,000

SPECIAL REVENUE FUND
   Expenditures—Personnel   80,000
      Revenue—Operating Grants   80,000

In addition, the capital asset accounted for in the Capital Projects Fund would have to be reflected in the General Fixed Assets Account Group.

Financial Statement

As suggested earlier, due to the custodial nature of an Agency Fund, no operating statement is prepared for the fund. A Statement of Changes in Assets and Liabilities should be prepared for an Agency Fund. An example of the Statement is presented in Exhibit III.

EXHIBIT III

Statement of Changes in Assets and Liabilities

City of Centerville
Statement of Changes in Assets and Liabilities
(Dual Recording) Agency Fund
For Year Ended June 30, 19X5

	Balance 7/1/X4	Additions	Deductions	Balance 6/30/X5
Assets				
Cash	$ 0	$400,000	$320,000	$80,000
Liabilities				
Due to capital projects fund	$ 0	$300,000	$240,000	$60,000
Due to special revenue fund	0	100,000	80,000	20,000
Total liabilities	$ 0	$400,000	$320,000	$80,000

When there is more than one Agency Fund, a Combining Statement of Changes in Assets and Liabilities must be prepared.

IRC Section 457 Deferred Compensation Plans Section 457(a) of the Internal Revenue Code reads as follows:

> In the case of a participant in an eligible State deferred compensation plan, any amount of compensation deferred under the plan, and any income attributable to the amounts so deferred, shall be includible in gross income only for the taxable year in which such compensation or other income is paid or otherwise made available to the participant or other beneficiary.

The term *State* in the above definition means a State, a political subdivision of a State, and an agency or instrumentality of a State, or political subdivision of a State.

IRC Section 457 deferred compensation plans may be administered by an independent plan administrator, or the governmental entity may administer the plan. The assets that represent the deferred compensation amounts and the related earnings legally belong to the employer. The plan administrator has a fiduciary responsibility to administer the plan; however, the participants in the plan generally assume the risk for losses that might arise from investments made by the plan administrator, assuming the administrator exercised due care in making the investments.

Participants in the plan and their beneficiaries do not have access to the assets until amounts are due and payable as specified in the plan agreement. Legally, the assets that represent the deferred compensation amounts and related earnings are accessible by the governmental entity and by its general creditors. If the assets and related earnings are placed in a trust or otherwise insulated so that the governmental entity or its general creditors are denied access to the resources, the deferred compensation amounts and related earnings are considered to be income to the participants and subject to taxation.

Compensation deferred under Section 457 presents a financial reporting problem for a governmental entity in that while the entity *owns* the related assets, it also has an obligation to pay participants their share of the assets at a later date. This financial reporting problem was addressed in GASB-2 (Financial Reporting of Deferred Compensation Plans Adopted under the Provisions of Internal Revenue Code Section 457). GASB-2 applies only to IRC Section 457 deferred compensation plans.

Depending upon the circumstances, the resources and obligations arising from an IRC Section 457 deferred compensation plan may be reported in an Agency Fund or as part of a proprietary fund.

Fiduciary Funds

Agency fund reporting The GASB concluded that rights and obligations related to an IRC Section 457 deferred compensation plan should be accounted for in an Agency Fund of the governmental employer that uses fund accounting and has legal access to the resources. The assets related to the plan itself may be held by a public employee retirement system (PERS), the governmental employer, a nongovernmental third party, or another governmental entity under a multiple-jurisdictional plan.

The Agency Fund would display assets held by the plan and obligations under the plan agreement. These two amounts would be stated at the same amount and consistent with the concept of an Agency Fund; no fund balance account would be presented. This presentation format emphasizes the fiduciary responsibility assumed by the governmental entity with respect to the participants and also discloses the economic substance of the deferred compensation plan. The economic substance recognizes that while the governmental unit has access to the plan assets, there is an obligation to make future payment to employees or their beneficiaries.

> **OBSERVATION:** *The GASB rejected the argument that IRC Section 457 deferred compensation plans be accounted for in a Trust Fund because the commitments to employees are better described as a liability rather than as equity (fund balance) of a fiduciary fund.*

To illustrate the basic entries related to an IRC Section 457 deferred compensation plan, assume that a governmental unit recognizes payroll expenditures of $700,000, of which $50,000 is deferred under the deferred compensation plan. The plan is administered by an insurance company (nongovernmental third party) and plan benefits are immediately funded. If it is assumed that the payroll expenditure is recorded in the governmental unit's General Fund, the following entries would be made:

AGENCY FUND
Property And Rights Held Under Deferred Compensation Plan	50,000	
Obligations To Employees Under Deferred Compensation Plan		50,000

GENERAL FUND
Expenditures—Payroll	700,000	
Accrued Payroll		700,000

Fiduciary Funds

Accrued Payroll	700,000	
Cash (Payment to Plan Administrator)		50,000
Cash (Payment To Employees—Net Payroll)		500,000
Liabilities (Various Liabilities For Payroll Deductions)		150,000

The cash received by the insurance company is not recorded by the governmental entity, because the plan administrator is not part of the governmental reporting entity.

Generally the plan administrator invests funds and accounts for investment income and benefit payments made to employees or their beneficiaries. As investment income or investment losses are recognized, the asset and obligation accounts in the Agency Fund are increased or decreased. When benefit payments are made, these account balances should be reduced. For example, if the plan administrator notifies the governmental unit that investment income for the period amounted to $80,000, the following entry would be made in the Agency Fund:

Property And Rights Held Under Deferred Compensation Plan	80,000	
Obligations To Employees Under Deferred Compensation Plan		80,000

If benefits payments totaled $45,000 for the period, the payments would be recognized in the Agency Fund in the following manner:

Obligations To Employees Under Deferred Compensation Plan	45,000	
Property And Rights Held Under Deferred Compensation Plan		45,000

The plan assets should be measured at market value by the plan administrator, and the market valuation should be the basis for measuring both the asset and obligation accounts reflected in the Agency Fund. If a measurement basis other than market is used, both the asset and obligation accounts in the Agency Fund must use the same measurement basis, since both accounts must have the same carrying values. Generally, a market valuation report should be obtained from the plan administrator and the valuation date should coincide with the governmental unit's reporting date. When it is impractical to obtain a report that measures plan assets as of the governmental unit's reporting date, the most recent report should be

Fiduciary Funds

used and adjusted for contributions and withdrawals subsequent to the date of the report. For example, if it is assumed that an Agency Fund has asset and obligation accounts with carrying values of $4,250,000, and the plan administrator reports at the end of the period that the market value of plan assets is $4,350,000, the appreciation of the plan assets would be recorded as follows in the Agency Fund:

Property And Rights Held Under Deferred Compensation Plan	100,000	
Obligations To Employees Under Deferred Compensation Plan		100,000

The GASB concluded that an Agency Fund should not be established to report unfunded plans, although the Internal Revenue Service does not prohibit unfunded deferred compensation plans. Funding occurs when the governmental employer transfers the deferred compensation to the plan administrator. If the plan is not currently funded, the liability for the eventual deferred compensation payment should be reported as an obligation of the payroll paying governmental fund. The amount of the obligation may include an amount greater than the initial deferred compensation amount, and the total amount to be paid must be accrued as an obligation under the deferred compensation plan. For example, the eventual payments may include the deferred compensation amount plus interest at a stated rate. The interest would be reflected as an obligation with the passage of time (accrued). It is important that no part of the unfunded liability arising from an IRC Section 457 deferred compensation plan be shown as part of the governmental unit's General Long-Term Debt Account Group, but rather be reported as a fund liability.

> **OBSERVATION:** *The requirements that (1) interest be accrued as part of the obligation when the deferred compensation is not funded and (2) no part of the obligation can be presented as part of the General Long-Term Debt Account Group are inconsistent with the basic governmental accounting model in that a fund liability should be recognized only when it is payable from current expendable resources of the fund.*

As noted earlier, a governmental entity has legal access to the assets related to an IRC Section 457 deferred compensation plan.

Fiduciary Funds

When a governmental unit uses assets of the plan for purposes other than paying for benefits related to the plan, the withdrawal should be recognized as a receivable in the Agency Fund. For example, if a governmental entity withdraws $150,000 from a deferred compensation plan to be used for (General Fund) operating purposes, the withdrawal would be recorded as follows:

AGENCY FUND
Receivable From General Fund   150,000
    Property And Rights Held Under
        Deferred Compensation Plan   150,000

GENERAL FUND
Cash   150,000
    Payable To Agency Fund   150,000

> **OBSERVATION:** *While the liability of the General Fund is actually payable to the plan administrator and not the Agency Fund, it should be classified as an interfund liability and adequately described in a note to the financial statements.*

In addition to presenting the economic substance of a deferred compensation plan as described above, the fiduciary relationship between the governmental entity and employees that participate in the plan should be made. The GASB requires that a note to the financial statements should include the following with respect to the fiduciary relationship:

- The requirement of IRC Section 457 that the assets in the plan remain the property of the employer until paid or made available to participants, subject only to the claims of the government's general creditors.
- A statement of the government's fiduciary responsibilities under the plan.
- If applicable, a description of how plan assets were used in the past for purposes other than to pay benefits.

Presented below is an example of a note describing a deferred compensation plan.

Fiduciary Funds

▶ Employees of the City of Centerville may participate in a deferred compensation plan adopted under the provisions of Internal Revenue Code Section 457 (Deferred Compensation Plans With Respect To Service For State and Local Governments).

The deferred compensation plan is available to all employees of the City. Under the plan, employees may elect to defer a portion of their salaries and avoid paying taxes on the deferred portion until the withdrawal date. The deferred compensation amount is not available for withdrawal by employees until termination, retirement, death, or unforeseeable emergency.

The deferred compensation plan is administered by an unrelated financial institution. Under the terms of an IRC Section 457 deferred compensation plan, all deferred compensation and income attributable to the investment of the deferred compensation amounts held by the financial institution, until paid or made available to the employees or beneficiaries, are the property of the City subject only to the claims of the City's general creditors. In addition, the participants in the plan have rights equal to those of the general creditors of the City, and each participant's rights are equal to his or her share of the fair market value of the plan assets. The City believes that it is unlikely that plan assets will be needed to satisfy claims of general creditors that might arise.

As part of its fiduciary role, the City has an obligation of due care in selecting the third party administrator. In the opinion of the City's legal counsel, the City has acted in a prudent manner and is not liable for losses that may arise from the administration of the plan. ◀

A governmental employer that records the rights and obligations of an IRC Section 457 deferred compensation plan in an Agency Fund may administer a multiple jurisdictions' plan. Under this circumstance, the amount of the asset and obligation shown in the Agency Fund should be the total for the plan and not just the portion applicable to its employees. In the note to the financial statements that describes the characteristics of the deferred compensation plan there should be a disclosure of the portion of the assets in the fund to which the governmental unit has access.

Proprietary fund reporting The GASB specifically identified "separately constituted governmental public utilities and public authorities" as governmental entities that should report assets and obligations arising from IRC Section 457 deferred compensation plans in their financial statements (proprietary fund reporting), rather than as part of an Agency Fund. The assets related to the deferred compensation plan may be held by a PERS, the governmental employer, a nongovernmental third party, or another governmental entity under a multiple-jurisdictional plan.

The governmental public utility or public authority would display assets held by the plan and obligations under the plan agreement in its balance sheet. The accounting and disclosure requirements for deferred compensation plans are the same as those applicable to agency fund reporting as described in the previous section.

To illustrate the accounting for a deferred compensation plan, assume that a public authority incurs payroll expense of $300,000, of which $30,000 is deferred under the deferred compensation plan. The plan is administered by a nongovernmental third party and plan benefits are immediately funded. The payroll expense would be recorded by the public authority (proprietary fund accounting) by making the following entries:

Expense—Payroll	300,000	
Accrued Payroll		300,000
Accrued Payroll	300,000	
Cash (Payment To Plan Administrator)		30,000
Cash (Payment To Employees—		
Net Payroll)		205,000
Liabilities (Various Liabilities		
For Payroll Deductions)		65,000
Property And Rights Held Under		
Deferred Compensation Plan	30,000	
Obligations To Employees Under		
Deferred Compensation Plan		30,000

Proprietary fund types and similar Trust Funds of a state or local government must report in a manner similar to governmental public utilities and public authorities only when these proprietary funds and Nonexpendable Trust Funds have separate plans for their employees. When the proprietary fund types and similar Trust Funds do not have separate plans for their employees, they must account for IRC Section 457 deferred compensation plans by using the agency fund reporting described earlier.

Plans administered by PERS A reporting problem arises when an IRC Section 457 deferred compensation plan is administered by a PERS. If it is concluded that the financial statements of the PERS (the component entity) should be combined with the general governmental entity's financial statements (oversight entity), there will be a duplication of reported assets. The GASB, in order to prevent

Fiduciary Funds

such a duplication, requires that the combined financial statements of the reporting entity reflect the following:

- Deferred compensation amounts applicable to the oversight unit should be included only once in the Trust and Agency Fund column of the combined financial statements.
- Deferred compensation amounts applicable to other component units of the entity should be included only in the appropriate columns applicable to those component units.

Thus, the amounts applicable to the deferred compensation plan as shown in the Agency Fund must be reported in the combined financial statements, and the financial statements of the PERS must be modified to remove the duplication.

In addition, a note to the financial statements should disclose the following for deferred compensation plans administered by the PERS but not considered part of the reporting entity:

- The IRC Section 457 requirement that assets in the plan remain the property of the employer until paid to or made available to participants, subject only to the government's general creditors.
- A statement of the government's fiduciary responsibilities under the plan.
- If applicable, a description of how plan assets were used in the past for purposes other than to pay benefits.

To illustrate the accounting for a deferred compensation plan when a PERS administers the plan, assume that the agency fund reporting example used earlier is administered by a PERS and not by a financial institution. The following entries would be made to record the payroll expenditures of $700,000:

PERS
PUBLIC EMPLOYEE RETIREMENT SYSTEM
  Cash   50,000
     Contributions—Employees   50,000

AGENCY FUND
  Property And Rights Held Under
    Deferred Compensation Plan   50,000
     Obligations To Employees Under
       Deferred Compensation Plan   50,000

GENERAL FUND

Expenditures—Payroll	700,000	
Accrued Payroll		700,000
Accrued Payroll	700,000	
Cash (Payment To Plan Administrator)		50,000
Cash (Payments To Employees—		
Net Payroll)		500,000
Liabilities (Various Liabilities		
For Payroll Deductions)		150,000

If the PERS financial statements are combined with the oversight entity, the assets and fund balance of the financial statements of the PERS would have to be reduced by the amount shown in the Agency Fund. The required adjustments to the PERS' financial statements are limited to the balance sheet because an Agency Fund does not present an activity statement.

Plans administered by oversight unit A reporting problem arises when an IRC Section 457 deferred compensation multiple-employer plan is administered by an oversight unit and some of those employers are part of the overall reporting entity. To avoid duplication of assets held under the plan, deferred compensation amounts applicable to other component units of the entity should be included only in the appropriate columns applicable to those component units.

LITERATURE REFERENCES

Material in this chapter is based on the following authoritative pronouncements and publications, which are grouped according to the major headings used within the chapter. A dual reference (both paragraph and page number) is used for NCGA-1 and NCGA-2 because the original pronouncements do not use paragraph numbers.

Introduction
NCGA-1 *Governmental Accounting and Financial Reporting Principles*, p. 6/ ¶ 18.

Expendable Trust Funds
NCGA-1 *Governmental Accounting and Financial Reporting Principles*, pp. 6, 10, and 14/¶¶ 18, 57, and 98.

Fiduciary Funds

Revenues and Other Sources of Financing
NCGA-1   *Governmental Accounting and Financial Reporting Principles*, pp. 11, 15, and 16/¶¶ 62 and 105.

Expenditures
NCGA-1   *Governmental Accounting and Financial Reporting Principles*, pp. 14, 16, and 17/¶¶ 91, 109, and 111-116.

Assets
NCGA-1   *Governmental Accounting and Financial Reporting Principles*, pp. 8 and 12/¶¶ 37 and 73.
NCGA INTERPRETATION-9   *Certain Fund Classifications and Balance Sheet Accounts*, ¶ 11.

Liabilities
NCGA-1   *Governmental Accounting and Financial Reporting Principles*, p. 9/ ¶¶ 42-44.

Financial Statements
NCGA-1   *Governmental Accounting and Financial Reporting Principles*, p. 21/ ¶ 143.

Nonexpendable Trust Funds
NCGA-1   *Governmental Accounting and Financial Reporting Principles*, pp. 6, 10, and 14/¶¶ 18, 57, and 98.

Revenues
NCGA-1   *Governmental Accounting and Financial Reporting Principles*, pp. 12, 15, and 16/¶¶ 74 and 105.
NCGA-2   *Grant, Entitlement, and Shared Revenue Accounting by State and Local Governments*, p. 2/¶¶ 11-13.
FASB:CS-6   *Elements of Financial Statements*, ¶ 78.
APB STATEMENT-4   *Basic Concepts and Accounting Principles Underlying Financial Statements of Business Enterprises*, ¶ 150.
APB OPINION-21   *Interest on Receivables and Payables*, ¶ 15.
APB OPINION-18   *The Equity Method of Accounting For Investments in Common Stock*, ¶¶ 14-20.
FASB-12   *Accounting for Certain Marketable Securities*, ¶¶ 7-21.

Expenses
NCGA-1   *Governmental Accounting and Financial Reporting Principles*, p. 12/ ¶ 74.
NCGA-2   *Grant, Entitlement, and Shared Revenue Accounting by State and Local Governments*, p. 3/¶ 18.

Assets
NCGA-1 *Governmental Accounting and Financial Reporting Principles*, p. 8/ ¶¶ 35 and 37.
FASB:CS-6 *Elements of Financial Statements*, ¶ 25.

Liabilities
NCGA-1 *Governmental Accounting and Financial Reporting Principles*, p. 9/¶ 42.
FASB:CS-6 *Elements of Financial Statements*, ¶ 35.

Financial Statements
NCGA-1 *Governmental Accounting and Financial Reporting Principles*, p. 21/¶ 143.

Agency Funds
NCGA-1 *Governmental Accounting and Financial Reporting Principles*, pp. 6, 8, 10, 11, 14, and 15/¶¶ 18, 30, 31, 57, and 98.

Pass Through Agency Fund
NCGA-2 *Grant, Entitlement, and Shared Revenue Accounting by State and Local Governments*, p. 2/¶ 8.

Discretionary Agency Fund
NCGA-2 *Grant, Entitlement, and Shared Revenue Accounting by State and Local Governments*, p. 2/¶ 9.

Dual Recording Agency Fund
NCGA-2 *Grant, Entitlement, and Shared Revenue Accounting by State and Local Governments*, p. 2/¶ 10.

Financial Statement
NCGA-1 *Governmental Accounting and Financial Reporting Principles*, p. 21/ ¶ 143.
IRC Section 457 *Deferred Compensation Plans.*
GASB-2 *Financial Reporting of Deferred Compensation Plans Adopted under the Provisions of Internal Revenue Code Section 457*, ¶¶ 9-14.

PENSION TRUST FUNDS

BASIC CONCEPTS AND STANDARDS

Currently, both the NCGA and the FASB have outstanding pronouncements that address the accounting and reporting issues of pension plans established by state and local governments. In June 1983, NCGA-6 (Pension Accounting and Financial Reporting: Public Employee Retirement Systems and State and Local Government Employers) was issued and in March 1980, FASB-35 (Accounting and Reporting by Defined Benefit Pension Plans) was issued. Because there are unresolved differences between the two pronouncements, both the NCGA and the FASB have extended the effective date of each pronouncement indefinitely. Until these differences are resolved, the GASB has concluded that pension accounting and reporting standards established by any one of the following pronouncements may be followed by a state or local government:

- NCGA-1 (The related material contained in the 1968 GAAFR may be considered illustrative of the principles of NCGA-1, to the extent such material is consistent with NCGA-1)
- NCGA-6
- FASB-35

This chapter discusses the accounting and reporting standards established by NCGA-6.

Disclosure standards for pension information were established by GASB-5 (Disclosure of Pension Information by Public Employee Retirement Systems and State and Local Governmental Employers) and these standards are discussed in Chapter 50 (Pension Disclosures).

GASB-4

In 1985, FASB-87 (Employers' Accounting for Pensions) was issued by the Financial Accounting Standards Board. FASB-87 superseded APB-8 (Accounting for the Cost of Pension Plans) and FASB-36 (Disclosure of Pension Information), thereby dramatically changing the manner in which pensions are accounted for and presented in financial statements. Without action by the GASB, proprietary funds would have had to change how they account for pension costs in order to conform to FASB-87. In addition, the GASB is currently studying pension accounting issues and it expects to issue perhaps two or three Statements that will provide accounting and reporting standards for governmental entities in this area of accounting.

In order to avoid still another change in accounting procedures used by proprietary funds at the time the GASB Statements are issued, GASB-4 (Applicability of FASB-87, "Employers' Accounting for Pensions," to State and Local Governmental Employers) was issued. GASB-4 concluded that "state and local governmental employers, including proprietary funds and similar Trust Funds, should not change their accounting and reporting of pension activities as a result of the issuance of FASB-87."

Objectives of Pension Fund Reporting

The scope of NCGA-6 is limited to financial reporting by defined benefit plans that are administered by Public Employee Retirement Systems (PERS) and state and local government employers. A defined benefit plan establishes the guaranteed benefits that will be paid to governmental employees at the time of their retirement. In a defined contribution plan the required contributions that must be paid by the state or local government are established and there is no guarantee of the level of benefits that will be paid when the governmental employees retire. NCGA-6 is not applicable to defined contribution plans.

Financial statements of a PERS will be used by a variety of parties, including the management of the governmental unit, employees, and taxpayers. The primary objective of financial reporting by a PERS as identified in GASB-5 is to provide interested parties who are familiar with financial reporting concepts with useful information that will enable them to accomplish the following:

- Assess the funding status of a PERS on the basis of a going concern
- Ascertain the progress made in accumulating assets that will be used to pay future pension obligations
- Assess the extent to which employers are making periodic contributions at actuarially determined rates

A PERS is created to receive contributions made by the employer government. These contributions are used to acquire various prudent investments including long-term investments in debt securities and equity securities as well as investments in short-term financial instruments. The employer and employee contributions and investment earnings are the basis for paying benefits due to governmental employees and their beneficiaries. The actual pension payments are made from the PERS.

Basis of Accounting

An entity's basis of accounting determines when transactions and economic events are to be recorded. The accrual basis of accounting is used by a PERS. FASB:CS-1 (Objectives of Financial Reporting by Business Enterprises) describes accrual accounting as follows:

> Accrual accounting attempts to record the financial effects on an enterprise of transactions and other events and circumstances that have cash consequences for an enterprise in the periods in which those transactions, events, and circumstances occur rather than only in the periods in which cash is received or paid by the enterprise. Accrual accounting is concerned with the process by which cash expended on resources and activities is returned as more (or perhaps less) cash to the enterprise, not just with the beginning and end of that process.

Accrual accounting encompasses accounting concepts such as the deferral of expenditures and the subsequent amortization of the deferred costs (prepaid expenses, supplies, etc.), and the capitalization of capital expenditures and the subsequent depreciation of the capitalized costs (depreciation of fixed operating assets).

Measurement Focus

While the basis of accounting determines when transactions and economic events should be reflected in a fund's financial statements, the measurement focus identifies what transactions and economic events should be recorded. The measurement focus is concerned with the inflow and outflow of resources that affect an entity. The balance sheet should reflect those resources that are available to meet obligations, and that are to be used in the payment of expenses of a PERS. The activity statement of a PERS should summarize those resources received and those consumed during the current period.

A PERS uses the same measurement focus as commercial enterprises, namely the *flow of economic resources*. The flow of economic resources refers to all of the assets available to a PERS for the purpose of paying benefits to those covered by the defined benefit plan. When the flow of economic resources and the accrual basis of accounting are combined, they provide the foundation for generally accepted accounting principles as applied by commercial enterprises. When the flow of economic resources is applied on an accrual basis for a PERS, all assets and liabilities, both current and long-term, would be presented on the fund's balance sheet. The activity statement of a PERS would include all costs incurred to provide retirement benefits during the period.

Budgetary System and Accounts

While the NCGA recommended that all funds adopt a budget for control purposes, there is a recognition that the nature of budgeting differs between that for a governmental fund and that for a fund accounted for in a manner similar to a commercial enterprise. Because the expenses that arise from the payment of retirement benefits are determined by the pension agreement, there is no need to adopt an operating budget for a PERS or to integrate budgetary accounts into its accounting system. Similarly, there is no need to utilize an encumbrance system.

ACCOUNTS AND TRANSACTIONS

While accounting for a PERS is similar to the manner in which a commercial enterprise is accounted for, there are unique accounting methods that differentiate accounting for a PERS from commercial accounting. These differences are discussed in various sections of the remainder of this chapter.

Revenues

FASB:CS-6 (Elements of Financial Statements) defines revenues as "inflows or other enhancements of assets of an entity or settlements of its liabilities (or a combination of both) during a period resulting

Pension Trust Funds

from delivering or producing goods, rendering services, or other activities that constitute the entity's ongoing major or central operations." A PERS should recognize revenue on an accrual basis, meaning that revenue is considered realized when (1) the earnings process is complete or virtually complete and (2) an exchange has taken place.

Investment Income An important function of a PERS is to invest resources and earn an adequate rate of return. Investments may include the acquisition of debt securities and equity securities.

Debt securities Interest income on investments in debt securities (fixed-income securities) should be determined by using the effective interest method. Under the effective interest method, income is recognized over the life of the investment so as to produce a constant rate of return on the carrying value of the investment. For example, assume that on June 30, 19X1, a PERS acquires 6% bonds with a par value of $1,000,000 that mature in five years, and the bonds are purchased for $920,143 in order to yield a rate of return of 8%. The investment would be recorded as follows on June 30, 19X1:

Investment In Bonds	920,143	
Cash		920,143

Since the bonds were purchased at a discount, the discount (through the investment account) must be amortized over the five-year life of the bonds. In order to facilitate the computation of periodic interest income, an amortization table similar to the following one may be prepared:

Date	Interest payment	Interest @ 8%	Amortization of discount	Carrying value of investment
6/30/X1				$ 920,143
6/30/X2	60,000	73,611	13,611	933,754
6/30/X3	60,000	74,700	14,700	948,454
6/30/X4	60,000	75,876	15,876	964,330
6/30/X5	60,000	77,146	17,146	981,476
6/30/X6	60,000	78,524[R]	18,524	1,000,000

[R] = Rounding error

Based on the amortization schedule shown above, the following entry would be made on June 30, 19X2, to record the receipt of the first interest payment and to amortize the bond discount:

Pension Trust Funds

Cash	60,000	
Investment In Bonds	13,611	
Bond Interest Income		73,611

Temporary changes, either increases or decreases, in the market value of investments in debt instruments should not be recognized as unrealized gains or losses in the financial statements of the PERS. However, permanent declines in market values must be treated as a realized loss (that is, reported on the Statement of Revenues, Expenses, and Changes in Fund Balance). Identifying a permanent decline in the market value of debt instruments is often difficult. FASB-12 (Accounting for Certain Marketable Securities) notes that the following factors should be considered in determining whether a market value decline is temporary or permanent:

- A realized gain or loss on the sale of the debt instrument after the balance sheet date but before the issuance of the current financial statements.
- A change in the market value of the debt instrument after the balance sheet date but before the issuance of the current financial statements.

If it is concluded that the market value decline is permanent (other than temporary), the writedown to market is recorded. For example, if an investment in 25-year bonds has a carrying value of $1,000,000 and a market value of $300,000, and the market value decline appears to be permanent, the following entry would be made:

Loss On Permanent Decline In Market		
Value Of Bond Investment	700,000	
Investment In Bonds		700,000

Subsequent increases in the value of bond investments that have been written down to market value should not be recognized. For example, if at the end of the following year the 25-year bonds had a market value of $350,000, no entry would be made.

Generally, the amount of the writedown due to a permanent market value decline is equal to the difference between the cost of the investment and the market value of the investment as of the balance sheet date. Further declines in the market value after the balance sheet date but before the issuance of the financial statements should not be recognized because those declines are based on events that occurred after the close of the current period and should be considered potential losses of the following period. However, footnote disclosure of such declines is appropriate. On the other hand, increases in the market value of the debt investment after the balance sheet date but before the issuance of the financial statements would suggest that the market value decline was temporary rather than permanent and for this reason subsequent increases in market value should be taken into consideration in determining the amount of the loss to be recognized in the current period's financial statements.

> **OBSERVATION:** It should be emphasized that market value declines after the date of the balance sheet are considered in determining whether the decline at the balance sheet date is permanent in nature, even though subsequent declines are not considered in determining the amount of the recognized loss in the current period.

When a PERS actively manages a portfolio of debt securities, the investment portfolio may be accounted for on a cost basis with no provision for the amortization of discount or premium.

Equity securities Dividend income from equity securities is accounted for on an accrual basis. Temporary changes in the market value of equity investments are not recognized in the Statement of Revenues, Expenses, and Changes in Fund Balance; however, market value declines that are other than temporary must be recorded as losses in the current period. (See previous section for a discussion of declines that are not considered temporary.)

Exchange of Debt Securities

In order to improve the rate of return earned by a PERS, debt investments may be sold before maturity and the proceeds reinvested in other debt instruments. Generally, the difference between the book value and market value of the old debt investment is recognized as gains or losses. For example, if a bond investment that has a book value of $750,000 is sold for $600,000 and the proceeds are invested in a new bond instrument, the following entry will be made to record the exchange:

Cash	600,000	
Loss On Sale Of Bond Investments	150,000	
Investment In Bonds		750,000
Investment In Bonds	600,000	
Cash		600,000

Pension Trust Funds

It may be argued that the generally accepted accounting principles that require the immediate recognition of a loss on the sale of fixed-income securities might discourage an investment manager from selling a debt investment in order to avoid that recognition of a loss on the fund's financial statements. Thus, in order to avoid an "accounting loss" (the economic loss has already occurred), it may be necessary to make a poor investment decision, namely to continue to hold the investment. NCGA-6 recognized this potential problem and concluded that gains and losses on certain exchanges of debt instruments may be recognized immediately or they may be deferred. The nonrecognition of gains and losses may be chosen when there has been an *exchange* of fixed-income securities. An exchange is the sale of one debt security for another debt security with the following additional characteristics:

- Both the sale and the purchase must be planned simultaneously, that is, each half undertaken in contemplation of the other and each half executed conditioned upon execution of the other.
- Both the sale and the purchase must be made on the same day, although settlement of the two transactions may occur on different dates.
- The sale and purchase must result in an increase in the net yield to maturity and/or an improvement in the quality of the bond held.
- The purchase must involve an investment graded bond that is better rated, equally rated, or no worse than one investment grade lower than the bond sold.

When all of these four criteria are satisfied, gains and losses on the exchange of debt investments may be accounted for under the (1) completed transaction method, (2) deferral/amortization method, or (3) cost pass-through method.

Completed transaction method When the completed transaction method is used to account for gains and losses from the exchange of fixed-income investments, gains and losses are recognized at the exchange date.

To illustrate the completed transaction method, assume that a bond investment that has a book value of $500,000 is sold for $425,000 and the proceeds are immediately used to invest in a higher quality bond. The exchange would be recorded as follows:

Cash	425,000	
Loss On Sale Of Bond Investments	75,000	
Investment In Bonds		500,000
Investment In Bonds	425,000	
Cash		425,000

Deferral/amortization method Under the deferral/amortization method, the gain or loss on the exchange is deferred at the date of the exchange. Subsequently, the deferred gain or loss is amortized over the lesser of the (1) maturity date of the debt instrument sold or (2) maturity date of the debt instrument purchased.

Using the previous example, the following entry would be made at the exchange date if the deferral/amortization method is used to account for gains and losses:

Cash	425,000	
Deferred Loss On Sale Of Bond		
Investments (Asset Account)	75,000	
Investment In Bonds		500,000
Investment In Bonds	425,000	
Cash		425,000

If it is assumed that the remaining lives of the securities sold and purchased were ten years and fifteen years, respectively, the following amortization entry would be made at the end of each of the next ten years:

Amortization Of Deferred Loss On Sale		
Of Bond Investments ($75,000/10 Years)	7,500	
Deferred Loss On Sale Of Bond		
Investments		7,500

If the deferral/amortization method is adopted, it must be used consistently from period to period. Also, NCGA-6 notes that transactions should not be deliberately timed in a manner that results in the immediate recognition of gains and the deferral of losses.

> **OBSERVATION:** *Based on the four criteria established by NCGA-6, gains and losses may be manipulated by selling a debt security and either (1) immediately buying another debt security (in order to defer a loss) or (2) temporarily delaying the purchase of another debt security (in order to recognize a gain).*

Pension Trust Funds

Cost pass-through method If the cost pass-through method is used to account for gains and losses arising from the exchange of debt investments, the book value of the old debt investment is used as the basis for recording the new debt investment.

Continuing with the previous example, the following entry would be made at the exchange date if the cost pass-through method is used to account for gains and losses:

Cash	425,000	
Investment In Bonds (New Investment)	75,000	
Investment In Bonds (Old Investment)		500,000
Investment In Bonds (New Investment)	425,000	
Cash		425,000

Note: The book value of the new investment is composed of two elements. Alternatively, the entries could be combined into a single entry to avoid two separate postings to the new investment account.

In order to avoid the more or less permanent deferral of losses arising from exchanges (and to a lesser extent gains arising from exchanges), there is a limit on the number of times an investment base (old investment) can be passed to a subsequent investment. NCGA-6 states that only two exchanges in the same investment stream may be deferred. If a third exchange takes place, the deferred gain or loss must be accounted for by using either the completed transaction method or the deferral/amortization method. For example, assume that Investment A is purchased at a cost of $110,000 and subsequently exchanged for $75,000, and the proceeds are immediately used to purchase Investment B. At a later date, Investment B is exchanged for $40,000 and Investment C is immediately acquired at a cost of $40,000. If Investment C is exchanged for $30,000 and Investment D is immediately acquired with the proceeds, the cost pass-through method cannot be used to account for the acquisition of Investment D. The loss of $80,000 ($110,000 − $30,000) on the third exchange (purchase of Investment D) must either be recognized immediately (completed transaction method) or deferred and amortized over the lesser of the remaining life of Investment C or Investment D.

Other Revenue Other revenue for a PERS will include pension contributions made by the state or local government and, if the plan is contributory, contributions from employees. The employer's contributions will be determined by contract and should be recognized as revenue by the PERS when the pension contribution is due to be paid. Contributions by employees will be based on payroll deductions and should be recognized as revenue when the governmental unit's payroll is subject to accrual.

Expenses

FASB-6 defines expenses as outflows or other using up of assets or incurrences of liabilities (or a combination of both) during a period resulting from delivering or producing goods, rendering services, or carrying out other activities that constitute the entity's ongoing major or central operations. Expenses of a PERS are determined by the pension agreement that exists between the governmental unit and employees. As pension benefits are paid as specified by the pension contract, operating expenses are recognized. These expenses may include payments for current pension benefits based on the pension formula, death benefits, disability benefits, and refunds to terminated employees. In addition, administrative expenses are recorded in a manner consistent with accounting practices used by a commercial enterprise. For example, administrative expenses may include depreciation expense, salaries and wages, and other overhead costs incurred to administer the pension plan.

Although an expense is recognized when a PERS makes payments to retirees or their beneficiaries, the expenditure for the pension plan is recorded in the governmental fund before actual pension benefit payments are made. The amount of the pension expenditure must be computed by employing an acceptable actuarial cost method. GASB-5 identifies the following as acceptable actuarial cost methods:

- Unit Credit Actuarial Cost Method
- Entry Age Actuarial Cost Method
- Attained Age Actuarial Cost Method
- Aggregate Actuarial Cost Method
- Frozen Entry Age Actuarial Cost Method
- Frozen Attained Age Actuarial Cost Method
- Individual Level Actuarial Cost Method
- Individual Spread Gain Actuarial Cost Method
- Project Actuarial Cost Method

Once the pension obligation for the current period is computed using an acceptable actuarial cost method, the portion of the obligation that is funded using expendable available financial resources of the governmental fund is recorded as an expenditure and a liability of the governmental fund, and the balance (the portion not requiring the use of expendable available financial resources) is reported as part of the General Long-Term Debt Account Group. For example, assume that a current pension obligation of $500,000 is computed using an acceptable actuarial cost method, and $150,000 of the amount is immediately funded. Assuming the current payment is made from the General Fund, the following entries would be made to recognize the current pension obligation:

GENERAL FUND
 Expenditures—Pensions   150,000
  Cash   150,000

GENERAL LONG-TERM DEBT ACCOUNT GROUP
 Amount To Be Provided For Pension
  Liability   350,000
   Long-Term Pension Liability   350,000

The pension expenditure should be disclosed in the financial statements of the governmental unit in the following manner:

Expenditures
 Employer pension contribution ($500,000 (total
 amount determined for the year by an acceptable
 actuarial cost method) less $350,000 (recorded
 as long-term obligations)) $150,000

Assets

Assets, as defined in FASB:CS-6, are "probable future economic benefits obtained or controlled by a particular entity as a result of past transactions or events." Fixed assets such as buildings, equipment, and fixtures used in the administration of the pension plan should be capitalized and depreciated in a manner consistent with accounting practices used by a commercial enterprise. The accounting for other assets of a PERS is summarized in the paragraph below.

Equity securities Investments in equity securities such as common and preferred stock should be accounted for on a cost basis; however, as discussed, market declines below cost that are other than temporary must be recognized. The total market value of the portfolio of equity securities should be disclosed parenthetically.

Fixed-income securities Fixed-income securities represent investments in debt instruments such as bonds and notes. These investments should be accounted for at amortized cost, except market declines below the book value of the investment that are not temporary must be recorded. When a PERS actively manages a fixed-income portfolio, the portfolio may be reported at cost. The total market value of the portfolio of fixed-income securities should be disclosed parenthetically, irrespective of whether the amortized cost or cost method is used.

Insurance contracts Allocated insurance contracts are not recorded as an asset of a PERS. Likewise, the value of future benefits insured through allocated insurance contracts is excluded from the actuarial present value of credited projected benefits. (The present value of credited projected benefits is discussed later in this chapter.) NCGA-6 notes that unallocated insurance contracts are reported at the value determined by the insurance company.

> *OBSERVATION:* NCGA-6 refers to FASB-35 (Accounting and Reporting by Defined Benefit Pension Plans), which states that "contracts with insurance companies shall be presented in the same manner as that contained in the annual report filed by the plan with certain governmental agencies pursuant to ERISA (Employee Retirement Income Security Act)." Plans not subject to ERISA should nonetheless follow the same valuation methods.

Securities subject to forced liquidation Under some circumstances it may be necessary to sell investments in equity securities or fixed-income securities in order to pay benefits required by the pension plan agreement. If it appears that the plan will be faced with forced liquidation of securities to cover these expenses, it may be appropriate to report the securities expected to be sold at market value rather than at cost, or amortized cost.

> *OBSERVATION:* A significant difference between NCGA-6 and FASB-35 is that NCGA-6 requires that pension plan assets be reported at cost while FASB-35 requires that fair value be used.

Pension Trust Funds

Liabilities

FASB:CS-6 defines liabilities as "probable future sacrifices of economic benefits arising from present obligations of a particular entity to transfer assets or provide services to other entities in the future as a result of past transactions or events." Although future pension liabilities constitute a liability of a PERS, NCGA-6 concluded that actuarial liabilities resulting from the pension plan agreement are not reported as a fund liability. (As discussed below, actuarial liabilities are reported as part of the fund balance.) Thus, liabilities of a PERS include obligations arising from the administration of the plan and may include such items as accrued operating expenses and payroll taxes withheld. In addition, pension benefits that are due and payable are classified as a liability of a PERS.

Designation of Fund Balances

Actuarial liabilities that arise from the defined benefit pension plan are reported as part of the fund balance section of the PERS financial statements. To compute the actuarial present value of future benefits, the unit credit actuarial cost method with benefits based on projected salary increases should be used. In addition, the computation may take into consideration the effects of step-rate benefits. The effects of step-rate benefits in computing the actuarial present value of credited projected benefits are part of the disclosure requirements established by GASB-5.

NCGA-6 requires that the fund balance section of the PERS financial statements include the following accounts:

- Actuarial present value of projected benefits payable to current retirants and beneficiaries
- Actuarial present value of projected benefits payable to terminated vested participants who have not reached the eligibility age for receiving benefits
- Actuarial present value of credited projected benefits payable to active participants with specific identification of the portion of this amount that comprises accumulated member contributions

Rather than present the three elements listed above, the following present-value elements that comprise the pension benefit obligation may be presented in the fund balance section of the PERS financial statements:

- Retirees and beneficiaries currently receiving benefits and terminated employees entitled to benefits but not yet receiving them
- Current employees
  — Accumulated employee contributions including allocated investment income, if any
  — Employer-financed vested
  — Employer-financed nonvested

These latter elements are consistent with the standard note disclosure requirements for all PERS as established by GASB-5. Whether the standards established by NCGA-6 or GASB-5 are followed, all the elements of the pension obligation should be added together and identified as the "Total Actuarial Present Value of Credited Projected Benefits."

Generally the net assets (total fund assets minus total fund liabilities) of the pension fund will be less than the total actuarial present value of credited projected benefits, in which case there is a deficit in the fund balance, which should be captioned "Unfunded actuarial present value of credited projected benefits." If the net assets of the fund exceed the total actuarial present value of credited projected benefits, a surplus exists and should be identified as "Net assets available for future benefit credits."

Disclosures

Disclosure requirements established by NCGA-6 were superseded by reporting standards established by GASB-5. GASB-5 reporting standards are applicable to all governmental employers that have pension activities. The specific reporting standards, which include both notes to the financial statements and required supplementary information, are determined by the characteristics of the pension plan and the reporting entity that includes the pension activity in its financial statements. A discussion of pension plan disclosures can be found in Chapter 50 (Pension Disclosures).

Disclosures as a Component Unit

The PERS should be evaluated to determine whether its financial statements should be combined with the state or local government's financial statements in order to report as a single reporting entity.

NCGA-3 (Defining the Governmental Reporting Entity) concludes that a component unit (PERS) should be combined with the oversight unit (state or local government) for financial reporting purposes when the latter exercises oversight responsibility over the former. Factors to be considered in determining whether oversight responsibility exists are the following:

- Financial interdependency
- Selection of governing authority
- Designation of management
- Ability to significantly influence operations
- Accountability for fiscal matters

These factors are discussed in Chapter 4 (The Governmental Reporting Entity).

When it is concluded that a PERS financial statement should be reported as a component unit of the reporting entity, the PERS financial statements are formatted to conform to the presentation used by other funds that compose the reporting entity. Thus, on the balance sheet the pension fund's assets are reported in a manner to equal its liabilities and fund balance (current liabilities are not subtracted from assets). The pension fund's fund balance is presented as a single item captioned *Reserved for employees' retirement system.* However, the detail of the fund balance—that is, (1) actuarial present value of projected benefits payable to current retirants and beneficiaries, (2) actuarial present value of projected benefits payable to terminated vested participants, (3) actuarial present value of credited projected benefits for active employees, and (4) the sum of these three elements—must be presented in notes to the reporting entity's general purpose financial statements and on the face of the individual fund statements in the Comprehensive Annual Financial Report.

In addition to the presentation of the PERS financial statements, supporting notes and required supplementary information must be presented in the reporting entity's financial report.

Financial Statements

A PERS financial statement should include a (1) Balance Sheet, (2) Statement of Revenues, Expenses, and Changes in Fund Balance, and (3) Statement of Changes in Financial Position.

The Balance Sheet should not differentiate between current and noncurrent assets and liabilities. Liabilities should be subtracted from total assets and the balance labeled "Net assets available for benefits." Also, the fund balance section of the Balance Sheet should include the following:

- The actuarial present value of projected benefits payable to current retirants and beneficiaries
- The actuarial present value of projected benefits payable to terminated vested participants who have not reached the eligibility age for receiving benefits
- The actuarial present value of credited projected benefits payable to active participants with specific identification of the portion of this amount that comprises accumulated member contributions

> **OBSERVATION:** *As noted earlier, the balance sheet presentation may conform to the note disclosure requirements established by GASB-5 whereby the categories presented in the fund balance for the pension benefit obligation would be (a) retirees and beneficiaries currently receiving benefits and terminated employees entitled to benefits but not yet receiving them and (b) current employee (i) accumulated employee contributions including allocated investment income, if any, (ii) employer-financed vested, and (iii) employer-financed nonvested.*

The three items listed above should be summed and labeled "Total actuarial present value of credited projected benefits." When this total is greater than the net assets available for benefits, the deficit should be labeled "Unfunded actuarial present value of credited projected benefits." On the other hand, when the total is less than the net assets available for benefits, the difference should be labeled "Net assets available for future benefit credits."

An example of a PERS financial statement is presented in Exhibits I, II, and III.

EXHIBIT I
Balance Sheet

City of Centerville Employees' Retirement System
Balance Sheet
June 30, 19X5

		in thousands of dollars
ASSETS		
Cash		$15,000
Accrued interest and dividends		40,000
Investments		
Common stock, at cost (market value, $222,000)	$200,000	
Preferred stock, at cost (market value, $125,000)	120,000	
Bonds, at amortized cost (market value, $276,000)	250,000	
Total investments		570,000
Furniture, fixtures, and equipment (net of accumulated depreciation, $15,000)		34,000
Total assets		659,000
LIABILITIES		
Accrued expenses	10,000	
Accounts payable	12,000	
Total liabilities		22,000
Net assets available for benefits		$637,000
FUND BALANCE		
Actuarial present value of projected benefits payable to current retirants and beneficiaries		250,000
Actuarial present value of projected benefits payable to terminated vested participants		10,000
Actuarial present value of credited projected benefits for active employees		
Member contributions	260,000	
Employer-financed portion	305,000	
Total actuarial present value of credited projected benefits		$825,000
Unfunded actuarial present value of credited projected benefits		(188,000)
Total fund balance		$637,000

EXHIBIT II
Statement of Revenues, Expenses, and Changes in Fund Balance

City of Centerville Employees' Retirement System
Statement of Revenues, Expenses, and Changes in Fund Balance
For Year Ended June 30, 19X5

	in thousands of dollars
Operating revenues	
Member contributions	$ 45,000
Employer contributions	65,000
Investment income	65,000
Total operating revenues	175,000
Operating expenses	
Benefits	16,000
Refunds	9,600
Administrative	2,400
Total operating expenses	28,000
Net operating income	147,000
Fund balance, July 1, 19X4	490,000
Fund balance, June 30, 19X5	$637,000

EXHIBIT III
Statement of Changes in Financial Position

City of Centerville Employees' Retirement System
Statement of Changes in Financial Position
For Year Ended June 30, 19X5

in thousands of dollars

Resources provided by	
Operations	
Net operating income	$147,000
Items not requiring current resources	
Depreciation expenses	1,000
Total resources provided	148,000
Resources used by	
Purchase of furniture, fixtures, and equipment	7,000
Net increase in working capital	$141,000

Elements of net increase (decrease) in working capital

	Year ended June 30		Working capital increase
	19X5	19X4	(decrease)
Current assets			
Cash	$15,000	$12,000	3,000
Accrued interest and dividends	40,000	45,000	(5,000)
Investments			
Common stock	200,000	150,000	50,000
Preferred stock	120,000	75,000	45,000
Bonds	250,000	200,000	50,000
Total current assets	625,000	482,000	143,000
Current liabilities			
Accrued expenses	10,000	9,000	(1,000)
Accounts payable	12,000	11,000	(1,000)
Total current liabilities	22,000	20,000	(2,000)
Working capital	$603,000	$462,000	$141,000

LITERATURE REFERENCES

Material in this chapter is based on the following authoritative pronouncements and publications, which are grouped according to the major headings used within the chapter. A dual reference (both paragraph and page number) is used for NCGA-1 and NCGA-2 because the original pronouncements do not use paragraph numbers.

Basic Concepts and Standards
GASB-1   *Authoritative Status of NCGA Pronouncements and AICPA Industry Audit Guide,* ¶ 9.
NCGA INTERPRETATION-8   *Certain Pension Matters,* ¶ 16.

GASB-4
GASB-4   *Applicability of FASB-87, "Employers' Accounting for Pensions,"* ¶¶ 10 and 11.

Objectives of Pension Fund Reporting
NCGA-6   *Pension Accounting and Financial Reporting: Public Employee Retirement Systems and State and Local Government Employers,* ¶ 4.
GASB-5   *Disclosure of Pension Information by Public Employee Retirement Systems and State and Local Governmental Employers,* ¶¶ 5 and 6.

Basis of Accounting
NCGA-1   *Governmental Accounting and Financial Reporting Principles,* pp. 6 and 12/ ¶¶ 18 and 74.
FASB:CS-1   *Objectives of Financial Reporting by Business Enterprises,* ¶ 44.

Measurement Focus
NCGA-1   *Governmental Accounting and Financial Reporting Principles,* p. 6/ ¶ 18.
GASB DISCUSSION MEMORANDUM   *Measurement Focus and Basis of Accounting—Governmental Funds* (nonauthoritative).

Budgetary System and Accounts
NCGA-1   *Governmental Accounting and Financial Reporting Principles,* pp. 13 and 14/ ¶¶ 78, 82, and 97.

Revenues
FASB:CS-6   *Elements of Financial Statements,* ¶ 78.
APB-4   *Basic Concepts and Accounting Principles Underlying Financial Statements of Business Enterprises,* ¶ 150.

Pension Trust Funds

Investment Income

NCGA-6   *Pension Accounting and Financial Reporting: Public Employee Retirement Systems and State and Local Government Employers,* ¶¶ 28 and 29.

APB-21   *Interest on Receivables and Payables,* ¶ 15.

FASB-12   *Accounting for Certain Marketable Securities,* ¶ 21.

FASB INTERPRETATION-11   *Changes in Market Values After Balance Sheet Date,* ¶¶ 3 and 4.

Exchange of Debt Securities

NCGA-6   *Pension Accounting and Financial Reporting: Public Employee Retirement Systems and State and Local Government Employers,* ¶¶ 47-50.

Other Revenue

NCGA-6   *Pension Accounting and Financial Reporting: Public Employee Retirement Systems and State and Local Government Employers,* Appendix p. 18 (nonauthoritative).

Expenses

FASB:CS-6   *Elements of Financial Statements,* ¶ 80.

NCGA-6   *Pension Accounting and Financial Reporting: Public Employee Retirement Systems and State and Local Government Employers,* ¶ 46.

NCGA INTERPRETATION-8   *Certain Pension Matters,* ¶¶ 9 and 11.

GASB-5   *Disclosure of Pension Information by Public Employee Retirement Systems and State and Local Governmental Employers,* Appendix E.

Assets

FASB:CS-6   *Elements of Financial Statements,* ¶ 25.

NCGA-6   *Pension Accounting and Financial Reporting: Public Employee Retirement Systems and State and Local Government Employers,* ¶¶ 28-31 and 34.

FASB-35   *Accounting and Reporting by Defined Benefit Pension Plans,* ¶ 12.

Liabilities

FASB:CS-6   *Elements of Financial Statements,* ¶ 35.

NCGA-6   *Pension Accounting and Financial Reporting: Public Employee Retirement Systems and State and Local Government Employers,* ¶ 32.

Designation of Fund Balances

NCGA-6   *Pension Accounting and Financial Reporting: Public Employee Retirement Systems and State and Local Government Employers,* ¶¶ 22, 35, and 36.

GASB-5   *Disclosure of Pension Information by Public Employee Retirement Systems and State and Local Governmental Employers,* ¶ 49.

Disclosures

GASB-5   *Disclosure of Pension Information by Public Employee Retirement Systems and State and Local Governmental Employers,* ¶ 4.

Disclosures as a Component Unit
NCGA-6   *Pension Accounting and Financial Reporting: Public Employee Retirement Systems and State and Local Government Employers,* ¶ 40.
NCGA-3   *Defining the Governmental Reporting Entity,* ¶ 9.

Financial Statements
NCGA-6   *Pension Accounting and Financial Reporting: Public Employee Retirement Systems and State and Local Government Employers,* ¶¶ 22, 27, 33, 35, and 36.
GASB-5   *Disclosure of Pension Information by Public Employee Retirement Systems and State and Local Governmental Employers,* ¶ 49.

GENERAL LONG-TERM DEBT ACCOUNT GROUP

A governmental unit may incur a variety of long-term debt obligations. The presentation of the noncurrent debt in a reporting entity's financial statements depends upon the nature of the obligation. Long-term obligations of proprietary funds and certain trust funds are presented as liabilities to each of the individual funds. Noncurrent debt that is not specifically the obligation of one of these three fund types must be accounted for in the General Long-Term Debt Account Group (GLTDAG).

The GLTDAG is not a fund because it does not account for available financial resources or current obligations. Financial resources are neither accumulated nor expended through the GLTDAG. This account group simply lists all long-term liabilities that are not presented as liabilities of a specific fund. Although the title of the account group refers to general long-term debt, the term is broader and encompasses various types of noncurrent liabilities that may be incurred by a governmental unit. Included in this broad definition of general long-term debt are the following liabilities:

- Debt instruments
- Bond anticipation notes
- Demand bonds
- Loss contingencies
- Compensated absences
- Special termination benefits
- Leases
- Pensions

Long-term liabilities presented in the GLTDAG are backed by the full faith and credit of the state or local government, which means that the debt is secured by the general taxing authority of the governmental unit.

Debt Instruments

A state or local government may acquire resources by issuing long-term debt instruments such as bonds or notes. The proceeds from the issuance of a debt instrument are recorded in the fund that receives the resources. The receipt of the resources is recorded as an other financing source (Proceeds from Issuance of Long-Term Debt) in the recipient fund's financial statements, while the liability is recorded in the GLTDAG. The segregation of general long-term debt in a separate account group, rather than reporting it as a fund liability, maintains the fundamental concept of governmental accounting, whereby a specific governmental fund presents only available expendable resources and liabilities that will use those resources. For example, if 8% serial bonds of $500,000 were issued and the proceeds were made available to the General Fund, the following entries would be made:

GLTDAG
Amount To Be Provided For Repayment Of Serial Bonds	500,000	
Serial Bonds Payable		500,000

GENERAL FUND
Cash	500,000	
Proceeds From Issuance Of Bonds		500,000

The account *amount to be provided for repayment of serial bonds* represents the amount of the unfunded liability and allows for the GLTDAG to have a set of self-balancing accounts. As resources are accumulated for the retirement of general obligation debt, the amount of the funding is reflected in the GLTDAG. For example, if in the current illustration $100,000 is transferred from the General Fund to a Debt Service Fund, and the transfer represents resources that will be used to eventually repay maturing serial bonds, the following entries would be made:

GLTDAG
Amount Available In Debt Service Fund	100,000	
Amount To Be Provided For Repayment Of Serial Bonds		100,000

GENERAL FUND
Transfers Out—Debt Service Fund	100,000	
Cash		100,000

General Long-Term Debt Account Group

DEBT SERVICE FUND
Cash   100,000
    Transfers In—General Fund   100,000

The account *amount available in Debt Service Fund* represents the amount of the long-term debt that has been funded. If future interest payments are funded in a Debt Service Fund, no entry is made in the GLTDAG for the funding of the interest.

> **OBSERVATION:** *Debt service transactions may be accounted for in a Debt Service Fund; however, unless required by law or by a covenant in the debt agreement, it is up to the discretion of the governmental unit whether a separate Debt Service Fund(s) should be created. NCGA-1 states that debt service transactions can be accounted for in the General Fund unless resources are being accumulated for principal and interest payments maturing in future years, or a separate Debt Service Fund is legally mandated.*

When general long-term debt becomes due and payable, the liability is removed from the GLTDAG and is shown as a liability of the Debt Service Fund (or the General Fund if no Debt Service Fund was established). The transfer of the liability from the GLTDAG to the Debt Service Fund occurs when the liability is due and payable and not when the debt becomes a current liability. For example, if $100,000 of the serial bonds referred to above were due and payable on July 1, 19X7, and the governmental unit's fiscal year ended June 30, no entry would be made on June 30, 19X7, even though a portion of the serial bonds ($100,000) represents a current liability. On July 1, 19X7, the following entries would be made, assuming the amount for the principal repayment is transferred from the General Fund to the Debt Service Fund:

GLTDAG
Amount Available In Debt Service Fund   100,000
    Amount To Be Provided For
      Repayment Of Serial Bonds   100,000

Serial Bonds Payable   100,000
    Amount Available In Debt Service
      Fund   100,000

GENERAL FUND
Transfers Out—Debt Service Fund   100,000
    Cash   100,000

Debt Service Fund

Cash	100,000	
Transfers In—General Fund		100,000
Expenditures—Principal	100,000	
Bonds Payable		100,000

Alternatively, if a maturing obligation (one that is due early in the following year) has been funded in a Debt Service Fund, the obligation may be removed from the GLTDAG. In the current example, if $100,000 were transferred from the General Fund to the Debt Service Fund on June 30, 19X7, the entries made immediately above would be made as of June 30 rather than July 1, even though the serial bonds are not due and payable until July 1.

> **OBSERVATION:** *Expenditures under the modified accrual basis of accounting are recognized when the related liability is incurred; however, as noted in NCGA-1 there is an exception for unmatured principal and interest on general long-term debt. These items, as demonstrated in the preceding example, are recorded as expenditures when they become due and payable.*

Bond Anticipation Notes

Bond anticipation notes are issued with the understanding that the notes will be liquidated within a short period of time when the actual bonds are sold to investors. Bond anticipation notes are classified as GLTDAG when the two criteria established by FASB-6 (Classification of Short-Term Obligations Expected to Be Refinanced) are satisfied. First, the governmental unit must intend to refinance the bond anticipation notes with the issuance of long-term bonds, and second, the intention to refinance must be substantiated either by a post-balance sheet issuance of the long-term bonds or the execution of an acceptable financing agreement. When the state or local government's intention to refinance the bond anticipation notes is substantiated through a financing agreement, FASB-6 established the following guidelines that must be satisfied:

- The agreement does not expire within one year from the date of the enterprise's balance sheet and during that period the agreement is not cancelable by the lender or the prospective lender

General Long-Term Debt Account Group

(and obligations incurred under the agreement are not callable during that period) except for violation of a provision with which compliance is objectively determinable.

- No violation of any provision in the financing agreement exists at the balance sheet date and no available information indicates that a violation has occurred thereafter but prior to the issuance of the balance sheet, or, if one exists at the balance sheet date or has occurred thereafter, a waiver has been obtained.

- The lender or the prospective lender or investor with which the enterprise has entered into the financing agreement is expected to be financially capable of honoring the agreement.

To illustrate, assume that $500,000 in bond anticipation notes is issued by a Capital Projects Fund. If the notes satisfy the two criteria established by FASB-6, the following entries would be made:

GLTDAG
Amount To Be Provided For Repayment Of Bond Anticipation Notes	500,000	
Bond Anticipation Notes Payable		500,000

CAPITAL PROJECTS FUND
Cash	500,000	
Proceeds From Issuance Of Bond Anticipation Notes		500,000

Subsequently, if bonds of $500,000 are issued and the bond anticipation notes are retired, the transactions would be recorded in the following manner, assuming that the debt is accounted for in a Debt Service Fund:

GLTDAG
Bond Anticipation Notes Payable	500,000	
Amount To Be Provided For Repayment Of Bond Anticipation Notes		500,000
Amount To Be Provided For Repayment Of Bonds	500,000	
Bonds Payable		500,000

General Long-Term Debt Account Group

DEBT SERVICE FUND
Expenditures—Repayment Of Bond Anticipation Notes	500,000	
Cash		500,000
Cash	500,000	
Proceeds From Issuance Of Bonds		500,000

The fund affected by the debt extinguishment must record both an expenditure (for the debt retirement) and an other source of financing (for the new debt proceeds).

Bond anticipation notes that do not satisfy the criteria established by FASB-6 cannot be recorded in the GLTDAG but rather must be reported as a specific fund liability.

> **OBSERVATION:** *Tax and revenue anticipation notes should not be reported as part of GLTDAG under any circumstance.*

Demand Bonds

Bonds issued by state or local governments may be due on demand. The demand feature is often referred to as a *put*. GASB Interpretation-1 (Demand Bonds Issued by State and Local Governmental Entities) concludes that demand bonds that have an exercisable provision for redemption at or within one year of the governmental unit's balance sheet date may not be reported as part of GLTDAG unless all of the following criteria are met:

- Before the financial statements are issued, the issuer has entered into an arm's-length financing (take out) agreement to convert bonds *put* but not resold into some other form of long-term obligation.
- The take out agreement does not expire within one year from the date of the issuer's balance sheet.
- The take out agreement is not cancelable by the lender or the prospective lender during that year, and obligations incurred under the take out agreement are not callable by the lender during that year.
- The lender or the prospective lender or investor is expected to be financially capable of honoring the take out agreement.

Demand bonds that do not satisfy the preceding criteria must be reported as a liability of the fund that received the proceeds from the sale of the bonds.

General Long-Term Debt Account Group

To illustrate, assume that $700,000 in demand bonds is issued and the proceeds are to be used by the General Fund. If the criteria established by GASB Interpretation-1 have been met, the issuance of the bonds would be recorded as follows:

GLTDAG
Amount To Be Provided For Repayment Of Demand Notes	700,000	
Demand Bonds Payable		700,000

GENERAL FUND
Cash	700,000	
Proceeds From Issuance Of Demand Bonds		700,000

If demand bonds are redeemed, the repayment is recorded as an expenditure of the fund from which debt service is normally paid. Continuing with the current illustration, assume that the demand bonds are redeemed and paid out of the Debt Service Fund from resources transferred from the General Fund. In addition, assume that as part of the take out agreement, long-term installment notes are issued to fund the payment for the demand bonds.

GLTDAG
Amount Available In Debt Service Fund For Redemption Of Demand Bonds	700,000	
Amount To Be Provided For Repayment Of Demand Bonds		700,000
Demand Bonds Payable	700,000	
Amount Available In Debt Service Fund For Redemption Of Demand Bonds		700,000
Amount To Be Provided For Repayment Of Long-Term Installment Notes	700,000	
Long-Term Installment Notes Payable		700,000

GENERAL FUND
Cash	700,000	
Proceeds From Issuance Of Long-Term Installment Notes To Finance Redemption Of Demand Bonds		700,000
Transfers Out—Debt Service Fund	700,000	
Cash		700,000

General Long-Term Debt Account Group

DEBT SERVICE FUND
Cash	700,000	
Transfers In—General Fund		700,000
Expenditures—Redemption Of		
Demand Bonds	700,000	
Cash		700,000

Loss Contingencies

Loss contingencies represent potential liabilities that may exist as of the governmental unit's balance sheet date. FASB-5 (Accounting for Contingencies) requires that a loss contingency be accrued when (1) it is probable, that is, the future loss is likely to occur, and (2) a reasonable estimate of the loss can be made. When an accrued loss contingency will not be liquidated with expendable available financial resources, it is recorded as part of the GLTDAG.

NCGA-4 (Accounting and Financial Reporting Principles for Claims and Judgments and Compensated Absences) concludes that FASB-5 should be applied to evaluate various governmental claims, such as the following:

- Worker compensation and unemployment claims
- Contractual claims arising from delays or inadequate specifications
- Claims arising from medical malpractice
- Claims arising from damage to property by government personnel
- Claims arising from personal injuries

To illustrate the accounting for claims, assume that a personal property claim is pending against a governmental unit and it is believed that the total payment for the claim will be approximately $100,000. Also, it is estimated that $20,000 of the claim will be paid from current expendable resources of the General Fund, and the balance will be paid in about eighteen months. The loss contingency would be recorded as follows:

GLTDAG
Amount To Be Provided For Payment		
Of Personal Property Claims	80,000	
Estimated Liabilities For Personal		
Property Claims		80,000

GENERAL FUND
   Expenditures—Personal Property Claims   20,000
      Estimated Liabilities For Personal
         Property Claims   20,000

NCGA-4 recommends that the governmental unit make the following presentation to show the relationship of the total loss contingency and the amount that is recognized as a long-term liability.

   Expenditures
      Claims and judgments ($100,000 (total amount
      determined for the year under FASB-5) less
      $80,000 (recorded as long-term obligations)) $20,000

In this example, the above disclosure would be made on the General Fund's Statement of Revenues, Expenditures, and Changes in Fund Balance.

 A separate Debt Service Fund may be, but is not required to be, established to account for the accumulation of resources to pay the claim and record the expenditure. When the long-term portion of the loss contingency becomes current, the debt is transferred to the governmental fund that will be responsible for payment of the claim. For example, if it is assumed that in the current illustration the General Fund (no Debt Service Fund was established) will pay the maturing claim, the following entries would be made when the claim is considered current:

GLTDAG
   Estimated Liabilities For Personal
      Property Claims   80,000
         Amount To Be Provided For Payment
           Personal Property Claims   80,000
GENERAL FUND
   Expenditures—Personal Property Claims   80,000
      Estimated Liabilities For Personal
         Property Claims   80,000

Loss contingencies related to proprietary funds and Nonexpendable Trust Funds are recorded in each specific fund, and no portion is presented as part of GLTDAG.

Compensated Absences

Benefits available to government employees may include compensation for absences that may arise from vacations, holidays, and illnesses. NCGA-4 requires that the accounting and reporting standards established by FASB-43 (Accounting for Compensated Absences) must be followed by state and local governments in accounting for compensated absences.

Compensated absences may create rights that vest or accumulate. FASB-43 defines these terms as follows:

- *Vested rights*—represent rights for which the employer has an obligation to make payment even if an employee terminates; thus, they are not contingent on an employee's future service.
- *Accumulated rights*—represent rights that are earned but unused rights to compensated absences that may be carried forward to one or more periods subsequent to that in which they are earned, even though there may be a limit to the amount that can be carried forward.

When all of the following four conditions exist, a governmental unit must accrue a liability for compensated absences:

- The employer's obligation relating to employees' rights to receive compensation for future absences is attributable to employees' service already rendered.
- The obligation relates to rights that vest or accumulate.
- Payment of the compensation is probable.
- The amount can be reasonably estimated.

The accrual for compensated absences is reflected in GLTDAG when their liquidation will not require the use of expendable available financial resources. For example, if at the end of a fiscal year it is estimated that the total cost of compensated absences is $55,000 and only $3,000 of this amount will use current expendable resources (from the General Fund), the following entries would be made to record the accrual for compensated absences:

GLTDAG

Amount To Be Provided For Payment Of Compensated Absences	52,000	
Estimated Liabilities For Compensated Absences		52,000

GENERAL FUND
    Expenditures—Compensated Absences   3,000
        Estimated Liabilities For
            Compensated Absences   3,000

To disclose the relationship between the total estimated liability for compensated absences and the amount that is recognized as a long-term liability, the following presentation may be made in the fund that recorded part of the liability as a current expenditure:

    Expenditures
        Compensated absences ($55,000 (total amount determined for the year under FASB-43) less $52,000 (recorded as long-term obligations))   <u>$3,000</u>

    A separate Debt Service Fund is not required to be established unless mandated. When a portion of the long-term liability for compensated absences becomes current, the obligation is transferred to the governmental fund that will liquidate the debt. In the current example, if it is assumed that $15,000 of the long-term obligation will be paid during the current period from the General Fund, the following entries would be made:

GLTDAG
    Estimated Liabilities For Compensated
        Absences   15,000
        Amount To Be Provided For Payment
            Of Compensated Absences   15,000

GENERAL FUND
    Expenditures—Compensated Absences   15,000
        Estimated Liabilities For
            Compensated Absences   15,000

    Compensated absences related to proprietary funds and Nonexpendable Trust Funds are recorded in each specific fund, and no portion is presented as part of GLTDAG.

Special Termination Benefits

In order to encourage employees to retire early, a governmental unit may offer to pay special termination benefits. When a special termination plan is offered, NCGA Interpretation-8 (Certain Pension Matters) requires that accounting and reporting standards established by FASB-74 (Accounting for Special Termination Benefits Paid to Employees) be observed.

The special termination plan must be offered for only a short period of time and may consist of both immediate payments and deferred payments. The total amount of the liability is the total of the current lump sum payments and the present value of the future period payments. The portion of the liability that will not be liquidated with current expendable financial resources is classified as part of GLTDAG. For example, if the total estimated cost of a special termination plan is $100,000, of which $25,000 is to be paid immediately from the General Fund, the following entries would be made:

GLTDAG
Amount To Be Provided For Payment Of
  Special Termination Benefits   75,000
    Special Termination Benefits Payable   75,000

GENERAL FUND
Expenditures — Special Termination
  Benefits   25,000
    Liabilities Under Special Termination
      Benefits Plan   25,000

NCGA Interpretation-8 recommends that the following information be disclosed with respect to the total liability created by the special termination benefits plan:

Expenditures
  Special termination benefits ($100,000 (total amount
  determined for the year by an acceptable actuarial
  cost method) less $75,000 (recorded as long-term
  obligations)) $25,000

No separate Debt Service Fund is required to be established unless mandated. When a portion of the long-term liability for special termination benefits becomes current, the obligation is transferred to the governmental fund that will liquidate the debt.

Special termination benefits related to proprietary funds and Nonexpendable Trust Funds are recorded in each specific fund and no portion is presented as part of GLTDAG.

Leases

A governmental unit may enter into a lease agreement that may create a long-term obligation if it is determined that the lease must be capitalized. NCGA-5 (Accounting and Financial Reporting Principles for Lease Agreements of State and Local Governments) requires that the accounting and reporting standards established by FASB-13 (Accounting for Leases, as amended) be observed to account for governmental leases.

FASB-13 requires that a lease be capitalized if any one of the following four criteria is a characteristic of the lease transaction:

- The lease transfers ownership of the property to the lessee by the end of the lease term.
- The lease contains a bargain purchase option.
- The lease term is equal to 75 percent or more of the estimated economic life of the lease property.
- The present value at the beginning of the lease term of the minimum lease payments, excluding that portion of the payments representing executory costs, to be paid by the lessor, including any profit thereon, equals or exceeds 90 percent of the excess of the fair value of the leased property to the lessor at the inception of the lease over any related investment tax credit retained by the lessor and expected to be realized by him.

When it is concluded that a lease should be capitalized, the lease obligation is equal to the present value of the minimum lease payments and the portion that will not use current expendable financial resources is recorded as part of the GLTDAG. For example, if a four-year lease agreement is signed on June 30, 19X1, and the annual lease payments are $10,000 for each year beginning on June 30, 19X2, the total amount of the long-term obligation is $33,121 as computed below (an implicit interest rate of 8% is assumed):

Annual lease payments	$10,000
Present value of an ordinary annuity, where the interest rate is 8% and the number of periods is 4	× 3.31213
Present value of minimum lease payments	$33,121

The capital lease would be recorded as follows on June 30, 19X1, assuming the lease represents equipment acquired for a Capital Projects Fund:

General Long-Term Debt Account Group

GLTDAG
  Amount To Be Provided For Lease
    Payments   33,121
    Obligations Under Capital Lease
      Agreements   33,121

GENERAL FIXED ASSETS ACCOUNT GROUP
  Assets Under Capital Leases   33,121
    Investment In General Fixed Assets—
      Capital Leases   33,121

CAPITAL PROJECTS FUND
  Expenditures—Capitalized Leases   33,121
    Other Financing Sources—
      Capitalized Leases   33,121

As portions of the lease obligation become a current liability in subsequent periods, the lease debt in the GLTDAG is reduced. The amount of the reduction is equal to the principal portion of the maturing lease payment and not to the full lease payment. To differentiate between the principal and interest portions, it may be helpful to prepare an amortization schedule. An illustration of an amortization schedule for the current example is presented below:

Amortization Schedule

	Payment	Interest expenditure @8%	Principal expenditure	Amount of general long-term debt
6/30/X1				$33,121
6/30/X2	$10,000	$2,650	$7,350	25,771
6/30/X3	10,000	2,062	7,938	17,833
6/30/X4	10,000	1,427	8,573	9,260
6/30/X5	10,000	740	9,260	-0-

Using the amortization schedule prepared above, the lease payment due on June 30, 19X2, would be recorded as follows:

GLTDAG
  Obligation Under Capital Lease
    Agreements   7,350
    Amount To Be Provided For Lease
      Payments   7,350

CAPITAL PROJECTS FUND
Expenditures—Capital Lease Principal
  Payments   7,350
Expenditures—Capital Lease Interest
  Payments   2,650
    Cash (Vouchers Payable)   10,000

> **OBSERVATION:** *This entry assumes that the governmental unit is not required to create a Debt Service Fund to account for service charges related to the lease obligation.*

Disclosures

As discussed in this chapter, the GLTDAG does not include long-term liabilities that are presented as part of a proprietary fund or Nonexpendable Trust Fund; however, when a governmental reporting entity is contingently liable for long-term debt of these types of funds, this fact should be disclosed as a contingent liability in notes to the general purpose financial statements.

NCGA-1 requires that the following disclosures with respect to liabilities and related transactions be presented in the general purpose financial statements:

- Significant contingent liabilities
- Encumbrances outstanding
- Pension plan obligations
- Accumulated unpaid employees benefits, such as vacation and sick leave
- Debt service requirements to maturity
- Commitments under noncapitalized leases
- Construction and other significant commitments
- Changes in general long-term debt

In addition, NCGA Interpretation-6 (Notes to the Financial Statements Disclosures) requires that the following liability-related disclosures be made:

- Claims and judgments
- Short-term debt instruments and liquidity
- Capital leases
- Contingencies

Other specific disclosures related to GLTDAG are summarized below.

Bond anticipation notes When a liability for bond anticipation notes meets the criteria for classification as part of GLTDAG, a note to the financial statements should present (1) a general description of the financing agreement, and (2) the terms of any new debt incurred or expected to be incurred as a result of the agreement.

Demand bonds When a governmental unit has demand bonds outstanding, irrespective of the exercisable date of the demand provision, the following information should be disclosed:

- General description of the demand bond program
- Terms of any letters of credit or other standby liquidity agreements outstanding
- Commitment fees to obtain the letters of credit
- Any amounts drawn on the letters of credit as of the balance sheet date
- A description of the take out agreement (expiration date, commitment fees to obtain the agreement, and terms of any new obligation under the take out agreement)
- Debt service requirements if take out agreement is exercised

Loss contingencies When a loss contingency arising from a claim is either not probable or not subject to reasonable estimation, the contingency must be disclosed in the financial statements when it is reasonably possible that a loss will eventually be incurred. The financial statement disclosure should describe the nature of the loss contingency and an estimate of the possible loss or range of loss. If an estimate of the loss cannot be made based on the available information, the disclosure should state that no estimate can be made.

Even though a claim has been accrued as a loss contingency, it may nonetheless be necessary to disclose the nature of the loss and the amount of the loss in order to avoid the issuance of misleading financial statements.

Compensated absences When all of the criteria for accrual of compensated absences exist, except for the fourth criterion (subject to reasonable estimation), the reason for the nonaccrual must be disclosed.

Leases The following information with respect to capitalized leases included in GLTDAG should be disclosed:

- Future minimum lease payments as of the date of the latest balance sheet presented, in the aggregate and for each of the five succeeding fiscal years, with separate deductions from the total for the amount representing executory costs, including any profit thereon, included in the minimum lease payments and for the amount of the imputed interest necessary to reduce the net minimum lease payments to present value.
- The total of minimum sublease rentals to be received in the future under noncancelable subleases as of the date of the latest balance sheet presented.
- Total contingent rentals actually incurred for each period for which an operating statement is presented.

In addition to the preceding disclosures, there should be a general description of the lease agreements, including such items as the existence of renewal or purchase options and restrictions imposed by the lease agreements.

Financial Statements

Although the GLTDAG is not a governmental fund, a Statement of General Long-Term Debt should be prepared. The Statement should disclose the amount of debt outstanding and the characteristics of the outstanding debt. The Statement of General Long-Term Debt is seldom presented as a separate financial statement but is usually displayed as a separate column in the reporting entity's Combined Balance Sheet—All Fund Types and Account Groups. An example of the Statement is presented in Exhibit I.

EXHIBIT I
Statement of General Long-Term Debt

City of Centerville
Statement of General Long-Term Debt
June 30, 19X5

Amounts available and to be provided for
the payment of general long-term debt:

8% Serial bonds		
Amount available in debt service fund	$100,000	
Amount to be provided	400,000	$500,000
9% Term bonds		
Amount available in debt service fund	150,000	
Amount to be provided	600,000	750,000
9% Bond anticipation notes		
Amount to be provided		450,000
Estimated liabilities for accrued loss contingencies		
Amount to be provided		75,000
Estimated liabilities for compensated absences		
Amount to be provided		40,000
Obligations for capitalized leases		
Amount to be provided		25,000
Total amount available and to be provided		$1,840,000
General long-term debt obligations:		
8% Serial bonds payable		$ 500,000
9% Term bonds payable		750,000
9% Bond anticipation notes payable		450,000
Estimated liabilities for accrued loss contingencies		75,000
Estimated liabilities for compensated absences		40,000
Obligations for capitalized leases		25,000
Total general long-term debt obligations		$1,840,000

The reporting entity should prepare a separate Statement of Changes in General Long-Term Debt unless adequate disclosures are made in notes to the financial statements. An example of this financial statement is presented in Exhibit II.

General Long-Term Debt Account Group

EXHIBIT II
Statement of Changes in General Long-Term Debt

City of Centerville
Statement of Changes in General Long-Term Debt
For Year Ended June 30, 19X5

	Balance July 1, 19X4	New issues	Principal repayments	Balance June 30, 19X5
General obligation debt:				
8% Serial bonds	$800,000	-0-	$300,000	$500,000
9% Term bonds	600,000	$150,000	-0-	750,000
9% Bond anticipation notes	-0-	450,000	-0-	450,000
Operating liabilities:				
Estimated liabilities for accrued loss contingencies	15,000	70,000	10,000	75,000
Estimated liabilities for compensated absences	35,000	10,000	5,000	40,000
Capital leases:				
General fund commitments	17,000	-0-	2,800	14,200
Capital projects fund commitments	-0-	12,100	1,300	10,800
Totals	$1,467,000	$692,100	$319,100	$1,840,000

General Long-Term Debt Account Group

LITERATURE REFERENCES

Material in this chapter is based on the following authoritative pronouncements and publications, which are grouped according to the major headings used within the chapter. A dual reference (both paragraph and page number) is used for NCGA-1 and NCGA-2 because the original pronouncements do not use paragraph numbers.

Introduction
NCGA-1 *Governmental Accounting and Financial Reporting Principles,* pp. 6, 8, and 9/ ¶¶ 19, 32, and 42-44.

Debt Instruments
NCGA-1 *Governmental Accounting and Financial Reporting Principles,* pp. 6, 8, 9, 12, and 16/ ¶¶ 19, 30, 44, 70, 72, 107, and 108.

Bond Anticipation Notes
NCGA Interpretation-9 *Certain Fund Classifications and Balance Sheet Accounts,* ¶ 12.
FASB-6 *Classification of Short-Term Obligations Expected to Be Refinanced,* ¶¶ 10-12 and 15.

Demand Bonds
GASB Interpretation-1 *Demand Bonds Issued by State and Local Governmental Entities,* ¶¶ 9-13.

Loss Contingencies
NCGA-4 *Accounting and Financial Reporting Principles for Claims and Judgments and Compensated Absences,* ¶¶ 9 and 16.
FASB-5 *Accounting for Contingencies,* ¶ 8.

Compensated Absences
NCGA-4 *Accounting and Financial Reporting Principles for Claims and Judgments and Compensated Absences,* ¶¶ 22, 23, and 25-28.
FASB-43 *Accounting for Compensated Absences,* ¶ 6.

Special Termination Benefits
NCGA Interpretation-8 *Certain Pension Matters,* ¶¶ 10 and 12.
FASB-74 *Accounting for Special Termination Benefits Paid to Employees,* ¶¶ 1 and 2.

Leases
NCGA-5 *Accounting and Financial Reporting Principles for Lease Agreements of State and Local Governments,* ¶¶ 11-14.
FASB-13 *Accounting for Leases,* as amended, ¶¶ 5, 7, and 10.

Disclosures

NCGA-1 *Governmental Accounting and Financial Reporting Principles,* p. 9/ ¶ 46.

NCGA INTERPRETATION-6 *Notes to the Financial Statements Disclosure,* ¶ 5.

FASB-6 *Classification of Short-Term Obligations Expected to Be Refinanced,* ¶ 15.

GASB INTERPRETATION-1 *Demand Bonds Issued by State and Local Governmental Entities,* ¶ 11.

FASB-5 *Accounting for Contingencies,* ¶¶ 9 and 10.

FASB-43 *Accounting for Compensated Absences,* ¶ 6.

FASB-13 *Accounting for Leases,* as amended, ¶¶ 13 and 16.

NCGA-5 *Accounting and Financial Reporting Principles for Lease Agreements of State and Local Governments,* ¶ 27.

Financial Statements

NCGA-1 *Governmental Accounting and Financial Reporting Principles,* pp. 21 and 22/ ¶¶ 141, 143, and 145.

GENERAL FIXED ASSETS ACCOUNT GROUP

A governmental unit may report its fixed assets in a specific fund or in the General Fixed Assets Account Group (GFAAG). Fixed assets utilized by Enterprise Funds, Internal Service Funds, and Nonexpendable Trust Funds are reported as fixed assets of each of these respective funds and are accounted for in the same manner as a commercial enterprise would account for its fixed assets. All other fixed assets of the governmental unit are considered general fixed assets and are recorded in the GFAAG.

The GFAAG is not a fund because it does not account for available financial resources or governmental obligations. Assets reported in the GFAAG are not available to finance current expenditures of the governmental unit and therefore should not be reported as available financial resources of a particular governmental fund. General fixed assets are available to the governmental unit as a whole rather than to specific funds of the governmental unit. The GFAAG may include a variety of general fixed assets such as land, land improvements, buildings, equipment, vehicles, and infrastructure assets.

Due to the measurement focus of the governmental fund (flow of current expendable resources), the accounting and reporting standards related to general fixed assets are unique when compared to commercial accounting standards.

Acquisition of General Fixed Assets

General fixed assets acquired by a state or local government should be recorded at cost. Cost is equal to either the fair value of the consideration given or consideration received, whichever is more objectively determinable. In most transactions, the fair value of the acquired property is equal to the amount of monetary assets and/or monetary liabilities exchanged. Thus, a general fixed asset that is acquired by expending $10,000 in cash and signing a $25,000 interest-bearing note is recorded at $35,000.

OBSERVATION: *Monetary assets and liabilities are assets and liabilities whose amounts are fixed in terms of future cash flows. Cash and accounts and notes receivable are examples of monetary assets. Monetary liabilities include accounts and notes payable.*

In addition to the consideration given up to acquire a general fixed asset, ancillary costs associated with preparing the property for its intended use should be capitalized. Some ancillary costs that may be incurred by a governmental unit are summarized below:

General fixed asset	Ancillary costs to be capitalized
Land	Title search costs, attorney's fees, liens assumed, taxes assumed, grading costs, and land improvements with an indefinite life
Buildings	Attorney's fees, architect's fees, and inspection and building permits
Machinery	Freight charges, installation costs, and setup costs

The acquisition of general fixed assets must be financed by expending resources of a governmental fund, such as the General Fund or a Capital Projects Fund. If the acquisition is financed by a current cash disbursement, the payment is recognized as an expenditure of the governmental fund whose financial resources are reduced. The general fixed asset is recorded in the GFAAG by debiting an appropriately descriptive asset account and crediting an account that identifies the financing source used to acquire the asset. For example, if an automobile costing $10,000 is purchased by expending cash from the General Fund, the acquisition would be recorded as follows:

GFAAG
   Automobiles   10,000
      Investment In General Fixed Assets—
         General Fund Revenues   10,000

GENERAL FUND
   Expenditures—Capital Outlays   10,000
      Vouchers Payable (Cash)   10,000

In some instances, the acquired cost of property may not be available and some alternative basis must be used to record the general fixed asset. For example, a governmental unit may not have documented the original cost of acquired or constructed property, and it may be impossible or time-consuming to reconstruct the actual cost of the property. Under this condition, the original cost of the property may be estimated and used as the basis for capitalization. When estimates are used, the financial statements should disclose the estimation methods employed and the extent to which estimates were used.

Generally, property acquired from delinquent taxpayers is sold to satisfy the liens against the property, in which case the temporarily acquired property is accounted for in the governmental fund that was responsible for levying the original tax or assessment against the property. Forfeited property that the governmental unit decides to retain and use to provide its services should be capitalized at an amount equal to the unpaid property taxes, penalty charges, and legal fees incurred to gain clear title to the property; however, the capitalized cost should not be greater than the fair market value of the forfeited property. For example, assume a governmental unit forecloses on land that has outstanding delinquent property taxes of $12,000. The land will be retained by the governmental unit and converted into a park. Assuming the property taxes were originally accounted for in the General Fund, the foreclosure on the property would be recorded as follows:

GFAAG
    Land   12,000
        Investment In General Fixed Assets—
        General Fund Property Tax
            Foreclosures   12,000

GENERAL FUND
    Expenditures—Capital Outlays   12,000
        Property Taxes Receivable—
            Delinquent   12,000

Through eminent domain, a governmental unit has the authority to acquire property without the consent of the property owner. The property owner must be paid a reasonable price for the property, and the price would be capitalized in the GFAAG.

There is, of course, no cost basis when property is donated to a state or local government. When property is acquired through donation, the fixed asset should be recorded at its estimated fair market value at the date the gift is made.

General fixed assets acquired from grants, entitlements, and shared revenues should be capitalized and presented as part of the GFAAG.

Infrastructure Fixed Assets

Infrastructure or public domain general fixed assets are immovable assets that are generally of value only to the state or local government. Included in this category of fixed assets are highways, bridges, sidewalks, drainage systems, and lighting systems. Because these assets are not portable, the reporting of infrastructure fixed assets in the GFAAG is optional; however, the accounting policy used to account for infrastructure general fixed assets must be disclosed in the governmental unit's financial statements.

When a governmental unit decides not to record infrastructure assets as part of the GFAAG, there is only a need to record the capital outlay expenditure in the governmental unit that paid for the fixed asset acquisition. For example, if a pedestrian mall in a downtown area is constructed at a cost of $125,000 and the capital outlay was accounted for in a Capital Projects Fund, the following entry would be made, assuming the local government does not record its infrastructure assets in the GFAAG:

CAPITAL PROJECTS FUND
    Expenditures—Capital Outlays   125,000
        Vouchers Payable/Cash   125,000

GFAAG
    No entry

On the other hand, if the governmental unit records infrastructure general fixed assets in the GFAAG, the following additional entry must be made:

GFAAG
    Infrastructure Assets—Pedestrian Mall   125,000
        Investment In General Fixed Assets—
            Capital Projects Fund   125,000

Construction in Progress

Generally, a Capital Projects Fund is used to account for the construction of a general fixed asset for a governmental unit. As construction progresses, the cumulative expenditures are capitalized as construction in progress in the GFAAG. Upon completion of the capital asset, the balance in the construction in progress account is transferred to an appropriate descriptive account title such as building or equipment.

General Fixed Assets Account Group

During the construction of general fixed assets, it is likely that interest costs will be incurred by the governmental unit either through short-term financing by governmental funds, or through general long-term debt issued by the governmental unit. Interest cost incurred during the construction of general fixed assets is subject to capitalization as part of the cost of construction when conditions identified by FASB-34 (Capitalization of Interest Cost) exist. To determine the amount of interest cost to be capitalized, the weighted-average amount of accumulated expenditures for the period is multiplied by the governmental unit's average borrowing rate for the period. Rather than using the overall average borrowing rate, the following approach can be used:

- The interest rate for the obligation incurred specifically to finance the construction of the capital asset may be used.
- The overall average borrowing rate would be used for any accumulated expenditures in excess of specific borrowings.

The amount of interest cost to be capitalized is limited to the actual amount of interest expenditures incurred by the governmental unit.

To illustrate the capitalization of interest cost, assume that equipment being constructed is accounted for in a Capital Projects Fund. The general fixed asset construction is entirely financed by a $100,000, 7% note. The weighted-average accumulated expenditures for the period amounted to $30,000 and total expenditures were $90,000. The amount of interest to be capitalized is $2,100 ($30,000 × 7%), assuming the governmental unit decides to use the interest rate related to the construction note. Assuming the construction note is accounted for in a Debt Service Fund, cost associated with the construction of the equipment during the period would be recorded as follows:

GFAAG
Construction In Progress	92,100	
Investment In General Fixed Assets—Capital Projects Fund Construction Note		92,100

CAPITAL PROJECTS FUND
Expenditures—Capital Outlays	90,000	
Vouchers Payable/Cash		90,000

DEBT SERVICE FUND
Expenditures—Interest ($100,000 × 7%)	7,000	
Cash		7,000

General Fixed Assets Account Group

Capital Lease Rights

NCGA-5 (Accounting and Financial Reporting Principles for Lease Agreements of State and Local Governments) requires a lease agreement that satisfies the criteria established by FASB-13 (Accounting for Leases, as amended) to be capitalized. Capitalized property rights must be recorded as part of the GFAAG when any one of the following criteria is satisfied:

- The lease transfers ownership of the property to the lessee by the end of the lease term.
- The lease term contains a bargain purchase option.
- The lease term is equal to 75% or more of the estimated economic life of the leased property.
- The present value at the beginning of the lease term of the minimum lease payments, excluding that portion of the payments representing executory costs, to be paid by the lessor, including any profit thereon, equals or exceeds 90% of the excess of the fair value of the leased property to the lessor at the inception of the lease over any related investment tax credit retained by the lessor and expected to be realized by him.

To illustrate the capitalization of capital lease rights, assume that machinery is leased and the present value of minimum lease payments is $25,000. In addition, appropriate criteria established by FASB-13 are satisfied. Assuming the machinery acquisition is accounted for in a Capital Projects Fund, the following entries would be prepared:

GFAAG
Assets Under Capital Leases	25,000	
Investment In General Fixed Assets—		
Capital Leases		25,000

GENERAL LONG-TERM DEBT ACCOUNT GROUP
Amount To Be Provided For Lease		
Payments	25,000	
Obligations Under Capital Lease		
Agreements		25,000

CAPITAL PROJECTS FUND
Expenditures—Capital Outlays	25,000	
Other Financing Sources—Execution		
Of Capital Lease		25,000

Subsequent periodic lease payments are recorded (1) as expenditures in the governmental fund making the disbursements and (2) as long-term debt reduction in the General Long-Term Debt Account Group, but those lease payments have no effect on the carrying value of the capitalized lease rights in the GFAAG.

Depreciation

A governmental fund's statement of operations reports only the sources and uses of current expendable financial resources. Depreciation is the allocation of the cost of a fixed asset over its estimated economic life. Even though depreciation of fixed assets occurs in a physical sense during each period, depreciation does not affect a fund's expendable financial resources. For these reasons depreciation is not recorded in a governmental fund's activity statement. The purchase of a fixed asset results in a reduction of a governmental fund's expendable financial resources (expenditure) in the period in which the asset is purchased. For example, if equipment is purchased using financial resources of the General Fund, an expenditure for capital outlays would be recorded by the General Fund. Even though the economic life of the equipment is, say, three years, no depreciation is recognized in the General Fund during this period.

While depreciation cannot be recorded in a governmental fund, NCGA-1 concludes that it may be recorded in the GFAAG. It should be noted that recording depreciation in the GFAAG is not mandatory. If the governmental unit decides to record depreciation, the conventional accounting standards with respect to acceptable depreciation methods, estimated economic life, and estimated salvage value should be observed. When the depreciation entry is made in the GFAAG, depreciation expense is not recorded but, rather, the investment in general fixed assets account is reduced and accumulated depreciation is increased. For example, if equipment purchased by the General Fund for $100,000 with an estimated salvage value of $10,000 and estimated economic life of four years is depreciated using the straight-line depreciation method, the following entry would be made:

GFAAG
   Investment In General Fixed Assets—
      General Fund Revenues   22,500
         Accumulated Depreciation—
            Equipment   22,500

Although depreciation is not recorded in a specific governmental fund, this does not preclude the governmental unit from considering depreciation calculations in evaluating various governmental activities and programs. For example, depreciation calculations may be an important cost element to consider in the following situations:

- Total cost of such activities as garbage collection, fire protection, etc.
- Make-or-buy decisions
- Reimburseable cost under a particular intergovernmental program
- Fee schedule establishment

Disposition and Exchange of General Fixed Assets

When general fixed assets are sold or otherwise disposed of, the asset's book value is removed from the GFAAG. If the capital asset is sold, the proceeds from the sale should be recorded in the governmental fund that by law or past practice is entitled to the funds. The sale proceeds should be identified as miscellaneous or other revenue. To illustrate, assume that equipment that originally cost $40,000 five years ago is sold for $6,500 and the proceeds from the sale are made available to the General Fund. The disposition would be recorded as follows, assuming that the asset was originally purchased by expending resources of the General Fund and the governmental unit does not record depreciation on its general fixed assets:

GFAAG
Investment In General Fixed Assets—
    General Fund Revenues   40,000
        Equipment   40,000

GENERAL FUND
Cash   6,500
    Other Revenues—Sale Of General
        Fixed Assets   6,500

If a governmental unit records depreciation on its general fixed assets, the related accumulated depreciation must be removed when the asset is sold.

General fixed assets of a governmental unit may be exchanged for other general fixed assets. When the transaction is a nonmonetary exchange, the accounting for the exchange is dependent upon whether dissimilar or similar property was exchanged.

> **OBSERVATION:** *Nonmonetary assets and liabilities are all other assets and liabilities that are not classified as monetary assets or monetary liabilities. General fixed assets of a governmental unit are classified as nonmonetary assets.*

Dissimilar Exchanges An exchange that involves dissimilar property should be recorded at the fair value of the property given or the fair value of the property received, whichever is more objectively determinable. The fair value of exchanged property may be determined by one of the following methods:

- Refer to estimated realizable values in cash transactions of the same or similar assets
- Refer to quoted market prices for the exchanged property
- Obtain independent appraisals of the exchanged property

A dissimilar exchange is accounted for by recording the fair value of the general fixed asset in the GFAAG. The book value (including accumulated depreciation, if depreciation is recognized) of the general fixed asset given up is removed from the GFAAG. Almost always there will be a difference between the fair value of the asset received and the book value of the asset given up; however, in governmental accounting there is no recognition of a gain or loss on the exchange. To illustrate, assume that a parcel of land with a cost basis of $20,000 is exchanged for equipment, and both assets have a fair value of $90,000. The exchange of these dissimilar assets would be recorded in the following manner:

GFAAG
Investment In General Fixed Assets—		
General Fund Revenues	20,000	
Land		20,000
Equipment	90,000	
Investment In General Fixed Assets—		
General Fund Revenues		90,000

Cash (or other monetary assets) received or paid as part of the exchange of dissimilar assets would be recorded as a revenue or an expenditure in the governmental fund affected by the transaction.

Under some circumstances, it may not be possible to determine a reasonable fair value of the property received or given up in the exchange. In this case the book value of the general fixed asset given up should be used to record the receipt of the new asset.

Similar Exchanges   An exchange of similar property involves an exchange of a general fixed asset for a similar asset or an equivalent interest in the same or similar asset. Assets are similar when they are of the same general type and perform the same function.

Unlike dissimilar exchanges, a similar exchange is accounted for by using the book value of the general fixed asset given up. The book value (including accumulated depreciation, if depreciation is recognized) of the asset given up becomes the basis of the new asset received. For example, if a governmental unit exchanges a parking lot that has a cost basis of $100,000 and a fair value of $350,000 for another parking lot, the exchange of similar property would be recorded as follows:

GFAAG
   Investment In General Fixed Assets—
      General Fund Revenues   100,000
         Land   100,000

   Land   100,000
      Investment In General Fixed Assets—
         General Fund Revenues   100,000

Of course the two entries are offsetting and have no net effect on the total value of general fixed assets; however, journal entries or memorandum entries should be made to provide a management trail for the executed transaction. In addition, the exchange will require that the subsidiary ledger that supports the *land* account be changed to reflect detail information relevant to the newly acquired asset.

Disclosures

With respect to general fixed assets, NCGA-1 requires that the following should be disclosed in a governmental unit's financial statements:

- Accounting policy used to account for infrastructure general fixed assets
- Accounting policy used to account for the capitalization of interest cost associated with self-constructed general fixed assets
- Methods and amounts used to estimate the cost of general fixed assets
- Disclosures required by FASB-13 with respect to noncapitalized lease commitments

The 1980 GAAFR (Governmental Accounting, Auditing, and Financial Reporting) suggests that it may be necessary to make the following disclosures in supplementary data schedules:

- General fixed assets by sources
- General fixed assets by function and activity classifications for each major asset class
- Changes in general fixed assets by functions and activities
- Changes in general fixed assets by major asset class

When a governmental unit has engaged in nonmonetary transactions during the period, disclosures in the financial statements should include a description of the transactions and the basis of accounting for assets transferred.

An example of a note disclosing certain information related to a governmental unit's general fixed assets accounting policies is presented below:

▶ General fixed assets have been acquired for general governmental purposes. Assets purchased are recorded as expenditures in the governmental funds and capitalized at cost in the General Fixed Assets Account Group. Contributed fixed assets are recorded as general fixed assets at estimated fair market value at the time received.

Fixed assets consisting of certain improvements other than buildings, including roads, bridges, curbs and gutters, streets and sidewalks, drainage systems, and lighting systems, have not been capitalized. Such assets normally are immovable and of value only to the City. Therefore, the purpose of stewardship for capital expenditures is satisfied without recording these assets.

No depreciation has been provided on general fixed assets. No interest has been capitalized on self-constructed assets because noncapitalization of interest does not have a material effect on the city's financial statements.

Property, plant, and equipment owned by proprietary funds of the City are stated at cost or estimated fair market value. Depreciation has been provided over the estimated useful lives using the straight-line depreciation method.

The City leases a significant amount of property and equipment from others. Certain leased properties that take on elements of ownership are classified as capital leases in the General Fixed Assets Account Group. The related obligations, in amounts equal to the present value of minimum lease payments during the lease terms, are recorded in the General Long-Term Debt Account Group. Other leased properties and all leased equipment are classified as operating leases. Both capital and operating lease payments are charged to expenditures when payable. Total expenditures on such leases for the year ended June 30, 19X5, amounted to $15,000,000. ◄

Financial Statements

Although the GFAAG is not a governmental fund, a Statement of General Fixed Assets should be prepared. The statement should disclose the general fixed assets of the governmental unit and the sources of these assets. The Statement of General Fixed Assets is seldom presented as a separate financial statement but is usually displayed as a separate column in the reporting entity's Combined Balance Sheet—All Fund Types and Account Groups. An example of a separate statement is presented in Exhibit I.

The reporting entity should prepare a separate Statement of Changes in General Fixed Assets, unless adequate disclosures are made in notes to the financial statements. An example of this financial statement is presented in Exhibit II. In addition, a Schedule of General Fixed Assets (By Function and Activity) may be presented. An example of this schedule is presented in Exhibit III.

EXHIBIT I
Statement of General Fixed Assets

City of Centerville
Statement of General Fixed Assets
June 30, 19X5

(in thousands of dollars)

General fixed assets	
Land	$ 700,000
Buildings	1,600,000
Equipment	750,000
Assets under capital leases	150,000
Construction in progress	300,000
Total general fixed assets	$3,500,000
Investments in general fixed assets from:	
Capital projects funds:	
General obligation bonds	$1,400,000
Federal grants	600,000
Capital lease obligations	110,000
General fund revenues	800,000
Special revenue fund revenues	300,000
Special assessments	250,000
Donations	40,000
Total investments in general fixed assets	$3,500,000

General Fixed Assets Account Group

EXHIBIT II
Statement of Changes in General Fixed Assets

City of Centerville
Statement of Changes in General Fixed Assets
(By Function and Activity)
For Year Ended June 30, 19X5

(in thousands of dollars)

Function and Activity	General fixed assets 7/1/X4	Additions	Deductions	General fixed assets 6/30/X5
General government control				
Legislative	$ 60	$ 20	$ 30	$ 50
Executive	180	40	10	210
Judicial	35	5	—	40
Total control	275	65	40	300
Staff functions				
General government buildings	970	200	70	1,100
Community improvements	250	50	—	300
Legal and finance	260	—	10	250
Other	60	20	30	50
Total staff functions	1,540	270	110	1,700
Total general government	1,815	335	150	2,000
Public safety				
Police	600	50	100	550
Fire	270	40	10	300
Inspection	55	5	10	50
Total public safety	925	95	120	900
Streets	120	20	40	100
Sanitation	60	30	20	70
Health and welfare	35	15	—	50
Libraries	30	25	15	40
Recreation	25	15	—	40
Total	270	105	75	300
Total general fixed assets allocated to functions and activities	$3,010	$535	$345	3,200
Under construction				300
Total general fixed assets				$3,500

68.14 / *GOVERNMENTAL GAAP GUIDE*

EXHIBIT III
Schedule of General Fixed Assets

City Of Centerville
Schedule of General Fixed Assets
(By Function and Activity)
For Year Ended June 30, 19X5

(in thousands of dollars)

Function and Activity	Land	Buildings	Equipment	Capital leases	Total
General government control					
Legislative	—	—	$50	—	$50
Executive	—	—	210	—	210
Judicial	—	—	40	—	40
Total control	—	—	300	—	300
Staff functions					
General government buildings	$300	$700	100	—	1,100
Community improvements	100	100	100	—	300
Legal and finance	—	—	100	$150	250
Other	—	—	50	—	50
Total staff functions	400	800	350	150	1,700
Total general government	400	800	650	150	2,000
Public safety	140	370	40	—	550
Police	50	220	30	—	300
Fire	10	30	10	—	50
Total public safety	200	620	80	—	900
Streets	30	65	5	—	100
Sanitation	20	45	5	—	70
Health and welfare	10	40	—	—	50
Libraries	10	25	5	—	40
Recreation	30	5	5	—	40
Total	100	180	20	—	300
Total general fixed assets allocated to functions and activities	$700	$1,600	$750	$150	3,200
Under construction					300
Total general fixed assets					$3,500

General Fixed Assets Account Group

LITERATURE REFERENCES

Material in this chapter is based on the following authoritative pronouncements and publications, which are grouped according to the major headings used within the chapter. A dual reference (both paragraph and page number) is used for NCGA-1 and NCGA-2 because the original pronouncements do not use paragraph numbers.

Introduction
NCGA-1 *Governmental Accounting and Financial Reporting Principles*, pp. 8 and 9/¶¶ 33-39 and 41.

Acquisition of General Fixed Assets
NCGA-1 *Governmental Accounting and Financial Reporting Principles*, pp. 9 and 10/¶¶ 47-50.
NCGA-2 *Grant, Entitlement, and Shared Revenue Accounting by State and Local Governments*, p. 3/¶ 15.
APB-29 *Accounting for Nonmonetary Transactions*, ¶¶ 1 and 3.
1980 GAAFR *Governmental Accounting, Auditing, and Financial Reporting*, p. 54.

Infrastructure Fixed Assets
NCGA-1 *Governmental Accounting and Financial Reporting Principles*, p. 9/ ¶ 40.

Construction in Progress
NCGA-1 *Governmental Accounting and Financial Reporting Principles*, p. 9/ ¶ 40.
FASB-34 *Capitalization of Interest Cost*, ¶¶ 13 and 17.

Capital Lease Rights
NCGA-5 *Accounting and Financial Reporting Principles for Lease Agreements of State and Local Governments*, ¶ 12.
FASB-13 *Accounting for Leases*, as amended, ¶¶ 7 and 8.

Depreciation
NCGA-1 *Governmental Accounting and Financial Reporting Principles*, p. 10/ ¶¶ 51-56.

Disposition and Exchange of General Fixed Assets
1980 GAAFR *Governmental Accounting, Auditing, and Financial Reporting*, pp. 54 and 55.
APB-29 *Accounting for Nonmonetary Transactions*, ¶¶ 3, 21, 25, and 26.

Disclosures
NCGA-1 *Governmental Accounting and Financial Reporting Principles*, pp. 9, 10, 21, and 22/¶¶ 40, 48, 49, and 143.
1980 GAAFR *Governmental Accounting, Auditing, and Financial Reporting*, p. 53.
APB-29 *Accounting for Nonmonetary Transactions*, ¶ 28.

Financial Statements
NCGA-1 *Governmental Accounting and Financial Reporting Principles*, pp. 21 and 22/¶¶ 141, 143, and 145.

Special Governmental Units and Agencies

HOSPITALS

BASIC CONCEPTS AND STANDARDS

Hospitals may be privately owned or owned by various governmental units at the federal, state, or local level. The financial statements of a hospital owned by a state or local government must be included in the governmental unit's combined financial statements when the governmental unit exercises oversight responsibility over the hospital, as described in NCGA-3 (Defining the Governmental Reporting Entity).

Accounting and reporting standards applicable to hospitals operated by governmental units are established by the following pronouncements:

- AICPA Hospital Audit Guide
- AICPA SOP (Auditing) (March 1978) (Clarification of Accounting, Auditing and Reporting Practices Relating to Hospital Malpractice Loss Contingencies)
- AICPA SOP 78-1 (Accounting by Hospitals for Certain Marketable Equity Securities)
- AICPA SOP 78-7 (Financial Accounting and Reporting by Hospitals Operated by a Governmental Unit)
- AICPA SOP 81-2 (Reporting Practices Concerning Hospital-Related Organizations)
- AICPA SOP 85-1 (Financial Reporting by Not-for-Profit Health Care Entities for Tax-Exempt Debt and Certain Funds Whose Use Is Limited)

Additional guidance for identifying accounting and reporting standards for hospitals can be found in the American Hospital Association's (AHA) *Chart of Accounts for Hospitals*.

> **OBSERVATION:** Although the AHA's Chart of Accounts for Hospitals *does not carry the same authoritative weight as the AICPA's Audit Guides and SOPs, it is a recognized source of authority under the GASB hierarchy of generally accepted accounting principles as described in Chapter 1 of this guide.*

GOVERNMENTAL GAAP GUIDE / 80.01

Basis of Accounting

An entity's accounting basis determines when transactions and economic events are reflected in its financial statements. NCGA-1 (Governmental Accounting and Financial Reporting Principles) states that a basis of accounting refers to "when revenues, expenditures, expenses, and transfers—and the related assets and liabilities—are recognized in the accounts and reported in the financial statements." SOP 78-7 concludes that hospitals operated by governmental units should be accounted for as an Enterprise Fund. Since an Enterprise Fund uses the accrual basis, hospitals must also use the accrual basis to determine when the economic consequences of transactions and events should be reflected in their financial statements.

In FASB:CS-1 (Objectives of Financial Reporting by Business Enterprises) accrual accounting is described in the following manner:

> Accrual accounting attempts to record the financial effects on an enterprise of transactions and other events and circumstances that have cash consequences for an enterprise in the periods in which those transactions, events, and circumstances occur rather than only in the periods in which cash is received or paid by the enterprise. Accrual accounting is concerned with the process by which cash expended on resources and activities is returned as more (or perhaps less) cash to the enterprise, not just with the beginning and end of the process.

The essential elements of the accrual accounting method include the (1) deferral of expenditures and the subsequent amortization of the deferred cost (prepaid expenses, supplies, etc.), (2) deferral of revenues until they are earned (governmental payments received in advance by a hospital), and (3) capitalization of certain expenditures and the subsequent depreciation of the capitalized cost (depreciation of diagnostic equipment). The *Chart of Accounts for Hospitals* defines accrual accounting as a system that "gives recognition to all revenues earned and to all expenses incurred in each time period, irrespective of the flow of cash between the hospital and other parties."

Although hospitals use the same basis of accounting as Enterprise Funds, transactions and events that affect hospitals are recorded in a variety of specialized funds in much the same manner as the various funds that are used by governmental units.

Measurement Focus

The measurement focus for an entity is concerned with the inflow and outflow of resources that affect the organization. The balance sheet should reflect those resources that are available both to meet current obligations and to be used in the delivery of the services provided by a hospital. The activity statement for the period should summarize those resources received and those consumed during the current period. The measurement focus of a hospital is the flow of economic resources.

The flow of economic resources refers to all of the assets available to the hospital for the purpose of providing its services to its patrons. When the flow of economic resources and the accrual basis of accounting are combined, they provide the foundation for generally accepted accounting principles used by business enterprises.

When the flow of economic resources is applied on an accrual basis for a hospital, all assets and liabilities, both current and long-term, would be presented in the hospital's balance sheet. The key differences between this approach and the accounting model used by governmental funds are summarized below:

- Fixed assets would be recorded in the hospital's balance sheet net of accumulated depreciation and not in the General Fixed Assets Account Group.
- Long-term debt would be recorded in the hospital's balance sheet and not in the General Long-Term Debt Account Group.
- The hospital's fund balance would represent the net assets (total assets minus total liabilities) available to the hospital, and not only those net assets available to pay current expenditures or debts arising from operations.

The hospital's activity statement would include all costs of providing medical services during the period. These costs would include depreciation, the cost of supplies consumed during the period, and other operating expenses. On the activity statement, revenues earned during the period should match the total cost of providing medical services.

Budgetary System and Accounts

A budget is a plan of financial operations which provides a basis for the planning, controlling, and evaluation of activities of a hospital.

A hospital should prepare a flexible budget, which changes as activity levels change. In a hospital, overall activity is measured in terms of revenues and expenses, and will in part fluctuate depending upon the demand of services by the patrons of the hospital. Generally, a flexible budget, unlike the adoption of a fixed budget by a governmental unit, is not considered a form of appropriations, but rather serves as an approved plan that can facilitate budgetary control and operational evaluations. A flexible budget approach allows the hospital to prepare several budgets at different activity levels in order to establish an acceptable comparative basis for planned activity and actual results.

> **OBSERVATION:** NCGA-1 discusses the preparation of several budgets based on anticipated activity levels. Even if several budgets are prepared, the budget ultimately used as a comparison with actual results should be based on the actual, not the anticipated level of activity. The preparation of the budget based on actual activity is feasible, since the flexible budgeting approach can be expressed in terms of a formula (Total Expenses = Fixed Expenses + Variable Expenses) and should be applicable at any activity level.

Generally, it is not appropriate to integrate the budgetary system into the hospital's accounting system when a flexible budget system is used; however, if a fixed budget is used, perhaps due to a legal requirement or preference, it may be useful to integrate the budgetary accounts into the accounting system. The basis of accounting used to prepare a budget for a hospital should be the same as the basis used to record the entity's actual transactions, namely the accrual basis.

ACCOUNTS AND TRANSACTIONS

A hospital records its transactions using the same accounting principles used by a commercial enterprise. Transactions accounted for by a hospital must be recorded in a manner consistent with FASB pronouncements, except when the GASB has addressed the accounting issue. When a hospital's financial statements are presented as part of the governmental unit's combined financial statements, GASB pronouncements must be observed.

Consistent with the basic governmental accounting model, transactions of a hospital are recorded in a variety of funds. The American

Hospital Association recommends the use of the following funds to account for a hospital's transactions:

- General Funds (Unrestricted Funds)
  - Operating Fund
  - Board-Designated Funds
- Restricted Funds
  - Specific-Purpose Funds
  - Endowment Funds
  - Plant Replacement and Expansion Funds

Presented below is a discussion of the typical transactions encountered by a hospital and the funds used to record these various transactions:

Revenues and Other Sources of Assets

FASB:CS-6 (Elements of Financial Statements) defines revenues as "inflows or other enhancements of assets of an entity, or settlements of its liabilities during a period from delivering or producing goods, rendering services, or other activities that constitute the entity's ongoing major or central operations." Revenues, as established in APB Statement-4 (Basic Concepts and Accounting Principles Underlying Financial Statements of Business Enterprises) should be recognized when the earning process is complete or virtually complete and an exchange has taken place. In general, revenues for medical services are accrued when the services are delivered. As described below there are a number of revenue sources for a hospital.

Patient Service Revenues Charges to patients for nursing services and other professional services rendered are the primary source of revenue for most hospitals. Professional service revenues arise from a multitude of services performed by the hospital staff, including general surgery, anesthesiology, electrocardiology, and respiratory therapy. Patient service revenues should be recognized on an accrual basis during the period in which the nursing or professional service is being performed.

> **OBSERVATION:** *Recognizing patient service revenues on the "discharge basis" is not a generally accepted accounting principle.*

The amount billed to a patient should be based on the hospital's established rate even though it may be unlikely that the hospital will eventually recover the total charge. The net amount of revenue expected to be realized is estimated by utilizing a number of contra revenue accounts as described below.

Provision for bad debts The provision for bad debts for a hospital is not classified as an expense, but rather is treated as an offset to gross patient service revenues. Although the provision is treated as a contra revenue account, it and the related allowance for uncollectible receivables account (contra asset account) are used in the same manner as a commercial enterprise would use them. Thus, the provision for bad debts, the writeoff of a bad account, and the recovery of an account previously written off are processed through these two related accounts.

Contractual adjustments Many hospital services will be paid by third-party reimbursers, such as the state or federal government and private or quasi-private health care insurance companies, such as Blue Cross or Health Maintenance Organization. These organizations will pay for the service based on an actual contract or regulations established by governmental agencies. The difference between the amount billed to the patient and the amount payable under the third-party reimbursement program is charged to a contra revenue account entitled "contractual adjustments." When payment is received from the third-party reimburser, the receivable is reduced by the amount billed to the patient, and the difference between the full billing and amount billed to the third party is charged to the allowance for uncollectible receivables, assuming the difference is not recoverable from the patient.

Charity services Certain charity patients may be billed at a reduced rate or not billed at all based on the policies established by the hospital. Nonetheless, as suggested earlier, the full charge for the service should be shown as patient service revenues. The difference between the full charge and the amount billed to the patient, if any, is debited to the account "charity service" (contra revenue account), with a corresponding credit being made directly to accounts receivable, since the amount of the charity discount usually is known when the patient is admitted to the hospital.

Other deductions Based on hospital policies, certain patients such as hospital employees may receive discounts or other courtesy allowances. These deductions from the established rates should be recorded as contra revenue, and charged directly to accounts receivable rather than to an allowance account.

Other Operating Revenues A hospital may receive significant revenues from other operating sources that are not related to the delivery of nursing services or other professional services. These other operating revenues may be broadly classified as transfers from restricted funds, nonprofessional services, and donated suppliers and assets.

Transfers from restricted funds Restricted funds are created when a donor imposes certain limitations on how contributed assets can be expended by the hospital. For example, restricted funds may be created to finance certain types of research, educational activities, or other specific operating expenses. The actual donor-restricted expense is recorded in the Operating Fund and resources are transferred from the restricted fund to finance the expense. To illustrate, assume that $100,000 is transferred from a restricted fund to finance actual expenses for an approved research project. The transfer between funds would be recorded as follows:

OPERATING FUND

Research Expenses	100,000	
Cash		100,000
Due From Restricted Fund	100,000	
Transfers From Restricted Funds For		
Research		100,000

RESTRICTED FUND

Transfers To Operating Fund For		
Operating Purposes	100,000	
Due To Unrestricted Fund		100,000

Nonprofessional services Revenues from nonprofessional services include such items as parking fees, vending machine commissions, television rentals, and nonpatient room rentals. These sources of revenue should be accrued as the service is delivered and recognized as other operating revenue.

Donated supplies and equipment When a hospital receives donated materials or supplies that are normally used in its operations, such as drugs and linens, these assets are recorded at their fair values, and other operating revenue is recognized. As these items are used, an operating expense will result through inventory reduction.

Property and equipment that are donated by outside parties should be recorded at their fair values; however, the receipt of these assets is not recorded as other operating revenue, but rather as a direct increase to the unrestricted fund balance account of the Operating Fund assuming there are no restrictions on how the assets are to be used.

Nonoperating Revenues A hospital's nonoperating revenues are usually generated through donated services, investment transactions, pledges, and unrestricted gifts.

Donated services Hospitals may receive donated services from parties or institutions that desire to support the hospital's mission. Donations of services should be recorded as revenue (nonoperating) only when (1) the equivalent of an employer-employee relationship exists and (2) an objective basis for determining fair value of the services received exists. (Generally, donated services are recognized as revenue only when the hospital is supported by a religious group.) If the two criteria for revenue recognition are satisfied, the donated services are recorded by simultaneously recognizing an operating expense (based on the nature of the donated services) and nonoperating revenue.

Unrestricted investment transactions Investment income from unrestricted investments and board-designated investments should be recognized as nonoperating revenue in the hospital's Statement of Revenues and Expenses for the Operating Fund. Likewise, any realized gains or losses incurred from the sale of unrestricted investments and board-designated investments should be recorded as nonoperating revenues or expenses.

Endowment fund investment transactions Investment income from Endowment Funds should be accounted for in a manner consistent with the donor's wishes. If the use of the income is unrestricted, the investment income should be recorded as nonoperating revenue in the Operating Fund's activity statement. If the income is restricted for specific operating purposes, the investment income should be included in the Endowment Fund's fund balance account. In the latter case, when resources are transferable from the Endowment Fund to the Operating Fund to finance the specified expenses, the Operating Fund recognizes the operating expense specified and also records an equivalent amount of other operating revenue.

If the income from Endowment Funds is available to the hospital for unrestricted purposes, the Operating Fund should recognize nonoperating revenue for the amount of the resources receivable from the Endowment Funds at the date the resources are transferable.

Realized gains and losses from the sale of Endowment Fund investments should be added or deducted from the Endowment Fund's fund balance account; however, realized gains and losses are recorded as nonoperating revenue (loss) on the Operating Fund's activity statement if legally available for other uses or chargeable against an unrestricted fund.

Other investment transactions Investment income and realized gains and losses on the sale of investments of restricted funds other than Endowment Funds should be added to or deducted from the restricted fund's fund balance account; however, if the resources are available for unrestricted purposes, the results of the investment transactions should be reported as nonoperating revenue in the Operating Fund's activity statement.

When investments are traded between unrestricted and restricted funds, gains and losses should be recognized. On the other hand, gains and losses arising from transactions between designated portions of the unrestricted fund balance should not be recorded.

Pledges All pledges should be reflected in the hospital's financial statements net of an estimate for uncollectibles. If pledges are restricted, they should be recorded as part of the appropriate restricted fund's fund balance account. Unrestricted pledges should be recorded as nonoperating revenue in the year the pledges are made, except that unrestricted pledges to be applied in future periods should be recorded as deferred revenue until applied.

Unrestricted gifts Gifts, grants, and bequests that are not restricted for use by donors are recorded as nonoperating revenue based on their estimated fair value. Unrestricted gifts may include such items as subsidies from governmental agencies, grants, and contributions from concerned citizens. Even though unrestricted gifts may be designated for a specific use by the hospital board, they are nonetheless recorded as nonoperating revenue.

Expenses

FASB:CS-6 defines expenses as "outflows or other using up of assets or incurrences of liabilities during a period from delivering or producing goods, rendering services, or carrying out other activities that constitute the entity's ongoing major or central operations." The recognition of an expense by a hospital, as described in APB Statement-4 and FASB:CS-5 (Recognition and Measurement in Financial Statements of Business Enterprises), should be consistent with the following guidelines:

- Associating cause and effect—Some expenses (such as cost of providing professional services) are recognized upon recognition of revenues that result directly and jointly from the same transactions or events as the expenses.
- Systematic and rational allocation—Some expenses (such as depreciation) are allocated by systematic and rational procedures to the periods during which the related assets are expected to provide benefit.
- Immediate recognition—Many expenses (such as administrative expenses) are recognized during the period in which cash is spent or liabilities are incurred for goods and services that are used up either simultaneously with acquisition or soon after.

Depreciation Expense Unlike other governmental funds, depreciation expense is recognized in a hospital's activity statement in the same manner as a commercial enterprise would account for depreciation.

The American Hospital Association recommends that a hospital account for depreciation on an historical cost basis adjusted for changes in the general price level. When price level adjusted depreciation is computed, the American Hospital Association suggests that the following guidelines be observed:

- Changes in the general price level should be determined by reference to an index of the general price level, not to an index of the price of a specific type of goods or service. The gross national product (GNP) Implicit Price Deflator is considered to be the most comprehensive indicator of the general price level in the United States and should normally be used.
- The general price level increments should be formally recorded in the appropriate accounts. Depreciation should be computed on the basis of general price levels. Adjustments in the amount

of depreciation recorded should be made for the portion of the assets currently being financed through debt.
- Full disclosure must be made in the financial statements on the basis of valuing fixed assets and of determining depreciation charges. The differences between those fixed assets and related depreciation charges that are based on historical cost, and those fixed assets and related depreciation charges that are restated for general price level changes must also be disclosed.

- Changes in the general price level should be determined and presented in terms of the general purchasing power of the dollar at the time the latest balance sheet is generated (not related to depreciation).

Although price-level depreciation is recommended by the American Hospital Association, the AICPA Audit Guide specifically notes that the computation of depreciation expense in such a manner is "not in accordance with generally accepted accounting principles."

A hospital's governing board may decide to set aside funds for the replacement or expansion of depreciable property. The accumulation of funds should be presented as a designation of the unrestricted fund balance and not as an expense in the Operating Fund's Statement of Revenues and Expenses.

Capital grants A hospital's depreciable assets that are financed by resources restricted for capital investment may be accounted for in one of two ways.

First, the depreciable property acquired through grants, entitlements, or shared revenues restricted for capital outlays may be accounted for in a manner similar to depreciable property owned by a commercial enterprise. Depreciation expense and accumulated depreciation are recorded, and the depreciation expense is presented as an operating expense and closed along with other expenses directly to the fund balance account.

Alternatively, depreciation expense and accumulated depreciation are recorded, but the depreciation expense at the end of the year is closed directly to the hospital's contributed capital account that was created when the restricted grants, entitlements, or shared revenue was received. On the Statement of Revenues and Expenses, the depreciation expense is presented as an operating expense and is used to compute the hospital's excess of revenues over expenses. Then, the depreciation expense is added to the excess of revenues over expenses figure to identify the net increase (decrease) in the

Hospitals

fund balance for the year and the latter amount is added to the beginning balance of the Operating Fund's fund balance account.

To illustrate the two methods of accounting for depreciable property acquired through a restricted grant, entitlement, or shared revenue, assume that a capital grant of $100,000 is received to finance the purchase of equipment for a hospital. The receipt of the grant and the purchase of the equipment would be recorded as follows:

PLANT REPLACEMENT AND EXPANSION FUND

Cash	100,000	
Fund Balance—Capital Grants		
(Receipt Of Cash)		100,000
Fund Balance—Capital Grants	100,000	
Cash (Purchase Of Equipment)		100,000

OPERATING FUND

Equipment	100,000	
Fund Balance—Capital Grants		100,000

Note: Alternatively, a cash transfer from the Plant Replacement and Expansion Fund could be made to the Operating Fund and the Operating Fund could make the equipment acquisition.

If it is assumed that the estimated economic life of the property is four years, that its residual value is a nominal amount, and that the straight-line method of depreciation is used, depreciation for the year is recorded in the hospital's accounting records by making the following conventional entry in the Operating Fund:

Depreciation Expense	25,000	
Accumulated Depreciation—		
Equipment		25,000

The manner in which depreciation expense is closed at the end of the year depends upon whether Alternative #1 or Alternative #2, as described above, is utilized. The following closing entry would be made in the Operating Fund if the first alternative is used by the hospital:

Revenue And Expense Summary (Fund Balance)	25,000	
Depreciation Expense		25,000

If Alternative #2 is used, the following closing entry would be made in the hospital's records:

Fund Balance—Capital Grants	25,000	
Depreciation Expense		25,000

The second alternative may be used for capital grants, entitlements, and shared revenues designated specifically for the acquisition of capital assets. The method is not applicable to interfund transactions, unrestricted resources received from other governments, or resources received from private contributors such as foundations or commercial enterprises.

Interest Cost Interest cost associated with the construction of a hospital's capital assets should be capitalized and reflected as part of property, plant, and equipment. FASB-34 (Capitalization of Interest Cost) concludes that the capitalization period begins when the following three conditions are present:

- Expenditures for the capital asset have been made.
- Activities that are necessary to get the capital asset ready for its intended use are in progress.
- Interest cost is being incurred.

To determine the amount of interest cost to be capitalized, the weighted-average amount of accumulated expenditures for the period are multiplied by the hospital's average borrowing rate for the period. Rather than using the overall average borrowing rate, the following approach can be employed:

- The interest rate for the obligation incurred specifically to finance the construction of the capital asset may be used and
- The overall average borrowing rate would be used for any accumulated expenditures in excess of specific borrowings.

The amount of interest cost to be capitalized is limited to the actual interest expense incurred for the period.

FASB-62 (Capitalization of Interest Cost in Situations Involving Certain Tax-Exempt Borrowings and Certain Gifts and Grants) concludes that the amount of initial cost to be capitalized on assets acquired with tax-exempt borrowings is equal to the cost of the borrowing less interest earned on related interest-bearing investments acquired with proceeds of the related tax-exempt borrowing. FASB-62 allows the offsetting of interest earned against interest cost in those situations "involving acquisition of qualifying assets financed with the proceeds of tax-exempt borrowings if those funds are externally restricted to finance acquisition of specified qualifying assets or to service the related debt."

Assets

FASB:CS-6 defines assets as "probable future economic benefit obtained or controlled by a particular entity as a result of past transactions or events and possessing the following essential characteristics:

- It embodies a probable future benefit that involves a capacity to contribute directly or indirectly to future net cash inflows.
- A particular enterprise can obtain the benefit and control others' access to it.
- The transaction or other event giving rise to the enterprise's right to control of the benefit has already occurred."

Assets acquired by hospitals are recorded at cost at the date an exchange takes place. When assets are received through donations from external parties, they should be recorded at their estimated fair value on the date the assets are transferred. In general, accounting principles followed by a commercial enterprise are also applicable to hospital asset accounting. The unique features of accounting for assets held by a hospital are discussed below.

Cash A hospital must maintain adequate accounting records to distinguish cash related to unrestricted funds and cash related to restricted funds. The proper classification of cash is based on the donor-imposed restrictions.

Marketable Equity Securities FASB-12 (Accounting for Certain Marketable Equity Securities) requires that marketable equity securities be accounted for on the lower of aggregate cost or market basis; however, FASB-12 was not applicable to not-for-profit hospitals. SOP 78-1 (Accounting by Hospitals for Certain Marketable Equity Securities) has been issued as an amendment to the AICPA *Hospital Audit Guide*. The SOP concluded that marketable equity securities held by a hospital should also be accounted for on the lower of aggregate cost or market basis.

OBSERVATION: *Although SOP 78-1 adopted the basic valuation method established by FASB-12, the Statement itself was not adopted in its entirety because of the somewhat unique nature of hospital accounting.*

Marketable equity securities held by a hospital (and all related entities whose financial statements are combined for reporting purposes with the hospital's financial statements) should be classified in one of the following five portfolios:

- Unrestricted Funds—current portfolio
- Unrestricted Funds—noncurrent portfolio
- Specific-Purpose Funds portfolio
- Endowment Funds portfolio
- Plant Replacement and Expansion Funds portfolio

Unrealized losses related to the valuation of marketable equity securities classified in the unrestricted funds' current portfolio should be recorded as nonoperating losses in the Operating Fund's Statement of Revenues and Expenses and recoveries of prior-years' writeoffs should be presented as nonoperating revenue. Unrealized losses from the valuation of marketable equity securities in the other four portfolios should be disclosed as a contra equity account in each fund's fund balance section. However, when the decline in a specific investment in one of these four portfolios is considered to be "other than temporary," the decline should be recorded in the Operating Fund's activity statement as a nonoperating loss. Securities reclassified from one portfolio to another should be valued at the lower of cost or market on the reclassification date, and any write-down should be charged to the Operating Fund's Statement of Revenues and Expenses as a nonoperating loss. However, gains or losses on transactions between board-designated funds of the unrestricted fund should not be recognized.

Significant net realized and net unrealized gains and losses that occur after the balance sheet date but before the financial statements are issued should not be recognized but should be disclosed in the financial statements.

The following disclosures with respect to investments in marketable equity securities should be made in the hospital's financial statements:

- As of the date of each balance sheet presented, aggregate cost and market values for each separate portfolio into which marketable equity securities were grouped to determine carrying amount, with identification of the carrying amount
- As of the date of the latest balance sheet presented, the following segregated by portfolio:
  - Gross unrealized gains representing the excess of market value over cost for all marketable equity securities having such an excess in the portfolio
  - Gross unrealized losses representing the excess of cost over market value for all marketable equity securities having such an excess in the portfolio
- For each period for which a statement of revenues and expenses is presented:
  - Net realized gain or loss included in nonoperating revenue
  - The basis on which cost was determined in computing realized gain or loss (average cost or other method)

Long-Term Securities Investments The accounting method that should be used to account for noncurrent investments in marketable equity securities was described in the previous section. Other long-term investments in equity securities should be accounted for on a cost basis if the percentage ownership is less than 20% of the investee corporation's outstanding voting stock. If there is a permanent decline in the value of the long-term investment in other equity securities, the investment should be written down to its estimated fair value. Investments in other equity securities that represent between 20% and 50% of the voting stock of another enterprise should be accounted for by using the equity method. When the investment percentage is greater than 50%, the financial statement of the subsidiary should be consolidated with the hospital's financial statements.

Investment in long-term bonds or other debt instruments should be accounted for on an amortized cost basis. Any premium or discount related to the debt security should be amortized using the effective interest method. Declines in the investment in long-term debt securities that are permanent should be recorded as a nonoperating loss in the hospital's Operating Fund's Statement of Revenues and Expenses.

The American Hospital Association recommends that all long-term security investments be accounted for on a current market value basis. The market value approach is suggested by the American Hospital Association for the following reasons:

- Use of costs serves no real purpose and could even be misleading.
- The current market value of an investment portfolio is the true indicator of its earning power and of the stewardship responsibility of management.
- Use of the current market value of securities facilitates accounting for pooled investments. (Records of the actual costs of long-term security investments should be maintained as supplemental information. As an alternative, hospitals can retain the historical cost in the formal accounting records and treat the current market value as supplemental information.)

The *Hospital Audit Guide* specifically notes that accounting for long-term security investments on a market basis "is not in accordance with generally accepted accounting principles."

Receivables As noted earlier, revenues should be determined by using the hospital's established billing rates regardless of whether it is likely that the full charge will be collected from the patient or a third party. Receivables should be presented net of allowances for estimated bad debts, contractual adjustments related to third-party reimbursers such as Blue Cross, Medicare, and Medicaid, estimated collection agency fees, and other items that may result in a collection of an amount less than the full charge for the service rendered by the hospital.

The allowance for contractual adjustments at the end of the period is an estimated amount and will differ when the final settlement amount is determined. Cost reimbursement adjustments should be treated as changes in estimates as described in APB-20 (Accounting Changes). The effects of a change in an estimate are accounted for in the period in which the change occurs, namely, the year in which the cost reimbursement settlement computation is made and agreed to by the hospital and the third-party reimburser.

Property, Plant, and Equipment Fixed assets of a hospital, such as land, buildings, major movable equipment, and fixed equipment, should be accounted for at cost and, with the exception of land, should be depreciated over the estimated useful life of each item. Property, plant, and equipment and related liabilities should be accounted for in the Operating Fund; however, if the use of the proceeds from the sale of fixed assets is restricted, this restriction should be disclosed in the hospital's financial statements.

Some third-party reimbursers may reimburse a hospital for depreciation, and restrict that portion of the reimbursement for the replacement or expansion of the hospital's fixed assets. In this case, the full amount of the reimbursement should be recognized as revenue in the Operating Fund, but the "depreciation portion" should be shown as a fund balance transfer from the Operating Fund to the Plant Replacement and Expansion Fund. When the resources are expended for the replacement or expansion of fixed assets, the amount is transferred from the Plant Replacement and Expansion Fund to the Operating Fund.

> **OBSERVATION:** *The American Hospital Association recommends that hospitals account for property, plant, and equipment in a manner that reflects inflation. Inflation accounting is not a generally accepted accounting principle for hospitals. (For a description of the AHA's proposal, see the earlier section of this chapter that discusses depreciation expense.)*

Liabilities

FASB:CS-6 defines liabilities as "probable future sacrifices of economic benefits arising from present obligations of a particular entity to transfer assets or provide services to other entities in the future as a result of past transactions or events." Liabilities embody the following fundamental characteristics:

- The present duty or responsibility to one or more other entities that entails settlement by probable future transfer or use of assets at a specified or determinable date, on occurrence of a specified event, or on demand
- The duty or responsibility obligates a particular enterprise, leaving it little or no discretion to avoid the future sacrifice
- The transaction or other event obligating the enterprise has already happened

The financial statements of a hospital present both current and long-term liabilities that are to be paid by the hospital. The current classification may be composed of a variety of debts such as accounts payable, deferred revenues, accruals for operating expenses, current portion of long-term debt, and amounts due to third-party reimbursers for over-reimbursements. Noncurrent liabilities may include debt instruments such as notes, bonds, and mortgage notes. A hospital's noncurrent liabilities may include liabilities other than those that arise from the issuance of a debt instrument. For example, a hospital may record obligations arising from capitalized leases, claims and judgments, and pension obligations. These as well as other liabilities of a hospital should be accounted for in a manner similar to the accounting and reporting standards followed by commercial enterprises.

General obligation bonds   General obligation bonds are full faith and credit bonds, which means that the debt is secured by the general taxing powers of the state or local government. If general obligation bonds are to be repaid (interest and principal) from earnings of the hospital, they should be reported as a liability of the hospital. On the other hand, general obligation bonds that are to be paid from general taxes and revenues of the governmental unit should be reported as part of the governmental unit's General Long-Term Debt Account Group. In the latter case, the proceeds from the issuance of the bonds that are made available to a hospital are treated as a capital contribution. When general obligation bonds are recorded as liabilities of a hospital, the General Long-Term Debt Account Group should report the outstanding debt as a contingent liability.

Revenue bonds   Principal and interest on revenue bonds are paid exclusively from the earnings of a hospital. If the debt is also secured by specific fixed assets of the hospital, they are referred to as mortgage revenue bonds. Revenue bonds are recorded as a liability of the hospital. Because revenue bonds are not full faith and credit bonds, they are not shown as a contingent liability in the governmental unit's General Long-Term Debt Account Group.

Contingent Liabilities   Malpractice risks arising from potential litigation are classified as loss contingencies and should be evaluated in the context of FASB-5 (Accounting for Contingencies) and FASB Interpretation-14 (Reasonable Estimation of the Amount of a Loss). Contingent liability concepts established by FASB-5 and Interpretation-14 are illustrated in the *Hospital Audit Guide*.

A loss contingency arises when there *appears* to be an impairment of an asset or the incurrence of a liability. Hospital malpractice litigation is an example of a loss contingency (incurrence of a liability) in that there is a degree of uncertainty as to whether the hospital will actually suffer an economic loss from the actions taken by third parties. The initial step in determining how to account for a loss contingency of a hospital is to assess the probability that an actual economic loss will eventually occur. FASB-5 identifies the following three possible outcomes of a loss contingency:

- Probable—The future event or events are likely to occur.
- Reasonably possible—The chance of the future event or events occurring is more than remote, but less than likely.
- Remote—The chance of the future event or events occurring is slight.

These three subjective probabilities are used to determine whether a loss contingency arising from a malpractice claim should be (1) accrued or (2) disclosed in the hospital's financial statements.

Accrual of loss contingency A loss contingency arising from a malpractice claim is accrued as of the balance sheet date when both of the following conditions exist:

- Information available prior to issuance of the financial statements indicates that it is *probable* that an asset has been impaired or liability has been incurred at the date of the most recent accounting period for which financial statements are being presented. (It is implicit in this condition that it be probable that one or more future events will occur confirming the fact of the loss.)
- The amount of the loss can be reasonably estimated.

If the above conditions exist, the loss contingency related to the malpractice suit is recorded as a liability of the hospital. In determining a reasonable estimate, the estimate may be in the form of a range rather than a single point estimate. FASB Interpretation-14 concludes that the existence of more than one reasonable estimate of a loss contingency does not preclude the accrual of the contingency. If the point estimates within the range have differing probabilities, the one with the greatest probability should be accrued, and the balance should be disclosed in a note to the hospital's financial statements.

For example, assume that malpractice claims of $15,000,000 exist at the balance sheet date, and that it is probable that some of the claims will be paid. Also, assume that the following reasonable estimates of possible payments have been made:

Estimate of possible malpractice payments	Probability of payment
$6,000,000	15%
$3,000,000	45%
$1,000,000	40%

In this situation, an accrual of $3,000,000 would be made in the hospital's financial statements, and disclosure of the nature of the contingency and the exposure to an additional loss of possibly $3,000,000 would be made in a note to the financial statements. On the other hand, if a reasonable estimate of the malpractice claims is between $1,000,000 and $6,000,000, and the probability of each loss ($6,000,000, $3,000,000, and $1,000,000) is equal (33 1/3%), an accrual of $1,000,000 would be made and the balance of a possible loss of $5,000,000 would be disclosed in a note.

The accrual of a loss contingency is not dependent upon whether an actual malpractice claim existed as of the date of the balance sheet. All that is needed is the occurrence of an event on or before the balance sheet date that may lead to a loss contingency. If the hospital becomes aware of the malpractice claim after the balance sheet date, but before the issuance of the financial statements, the claim must be evaluated for possible accrual. FASB-5 lists the following as factors that should be considered in determining whether a claim is the basis for a loss contingency accrual:

- The nature of the claim
- The progress of the case (including progress after the date of the financial statements but before the statements are issued)
- Opinion or view of legal counsel and other advisers
- Experience of hospitals in similar cases
- Decisions by the hospital on how to respond to the claim

If legal counsel is unable to express an opinion that the malpractice claim will be resolved without liability, this does not automatically imply that the claim should be accrued. Likewise, the filing of a lawsuit or a claim does not automatically require that a loss contingency be accrued. On the other hand, a loss contingency may have to be accrued even if a claim has not been asserted as of the date of the financial statements or the date when the financial statements are distributed. Unasserted malpractice claims must be accrued when (1) it is probable that the claim will eventually be asserted, (2) it is probable that the unasserted claim will lead to an actual incurrence of a liability, and (3) a reasonable estimate of the loss can be made.

Hospitals

Disclosure of loss contingency When a loss contingency arising from a malpractice claim is either not probable or not subject to reasonable estimation, the contingency must be disclosed in the financial statements when it is *reasonably possible* that a loss will eventually be incurred. The financial statement disclosure should describe the nature of the loss contingency and an estimate of the possible loss or range of loss. If an estimate of the loss cannot be made based on the available information, the disclosure should state that no estimate of the loss can be made.

Events may occur subsequent to the balance sheet date, but before the financial statements are issued, that should be evaluated in in the context of FASB-5. These events may suggest that (1) it is probable that a liability was incurred after the balance sheet date, or (2) it is reasonably possible that a liability was incurred after the balance sheet date. In neither case should a loss contingency be accrued because the liability did not exist as of the balance sheet date; however, it may be necessary to disclose the subsequent event so as to avoid issuing misleading financial statements. If the subsequent event is disclosed, the nature of the claim and the estimate of the loss or range of loss resulting from the claim should be described in the financial statements of the hospital. If an estimate of the loss cannot be made, this fact should be part of the disclosure.

The *Hospital Audit Guide* presents the following as an example of a disclosure of a loss contingency:

> Malpractice claims in excess of insurance coverage have been asserted against the hospital by various claimants. The claims are in various stages of processing and some may ultimately be brought to trial. Counsel is unable to conclude about the ultimate outcome of the actions. There are known incidents occurring through (balance sheet date) that may result in the assertion of additional claims, and other claims may be asserted arising from services provided to patients in the past. The hospital is unable to estimate the ultimate cost, if any, of the settlement of such potential claims and, accordingly, no accrual has been made for them.

The disclosure of a subsequent event that did not result in a liability as of the balance sheet date may be presented in the form of pro forma financial data. If a reasonable estimate of the loss arising from the claim can be made, the financial statements as of the balance sheet date can be modified on a pro forma basis only, to reflect the subsequent event. The pro forma financial statements serve as a supplement to, and not a substitute for, the historical cost financial statements, and may be presented in columnar form on the face of the hospital's historical cost financial statements.

FASB-5 does not require the disclosure of unasserted claims if "there has been no manifestation by a potential claimant of an awareness of a claim or assessment unless it is considered probable that a claim will be asserted and there is a reasonable possibility that the outcome will be unfavorable."

Disclosure of loss contingency accrued Even though a malpractice claim has been accrued as a loss contingency, it may nonetheless be necessary to disclose the nature of the loss and the amount of the loss in order to avoid the issuance of misleading financial statements.

Other disclosures With respect to malpractice claims and insurance coverage, the following should be considered for possible disclosure in a hospital's financial statements in order to satisfy the reporting objective of adequate disclosure:

- Hospital's policy for malpractice insurance coverage and any changes in the policy
- Change in the malpractice insurance coverage from an occurrence basis policy to a claims made policy
- Description of facts and circumstances related to a hospital's material uninsured malpractice risks (for the first year a hospital is uninsured)
- Insurance premiums determined on a retrospective basis

Nontransfer of Malpractice Risk The amount of loss contingency from malpractice claims to be accrued or disclosed is reduced by the amount of the loss that will be covered by malpractice insurance policies. In some instances the insurance coverage may exist in form but not in substance. When the insurance contract does not transfer the risk of loss to the insurance company, the accrual or disclosure of the loss contingency must take this fact into consideration. For example, if the insurance premiums paid by the hospital represent a deposit with the insurance company, the premium payment less any amount retained by the insurance company should be treated as a deposit.

Some hospitals may join together to form a captive or joint insurance company in order to shift the burden of possible malpractice claims. The arrangement must be carefully scrutinized to determine whether an individual hospital has in fact transferred the risk of mal-

Hospitals

practice cost to the related insurance company. If there is a transfer of risk, the insurance coverage is treated like insurance coverage from an independent insurance company; however, if the risk has not been transferred, the premium payments may be treated as a deposit and the consequences of the nontransfer of risk must be considered in evaluating the accrual or disclosure of malpractice claims.

Asserted and Unasserted Claims for Health Care Providers

FASB-5 and FASB Interpretation-14 provide general guidelines for the evaluation of contingent liabilities. In 1987, the AICPA issued SOP 87-1 (Accounting for Asserted and Unasserted Medical Malpractice Claims of Health Care Providers and Related Issues) to address contingent liabilities in the context of health care providers. A health care provider is defined as "a person or other entity or group of entities under common control that delivers health care services, including, but not limited to, hospitals, nursing homes, and practices of physicians, dentists, or other health care specialists." SOP 87-1 applies to all health care providers and their wholly owned and multi-provider-owned captive insurance companies. A multiprovider captive insurance company provides malpractice insurance for two or more health care providers that also own the insurance company. SOP 87-1 addressed a number of accounting issues, which are summarized below.

Asserted and unasserted claims Malpractice loss contingencies may be characterized as asserted claims and unasserted claims. Asserted claims are actual claims asserted against the health care provider, while unasserted claims are based on an incident of alleged malpractice, although an actual claim has not been asserted. Unasserted claims may be based on reported incidents that have been identified by the health care provider, or unreported incidents that have not been identified by the health care provider.

SOP 87-1 reiterates standards established by FASB-5 by concluding that the cost (settlement cost and legal cost) of malpractice claims should be recognized as a liability in the period in which the malpractice incident occurred assuming that (1) it is *probable* that a liability has been incurred and (2) a *reasonable estimate* of the liability can be made. Asserted claims and unasserted claims arising from reported incidents should be evaluated individually or on a group basis to determine the best estimate for malpractice losses. In determining the

Hospitals

amount of estimated losses, all relevant information should be considered, including industry experience.

Unasserted claims related to unreported incidents should be evaluated with respect to the probability that an incident has occurred and the probability that a loss may arise from an unreported incident. SOP 87-1 suggests that to evaluate these two elements, all relevant information should be used in the analysis, including the following factors:

- Industry experience
- Historical experience of the health care provider
- Existing asserted claims and reported incidents

> **OBSERVATION:** *FASB-5 concludes that initially unasserted claims must be evaluated from two perspectives to determine (1) the probability that an unasserted claim will eventually be asserted and (2) if the unasserted claim is asserted, the probability that the resulting asserted claim will result in a loss. Thus, for unasserted claims, the criteria for accrual of a loss contingency are (1) it is probable that an unasserted claim will eventually be asserted, (2) it is probable that a loss will materialize and (3) a reasonable estimate of the loss can be made. SOP 87-1 does not specifically address the evaluation of unasserted claims in a manner consistent with the criteria established in FASB-5.*

Industry information used to evaluate malpractice losses must be carefully assessed to ensure that the results of the evaluation are consistent with concepts established in FASB-5. FASB-5 does not allow for the *smoothing* of loss contingencies over several years. A loss contingency occurs only when an identifiable event has occurred that will probably result in a loss. The accrual of malpractice losses should not be *managed* so that recorded losses approximate the average losses recognized in the industry or by a portion of the industry.

If a health care provider cannot make a reasonable estimate of losses arising from asserted or unasserted claims, the contingency should be described in a note to the financial statements in accordance with the disclosure requirements established by FASB-5.

Valuation of malpractice claims Once it is decided that a loss contingency should be accrued, it may be argued that the liability should be measured at its present value because an actual cash payment may be deferred for several accounting periods. Current accounting practice allows for the liability to be measured at either (1) the expected future cash payment or (2) the present value of the expected future cash payment. If the present value basis is used to measure the liability, the value of the liability before it is discounted and the interest rate(s) used to determine the present value of the liability should be disclosed in the health care provider's financial statements.

Claims-made policies Under a claims-made policy, an insurance carrier is responsible for only those claims that were reported during the period covered by the policy. If an incident occurred during the covered period but was not reported until after the coverage expired or the policy was terminated, the insurance carrier is not responsible for the unreported claims. SOP 87-1 concludes that claims and incidents not reported to an insurance carrier under a claims-made policy must be evaluated like other loss contingencies to determine whether accrual or disclosure is appropriate. However, no such analysis is necessary if the following conditions exist:

- Tail coverage insurance has been obtained by the health care provider (tail coverage insurance provides coverage of claims not reported during the period covered by a claims-made policy).
- The cost of the tail coverage insurance premium has been treated as an expense by the health care provider.

Retrospectively rated premiums Insurance premiums for a retrospectively rated policy are adjusted to reflect the actual loss experience of a health care provider or a group of health care providers. Generally, the health care provider pays an insurance deposit premium which represents a minimum premium plus an amount for estimated claim experience losses. The minimum premium is based upon the insurance carrier's expenses and profits.

When the total retrospective premium is based primarily on the experience of the health care provider, the payment representing the minimum premium should be amortized over the life of the policy. Estimated malpractice claims in excess of the minimum premium should be accrued when criteria established by FASB-5 are satisfied; however, the accrual should be no greater than the stipulated maximum premium.

When the total retrospective premium is based primarily on the experience of a group of health care providers, the initial premium should be amortized over the life of the policy. Additional premiums or refunds that are estimated based on the experience of the group should be used to compute the current cost of insurance coverage. In addition, the health care provider should disclose the following:

- Insurance coverage is based on a retrospectively rated policy.
- Premiums reflect the experience of the group of health care providers as of the date of the balance sheet.

Coverage through captive insurance companies   A health care provider may obtain malpractice insurance coverage through a wholly owned or multiprovider-owned captive insurance company.

> **OBSERVATION:** *Wholly owned and multiprovider-owned captive insurance companies must observe the accounting and reporting standards established by FASB-60 (Accounting and Reporting by Insurance Enterprises).*

When a health care provider is insured through a wholly owned captive insurance subsidiary, losses related to malpractice asserted and unasserted claims must be accounted for in accordance with FASB-5 and SOP 87-1 (as discussed earlier in the section entitled Asserted and Unasserted Claims). The results of applying FASB-5 and SOP 87-1 may be shown directly on the health care provider's financial statements or in the consolidated financial statements that include the financial statements of the wholly owned captive insurance subsidiary.

A health care provider may be insured through a multiprovider captive insurance company under a retrospectively rated insurance policy. If the retrospective premium is based upon the experience of the health care provider, the minimum premium should be amortized over the life of the policy. Estimated malpractice claims in excess of the minimum premium should be accrued when criteria established by FASB-5 are satisfied; however, the accrual should not be greater than the stipulated maximum premium. If the retrospective premium is based upon the experience of a group of health care providers, the initial premium should be amortized over the life of the policy and additional premiums or refunds should be used to compute the current cost of insurance coverage. Also, the following disclosures should be made by the health care provider:

- Insurance coverage is based on a retrospectively rated policy.
- Premiums reflect the experience of the group of health care providers as of the date of the balance sheet.

Hospitals

All health care providers that are insured by multiprovider captive insurance companies should make the following disclosures:

- Malpractice insurance coverage provided through a multiprovider captive insurance company
- Percentage ownership in the multiprovider captive insurance company
- Method used to account for investment in multiprovider captive insurance company

Trust funds Some health care providers may establish a separate trust fund to pay malpractice claims and related expenses. For a governmental entity, the trust fund may be established as an Internal Service Fund. The use of a trust fund in this instance does not limit the health care provider's legal liability for malpractice claims even if the trust fund is irrevocable.

The financial accounts of a trust fund should be included in the health care provider's financial statements and the following guidelines should be observed:

- Fund assets equal to the amount of malpractice claims classified as current liabilities should be classified as current assets.
- Trust fund revenues should be classified as other operating revenues.
- Trust fund administrative expenses should be classified as other administrative expenses.

In some circumstances, it may not be possible to include the financial accounts of the trust fund in the health care provider's financial statements. For example, regulatory or other restrictions may not allow the combining of the accounts. When the financial accounts of the trust fund cannot be combined with the health care provider's financial statements, the estimated losses from asserted and unasserted claims must be accounted for in the health care provider's financial statements in accordance with FASB-5 and SOP 87-1 (as discussed earlier in the section entitled Asserted and Unasserted Claims). Payments to the trust fund should not be treated as an expense on the health care provider's financial statements. Also, it should be disclosed that a trust fund has been established to pay malpractice related claims and expenses. If the trust fund is irrevocable, that fact too should be disclosed.

Tax-Exempt Debt Restrictions Some hospitals are not allowed to issue tax-exempt revenue bonds and, therefore, are unable to take advantage of financial projects at a relatively low interest rate. This restriction has been circumvented in many states by creating a financial authority that issues tax-exempt debt and passes the funds to a health care institution. In order to reduce the diversity of accounting practices that have arisen from the latter arrangement, the AICPA issued SOP 85-1 (Financial Reporting by Not-for-Profit Health Care Entities for Tax-Exempt Debt and Certain Funds Whose Use Is Limited), in which the following issues were addressed:

- Classification of the debt
- Classification of restricted assets
- Classification of income and expenses

Classification of the debt Although the state financing authority directly issues the tax-exempt debt, the health care institution is responsible for the repayment of the debt. The health care entity should report the debt issued through the state financing authority in its unrestricted fund section of the balance sheet.

Classification of restricted assets Although the proceeds from the debt issued by the state authority can be used only for the construction of a particular project, the restriction imposed by the debt agreement is not considered a restriction by a donor or grantor. Thus, the proceeds from the debt issuance should be reported in the unrestricted section of the hospital's balance sheet and not in the donor-restricted fund section. The limited use of the assets should be disclosed.

Classification of income and expenses Interest expense on the debt and interest income on the investment of the proceeds may be presented in either of the following ways:

- Interest expense and interest income may be reported separately as an operating expense and an operating revenue. (This assumes that the amounts are not subject to capitalization under the provisions of FASB-62, Capitalization of Interest Cost in Situations Involving Certain Tax-Exempt Borrowings and Certain Gifts and Grants.)
- Interest expense and interest income may be netted and reported as an operating expense, or income, with the offsetting amount noted parenthetically.

Hospitals

SOP 85-1 rejected the practice of reporting interest expense and interest income as nonoperating items; however, investment income arising from "funds whose use is limited under third-party reimbursement arrangements and unrestricted funds held by a trustee that are not borrowed funds" are reported as nonoperating income.

Deferred Revenue—Third-Party Reimbursements A hospital may enter into a contract with a third-party reimburser and the reimbursement payments may be based in part on the hospital's use of an accelerated depreciation method. If the hospital does not use the same (accelerated) depreciation method for financial statement reporting purposes, there is a timing difference that must be recognized in the statements. The difference between the accelerated depreciation recognized in the reimbursement computation and the depreciation recorded in the financial statements is recorded as deferred revenue. The deferred revenue amount is amortized as revenue as the depreciation timing difference reverses in subsequent accounting periods. When depreciation is not directly used to determine the amount of reimbursement under the third-party contract, no timing difference arises and there is no need to defer part of the payments received from the third party.

To illustrate the accounting for timing differences, assume that during 19X5, a hospital billed $4,000,000 for services that will be reimbursed under a third-party reimbursement contract. The performance of the professional services would result in the following entry:

Accounts Receivable (Billed To Third-Party)	4,000,000	
Professional Services Revenue		4,000,000

The reimbursement contract directly takes into consideration accelerated depreciation in computing the amount to be reimbursed but the hospital uses the straight-line depreciation method for financial reporting purposes. For the current year the difference between accelerated depreciation and straight depreciation is $200,000. To recognize this timing difference the following entry would be made at the end of the year:

Professional Services Revenue	200,000	
Deferred Revenue—Third-Party Reimbursements		200,000

If it is assumed that $40,000 of the $200,000 difference in computing depreciation under the two methods reverses the following year, the reversal would be recorded as illustrated below:

Deferred Revenue—Third-Party Reimbursements	40,000	
Professional Services Revenue		40,000

Other timing differences, such as the accounting for pension cost, may occur and should be properly reflected in the hospital's financial statements.

Interfund Transfers and Restricted Resources

Resources received from donors should be accounted for in the manner determined under the donor agreement. Donor-contributed resources that are restricted for use may be classified as those available for specific operating purposes, additions to property, plant and equipment, and endowment funds.

When resources are received by a hospital for a specific operating purpose, the receipt of the resources is recorded in a Specific-Purpose Fund's fund balance account. For example, the following entry would be made in the Specific-Purpose Fund to record the receipt of $100,000 to be used to finance certain research expenses related to birth defects:

Cash	100,000	
Fund Balance		100,000

When actual expenses for the fund's specified purposes are incurred, the expense is recorded in the Operating Fund, and an appropriate transfer is made from the Specific-Purpose Fund to the Operating Fund. In the current example, if it is assumed that the hospital incurred $75,000 of qualifying birth defect research expenses, the following entries would be made:

OPERATING FUND

Research Expenses	75,000	
Cash		75,000
Due From Specific-Purpose Fund	75,000	
Transfers From Restricted Funds For Research (Other Operating Revenue)		75,000

SPECIFIC-PURPOSE FUND
  Transfers To Operating Fund For
    Operating Purposes   75,000
      Due To Operating Fund   75,000

Restricted resources contributed for the purpose of additions to property, plant, and equipment should be recorded in the Plant Replacement and Expansion Fund as part of the hospital's permanent capital. For example, if a donor made a restricted gift of $400,000 that was to be used to purchase certain items of major movable equipment, the following entry would be made in the Plant Replacement and Expansion Fund:

  Cash   400,000
    Fund Balance   400,000

The purchase of the qualifying property, plant, and equipment would be recorded in the Operating Fund even though the financing, or part of the financing, comes from the Plant Replacement and Expansion Fund. Once the approved expenditures are incurred, a transfer from the Plant Replacement and Expansion Fund to the Operating Fund is recorded. The transfer is recorded as a fund balance transaction and is not classified as other operating revenue by the Operating Fund; therefore, the transfer is not used to compute the Operating Fund's excess of revenues over expenses amount that would appear on the hospital's Statement of Revenues and Expenses. In the current example, if it is assumed that major movable equipment of $350,000 is acquired, the following entries would be made:

OPERATING FUND
  Major Movable Equipment   350,000
    Accounts Payable   350,000

  Due From Plant Replacement And
    Expansion Fund   350,000
      Fund Balance—Transfer From Plant
        Replacement And Expansion Fund
        For Capital Outlays   350,000

PLANT REPLACEMENT AND EXPANSION FUND
  Fund Balance—Transfer to Operating
    Fund   350,000
      Due To Operating Fund   350,000

Restricted resources may be recorded in Endowment Funds where (1) only the income from the endowment may be expended (Permanent Endowment Fund), or (2) both the income and the principal, under certain conditions, can be expended (Term Endowment Fund). The receipt of resources for a Permanent Endowment Fund and a Term Endowment Fund is recorded as an addition to the Endowment Fund's fund balance account. For example, the receipt of a $600,000 gift under a Permanent Endowment Fund arrangement and a $200,000 gift under a Term Endowment Fund arrangement would be recorded as follows:

Cash	600,000	
Fund Balance—Permanent Endowment		600,000
Cash	200,000	
Fund Balance—Term Endowment		200,000

Income from Permanent Endowment Funds and Term Endowment Funds may be unrestricted or restricted. If the income is unrestricted, the amount transferable to the Operating Fund is recorded as nonoperating revenue by the Operating Fund. If the income is restricted, the amount transferable to the restricted fund is treated as a fund balance transfer and no revenue is recorded. For example, if it is assumed that $45,000 is earned by the Permanent Endowment Fund, which is available for unrestricted use by the hospital, the following entries would be made:

OPERATING FUND

Due From Permanent Endowment Fund	45,000	
Transfers Of Unrestricted Income From Endowment Fund (Nonoperating Revenue)		45,000

PERMANENT ENDOWMENT FUND

Cash	45,000	
Due To Operating Fund		45,000

On the other hand, if it is assumed that the $45,000 earned by the Permanent Endowment is restricted for the purpose of plant expansion, the following entries would be made:

PERMANENT ENDOWMENT FUND

Cash	45,000	
Due To Plant Replacement And Expansion Fund		45,000

PLANT REPLACEMENT AND EXPANSION FUND
  Due From Permanent Endowment Fund   45,000
    Transfers From Restricted Funds For
      Capital Outlays (Fund Balance)   45,000

When the principal of a Term Endowment Fund becomes available for expenditure, the use of the principal amount may be unrestricted or restricted. If the principal balance is available to the hospital for unrestricted purposes, the Operating Fund should record the transferable amount as nonoperating revenue. If the principal balance is restricted, the transferable amount should be recorded in the appropriate restricted fund (Specific-Purpose Fund, Plant Replacement and Expansion Fund, or another Endowment Fund) as an addition to its fund balance.

HOSPITAL FUNDS

Although a hospital uses the same basis of accounting and measurement focus as a commercial enterprise, transactions and events that affect a hospital are accounted for in several different funds. There are two basic fund groups, namely, (1) General Funds, composed of an Operating Fund and Board-Designated Funds and (2) restricted funds, comprised of Specific-Purpose Funds, Endowment Funds, and Plant Replacement and Expansion Funds.

Operating Fund (General Fund)

An Operating Fund is used to account for all resources of the hospital that are not restricted by a donor or designated for a specified use by the hospital's Board of Directors. These assets include the hospital's fixed assets and investments, as well as the various current assets, such as receivables, prepayments, and inventories that arise from operations. Liabilities, both current and noncurrent, incurred by the hospital would be accounted for directly in the Operating Fund.

The day-to-day operations of a hospital would generate a variety of nominal accounts that would be reflected in the Operating Fund. These transactions would include those related to revenues arising from nursing and other professional services, other operating services (such as tuition fees, nonprofessional sources of revenue, and transfers from other funds), and nonoperating revenues (such as certain donated services and investment income). Operating expenses associated with the hospital's normal operations would include expenses related to the performance of nursing and professional services, other services such as research cost and nursing education expenses, general and administrative services, and nonoperating expenses such as losses from the sale of fixed assets and investments.

To illustrate the routine transactions that are accounted for in a hospital's Operating Fund, assume that at the beginning of the fiscal year a hospital had the following trial balance. (Unless otherwise noted, all entries are recorded in the hospital's Operating Fund.):

Centerville Hospital
Operating Fund
Trial Balance
July 1, 19X4

	Dr.	Cr.
Cash	$ 3,000,000	
Accounts/notes receivable	4,000,000	
Allowance for bad debts		$ 500,000
Allowance for contractual adjustments		300,000
Pledges receivable	100,000	
Allowance for uncollectible pledges		20,000
Inventory—pharmacy	100,000	
Investment—equity securities (current)	400,000	
Allowance to reduce cost to market (current)		30,000
Investment—equity securities (noncurrent)	500,000	
Allowance to reduce cost to market (noncurrent)		20,000
Land	2,000,000	
Buildings	10,000,000	
Fixed equipment	3,000,000	
Major movable equipment	5,000,000	
Minor equipment	1,000,000	
Construction in progress	100,000	
Accumulated depreciation		4,000,000
Accounts payable		50,000
Accrued expenses		100,000
Long-term notes payable		15,000,000
Fund balance (net of $20,000 unrealized loss on noncurrent marketable equity securities)		9,180,000
	$29,200,000	$29,200,000

Hospitals

During the fiscal year the following transactions occurred and were recorded in the hospital's Operating Fund as described below:

Patient service revenues Billings for nursing services amounted to $12,000,000, and other professional services totaled $26,000,000.

Accounts And Notes Receivable	38,000,000	
Revenues—Nursing Services		12,000,000
Revenues—Other Professional Services		26,000,000

Deductions from revenues The following provisions for deductions from billed revenues were made during the year: provision for bad debts ($1,000,000), contractual adjustments ($3,000,000), and charity services ($200,000).

Provision For Bad Debts	1,000,000	
Contractual Adjustments	3,000,000	
Charity Services	200,000	
Allowance For Bad Debts		1,000,000
Allowance For Contractual Adjustments		3,000,000
Accounts And Notes Receivable		200,000

Cash collections on account during the year were $31,000,000, net of contractual adjustments of $2,500,000.

Cash	31,000,000	
Allowance For Contractual Adjustments	2,500,000	
Accounts And Notes Receivable		33,500,000

Accounts written off during the year as uncollectible amounted to $800,000.

Allowance For Bad Debts	800,000	
Accounts And Notes Receivable		800,000

Other operating revenues During the period, cash receipts from nonprofessional services amounted to $100,000, consisting of receipts from the cafeteria ($70,000), television rentals ($20,000), and nonpatient room rentals ($10,000).

Cash	100,000	
Revenues—Nonprofessional Services		100,000

Donations of medicine ($20,000) and fixed equipment ($120,000) were received from various outside parties.

Inventory—Pharmacy	20,000	
Fixed Equipment	120,000	
Revenues—Donated Supplies And Materials		20,000
Fund Balance—Value Of Donated Property, Plant, And Equipment		120,000

Nonoperating revenues Unsolicited gifts of cash amounting to $30,000 were received. These gifts were unrestricted.

Cash	30,000	
Revenues—General Contributions		30,000

During the year solicited pledges (unrestricted) of $500,000 were made by various interested parties. It is estimated that approximately 10% of the pledges will not be honored.

Pledges Receivable	500,000	
Allowance For Uncollectible Pledges		50,000
Revenues—General Contributions		450,000

Pledges of $420,000 were collected, and $45,000 of the outstanding pledges were considered dishonored.

Cash	420,000	
Allowance For Uncollectible Pledges	45,000	
Pledges Receivable		465,000

Marketable equity securities (current portfolio) At the beginning of the year, the hospital's current portfolios of marketable equity securities for unrestricted funds comprised the following investments:

Hospitals

	Cost	Market
Current portfolios		
Operating fund:		
Alpha Company	$200,000	$180,000
Beta Company	150,000	130,000
Rho Company	50,000	60,000
Total operating portfolio	400,000	370,000
Board-designated fund:		
Omega Company	70,000	60,000
Sigma Company	50,000	60,000
Theta Company	40,000	20,000
Total board-designated portfolio	160,000	140,000
Total cost of portfolios	560,000	
Balance in allowance account necessary to reduce aggregate cost to aggregate market	(50,000)	
Lower of aggregate cost or market	$510,000	$510,000

During the period, dividend income from the investments in marketable equity securities amounted to $30,000 from the Operating Fund's portfolio, and $10,000 from the Board-Designated Fund's portfolio.

OPERATING FUND
Cash	30,000	
Income And Gains (Losses) From		
Operating Fund Investments		30,000

BOARD-DESIGNATED FUND
Cash	10,000	
Income And Gains (Losses) From		
Board-Designated Fund		10,000

On April 15, 19X5, the investment in Beta Company's common stock was reclassified as part of the Operating Fund's noncurrent portfolio. The fair market value of the investment at the date of the reclassification was $120,000.

Investments In Marketable Securities (Noncurrent)	120,000	
Income And Gain (Loss) From Operating Fund Investments	30,000	
Investments In Marketable Securities (Current)		150,000

Hospitals

At the end of the year, the hospital's current portfolios of marketable equity securities for unrestricted funds were composed of the following investments:

	Cost	Market
Current portfolios		
Operating fund:		
Alpha Company	$200,000	$170,000
Rho Company	50,000	40,000
Total operating portfolio	250,000	210,000
Board-designated fund:		
Omega Company	70,000	40,000
Sigma Company	50,000	30,000
Theta Company	40,000	30,000
Total board-designated portfolio	160,000	100,000
Total cost of portfolios	410,000	
Required balance in allowance account necessary to reduce aggregate cost to aggregate market	(100,000)	
Lower of aggregate cost or market	$310,000	$310,000

Based on the above analysis, the year-end adjustments to reduce the aggregate cost of the combined current portfolios to market would be as follows:

OPERATING FUND
Income And Gains (Losses) From
  Operating Fund Investments
  ($100,000 – $50,000)   50,000
    Allowance Valuation To Reduce
    Aggregate Cost To Aggregate
    Market For Marketable Equity
    Securities—Current Portfolio
    ($40,000 – $30,000)   10,000
    Fund Balance—Transfer Of Market
    Valuation Loss From Board-
    Designated Fund's Portfolio
    Investments ($60,000 – $20,000)   40,000

BOARD-DESIGNATED FUND
Fund Balance—Transfer Of Market
  Valuation Loss To Operating Fund   40,000
    Allowance Valuation To Reduce
    Aggregate Cost To Aggregate
    Market For Marketable Equity
    Securities—Current Portfolio   40,000

Hospitals

Because the total valuation loss must be recorded in the Operating Fund's Statement of Revenues and Expenses, the portion of the loss that represents the valuation of the Board-Designated Fund's current portfolio must be treated as a fund balance transfer.

> **OBSERVATION:** Because the portfolios of the Operating Fund and the Board-Designated Funds are combined for making the adjustment to the lower of aggregate cost or market and a separate allowance account (contra asset account) must be related to each unrestricted fund's investment portfolio, an allocation problem for the overall allowance balance may arise. When there is an aggregate cost in excess of market for the combined unrestricted funds, but one portfolio has a total cost in excess of market while the other portfolio has a total market in excess of cost, the overall required balance in the allowance account is not large enough to reduce the investment portfolio of the unrestricted fund that has the cost in excess of market position. In order not to overstate the net assets of the latter fund, it may be necessary to treat the two portfolios as separate portfolios for valuation purposes and record the larger unrealized loss, even though this violates the accounting standards established by SOP 78-1. At the minimum, the valuation issue should be described in a note to the financial statements.

Marketable equity securities (noncurrent portfolio)   At the beginning of the year, the hospital's noncurrent portfolios of marketable equity securities for unrestricted funds were comprised of the following investments:

	Cost	Market
Noncurrent portfolio		
Operating fund:		
Lambda Company	$400,000	$390,000
Tau Company	100,000	90,000
Total operating portfolio	500,000	480,000
Board-designated fund:		
Mu Company	150,000	160,000
Gamma Company	100,000	80,000
Delta Company	50,000	40,000
Total board-designated portfolio	300,000	280,000
Total cost of portfolios	800,000	
Balance in allowance account necessary to reduce aggregate cost to aggregate market	(40,000)	
Lower of aggregate cost or market	$760,000	$760,000

During the period, dividend income from investments in marketable equity securities amounted to $45,000 from the Operating Fund's portfolio, and $30,000 from the Board-Designated Fund's portfolio.

OPERATING FUND
Cash	45,000	
Income And Gains (Losses) From		
Operating Fund Investments		45,000

BOARD-DESIGNATED FUND
Cash	30,000	
Income And Gains (Losses) From		
Board-Designated Fund		30,000

On April 15, 19X5, the investment in Beta Company's common stock, which was classified as part of the current portfolio, was reclassified as a noncurrent investment. (This entry was recorded in the previous section.)

On May 1, 19X5, it was concluded that there was a reduction in the value of the investment in Lambda Company that was not a temporary decrease. The nontemporary reduction (from cost) was estimated to be $35,000.

Income And Gains (Losses) From		
Operating Fund Investments	35,000	
Investments In Marketable Securities		
(Noncurrent)		35,000

On June 1, 19X5, the investment in Tau Company's common stock was sold for $130,000.

Cash	130,000	
Investment In Marketable Securities		
(Noncurrent)		100,000
Income And Gains (Losses) From		
Operating Fund Investments		30,000

At the end of the year, the hospital's noncurrent portfolios of marketable equity securities for unrestricted funds were composed of the following investments:

Hospitals

	Cost	Market
Noncurrent portfolio		
Operating fund:		
Lambda Company	$365,000	$360,000
Beta Company	120,000	100,000
Total operating portfolio	485,000	460,000
Board-designated fund:		
Mu Company	150,000	170,000
Gamma Company	100,000	60,000
Delta Company	50,000	40,000
Total board-designated portfolio	300,000	270,000
Total cost of portfolios	785,000	
Required balance in allowance account necessary to reduce aggregate cost to aggregate market	(55,000)	
Lower of aggregate cost or market	$730,000	$730,000

Based on the above analysis the year-end adjustments to reduce the aggregate cost of the combined current portfolios to market would be as follows:

OPERATING FUND

Fund Balance—Reduction Of Noncurrent Marketable Equity Securities Portfolio From Aggregate Cost To Aggregate Market ($25,000 – $20,000)   5,000
    Allowance Valuation To Reduce Aggregate Cost To Aggregate Market For Marketable Equity Securities—Noncurrent Portfolio   5,000

BOARD-DESIGNATED FUND

Fund Balance—Reduction On Noncurrent Marketable Equity Securities From Aggregate Cost To Aggregate Market ($30,000 – $20,000)   10,000
    Allowance Valuation To Reduce Aggregate Cost To Aggregate Market For Marketable Equity Securities—Noncurrent Portfolio   10,000

OBSERVATION: *Because the portfolios of the Operating Fund and the Board-Designated Funds are combined for making the adjustment to the lower of aggregate cost or market, and a separate reporting analysis must be made of each unrestricted fund's fund balance account at the end of the year, an allocation problem for the overall unrealized loss may arise. When there is an aggregate cost in excess of market for the combined unrestricted funds, but one portfolio has a total cost in excess of market while the other portfolio has a total market in excess of cost, the overall unrealized loss (contra equity account) is not large enough to reduce the fund balance of the unrestricted fund that has the cost in excess of market position. In order not to overstate the net assets of the latter fund, it may be necessary to treat the two portfolios as separate portfolios for valuation purposes and record the larger unrealized loss even though this violates the accounting standards established by SOP 78-1. At the minimum, the valuation issue should be described in a note to the financial statements.*

Long-term security investments On July 1, 19X4, 10-year bonds with a face value of $500,000 and a stated interest rate of 6% were acquired for $432,897. The investment yields an effective interest rate of 8%, and interest is paid annually on June 30.

Investments In Long-Term Securities	432,897	
Cash		432,897

On June 30, 19X5, the bond interest payment is received and the investment is amortized to reflect an 8% effective yield.

Cash	30,000	
Investments In Long-Term Securities	4,632	
Income And Gains (Losses) From		
Operating Fund Investments		
[$432,897 × 8%]		34,632

Property, plant, and equipment A building having a cost basis of $700,000 and related accumulated depreciation of $300,000 was sold for $500,000.

Cash	500,000	
Accumulated Depreciation	300,000	
Building		700,000
Gain On Sale Of Fixed Assets		100,000

Hospitals

Major movable equipment was purchased at a cost of $600,000. The purchase was financed with funds from current operations.

Major Movable Equipment	600,000	
Cash		600,000

Expenses The following operating expenses were paid during the year:

Nursing services	$17,000,000
Other professional services	6,000,000
General services	5,000,000
Fiscal and administrative services	1,900,000
Accrued expenses (beginning of year)	100,000
	$30,000,000

Nursing Services	17,000,000	
Other Professional Services	6,000,000	
General Services	5,000,000	
Fiscal And Administrative Services	1,900,000	
Accrued Expenses	100,000	
Cash		30,000,000

At the end of the year accrued expenses for general services amounted to $200,000.

General Services	200,000	
Accrued Expenses		200,000

Depreciation expense for the year totaled $1,500,000.

Depreciation Expense	1,500,000	
Accumulated Depreciation		1,500,000

During the year the construction of a new wing for the hospital was begun and the cost to date amounted to $750,000.

Construction In Progress	750,000	
Cash		750,000

The average accumulated expenditures for the year were $250,000 and the interest rate used to capitalize interest cost was 8% (the only debt outstanding during the year was a long-term note that carries an 8% interest rate).

Hospitals

Construction In Progress ($250,000 × 8%)	20,000	
Interest Expense		20,000

Liabilities The interest on the 8% long-term notes ($15,000,000), which mature in four years, was paid.

Interest Expense ($15,000,000 × 8%)	1,200,000	
Cash		1,200,000

On June 30, 19X5, general obligation bonds of $2,000,000 were issued at par. The interest and principal are to be paid from future earnings of the hospital.

Cash	2,000,000	
Bonds Payable		2,000,000

The beginning balance in accounts payable arose from the purchase of pharmacy supplies. During the year, $400,000 was paid to vendors for pharmacy supplies purchased.

Inventory—Pharmacy	350,000	
Accounts Payable	50,000	
Cash		400,000

At the end of the year, accounts payable for the purchase of pharmacy supplies amounted to $70,000.

Inventory—Pharmacy	70,000	
Accounts Payable		70,000

Pharmacy supplies on hand at the end of the period amounted to $90,000.

Other Professional Services	450,000	
Inventory—Pharmacy		450,000

Beginning balance	$100,000
Purchases for the year	420,000
Donations for the year	20,000
Ending balance	(90,000)
Inventory consumed during year	$450,000

Hospitals

Interfund transactions During the year, the Operating Fund incurred research expenses of $600,000, of which $200,000 is reimbursable from a Specific-Purpose Fund.

OPERATING FUND
Expenses—Research	600,000	
Cash		600,000
Due From Specific-Purpose Fund	200,000	
Transfers From Specific-Purpose Fund		200,000

SPECIFIC-PURPOSE FUND
Fund Balance	200,000	
Due To Operating Fund		200,000

By the end of the year, the Specific-Purpose Fund had transferred cash of $180,000 to reimburse the Operating Fund for the qualifying research expenses incurred.

OPERATING FUND
Cash	180,000	
Due From Specific-Purpose Fund		180,000

SPECIFIC-PURPOSE FUND
Due To Operating Fund	180,000	
Cash		180,000

During the year the Plant Replacement and Expansion Fund purchased major movable equipment for $90,000.

OPERATING FUND
Major Movable Equipment	90,000	
Fund Balance—Transfer From Plant Replacement And Expansion Fund For Capital Outlays		90,000

PLANT REPLACEMENT AND EXPANSION FUND
Fund Balance	90,000	
Cash		90,000

Note: These interfund transactions are also illustrated as part of the discussion of Restricted Funds.

After taking into account the transactions described above, the trial balance for the Operating Fund for the year ended June 30, 19X5, would be as follows.

Centerville Hospital
Operating Fund
Trial Balance
June 30, 19X5

	Dr.	Cr.
Cash	$ 3,482,103	
Accounts/notes receivable	7,500,000	
Allowance for uncollectibles		$ 700,000
Allowance for contractual adjustments		800,000
Pledges receivable	135,000	
Allowance for uncollectible pledges		25,000
Inventory—pharmacy	90,000	
Investments—equity securities (current)	250,000	
Allowance to reduce cost to market (current)		40,000
Due from specific-purpose fund	20,000	
Land	2,000,000	
Buildings	9,300,000	
Fixed equipment	3,120,000	
Major movable equipment	5,690,000	
Minor equipment	1,000,000	
Construction in progress	870,000	
Accumulated depreciation		5,200,000
Investments—equity securities (noncurrent)	485,000	
Allowance to reduce cost to market (noncurrent)		25,000
Investments in government bonds	437,529	
Accounts payable		70,000
Accrued expenses		200,000
Bonds payable		2,000,000
Long-term notes payable		15,000,000
Fund balance		9,180,000
Fund balance—value of donated property, plant, and equipment		120,000
Fund balance—transfer of market valuation loss from board-designated fund's portfolio investments		40,000
Fund balance—reduction on noncurrent marketable equity securities portfolio from cost to market	5,000	

Hospitals

	Dr.	Cr.
Fund balance—transfer from plant replacement and expansion fund for capital outlays		90,000
Revenues—nursing services		12,000,000
Revenues—other professional services		26,000,000
Provision for bad debts	1,000,000	
Contractual adjustments	3,000,000	
Charity services	200,000	
Nonprofessional services		100,000
Transfers from specific-purpose fund		200,000
Nursing services	17,000,000	
Other professional services	6,450,000	
General services	5,200,000	
Fiscal and administrative services	1,900,000	
Research	600,000	
Depreciation	1,500,000	
Interest	1,180,000	
General contributions		480,000
Gain on sale of fixed assets		100,000
Income and gains (losses) from operating fund investments		24,632
Donated supplies and material		20,000
	$72,414,632	$72,414,632

Board-Designated Funds

A hospital's Board of Directors may designate resources for a specified purpose. The board-designated resources should be accounted for in an unrestricted fund because the board can at its discretion rescind the designation and use the resources in any manner it deems appropriate. For this reason, the resources are not considered restricted. Transactions affecting a Board-Designated Fund should be accounted for separately from the hospital's Operating Fund in order to provide a basis for adequately disclosing those resources that have been designated by the board for a particular purpose.

To illustrate the routine transactions that are accounted for in a Board-Designated Fund, assume that assets are being accumulated for the possible purchase of land adjacent to the hospital. At the beginning of the fiscal year, the hospital prepared the following trial balance for the Board-Designated Fund:

Hospitals

Centerville Hospital
Board-Designated Fund
Trial Balance
July 1, 19X4

	Dr.	Cr.
Cash	$ 10,000	
Investments in marketable equity securities (current)	160,000	
Allowance valuation to reduce aggregate cost to aggregate market for marketable equity securities (current portfolio)		$ 20,000
Investments in marketable equity securities (noncurrent)	300,000	
Allowance valuation to reduce aggregate cost to aggregate market for marketable equity securities (noncurrent portfolio)		20,000
Fund balance		430,000
	$470,000	$470,000

The transactions of the Board-Designated Fund were illustrated in conjunction with the analysis of the Operating Fund's transactions. These transactions included (1) the receipt of dividend income of $40,000 (for both the current and noncurrent portfolios), (2) the increase in the allowance valuation account for the current portfolio for $40,000, and (3) the increase in the allowance valuation account for the noncurrent portfolio for $10,000. After considering these transactions, the trial balance for the Board-Designated Fund at the end of the year would be as follows:

Hospitals

Centerville Hospital
Board-Designated Fund
Trial Balance
June 30, 19X5

	Dr.	Cr.
Cash	$50,000	
Investments in marketable equity securities (current)	160,000	
Allowance valuation to reduce aggregate cost to aggregate market for marketable equity securities (current portfolio)		$60,000
Investments in marketable equity securities (noncurrent)	300,000	
Allowance valuation to reduce aggregate cost to aggregate market for marketable equity securities (noncurrent portfolio)		30,000
Fund balance		420,000
	$510,000	$510,000

Specific-Purpose Funds

Resources from donors that are restricted for a particular use should be accounted for in a Specific-Purpose Fund. The receipt of the resources is recorded as an increase to the Specific-Purpose Fund's fund balance account. When qualifying expenses are incurred, the expenses are recorded in the hospital's Operating Fund, and an amount equal to the qualifying expenses is transferred from the Specific-Purpose Fund to the Operating Fund. The Operating Fund records the transfer as other operating revenue.

A Specific-Purpose Fund generally acquires various investments with excess resources. Related investment income, gains and losses from the disposition of investments, and unrealized losses related to the valuation of marketable equity securities, should be recorded as part of the Specific-Purpose Fund's fund balance account.

To illustrate the routine transactions that are accounted for in a Specific-Purpose Fund, assume that restricted resources have been donated to support heart disease research. At the beginning of the fiscal year, the hospital prepared the following trial balance for the fund:

Hospitals

Centerville Hospital
Specific-Purpose Fund
Trial Balance
July 1, 19X4

	Dr.	Cr.
Cash	$100,000	
Investments in marketable equity securities	650,000	
Allowance valuation to reduce aggregate cost to aggregate market for marketable equity securities		$40,000
Fund balance		710,000
	$750,000	$750,000

Restricted donations During the year restricted donations of $70,000 were received and pledges of $50,000 were made. It is estimated that approximately 10% of the pledges will not be honored.

Cash	70,000	
Pledges Receivable	50,000	
Allowance For Uncollectible Pledges		5,000
Fund Balance		115,000

By the end of the year, $35,000 of the pledges had been collected, while specific pledges of $3,000 were written off.

Cash	35,000	
Allowance For Uncollectible Pledges	3,000	
Pledges Receivable		38,000

Marketable equity securities At the beginning of the year, the hospital's portfolio of marketable securities (includes both current and noncurrent) for the Specific-Purpose Fund was composed of the following investments:

	Cost	Market
Epsilon Company	$300,000	$310,000
Eta Company	200,000	180,000
Nu Company	150,000	120,000
Total cost	650,000	
Required balance in allowance account necessary to reduce aggregate cost to aggregate market	(40,000)	
Lower of aggregate cost or market	$610,000	$610,000

Hospitals

Dividend income from the investments in marketable equity securities amounted to $45,000 during the year.

Cash	45,000	
Fund Balance		45,000

On June 1, 19X5, the investment in Eta Company was sold for $190,000.

Cash	190,000	
Fund Balance	10,000	
Investments In Marketable Equity Securities		200,000

At the end of the year, the Specific-Purpose Fund's investment in marketable equity securities was composed of the following securities:

	Cost	Market
Epsilon Company	$300,000	$290,000
Nu Company	150,000	110,000
Total cost	450,000	
Required balance in allowance account necessary to reduce aggregate cost to aggregate market	(50,000)	
Lower of aggregate cost or market	$400,000	$400,000

Based on the above analysis, the year-end adjustment to reduce the aggregate cost of the portfolio to market would be as follows:

Fund Balance	10,000	
Allowance Valuation To Reduce Aggregate Cost To Market For Marketable Equity Securities ($50,000 – $40,000)		10,000

Interfund transactions During the year, the Operating Fund incurred research expenses of $200,000 that qualify for financing from the Specific-Purpose Fund.

OPERATING FUND

Expenses—Research	200,000	
Cash		200,000

Hospitals

Due From Specific-Purpose Fund	200,000	
Transfers From Specific-Purpose Fund		200,000

SPECIFIC-PURPOSE FUND

Fund Balance	200,000	
Due To Operating Fund		200,000

By the end of the year, the Specific-Purpose Fund had transferred cash of $180,000 to reimburse the Operating Fund for the qualifying research expenses incurred.

OPERATING FUND

Cash	180,000	
Due From Specific-Purpose Fund		180,000

SPECIFIC-PURPOSE FUND

Due To Operating Fund	180,000	
Cash		180,000

Note: The entries for interfund transactions are also illustrated as part of the discussion of the Operating Fund.

After taking into account the transactions described above, the trial balance for the Specific-Purpose Fund at the end of the year would be as follows:

Centerville Hospital
Specific-Purpose Fund
Trial Balance
June 30, 19X5

	Dr.	Cr.
Cash	$260,000	
Investments in marketable equity securities	450,000	
Allowance valuation to reduce aggregate cost to aggregate market for marketable equity securities		$ 50,000
Pledges receivable	12,000	
Allowance for uncollectible pledges		2,000
Due to operating fund		20,000
Fund balance		650,000
	$722,000	$722,000

Hospitals

Endowment Funds

Resources may be given by a donor, whereby only the income from the contributed amount is available for expenditure (Permanent Endowment Fund), or whereby both the income and the contributed amount can be expended (Term Endowment Fund). The accounting for contributions and earnings for these two types of Endowment Funds was discussed earlier in this chapter (see Operating Fund—Interfund Transfers and Restricted Resources).

In order to facilitate compliance with the donor agreement, the Endowment Fund's fund balance account should be titled as either restricted or unrestricted.

To illustrate the routine transactions that are accounted for in an Endowment Fund, assume that restricted resources have been donated and the income is to be used for the purchase of specialized equipment. At the beginning of the fiscal year, the hospital prepared the following trial balance for the fund:

Centerville Hospital
Permanent Endowment Fund
Trial Balance
July 1, 19X4

	Dr.	Cr.
Cash	$ 3,000	
Investment in government bonds	100,000	
Fund balance—restricted		$103,000
	$103,000	$103,000

Restricted donations Restricted donations of $50,000, to be used to acquire certain specialized equipment, were received during the year.

Cash	50,000	
Fund Balance—Restricted		50,000

Investments During the year additional governmental bonds were purchased for $52,000.

Investment In Government Bonds	52,000	
Cash		52,000

Hospitals

Interfund transfers Interest income from the investment in governmental bonds amounted to $9,000.

PERMANENT ENDOWMENT FUND
Cash   9,000
    Due To Plant Replacement And
        Expansion Fund   9,000

PLANT REPLACEMENT AND EXPANSION FUND
Due From Permanent Endowment Fund   9,000
    Transfers From Restricted Funds For
        Capital Outlays   9,000

After taking into account the transactions described above, the trial balance for the Permanent Endowment Fund at the end of the year would be as follows:

Centerville Hospital
Permanent Endowment Fund
Trial Balance
June 30, 19X5

	Dr.	Cr.
Cash	$ 10,000	
Investment in government bonds	152,000	
Due to plant replacement and expansion fund		$ 9,000
Fund balance—restricted		153,000
	$162,000	$162,000

Plant Replacement and Expansion Fund

When donations are made that can be used only for the purchase of property, plant, and equipment, the restricted gifts should be accounted for in the restricted fund entitled Plant Replacement and Expansion Fund. The receipts of restricted donations are recorded as an increase to the Plant Replacement and Expansion Fund's fund balance account. The subsequent purchase of fixed assets is recorded as a reduction of the Plant Replacement and Expansion Fund's fund balance account. The asset acquired is recorded in the hospital's Operating Fund by recognizing a transfer that is considered a direct increase to the Operating Fund's fund balance account.

Hospitals

Investment transactions, such as gains and losses from sale of investments and interest income, are accounted for in the Plant Replacement and Expansion Fund as an increase (decrease) to its fund balance account.

To illustrate the routine transactions that are accounted for in a Plant Replacement and Expansion Fund, assume that restricted resources have been donated for the purpose of acquiring certain fixed assets. At the beginning of the fiscal year, the hospital prepared the following trial balance for the fund:

Centerville Hospital
Plant Replacement and Expansion Fund
Trial Balance
July 1, 19X4

	Dr.	Cr.
Cash	$30,000	
Investments in marketable equity securities	450,000	
Allowance valuation to reduce aggregate cost to aggregate market for marketable equity securities		$25,000
Pledges receivable	20,000	
Allowance for uncollectible pledges		5,000
Fund balance		470,000
	$500,000	$500,000

Restricted donations During the year, restricted donations of $50,000 were received and pledges of $20,000 were made. It is estimated that approximately $5,000 of the pledges will not be honored.

Cash	50,000	
Pledges Receivable	20,000	
Allowance For Uncollectible Pledges		5,000
Fund Balance		65,000

Of the pledges outstanding at the beginning of the year, $15,000 of them were collected and the balance was written off.

Cash	15,000	
Allowance For Uncollectible Pledges	5,000	
Pledges Receivable		20,000

By the end of the year, $10,000 of the pledges made during the year were collected, while specific pledges of $2,000 were written off as dishonored.

Cash	10,000	
Allowance For Uncollectible Pledges	2,000	
Pledges Receivable		12,000

Marketable equity securities At the beginning of the year, the hospital's Plant Replacement and Expansion Fund had the following investments:

	Cost	Market
Phi Company	$250,000	$240,000
Chi Company	150,000	125,000
Iota Company	50,000	60,000
Total cost	450,000	
Required balance in allowance account necessary to reduce aggregate cost to aggregate market	(25,000)	
Lower of aggregate cost or market	$425,000	$425,000

During the year, dividend income of $30,000 was received.

Cash	30,000	
Fund Balance		30,000

On April 12, 19X5, $100,000 of Upsilon Company's common stock was purchased.

Investments In Marketable Equity Securities	100,000	
Cash		100,000

On the same date the investment in Chi Company's common stock was sold for $115,000.

Cash	115,000	
Fund Balance	35,000	
Investments In Marketable Equity Securities		150,000

At the end of the year, the Plant Replacement and Expansion Fund held the following marketable equity securities:

Hospitals

	Cost	Market
Phi Company	$250,000	$260,000
Iota Company	50,000	30,000
Upsilon Company	100,000	80,000
Total cost	400,000	
Required balance in allowance account necessary to reduce aggregate cost to aggregate market	(30,000)	
Lower of aggregate cost or market	$370,000	$370,000

Based on the above analysis, the year-end adjustment to reduce the aggregate cost of the investments to market would be as follows:

Fund Balance	5,000	
Allowance Valuation To Reduce Aggregate Cost To Aggregate Market For Marketable Equity Securities ($30,000 − $25,000)		5,000

Interfund transactions During the year the Plant Replacement and Expansion Fund purchased major movable equipment for $90,000.

OPERATING FUND
Major Movable Equipment	90,000	
Fund Balance—Transfer From Plant Replacement And Expansion Fund For Capital Outlays		90,000

PLANT REPLACEMENT AND EXPANSION FUND
Fund Balance	90,000	
Cash		90,000

Interest income of $9,000 earned by a Permanent Endowment Fund was transferable during the year, although the actual cash has not been received.

PLANT REPLACEMENT AND EXPANSION FUND
Due From Permanent Endowment Fund	9,000	
Transfers From Restricted Fund For Capital Outlays		9,000

PERMANENT ENDOWMENT FUND
Cash	9,000	
Due To Plant Replacement And Expansion Fund		9,000

Note: These interfund transactions are also illustrated as part of the discussion of the related restricted fund and the operating fund.

After taking into account the transactions described above, the trial balance for the Plant Replacement and Expansion Fund would be as follows:

Centerville Hospital
Plant Replacement and Expansion Fund
Trial Balance
June 30, 19X5

	Dr.	Cr.
Cash	$ 60,000	
Investments in marketable equity securities	400,000	
Allowance valuation to reduce aggregate cost to aggregate market for marketable equity securities		$ 30,000
Pledges receivable	8,000	
Allowance for uncollectible pledges		3,000
Due from permanent endowment fund	9,000	
Transfers from restricted fund for capital outlays		9,000
Fund balance		435,000
	$477,000	$477,000

FINANCIAL STATEMENTS

A hospital's financial statements should be presented in a governmental unit's financial statements as an Enterprise Fund. The governmental unit's general purpose financial statements would incorporate a hospital's financial statements into the (1) Combined Balance Sheet—All Fund Types and Account Groups, (2) Combined Statement of Revenues, Expenses, and Changes in Retained Earnings (or Equity)—All Proprietary Fund Types, (3) Combined Statement of Changes in Financial Position—All Proprietary Fund Types, and (4) Notes to the Financial Statements.

Hospitals

The financial statements of a nonprofit hospital should include the following:

- Balance Sheet
- Statement of Revenues and Expenses
- Statement of Changes in Fund Balances
- Statement of Changes in Financial Position

These financial statements are illustrated below and reflect the accounts and transactions developed earlier in the chapter (see section entitled Hospital Funds).

Balance Sheet A hospital's Balance Sheet should include the balance sheets for all unrestricted and restricted funds; however, the balance sheets should not be combined. The individual assets, liabilities, and fund balances for each individual fund type should be presented separately, although the hospital's Operating Fund and Board-Designated Funds, both unrestricted funds, may be combined. Only the Operating Fund's Balance Sheet is classified by major asset and liability categories.

An example of a Balance Sheet for all hospital fund types is presented in Exhibit I.

Statement of Revenues and Expenses Revenue and expense transactions are recorded only in a hospital's Operating Fund. The statement of operations should be classified to identify patient services revenue, other operating revenue, and nonoperating revenue. The final line item in the statement should be identified as the excess of revenues over expenses (or the excess of expenses over revenues). Other financial reporting standards should be observed in formatting the activity statement, including the identification of extraordinary items (APB-30—Reporting the Results of Operations) and the effects of changes in accounting principles (APB-20—Accounting Changes).

An example of a Statement of Revenues and Expenses is presented in Exhibit II.

Statement of Changes in Fund Balances As noted earlier, only the Operating Fund reflects revenues earned and expenses incurred by the hospital in an activity statement. Restricted funds and some transactions that affect Board-Designated Funds are summarized in

EXHIBIT I
Balance Sheet

Centerville Hospital
Balance Sheet
June 30, 19X5

ASSETS

UNRESTRICTED FUNDS

Operating fund:
Current assets
Cash	$3,482,103
Accounts/notes receivable	7,500,000
Allowance for uncollectibles	(700,000)
Allowance for contractual adjustments	(800,000)
Pledges receivable	135,000
Allowance for uncollectibles	(25,000)
Inventory—pharmacy	90,000
Investments—equity securities	250,000
Allowance to reduce cost to market	(40,000)
Due from specific-purpose fund	20,000
Total current assets	9,912,103

LIABILITIES AND FUND BALANCES

Current liabilities		
Accounts payable	$ 70,000	
Accrued expenses	200,000	
Total current liabilities		270,000
Long-term debt		
Bonds payable	2,000,000	
Notes payable	15,000,000	
Total long-term debt		17,000,000
Total liabilities		17,270,000
Fund balance (net of $25,000 unrealized losses on valuation of investments in non-current marketable equity securities)		10,319,632

Hospitals

GOVERNMENTAL GAAP GUIDE / 80.61

EXHIBIT I
(continued)

ASSETS

UNRESTRICTED FUNDS

Property, plant, and equipment		
Land	2,000,000	
Buildings	9,300,000	
Fixed equipment	3,120,000	
Major movable equipment	5,690,000	
Minor equipment	1,000,000	
Construction in progress	870,000	
Less accumulated depreciation	(5,200,000)	
Net property, plant, and equipment		16,780,000
Investments		
Investments — equity securities	485,000	
Allowance to reduce cost to market	(25,000)	
Other	437,529	
Total investments		897,529
Total assets		27,589,632

LIABILITIES AND FUND BALANCES

Total liabilities and fund balance	27,589,632

EXHIBIT I
(continued)

UNRESTRICTED FUNDS

ASSETS		
Board-designated funds:		
Cash		50,000
Investments—equity securities current portfolio	160,000	
Allowance to reduce cost to market	(60,000)	
Investments—equity securities noncurrent portfolio	300,000	
Allowance to reduce cost to market	(30,000)	
Total assets		420,000
Total for unrestricted funds		$28,009,632

LIABILITIES AND FUND BALANCES		
Fund balance (net of $30,000 unrealized losses on valuation of investments in non-current marketable equity securities)		420,000
Total fund balance		420,000
Total for unrestricted funds		$28,009,632

EXHIBIT I
(continued)

RESTRICTED FUNDS

ASSETS			LIABILITIES AND FUND BALANCES	
Specific-purpose funds:				
Cash	$ 260,000		Due to operating fund	$ 20,000
Investments—equity securities	450,000		Fund balance (net of $50,000 unrealized losses on valuation of investments in marketable equity securities)	650,000
Allowance to reduce cost to market	(50,000)			
Pledges receivable	12,000			
Allowance for uncollectibles	(2,000)			
Total assets	$ 670,000		Total liabilities and fund balance	$ 670,000
Endowment funds:				
Cash	$ 10,000		Due to plant replacement and expansion fund	$ 9,000
Investments in bonds	152,000		Fund balance	153,000
Total assets	$ 162,000		Total liabilities and fund balance	$ 162,000
Plant replacement and expansion funds:				
Cash	$ 60,000		Fund balance (net of $30,000 unrealized losses on valuation of investments in marketable equity securities)	$ 444,000
Investments—equity securities	400,000			
Allowance to reduce cost to market	(30,000)			
Pledges receivable	8,000			
Allowance for uncollectibles	(3,000)			
Due from permanent endowment fund	9,000			
Total assets	$ 444,000		Total liabilities and fund balance	$ 444,000

EXHIBIT II
Statement of Revenues and Expenses

Centerville Hospital
Statement of Revenues and Expenses
For Year Ended June 30, 19X5

Patient services revenue	
Nursing services	$12,000,000
Other professional services	26,000,000
Total patient services	38,000,000
Deductions from patient services revenue	
Provision for bad debts	1,000,000
Contractual adjustments	3,000,000
Charity services	200,000
Total deductions from patient services revenue	4,200,000
Net patient services revenue	33,800,000
Other operating revenue	
Nonprofessional services	100,000
Transfers from specific-purpose fund	200,000
Total other operating revenue	300,000
Total operating revenue	34,100,000
Operating expenses	
Nursing services	17,000,000
Other professional services	6,450,000
General services	5,200,000
Fiscal and administrative services	1,900,000
Research	600,000
Depreciation	1,500,000
Interest	1,180,000
Total operating expenses	33,830,000
Income from operations	270,000
Nonoperating revenue	
Income and gains (losses) from board-designated fund	40,000
General contributions	480,000
Gain on sale of fixed assets	100,000
Income and gains (losses) from operating fund investments	24,632
Donated supplies and material	20,000
Total nonoperating revenue	664,632
Excess of revenues over expenses	$ 934,632

Hospitals

separate analyses of each fund type's changes in fund balance during the period. For example, certain "operating activities" (such as investment earnings and equity transactions) and interfund transfers are included in the analysis of each fund balance. The fund balance analysis should reconcile the beginning balance of the account to the ending balance in the account.

An example of a Statement of Changes in Fund Balances is presented in Exhibit III.

EXHIBIT III
Statement of Changes in Fund Balances

Centerville Hospital
Statement of Changes in Fund Balances
For Year Ended June 30, 19X5

UNRESTRICTED FUNDS
Operating fund:

Balance at beginning of year	$9,180,000
Excess of revenues over expenses ($934,632 less $40,000 to board-designated fund)	894,632
Value of donated property, plant, and equipment	120,000
Transfer of market valuation loss from board-designated fund's portfolio investment	40,000
Increase of unrealized losses on valuation of investments in noncurrent marketable equity securities	(5,000)
Transfer from plant replacement and expansion fund for capital outlays	90,000
Balance at end of year	10,319,632
Board-designated funds:	
Balance at beginning of year	430,000
Investment income	40,000
Transfer of market valuation loss related to portfolio investment to operating fund	(40,000)
Increase of unrealized losses on valuation of investments in noncurrent marketable equity securities	(10,000)
Balance at end of year	420,000
Fund balance at end of year—all unrestricted funds	$10,739,632

EXHIBIT III
(continued)

RESTRICTED FUNDS

Specific-purpose funds:
Balance at beginning of year	$710,000
Restricted donations	115,000
Investment income	45,000
Realized loss on sale of investments	(10,000)
Increase of unrealized loss on valuation of investments in marketable equity securities	(10,000)
Transfers to operating fund	(200,000)
Balance at end of year	$650,000

Endowment funds:
Balance at beginning of year	$103,000
Restricted donations	50,000
Balance at end of year	$153,000

Plant replacement and expansion funds:
Balance at beginning of year	$470,000
Restricted donations	65,000
Investment income	30,000
Realized loss on sale of investments	(35,000)
Increase of unrealized losses on valuation of investments in marketable equity securities	(5,000)
Transfers to operating fund	(90,000)
Transfers from permanent endowment fund	9,000
Balance at end of year	$444,000

Statement of Changes in Financial Position Because only operating activities related to the Operating Fund are reflected in a hospital's activity statement, a Statement of Changes in Financial Position is prepared only to summarize financing and investing activities of the Operating Fund. In preparing the Statement of Changes in Financial Position, reporting standards established by APB-19 (Reporting Changes in Financial Position) should be observed.

An example of a Statement of Changes in Financial Position is presented in Exhibit IV.

Hospitals

EXHIBIT IV
Statement of Changes in Financial Position

Centerville Hospital
Statement of Changes in Financial Position
(Operating Fund)
For Year Ended June 30, 19X5

Sources of funds	
From operations	
Income from operations	$ 270,000
Add (deduct) items not requiring funds	
Depreciation	1,500,000
Funds from operations	1,770,000
From nonoperating activities	
Nonoperating revenues ($664,632 less $40,000 to board-designated fund)	624,632
Add (deduct) items not requiring funds	
Gain on sale of fixed assets	(100,000)
Transfer of market valuation loss from board-designated fund's portfolio investments	40,000
Writedown of nontemporary loss in noncurrent marketable equity security investments	35,000
Amortization of discount on long-term investments	(4,632)
Funds from nonoperating activities	595,000
Funds from operations and nonoperating activities	2,365,000
Other sources	
Sale of noncurrent marketable equity securities	130,000
Sale of property, plant, and equipment	500,000
Issuance of long-term bonds	2,000,000
Total other sources	2,630,000
Total sources of fund	4,995,000
Application of funds	
Acquisition of long-term investments	432,897
Reclassification of marketable equity securities from current to noncurrent portfolio	150,000

EXHIBIT IV
(continued)

Acquisition of major movable equipment	600,000
Construction in progress (including capitalization of interest)	770,000
Total application of funds	1,952,897
Increase in working capital	$3,042,103
Financing and investing activities not affecting working capital	
Value of property, plant, and equipment donated to hospital during the period	$ 120,000
Transfers from plant replacement and expansion fund for acquisition of property, plant, and equipment during the period	$ 90,000

Elements of net increase (decrease) to working capital

Cash	$ 482,103
Accounts/notes receivable	3,500,000
Allowance for uncollectibles	(200,000)
Allowance for contractual adjustments	(500,000)
Pledges receivable	35,000
Allowance for uncollectibles	(5,000)
Inventory—pharmacy	(10,000)
Investments—equity securities	(150,000)
Allowance to reduce cost to market	(10,000)
Due from specific-purpose fund	20,000
Accounts payable	(20,000)
Accrued expenses	(100,000)
Net increase (decrease) to working capital	$3,042,103

Separate Trust Funds

Resources that may become available to a hospital may be held in a separate trust fund administered by trustees neither directly nor indirectly controlled by the hospital. The financial resources held by such separate trust funds should not be reported as part of the financial resources of the hospital, although the existence of the funds may be disclosed in the hospital's financial statements. Accrual accounting should be used to record nondiscretionary distributions from the separate trust funds, and the distributions should be recorded as endowment income (nonoperating revenue). When the distributions to the hospital are discretionary, the distributions should be recorded as a donation (nonoperating revenue) or in accordance with the terms of the restricted gift.

Consolidated or Combined Financial Statements

The *Hospital Audit Guide* notes that organizations, such as fund-raising groups, often provide assistance to a hospital. When these organizations are not controlled by a hospital, they should prepare financial statements that are separate from those of the hospital; however, if these organizations provide significant resources to or services for the hospital, appropriate disclosures should be made in the hospital's financial statements.

On the other hand, when these organizations are under the control of a hospital, their financial statements should be combined or consolidated with the financial statements of the hospital. SOP 81-2 (Reporting Practices Concerning Hospital-Related Organizations) proposed the following criteria for determining whether a separate organization is related to a hospital:

a. The hospital controls the separate organization through contracts or other legal documents that provide the hospital with the authority to direct the separate organization's activities, management, and policies; or
b. The hospital is for all practical purposes the sole beneficiary of the organization. The hospital should be considered the organization's sole beneficiary if any one of the three following circumstances exist:

1. The organization has solicited funds in the name of the hospital, and with the expressed or implied approval of the hospital, and substantially all the funds solicited by the organization were intended by the contributor, or were otherwise required, to be transferred to the hospital or used at its discretion or direction.
2. The hospital has transferred some of its resources to the organization, and substantially all of the organization's resources are held for the benefit of the hospital.
3. The hospital has assigned certain of its functions (such as the operation of a dormitory) to the organization, which is operating primarily for the benefit of the hospital.

Hospitals

When it is concluded that the separate organization's financial statements should not be consolidated or combined with the hospital because the criteria described above do not exist, the hospital's financial statements should disclose the existence and nature of the two entity's relationships if either of the following conditions exist:

- Material resources that have been designated for the benefit of the hospital are being held by the separate entity.
- Material transactions have occurred between the two entities.

If material transactions have occurred between the separate organization and the hospital, the following additional disclosures should be made:

- A description of the transactions, summarized if appropriate, for the period reported on, including dollar amounts, if any, and any other information deemed necessary for understanding the effects of the transactions on the hospital's financial statements
- The dollar volume of transactions and the effects of any change in the terms from the preceding period
- Amounts due from or to the related organization, and, if not otherwise apparent, the terms and manner of settlement

> **OBSERVATION:** *These disclosure requirements are consistent with the reporting standards established by FASB-57 (Related Party Disclosures).*

When the separate organization's financial statements are not consolidated or combined with the hospital, and condition (a) and at least one of the three conditions that compose condition (b) exist, the hospital's financial statements should contain the following disclosures:

- Summarized financial information of the separate organization
- Nature of relationships between the separate organization and the hospital

LITERATURE REFERENCES

Material in this chapter is based on the following authoritative pronouncements and publications, which are grouped according to the major headings used within the chapter. A dual reference (both paragraph and page number) is used for NCGA-1 and NCGA-2 because the original pronouncements do not use paragraph numbers.

Basic Concepts and Standards
NCGA-1   *Governmental Accounting and Financial Reporting Principles,* p. 27, footnote 4.
NCGA-3   *Defining the Governmental Reporting Entity,* ¶¶ 9-14.
SOP 78-7   *Financial Accounting and Reporting by Hospitals Operated by a Governmental Unit,* p. 86 (as reproduced in the *Hospital Audit Guide*).

Basis of Accounting
NCGA-1   *Governmental Accounting and Financial Reporting Principles,* p. 11/ ¶ 58.
SOP 78-7   *Financial Accounting and Reporting by Hospitals Operated by a Governmental Unit,* p. 86 (as reproduced in the *Hospital Audit Guide*).
FASB:CS-1   *Objectives of Financial Reporting by Business Enterprises,* ¶ 44.
AMERICAN HOSPITAL ASSOCIATION-1976   *Chart of Accounts for Hospitals,* p. 9.

Measurement Focus
GASB Discussion Memorandum, *Measurement Focus and Basis of Accounting—Governmental Funds,* (nonauthoritative).

Budgetary System and Accounts
NCGA-1   *Governmental Accounting and Financial Reporting Principles,* pp. 13 and 14/¶¶ 78 and 94-97.
AMERICAN HOSPITAL ASSOCIATION-1976   *Chart of Accounts for Hospitals,* p. 6.

Accounts and Transactions
GASB-1   *Authoritative Status of NCGA Pronouncements and AICPA Industry Audit Guides,* Appendix B, pp. 9 and 10.
AMERICAN HOSPITAL ASSOCIATION-1976   *Chart of Accounts for Hospitals,* pp. 10 and 11.

Revenues and Other Sources of Assets
FASB:CS-6   *Elements of Financial Statements,* ¶ 78.
APB Statement-4   *Basic Concepts and Accounting Principles Underlying Financial Statements of Business Enterprises,* ¶ 150.

Hospitals

Patient Service Revenues
AICPA INDUSTRY AUDIT GUIDE   *Hospital Audit Guide*, pp. 5 and 6.
AMERICAN HOSPITAL ASSOCIATION-1976   *Chart of Accounts for Hospitals*, pp. 80-82.

Other Operating Revenues
AICPA INDUSTRY AUDIT GUIDE   *Hospital Audit Guide*, pp. 6 and 7.
AMERICAN HOSPITAL ASSICIATION-1976   *Chart of Accounts for Hospitals*, pp. 78-80.

Nonoperating Revenues
AICPA INDUSTRY AUDIT GUIDE   *Hospital Audit Guide*, pp. 7, 8, and 10.
AMERICAN HOSPITAL ASSOCIATION-1976   *Chart of Accounts for Hospitals*, pp. 11 and 93.

Expenses
FASB:CS-6   *Elements of Financial Statements*, ¶ 80.
FASB:CS-5   *Recognition and Measurement in Financial Statements of Business Enterprises*, ¶ 86.
APB Statement-4   *Basic Concepts and Accounting Principles Underlying Financial Statements of Business Enterprises*, ¶¶ 157-160 and 181.

Depreciation Expense
AICPA INDUSTRY AUDIT GUIDE   *Hospital Audit Guide*, pp. 4 and 5.
AMERICAN HOSPITAL ASSOCIATION-1976   *Chart of Accounts for Hospitals*, p. 4.
NCGA-2   *Grant, Entitlement, and Shared Revenue Accounting and Reporting by State and Local Governments*, ¶¶ 2 and 18.

Interest Cost
FASB-34   *Capitalization of Interest Cost*, ¶¶ 13 and 17.
FASB-62   *Capitalization of Interest Cost in Situations Involving Certain Tax-Exempt Borrowings and Certain Gifts and Grants*, ¶¶ 3 and 4.

Assets
FASB:CS-6   *Elements of Financial Statements*, ¶¶ 25 and 26.
AICPA INDUSTRY AUDIT GUIDE   *Hospital Audit Guide*, p. 7.
AMERICAN HOSPITAL ASSOCIATION-1976   *Chart of Accounts for Hospitals*, p. 8.

Cash
AICPA INDUSTRY AUDIT GUIDE   *Hospital Audit Guide*, p. 17.

Marketable Equity Securities
SOP 78-1   *Accounting by Hospitals for Certain Marketable Equity Securities*, pp. 75-79 (as reproduced in the *Hospital Audit Guide*).

Long-Term Securities Investments
AICPA INDUSTRY AUDIT GUIDE   *Hospital Audit Guide*, p. 4.
AMERICAN HOSPITAL ASSOCIATION-1976   *Chart of Accounts for Hospitals*, pp. 8 and 9.
ARB-43   *Restatement and Revision of Accounting Research Bulletins*, Chapter 3A, ¶ 9.
APB-21   *Interest on Receivables and Payables*, ¶ 15.
APB-18   *The Equity Method of Accounting for Investments in Common Stock*, ¶¶ 14-17.

Receivables
AICPA INDUSTRY AUDIT GUIDE   *Hospital Audit Guide*, pp. 5 and 6.
APB-20   *Accounting Changes*, ¶¶ 31-33.

Property, Plant, and Equipment
AICPA INDUSTRY AUDIT GUIDE   *Hospital Audit Guide*, pp. 5 and 6.
AMERICAN HOSPITAL ASSOCIATION-1976   *Chart of Accounts for Hospitals*, pp. 7 and 8.

Liabilities
FASB:CS-6   *Elements of Financial Statements*, ¶¶ 35 and 36.
AICPA INDUSTRY AUDIT GUIDE   *Hospital Audit Guide*, p. 24.
1980 GAAFR   *Governmental Accounting, Auditing, and Financial Reporting*, p. 57.

Contingent Liabilities
SOP (1978)   *Clarification of Accounting, Auditing, and Reporting Practices Relating to Hospital Malpractice Loss Contingencies*, pp. 67-79 (as reproduced in the *Hospital Audit Guide*).
FASB-5   *Accounting for Contingencies*, ¶¶ 3, 8-11, 35-38, 44, and 45.
FASB INTERPRETATION-14   *Reasonable Estimation of the Amount of a Loss*, ¶¶ 2 and 3.

Nontransfer of Malpractice Risk
SOP (1978)   *Clarification of Accounting, Auditing, and Reporting Practices Relating to Hospital Malpractice Loss Contingencies*, p. 67 (as reproduced in the *Hospital Audit Guide*).
FASB-5   *Accounting for Contingencies*, ¶¶ 44 and 45.

Asserted and Unasserted Claims for Health Care Providers
SOP 87-1   *Accounting for Asserted and Unasserted Medical Malpractice Claims of Health Care Providers and Related Issues*.

Hospitals

Tax-Exempt Debt Restrictions
SOP 85-1 *Financial Reporting by Not-for-Profit Health Care Entities for Tax-Exempt Debt and Certain Funds Whose Use Is Limited.*

Deferred Revenue—Third-Party Reimbursements
AICPA INDUSTRY AUDIT GUIDE *Hospital Audit Guide*, p. 5.
AMERICAN HOSPITAL ASSOCIATION-1976 *Chart of Accounts for Hospitals*, p. 9.

Interfund Transfers and Restricted Resources
AICPA INDUSTRY AUDIT GUIDE *Hospital Audit Guide*, pp. 8 and 9.
AMERICAN HOSPITAL ASSOCIATION-1976 *Chart of Accounts for Hospitals*, p. 10.

Hospital Funds
AICPA INDUSTRY AUDIT GUIDE *Hospital Audit Guide*, pp. 8 and 9.
AMERICAN HOSPITAL ASSOCIATION-1976 *Chart of Accounts for Hospitals*, p. 10.

Operating Fund (General Fund)
AICPA INDUSTRY AUDIT GUIDE *Hospital Audit Guide*, p. 8.
AMERICAN HOSPITAL ASSOCIATION-1976 *Chart of Accounts for Hospitals*, pp. 10 and 11.

Board-Designated Funds
AICPA INDUSTRY AUDIT GUIDE *Hospital Audit Guide*, p. 8.
AMERICAN HOSPITAL ASSOCIATION-1976 *Chart of Accounts for Hospitals*, p. 11.

Specific-Purpose Funds
AICPA INDUSTRY AUDIT GUIDE *Hospital Audit Guide*, pp. 8 and 9.
AMERICAN HOSPITAL ASSOCIATION-1976 *Chart of Accounts for Hospitals*, p. 10.

Endowment Funds
AICPA INDUSTRY AUDIT GUIDE *Hospital Audit Guide*, pp. 8 and 9.
AMERICAN HOSPTIAL ASSOCIATION-1976 *Chart of Accounts for Hospitals*, p. 10.

Plant Replacement and Expansion Fund
AICPA INDUSTRY AUDIT GUIDE *Hospital Audit Guide*, p. 9.
AMERICAN HOSPITAL ASSOCIATION-1976 *Chart of Accounts for Hospitals*, p. 10.

Hospitals

Financial Statements
NCGA-1   *Governmental Accounting and Financial Reporting Principles*, p. 20/¶ 141.
AICPA Industry Audit Guide   *Hospital Audit Guide*, pp. 38-52.
AMERICAN HOSPITAL ASSOCIATION-1976   *Chart of Accounts for Hospitals*, p. 11.
SOP 78-7   *Financial Accounting and Reporting by Hospitals Operated by a Governmental Unit*, p. 86 (as reproduced in the *Hospital Audit Guide*).

Separate Trust Funds
AICPA Industry Audit Guide   *Hospital Audit Guide*, p. 11.

Consolidated or Combined Financial Statements
SOP 81-2   *Reporting Practices Concerning Hospital-Related Organizations*.

COLLEGES AND UNIVERSITIES

BASIC CONCEPTS AND STANDARDS

Colleges and universities may be private or public institutions. When a college or university is publicly owned, its financial statements may have to be included in the financial statements of the governmental unit that exercises oversight responsibility over the institution. NCGA-3 (Defining the Governmental Reporting Entity), discussed in Chapter 4, established criteria that should be used to determine whether a state or local governmental unit (oversight unit) has oversight responsibility over another governmental entity (component unit).

Accounting and reporting standards applicable to colleges and universities controlled by governmental units are established by the following pronouncements:

- AICPA Audits of Colleges and Universities
- AICPA SOP 74-8 (Financial Accounting and Reporting by Colleges and Universities)

In addition, accounting and reporting standards are established by *College and University Business Administration: Administrative Service* (CUBA), which is published by the National Association of College and University Business Officers (NACUBO). This publication is a looseleaf service that addresses financial and nonfinancial topics relevant to the administration of a college or university. The accounting and financial reporting standards are discussed in Section 5 of the publication.

> **OBSERVATION:** *Although the NACUBO publication does not carry the same authoritative weight as the AICPA's Audit Guide and SOP, it is a recognized source of authority under the GASB hierarchy of generally accepted accounting principles as described in Chapter 1 of this guide.*

Basis of Accounting

The selection of an accounting basis determines when transactions and economic events are reflected in an entity's financial statements. In NCGA-1 (Governmental Accounting and Financial Reporting Principles), it is noted that a basis of accounting refers to "when revenues, expenditures, expenses, and transfers—and related assets and liabilities—are recognized in the accounts and reported in the financial statements."

The accrual basis of accounting, with some modifications, should be used by colleges and universities in preparing their financial statements. FASB:CS-1 (Objectives of Financial Reporting by Business Enterprises) defines accrual accounting as follows:

> Accrual accounting attempts to record the financial effects on an enterprise of transactions and other events and circumstances that have cash consequences for an enterprise in the periods in which those transactions, events, and circumstances occur rather than only in the periods in which cash is received or paid by the enterprise. Accrual accounting is concerned with the process by which cash expended on resources and activities is returned as more (or perhaps less) cash to the enterprise, not just with the beginning and end of the process.

The accrual basis as applied by a commercial enterprise is not fully applicable to financial reporting by a college or university. NACUBO draws the following conclusion:

> Since service, in which resources are consumed, is the objective of the college or university, the accounting and reporting process must address itself to accounting for resources received and used rather than to the determination of net income.

The single most significant modification to the accrual basis when applied to college and university accounting is the treatment of depreciation. As discussed later, depreciation is not recorded as an expense by a college or university. Consistent with fundamental governmental accounting principles, the purchase of a fixed asset may be treated as a current expenditure and not capitalized for later amortization over the life of the property.

Colleges and Universities

> **OBSERVATION:** *While the treatment of depreciation for colleges and universities is consistent with fundamental governmental accounting principles, it is not consistent with the treatment employed by hospitals. As discussed in Chapter 80, hospitals capitalize purchases of fixed assets and recognize depreciation in their Operating Funds. It is difficult to explain how the mission of each type of institution differs to such an extent to justify the completely different treatment of capital expenditures.*

Measurement Focus

The measurement focus for an entity is concerned with the inflow and outflow of resources that affect the organization. The balance sheet should reflect those resources that are available to meet current obligations and that are to be used in the delivery of the services provided by a college or university. The statement of operations for the period should summarize those resources received and those consumed during the current period.

For a college or university the results of operations are recorded in the Current Funds (Unrestricted and Restricted). The measurement focus for these funds is, for the most part, the flow of current financial resources. Thus in the Current Fund, expenditures are recognized that require the use of current financial resources available to the institution. As noted earlier, depreciation is not recorded in the Current Funds because the acquisition of a fixed asset results in the use of financial resources when the asset is paid for, not when the cost of the asset is allocated to future accounting periods.

Although the measurement focus for a college or university is similar to the measurement focus used by a governmental unit, there are significant differences. Fixed assets of a college or university are recorded in a separate fund group, whereas a governmental unit would record its fixed assets in its General Fixed Assets Account Group. In addition, long-term debt of a college or university is recorded in various funds, while similar debt of a governmental unit would be recorded in the unit's General Long-Term Debt Account Group.

Budgetary System and Accounts

A budget represents a plan of financial operations that establishes a basis for the control and evaluation of activities financed through the Current Funds of the college or university. Generally, the type of budget prepared by a college or university will more closely resemble a budget prepared by a commercial enterprise than a budget prepared by a governmental unit. For this reason, a college or university usually will find it unnecessary to integrate the adoption of its budget into its formal accounting records; however, formal integration may be legally mandated in some jurisdictions (for example, when a state legislature or local council appropriates funds for an institution).

If a college or university records its budget, the recording is similar to the recording of a governmental unit's budget. Presented below is the general format for recording a budget:

Estimated Revenues	X	
Estimated Expenditures		X
Budget Balance (surplus)		X

The estimated revenues and expenditures accounts are control accounts and would be supported by appropriate subsidiary ledgers.

Because the three accounts illustrated above are budgetary accounts, at the end of the period the entry to close the budget would reverse the entry that recorded the budget, and therefore the recording of the budget would have no effect on the institution's operating accounts.

In addition to recording an institution's budget, a college or university should use an encumbrance system to control expenditures for the period. Encumbrances do not represent expenditures for a period, and those encumbrances outstanding at the end of a period must be closed so that neither an expenditure nor a liability is shown on the institution's financial statements.

Accounts and Transactions

Transactions accounted for by a college or university must be recorded in a manner consistent with FASB pronouncements, except when the GASB has addressed the accounting issue. When the financial statements of a college or university are presented as part of a governmental unit's financial statements, GASB pronouncements must be followed.

Consistent with the basic governmental accounting model, transactions of a college or university are recorded in a variety of separate

Colleges and Universities

funds. Generally, the following funds are used by a college or university:

- Current Fund
  - Unrestricted
  - Restricted
- Loan Funds
- Endowment and Similar Funds
- Annuity and Life Income Funds
- Plant Funds
- Agency Funds

Presented below is a discussion of the basic accounts and transactions that are part of the fund accounting system employed by a college or university.

Revenues and Other Sources of Assets

FASB:CS-6 (Elements of Financial Statements) defines revenues as "inflows or other enhancements of assets of an entity or settlements of its liabilities during a period from delivering or producing goods, rendering services, or other activities that constitute the entity's on-going major or central operations." Revenues, as established in APB Statement-4 (Basic Concepts and Accounting Principles Underlying Financial Statements of Business Enterprises), should be recognized when the earning process is complete, or virtually complete, and an exchange has taken place. The AICPA's Audit Guide simply states that revenues of a college or university should be reported when earned. Revenues earned or received by a college or university must be recorded in a Current Fund. Generally, revenues of a college or university include all resources earned during the period, unrestricted gifts and grants, and restricted resources that were expended during the period. The primary sources of revenues for a college or university are described below.

Tuition and Fees Student tuition and fees should be recorded as unrestricted current fund revenue. The amount recognized should be equal to the full charge, even though part or all of the billed amount will not be collected. Amounts not collected should be charged to appropriate expenditure accounts, such as scholarships and fellowships, or to the allowance for uncollectible accounts. Fees that are assessed based on a binding external restriction, such as debt service, should not be recognized as unrestricted current fund revenue but, rather, should be shown as an addition to the appropriate college or university fund that will utilize the resources. To be considered a binding external restriction, the fee must be explicitly represented on the student bill as available for a specific nonoperating purpose.

Tuition and fees that encompass two fiscal years should be recorded as revenue in the year in which the majority of the program is completed. When a single billing represents various charges, such as tuition and room and board, a reasonable basis should be established to allocate the total billing to that portion representing tuition and that portion representing sales and services for auxiliary enterprises.

Pledged tuition and fees When tuition and fees are pledged as part of a bond indenture agreement, the total amount billed is recorded as unrestricted current fund revenue; however, the pledged amount should then be recorded as a mandatory transfer to the Plant Fund which carries the bonded debt.

Allocated tuition and fees When a portion of tuition and fees is allocated by the governing board for other operating purposes, the total amount billed is recorded as Unrestricted Current Fund revenue; however, the allocated portion should then be recorded as a nonmandatory transfer to the appropriate other fund.

To illustrate, assume that tuition and fees of $3,000,000 were billed. A portion of the total ($400,000) is pledged under a bond indenture agreement, while another portion ($200,000) is allocated by the governing board to finance the construction of a classroom building. The billing of the tuition and fees would be recorded as follows:

CURRENT FUND (UNRESTRICTED)
Accounts Receivable	3,000,000	
Revenues—Tuition And Fees		3,000,000
Mandatory Transfers—Principal		
And Interest	400,000	
Fund Balance (Nonmandatory Transfer)	200,000	
Due To Retirement Of Indebted-		
ness Fund (Plant Fund)		400,000
Due To Unexpended Plant Fund		
(Plant Fund)		200,000

PLANT FUND—RETIREMENT OF INDEBTEDNESS
   Due From Current Fund (Unrestricted)   400,000
      Fund Balance—Restricted   400,000

PLANT FUND—UNEXPENDED
   Due From Current Fund (Unrestricted)   200,000
      Fund Balance—Restricted   200,000

Governmental Appropriations A college or university may receive appropriations from the federal, state, or local government. These appropriations would be recorded as Current Fund revenues if they are unrestricted and therefore available to finance current operations, or if they are restricted amounts that are to be expended for current operations (educational and general support). Resources are considered restricted only when "the restrictions are so specific that they substantially reduce the institutions' flexibility in financial operations."

Disbursements made by a governmental agency on behalf of a college or university, such as payments to a state retirement system, are recorded as unrestricted revenues of the college or university.

Governmental appropriations should be identified as being received from the federal, state, or local government. When resources flow from one governmental level to another level and ultimately to a college or university, the source of the revenue is determined by the level of government that decided how the resources would be utilized.

Governmental Grants and Contracts Federal, state, or local governments may provide resources to colleges and universities through various grant or contract arrangements. These resources would be considered Current Fund revenue if they are unrestricted and therefore available to finance current operations, or if they are restricted amounts that are to be expended for current operations.

When resources are recorded under restricted grant or contract arrangements, the amounts received should be recorded as revenue only when appropriate expenditures are incurred. The initial receipts of the restricted resources would be recorded as an increase to the fund balance account of the Restricted Current Fund. For example, assume that a college or university receives a restricted state grant of $250,000 that is to be used for a particular type of research. The receipt of the grant would be recorded as follows:

CURRENT FUND (RESTRICTED)
   Cash   250,000
      Fund Balance   250,000

The following entry would be made if it is assumed that $100,000 of qualifying research expenditures are incurred under the grant:

CURRENT FUND (RESTRICTED)

Expenditures—Research	100,000	
Cash		100,000
Fund Balance	100,000	
Revenues—State Grants And		
Contracts		100,000

Amounts equal to direct cost incurred under a governmental grant or contract should be recorded as restricted revenue (Current Fund—Restricted), while amounts equal to indirect cost incurred should be recorded as unrestricted revenue (Current Fund—Unrestricted).

Governmental grants and contracts should be identified by source (federal, state, or local).

Private Gifts and Grants Revenue should be recorded when unrestricted gifts, grants, and bequests are received from nongovernmental sources. Restricted gifts, grants, and contracts would be recognized as revenue when they are expended for current operations. Restricted resources are recorded as revenue of Current Funds (Restricted) when direct costs are incurred. Restricted resources are recognized as revenue of the Current Fund (Unrestricted) when indirect costs of the Restricted Current Fund are incurred.

When resources are received from funds that are held in a revocable trust or that are distributable at the discretion of the trustees of the trust, revenue should be recorded and adequately disclosed in the Current Fund (Unrestricted and Restricted).

Endowment Income A Current Fund recognizes endowment income for (1) unrestricted income from the Endowment Fund and similar funds, (2) restricted income from the Endowment Fund and similar funds to the extent it is expended for current operations, and (3) income from funds held by others under irrevocable trusts.

The amount of unrestricted income from Endowment Funds to be recorded in the Current Fund is equal to the ordinary income. Gains and losses from the sale of trust assets and any income that must be added to the principal, based on the terms of the endowment agreement, would not be recorded as endowment income. For example, if an Endowment Fund receives $50,000 of dividend income and the earnings from the trust are to be used for unrestricted purposes, the following entries would be made:

CURRENT FUND—UNRESTRICTED
   Due From Endowment Fund   50,000
      Revenues—Endowment Income   50,000

ENDOWMENT FUND
   Cash   50,000
      Due To Current Fund (Unrestricted)   50,000

The actual gain or loss from the sale of assets of Endowment Funds is recorded only in the Endowment Fund; however, if all or part of a gain is used for operating purposes, that portion should be accounted for as a transfer from the Endowment Fund to the Current Fund and not as a revenue transaction.

An endowment income stabilization reserve may be established to reduce the fluctuation of endowment income available from year to year to the various funds of the college or university. The total income from endowment investment pools should be accounted for so that all income is allocated to all participating funds. The full amount allocable to the Current Fund (Unrestricted) should be recorded as endowment income, and amounts added to the stabilization reserve should be reported as a separate item in the fund balance account of the Current Fund (Unrestricted). Amounts due to the Current Fund (Restricted) should be shown as an addition to its fund balance account. To illustrate, assume that pooled investments earn an actual return of 7%, but only 6% is distributed to participating funds and 1% is added to the stabilization reserve. The following entries would be made if the Current Fund (Unrestricted) earned income amounted to $7,000 but only $6,000 is currently distributable, and the Current Fund (Restricted) earned income amounted to $14,000 but only $12,000 is currently distributable.

CURRENT FUND—UNRESTRICTED
   Cash   6,000
   Due From Endowment Fund   1,000
      Revenues—Endowment Income   7,000

   Fund Balance   1,000
      Fund Balance—Allocated For
          Endowment Income Stabilization
          Reserve   1,000

Colleges and Universities

CURRENT FUND—RESTRICTED
Cash	12,000	
Due From Endowment Fund	2,000	
Fund Balance		14,000

ENDOWMENT FUND
Cash (Dividends Receivable, Etc.)	21,000	
Due To Current Fund—Unrestricted		7,000
Due To Current Fund—Restricted		14,000
Due To Current Fund—Unrestricted	6,000	
Due To Current Fund—Restricted	12,000	
Cash		18,000

Sales and Services of Educational Activities This revenue classification is generally recorded in the Current Fund (Unrestricted) and includes the following broad types of income:

- Revenues related incidentally to instruction, research, and public service (such as sales of scientific publications and revenues from testing services)
- Revenues related to student instructional and laboratory experience that incidentally creates goods or services (such as income generated from poultry farms and fees generated from health clinics)

When activities are undertaken for the purpose of selling services or products, the revenue should be reported as income from auxiliary enterprises or hospitals.

Sales and Services of Auxiliary Enterprises This revenue category includes income from an entity that is organized to provide goods or services to students, faculty, or staff at a fee directly related to the cost of the goods or services provided. Included in this group would be receipts from food services, residence halls, and college book stores.

Sales and Services of Hospitals Revenues from a hospital and its health clinics should be recorded as Current Fund revenue. The amount recognized as revenue should be net of discounts, estimated doubtful accounts, and other allowances.

Independent Operations Revenues from operations that enhance, but are unrelated to, the main mission of the college or university (instruction, research, and public service) should be recorded as revenue from independent operations. Included in this category would be federally funded research laboratories and other activities that are not otherwise classified as part of the entity's educational, auxiliary, or hospital activities.

Other Revenue Sources   Revenues not classified in one of the previously discussed categories should be designated as other revenue sources. This grouping would include such items as expired term endowments, miscellaneous sales, and transactions related to investments held by Current Funds.

Fund Balance Additions   Only the Current Fund (Unrestricted) records revenue when resources are received. The Current Fund (Restricted) records the receipt of resources as *addition* to the fund balance rather than as revenue. As noted earlier, the Current Fund (Restricted) recognizes revenue at the time qualifying expenditures are incurred. Funds other than the Current Fund group record the receipt of resources as increases (additions) in their fund balance account.

Expenditures

A college or university records expenditures only in its Current Funds (Unrestricted and Restricted). When resources in other funds are disbursed, the transaction is accounted for as a direct reduction to the fund's fund balance account.

Expenditures are defined as the "recognition of the expending of resources of the Current Funds group toward objectives of each of the respective funds of that group." An expenditure is recognized when an entity is committed to expending resources. On the other hand, an expense is recognized in an attempt to match the consumption of goods and services with the earning of income. Because a college or university is a nonprofit organization, there is no need to match revenues and expenses, or to compute net income for the period.

Although a college or university recognizes expenditures rather than expenses, the basis for the recognition of expenditures is not as narrow as that used in governmental fund accounting. In governmental fund accounting, an expenditure is recognized if the related liability will be met by expending currently available financial resources. A college or university recognizes an expenditure at the time the related liability is incurred, with no stipulation that the liability must be met by expending available current resources. In practice there is a very close symmetry between the recording of expenditures by a college or university and the recognition of expenses by a commercial enterprise. The significant difference between the two measurement focuses is the treatment of capital expenditures.

Capital Expenditures Capital expenditures result in the acquisition of capital assets. A capital asset is defined as "any physical resource that benefits a program for more than one year," and includes expenditures for land, buildings, improvements, equipment, and library books. Capital assets are not recognized as assets in the Current Funds of a college or university but, rather, are recorded as part of the institution's Plant Fund (Investment in Plant). Because depreciation is an expense rather than an expenditure, no depreciation of capital assets is reflected in the Current Funds of a college or university. Depreciation may be reflected in the Plant Fund (Investment in Plant) by crediting an appropriate accumulated depreciation account and debiting the fund's equity account.

Capital assets may be financed directly from resources accumulated in the Plant Fund. Under this arrangement no expenditure is recognized, because expenditures can only be recorded in the Current Funds. When capital assets are financed directly from Current Funds, they are reported as expenditures in the year of acquisition by that fund group.

Although depreciation expense is not recorded in the accounts of a college or university, there is, of course, a need for the institution to consider depreciation as a cost factor when determining the amount that is reimbursable under a grant or contract.

With the issuance of FASB-93 (Recognition of Depreciation by Not-for-Profit Organizations), public colleges and universities that prepare their financial statements in accordance with accounting and reporting standards established by the AICPA Audit Guide entitled "Audits of Colleges and Universities" were required to change their accounting for and reporting of depreciable assets. In order to allow the GASB to continue its research in this area, and to avoid the adoption of new rules established by the FASB that may be changed once again based on action subsequently taken by the GASB, the GASB issued GASB-8 (Applicability of FASB Statement No. 93, Recognition of Depreciation by Not-for-Profit Organizations, to Certain State and Local Governmental Entities). GASB-8 exempts public colleges and universities from requirements established by FASB-93.

Contributed Services Services contributed to a college or university by members of a religious group should be recorded as an expenditure, based on the estimated fair value of the services performed. The value of the services received should be recorded as gift revenue. The amount of the gift revenue should be reduced by expenditures paid by the college or university for benefits that are not generally part of an employer compensation plan, such as room and board allowances.

Expenditure and Transfer Classification CUBA recommends that expenditures and transfers of a college or university be classified for financial reporting purposes using the following functional categories:

- Education and General
  - Expenditures
    - Instruction
    - Research
    - Public Service
    - Academic Support
    - Student Services
    - Institutional Support
    - Operation and Maintenance of Plant
    - Scholarships and Fellowships
  - Mandatory Transfers
  - Nonmandatory Transfers
- Auxiliary Enterprises
  - Expenditures
  - Mandatory Transfers
  - Nonmandatory Transfers
- Hospitals
  - Expenditures
  - Mandatory Transfers
  - Nonmandatory Transfers
- Independent Operations
  - Expenditures
  - Mandatory Transfers
  - Nonmandatory Transfers

Fund Balance Deductions Deductions from a fund balance of a Current Fund are not considered expenditures. Included in this category are such items as refunds to donors and grantors and unexpended resources that have been or must be returned to a governmental unit.

Assets

FASB:CS-6 defines assets as probable future economic benefits obtained or controlled by a particular entity as a result of past transactions or events and possessing the following essential characteristics:

- It embodies a probable future benefit that involves a capacity to contribute directly or indirectly to future net cash inflows.
- A particular enterprise can obtain the benefit and control others' access to it.
- The transaction or other event giving rise to the enterprise's right to control of the benefit has already occurred.

Assets acquired by a college or university are recorded at cost, while assets received as donations are recorded at their estimated fair value at the date of transfer. For the most part, accounting principles followed by a commercial enterprise are also applicable to assets owned by a college or university. The unique features of accounting for assets held by a college or university are described below.

Inventories and Deferred Charges Generally, inventories and deferred charges can be accounted for as expenditures when the related liabilities are incurred. However, CUBA concludes that inventories and deferred charges that are material in amount should be capitalized and treated as expenditures when they are consumed or expire.

Investments Various funds of a college or university may purchase investments or receive investments as gifts. Investments should initially be recorded at cost or estimated fair value if received as a gift. Subsequently, the investment may be accounted for on a cost basis or a current market value basis. The current market value basis may be used only when all investments in all funds are accounted for on the current market value basis.

> **OBSERVATION:** FASB-12 (Accounting for Certain Marketable Securities) requires that marketable equity securities be accounted for on the lower aggregate cost or market basis; however, FASB-12 is not applicable to nonprofit entities.

When the cost basis is used, investments in equity securities are not adjusted unless there is a decline in market value that is below cost and the decline is considered to be other than temporary. If the investment represents ownership of debt securities and the investment is considered long-term by the educational institution, any premiums or discounts that are reflected in the original purchase of the investment should be amortized using the effective interest method.

If the current market value method is used to account for investments, unrealized gains and losses should be (1) recognized as other revenues and expenditures if the investments are held by the Unrestricted Current Fund, or (2) recognized as a direct item to the fund balance account for all other funds. For example, if investments with a cost basis of $100,000 held by the Unrestricted Current Fund are worth $150,000, and investments with a cost basis of $50,000 held by a Restricted Current Fund are worth $90,000, the following adjustments would be made at the end of the accounting period:

CURRENT FUND—UNRESTRICTED
Investments   50,000
    Revenues—Other Sources   50,000

CURRENT FUND—RESTRICTED
Investments   40,000
    Fund Balance   40,000

There may be sales of investments among various funds. Such transactions should be recorded at fair market or appraised values at the date of sale, and gains or losses should be reflected in the appropriate fund. The Unrestricted Current Fund would record gains and losses as revenues and expenditures, while all other funds would adjust their fund balance accounts.

> **OBSERVATION:** Because the sale of an investment between funds would be considered a related party transaction, the disclosure requirements of FASB-57 (Related Party Disclosures) should be followed.

Colleges and Universities

Investments held by various funds may be pooled if not prohibited by donor agreements or statute. When investments are pooled, current market values of the investments held for each fund should be used to determine the amount of income distributable to each fund and the equity basis of each fund in the investment pool. Using current market values in this manner does not require that the current market value basis be used to account for investments, since memorandum records can be used to reflect market values.

Plant Assets and Related Liabilities A college or university records transactions related to its fixed assets in its Plant Funds. As noted in CUBA, the following are the general sources of assets for Plant Funds:

- Funds from external agencies
- Student fees and assessments for debt service or other plant purposes, which create an obligation equivalent to an externally imposed restriction and which are not subject to the discretionary right of the governing board to use for other purposes
- Transfers, both mandatory and nonmandatory, from other fund groups
- Borrowings from external sources for plant purposes
- Borrowings by advances from other fund groups
- Income and net gains from investments in the unrestricted and restricted elements of each of the subgroups of the Plant Funds

When resources are received from external parties and are to be used only for Plant Fund purposes, the receipt of the resources should be recorded in the appropriate Plant Fund as an increase to the fund balance. No entry should be made in the Current Fund group. The fund balances of the Plant Fund group should be properly designated as restricted or unrestricted depending upon the terms governing the receipt of the resources.

The Plant Fund group is comprised of four self-balancing subgroups, namely, Unexpended Plant Fund, Fund for Renewals and Replacements, Fund for Retirement of Indebtedness, and Investment in Plant.

Plant Fund—Unexpended The Unexpended Plant Fund accounts for resources received and liabilities incurred to finance the acquisition of property, plant, and equipment. When a liability such as bonds payable or mortgages payable is issued, the liability is recorded in the Unexpended Plant Fund. When resources are received from nondebt transactions, the receipt is recorded as an increase to the unrestricted or restricted fund balance account. For example, assume that a gift of $400,000 is received and is to be used to assist in the financing of a classroom building, and a nonmandatory transfer of $100,000 is received from the Unrestricted Current Fund for the same purpose. These transactions would be recorded as follows:

PLANT FUND—UNEXPENDED
Cash   500,000
    Fund Balance—Unrestricted   100,000
    Fund Balance—Restricted   400,000

CURRENT FUND—UNRESTRICTED
Fund Balance (Nonmandatory Transfer)   100,000
    Cash   100,000

The transfer from the Unrestricted Current Fund is identified as unrestricted because the institution's board of governors has the authority to rescind a nonmandatory transfer and to use the resources for other purposes.

As capital assets are purchased by the unexpended plant fund, the payments are charged to its fund balance account; however, the acquired asset is recorded directly in the Plant Fund—Investment in Plant. For example, if equipment costing $40,000 is acquired by the Unexpended Plant Fund, the following entries would be made.

PLANT FUND—UNEXPENDED
Fund Balance—Unrestricted   40,000
    Cash   40,000

PLANT FUND—INVESTMENT IN PLANT
Equipment   40,000
    Net Investment In Plant   40,000

Assets under construction by the college or university may be accounted for in the Unexpended Plant Fund (or the Plant Fund—Investment in Plant). Costs are accumulated in a construction-in-progress account, and related liabilities, such as mortgages, are recorded. Interest cost associated with the construction of capital assets should be capitalized and reflected as part of the cost of the property, plant, and equipment. FASB-34 (Capitalization of Interest Cost) concludes that the capitalization period begins when the following three conditions are present:

Colleges and Universities

- Expenditures for the capital asset have been made.
- Activities that are necessary to get the capital asset ready for its intended use are in progress.
- Interest cost is being incurred.

To determine the amount of interest cost to be capitalized by a college or university, the weighted-average amount of accumulated expenditures for the period is multiplied by the institution's average borrowing rate for the period. Rather than use the overall average borrowing rate, the following approach can be employed:

- The interest rate the obligation incurred specifically to finance the construction of the capital asset may be used, and
- The overall average borrowing rate would be used for any accumulated expenditures in excess of specific borrowings.

The amount of interest cost to be capitalized is limited to the actual interest expenditures incurred for the period.

FASB-62 (Capitalization of Interest Cost in Situations Involving Certain Tax-Exempt Borrowings and Certain Gifts and Grants) concludes that the amount of initial cost to be capitalized on assets acquired with tax-exempt borrowings is equal to the cost of the borrowing less interest earned on related interest-bearing investments acquired with proceeds of the related tax-exempt borrowing. FASB-62 allows the offsetting of interest earned against interest cost in those situations "involving acquisition of qualifying assets financed with the proceeds of tax-exempt borrowings if those funds are externally restricted to finance acquisition of specified qualifying assets or to service the related debt."

When the capital asset is completed, the total cost of construction, including capitalized interest cost, is transferred from the Unexpended Plant Fund to the Plant Fund—Investment in Plant. Liabilities related to the financing of the constructed asset are also transferred to the Plant Fund—Investment in Plant. Alternatively, the cost of construction to date can be transferred at the end of each reporting period.

Plant Fund—Renewals and Replacements This subgroup fund is used to account for resources that are accumulated for the purpose of renewing or replacing property, plant, and equipment. The receipts of resources are credited to the fund balance account and should be designated as unrestricted or restricted depending upon the circumstances surrounding the transactions. Generally, nonmandatory transfers from the Unrestricted Current Fund would be recorded as additions to the unrestricted fund balance while restricted grants and gifts would be designated as such.

Expenditures for the Plant Fund—Renewals and Replacements are recorded as reductions to the fund balance account. Because the fund is used to account for the maintenance of the institution's physical plant, expenditures are not usually capitalized in the Plant Fund—Investment in Plant. If it is concluded that an expenditure represents an addition or improvement to the plant facilities, it should be capitalized in the Plant Fund—Investment in Plant, in a manner similar to the accounting treatment used in the unexpended plant fund.

Plant Fund—Retirement of Indebtedness This plant fund subgroup is used to account for resources that are accumulated for the payment of debt and interest related to the financing of plant assets. Resources received are recorded as additions to the fund balance accounts (unrestricted or restricted). Expenditures are charged against the fund balance account, and any payment that represents a decrease in the debt principal is also recorded in the Plant Fund—Investment in Plant. For example, if a $150,000 payment is made from the Plant Fund—Retirement of Indebtedness to retire bonds, the following entries would be made:

PLANT FUND—RETIREMENT OF INDEBTEDNESS
Fund Balance—Restricted	150,000	
Cash		150,000

PLANT FUND—INVESTMENT IN PLANT
Bonds Payable	150,000	
Net Investment In Plant		150,000

Plant Fund—Investment in Plant All property, plant, and equipment, except for those capital assets held by endowment and similar funds or construction in progress in the Plant Fund—Unexpended or Plant Fund—Renewals and Replacements, are recorded in the Plant Fund—Investment in Plant. Included in this fund would be land, land improvements, buildings, equipment, and library books. Also, any outstanding liabilities that were used to finance the acquisition of plant assets may be reported in this fund.

CUBA notes that property, plant, and equipment recorded in the Plant Fund—Investment in Plant may be received from the following sources:

Colleges and Universities

- The capitalized completion costs of projects transferred from the Plant Fund—Unexpended and Plant Fund—Renewals and Replacements
- Capitalized costs of construction in progress transferred from the Plant Fund—Unexpended and Plant Fund—Renewals and Replacements at the reporting date, unless held in those subgroups until completion of the project
- Donation (at fair market value on date of gift) of plant assets
- The cost of long-lived assets financed by expenditures of current and other funds, except endowment and similar funds

The difference between the cost of property, plant, and equipment received and the related liabilities is recorded as an increase in the account entitled net investment in plant, which represents the equity balance in the fund. As liabilities associated with plant assets are repaid by other funds, the net investment in plant account is increased. As suggested earlier, depreciation expense is not recorded in the operating statement of a college or university. Depreciation may be recognized in the Plant Fund—Investment in Plant by making the following entry:

Net Investment In Plant	X	
Accumulated Depreciation		X

When plant assets are sold, the asset and related liability, if any, are removed from the Plant Fund—Investment in Plant. Any proceeds from the sale of plant assets must be reported in the fund that is entitled to the proceeds. Identifying the fund entitled to the proceeds may be based on such factors as (1) source of funds for the initial purchase of the plant asset, (2) laws and administrative regulations, and (3) terms of donor agreements. For example, assume that equipment with an original cost of $100,000 is sold for $15,000. If it is assumed that the Unexpended Plant Fund is entitled to the proceeds, the following entries would be made:

PLANT FUND—INVESTMENT IN PLANT

Net Investment In Plant	100,000	
Equipment		100,000

PLANT FUND—UNEXPENDED

Cash	15,000	
Fund Balance—Restricted		15,000

No gain or loss is recorded on the disposition of plant assets.

Assets Held by Sponsoring Religious Groups

Religious groups that support a college or university may make available to the educational institution certain facilities. Since these facilities are owned by the religious group, they should not be reported as assets of the college or university; however, the facilities made available along with any related debt should be disclosed in the financial statements of the college or university.

Liabilities

FASB:CS-6 defines liabilities as "probable future sacrifices of economic benefits arising from present obligations of a particular entity to transfer assets or provide services to other entities in the future as a result of past transactions or events." A liability embodies the following fundamental characteristics:

- The present duty or responsibility to one or more entities that entails settlement by probable future transfer or use of assets at a specified or determinable date, on occurrence of a specified event or on demand
- The duty or responsibility to obligate a particular enterprise, leaving it little or no discretion to avoid the future sacrifice
- The transaction or other event obligating the enterprise has already happened

The financial statements of a college or university reflect both current and noncurrent liabilities; however, the balance sheet presentation does not distinguish between short-term and long-term liabilities. Unlike governmental units, the issuance of debt by a college or university is not recorded as an other source of financing and, therefore, the proceeds are not shown on the institution's operating statement. Liabilities are recorded in the fund that will ultimately be responsible for the payment of the debt. Current Funds generally record liabilities that arise from current operations such as accounts payable, accrued expenses, and deferred revenue transactions. Long-term debt that is related to the financing of the acquisition of property, plant, and equipment is presented in the Plant Funds. If long-term debt is issued to finance current operations, the debt should be presented as a liability of the Current Fund—Unrestricted.

In order to control the level of expenditures, a college or university should use an encumbrance system. The resources of a college or university are committed for future expenditure when executory contracts such as purchase orders and specific contracts for goods and services are signed. An actual expenditure is not recorded until the contract is executed; however, control over executory contracts should be established to make sure disbursement commitments do not exceed the amount budgeted.

When a purchase order is issued or a contract is signed, an encumbrance should be established. For example, if a college or university signs purchase orders of $100,000, the following entry would be made:

Encumbrances	100,000	
Reserve For Encumbrances		100,000

The encumbrances account is a budgetary account and does not represent an actual expenditure for financial reporting purposes. Similarly, the account reserve for encumbrances is not a liability but, rather, a budgetary account. When the actual goods and services are received by the college or university, an expenditure and related liability account would be recorded. For example, if it is assumed that the previous encumbrances of $100,000 are vouchered for $99,000, the following entries would be made to record the expenditures and reduce the encumbrances:

Expenditures	99,000	
Accounts Payable		99,000
Reserve For Encumbrances	100,000	
Encumbrances		100,000

Encumbrances are initially recorded at their expected cost, while expenditures are vouchered based on actual invoices received from vendors.

Encumbrances that are not vouchered by the end of the accounting period must be reversed by debiting the reserve for encumbrances account and crediting the encumbrances account. The amount of the outstanding encumbrances at the end of the year should be shown as a designation or allocation of the fund balance account or adequately disclosed in notes to the financial statements.

Interfund and Interdepartmental Transactions

Each fund that accounts for transactions of a college or university is a separate accounting entity. Transactions between funds must be accounted for in a manner that adequately discloses the nature and extent of interfund transactions. Interfund transactions may be classified as nonmandatory transfers, mandatory transfers, and interfund borrowings. In a similar manner, interdepartmental transactions must be accounted for to present financial statements that are not misleading. These transactions are discussed below.

Nonmandatory Transfers When transfers are made from the Current Funds to other funds based on the discretion of the institution's governing board, they are referred to as nonmandatory transfers. Examples of nonmandatory transfers include discretionary transfers for provision for debt service on the educational plant, matching grants for Loan Funds, and additions to Endowment Funds. Nonmandatory transfers that are made to other funds may be related to auxiliary enterprises, hospitals, and independent operations, and should be distinguished from transfers for educational and general operations purposes. Nonmandatory transfers are reported on the Statement of Changes in Fund Balances.

A nonmandatory transfer is recorded in the recipient fund by increasing the recipient fund's fund balance account. For example, the following entries would be made to record a nonmandatory transfer of $50,000 from the Unrestricted Current Fund to an Endowment Fund:

CURRENT FUND—UNRESTRICTED
  Fund Balance (Nonmandatory Transfer)   50,000
    Cash   50,000

ENDOWMENT FUND
  Cash   50,000
    Fund Balance—Quasi-Endowment   50,000

When unrestricted resources are transferred to the Current Fund from other funds, the transfer is classified as a nonmandatory transfer rather than as Current Fund revenue. An example of this type of transaction is the return of resources from an Endowment Fund that may be used by the Unrestricted Current Fund to finance educational and general operations.

Mandatory Transfers Transfers that are not subject to control by the institution's governing board are referred to as mandatory transfers. CUBA notes that mandatory transfers arise from the following situations:

- Binding legal agreements related to the financing of educational plant, such as amounts for debt retirement, interest, and required provisions for renewals and replacements of plant not financed from other sources
- Grant agreements with agencies of the federal government, donors, and other organizations to match gifts and grants to loan and other funds

Mandatory transfers that are made to other funds may be related to auxiliary enterprises, hospitals, and independent operations, and should be distinguished from transfers for educational and general operations purposes. In addition, they should be reported on the Statement of Current Funds Revenues, Expenditures, and Other Changes, identified separately from expenditures, and classified as either (1) provision for debt service on educational plant, (2) loan fund matching grants, or (3) other mandatory transfers.

Interfund Borrowing Transfers between fund groups that are temporary in nature should be recorded as interfund borrowings, rather than as nonmandatory or mandatory transfers. What constitutes a temporary movement of resources between fund types is judgmental, but interfund borrowing would be suggested when there is a definite plan of repayment and interest payments are involved. When a transaction is considered interfund borrowing, the recipient fund would record a liability and the transferring fund would record a receivable.

The same guidelines used to identify interfund borrowing between fund groups should also be used to determine whether a liability should be recognized when separate funds within the Current Fund group are involved in the transfer of resources. For example, a movement of resources from the Unrestricted Current Fund to a Restricted Current Fund would be recorded as interfund borrowing if the criteria described in the previous paragraph are satisfied.

Interdepartmental Transactions Goods and services may be provided by one department and consumed by another department of the same institution. The department providing the goods and services should not record revenue but, rather, should reduce its expenditures by the cost of the goods and services provided to the other department. On the other hand, the department receiving the goods and services should record an expenditure based on the billing price established by the department providing the goods and services. If there is a difference between the cost of the goods and services provided and the amount billed, the difference should be shown in the department providing the goods and services as an increase or decrease to the expenditure classification entitled institutional support. For example, if the Art Department bills the Department of Accounting $1,200 for the preparation of certain posters that cost $1,000 to prepare, the following entries would be made in the Unrestricted Current Fund:

SERVICE DEPARTMENT (ART DEPARTMENT)
Due From Department Of Accounting 1,200
   Expenditures—Academic Support 1,000
   Expenditures—Institutional Support 200

USER DEPARTMENT (DEPARTMENT OF ACCOUNTING)
Expenditures—Instruction 1,200
   Due To Art Department 1,200

Interdepartmental transactions are accounted for in this manner to avoid recording expenditures at an inflated amount.

The following interdepartmental transactions should be treated as revenue by the service department and as expenditures by the user department:

- Sales of materials or services by an instructional department that are created as a by-product of the instructional program to other departments (including auxiliary enterprises and hospitals). (An example would be the sale of milk by the dairy department to the food services unit.)
- Sales of materials or services by an auxiliary enterprise to other departments. (An example would be the sale of supplies by the college book store to instructional departments.)

COLLEGE AND UNIVERSITY FUNDS

As suggested earlier, a college or university records its transactions in a variety of separate funds. There are two basic fund groups, namely, (1) Current Funds, comprised of an Unrestricted Current Fund and various Restricted Current Funds, and (2) Restricted Funds, comprised of Loan Funds, Endowment Funds, Annuity and Life Income Funds, Plant Funds, and Agency Funds.

Current Fund—Unrestricted

The Unrestricted Current Fund of a college or university is used to account for transactions related to the primary and supporting missions of an educational institution. Assets of the Unrestricted Current Fund include all resources that are not restricted to use by either a donor or an external agency. Educational and general revenues (student tuition and fees, governmental appropriations, governmental grants and contracts, gifts and private grants, endowment income, and other sources) are recorded in the Unrestricted Current Fund. Expenditures related to the delivery of educational and support services (instruction, research, public support, academic support, student services, institutional support, operation and maintenance of plant, and student aid) are recorded in the Unrestricted Current Fund. Generally, auxiliary enterprises and hospitals are accounted for in the Unrestricted Current Fund while independent operations are usually accounted for in a Restricted Current Fund.

To illustrate the routine transactions that are accounted for in the Current Fund—Unrestricted, assume that at the beginning of the fiscal year a community college had the following trial balance. Unless otherwise noted, all entries are recorded in the Current Fund—Unrestricted.

Centerville Community College
Current Fund—Unrestricted
Trial Balance
July 1, 19X4

	Dr.	Cr.
Cash	$ 200,000	
Accounts receivable	700,000	
Allowance for uncollectible accounts		$ 150,000
Inventories	120,000	
Accrued investment revenue	5,000	
Temporary investments	205,000	
Investments	120,000	
Accounts payable		50,000
Accrued liabilities		100,000
Fund balance—reserved for encumbrances		50,000
Fund balance		1,000,000
	$1,350,000	$1,350,000

During the fiscal year the following transactions occurred and were recorded in the community college's Unrestricted Current Fund as described below:

Colleges and Universities

Approval of operating budget The community college's governing board approved a budget that included estimated revenues of $10,000,000 and estimated expenditures of $9,000,000.

Estimated Revenues	10,000,000	
Estimated Expenditures		9,000,000
Budget Balance (Surplus)		1,000,000

Tuition and fees During the fiscal year student tuition and fees in the amount of $6,000,000 were billed. Of this amount, 10% is expected to be uncollectible and 25% represents scholarships. In addition, $200,000 of the total billings is legally pledged for the payment of bonds outstanding, and the governing board allocated $100,000 for the purchase of personal computers.

CURRENT FUND—UNRESTRICTED

Accounts Receivable	6,000,000	
Allowance For Uncollectible		
Accounts		600,000
Revenues—Tuition And Fees		5,400,000
Expenditures—Scholarships And		
Fellowships	1,500,000	
Accounts Receivable		1,500,000
Fund Balance	100,000	
Mandatory Transfers—Debt		
Retirement And Interest	200,000	
Due To Unexpended Plant Fund		
(Plant Fund)		100,000
Due To Retirement Of Indebted-		
ness Fund (Plant Fund)		200,000

PLANT FUND—UNEXPENDED

Due From Current Fund—Unrestricted	100,000	
Fund Balance—Unrestricted		100,000

PLANT FUND—RETIREMENT OF INDEBTEDNESS

Due From Current Fund—Unrestricted	200,000	
Fund Balance—Restricted		200,000

Cash collections from students amounted to $3,800,000, and $450,000 of accounts was written off during the year.

Cash	3,800,000	
Allowance For Doubtful Accounts	450,000	
Accounts Receivable		4,250,000

Colleges and Universities

Governmental appropriations Appropriations were received from the federal government ($400,000), state government ($1,200,000), and county government ($2,000,000).

Cash	3,600,000	
Revenues—Governmental		
Appropriations—Federal		400,000
Revenues—Governmental		
Appropriations—State		1,200,000
Revenues—Governmental		
Appropriations—Local		2,000,000

Governmental grants and contracts Unrestricted governmental grants were received from the federal government ($200,000) and state government ($100,000).

Cash	300,000	
Revenues—Governmental Grants		
And Contracts—Federal		200,000
Revenues—Governmental Grants		
And Contracts—State		100,000

Private gifts and grants Unrestricted gifts of $500,000 were received from private donations.

Cash	500,000	
Revenues—Private Gifts, Grants,		
And Contracts		500,000

Endowment income During the year $120,000 (all unrestricted) was earned by Endowment Funds, of which $100,000 has been distributed to the Unrestricted Current Fund.

CURRENT FUND—UNRESTRICTED

Cash	100,000	
Due From Endowment Fund	20,000	
Revenues—Endowment Income		120,000

ENDOWMENT FUND

Cash	120,000	
Due To Current Fund (Unrestricted)		120,000
Due To Current Fund (Unrestricted)	100,000	
Cash		100,000

Auxiliary enterprises Receipts from the college book store amounted to $650,000 for the fiscal year.

Cash	650,000	
Revenues—Auxiliary Enterprises		650,000

Capital expenditures Equipment ($50,000) and books ($30,000) were purchased for the library during the fiscal year from unrestricted funds.

CURRENT FUND—UNRESTRICTED
Expenditures—Academic Support	80,000	
Cash		80,000

PLANT FUND—INVESTMENT IN PLANT
Equipment	50,000	
Library Books	30,000	
Net Investment In Plant		80,000

Expenditures The following expenditures were made during the community college's fiscal year:

Instruction	$4,800,000
Research	300,000
Public service	200,000
Academic support	400,000
Student services	250,000
Institutional support	150,000
Operation and maintenance of plant	300,000
Scholarships and fellowships	50,000
Auxiliary enterprises	600,000
Accrued liabilities (beginning of year)	100,000
	$7,150,000

Expenditures—Instruction	4,800,000	
Expenditures—Research	300,000	
Expenditures—Public Service	200,000	
Expenditures—Academic Support	400,000	
Expenditures—Student Services	250,000	
Expenditures—Institutional Support	150,000	
Expenditures—Operations And Maintenance Of Plant	300,000	
Expenditures—Scholarships And Fellowships	50,000	
Expenditures—Auxiliary Enterprises	600,000	
Accrued Liabilities	100,000	
Cash		7,150,000

Colleges and Universities

At the end of the fiscal year, accrued expenditures amounted to $150,000 and were comprised of accruals for instruction ($100,000), academic support ($30,000), and institutional support ($20,000).

Expenditures—Instruction	100,000	
Expenditures—Academic Support	30,000	
Expenditures—Institutional Support	20,000	
Accrued Liabilities		150,000

Fund balance deductions Unexpended resources of $20,000 were returned to the county government during the fiscal year.

Fund Balance	20,000	
Cash		20,000

Inventories The beginning balance in accounts payable arose from the purchase of inventories. During the year, $300,000 was paid to vendors for inventory purchased.

Inventories	250,000	
Accounts Payable	50,000	
Cash		300,000

At the end of the year, accounts payable for the purchase of inventories amounted to $100,000.

Inventories	100,000	
Accounts Payable		100,000

Inventories on hand at the end of the year amounted to $70,000. Inventories were used for instruction (60%), research (20%), academic support (10%), and institutional support (10%).

Expenditures—Instruction		
($400,000 × 60%)	240,000	
Expenditures—Research		
($400,000 × 20%)	80,000	
Expenditures—Academic support		
($400,000 × 10%)	40,000	
Expenditures—Institutional Support		
($400,000 × 10%)	40,000	
Inventories		400,000

Beginning balance	$120,000	
Purchases for the year	350,000	
Ending balance	(70,000)	
Inventories consumed during the year	$400,000	

Investments Certain temporary investments are made with excess cash held by the Unrestricted Current Fund. During the period, investment income earned amounted to $17,000, of which $13,000 was collected.

Cash	13,000	
Accrued Investment Revenue	4,000	
Revenues—Other Sources		17,000

Accrued investment income at the beginning of the year was collected.

Cash	5,000	
Accrued Investment Revenue		5,000

Temporary investments of $420,000 matured during the fiscal year.

Cash	420,000	
Temporary Investments		420,000

Additional temporary investments of $400,000 were acquired during the fiscal year.

Temporary Investments	400,000	
Cash		400,000

Nonmandatory transfers A nonmandatory transfer of $90,000 was made from the Unrestricted Current Fund to the Plant Fund—Unexpended.

CURRENT FUND—UNRESTRICTED

Fund Balance (Nonmandatory Transfer)	90,000	
Cash		90,000

PLANT FUND—UNEXPENDED

Cash	90,000	
Fund Balance—Unrestricted		90,000

Colleges and Universities

A nonmandatory transfer of $80,000 from the Unrestricted Current Fund to the Plant Fund—Renewals and Replacements was made during the fiscal year.

CURRENT FUND—UNRESTRICTED
Fund Balance (Nonmandatory Transfer) 80,000
 Cash   80,000

PLANT FUND—RENEWALS AND REPLACEMENTS
Cash   80,000
 Fund Balance—Unrestricted   80,000

The community college's governing board transferred $40,000 from the Unrestricted Current Fund to the Loan Fund. Of this amount, $10,000 must be repaid within six months.

CURRENT FUND—UNRESTRICTED
Due From Loan Fund   10,000
Fund Balance (Nonmandatory Transfer) 30,000
 Cash   40,000

LOAN FUND
Cash   40,000
 Due To Current Fund (Unrestricted)   10,000
 Fund Balance—Unrestricted   30,000

The community college's governing board transferred $50,000 to Endowment Funds from the Unrestricted Current Fund. The amount is to be invested indefinitely, and the income is to be used to encourage faculty research.

CURRENT FUND—UNRESTRICTED
Fund Balance (Nonmandatory Transfer) 50,000
 Cash   50,000

ENDOWMENT FUND
Cash   50,000
 Fund Balance—Quasi-Endowment   50,000

Mandatory transfers Mandatory transfers for principal and interest payments from the Unrestricted Current Fund totaled $650,000 during the year.

CURRENT FUND—UNRESTRICTED
   Mandatory Transfers—Principal And
      Interest   650,000
        Cash   650,000

PLANT FUND—RETIREMENT OF INDEBTEDNESS
   Cash   650,000
     Fund Balance—Restricted   650,000

Terminated agreements During the year a commitment under one annuity agreement was fully satisfied and the remaining investments of $35,000 were transferred to the Unrestricted Current Fund. The fair market value of the transferred investments is $40,000.

CURRENT FUND—UNRESTRICTED
   Investments   40,000
     Revenues—Expired Annuity
       Agreements   40,000

ANNUITY FUND
   Fund Balance   35,000
     Investments   35,000

During the year a commitment under one life income agreement was fully satisfied and the principal of $50,000 was transferred to the Unrestricted Current Fund. The fair market value of the transferred investments was $75,000.

CURRENT FUND—UNRESTRICTED
   Investments   75,000
     Revenues—Expired Life Income
       Agreement   75,000

LIFE INCOME FUND
   Fund Balance   50,000
     Investments   50,000

Encumbrances At the end of the current fiscal year unvouchered encumbrances of the Unrestricted Current Fund in the amount of $70,000 were outstanding.

   Fund Balance   20,000
     Fund Balance—Reserve For
       Encumbrances [$70,000 – $50,000]   20,000

Colleges and Universities

Note: The recording of encumbrances would be made as purchase orders and contracts are signed and would be reversed as invoices are received and vouchered. In the example, the recording of the encumbrances has been omitted, except for the net amount outstanding at the end of the year.

Reversal of budget The budgetary accounts used to record the operating budget are closed.

Budget Balance (Surplus)	1,000,000	
Estimated Expenditures	9,000,000	
Estimated Revenues		10,000,000

Note: Transactions that affect more than one fund group are also reproduced as illustrative entries in the other fund group.

After taking into account the transactions described above, the trial balance for the Unrestricted Current Fund for the year ended June 30, 19X5, would be as follows:

Centerville Community College
Current Fund—Unrestricted
Trial Balance
June 30, 19X5

	Dr.	Cr.
Cash	$ 728,000	
Accounts receivable	950,000	
Allowance for uncollectible accounts		$ 300,000
Inventories	70,000	
Accrued investment revenue	4,000	
Temporary investments	185,000	
Investments	235,000	
Due to endowment fund	20,000	
Due to loan fund	10,000	
Accounts payable		100,000
Accrued liabilities		150,000
Due to unexpended plant fund		100,000
Due to retirement of indebtedness plant fund		200,000
Revenues—tuitions and fees		5,400,000
Revenues—governmental appropriations—federal		400,000
Revenues—governmental appropriations—state		1,200,000
Revenues—governmental appropriations—local		2,000,000
Revenues—governmental grants and contracts—federal		200,000

Colleges and Universities

	Dr.	Cr.
Revenues—governmental grants and contracts—state		100,000
Revenues—private gifts, grants, and contracts		500,000
Revenues—endowment income		120,000
Revenues—auxiliary enterprises		650,000
Revenues—other sources		17,000
Revenues—expired annuity and life income agreements		115,000
Expenditures—instruction	5,140,000	
Expenditures—research	380,000	
Expenditures—public service	200,000	
Expenditures—academic support	550,000	
Expenditures—student services	250,000	
Expenditures—institutional support	210,000	
Expenditures—operations and maintenance of plant	300,000	
Expenditures—scholarships and fellowships	1,550,000	
Expenditures—auxiliary enterprises	600,000	
Mandatory transfers—debt retirement and interest	850,000	
Fund balance—reserved for encumbrances		70,000
Fund balance		610,000
	$12,232,000	$12,232,000

Current Fund—Restricted

The Restricted Current Fund accounts for resources that are available to finance current operations of a college or university but whose use has been restricted to some designated activity by donors and other external agencies. When resources have been designated for a particular use by the institution's governing board, the resources are accounted for in the Unrestricted Current Fund not in the Restricted Current Fund because the board could reverse its designation and use the resources for other than the designated purpose.

Resources received by a Restricted Current Fund are recorded as increases to the fund balance account. Revenue is recognized when qualifying expenditures are incurred by the Restricted Current Fund. Thus, total revenues and total expenditures are always equal in the Restricted Current Fund's Statement of Revenues, Expenditures, and Other Changes.

To illustrate the routine transactions that are accounted for in the Current Fund—Restricted, assume that at the beginning of the fiscal year a community college had the following trial balance. Unless

Colleges and Universities

otherwise noted, all entries are recorded in the Current Fund—Restricted.

Centerville Community College
Current Fund—Restricted
Trial Balance
July 1, 19X4

	Dr.	Cr.
Cash	$ 60,000	
Investments	350,000	
Fund balance		$410,000
	$410,000	$410,000

During the fiscal year the following transactions occurred and were recorded in the community college's Restricted Current Fund as described below.

Governmental grants and contracts Federal ($300,000) and state ($100,000) grants were received during the year to be used to finance scholarships. Scholarship expenditures financed by the grants amounted to $370,000 ($280,000, federal; $90,000, state).

Cash	400,000	
Fund Balance		400,000
Expenditures—Scholarships And		
Fellowships	370,000	
Cash		370,000
Fund Balance	370,000	
Revenues—Governmental Grants		
And Contracts—Federal		280,000
Revenues—Governmental Grants		
And Contracts—State		90,000

State grants of $250,000 were received during the year to fund faculty research. Expenditures financed by the state grants for research totaled $235,000.

Cash	250,000	
Fund Balance		250,000
Expenditures—Research	235,000	
Cash		235,000

Colleges and Universities

Fund Balance	235,000	
Revenues—Governmental Grants		
And Contracts—State		235,000

Private gifts and grants Private gifts of $130,000 were received and were restricted for certain expenditures. Qualifying expenditures of $140,000 (academic support, $90,000; student service, $50,000) were incurred.

Cash	130,000	
Fund Balance		130,000
Expenditures—Academic Support	90,000	
Expenditures—Student Services	50,000	
Cash		140,000
Fund Balance	140,000	
Revenues—Private Gifts, Grants,		
And Contracts		140,000

Note: Although only $130,000 in private gifts was received currently, it is appropriate to recognize $140,000 as revenue assuming the fund balance includes prior year private restricted receipts.

Endowment income During the year $70,000 (all restricted for operations) was earned by Endowment Funds, of which $50,000 has been distributed to the Restricted Current Fund. The resources are restricted for the payment of student financial aid. Qualifying expenditures for the year amounted to $40,000.

CURRENT FUND—RESTRICTED

Cash	50,000	
Due From Endowment Fund	20,000	
Fund Balance		70,000
Expenditures—Scholarships And		
Fellowships	40,000	
Cash		40,000
Fund Balance	40,000	
Revenues—Endowment Income		40,000

ENDOWMENT FUND

Cash	70,000	
Due To Current Fund—Restricted		70,000
Due To Current Fund—Restricted	50,000	
Cash		50,000

Colleges and Universities

Fund balance deductions During the year $15,000 was returned to grantors because certain expenditures were not made within a specified period of time.

Fund Balance	15,000	
Cash		15,000

Investment transactions Investment income (cash) totaled $25,000 for the year.

Cash	25,000	
Fund Balance		25,000

Note: Transactions that affect more than one fund group are also reproduced as illustrative entries in the other fund group. Also, although all transactions included in the above series of Current Fund—Restricted revenues and expenditures transactions involved cash flows, it should be recognized that revenues and expenditures could have occurred on an accrual basis as well. That is, expenditures and revenues would be recognized without immediate cash flow effect.

After taking into account the transactions described above, the trial balance for the Restricted Current Fund for the year ended June 30, 19X5, would be as follows:

Centerville Community College
Current Fund—Restricted
Trial Balance
June 30, 19X5

	Dr.	Cr.
Cash	$ 115,000	
Investments	350,000	
Due from endowment fund	20,000	
Revenues—governmental grants and contracts—federal		$ 280,000
Revenues—governmental grants and contracts—state		325,000
Revenues—private gifts, grants, and contracts		140,000
Revenues—endowment income		40,000
Expenditures—scholarships and fellowships	410,000	
Expenditures—research	235,000	
Expenditures—academic support	90,000	
Expenditures—student services	50,000	
Fund balance		485,000
	$1,270,000	$1,270,000

Loan Funds

A college or university may establish Loan Funds to make resources available to students, and perhaps faculty and staff. Loan Funds are self-perpetuating (revolving), in that loans made to various parties are expected to be repaid along with the interest, and eventually made available for future lending purposes. Both the principal and the interest are available for lending in a Loan Fund. If only the income is available, the transactions should be accounted for in an Endowment Fund.

CUBA notes that resources to finance loans may originate from a variety of sources such as the following:

- Gifts of funds that are to be operated on a revolving basis, whereby repayments of principal and interest may be loaned to other individuals
- Gifts and grants that provide that, on repayment of principal and interest, the proceeds are to be refunded to the donors or grantors
- Endowment Fund income restricted to Loan Fund purposes
- Refundable grants by the U.S. government to be matched with institutional funds for loans to students
- Institutional funds transferred from Current Funds to match refundable U.S. government grants
- Unrestricted Current Funds designated by the governing board to function as Loan Funds
- Income and gains from investments of Loan Funds
- Interest on loans

With the exception of liabilities, the fund balance account is increased as resources are received. The fund balance account should be identified as unrestricted and restricted. Unrestricted resources are generally the result of transfers that have been designated by the institution's governing board and therefore are subject to reversal.

Decreases in the fund balance account result from the incurrence of administrative costs, losses from the sale of investments, and writeoffs of uncollectible loans.

A Loan Fund's assets generally consist of cash, investments, net receivables, accrued interest and investment income, and amounts due from other funds. Liabilities include accrued expenditures, refunds due to donors, and refundable Loan Funds. Refundable grants are not classified as liabilities but, rather, as part of the fund

Colleges and Universities

balance account if the date or repayment to the grantor is uncertain.

To illustrate the routine transactions that are accounted for in Loan Funds, assume that at the beginning of the fiscal year a community college had the following trial balance. Unless otherwise noted, all entries are recorded in the Loan Fund.

Centerville Community College
Loan Funds
Trial Balance
July 1, 19X4

	Dr.	Cr.
Cash	$ 113,000	
Student loans receivable	3,712,000	
Allowance for uncollectible accounts		$ 417,000
Accrued interest receivable	15,000	
Investments	150,000	
Refundable grants—federal government		200,000
Fund balance—restricted		3,347,000
Fund balance—unrestricted		26,000
	$3,990,000	$3,990,000

During the fiscal year the following transactions occurred and were recorded in the community college's Loan Fund:

Nonrefundable gifts and grants Private gifts of $370,000 were given to the college in order to make loans to qualifying students.

Cash	370,000	
Fund Balance—Restricted		370,000

Refundable grants Refundable grants of $200,000 were received from the federal government. These grants are to be used for student aid and are refundable to the federal government as the student loans are repaid.

Cash	200,000	
Refundable Grants—Federal Government		200,000

During the year, the college returned $45,000 to the federal government based on repaid student loans.

Colleges and Universities

Refundable Grants—Federal Government	45,000	
Cash		45,000

Transfers The community college's governing board transferred $40,000 from the Unrestricted Current Fund to the Loan Fund. Of this amount, $10,000 must be repaid within six months.

LOAN FUND
Cash	40,000	
Due To Current Fund (Unrestricted)		10,000
Fund Balance—Unrestricted		30,000

CURRENT FUND—UNRESTRICTED
Due From Loan Fund	10,000	
Fund Balance (Nonmandatory Transfer)	30,000	
Cash		40,000

Endowment income During the year $70,000 (restricted for student loans) was earned by Endowment Funds, of which $55,000 has been distributed to the Loan Fund for the purpose of financing student loans.

LOAN FUND
Cash	55,000	
Due From Endowment Fund	15,000	
Fund Balance—Restricted		70,000

ENDOWMENT FUND
Cash	70,000	
Due To Loan Fund		70,000
Due To Loan Fund	55,000	
Cash		55,000

Investment transactions Investment and related activity for the fiscal year are summarized below:

Investment income (cash)	$11,000
Investments sold	
Proceeds	60,000
Cost basis	63,000
Investments purchased	40,000

Cash	11,000	
Fund Balance—Restricted		11,000

Colleges and Universities

Cash	60,000	
Fund Balance—Restricted	3,000	
Investments		63,000
Investments	40,000	
Cash		40,000

Student loan activity Student loans of $620,000 were made during the year. Uncollectible accounts are expected to be 10% of the total loans.

Student Loans Receivable	620,000	
Fund Balance—Restricted	62,000	
Cash		620,000
Allowance For Uncollectible		
Accounts		62,000

During the year collections on student loans amounted to $145,000 and loans of $40,000 were written off as uncollectible.

Cash	145,000	
Allowance For Uncollectible Accounts	40,000	
Student Loans Receivable		185,000

Interest earned on student loans amounted to $35,000 and $25,000 was collected (includes $15,000 balance accrued at the beginning of the year).

Cash	25,000	
Accrued Interest Receivable	10,000	
Fund Balance—Restricted		35,000

Administrative costs Administrative costs amounted to $12,000 and were accrued at the end of the year.

Fund Balance—Restricted	12,000	
Accrued Liabilities		12,000

Note: Transactions that affect more than one fund group are also reproduced as illustrative entries in the other fund group.

After taking into account the transactions described above, the trial balance for the Loan Fund for the year ended June 30, 19X5, would be as follows:

Centerville Community College
Loan Fund
Trial Balance
June 30, 19X5

	Dr.	Cr.
Cash	$ 314,000	
Student loans receivable	4,147,000	
Allowance for uncollectible accounts		$ 439,000
Due from endowment fund	15,000	
Accrued interest receivable	25,000	
Investments	127,000	
Accrued liabilities		12,000
Refundable grants—federal government		355,000
Due to unrestricted current fund		10,000
Fund balance—restricted		3,756,000
Fund balance—unrestricted		56,000
	$4,628,000	$4,628,000

Endowment and Similar Funds

Endowment Funds and Similar Funds may be classified as (True) Endowment Funds, Term Endowment Funds, and Quasi-Endowment Funds. CUBA describes these three funds in the following manner:

- *(True) Endowment Funds*—Funds for which donors or other external agencies have stipulated under the terms of the gift instrument creating the fund that the principal of the fund is not expendable—that is, it is to remain inviolate in perpetuity and is to be invested for the purpose of producing present and future income, which may be expended or added to principal.
- *Term Endowment Funds*—Funds that are like Endowment Funds, except that all or part of the principal may be used after a stated period of time or on the occurrence of a certain event.
- *Quasi-Endowment Funds*—Funds that the governing board of the institution, rather than a donor or other external agency, has determined are to be retained and invested. Since these funds are not required by the donor to be retained and invested, the principal as well as the income may be totally utilized at the discretion of the governing board, subject to any donor-imposed restrictions on use.

(Temporarily invested assets belonging to current and other funds should not be classified as Quasi-Endowment but should be shown as investments of the Current or other appropriate fund.) Quasi-Endowment Funds should be identified as unrestricted or restricted.

Endowment and similar funds may receive or hold a variety of assets such as investments in equity and debt securities, real estate, copyrights, and patents. CUBA concludes that income from these investments should be accounted as follows:

- Restricted purposes—Credited to the respective unexpended endowment income accounts in Restricted Current Funds or to fund balance such as Loan, Endowment, or Plant Funds as specified by the terms of the gift instrument.

- Unrestricted—Credited to Unrestricted Current Funds revenues.

There is no universally accepted definition of what constitutes income that is eventually distributable to other funds. Generally, colleges and universities accept the trust fund theory, which argues that only the "yield" from investments is considered distributable income. Yield includes such items as interest, dividends, royalties, and rents. Capital appreciation is considered to be an enhancement of the corpus and not available for distribution.

Alternatively, the corporate law concept treats the appreciation or depreciation of investments as part of the computation of distributable income.

> **OBSERVATION:** *Another alternative is referred to as the total return theory, which allows for a "prudent portion" of the capital appreciation to be distributed. Because there is no acceptable definition of what constitutes a prudent portion, CUBA concludes that distributions of capital based on the total return theory should be treated as a fund balance transfer.*

Additions to and deductions from an Endowment Fund's fund balance account would include such items as the following:

Additions— Gifts and bequests restricted to endowment
Income added to the principal as provided by the donor agreement

> Gains on dispositions of investments
> Transfers to Quasi-Endowment Funds from other fund groups

Deductions— Losses on disposition of investments
Writedowns on investments
Withdrawals and transfers to other funds

Generally, expenditures related to the management of endowment investments should be recorded as expenditures (institutional support) of the Unrestricted Current Fund or the Restricted Current Fund, whichever is more appropriate. Alternatively, expenditures may be netted against endowment income recognized in the Current Funds. Commissions on the purchase and sale of investments and expenditures related to the management of real estate investments should be accounted for in the Endowment Fund. Income from real estate investments should be reported on a net basis (income and related expenditures netted). Expenditures related to fund raising should be accounted for in the Unrestricted Current Fund, unless the expenditures are directly related to the proceeds from a fund-raising campaign. Fund-raising expenditures incurred by an Endowment Fund should be shown as a separate item (a change to the fund balance account) and not netted against gift proceeds.

In addition to investments, the assets of an Endowment Fund may include such items as cash, prepayments, deferrals, accounts receivable, and amounts due from other funds. Liabilities may include items such as debts related to endowment investments and amounts due to other funds.

When all or a portion of the principal of a Term Endowment Fund is distributed to another fund, the fund receiving the resources should clearly label the transaction so as not to infer that another gift has been received by the college or university. If the Unrestricted Current Fund is entitled to the resources, revenue is recorded and should be identified as expired term endowment revenue. If a restricted fund receives the assets, the receipt should be recorded as an increase to the fund's fund balance account.

Principal distributions from Quasi-Endowment Funds should be recorded as a nonmandatory transfer.

To illustrate the routine transactions that are accounted for in Endowment Funds, assume that at the beginning of the fiscal year a community college had the following trial balance. Unless otherwise noted, all entries are recorded in the Endowment Fund.

Centerville Community College
Endowment Funds
Trial Balance
July 1, 19X4

	Dr.	Cr.
Cash	$ 126,000	
Investments	3,824,000	
Fund balance—endowment		$2,400,000
Fund balance—term		1,380,000
Fund balance—quasi-endowment		170,000
	$3,950,000	$3,950,000

During the fiscal year the following transactions occurred and were recorded in the community college's Endowment Funds:

Unrestricted endowment income During the year $120,000 (all unrestricted) was earned by Endowment Funds, of which $100,000 has been distributed to the Unrestricted Current Fund.

ENDOWMENT FUND
Cash	120,000	
Due To Current Fund (Unrestricted)		120,000
Due To Current Fund (Unrestricted)	100,000	
Cash		100,000

CURRENT FUND—UNRESTRICTED
Cash	100,000	
Due From Endowment Fund	20,000	
Revenues—Endowment Income		120,000

Restricted endowment income During the year $70,000 (all restricted for operations) was earned by Endowment Funds, of which $50,000 has been distributed to the restricted current fund. The resources are restricted for the payment of student aid.

ENDOWMENT FUND
Cash	70,000	
Due To Current Fund (Restricted)		70,000
Due To Current Fund (Restricted)	50,000	
Cash		50,000

Colleges and Universities

CURRENT FUND—RESTRICTED
Cash	50,000	
Due From Endowment Fund	20,000	
Fund Balance		70,000

During the year $70,000 (restricted for student loans) was earned by Endowment Funds, of which $55,000 has been distributed to the Loan Fund for the purpose of financing student loans.

ENDOWMENT FUND
Cash	70,000	
Due To Loan Fund		70,000
Due To Loan Fund	55,000	
Cash		55,000

LOAN FUND
Cash	55,000	
Due From Endowment Fund	15,000	
Fund Balance—Restricted		70,000

Private donations Donations from private parties were received and, based on donations agreements, $200,000 was considered True Endowment and $100,000 was classified as Term Endowment.

Cash	300,000	
Fund Balance—Endowment		200,000
Fund Balance—Term Endowment		100,000

Board-designated transfers The community college's governing board transferred $50,000 to Endowment Funds from the Unrestricted Current Fund. The amount is to be invested indefinitely and the income is to be used to encourage faculty research.

ENDOWMENT FUND
Cash	50,000	
Fund Balance—Quasi-Endowment		50,000

CURRENT FUND—UNRESTRICTED
Fund Balance (Nonmandatory Transfer)	50,000	
Cash		50,000

Investment transactions Investment and related activity for the fiscal year are summarized below. (It is assumed that the college

Colleges and Universities

treats [realized] capital appreciation as an increase to the endowment principal.)

	Endowment Funds			
	True	Term	Quasi	Total
Investments sold				
Proceeds	$300,000	$250,000	$50,000	$600,000
Cost basis	280,000	200,000	40,000	520,000
Investments purchased	510,000	330,000	120,000	960,000

```
Cash                                   600,000
  Investments                                      520,000
  Fund Balance—Endowment                            20,000
  Fund Balance—Term Endowment                       50,000
  Fund Balance—Quasi-Endowment                      10,000

Investments                            960,000
  Cash                                             960,000
```

Note: Transactions that affect more than one fund group are also reproduced as illustrative entries in the other fund group.

After taking into account the transactions described above, the trial balance for the Endowment Funds for the year ended June 30, 19X5, would be as follows:

Centerville Community College
Endowment Funds
Trial Balance
June 30, 19X5

	Dr.	Cr.
Cash	$ 171,000	
Investments	4,264,000	
Due to unrestricted current fund		$ 20,000
Due to restricted current fund		20,000
Due to loan fund		15,000
Fund balance—endowment		2,620,000
Fund balance—term		1,530,000
Fund balance—quasi-endowment		230,000
	$4,435,000	$4,435,000

81.48 / GOVERNMENTAL GAAP GUIDE

Annuity and Life Income Funds

When a college or university receives an endowment with the stipulation that a portion of the principal and/or earnings of the endowment be paid to the donor or another beneficiary designated by the donor, the contributed resources should be accounted for in either an Annuity Fund or a Life Income Fund. Although these funds are accounted for separately, they are generally combined for financial reporting purposes. Insignificant annuity and life income funds can be combined with the Endowment Fund group for financial reporting purposes.

Annuity Funds An Annuity Fund should be established when a college or university receives resources under the condition that the donor or another designated individual will receive periodic payments for a length of time specified by the donor agreement.

The assets and any related liabilities received are recorded at estimated fair market value. Also, a liability based on the actuarially computed present value of future annuity payments should be recorded (annuities payable). Any difference between the recorded value of assets donated and liabilities recorded should be reported as an increase or decrease to the fund balance account. Investment income, and gains and losses from the sale of investments are recorded in the fund balance account. When stipulated payments are made under the annuity agreement, the annuities payable account is reduced by the original present value of the payment and the difference is charged against the fund balance account.

Periodically, the actuarially computed present value of the annuities payable account should be evaluated based on possible changes in anticipated returns on investments and revised life expectancies of the donor or other beneficiary. Changes would be charged or credited to the fund balance account.

Assets of an Annuity Fund would usually consist of cash and various investments. Liabilities would include debts related to donated or acquired investments, the liability for the annuity payments, and amounts due other funds.

When an Annuity Fund is terminated, the remaining resources would be transferred to the fund group designated by the donor agreement. If no designation was made in the agreement and the distribution of the resources is not otherwise restricted, then the resources should be transferred to the Unrestricted Current Fund and identified in the latter fund in a way that does not imply that a new gift has been received by the college or university. The fund receiv-

Colleges and Universities

ing the transferred property should record the assets at their estimated fair market value.

Some states have adopted statutes or regulations that dictate the circumstances under which annuities are to be established and administered by nonprofit organizations.

To illustrate the routine transactions that are accounted for in Annuity Funds, assume that at the beginning of the fiscal year a community college had the following trial balance. Unless otherwise noted, all entries are recorded in the Annuity Funds.

Centerville Community College
Annuity Funds
Trial Balance
July 1, 19X4

	Dr.	Cr.
Cash	$ 10,000	
Investments	400,000	
Annuities payable		$330,000
Fund balance		80,000
	$410,000	$410,000

During the fiscal year the following transactions occurred and were recorded in the community college's Annuity Funds:

Donations During the year the community college and a private donor agreed to the terms of an annuity contract. The donor transferred property with an estimated fair market value of $150,000. The actuarially computed present value of the future annuities is $70,000.

Investments	150,000	
Annuities Payable		70,000
Fund Balance		80,000

Annuity payments Based on donor agreements, annuity payments totaled $25,000 and the original present value of these payments was $19,000.

Annuities payable	19,000	
Fund balance	6,000	
Cash		25,000

81.50 / GOVERNMENTAL GAAP GUIDE

Investment transactions Investment and related activity for the fiscal year are summarized below:

Investment income (cash)	$32,000	
Investments sold		
Proceeds	12,000	
Cost basis	10,000	
Investments purchased	18,000	

Cash	32,000	
Fund Balance		32,000
Cash	12,000	
Investments		10,000
Fund Balance		2,000
Investments	18,000	
Cash		18,000

Evaluation of annuity agreement At the end of the year, the college decided to decrease the actuarially computed present value of annuities payable by $15,000, based on anticipated changes in the returns on certain investments.

Annuities Payable	15,000	
Fund Balance		15,000

Terminated agreement During the year a commitment under one annuity agreement was fully satisfied and the remaining investments of $35,000 were transferred to the Unrestricted Current Fund. The fair market value of the investments is $40,000.

ANNUITY FUND

Fund Balance	35,000	
Investments		35,000

CURRENT FUND—UNRESTRICTED

Investments	40,000	
Revenues—Expired Annuity Agreements		40,000

Note: Transactions that affect more than one fund group are also reproduced as illustrative entries in the other fund group.

Colleges and Universities

After taking into account the transactions described above, the trial balance for Annuity Funds for the year ended June 30, 19X5, would be as follows:

Centerville Community College
Annuity Funds
Trial Balance
June 30, 19X5

	Dr.	Cr.
Cash	$ 11,000	
Investments	523,000	
Annuities payable		$366,000
Fund balance		168,000
	$534,000	$534,000

Life Income Funds A Life Income Fund should be established when a college or university receives resources under the condition that the donor or another designated individual will receive all income earned from the donated assets for a period of time specified by the donor agreement.

The assets and related liabilities, if any, received from the donor are recorded at their estimated fair market value. Because the amount of income earned each period will vary from year to year, no liability is established for the payments of future income that will be earned. Thus, the value of the net assets received is credited to the fund balance account. Investment income as earned is recorded as a liability (income payable). Gains and losses on investment activity are recorded in the fund balance account unless the donor agreement stipulates otherwise.

Assets of a Life Income Fund would usually consist of cash and various investments, while liabilities would include debts related to donated or acquired investments and the life income payable to the donor or designated beneficiary.

When a Life Income Fund is terminated, the principal would be transferred to the fund group designated by the donor agreement. If no designation was made in the agreement and the distribution of the resources is not otherwise restricted, the resources should be transferred to the Unrestricted Current Fund and identified in the latter fund in a way that does not imply that a new gift has been received by the college or university. The fund receiving the transferred property should record the assets at estimated fair market value.

Colleges and Universities

Federal tax law and state laws must be observed in the establishment and administration of Life Income Funds. Generally, income from these funds is tax exempt; however, when federal or state taxes must be paid by the fund, they should be treated as a reduction to the amount due to the donor or designated beneficiary, unless otherwise stipulated in the donor agreement.

To illustrate the routine transactions that are accounted for in Life Income Funds, assume that at the beginning of the fiscal year a community college had the following trial balance. Unless otherwise noted, all entries are made in the Life Income Funds.

Centerville Community College
Life Income Funds
Trial Balance
July 1, 19X4

	Dr.	Cr.
Cash	$ 20,000	
Investments	250,000	
Income payable		$ 15,000
Fund balance		255,000
	$270,000	$270,000

During the fiscal year the following transactions occurred and were recorded in the community college's Life Income Funds.

Donations During the year the community college and a private donor agreed to the terms of a life income contract. The donor transferred property valued at $100,000.

Investments	100,000	
Fund Balance		100,000

Investment income Investment income of $20,000 was earned and received during the year.

Cash	20,000	
Income Payable		20,000

Income payments All amounts due donors were paid (including the amount due at the beginning of the year) except for $5,000.

Income Payable	30,000	
Cash		30,000

GOVERNMENTAL GAAP GUIDE / 81.53

Colleges and Universities

Investment transactions During the year, investments with a cost basis of $20,000 were sold for $35,000 and additional investments of $35,000 were made.

Cash	35,000	
Investments		20,000
Fund Balance		15,000
Investments	35,000	
Cash		35,000

Terminated agreement During the year a commitment under one life income agreement was fully satisfied and the principal of $50,000 was transferred to the Unrestricted Current Fund. The fair market value of the transferred investments was $75,000.

LIFE INCOME FUND

Fund Balance	50,000	
Investments		50,000

CURRENT FUND—UNRESTRICTED

Investments	75,000	
Revenues—Expired Life Income Agreement		75,000

Note: Transactions that affect more than one fund group are also reproduced as illustrative entries in the other fund group.

After taking into account the transactions described above, the trial balance for Life Income Funds for the year ended June 30, 19X5, would be as follows:

Centerville Community College
Life Income Funds
Trial Balance
June 30, 19X5

	Dr.	Cr.
Cash	$ 10,000	
Investments	315,000	
Income payable		$ 5,000
Fund balance		320,000
	$325,000	$325,000

Plant Funds

As noted earlier, a college or university records transactions related to its plant assets in its Plant Funds. The Plant Fund group is comprised of four self-balancing subgroups, namely Plant Fund—Unexpended, Plant Fund—Renewals and Replacements, Plant Fund—Retirement of Indebtedness and Plant Fund—Investment in Plant.

The plant assets, such as land, land improvements, buildings, equipment, and library books, are recorded in the subgroup entitled Plant Fund—Investment in Plant. The assets are recorded at cost when they are purchased or at estimated fair market value when they are received as a gift. The subgroup is self-balancing by recording the source of the fixed assets. If the fixed asset is being financed, an appropriate liability such as bonds payable is recorded. As the liability is reduced, there is an equal increase in the equity account entitled net investment in plant. Resources may be accumulated to retire debt and make interest payments related to the financing of plant assets. These resources are accumulated in the Plant Fund—Retirement of Indebtedness.

With the exception of the Plant Fund—Investment in Plant, the assets of the Plant Fund group may include cash, investments, receivables, amounts due from other fund groups, and deposits with others. Liabilities recorded in Plant Fund groups may consist of accounts payable, accrued liabilities for operating expenditures, amounts due to other fund groups, and debts related to assets carried in the individual fund subgroups. The difference between the recorded assets and liabilities is identified as the fund balance (unrestricted and restricted), except the equity account in the Plant Fund—Investment in Plant is referred to as net investment in plant.

To illustrate the routine transactions that are accounted for in the Plant Funds, assume that at the beginning of the fiscal year a community college had the following trial balances:

Colleges and Universities

Centerville Community College
Plant Fund Group
Trial Balances
July 1, 19X4

	Dr.	Cr.
Plant Fund—Unexpended		
Cash	$ 750,000	
Investments	2,000,000	
Fund balance—restricted		$ 2,710,000
Fund balance—unrestricted		40,000
	$ 2,750,000	$ 2,750,000
Plant Fund—Renewals and Replacements		
Cash	$ 25,000	
Investments	1,000,000	
Fund balance—restricted		$ 1,013,000
Fund balance—unrestricted		12,000
	$ 1,025,000	$ 1,025,000
Plant Fund—Retirement of Indebtedness		
Cash	$ 235,000	
Fund balance—restricted		$ 235,000
	$ 235,000	$ 235,000
Plant Fund—Investment in Plant		
Land	$ 6,000,000	
Land improvements	435,000	
Buildings	17,000,000	
Equipment	3,600,000	
Library books	1,400,000	
Notes payable		$ 800,000
Bonds payable		4,000,000
Mortgages payable		1,000,000
Net investment in plant		22,635,000
	$28,435,000	$28,435,000

During the fiscal year the following transactions occurred and were recorded in the community college's Plant Funds as described below.

Appropriations, grants, and gifts Grants of $70,000 were received from the federal government and a gift of $50,000 was received from a private foundation. The resources received must be used for the acquisition of plant assets.

PLANT FUND—UNEXPENDED
Cash   120,000
    Fund Balance—Restricted   120,000

Also, a nonmandatory transfer of $90,000 was made from the Unrestricted Current Fund to the Plant Fund—Unexpended.

PLANT FUND—UNEXPENDED
Cash 90,000
    Fund Balance—Unrestricted   90,000

CURRENT FUND—UNRESTRICTED
Fund Balance (Nonmandatory) 90,000
    Cash   90,000

A portion of tuition and fees billed during the fiscal year is legally pledged for the payment of bonds outstanding ($200,000), and the governing board allocated $100,000 for the purchase of personal computers.

PLANT FUND—RETIREMENT OF INDEBTEDNESS
Due From Current Fund (Unrestricted) 200,000
    Fund Balance—Restricted   200,000

PLANT FUND—UNEXPENDED
Due From Current Fund (Unrestricted) 100,000
    Fund Balance—Unrestricted   100,000

CURRENT FUND—UNRESTRICTED
Fund Balance (Nonmandatory Transfer) 100,000
Mandatory Transfers—Debt Retirement
  And Interest 200,000
    Due To Unexpended Plant Fund   100,000
    Due To Retirement Of Indebted-
      ness Fund (Plant Fund)   200,000

Capital asset acquisitions Equipment ($300,000) and library books ($200,000) were acquired by using restricted resources of the Plant Fund—Unexpended.

PLANT FUND—UNEXPENDED
Fund Balance—Restricted 500,000
    Cash   500,000

PLANT FUND—INVESTMENT IN PLANT
Equipment 300,000
Library Books 200,000
    Net Investment In Plant   500,000

Colleges and Universities

In addition, equipment ($50,000) and books ($30,000) were purchased for the library during the fiscal year from the Unrestricted Current Fund.

PLANT FUND—INVESTMENT IN PLANT
Equipment   50,000
Library Books   30,000
    Net Investment In Plant   80,000

CURRENT FUND—UNRESTRICTED
Expenditures—Academic Support   80,000
    Cash   80,000

During the fiscal year, land and a building were given to the college to be used as a classroom facility. The land had an estimated fair market value of $600,000 while the building was valued at $250,000. The college also assumed responsibility for a mortgage of $70,000 related to the transferred real estate.

PLANT FUND—INVESTMENT IN PLANT
Land   600,000
Building   250,000
    Mortgages Payable   70,000
    Net Investment In Plant   780,000

Construction in progress During the year, the governing board of the college approved the construction of a major addition to the library. Bonds with a 6% stated interest rate and a par value of $2,000,000 were issued at par to finance the construction of the new wing (the construction of the addition to the library is to be accounted for in the Plant Fund—Unexpended).

PLANT FUND—UNEXPENDED
Cash   2,000,000
    Bonds Payable   2,000,000

Construction costs of $1,400,000 were incurred, and cash payments for these costs amounted to $1,000,000.

PLANT FUND—UNEXPENDED
Construction In Progress   1,400,000
    Cash   1,000,000
    Accounts Payable   400,000

Colleges and Universities

The average accumulated expenditures for the year were $800,000, and it is decided to use the specific borrowing rate on the bonds (6%) to compute the amount of interest to be capitalized. Bond interest expenditures, as illustrated later, were paid from the Plant Fund—Retirement of Indebtedness.

PLANT FUND—UNEXPENDED
   Construction In Progress
     ($800,000 × 6%)   48,000
       Fund Balance—Restricted   48,000

> **OBSERVATION:** *The restricted fund balance account is increased by the amount of the capitalized interest. This amount, along with other capitalized cost and the related liability, will be transferred to the Plant Fund—Investment in Plant when the project is completed or at the end of the period. When the transfer occurs, the capitalized interest, as reflected in the restricted fund balance account, will become part of the Plant Fund—Investment in Plant's net investment in plant account (equity account). The transfer will occur for purposes of this example in a later period when the project is completed.*

Renewals and replacements Expenditures related to the maintenance of plant assets amounted to $70,000 and were paid from the Plant Fund—Renewals and Replacements. None of the expenditures resulted in improvements or additions to the college's plant assets.

PLANT FUND—RENEWALS AND REPLACEMENTS
   Fund Balance—Restricted   70,000
      Cash   70,000

Also, $80,000 was transferred from the Unrestricted Current Fund to the Plant Fund—Renewals and Replacements during the fiscal year.

PLANT FUND—RENEWALS AND REPLACEMENTS
   Cash   80,000
      Fund Balance—Unrestricted   80,000
CURRENT FUND—UNRESTRICTED
   Fund Balance (Nonmandatory Transfer)   80,000
      Cash   80,000

Colleges and Universities

Debt service During the year the following payments were made by the Plant Fund—Retirement of Indebtedness:

	Principal	Interest	Total
Bonds payable		$250,000	$250,000
Mortgages payable	$ 40,000	70,000	110,000
Notes payable	400,000	50,000	450,000
	$440,000	$370,000	$810,000

PLANT FUND—RETIREMENT OF INDEBTEDNESS
    Fund Balance—Restricted   810,000
        Cash   810,000

PLANT FUND—INVESTMENT IN PLANT
    Mortgages Payable   40,000
    Notes Payable   400,000
        Net Investment In Plant   440,000

Mandatory transfers for principal and interest payments from the Unrestricted Current Fund totaled $650,000 during the year.

PLANT FUND—RETIREMENT OF INDEBTEDNESS
    Cash   650,000
        Fund Balance—Restricted   650,000

CURRENT FUND—UNRESTRICTED
    Mandatory Transfers—Principal
      And Interest   650,000
        Cash   650,000

Disposition of plant assets Equipment with an original cost of $120,000 was sold for $30,000 (assume that state regulation requires that proceeds from the sale of plant assets must be made available to the Unexpended Plant Fund).

PLANT FUND—INVESTMENT IN PLANT
    Net Investment In Plant   120,000
        Equipment   120,000

PLANT FUND—UNEXPENDED
    Cash   30,000
        Fund Balance—Restricted   30,000

Colleges and Universities

Investment transactions Investment and related activity for the fiscal year are summarized below:

	Plant Funds	
	Unexpended	Renewals and Replacements
Investment income (cash)	$140,000	$70,000
Investments sold		
Proceeds	700,000	200,000
Cost basis	600,000	250,000
Investments purchased	800,000	240,000

PLANT FUND—UNEXPENDED

Cash	140,000	
Fund Balance—Restricted		140,000
Cash	700,000	
Investments		600,000
Fund Balance—Restricted		100,000
Investments	800,000	
Cash		800,000

PLANT FUND—RENEWALS AND REPLACEMENTS

Cash	70,000	
Fund Balance—Restricted		70,000
Cash	200,000	
Fund Balance—Restricted	50,000	
Investments		250,000
Investments	240,000	
Cash		240,000

Note: Transactions that affect more than one fund group are also reproduced as illustrative entries in the other fund group.

After taking into account the transactions described above, the trial balance for the Plant Funds for the year ended June 30, 19X5, would be as follows:

GOVERNMENTAL GAAP GUIDE / **81.61**

Colleges and Universities

Centerville Community College
Plant Funds—Restricted
Trial Balance
June 30, 19X5

	Dr.	Cr.
Plant Fund-Unexpended		
Cash	$ 1,530,000	
Due from restricted current fund	100,000	
Construction in progress	1,448,000	
Investments	2,200,000	
Accounts payable		$ 400,000
Bonds payable		2,000,000
Fund balance—restricted		2,648,000
Fund balance—unrestricted		230,000
	$ 5,278,000	$ 5,278,000
Plant Fund—Renewals and Replacements		
Cash	$ 65,000	
Investments	990,000	
Fund balance—restricted		$ 963,000
Fund balance—unrestricted		92,000
	$ 1,055,000	$ 1,055,000
Plant Fund—Retirement of Indebtedness		
Cash	$ 75,000	
Due from unrestricted current fund	200,000	
Fund balance—restricted		$ 275,000
	$ 275,000	$ 275,000
Plant Fund—Investment in Plant		
Land	$ 6,600,000	
Land improvements	435,000	
Buildings	17,250,000	
Equipment	3,830,000	
Library books	1,630,000	
Notes payable		$ 400,000
Bonds payable		4,000,000
Mortgages payable		1,030,000
Net investment		24,315,000
	$29,745,000	$29,745,000

Agency Funds

A college or university may take temporary custody of resources that belong to others. If the amount of the assets held in this manner is immaterial, the transactions may be accounted for as part of the Unrestricted Current Fund, otherwise an Agency Fund should be used.

Assets may be held for students, faculty, staff members, and various organizations. Because the college or university simply acts as a custodian for the assets, an Agency Fund has no fund balance account.

Assets in an Agency Fund may include cash, receivables, temporary investments and amounts due from other funds. Liabilities are composed of the specific amounts due to individuals, organizations, or other fund groups.

To illustrate the routine transactions that are accounted for in Agency Funds, assume that at the beginning of the fiscal year a community college had the following trial balance:

Centerville Community College
Agency Funds
Trial Balance
July 1, 19X4

	Dr.	Cr.
Cash	$12,000	
Deposits held in custody for others		$12,000
	$12,000	$12,000

During the fiscal year the following transactions occurred and were recorded in the community college's Agency Funds:

Receipt of custodial assets Assets of $34,000 were received from various parties and were temporarily under custody control of the community college.

Cash	34,000	
Deposits Held In Custody For Others		34,000

Disbursement of custodial assets Assets held for others of $32,000 were distributed to the appropriate parties.

Deposits Held In Custody For Others	32,000	
Cash		32,000

After taking into account the transactions described above, the trial balance for Agency Funds for the year ended June 30, 19X5, would be as follows:

Centerville Community College
Agency Funds
Trial Balance
June 30, 19X5

	Dr.	Cr.
Cash	$14,000	
Deposits held in custody for others		$14,000
	$14,000	$14,000

FINANCIAL STATEMENTS

A governmental unit's (the reporting entity's) general purpose financial statements should incorporate the financial statements of a college or university (the component entity) into the unit's (1) Combined Balance Sheet—All Fund Types and Account Groups, (2) Combined Statement of Revenues, Expenditures, and Changes in Fund Balances—All Governmental Fund Types, and (3) notes to the financial statements. The financial statements of a college or university should be shown as a discrete presentation rather than combined with one of the five governmental fund types.

The financial statements of a college or university should provide a basis for evaluating management's effectiveness in advancing goals of the institution. CUBA concludes that separately incorporated units for which the institution is responsible should be either (1) included in separate statements, accompanied by and cross-referenced to the basic institutional statements, (2) disclosed by footnotes, or (3) included in the financial statements of the institution.

The financial statements of a college or university should include the following:

- Balance Sheet
- Statement of Changes in Fund Balances

- Statements of Current Funds Revenues, Expenditures, and Other Changes

These financial statements are illustrated below and they reflect the accounts and transactions developed earlier in the chapter (see section entitled College and University Funds).

Balance Sheet A college or university presents a single balance sheet, but the format of the statement must be organized in a manner that will enable the reader to identify the net resources and fund balances of each major fund group. The format may be a vertical presentation or a columnar presentation. When a columnar format is used, there should be no total column, unless all necessary disclosures are made, including interfund borrowings. Because the various fund groups are restricted, fair presentation would not be achieved by combining the assets, liabilities, and fund balance accounts of all fund groups.

An example of a Balance Sheet for a college or university is presented in Exhibit I. The presentation uses a vertical format.

Statement of Changes in Fund Balances

Although a Statement of Changes in Financial Position is not presented for a college or university, a Statement of Changes in Fund Balances serves basically the same purpose. CUBA adopts the philosophy that "when significant resources or expenditures such as financing activities and investments in plant are not included in the Statement of Changes in Fund Balances, such activities may be disclosed separately in a note or elsewhere in the financial statements." This approach is similar to the "all financial resources" philosophy which is adopted by APB-19 (Reporting Changes in Financial Position).

A single Statement of Changes in Fund Balances is presented, but the statement is organized so that the significant increases and decreases of each fund group's fund balance account are disclosed. The format may be a vertical or columnar presentation. When a columnar presentation is made there should not be a total column, unless care is taken so that the totals are not mislabeled and changes in fund balances are not duplicated.

An example of a Statement of Changes in Fund Balances is presented in Exhibit II. The presentation uses a vertical format.

EXHIBIT I

Balance Sheet

Centerville Community College
Balance Sheet
June 30, 19X5

ASSETS

Current Funds

Unrestricted

Cash	$ 728,000	
Accounts receivable	950,000	
Allowance for uncollectible accounts	(300,000)	
Inventories	70,000	
Accrued investment revenue	4,000	
Temporary investments	185,000	
Investments	235,000	
Due to endowment fund	20,000	
Due to loan fund	10,000	
Total unrestricted		1,902,000

Restricted

Cash	115,000	
Investments	350,000	
Due from endowment fund	20,000	
Total restricted		485,000
Total current funds		$ 2,387,000

LIABILITIES AND FUND BALANCES

Unrestricted

Accounts payable	$ 100,000	
Accrued liabilities	150,000	
Due to unexpended plant fund	100,000	
Due to retirement of indebtedness plant fund	200,000	
Fund balance—reserved for encumbrances	70,000	
Fund balance	1,282,000	
Total unrestricted		1,902,000

Restricted

Fund balances		485,000
Total restricted		485,000
Total current funds		$ 2,387,000

Colleges and Universities

Loan Funds			Loan Funds		
Cash	$	314,000	Accrued liabilities	$	12,000
Student loans receivable		4,147,000	Refundable grants—federal government		355,000
Allowance for uncollectible accounts		(439,000)	Due to unrestricted current fund		10,000
Accrued interest receivable		25,000	Fund balances—restricted		3,756,000
Investments		127,000	Fund balances—unrestricted		56,000
Due from endowment fund		15,000	Total loan funds	$	4,189,000
Total loan funds	$	4,189,000			
Endowment and Similar Funds			Endowment and Similar Funds		
Cash	$	171,000	Due to unrestricted current fund	$	20,000
Investments		4,264,000	Due to restricted current fund		20,000
			Due to loan fund		15,000
			Fund balances		
			Endowment		2,620,000
			Term endowment		1,530,000
			Quasi-endowment		230,000
Total endowment and similar funds	$	4,435,000	Total endowment and similar funds	$	4,435,000

GOVERNMENTAL GAAP GUIDE / 81.67

Colleges and Universities

Annuity and Life Income Funds

Annuity Funds
Cash	$	11,000
Investments		523,000
Total annuity funds		534,000

Life Income Funds
Cash		10,000
Investments		315,000
Total life income funds		325,000
Total annuity and life income funds	$	859,000

Annuity and Life Income Funds

Annuity Funds
Annuities payable	$	366,000
Fund balance		168,000
Total annuity funds		534,000

Life Income Funds
Income payable		5,000
Fund balances		320,000
Total life income funds		325,000
Total annuity and life income funds	$	859,000

Colleges and Universities

Plant Funds		Plant Funds	
Unexpended		Unexpended	
Cash	$ 1,530,000	Accounts payable	$ 400,000
Construction in progress	1,448,000	Bonds payable	2,000,000
Investments	2,200,000	Fund balance—restricted	2,648,000
Due from restricted current fund	100,000	Fund balance—unrestricted	230,000
Total unexpended	5,278,000	Total unexpended	5,278,000
Renewals and Replacements		Renewals and Replacements	
Cash	65,000	Fund balance—restricted	963,000
Investments	990,000	Fund balance—unrestricted	92,000
Total renewals and replacements	1,055,000	Total renewals and replacements	1,055,000
Retirement of Indebtedness		Retirement of Indebtedness	
Cash	75,000	Fund balance—restricted	275,000
Due from unrestricted current fund	200,000		
Total retirement of indebtedness	275,000	Total retirement of indebtedness	275,000
Investment in Plant		Investment in Plant	
Land	6,600,000	Notes payable	400,000
Land improvements	435,000	Bonds payable	4,000,000
Buildings	17,250,000	Mortgages payable	1,030,000
Equipment	3,830,000	Net investment in plant	24,315,000
Library books	1,630,000		
Total investment in plant	29,745,000	Total investment in plant	29,745,000
Total plant funds	$36,353,000	Total plant funds	$36,353,000
Agency Funds		Agency Funds	
Cash	$ 14,000	Deposits held in custody for others	$ 14,000
Total agency funds	$ 14,000	Total agency funds	$ 14,000

GOVERNMENTAL GAAP GUIDE / 81.69

EXHIBIT II
Statement of Changes in Fund Balances

Centerville Community College
Statement of Changes in Fund Balances
Year Ended, June 30, 19X5

	Current Funds Unrestricted	Current Funds Restricted	Loan Funds
Revenues and other additions			
Unrestricted current fund revenues	$10,702,000		
Federal grants and contracts—restricted		$300,000	
State grants and contracts—restricted		350,000	
Private gifts, grants, and contracts—restricted		130,000	$ 370,000
Investment income—restricted		95,000	81,000
Realized gains on investment—unrestricted			
Realized gains on investments—restricted			
Interest on loans receivable			35,000
Expended for plant facilities			
Retirement of indebtedness			
Adjustment of actuarial liability for annuities payable			
Proceeds from sale of plant assets			
Capitalization of interest cost			
Total revenues and other additions	10,702,000	875,000	486,000
Expenditures and other deductions			
Educational and general expenditures	8,580,000	785,000	
Auxiliary enterprises expenditures	600,000		
Loan cancellations and writeoffs			62,000
Administrative costs			12,000
Payments to annuitants			
Expended for plant facilities			
Retirement of indebtedness			
Interest on debt			
Disposal of plant facilities			
Matured annuity and life income funds—unrestricted			
Realized loss on investments—restricted			3,000
Total expenditures and other deductions	9,180,000	785,000	77,000
Mandatory transfers			
Principal and interest	850,000		
Nonmandatory transfers			
Plant acquisitions—unrestricted	190,000		
Plant renewals and replacements—unrestricted	80,000		
Student loans—unrestricted	30,000		(30,000)
Research endowment—unrestricted	50,000		
Total nonmandatory transfers	350,000		(30,000)
Fund balance additions/(deductions)			
Resources returned to grantors	(20,000)	(15,000)	
Increase in encumbrances reserve	(20,000)		
Total additions/(deductions)	(40,000)	(15,000)	
Net increase/(decrease) for the year	282,000	75,000	439,000
Fund balance—beginning of year	1,000,000	410,000	3,373,000
Fund balance—end of year	$ 1,282,000	$485,000	$3,812,000

Colleges and Universities

Endowment & Similar Funds	Annuity & Life Income Funds	Plant Funds Unexpended	Renewals & Replacements	Retirement of Indebtedness	Investment in Plant
		$ 70,000			
$ 300,000					
	$180,000	50,000			$ 780,000
10,000	34,000	140,000	$ 70,000		
70,000		100,000			
	15,000				580,000
					440,000
	15,000	30,000			
		48,000			
380,000	244,000	438,000	70,000		1,800,000
	6,000				
		500,000	70,000		
				$440,000	
				370,000	
					120,000
	85,000		50,000		
	91,000	500,000	120,000	810,000	120,000
				(850,000)	
		(190,000)			
			(80,000)		
(50,000)					
(50,000)		(190,000)	(80,000)		
430,000	153,000	128,000	30,000	40,000	1,680,000
3,950,000	335,000	2,750,000	1,025,000	235,000	22,635,000
$4,380,000	$488,000	$2,878,000	$1,055,000	$275,000	$24,315,000

GOVERNMENTAL GAAP GUIDE / **81.71**

Statement of Revenues, Expenditures, and Other Changes

A Statement of Revenues, Expenditures and Other Changes is presented only for the Current Funds. A columnar presentation is to be used in order to present individually the activities of the Unrestricted Current Fund and Restricted Current Funds. The statement should include, in addition to operational activities (revenues, expenditures, and mandatory transfers), other changes that result in the identification of the net increase or decrease of each Current Fund's fund balance account. The net increase or decrease should be the same as the amounts shown for the Current Funds in the Statement of Changes in Fund Balances.

An example of a Statement of Revenues, Expenditures, and Other Changes is presented in Exhibit III.

> **OBSERVATION:** *The conventional format of a Statement of Revenues, Expenditures, and Other Changes has a deficiency in that there is no identification of the excess of revenues over expenditures or the excess of expenditures over revenues. Even though a college or university is not in business to generate a profit (therefore it has no need to identify "net income"), other nonprofit organizations highlight the relationship between operational resources and operational expenditures. There is no obvious reason why a college or university should not do the same.*

Supplementary Material and Schedules

In order to enhance the understanding of the basic financial statements of a college or university, CUBA concludes that interpretative material such as the following may be presented:

- A more complete statement of the principles and objectives of fund accounting and the relationships among fund groups.
- An explanation of accrual accounting and its objectives; its application to the various fund groups.
- Definitions of commonly used terms such as expenditures, expenses, mandatory transfers, nonmandatory transfers, other changes, encumbrances, and allocations.

Colleges and Universities

EXHIBIT III
Balance Sheet
Centerville Community College
Statement of Revenues, Expenditures,
and Other Changes
Year Ended, June 30, 19X5

	Current Funds		
	Unrestricted	Restricted	Total
Revenues			
Tuition and fees	$ 5,400,000		$ 5,400,000
Federal appropriations	400,000		400,000
State appropriations	1,200,000		1,200,000
Local appropriations	2,000,000		2,000,000
Federal grants and contracts	200,000	$280,000	480,000
State grants and contracts	100,000	325,000	425,000
Private gifts, grants, and contracts	500,000	140,000	640,000
Endowment income	120,000	40,000	160,000
Sales and services of auxiliary enterprises	650,000		650,000
Expired term endowment	115,000		115,000
Other sources	17,000		17,000
Total current revenues	10,702,000	785,000	11,487,000
Expenditures and mandatory transfers			
Educational and general			
Instruction	5,140,000		5,140,000
Research	380,000	235,000	615,000
Public service	200,000		200,000
Academic support	550,000	90,000	640,000
Student services	250,000	50,000	300,000
Institutional support	210,000		210,000
Operation and maintenance of plant	300,000		300,000
Scholarships and fellowships	1,550,000	410,000	1,960,000
Educational and general expenditures	8,580,000	785,000	9,365,000

Colleges and Universities

- An interpretation of the financial statements, schedules, and exhibits, referenced to charts, graphs, and other illustrative material. This interpretative material may include nonfinancial data associated with financial information to show trends in relationships such as:
  - Educational and general expenditures per full-time-equivalent student.
  - Expenditures for operations and maintenance of plant per square foot of floor space.
  - Average full-time faculty compensation, including staff benefits, by ranks within colleges and other major academic division.
  - Direct educational and general expenditures for instruction per semester or quarter hour by colleges and other academic divisions.

In addition, CUBA notes that supplementary schedules such as the following may be useful by some external parties in evaluating the effectiveness of the institution's management:

- Schedule of Current Fund expenditures and mandatory transfers and resources utilized
- Schedule of Current Fund revenues
- Schedule of Current Fund expenditures
- Summary of gifts received—by source and purpose
- Summary of property, plant, and equipment
- Schedule of long-term debt
- Details of balances of each fund and changes therein during the period
- Schedule of operations of auxiliary enterprises
- Schedule of operations of hospitals
- Schedule of operations of independent operations

Accounting Changes

Generally, a change in accounting principles, including accounting practices and methods, should be accounted for in the following manner:

- Financial statements of prior periods should be presented as they were originally.

Colleges and Universities

- The effect of the change of the reporting of current and prior periods should be disclosed in the financial statements or in the notes thereto. The cumulative effect of the change should be disclosed in the Statement of Changes in Fund Balances.

    OBSERVATION: *The reporting of a change in accounting principles for the current funds of a college or university is significantly different from the reporting format used by commercial enterprises. APB Opinion-20 (Accounting Changes) requires, with some specified exceptions, that the cumulative effects of a change in accounting principles be reported in the enterprise's statement of operations.*

	Current Funds		
	Unrestricted	Restricted	Total
Mandatory transfers for Principal and interest	850,000		850,000
Total education and general and mandatory transfers	9,430,000	785,000	10,215,000
Auxiliary enterprises Expenditures	600,000		600,000
Total expenditures and mandatory transfers	10,030,000	785,000	10,815,000
Other transfers and additions (deductions) Nonmandatory transfers	(350,000)		(350,000)
Excess of restricted receipts over transfers to revenue		90,000	90,000
Resources returned to grantors	(20,000)	(15,000)	(35,000)
Increase in encumbrances reserve	(20,000)		(20,000)
Net increase in fund balance	$ 282,000	$ 75,000	$ 357,000

Resources Held by Others

A college or university may benefit from resources held in trust by others. The financial statements of such trusts should not be presented as part of the financial statements of the college or university; however, they should be presented in notes to the financial statements or disclosed parenthetically in the Endowment and similar funds' balance sheet.

When the college or university has legally enforceable rights or claims to the assets and earnings of trusts, the assets and related accounts may be incorporated into the financial statements of the college or university. Income from irrevocable trusts (trustees have no power over the distribution of income) should be reported as endowment income or presented separately. Income from revocable trusts (trustees have power over the distribution of income), should be reported as gifts or presented separately.

LITERATURE REFERENCES

Material in this chapter is based on the following authoritative pronouncements and publications, which are grouped according to the major headings used within the chapter. A dual reference (both paragraph and page number) is used for NCGA-1 and NCGA-2 because the original pronouncements do not use paragraph numbers.

Basic Concepts and Standards
NCGA-3   *Defining the Governmental Reporting Entity,* ¶¶ 9-14.

Basis of Accounting
NCGA-1   *Governmental Accounting and Financial Reporting Principles,* p. 11/¶ 58.
AICPA INDUSTRY AUDIT GUIDE   *Audits of Colleges and Universities,* p. 7.
COLLEGE AND UNIVERSITY BUSINESS ADMINISTRATION: ADMINISTRATIVE SERVICE   *National Association of College and University Business Officers,* Chapter 5:1, pp. 2 and 5.
FASB:CS-1   *Objectives of Financial Reporting by Business Enterprises,* ¶ 44.

Measurement Focus
GASB DISCUSSION MEMORANDUM   *Measurement Focus and Basis of Accounting—Governmental Funds* (nonauthoritative).
COLLEGE AND UNIVERSITY BUSINESS ADMINISTRATION: ADMINISTRATIVE SERVICE   *National Association of College and University Business Officers,* Chapter 5:1, p. 5.

Colleges and Universities

Budgetary System and Accounts
NCGA-1   *Governmental Accounting and Financial Reporting Principles*, pp. 13 and 14/¶¶ 77 and 89-92.

Accounts and Transactions
AICPA Industry Audit Guide   *Audits of Colleges and Universities*, p. 6.
COLLEGE AND UNIVERSITY BUSINESS ADMINISTRATION: Administrative Service   *National Association of College and University Business Officers*, Chapter 5:1, p. 4.

Revenues and Other Sources of Assets
FASB:CS-6   *Elements of Financial Statements*, ¶ 78.
APB-4   *Basic Concepts and Accounting Principles Underlying Financial Statements of Business Enterprises*, ¶ 150.
AICPA Industry Audit Guide   *Audits of Colleges and Universities*, pp. 7 and 20.
COLLEGE AND UNIVERSITY BUSINESS ADMINISTRATION: Administrative Service   *National Association of College and University Business Officers*, Chapter 5:1, p. 5 and Chapter 5:2, p. 2.

Tuition and Fees
AICPA Industry Audit Guide   *Audits of Colleges and Universities*, pp. 20 and 21.
COLLEGE AND UNIVERSITY BUSINESS ADMINISTRATION: Administrative Service   *National Association of College and University Business Officers*, Chapter 5:2, pp. 2 and 3.

Governmental Appropriations
AICPA Industry Audit Guide   *Audits of Colleges and Universities*, p. 21.
COLLEGE AND UNIVERSITY BUSINESS ADMINISTRATION: Administrative Service   *National Association of College and University Business Officers*, Chapter 5:2, pp. 3 and 4.

Governmental Grants and Contracts
AICPA Industry Audit Guide   *Audits of Colleges and Universities*, p. 21.
COLLEGE AND UNIVERSITY BUSINESS ADMINISTRATION: Administrative Service   *National Association of College and University Business Officers*, Chapter 5:2, pp. 3 and 4.

Private Gifts and Grants
AICPA Industry Audit Guide   *Audits of Colleges and Universities*, pp. 21 and 22.
COLLEGE AND UNIVERSITY BUSINESS ADMINISTRATION: Administrative Service   *National Association of College and University Business Officers*, Chapter 5:2, p. 4.

Colleges and Universities

Endowment Income
AICPA INDUSTRY AUDIT GUIDE   *Audits of Colleges and Universities*, p. 22.
COLLEGE AND UNIVERSITY BUSINESS ADMINISTRATION: ADMINISTRATIVE SERVICE   *National Association of College and University Business Officers*, Chapter 5:2, p. 4.

Sales and Services of Educational Activities
AICPA INDUSTRY AUDIT GUIDE   *Audits of Colleges and Universities*, p. 23.
COLLEGE AND UNIVERSITY BUSINESS ADMINISTRATION: ADMINISTRATIVE SERVICE   *National Association of College and University Business Officers*, Chapter 5:2, pp. 4 and 5.

Sales and Services of Auxiliary Enterprises
AICPA INDUSTRY AUDIT GUIDE   *Audits of Colleges and Universities*, pp. 23 and 24.
COLLEGE AND UNIVERSITY BUSINESS ADMINISTRATION: ADMINISTRATIVE SERVICE   *National Association of College and University Business Officers*, Chapter 5:2, p. 5.

Sales and Services of Hospitals
COLLEGE AND UNIVERSITY BUSINESS ADMINISTRATION: ADMINISTRATIVE SERVICE   *National Association of College and University Business Officers*, Chapter 5:2, p. 5.

Independent Operations
COLLEGE AND UNIVERSITY BUSINESS ADMINISTRATION: ADMINISTRATIVE SERVICE   *National Association of College and University Business Officers*, Chapter 5:2, p. 5.

Other Revenue Sources
COLLEGE AND UNIVERSITY BUSINESS ADMINISTRATION: ADMINISTRATIVE SERVICE   *National Association of College and University Business Officers*, Chapter 5:2, p. 5.

Fund Balance Additions
COLLEGE AND UNIVERSITY BUSINESS ADMINISTRATION: ADMINISTRATIVE SERVICE   *National Association of College and University Business Officers*, Chapter 5:2, p. 5.

Expenditures
NCGA-1   *Governmental Accounting and Financial Reporting Principles*, pp. 12 and 16/¶¶ 70 and 109.
COLLEGE AND UNIVERSITY BUSINESS ADMINISTRATION: ADMINISTRATIVE SERVICE   *National Association of College and University Business Officers*, Chapter 5:2, pp. 5 and 6.

Colleges and Universities

Capital Expenditures
AICPA INDUSTRY AUDIT GUIDE   *Audits of Colleges and Universities*, pp. 9 and 10.
COLLEGE AND UNIVERSITY BUSINESS ADMINISTRATION: ADMINISTRATIVE SERVICE   *National Association of College and University Business Officers*, Chapter 5:2, pp. 5 and 6 and Chapter 5:1, p. 6.
GASB-8   *Applicability of FASB Statement No. 93, Recognition of Depreciation by Not-for-Profit Organizations, to Certain State and Local Governmental Entities*, ¶¶ 10 and 11.

Contributed Services
AICPA INDUSTRY AUDIT GUIDE   *Audits of Colleges and Universities*, p. 11.
COLLEGE AND UNIVERSITY BUSINESS ADMINISTRATION: ADMINISTRATIVE SERVICE   *National Association of College and University Business Officers*, Chapter 5:1, pp. 6 and 7.

Expenditure and Transfer Classification
COLLEGE AND UNIVERSITY BUSINESS ADMINISTRATION: ADMINISTRATIVE SERVICE   *National Association of College and University Business Officers*, Chapter 5:2, pp. 7-14.

Fund Balance Deductions
COLLEGE AND UNIVERSITY BUSINESS ADMINISTRATION: ADMINISTRATIVE SERVICE   *National Association of College and University Business Officers*, Chapter 5:2, p. 14.

Assets
FASB:CS-6   *Elements of Financial Statements*, ¶¶ 25 and 26.

Inventories and Deferred Charges
COLLEGE AND UNIVERSITY BUSINESS ADMINISTRATION: ADMINISTRATIVE SERVICE   *National Association of College and University Business Officers*, Chapter 5:2, p. 6.

Investments
AICPA INDUSTRY AUDIT GUIDE   *Audits of Colleges and Universities*, pp. 8 and 9.
COLLEGE AND UNIVERSITY BUSINESS ADMINISTRATION: ADMINISTRATIVE SERVICE   *National Association of College and University Business Officers*, Chapter 5:1, p. 6.
ACCOUNTING RESEARCH BULLETIN NO. 43   *Restatement and Revision of Accounting Research Bulletins*, Chapter 3A, ¶ 9.
APB-21   *Interest on Receivables and Payables*, ¶ 15.
FASB-57   *Related Party Disclosures*.

Plant Assets and Related Liabilities
AICPA INDUSTRY AUDIT GUIDE   *Audits of Colleges and Universities*, p. 8.
COLLEGE AND UNIVERSITY BUSINESS ADMINISTRATION: ADMINISTRATIVE SERVICE   *National Association of College and University Business Officers*, Chapter 5:4, pp. 1-3.
FASB-34   *Capitalization of Interest Cost*, ¶¶ 13 and 17.
FASB-62   *Capitalization of Interest Cost in Situations Involving Certain Tax Exempt Borrowings and Certain Gifts and Grants*, ¶¶ 3 and 4.

Assets Held by Sponsoring Religious Groups
COLLEGE AND UNIVERSITY BUSINESS ADMINISTRATION: ADMINISTRATIVE SERVICE   *National Association of College and University Business Officers*, Chapter 5:1, pp. 6 and 7.

Liabilities
FASB:CS-6   *Elements of Financial Statements*, ¶¶ 35 and 36.
AICPA INDUSTRY AUDIT GUIDE   *Audits of Colleges and Universities*, p. 7.
COLLEGE AND UNIVERSITY BUSINESS ADMINISTRATION: ADMINISTRATIVE SERVICE   *National Association of College and University Business Officers*, Chapter 5:1, p. 5.

Interfund and Interdepartmental Transactions
COLLEGE AND UNIVERSITY BUSINESS ADMINISTRATION: ADMINISTRATIVE SERVICE   *National Association of College and University Business Officers*, Chapter 5:1, p. 4.

Nonmandatory Transfers
SOP 74-8   *Financial Accounting and Reporting by Colleges and Universities*, p. 104 as reproduced in Audits of Colleges and Universities.
COLLEGE AND UNIVERSITY BUSINESS ADMINISTRATION: ADMINISTRATIVE SERVICE   *National Association of College and University Business Officers*, Chapter 5:2, pp. 5 and 12-14.

Mandatory Transfers
SOP 74-8   *Financial Accounting and Reporting by Colleges and Universities*, p. 104 as reproduced in Audits of Colleges and Universities.
COLLEGE AND UNIVERSITY BUSINESS ADMINISTRATION: ADMINISTRATIVE SERVICE   *National Association of College and University Business Officers*, Chapter 5:2, pp. 5 and 12-14.

Interfund Borrowing
COLLEGE AND UNIVERSITY BUSINESS ADMINISTRATION: ADMINISTRATIVE SERVICE   *National Association of College and University Business Officers*, Chapter 5:1:1, p. 1.

Interdepartmental Transactions
SOP 74-8   *Financial Accounting and Reporting by Colleges and Universities*, pp. 89, 90, and 98 as reproduced in Audits of Colleges and Universities.
COLLEGE AND UNIVERSITY BUSINESS ADMINISTRATION: ADMINISTRATIVE SERVICE   *National Association of College and University Business Officers*, Chapter 5:2, pp. 2 and 6.

College and University Funds
AICPA INDUSTRY AUDIT GUIDE   *Audits of Colleges and Universities*, p. 6.
COLLEGE AND UNIVERSITY BUSINESS ADMINISTRATION: ADMINISTRATIVE SERVICE   *National Association of College and University Business Officers*, Chapter 5:1, p. 4.

Current Fund—Unrestricted
SOP 74-8   *Financial Accounting and Reporting by Colleges and Universities*, pp. 87-106 as reproduced in Audits of Colleges and Universities.
COLLEGE AND UNIVERSITY BUSINESS ADMINISTRATION: ADMINISTRATIVE SERVICE   *National Association of College and University Business Officers*, Chapter 5:2, pp. 1-14.

Current Fund—Restricted
SOP 74-8   *Financial Accounting and Reporting by Colleges and Universities*, pp. 87-106 as reproduced in Audits of Colleges and Universities.
COLLEGE AND UNIVERSITY BUSINESS ADMINISTRATION: ADMINISTRATIVE SERVICE   *National Association of College and University Business Officers*, Chapter 5:2, pp. 1-14.

Loan Funds
AICPA INDUSTRY AUDIT GUIDE   *Audits of Colleges and Universities*, pp. 32 and 33.
COLLEGE AND UNIVERSITY BUSINESS ADMINISTRATION: ADMINISTRATIVE SERVICE   *National Association of College and University Business Officers*, Chapter 5:3, pp. 1 and 2.

Endowment and Similar Funds
AICPA INDUSTRY AUDIT GUIDE   *Audits of Colleges and Universities*, pp. 36-42.
COLLEGE AND UNIVERSITY BUSINESS ADMINISTRATION: ADMINISTRATIVE SERVICE   *National Association of College and University Business Officers*, Chapter 5:3, pp. 2-4.

Annuity and Life Income Funds
AICPA INDUSTRY AUDIT GUIDE   *Audits of Colleges and Universities*, pp. 50-53.

COLLEGE AND UNIVERSITY BUSINESS ADMINISTRATION: ADMINISTRATIVE SERVICE *National Association of College and University Business Officers*, Chapter 5:3, pp. 4 and 5.

Plant Funds
AICPA INDUSTRY AUDIT GUIDE *Audits of Colleges and Universities*, pp. 44-48.
COLLEGE AND UNIVERSITY BUSINESS ADMINISTRATION: ADMINISTRATIVE SERVICE *National Association of College and University Business Officers*, Chapter 5:4, pp. 1-3.

Agency Funds
AICPA INDUSTRY AUDIT GUIDE *Audits of Colleges and Universities*, pp. 53 and 54.
COLLEGE AND UNIVERSITY BUSINESS ADMINISTRATION: ADMINISTRATIVE SERVICE *National Association of College and University Business Officers*, Chapter 5:3, pp. 5 and 6.

Financial Statements
AICPA INDUSTRY AUDIT GUIDE *Audits of Colleges and Universities*, pp. 55-59.
COLLEGE AND UNIVERSITY BUSINESS ADMINISTRATION: ADMINISTRATIVE SERVICE *Administrative Service National Association of College and University Business Officers*, Chapter 5:7.

Supplementary Material and Schedules
AICPA INDUSTRY AUDIT GUIDE *Audits of Colleges and Universities*, p. 58.

Accounting Changes
AICPA INDUSTRY AUDIT GUIDE *Audits of Colleges and Universities*, pp. 58 and 59.

Resources Held by Others
AICPA INDUSTRY AUDIT GUIDE *Audits of Colleges and Universities*, pp. 10 and 11.
COLLEGE AND UNIVERSITY BUSINESS ADMINISTRATION: ADMINISTRATIVE SERVICE *National Association of College and University Business Officers*, Chapter 5:3, p. 6.

CERTAIN NONPROFIT ORGANIZATIONS

BASIC CONCEPTS AND STANDARDS

There are a variety of nonprofit organizations that may be subject to some degree of control by a governmental unit. In addition to hospitals (see Chapter 80) and colleges and universities (see Chapter 81), a governmental unit (oversight unit) may exercise oversight responsibility over nonprofit organizations such as libraries, museums, other cultural institutions, performing arts organizations, public broadcasting stations, and research and scientific organizations. NCGA-3 (Defining the Governmental Reporting Entity), which is discussed in Chapter 4, established criteria that should be used to determine whether a governmental unit has oversight responsibility over a nonprofit organization.

Rather than attempt to address the accounting and reporting issues of each individual organization, the AICPA has grouped these various nonprofit organizations into a broad category referred to as "certain nonprofit organizations." Accounting and reporting standards applicable to certain nonprofit organizations controlled by state or local governments are established by the following pronouncements:

- AICPA Audit and Accounting Guide (Audits of Certain Nonprofit Organizations)
- AICPA SOP 78-10 (Accounting Principles and Reporting Practices for Certain Nonprofit Organizations)

The guidelines established in these two publications are broader than the guidelines established for hospitals and colleges and universities because of the diverse nonprofit organizations covered by the publications just listed.

> **OBSERVATION:** *The AICPA has recommended accounting and reporting standards for voluntary health and welfare organizations (Audits of Voluntary Health and Welfare Organizations), but these organizations would not fall under the influence of a state or local government and, therefore, are not discussed in this guide.*

SOP 78-10 was issued in 1978, but no effective date was established for the promulgation. FASB-32 (Specialized Accounting and Reporting Principles and Practices in AICPA Statements of Position and Guides on Accounting and Auditing Matters) identifies AICPA SOPs as sources for preferable accounting principles for purposes of justifying a change in accounting principles as required by APB-20 (Accounting Changes).

Basis of Accounting

An organization's accounting basis determines when transactions and economic events are reflected in the entity's financial statements. In NCGA-1 (Governmental Accounting and Financial Reporting Principles) it is noted that a basis of accounting refers to "when revenues, expenditures, expenses, and transfers—and related assets and liabilities—are recognized in the accounts and reported in the financial statements." SOP 78-10 concludes that certain nonprofit organizations should use the accrual accounting method as their basis of accounting.

In FASB:CS-1 (Objectives of Financial Reporting by Business Enterprises), accrual accounting is described in the following manner:

> Accrual accounting attempts to record the financial effects on an enterprise of transactions and other events and circumstances that have cash consequences for an enterprise in the periods in which those transactions, events, and circumstances occur, rather than only in the periods in which cash is received or paid by the enterprise. Accrual accounting is concerned with the process by which cash expended on resources and activities is returned as more (or perhaps less) cash to the enterprise, not just with the beginning and end of the process.

The accrual accounting basis includes such essential elements as the (1) deferral of expenditures and the subsequent amortization of the deferred cost (prepaid expenses, deferred cost, etc.), (2) deferral of revenues until they are earned (grants and restricted gifts), and (3) capitalization of certain expenditures and the subsequent depreciation of the capitalized cost. SOP 78-10 describes accrual accounting as the recognition of goods and services purchased as assets or expenses at the time the related liabilities arise, which is normally when title to the goods passes or when the services are received.

Although certain nonprofit organizations should use the accrual

Certain Nonprofit Organizations

basis of accounting, transactions and events that affect these organizations are usually recorded in a variety of specialized funds in much the same manner as the various funds used by governmental units. Fund accounting facilitates the accounting for resources and transactions that are restricted in some manner by external parties or donor agreements. SOP 78-10 does not require the use of a fund accounting format for financial reporting; however, when an organization decides not to report on a fund basis, all material restrictions must be disclosed and reporting requirements established by the SOP must be followed. Financial reporting requirements are discussed later in the chapter (see section entitled Financial Statements).

Measurement Focus

The measurement focus for an entity is concerned with the inflow and outflow of all resources that affect the organization during an accounting period. The entity's balance sheet should reflect those resources that are available to meet current obligations and that are to be used in the delivery of the service provided by the nonprofit entity. The activity statement of the nonprofit organization should summarize those resources received and those consumed during the period.

The measurement focus of those entities grouped by the AICPA in the certain nonprofit organization category is the flow of economic resources. The flow of economic resources refers to all of the assets available to the nonprofit organization for the purpose of providing its services to the group it serves. When the flow of economic resources is applied on an accrual basis for a nonprofit organization, all assets and liabilities, both current and long-term, would be presented in the organization's balance sheet. The key differences between the measurement focus/basis of accounting used by certain nonprofit organizations and the accounting model used by governmental funds are summarized as follows:

- Fixed assets would be recorded in the entity's balance sheet net of accumulated depreciation and not in the General Fixed Assets Account Group.
- Long-term debt would be recorded in the entity's balance sheet and not in the General Long-Term Debt Account Group.
- The entity's fund balance would represent the net assets (total assets minus total liabilities) available to the entity, and not only the net assets available to pay current expenditures or existing debt arising from operations.

Certain Nonprofit Organizations

The nonprofit organization's activity statement would include all costs of providing its services during the period. These costs would include depreciation, the cost of supplies consumed during the period, and other operating expenses. There would be a matching on the activity statement of revenues earned and support received during the period, with the total cost of providing the entity's services. Although there is no attempt to measure net income for a nonprofit organization, the excess of resources received over resources consumed (or vice versa) should be identified on the activity statement.

Budgetary System and Accounts

A budget of a nonprofit organization is a strategy for financial operations which provides a basis for the planning, controlling, and evaluating activities of a nonprofit organization. Neither the AICPA Audit and Accounting Guide nor the AICPA SOP require that a nonprofit organization adopt a budget or integrate budgetary accounts into its financial accounting system. Nonetheless, as described in NCGA-1 (Governmental Accounting and Financial Reporting Principles), the use of a budget by an entity is obviously a recognized method of controlling an organization's expenditures and evaluating the effectiveness of its management. Thus, if deemed necessary, a nonprofit organization may integrate its budget into its financial accounting system.

> **OBSERVATION:** *Although the two AICPA publications do not discuss the need to use an encumbrance system, there are general references to an encumbrance system in the two publications. Thus, each nonprofit organization must determine whether an encumbrance system is a necessary part of its accounting control procedures. Whether or not an encumbrance system is used has no financial reporting consequences, since encumbrances do not represent expenses of the period. Significant commitments outstanding at the end of a period, whether or not represented by an outstanding encumbrance, should be disclosed in an organization's financial statements.*

ACCOUNTS AND TRANSACTIONS

A nonprofit organization records transactions and events in a manner that is basically consistent with accounting principles used by commercial enterprises. Transactions and events should be recorded based on the accounting standards established by FASB pronouncements except when the GASB has addressed the accounting issue. When a nonprofit organization's financial statements are presented as part of the governmental unit's combined financial statements, GASB pronouncements must be observed.

Transactions and events that affect a nonprofit organization are generally recorded in a variety of funds, in a manner consistent with the basic governmental accounting model. Because of the diversity of entities that may be classified in the certain nonprofit organization category, there is no complete list of fund groups that should be used by these organizations. The following is a series of fund groups that generally would be sufficient to record most of the routine transactions and events that would affect a nonprofit entity:

- Operating Funds
  - Unrestricted
  - Restricted
- Endowment Funds
- Plant Funds

Routine transactions and events of certain nonprofit organizations are discussed below, along with the fund groups used to account for the transactions and events.

Revenues and Other Sources of Assets

FASB:CS-6 (Elements of Financial Statements) defines revenues as "inflows or other enhancements of assets of an entity, or settlements of its liabilities from delivering or producing goods, rendering services, or other activities that constitute the entity's ongoing major or central operations." Revenues, as established in APB Statement-4 (Basic Concepts and Accounting Principles Underlying Financial Statements of Business Enterprises), should be recognized when the earnings process is complete, or virtually complete, and an exchange has taken place. In general, revenues for nonprofit organizations should be accrued when the services are delivered. As described below there are a number of revenue sources and other sources of assets for nonprofit organizations.

There are three broad external sources of financing for nonprofit organizations. These categories, which should be used as captions on the entity's activity statement, are (1) revenues, (2) support, and (3) capital additions. (On the activity statement, the categories *revenues* and *support* may be combined into a single caption.)

Revenues   The Audit and Accounting Guide defines revenues as follows:

> Gross increases in assets, gross decreases in liabilities, or a combination of both from delivering or producing goods, rendering services, or other earning activities of an organization during any period.

Many nonprofit organizations generate revenue in much the same manner as a commercial enterprise. The general revenue sources include (1) fees from the performance of services (membership dues, admission fees, etc.), (2) sales of publications and other items (subscriptions to periodicals, advertising space fees, sales of records, etc.), (3) income, and gains and losses from investments, and (4) reimbursements from third parties for services provided to others. Generally, nonprofit organizations should use the accrual method to account for revenues. (For the exception to this generalization, see the following section entitled Accounting for Investments.)

Specific guidance for the recognition of revenue, as suggested by the Audit and Accounting Guide, is summarized below:

Nature of revenue activity	Accounting treatment
Subscriptions, sale of goods, and sale of services	Recognize as revenue in the period the good is sold or the service is provided
Membership dues	Recognize (amortize) as revenue over the term of the membership
Nonrefundable initiation and life membership fees (where future dues will cover the cost of future services or no future service will be provided)	Recognize as revenue when due
Nonrefundable initiation and life membership fees (where future dues will not cover the cost of future services)	Recognize (amortize) as revenue over the expected life of the membership

Certain Nonprofit Organizations

Support The Audit and Accounting Guide differentiates between revenues and support. Support is defined as "the conveyance of property from one person or organization to another without consideration," and includes donations, gifts, grants, and bequests. Support received from external sources may be classified as unrestricted or restricted resources.

Unrestricted support Unrestricted resources that are received have no external restrictions and may be used for any purpose as determined by the governing board of the nonprofit organization. Gifts, grants, and bequests, should be recorded at their estimated fair market value and reported as support in the entity's Unrestricted Operating Fund. For example, if investments of $50,000 are received and can be used in any manner deemed appropriate by the nonprofit organization, the gift would be recorded as follows:

OPERATING FUND—UNRESTRICTED
Investments   50,000
    Support—Private Gifts, Grants,
        And Bequests   50,000

Restricted support Current restricted resources may be used for current operations but they must be expended in a way that satisfies restrictions imposed by the donor or grant agreement. Restricted gifts, grants, and bequests should be recorded at their estimated fair market value, and initially reported as deferred support in the Restricted Operating Fund. The deferred support account is a liability and should not be reported as part of the fund balance section of the nonprofit organization's balance sheet. When expenses specified by the donor or grantor are incurred, an amount equal to the incurred expenses should be recognized as support.

To illustrate the accounting for current restricted support, assume that a nonprofit organization receives $100,000 as a gift that is to be used for specific operating expenses. The following entry would be made to record the receipt of the restricted resources:

OPERATING FUND—RESTRICTED
Cash   100,000
    Deferred Support   100,000

Subsequently, if it is assumed that qualifying expenses of $80,000 are incurred, the following entries would be made:

OPERATING FUND—RESTRICTED

Expenses	80,000	
Cash		80,000
Deferred Support	80,000	
Support—Private Gifts, Grants,		
And Bequests		80,000

Capital Additions The Audit and Accounting Guide defines capital additions for nonprofit organizations as follows:

> Gifts, grants, bequests, investment income, and gains and losses on investments, restricted either permanently or for a period of time by parties outside of the organization to Endowment and Loan Funds. Capital additions also include similar resources restricted for fixed asset additions, but only to the extent expended during the year.

Typical restrictions imposed by the donor or grant agreement may include such items as (1) requirements that the resources not be used for a stated period of time, or until after the occurrence of a specific event, (2) stipulation that only property, plant, and equipment may be acquired, or (3) establishment of a permanent capital amount, whereby only the related investment income is available for expenditures.

Gifts, grants, bequests, and related investment transactions that are classified as capital additions should be recorded at their estimated fair market value. Due to the nature of capital additions, they should not be used to compute the "excess (deficiency) of revenue and support over (under) expenses" as reported on the entity's activity statement.

To illustrate the accounting for capital additions, assume that a nonprofit organization receives as a gift securities that have an estimated fair market value of $75,000. The gift cannot be expended; however, income related to the investment can be used to finance current operations of the entity. The receipt of the gift would be recorded as follows:

ENDOWMENT FUND

Investments	75,000	
Capital Additions—Private Gifts,		
Grants, And Bequests		75,000

Certain Nonprofit Organizations

Restricted gifts, grants, bequests, or gains on the sale of assets that can be used for current operations, but have not been used in this manner because qualifying expenses have not been incurred, should be recorded as restricted support and not as capital additions. Also, unrestricted amounts that have been designated as nonexpendable by the entity's governing board should not be recorded as capital additions; however, such designations should be adequately disclosed in the entity's financial statements.

Resources that are received and restricted to the purchase of property, plant, and equipment should be initially recorded as deferred capital support (liability account). Subsequently, when qualifying capital expenditures are incurred, an amount equal to the expenditure should be recorded as a capital addition. For example, if $70,000 is received as a gift and the amount is restricted for the purchase of equipment, the following entry would be made:

PLANT FUND
Cash	70,000	
Deferred Capital Support		70,000

If $50,000 of equipment is acquired that satisfies the restrictions imposed by the donor agreement, the following entries would be made:

PLANT FUND
Equipment	50,000	
Cash		50,000
Deferred Capital Support	50,000	
Capital Additions—Private Gifts,		
Grants, And Bequests		50,000

Pledges Nonprofit organizations often obtain pledges of support from various external parties. Pledges that are legally enforceable should be accrued, net of an estimate for uncollectible pledges. If the expected resources from pledges are to be used for current operations and are not restricted, they should be reported as support in the entity's Unrestricted Operating Fund. On the other hand, if the resources to be received are restricted for specific current operations, they should be recorded as deferred support in the entity's Restricted Operating Fund. For example, if pledges for current opera-

Certain Nonprofit Organizations

tions total $70,000, and for restricted current operations total $50,000, and it is estimated that 10% of the pledges will be dishonored, the pledges would be recorded as follows:

OPERATING FUND — UNRESTRICTED
Pledges Receivable   70,000
    Allowance For Uncollectible Pledges   7,000
    Support — Private Gifts, Grants,
      And Bequests   63,000

OPERATING FUND — RESTRICTED
Pledges Receivable   50,000
    Allowance For Uncollectible Pledges   5,000
    Deferred Support   45,000

Pledges should be recognized as support in the period designated by the donor. When the designated period extends beyond the balance sheet date, the pledged amount should be recognized as deferred support rather than as support. When no period has been designated by the donor, support should be recognized in the period in which the entity expects to realize the pledge.

Pledges that are restricted to the purchase of property, plant, and equipment should be recorded as deferred capital support. When the plant assets are acquired, the deferred capital support should be reclassified as a capital addition for the period.

Contributed Services   Many nonprofit organizations receive a considerable amount of support through services contributed by volunteers. From an accounting perspective it is difficult to assign a fair value to these services and the Audit and Accounting Guide generally concludes that contributed services should not be recorded as support by a nonprofit organization. However, support can be recognized if all of the following conditions exist:

- The services performed are significant and form an integral part of the efforts of the organization as it is presently constituted; the services would be performed by salaried personnel if donated or contributed services were not available for the organization to accomplish its purpose, and the organization would continue this program or activity.

- The organization controls the employment and duties of the service donors. The organization is able to influence their activities in a way comparable to the control it would exercise over employees with similar responsibilities. This includes control over time, location, nature, and performance of donated or contributed services.
- The organization has a clearly measurable basis for the amount to be recorded.
- The services of the reporting organization are not principally intended for the benefit of its members. Accordingly, donated and contributed services would not normally be recorded by organizations such as religious communities, professional and trade associations, labor unions, political parties, fraternal organizations, and social and country clubs.

When contributed services are received by a nonprofit organization, the organization should describe in its notes to the financial statements the methods used to value, record, and report such services. There should also be a description of contributed services that were recorded and those that were not recorded.

Contributed Materials and Facilities In addition to receiving services from volunteers, a nonprofit organization may receive free materials and the use of certain facilities.

Materials should be recorded as support (and eventually as an expense) based on their estimated fair market value. When a reasonable fair market value cannot be determined, no support should be recognized. On the other hand, if the nonprofit organization simply receives materials for the purpose of passing them on to charitable beneficiaries, no support should be recognized.

The use of facilities should be recorded as support based on the estimated fair market value of the use of the property. The support should be recorded in the period in which the property is in use by the nonprofit organization.

Investment Income and Realized Gains and Losses Various funds of a nonprofit organization may hold investments and the related income. Realized gains and losses from the disposition of these investments may either be unrestricted or restricted. As summarized below the accounting treatment of investment related transactions depends upon a number of factors:

Nature of investment transaction	Accounting treatment
Unrestricted investment income for all funds	Report as revenue in the current operating fund's activity statement as investment revenue
Unrestricted gains and losses for unrestricted and restricted current funds	Report in the current operating fund's activity statement as an element in computing the excess (deficiency) of revenues and support over (under) expenses
Restricted investment income and restricted gains and losses for investments of current restricted funds and restricted plant funds	Report as deferred amount in the fund's balance sheet
Restricted expendable income from investments of endowment funds	Report as deferred amount in the fund's balance sheet
Investment income from endowment funds that must be added to principal per donor agreement	Report as capital additions
Gains and losses on endowment fund investments	Report as capital additions or deductions

Expenses

FASB:CS-6 defines expenses as "outflows or other using up of assets or incurrences of liabilities from delivering or producing goods, rendering services, or carrying out other activities that constitute the entity's ongoing major or central operations." The recognition of an expense by a nonprofit organization as described in APB Statement-4 and FASB:CS-5 (Recognition and Measurement in Financial Statements of Business Enterprises) should be consistent with the following guidelines:

- Associating cause and effect—Some expenses (such as cost of providing services for a fee) are recognized upon recognition of revenues that result directly and jointly from the same transactions or events as the expenses.

- Systematic and rational allocation—Some expenses (such as depreciation) are allocated by systematic and rational procedures to the period during which the related assets are expected to provide benefits.
- Immediate recognition—Many expenses (such as administrative expenses) are recognized during the period in which cash is spent or liabilities are incurred for goods and services that are used up either simultaneously with acquisition or soon after.

Expenses of a nonprofit organization should be reported on the entity's activity statement and may be classified on a functional basis or on a natural (or some other) basis.

Functional Classification Basis Nonprofit organizations that receive significant support from the general public or federated fund-raising, or similar groups, should report their expenses on a functional classification basis.

Program services Expenses should be classified in a manner that describes the nonprofit organization's service activities. The specific identification of the program services is dependent upon the nature of the nonprofit organization. For example, a nonprofit museum's classifications may include program services such as exhibits, education, and curatorial and conservation. For a nonprofit library program, services may include research library, educational services, and community services. Each program service should be adequately described and should include all related service costs.

When an organization is required to remit a portion of its support to its affiliated state or national organization, the remittance should be treated as a reduction of support and not as an expense. Other remittances should be treated as a program service expense.

Management and general costs Costs that cannot be related to a specific program or fund-raising activity should be classified as management and general costs. These costs may include budgeting and accounting expenses, and salaries and related expenses of the chief executive and his or her staff. General costs related to the supervision of program services and supporting services should be prorated among those services.

Fund-raising and other supporting services All direct and indirect costs of fund-raising should be reported as a fund-raising expense. When unsolicited merchandise is sent to prospective contributors, the cost of the merchandise should be separately disclosed as a fund-raising expense. If an organization sells merchandise or stages events (theatre parties, etc.) in order to raise funds, the cost of the merchandise or event should be offset against the proceeds of the endeavor and not categorized as a fund-raising expense; however, the cost of the merchandise or event should be disclosed in the financial statements.

Generally, fund-raising costs are not subject to deferral and must be expensed immediately. Fund-raising costs may be deferred under the following conditions:

- Costs of printed materials and other items that will be used in future fund-raising campaigns
- Costs specifically related to pledges or restricted contributions that have already been received and recorded as deferred revenue and support, if it is clear that the contributor intended the donation to be used to cover such costs

Potential contributors and other users of financial statements for certain nonprofit organizations are particularly interested in the amount of resources an organization devotes to fund-raising activities. A difficult allocation problem arises when fund-raising activities are conducted jointly with other activities. The allocation of joint costs for fund-raising and information material and activities was addressed in SOP 87-2 (Accounting for Joint Costs of Informational Materials and Activities for Not-for-Profit Organizations that Include a Fund-Raising Appeal).

SOP 87-2 establishes the basic standard that unless it can be otherwise demonstrated *all joint costs of informational materials and services that include a fund-raising appeal should be reported as fund-raising expense.* When it can be demonstrated that a program or management and general expense has been incurred, the joint costs should be allocated among fund-raising expense, program expense, and management and general expense.

> **OBSERVATION:** *SOP 87-2 does not discuss methods that could be used to allocate joint costs among various expense classifications.*

Factors that should be considered in determining whether a program or management and general function activity has taken place include the following:

- Content of the non-fund-raising part of the activity
- Audience being addressed by the activity
- Written instructions to external party that conducted the activity
- Minutes of the meeting of the board of directors in which the purpose of the activity was discussed

All of these factors, plus other relevant facts, should be considered in determining whether all or a portion of the joint costs of an activity should be classified as fund-raising expense.

When joint costs of informational materials and activities that include fund-raising appeals have been incurred based on the criteria established in SOP 87-2, the following disclosures should be made in the financial statements:

- Joint costs for informational material and activities have included fund-raising appeals
- Amount of the joint costs allocated
- Amount of joint costs allocated to (1) fund-raising expenses, (2) specific program(s), and (3) management and general expenses

Allocation of common costs All organizations incur common costs that are not specifically identifiable with a particular function. Such costs might include rental costs, general fund-raising costs, and salaries of personnel that are involved in a variety of activities during an accounting period. Reasonable allocation methods should be adopted to apportion such common costs to the various functional categories. The methods used to allocate these costs should be disclosed in the nonprofit organization's financial statements.

While the Audit and Accounting Guide does not promulgate specific allocation methods for multiple function expenses and common costs, the following procedures are described in an appendix to the publication as illustrations of schemes that ordinarily would result in a reasonable allocation of common costs:

- A study of the organization's activities may be made at the start of each fiscal year to determine the best practicable allocation methods. The study should include an evaluation of the preceding year's time records or activity reports of key personnel, the use of space, the consumption of supplies and postage, and so forth. The results of the study should be reviewed periodically, and the allocation methods should be revised, if necessary, to reflect significant changes in the nature or level of the organization's current activities.

- Periodic time and expense records may be kept by employees who spend time on more than one function as a basis for allocating salaries and related costs. The records should indicate the nature of the activities in which the employee is involved. If the functions do not vary significantly from period to period, the preparation of time reports for selected test periods during the year might be sufficient.
- Automobile and travel costs may be allocated on the basis of the expense or time reports of the employees involved.
- Telephone expense may be allocated on the basis of use by extensions, generally following the charge assigned to the salary of the employee using the telephone, after making direct charges for the toll calls or other service attributable to specific functions.
- Stationery, supplies, and postage costs may be allocated based on a study of their use.
- Occupancy costs may be allocated on the basis of a factor determined from a study of the function of the personnel using the space involved.
- Depreciation and rental of equipment may be allocated based on asset usage.

Natural (or Some Other) Classification Basis Nonprofit organizations that receive no significant support from contributions from the general public or federated fund-raising, or similar groups, are encouraged by the Audit and Accounting Guide to report expenses on a functional basis; however, a natural classification basis or some other basis is permitted. Expense items that would compose the natural classification basis include such items as salaries, depreciation, insurance, and supplies. When a basis other than the functional classification approach is used to categorize expenses, notes to the financial statements should include adequate descriptions of the nonprofit organization's basic programs.

Depreciation A nonprofit organization's property, plant, and equipment that is exhaustible should be depreciated over their estimated useful lives. Depreciation is computed in the same manner as a commercial enterprise would determine its depreciation expense. Depreciation expense should be shown in the fund group that includes the organization's property, plant, and equipment. For example, if a separate Plant Fund is used by an organization, depreciation expense would be shown as an expense of the Plant Fund and should be classified on a functional basis like any other expense.

The Audit and Accounting Guide concludes that the following exhaustible assets need not be depreciated:

- Landmarks
- Monuments
- Cathedrals
- Historical treasures
- Structures used primarily as houses of worship

Collections owned by museums, art galleries, and the like that have a limited display life should be depreciated if they are capitalized (for guidelines on capitalizing collections, see a later section of this chapter entitled Assets—Collections).

With the issuance of FASB-93 (Recognition of Depreciation by Not-for-Profit Organizations), certain nonprofit organizations that prepare their financial statements in accordance with accounting and reporting standards established by the AICPA SOP 78-10 (Accounting Principles and Reporting Practices for Certain Nonprofit Organizations) were required to change their accounting for and reporting of depreciable assets. In order to allow the GASB to continue its research in this area and to avoid the adoption of new rules established by the FASB that may be changed once again based on action subsequently taken by the GASB, the GASB issued GASB-8 (Applicability of FASB Statement No. 93, Recognition of Depreciation by Not-for-Profit Organizations, to Certain State and Local Governmental Entities). GASB-8 exempts certain public nonprofit organizations from requirements established by FASB-93.

Grants Grants made by nonprofit organizations to other organizations should be recorded as an expense when the recipient organization is entitled to the grant. Accrual usually occurs when the governing board of the nonprofit organization approves the grant or notifies the recipient organization that it is entitled to the grant.

Grants that extend over more than one year and require no subsequent review or approval, other than routine performance on the part of the recipient organization, should be recorded as an expense and liability at the point of the initial approval of the grant. When the multi-year grant is subject to revocation regardless of performance by the recipient organization, the grant should not be accrued. Grants subject to periodic review and approval should be recorded as an expense when reapproval occurs; however, the nature of the remaining but unrecorded grants should be described in notes to the financial statements.

Assets

FASB:CS-6 defines assets as "probable future economic benefits obtained or controlled by a particular entity as a result of past transactions or events and possessing the following essential characteristics:

- It embodies a probable future benefit that involves a capacity to contribute directly or indirectly to future net cash inflows.
- A particular enterprise can obtain the benefit and control others' access to it.
- The transaction or other event giving rise to the enterprise's right to control of the benefit has already occurred."

Assets acquired by certain nonprofit organizations should be recorded at their cost. Generally, when assets are donated by external parties, they should be recorded at their estimated fair market value at the date of the gift. For the most part, accounting principles applicable to commercial enterprises should be observed by nonprofit organizations identified in the Audit and Accounting Guide. The unique features of accounting for assets held by these nonprofit organizations are discussed below.

Investments A nonprofit organization should record the purchase of investments at their cost. When investments are given to a nonprofit organization, they should be recorded at their estimated fair market value. Subsequent to the acquisition or receipt of investments, the following accounting methods should be used to account for the various investments that may be held by a nonprofit organization:

Type of investment	Accounting methods
Noncurrent marketable debt securities	(1) Amortized cost, (2) market value, or (3) lower of amortized cost or market
Current and noncurrent marketable equity securities and current marketable debt securities	(1) Market value or (2) lower of cost or market
Other investments (such as real estate, or oil and gas interests)	(1) Fair value or (2) lower of cost or fair value

The same accounting method should be used for all investments in a particular investment group. For example, all current marketable equity securities must be accounted for using a single accounting method. If investments are accounted for using a method other than market value, the market value for a particular investment group should be disclosed in the financial statements.

When investments are carried at market values, the change in the investment valuation from period to period should be accounted for in the following manner:

Investments of	Accounting treatment
Unrestricted and current restricted funds (where capital changes are unrestricted)	Increase or decrease should be used to compute excess (deficiency) of revenue and support over (under) expenses
Current restricted funds (where capital changes are restricted) and unrestricted plant funds	Increase or decrease should be reported as a deferred amount
Endowment funds	Increase or decrease should be reported as a capital addition or deduction

Investments carried at the lower of (amortized) cost or market should be based on the aggregate cost and market value of the fund group's investments. Writeoffs may be recovered in subsequent periods, but investments should not be stated at an amount greater than original (amortized) cost. Writeoffs and recoveries related to noncurrent investments should be added or subtracted from the fund balance account. Writeoffs and recoveries related to current investments should be accounted for in the activity statement in the same way that the fund accounts for realized gains and losses. (Investments in Current Restricted Funds should be considered current investments when accounting for writeoffs and recoveries.)

Except for Life Income and Custodial Funds, notes to the financial statements should summarize all realized and unrealized gains and losses and investment income for the period.

Separate funds of a nonprofit organization may combine their resources in a single investment pool. Once the pooling occurs, specific identification of a fund's investments is lost, and investment units, or some other method, must be devised to periodically identify and allocate the equity interest of each fund and the related investment income and investment gains and losses.

Fixed Assets Property, plant, and equipment owned by a nonprofit organization should be recorded at original cost if purchased by the organization, and at fair market value if received as a donation.

> **OBSERVATION:** *FASB-32 (Specialized Accounting and Reporting Principles and Practices in AICPA Statements of Position and Guides on Accounting and Auditing Matters) identifies AICPA SOPs as preferable accounting principles for purposes of justifying a change in accounting principle as discussed in APB Statement-20 (Accounting Changes). This means that a nonprofit organization can, but is not required to, adopt an accounting method endorsed by an SOP. If historical cost or fair value information is not available, other bases such as insurance appraisals and estimated replacement cost may be used to value fixed assets; however, these alternative valuation methods can be used only at the time a nonprofit organization adopts the accounting methods endorsed by SOP 78-10.*

Rental agreements that represent property leased by nonprofit organizations should be evaluated to determine whether the lease should be capitalized by applying standards established by FASB-13 (Accounting for Leases, as amended).

As discussed earlier in this chapter, nonprofit organizations should depreciate their fixed assets over the estimated useful lives of the property.

The financial statements should disclose the basis of valuation, depreciation methods used, and the amount, if any, of fixed assets pledged as security for external financing.

Collections Nonprofit organizations may own inexhaustible collections of works of art and other similar items. Generally these collections need not be capitalized because it is often difficult to value them. If the original cost or fair market value of the items can be substantiated, the collection should be capitalized. Also, if other reasonable estimates of cost or value can be made, such as appraised value, the collection should be capitalized. When collections are not capitalized, they nonetheless should appear as a line item on the organization's balance sheet with no assigned value, but with a reference to a note which adequately describes the collections.

Whether capitalized or not, inexhaustible collections of works of art and other similar items should not be depreciated. Additions to a particular collection during an accounting period should be disclosed in the financial statements, including the cost or fair value of the enhancements. Likewise, there should be adequate disclosures when a collection or part of a collection is sold or otherwise disposed of.

Liabilities

FASB:CS-6 defines liabilities as "probable future sacrifices of economic benefits arising from present obligations of a particular entity to transfer assets or provide services to other entities in the future as a result of past transactions or events." Liabilities embody the following fundamental characteristics:

- The present duty or responsibility to one or more other entities that entails settlement by probable future transfer or use of assets at a specified or determinable date, on occurrence of a specified event, or on demand
- The duty or responsibility obligates a particular enterprise, leaving it little or no discretion to avoid the future sacrifice
- The transaction or other event obligating the enterprise has already happened

The financial statements of certain nonprofit organizations present both current and noncurrent liabilities that must be paid by the organization. The current liabilities may be composed of debts such as accounts payable, deferred revenue or support, accrued expenses, and the current portion of long-term debt. Noncurrent debt may include debt instruments such as notes and bonds, and in addition, a nonprofit organization's noncurrent liabilities may include liabilities other than those that are represented by a debt instrument. For example, long-term liabilities may include capitalized leases, claims and judgments, and pension obligations. These as well as other liabilities of a nonprofit organization should be accounted for in a manner similar to the accounting and reporting standards that must be observed by commercial enterprises.

Encumbrances In order to control the level of expenses in any one period, a nonprofit organization may, but is not required to, use an encumbrance system. The resources of a nonprofit organization are committed for future payment when executory contracts such as purchase orders and specific contracts for goods and services are signed. An actual expense is not recorded until the goods are received or the service is rendered; however, control over executory contracts may be established to make sure disbursement commitments do not exceed the amount approved by the governing board of the nonprofit organization.

Encumbrances that are outstanding (unvouchered) at the end of the accounting period should be reversed by debiting the reserve for encumbrances account and crediting the encumbrances account. The amount of the outstanding encumbrances does not represent liabilities or expenses of the organization for the period; however, significant commitments should be adequately disclosed in notes to the financial statements. Disclosure may be achieved by identifying a portion of the fund balance account as designated for outstanding encumbrances.

Deferred Revenue and Support Certain resources received by or commitments made to a nonprofit organization should be classified as deferred revenue and support, and presented as a fund liability. The Audit and Accounting Guide defines deferred revenue and support as revenue or support received or recorded before it is earned, that is, before the conditions are met, in whole or in part, for which the revenue or support is received or is to be received. This classification would include the following items:

- Membership dues
- Nonrefundable initiation and life membership fees where future dues will not cover the cost of future services
- Unexpended restricted gifts, grants, and bequests
- Pledges of restricted resources to be received for current operations
- Pledges that are designated by donors for future use
- Pledges to be realized in future periods
- Restricted investment income and restricted gains and losses for investments of Current Restricted Funds and Restricted Plant Funds
- Restricted expendable income from investments of Endowment Funds

Deferred Taxes Some nonprofit organizations may engage in unrelated business activities that may be subject to federal or state taxes. When there is a difference between the timing of revenues and expenses for financial reporting purposes and tax purposes, interperiod income tax allocation procedures as established by FASB-96

(Accounting for Income Taxes) must be observed. If the income base subject to taxation is less than pretax financial income, a deferred tax credit is created and should be reported as a liability. If the income base subject to taxation is greater than pretax financial income, a deferred tax charge is created and should be reported as an asset.

Transfers and Interfund Transactions

Transfers among funds do not represent revenues, expenses, capital additions, or capital deductions for the funds involved in the transfer. Interfund transfers should be reported as additions or subtractions from the beginning balance of the fund account. Mandatory transfers (transfers made to comply with contractual agreements with external parties) should be differentiated from nonmandatory transfers (board-designated transfers). Also, transfers due to the expiration of a Term Endowment Fund should be separately identified.

Interfund Investment Transactions   Interfund investment transactions that involve a Restricted Fund should be accounted for at the fair market value of the investment sold or exchanged. The fund disposing of the investment should record any gains or losses in the same manner as it would record realized gains and losses arising from external party transactions.

Interfund Borrowings   Loans among funds should be recorded as interfund liabilities and receivables; however, if the transaction is of a permanent nature and it appears that the loan will not be repaid, the exchange should be treated as a transfer and not as a debt transaction. Differentiating between a transfer and a loan is subjective, but when a recipient fund does not have the resources to repay the disbursing fund, the transaction should be treated as a transfer.

The following should be disclosed in the financial statements for the current year and for the prior periods presented (including summary financial information presented for prior years), if applicable:

- Loans or transfers that are prohibited by law
- Material interfund borrowings involving a Restricted Fund
- Material interfund borrowings involving a fund that has a liquidity problem

NONPROFIT ORGANIZATION FUNDS

Although nonprofit organizations subject to the Audit and Accounting Guide use the same basis of accounting and measurement focus as a commercial enterprise, transactions and events that affect these organizations are accounted for in several different funds. There are two basic fund groups, namely (1) Operating Funds, that may include Current Operating Funds and Restricted Operating Funds and (2) Restricted Funds, that may include Loan Funds, Endowment Funds, Annuity and Life Income Funds, Plant Funds, and Agency Funds. It should be noted that there is no list of funds in the Audit and Accounting Guide. The circumstances surrounding the nonprofit organization and donor agreements dictate the fund that would account for specific transactions and events. Discussed and illustrated below are the more typical funds that would be used by a nonprofit organization.

Operating Funds—Unrestricted

An organization's Unrestricted Operating Fund is used to account for all unrestricted resources that are available to be expended for any current operating expenses. The sources of unrestricted resources include revenues earned by the organization (fees, sales, and investment transactions) and support received from external parties (unrestricted gifts, grants, and bequests). The uses of unrestricted resources include all direct and indirect current operational expenses related to the services provided by the nonprofit organization.

To illustrate the routine transactions that are accounted for in an Unrestricted Operating Fund of a nonprofit organization, assume that at the beginning of the fiscal year an organization had the following trial balance. Unless otherwise noted, all entries are recorded in the organization's Operating Fund—Unrestricted.

Centerville Museum
Operating Fund—Unrestricted
Trial Balance
July 1, 19X4

	Dr.	Cr.
Cash	$180,000	
Membership dues receivable	50,000	
Allowance for uncollectible dues		$ 10,000
Pledges receivable	85,000	
Allowance for uncollectible pledges		8,000
Prepaid expenses	10,000	
Investments (noncurrent)	120,000	
Accrued expenses		30,000
Notes payable (noncurrent)		800,000
Fund balance (deficit)	403,000	
	$848,000	$848,000

During the fiscal year the following transactions occurred and were recorded in the museum's Unrestricted Operating Fund as described below:

Revenues from members During the fiscal year general membership dues for 19X5 (membership year coincides with fiscal year) of $230,000 were billed, of which 10% were expected to be canceled.

Membership Dues Receivable	230,000	
Revenues—Memberships		207,000
Allowance For Uncollectible Dues		23,000

Cash collections for membership dues amounted to $220,000 and receivables of $20,000 were written off.

Cash	220,000	
Allowance For Uncollectible Dues	20,000	
Membership Dues Receivable		240,000

Revenues from admissions Admissions from individuals that visited the museum totaled $410,000.

Cash	410,000	
Revenues—Admissions		410,000

Revenues from auxiliary activities Revenues from the museum's coffee and gift shop were $278,000, and related expenses and cost of goods sold were $215,000, of which $20,000 were unpaid at the end of the fiscal year.

Cash	278,000	
Revenues—Auxiliary Activities		278,000
Expenses—Auxiliary Activities	215,000	
Cash		195,000
Accounts Payable		20,000

Unrestricted support During the fiscal year the museum received unrestricted gifts of cash ($70,000) and investments ($150,000).

Cash	70,000	
Investments (Noncurrent)	150,000	
Support—Private Gifts, Grants,		
And Bequests		220,000

Pledges of support Individuals and the business community pledged support of $400,000 which can be used for current operating expenses. It is estimated that 20% of the pledges will be dishonored.

Pledges Receivable	400,000	
Allowance For Uncollectible Pledges		80,000
Support—Private Gifts, Grants,		
And Bequests		320,000

During the year pledges of $350,000 were collected, and receivables of $65,000 were written off as dishonored.

Cash	350,000	
Allowance For Uncollectible Pledges	65,000	
Pledges Receivable		415,000

Contributed services During the fiscal year, once again certain educational services were contributed by a group of local high school teachers. The value of these services was approximately $45,000 (assume that the revenue recognition criteria established by SOP 78-10 were satisfied).

Expenses—Education	45,000	
Support—Contributed Services		45,000

Program and supporting services expenses The following expenses were paid during the year:

Program expenses		
Curatorial and conservation	$ 340,000	
Exhibits	260,000	
Education	120,000	
Supporting services expenses		
Management and general	220,000	
Fund raising	110,000	
Accrued expenses (beginning of year)	30,000	
	$1,080,000	

Expenses—Curatorial And Conservation	340,000	
Expenses—Exhibits	260,000	
Expenses—Education	120,000	
Expenses—Management And General	220,000	
Expense—Fund Raising	110,000	
Accrued Expenses	30,000	
Cash		1,080,000

At the end of the fiscal year accrued expenses representing management and general expenses amounted to $35,000.

Expenses—Management And General	35,000	
Accrued Expenses		35,000

Investment transaction (noncurrent) Investment income for the year amounted to $20,000.

Cash	20,000	
Revenues—Investment Income		20,000

Investments having a cost basis of $40,000 were sold for $65,000.

Cash	65,000	
Investments		40,000
Revenues—Net Realized Investment		
Gains (Losses)		25,000

Investments are accounted for on the lower of aggregate cost or market. At the end of the fiscal year aggregate cost was less than aggregate market for the investment portfolio.

Certain Nonprofit Organizations

Other current assets Payments for prepaid expenses totaled $25,000, and amortization of prepaid expenses amounted to $20,000 (curatorial and conservation, 30%; exhibits, 50%; management and general, 20%).

Prepaid Expenses	25,000	
Cash		25,000
Expenses—Curatorial And Conservation	6,000	
Expenses—Exhibits	10,000	
Expenses—Management And General	4,000	
Prepaid Expenses		20,000

Collections The museum owns a number of valuable collections whose cost or fair value cannot be substantiated. During the year certain existing collections were enhanced through purchases ($220,000) and donations (fair value cannot be substantiated). Part of a collection was sold during the year for $140,000.

Collections Accession (Expense Item)	220,000	
Cash		220,000
Cash	140,000	
Collections Deaccession (Revenue Item)		140,000

Liabilities During the fiscal year, early principal repayments on long-term notes totaled $140,000, while interest amounted to $70,000.

Expenses—Management And General	70,000	
Notes Payable (Noncurrent)	140,000	
Cash		210,000

Interfund transfers At the end of the fiscal year, $15,000 was transferred from the Unrestricted Operating Fund to the Plant Fund. The transfer is to be used for principal indebtedness and is a required transfer based on the mortgage agreement between the museum and a financial institution.

OPERATING FUND—UNRESTRICTED

Mandatory Transfers—Principal Indebtedness	15,000	
Cash		15,000

PLANT FUND
   Cash   15,000
      Mandatory Transfers—Principal
        Indebtedness   15,000

Equipment costing $35,000 was purchased by using resources of the Unrestricted Operating Fund (plant assets are accounted for by the museum in its Plant Fund).

OPERATING FUND—UNRESTRICTED
   Transfers—Acquisition Of Plant Assets
     By Unrestricted Operating Fund   35,000
       Cash   35,000

PLANT FUND
   Equipment   35,000
     Transfers—Acquisition Of Plant
       Assets By Unrestricted Operating
       Fund   35,000

A term endowment consisting of investments of $50,000 expired during the year and was transferred to the Unrestricted Operating Fund.

OPERATING FUND—UNRESTRICTED
   Investments (Noncurrent)   50,000
     Transfers—Expiration Of Term
       Endowments   50,000

ENDOWMENT FUND
   Transfers—Expiration Of Term
     Endowments   50,000
       Investments   50,000

Unrestricted investment income earned and received for the year by an Endowment Fund amounted to $70,000, of which $65,000 was transferred to the Unrestricted Operating Fund.

OPERATING FUND—UNRESTRICTED
   Due From Endowment Fund   70,000
     Revenues—Investment Income   70,000

   Cash   65,000
     Due from Endowment Fund   65,000

Certain Nonprofit Organizations

ENDOWMENT FUND

Cash	70,000	
Due To Unrestricted Operating Fund		70,000
Due To Unrestricted Operating Fund	65,000	
Cash		65,000

Note: Transactions that affect more than one fund group are also reproduced as illustrative entries in the other fund group.

After taking into account the transactions described above, the trial balance for the Unrestricted Operating Fund for the year ended June 30, 19X5, would be as follows:

Centerville Museum
Operating Fund—Unrestricted
Trial Balance
June 30, 19X5

	Dr.	Cr.
Cash	$ 18,000	
Membership dues receivable	40,000	
Allowance for uncollectible dues		$ 13,000
Pledges receivable	70,000	
Allowance for uncollectible pledges		23,000
Prepaid expenses	15,000	
Due from endowment fund	5,000	
Investments (noncurrent)	280,000	
Accounts payable		20,000
Accrued expenses		35,000
Notes payable (noncurrent)		660,000
Revenues—membership		207,000
Revenues—admissions		410,000
Revenues—investment income		90,000
Revenues—net realized investment gains (losses)		25,000
Revenues—auxiliary activities		278,000
Support—private gifts, grants, and bequests		540,000
Support—contributed services		45,000
Expenses—curatorial and conservation	346,000	
Expenses—exhibits	270,000	
Expenses—education	165,000	

Expenses—management and general	329,000	
Expenses—fund raising	110,000	
Expenses—auxiliary activities	215,000	
Collections accession	220,000	
Collections deaccession		140,000
Mandatory transfers—principal indebtedness	15,000	
Transfers—acquisition of plant assets by unrestricted fund	35,000	
Transfers—expiration of term endowments		50,000
Fund balance (deficit)	403,000	
	$2,536,000	$2,536,000

Operating Funds—Restricted

Restricted Operating Funds are created to account for resources that may be expended for specified current operating expenses as determined by the donor or grantor agreement. For this reason, the initial receipts of restricted resources would be recorded as deferred support (liability). When qualifying expenses are incurred, an equal amount of support is recognized.

To illustrate the routine transactions that are accounted for in a Restricted Operating Fund of a nonprofit organization, assume that at the beginning of the fiscal year an organization had the following trial balance. Unless otherwise noted, all entries are recorded in the organization's Operating Fund—Restricted:

Centerville Museum
Operating Fund—Restricted
Trial Balance
July 1, 19X4

	Dr.	Cr.
Cash	$150,000	
Pledges receivable	32,000	
Allowance for uncollectible pledges		$ 7,000
Investments	240,000	
Deferred support		410,000
Deferred investment income		5,000
	$422,000	$422,000

During the fiscal year the following transactions occurred and were recorded in the museum's Restricted Operating Fund:

Restricted support During the fiscal year, $200,000 of private gifts were received.

Cash	200,000	
Deferred Support		200,000

Qualifying current operating expenses of $330,000 as defined by various donor and grant agreements were incurred (education, $220,000; exhibits, $110,000).

Expenses—Education	220,000	
Expenses—Exhibits	110,000	
Cash		330,000
Deferred Support	330,000	
Support—Private Gifts, Grants, And Bequests		330,000

Pledges of support Individuals and the business community pledged support of $150,000, which can be used only for specified current operating expenses. It is estimated that 10% of the pledges will be dishonored.

Pledges Receivable	150,000	
Allowance For Uncollectible Pledges		15,000
Deferred Support		135,000

During the year, pledges of $120,000 were collected, and receivables of $18,000 were written off as dishonored.

Cash	120,000	
Allowance For Uncollectible Pledges	18,000	
Pledges Receivable		138,000

Current operating expenses of $125,000 that were financed by the pledge campaign were incurred (all related to curatorial and conservation programs).

Expenses—Curatorial And Conservation	125,000	
Cash		125,000

Certain Nonprofit Organizations

Deferred Support	125,000	
Support—Private Gifts, Grants, And Bequests		125,000

Investment transactions Investment income, which is restricted for financing specified current operating expenses, amounted to $20,000.

Cash	20,000	
Deferred Investment Income		20,000

Current operating expenses of $18,000, which qualify for financing from investment income, are incurred (all related to education programs).

Expenses—Education	18,000	
Cash		18,000
Deferred Investment Income	18,000	
Revenues—Investment Income		18,000

After taking into account the transactions described above, the trial balance for the Restricted Operating Fund for the year ended June 30, 19X5, would be as follows:

Centerville Museum
Operating Fund—Restricted
Trial Balance
June 30, 19X5

	Dr.	Cr.
Cash	$ 17,000	
Pledges receivable	44,000	
Allowance for uncollectible pledges		$ 4,000
Investments	240,000	
Deferred support		290,000
Deferred investment income		7,000
Revenues—investment income		18,000
Support—private gifts, grants, and bequests		455,000
Expenses—exhibits	110,000	
Expenses—education	238,000	
Expenses—curatorial and conservation	125,000	
	$ 774,000	$ 774,000

GOVERNMENTAL GAAP GUIDE / 82.33

Endowment Funds

When resources are received and only the income from the assets may be used to finance operations or capital acquisitions of an entity, the resources should be accounted in either (True) Endowment Funds, Term Endowment Funds, or Quasi-Endowment Funds.

(True) Endowment Funds—Funds for which donors or other external parties have stipulated under the terms of the gift instrument creating the fund that the principal of the fund is not expendable—that is, it is to remain inviolate in perpetuity and is to be invested for the purpose of producing present and future income, which may be expended or added to the endowment principal.

Term Endowment Funds—Funds that are like Endowment Funds, except that all or part of the principal may be used after a stated period of time or on the occurrence of a certain event.

Quasi-Endowment Funds—Funds that the governing board of the institution, rather than a donor or other external party, has determined are to be retained and invested. Since these funds are not required by the donor to be retained and invested, the principal as well as the income may be totally utilized at the discretion of the governing board, subject to any donor imposed restrictions on use.

The initial receipt of gifts, grants, or bequests under an endowment agreement should be recorded as a capital addition based on the fair market value of the property received.

Unrestricted investment income from Endowment Funds and Term Endowment Funds should be recorded as investment income in the Unrestricted Operating Fund. Restricted expendable investment income should be accounted for as deferred revenue. Investment income that must be added to the principal balance as required by a donor or grantor agreement should be reported as a capital addition. Also, gains and losses from investments should be reported as capital additions or deductions.

Transactions of a Quasi-Endowment Fund should be accounted for as a Current Fund, (either as a separate Current Fund or as part of the Unrestricted Operating Fund, but shown as a designation of the fund balance account).

When a Term Endowment Fund expires, the resources should be transferred to the Unrestricted Operating Fund or to a fund specifically designated in the donor or grantor agreement. The transfer must be separately disclosed in the nonprofit organization's financial statements.

To illustrate the routine transactions that are accounted for in an Endowment Fund of a nonprofit organization, assume that at the beginning of the fiscal year an organization had the following trial balance. Unless otherwise noted, all entries are recorded in the organization's Endowment Fund.

Centerville Museum
Endowment Fund
Trial Balance
July 1, 19X4

	Dr.	Cr.
Cash	$ 30,000	
Investments	800,000	
Deferred revenue		$ 20,000
Fund balance—endowments		500,000
Fund balance—term endowments		310,000
	$830,000	$830,000

During the fiscal year, the following transactions occurred and were recorded in the museum's Endowment Fund as described below:

Gifts, donations, and bequests During the fiscal year, investments of $200,000 (true endowments) and $100,000 (term endowments) were received.

Investments	300,000	
Capital Additions—Contributions		
(Endowment)		200,000
Capital Additions—Contributions		
(Term Endowment)		100,000

Investment transactions Unrestricted investment income earned and received for the year amounted to $70,000, of which $65,000 was transferred to the Unrestricted Operating Fund.

ENDOWMENT FUND

Cash	70,000	
Due To Unrestricted Operating Fund		70,000
Due To Unrestricted Operating Fund	65,000	
Cash		65,000

Certain Nonprofit Organizations

OPERATING FUND—UNRESTRICTED
Due From Endowment Fund 70,000
    Revenues—Investment Income   70,000

Cash 65,000
    Due From Endowment Fund   65,000

In addition, $40,000 of investment income was earned and received. Of this amount, $30,000 represents restricted expendable investment income and $10,000 represents earned income that must be added to the principal balance for an Endowment Fund as required by the donor agreement.

Cash 40,000
    Deferred Revenue   30,000
    Capital Additions—Investment
      Income (Endowment)   10,000

Investments from (true) endowments that had a cost basis of $55,000 were sold for $50,000.

Cash 50,000
Capital Deductions—Realized Investment
    Losses (Endowment) 5,000
      Investments   55,000

Expiration of term endowment A term endowment consisting of investments of $50,000 expired during the year and was transferred to the Unrestricted Operating Fund.

ENDOWMENT FUND
Transfers—Expiration Of Term
    Endowments 50,000
      Investments   50,000

OPERATING FUND—UNRESTRICTED
Investments 50,000
    Transfers—Expiration Of Term
      Endowments   50,000

Note: Transactions that affect more than one fund group are also reproduced as illustrative entries in the other fund group.

After taking into account the transactions just described, the trial balance for the Endowment Fund for the year ended June 30, 19X5, would be as follows:

Centerville Museum
Endowment Fund
Trial Balance
June 30, 19X5

	Dr.	Cr.
Cash	$ 125,000	
Investments	995,000	
Due to unrestricted operating fund		$ 5,000
Deferred revenue		50,000
Capital additions—contributions (endowment)		200,000
Capital additions—contributions (term endowment)		100,000
Capital additions—investment income (endowment)		10,000
Capital deductions—realized investment losses (endowment)	5,000	
Transfers—expiration of term endowments	50,000	
Fund balance—endowments		500,000
Fund balance—term endowments		310,000
	$1,175,000	$1,175,000

Plant Funds

A nonprofit organization may account for its property, plant, and equipment in a Plant Fund. The initial receipt of the assets is recorded at cost when purchased, and at fair market value when received through donation. Debt instruments related to the receipt of plant assets, such as mortgages and notes, should be recorded in the Plant Fund. Debt service transactions may be accounted for in the Plant Fund. Depreciation expense should be recorded in the same fund in which the organization's plant assets are recorded, and classified on a functional, natural, or some other reasonable expense basis.

Gifts, grants, and bequests that are received for the purpose of purchasing plant assets should be recorded as deferred capital support. When the restricted resources are expended to acquire fixed assets, the deferred capital support accounts should be reduced and a capital addition recorded. Likewise, pledges that are restricted to the purchase of plant assets should be recorded as deferred capital support until the resources from the pledges are used to acquire specific fixed assets. When plant assets are acquired by using resources of the Unrestricted Operating Fund, a transfer from the Unrestricted Operating Fund to the Plant Fund should be recognized for the amount of the purchase. Gains and losses from the disposition of property, plant, and equipment should be recorded as capital additions or deductions. The proceeds from the disposition should be recorded in the Plant Fund if such proceeds must legally be used to reinvest in plant assets. Proceeds that are unrestricted with respect to use should be treated as a transfer to the Unrestricted Operating Fund.

Restricted investment income and investment gains and losses should be recorded as deferred amounts in the Plant Fund's balance sheet. When plant assets are purchased from restricted revenues arising from investment income and investment gains, a capital addition should be recorded. Unrestricted investment income of the Plant Fund should be recorded as investment revenue in the Unrestricted Operating Fund.

The cost or fair market value of collections of works of art and other similar items may be capitalized and may also be recorded as part of the Plant Fund. When these items are capitalized, they should not be subject to depreciation.

To illustrate the routine transactions that are accounted for in a Plant Fund of a nonprofit organization, assume that at the beginning of the fiscal year an organization had the following trial balance. Unless otherwise noted, all entries are recorded in the Plant Fund.

Centerville Museum
Plant Fund
Trial Balance
July 1, 19X4

	Dr.	Cr.
Cash	$ 40,000	
Land	700,000	
Buildings	600,000	
Equipment	220,000	
Accumulated depreciation		$ 410,000
Investments	800,000	
Deferred support		70,000
Deferred revenue		30,000
Mortgage payable		340,000
Fund balance		1,510,000
	$2,360,000	$2,360,000

Certain Nonprofit Organizations

During the fiscal year, the following transactions occurred and were recorded in the museum's Plant Fund:

Acquisition and donation of plant assets Equipment costing $30,000 was purchased with funds from the Plant Fund, and equipment with a fair market value of $20,000 was received as a gift.

Equipment	50,000	
Cash		30,000
Capital Additions—Contributed		
Plant Assets		20,000

In addition, equipment of $35,000 was purchased by using resources of the Unrestricted Operating Fund.

PLANT FUND

Equipment	35,000	
Transfers—Acquisition Of Plant		
Assets By Unrestricted Operating		
Fund		35,000

OPERATING FUND—UNRESTRICTED

Transfers—Acquisition Of Plant Assets		
By Unrestricted Operating Fund	35,000	
Cash		35,000

Gifts, grants, and bequests During the fiscal year, gifts from private donations that were restricted for the purchase of plant assets amounted to $100,000.

Cash	100,000	
Deferred Support		100,000

Equipment costing $80,000 was acquired and financed from restricted resources donated to the museum.

Equipment	80,000	
Deferred Support	80,000	
Cash		80,000
Capital Additions—Gifts, Grants,		
And Bequests		80,000

Disposition of plant assets Equipment having an original cost of $75,000 and accumulated depreciation of $60,000 was sold for

Certain Nonprofit Organizations

$20,000. Legally, all proceeds and gains on the disposition of plant assets must be reinvested in plant assets.

Cash	20,000	
Accumulated Depreciation	60,000	
Equipment		75,000
Deferred Revenue		5,000

Debt transactions At the end of the fiscal year, $15,000 was transferred from the Unrestricted Operating Fund to the Plant Fund. The transfer is to be used for principal indebtedness and is required by the mortgage agreement between the museum and a financial institution.

PLANT FUND

Cash	15,000	
Mandatory Transfers—Principal Indebtedness		15,000

OPERATING FUND—UNRESTRICTED

Mandatory Transfers—Principal Indebtedness	15,000	
Cash		15,000

Debt service payments for the fiscal year amounted to $22,000, representing interest payments of $17,000 and early principal repayments of $5,000.

Expenses—Management And General	17,000	
Mortgage Payable	5,000	
Cash		22,000

Depreciation Depreciation expense amounted to $80,000 and was allocated to curatorial and conservation (10%), exhibits (60%), education (20%), and management and general (10%).

Expenses—Curatorial And Conservation	8,000	
Expenses—Exhibits	48,000	
Expenses—Education	16,000	
Expenses—Management And General	8,000	
Accumulated Depreciation		80,000

Investment transactions Restricted investment income earned and received during the fiscal year was $65,000.

Cash	65,000	
Deferred Revenue		65,000

Equipment purchased from restricted investment income totaled $48,000.

Equipment	48,000	
Deferred Revenue	48,000	
Cash		48,000
Capital Additions—Plant Assets Acquired From Restricted Investment Income		48,000

Note: Transactions that affect more than one fund group are also reproduced as illustrative entries in the other fund group.

After taking into account the transactions described above, the trial balance for the Plant Fund for the year ended, June 30, 19X5, would be as follows:

Centerville Museum
Plant Fund
Trial Balance
June 30, 19X5

	Dr.	Cr.
Cash	$ 60,000	
Land	700,000	
Building	600,000	
Equipment	358,000	
Accumulated depreciation		$ 430,000
Investments	800,000	
Deferred support		90,000
Deferred revenue		52,000
Mortgage payable		335,000
Expenses—curatorial and conservation	8,000	
Expenses—exhibits	48,000	
Expenses—education	16,000	
Expenses—management and general	25,000	
Capital additions—contributed plant assets		20,000
Capital additions—gifts, grants, and bequests		80,000
Capital additions—plant assets acquired from restricted investment income		48,000
Mandatory transfers—principal indebtedness		15,000
Transfers—acquisition of plant assets by unrestricted operating fund		35,000
Fund balance		1,510,000
	$2,615,000	$2,615,000

Certain Nonprofit Organizations

FINANCIAL STATEMENTS

The financial statements of certain nonprofit organizations identified in the AICPA's Audit and Accounting Guide should be incorporated into the governmental unit's (the reporting entity's) general purpose financial statements. The nonprofit organization's financial statements would be combined with the governmental unit's (1) Combined Balance Sheet—All Fund Types and Account Groups, (2) Combined Statement of Revenues, Expenses, and Changes in Retained Earnings (or Equity)—All Fund Types and Account Groups, (3) Combined Statement of Changes in Financial Position—All Proprietary Fund Types, and (4) notes to the financial statements.

The financial statement of a nonprofit organization should include the following:

- Balance Sheet
- Statement of Activity
- Statement of Changes in Financial Position

Although these three basic financial statements should be presented, titles for the statements and formats for the statements are not established by the Audit and Accounting Guide.

Each nonprofit organization should select the format presentation that best reflects the organization's financial position and activity for the period. Two possible formats include the multicolumn format and the layered format. In the multicolumn format, each fund group is presented in an appropriately identified column. In the layered format, each fund group is horizontally presented one after another. The Audit and Accounting Guide encourages, but does not require, (1) the presentation of totals of all fund groups and (2) the comparative presentation of current and prior period financial statements.

> **OBSERVATION:** *From a practical perspective it is difficult to present both* total *information and comparative information. The multicolumn format is the better format when total information is presented, while the layered format is the better format when comparative information is presented.*

There is no requirement that a nonprofit organization report its financial statements in the conventional fund accounting format. Formats such as (1) unrestricted and restricted format presentation and (2) expendable and nonexpendable format presentation may be used if the disclosures in the financial statements are sufficient to adequately describe the nature of account balances and transactions and related restrictions.

The three financial statements listed above are discussed and illustrated below. The illustrations reflect the accounts and transactions developed earlier in the chapter (see section entitled Nonprofit Organization Funds). The multicolumn format is used; however, no comparative information is presented.

Balance Sheet The balance sheet of a nonprofit organization should reflect all of the assets and liabilities of the entity, and should be presented in a manner so that assets and liabilities can be evaluated as either current or noncurrent. Due to the presentation of separately identified funds, the liquidity of resources and the maturity date of liabilities are often obvious; however, when the classification cannot be implied from the presentation, a classified balance sheet should be prepared.

The fund balances for a nonprofit organization should be identified as unrestricted, restricted, or designated. The unrestricted fund balance is available to finance any legitimate expenditure as determined by the governing board. The fund balance portion that is restricted, usually by donor or grantor agreements, can be expended only for specified purposes. The designated fund balance is identified by the governing board for a particular program, but a designated amount is significantly different from a restriction in that a designation can simply be removed by the governing board without consent from an external party.

> **OBSERVATION:** *Although the fund balance accounts should be appropriately identified, the Audit and Accounting Guide notes that this may not be feasible for Plant Funds. Plant assets may be purchased with unrestricted and restricted resources and, based on the restriction agreements, it may not be clear whether the restrictions continue to apply to the acquired assets. For this reason, a Plant Fund may be presented as a separate fund or combined with an Unrestricted Operating Fund or the Restricted Fund.*

An example of a classified Balance Sheet for a nonprofit organization is presented in Exhibit I.

EXHIBIT I
Balance Sheet

Centerville Museum
Balance Sheet
June 30, 19X5

	Operating Fund— Unrestricted	Operating Fund— Restricted	Endowment Fund	Plant Fund	Total
ASSETS					
Current assets					
Cash	$ 18,000	$ 17,000	$ 125,000	$ 60,000	$ 220,000
Membership dues receivable	40,000				40,000
Allowance for uncollectible dues	(13,000)				(13,000)
Pledges receivable	70,000	44,000			114,000
Allowance for uncollectible pledges	(23,000)	(4,000)			(27,000)
Prepaid expenses	15,000				15,000
Due from endowment fund	5,000				5,000
Total current assets	112,000	57,000	125,000	60,000	354,000
Investments	280,000	240,000	995,000	800,000	2,315,000
Property, plant, and equipment					
Land				700,000	700,000
Buildings				600,000	600,000
Equipment				358,000	358,000
Less accumulated depreciation				1,658,000	1,658,000
				430,000	430,000
Net property, plant, and equipment				1,228,000	1,228,000
Inexhaustible collections (not subject to valuation)					
Total assets	$ 392,000	$297,000	$1,120,000	$2,088,000	$3,897,000

	Operating Fund— Unrestricted	Operating Fund— Restricted	Endowment Fund	Plant Fund	Total
LIABILITIES AND FUND BALANCES					
Current liabilities					
Accounts payable	$ 20,000				$ 20,000
Accrued expenses	35,000				35,000
Due to unrestricted operating fund			$ 5,000		5,000
Deferred support		$290,000		$ 90,000	380,000
Deferred investment income		7,000			7,000
Deferred revenue			50,000	52,000	102,000
Total current liabilities	55,000	297,000	55,000	142,000	549,000
Long-term debt					
Notes payable	660,000				660,000
Mortgage payable				335,000	335,000
Total long-term debt	660,000			335,000	995,000
Fund balances					
Unrestricted (deficit)	(323,000)				(323,000)
Restricted—endowments			705,000		705,000
Restricted—term endowments			360,000		360,000
Restricted—acquisition of plant assets				1,611,000	1,611,000
Total fund balances	(323,000)		$1,065,000	1,611,000	2,353,000
Total liabilities and fund balances	$ 392,000	$297,000	$1,120,000	$2,088,000	$3,897,000

Statement of Activity A nonprofit organization's Statement of Activity should include all operational, financing, and support activity for the period, and provide a reconciliation between the beginning and ending balance of the fund balance accounts. Alternatively, a separate financial statement can be prepared to summarize the analysis of fund balance changes.

The Audit and Accounting Guide does not establish a single format for the Statement of Activity, but the Statement should identify the significant sources of revenue and support and related expenses. The Statement should also identify the excess (deficiency) of revenue and support over (under) expenses. Alternatively, when capital additions are shown on the Statement, rather than in a separate analysis of changes in fund balances, the Statement should separately identify (1) excess (deficiency) of revenue and support over (under) expenses before capital additions and deductions and (2) excess (deficiency) of revenue and support over (under) expenses after capital additions and deductions.

Presented in Exhibit II is an example of a Statement of Activity which combines both current activity and the analysis of change in fund balance accounts.

Statement of Changes in Financial Position A comprehensive Statement of Changes in Financial Position should be prepared for all funds of a nonprofit organization. In preparing the Statement, reporting standards established by APB-19 (Reporting Changes in Financial Position) should be observed. The Statement should include funds generated from operations, financing and investing activities, capital additions and deductions, and changes in deferred support and revenue.

An example of a Statement of Changes in Financial Position is presented in Exhibit III.

Combined Financial Statements

A nonprofit organization (reporting organization) may control another entity, in which case it may be necessary to combine the financial statements of the other entity with the financial statements of the nonprofit organization. The Audit and Accounting Guide defines control as the direct or indirect ability to determine the direction of the management and policies through ownership, by contact or otherwise. When controls exist and any one of the following criteria is satisfied, the financial statements of the other entity should be combined with those of the nonprofit organization:

- Separate entities solicit funds in the name of and with the expressed or implicit approval of the reporting organization, and substantially all of the funds solicited are intended by the contributor or are otherwise required to be transferred to the organization or used at its discretion or direction.
- A reporting organization transfers some of its resources to another separate entity whose resources are held for the benefit of the reporting organization.
- A reporting organization assigns functions to a controlled entity whose funding is primarily derived from sources other than public contributions.

If after applying the above criteria it is concluded that affiliated organizations (for example, a national organization with state chapters) should not be combined with the nonprofit organization, the financial statements should include a description of the affiliates and their relationships with the nonprofit organization.

> **OBSERVATION:** *The Audit and Accounting Guide notes that the application of the combining criteria must result in meaningful financial statements. If meaningful information is not created, combined financial statements should not be prepared even though the criteria are satisfied. For example, it is noted that due to the unique and complex interrelationships of religious organizations, it may not be useful to prepare combined financial statements.*

When the financial statements of the other entity are combined with the nonprofit organization, it should be determined whether it may be more appropriate to report all of the other entity's resources as restricted.

EXHIBIT II
Statement of Revenue, Support and Expenses, and Changes in Fund Balances

Centerville Museum
Statement of Revenue, Support and Expenses, and Changes in Fund Balances
For Year Ended June 30, 19X5

	Operating Fund— Unrestricted	Operating Fund— Restricted	Endowment Fund	Plant Fund	Total
Revenue and support					
Revenue					
Membership	$ 207,000				$ 207,000
Admissions	410,000				410,000
Investment income	90,000	$ 18,000			108,000
Net realized investment gains (losses)	25,000				25,000
Auxiliary activities	278,000				278,000
Total revenue	1,010,000	18,000			1,028,000
Support					
Private gifts, grants, and bequests	540,000	455,000			995,000
Contributed services	45,000				45,000
Total support	585,000	455,000			1,040,000
Total revenue and support	1,595,000	473,000			2,068,000
Expenses					
Program services					
Curatorial and conservation	346,000	125,000		$ 8,000	479,000
Exhibits	270,000	110,000		48,000	428,000
Education	165,000	238,000		16,000	419,000
Accession of collections (net of deaccessions)	80,000				80,000
Total program services	861,000	473,000		72,000	1,406,000

Certain Nonprofit Organizations

	Operating Fund— Unrestricted	Operating Fund— Restricted	Endowment Fund	Plant Fund	Total
Supporting services					
Management and general	329,000			25,000	354,000
Fund raising	110,000				110,000
Auxiliary activities	215,000				215,000
Total supporting services	654,000			25,000	679,000
Total expenses	1,515,000	473,000		97,000	2,085,000
Excess (deficiency) of revenue and support over (under) expenses before capital additions and deductions	80,000			(97,000)	(17,000)
Capital additions (deductions)					
Contributions (endowments)			200,000		200,000
Contributions (term endowments)			100,000		100,000
Investment income (endowments)			10,000		10,000
Realized investment losses (endowments)			(5,000)		(5,000)
Contributed plant assets				20,000	20,000
Plant assets acquired from restricted investment income and deferred support				128,000	128,000
Total capital additions (deductions)			305,000	148,000	453,000
Excess (deficiency) of revenue and support over (under) expenses after capital additions and deductions	80,000		305,000	51,000	436,000
Fund balance—beginning of year (deficit)	(403,000)		810,000	1,510,000	1,917,000
Mandatory transfers—principal indebtedness	(15,000)			15,000	
Other transfers					
Acquisition of plant assets by operating fund	(35,000)			35,000	
Expiration of term endowments	50,000		(50,000)		
Fund balance—end of year (deficit)	$ (323,000)		$1,065,000	$1,611,000	$2,353,000

GOVERNMENTAL GAAP GUIDE / **82.49**

Certain Nonprofit Organizations

EXHIBIT III
Statement of Changes in Financial Position

Centerville Museum
Statement of Changes in Financial Position
For Year Ended June 30, 19X5

	Operating Fund— Unrestricted	Operating Fund— Restricted
Sources of working capital		
From operations		
Excess (deficiency) of revenue and support over (under) expenses before capital additions and deductions	$ 80,000	
Capital additions and deductions		
Excess (deficiency) of revenue and support over (under) expenses after capital additions and deductions	80,000	
Add (deduct) items not using (providing) working capital		
Depreciation		
Gain on sale of investments	(25,000)	
Contributed investments	(150,000)	
Contributed plant assets		
Plant asset acquired from Restricted investment income and deferred support		
Realized loss on sale of investments		
Working capital from operations	(95,000)	
Other sources		
Sale of investments	65,000	
Deferred restricted contributions and investment income received		$ 473,000
Total sources of working capital	(30,000)	473,000
Applications of working capital		
Retirement of notes and mortgage	140,000	
Deferred restricted contributions and investment income recognized as support		473,000
Purchase of plant assets	35,000	
Mandatory transfers	15,000	
Total applications of working capital	190,000	473,000
Increase (decrease) in working capital	$(220,000)	
Elements of net increase (decrease) in working capital		
Cash	$(162,000)	$(133,000)
Membership dues receivable	(10,000)	
Allowance for uncollectible dues	(3,000)	
Pledges receivable	(15,000)	12,000
Allowance for uncollectible pledges	(15,000)	3,000
Prepaid expenses	5,000	
Due from endowment fund	5,000	
Accounts payable	(20,000)	
Accrued expenses	(5,000)	
Due to unrestricted operating fund		
Deferred support		120,000
Deferred investment income		(2,000)
Deferred revenue		
Net increase (decrease) in working capital	$(220,000)	—

Certain Nonprofit Organizations

Endowment Fund	Plant Fund	Total
	$ (97,000)	$ (17,000)
$ 305,000	148,000	453,000
305,000	51,000	436,000
	80,000	80,000
		(25,000)
(300,000)		(450,000)
	(20,000)	(20,000)
	(128,000)	(128,000)
5,000		5,000
10,000	(17,000)	(102,000)
50,000	15,000	130,000
		473,000
60,000	(2,000)	501,000
	5,000	145,000
		473,000
	30,000	65,000
	(15,000)	
	20,000	683,000
$ 60,000	$ (22,000)	$(182,000)
$ 95,000	$ 20,000	$(180,000)
		(10,000)
		(3,000)
		(3,000)
		(12,000)
		5,000
		5,000
		(20,000)
		(5,000)
(5,000)		(5,000)
	(20,000)	100,000
		(2,000)
(30,000)	(22,000)	(52,000)
$ 60,000	$ (22,000)	$(182,000)

LITERATURE REFERENCES

Material in this chapter is based on the following authoritative pronouncements and publications, which are grouped according to the major headings used within the chapter. A dual reference (both paragraph and page number) is used for NCGA-1 and NCGA-2 because the original pronouncements do not use paragraph numbers.

Basic Concepts and Standards
NCGA-3   *Defining the Governmental Reporting Entity,* ¶¶ 9-14.
AICPA AUDIT AND ACCOUNTING GUIDE   *Audits of Certain Nonprofit Organizations,* pp. 1-3.
AICPA SOP 78-10   *Accounting Principles and Reporting Practices for Certain Nonprofit Organizations,* ¶¶ 1, 2, 5, and 6.

Basis of Accounting
NCGA-1   *Governmental Accounting and Financial Reporting Principles,* p. 11/¶ 58.
FASB:CS-1   *Objectives of Financial Reporting by Business Enterprises,* ¶ 44.

Measurement Focus
GASB DISCUSSION MEMORANDUM   *Measurement Focus and Basis of Accounting—Governmental Funds,* (nonauthoritative).

Budgetary System and Accounts
NCGA-1   *Governmental Accounting and Financial Reporting Principles,* pp. 13 and 14/¶¶ 78 and 94-97.
AICPA SOP 78-10   *Accounting Principles and Reporting Practices for Certain Nonprofit Organizations,* ¶ 12.

Accounts and Transactions
GASB-1   *Authoritative Status of NCGA Pronouncements and AICPA Industry Audit Guide,* Appendix B, pp. 9 and 10.

Revenues and Other Sources of Assets
FASB:CS-6   *Elements of Financial Statements,* ¶ 78.
APB STATEMENT-4   *Basic Concepts and Accounting Principles Underlying Financial Statements of Business Enterprises,* ¶ 150.
AICPA SOP 78-10   *Accounting Principles and Reporting Practices for Certain Nonprofit Organizations,* ¶ 12.

Revenues
AICPA AUDIT AND ACCOUNTING GUIDE   *Audits of Certain Nonprofit Organizations,* pp. 11-14.

AICPA SOP 78-10 *Accounting Principles and Reporting Practices for Certain Nonprofit Organizations,* ¶ 84.

Support
AICPA AUDIT AND ACCOUNTING GUIDE *Audits of Certain Nonprofit Organizations,* p. 17.
AICPA SOP 78-10 *Accounting Principles and Reporting Practices for Certain Nonprofit Organizations,* pp. 54-63.

Capital Additions
AICPA AUDIT AND ACCOUNTING GUIDE *Audits of Certain Nonprofit Organizations,* pp. 17 and 18.
AICPA SOP 78-10 *Accounting Principles and Reporting Practices for Certain Nonprofit Organizations,* ¶¶ 28, 29, and 52.

Pledges
AICPA SOP 78-10 *Accounting Principles and Reporting Practices for Certain Nonprofit Organizations,* ¶¶ 64-66.

Contributed Services
AICPA SOP 78-10 *Accounting Principles and Reporting Practices for Certain Nonprofit Organizations,* ¶¶ 67-70.

Contributed Materials and Facilities
AICPA SOP 78-10 *Accounting Principles and Reporting Practices for Certain Nonprofit Organizations,* ¶ 71.

Investment Income and Realized Gains and Losses
AICPA SOP 78-10 *Accounting Principles and Reporting Practices for Certain Nonprofit Organizations,* ¶¶ 72 and 73.

Expenses
FASB:CS-6 *Elements of Financial Statements,* ¶ 80.
FASB:CS-5 *Recognition and Measurement in Financial Statements of Business Enterprises,* ¶ 86.
APB STATEMENT-4 *Basic Concepts and Accounting Principles Underlying Financial Statements of Business Enterprises,* ¶¶ 147-160 and 181.

Functional Classification Basis
AICPA SOP 78-10 *Accounting Principles and Reporting Practices for Certain Nonprofit Organizations,* ¶¶ 85-96 and 98-100 and Appendix B.
AICPA SOP 87-2 *Accounting for Joint Costs of Informational Materials and Activities of Not-for-Profit Organizations that Include a Fund-Raising Appeal,* ¶¶ 15-22.

Certain Nonprofit Organizations

Natural (or Some Other) Classification Basis
AICPA SOP 78-10 *Accounting Principles and Reporting Practices for Certain Nonprofit Organizations,* ¶ 85.

Depreciation
AICPA SOP 78-10 *Accounting Principles and Reporting Practices for Certain Nonprofit Organizations,* ¶¶ 106-115.
GASB-8 *Applicability of FASB Statement No. 95, Recognition of Depreciation by Not-for-Profit Organizations, to Certain State and Local Governmental Entities,* ¶¶ 10 and 11.

Grants
AICPA SOP 78-10 *Accounting Principles and Reporting Practices for Certain Nonprofit Organizations,* ¶¶ 101 and 102.

Assets
FASB:CS-6 *Elements of Financial Statements,* ¶ 25 and 26.
AICPA AUDIT AND ACCOUNTING GUIDE *Audits of Certain Nonprofit Organizations,* p. 29.

Investments
AICPA AUDIT AND ACCOUNTING GUIDE *Audits of Certain Nonprofit Organizations,* p. 30.
AICPA SOP 78-10 *Accounting Principles and Reporting Practices for Certain Nonprofit Organizations,* ¶¶ 72, 73, 77-83, 116, and 117.

Fixed Assets
AICPA AUDIT AND ACCOUNTING GUIDE *Audits of Certain Nonprofit Organizations,* p. 31.
AICPA SOP 78-10 *Accounting Principles and Reporting Practices for Certain Nonprofit Organizations,* ¶ 105.

Collections
AICPA AUDIT AND ACCOUNTING GUIDE *Audits of Certain Nonprofit Organizations,* p. 32.
AICPA SOP 78-10 *Accounting Principles and Reporting Practices for Certain Nonprofit Organizations,* ¶¶ 113-115.

Liabilities
FASB:CS-6 *Elements of Financial Statements,* ¶ 35 and 36.
AICPA AUDIT AND ACCOUNTING GUIDE *Audits of Certain Nonprofit Organizations,* p. 33.

Certain Nonprofit Organizations

Encumbrances
NCGA-1   *Governmental Accounting and Financial Reporting Principles,* p. 14/¶¶ 91 and 92.
AICPA SOP 78-10   *Accounting Principles and Reporting Practices for Certain Nonprofit Organizations,* ¶ 12.

Deferred Revenue and Support
AICPA SOP 78-10   *Accounting Principles and Reporting Practices for Certain Nonprofit Organizations,* ¶¶ 62, 65, 73, 85, and Appendix A.

Deferred Taxes
AICPA AUDIT AND ACCOUNTING GUIDE   *Audits of Certain Nonprofit Organizations,* p. 35.
AICPA SOP 78-10   *Accounting Principles and Reporting Practices for Certain Nonprofit Organizations,* ¶ 103.

Transfers and Interfund Transactions
AICPA SOP 78-10   *Accounting Principles and Reporting Practices for Certain Nonprofit Organizations,* ¶ 104.

Interfund Investment Transactions
AICPA SOP 78-10   *Accounting Principles and Reporting Practices for Certain Nonprofit Organizations,* ¶ 82.

Interfund Borrowings
AICPA AUDIT AND ACCOUNTING GUIDE   *Audits of Certain Nonprofit Organizations,* p. 34.
AICPA SOP 78-10   *Accounting Principles and Reporting Practices for Certain Nonprofit Organizations,* ¶¶ 118 and 119.

Nonprofit Organization Funds
AICPA SOP 78-10   *Accounting Principles and Reporting Practices for Certain Nonprofit Organizations,* ¶¶ 14 and 15.

Operating Fund—Unrestricted
AICPA AUDIT AND ACCOUNTING GUIDE   *Audits of Certain Nonprofit Organizations,* pp. 11-15, 17-24, 30, and 33-37.
AICPA SOP 78-10   *Accounting Principles and Reporting Practices for Certain Nonprofit Organizations,* ¶¶ 63-104 and Appendix A.

Operating Funds—Restricted
AICPA AUDIT AND ACCOUNTING GUIDE   *Audits of Certain Nonprofit Organizations,* pp. 29-30 and 35.

AICPA SOP 78-10 *Accounting Principles and Reporting Practices for Certain Nonprofit Organizations,* ¶¶ 54-62 and 72-83.

Endowment Funds
AICPA SOP 78-10 *Accounting Principles and Reporting Practices for Certain Nonprofit Organizations,* ¶¶ 28 and 76.

Plant Funds
AICPA SOP 78-10 *Accounting Principles and Reporting Practices for Certain Nonprofit Organizations,* ¶¶ 22, 28, 52, and 66.

Financial Statements
AICPA SOP 78-10 *Accounting Principles and Reporting Practices for Certain Nonprofit Organizations,* ¶¶ 16-41.

Combined Financial Statements
AICPA SOP 78-10 *Accounting Principles and Reporting Practices for Certain Nonprofit Organizations,* ¶¶ 42-48.

APPENDIX

ILLUSTRATION OF COMPREHENSIVE ANNUAL FINANCIAL REPORT

CITY OF CENTERVILLE
NEW JERSEY

COMPREHENSIVE ANNUAL FINANCIAL REPORT
Fiscal Year Ended June 30, 19X5

Prepared by: Department of Finance

CITY OF CENTERVILLE
NEW JERSEY
COMPREHENSIVE ANNUAL FINANCIAL REPORT
FOR FISCAL YEAR ENDED
JUNE 30, 19X5

TABLE OF CONTENTS

	Page
INTRODUCTORY SECTION	1
Table of Contents	1
Letter from Director of Finance	4
Certificate of Achievement for Excellence in Financial Reporting	16
FINANCIAL SECTION	17
GENERAL PURPOSE FINANCIAL STATEMENTS	19
Auditor's Report	20
Combined Statements—Overview	21
• Combined Balance Sheet—All Fund Types and Account Groups	22
• Combined Statement of Revenues, Expenditures, and Changes in Fund Balances—All Governmental Fund Types and Expendable Trust Funds	26
• Combined Statement of Revenues, Expenditures, and Changes in Fund Balances—Budget (GAAP Basis) and Actual (General, Special Revenue, and Capital Projects Funds)	28
• Combined Statement of Revenues, Expenses, and Changes in Retained Earnings/Fund Balances—All Proprietary Fund Types and Similar Trust Funds	30

	Page
● Combined Statement of Changes in Financial Position—All Proprietary Fund Types and Similar Trust Funds	31
● Notes to the Financial Statements	33

COMBINING STATEMENTS ... 59

Combining Statements—Governmental Fund Types ... 61

- ● Combining Balance Sheet—Special Revenue Funds ... 62
- ● Combining Statement of Revenues, Expenditures, and Changes in Fund Balances—Special Revenue Funds ... 63
- ● Combining Statement of Revenues, Expenditures, Encumbrances, and Changes in Fund Balances—Budget (GAAP Basis) and Actual—Special Revenue Funds ... 64
- ● Combining Balance Sheet—Debt Service Funds ... 66
- ● Combining Statement of Revenues, Expenditures, and Changes in Fund Balances—Debt Service Funds ... 67
- ● Combining Balance Sheet—Capital Projects Funds ... 68
- ● Combining Statement of Revenues, Expenditures, and Changes in Fund Balances—Capital Projects Funds ... 69
- ● Combining Statement of Revenues, Expenditures, Encumbrances, and Changes in Fund Balances—Budget (GAAP Basis) and Actual—Capital Projects Funds ... 70

Combining Statements—Proprietary Fund Types ... 73

- ● Combining Balance Sheet—Enterprise Funds ... 74
- ● Combining Statement of Revenues, Expenses, and Changes in Retained Earnings—Enterprise Funds ... 76
- ● Combining Statement of Changes in Financial Position—Enterprise Funds ... 77
- ● Combining Balance Sheet—Internal Service Funds ... 78

	Page
• Combining Statement of Revenues, Expenses, and Changes in Retained Earnings—Internal Service Funds	79
• Statement of Changes in Financial Position—Internal Service Funds	80
Combining Statements—Fiduciary Fund Types	81
• Combining Balance Sheet—Fiduciary Funds	82
ACCOUNT GROUPS	85
• Statement of General Fixed Assets	86
• Schedule of General Fixed Assets (By Function and Activity)	87
• Schedule of Changes in General Fixed Assets (By Function and Activity)	88
• Statement of General Long-Term Debt	89
• Schedule of Changes in Long-Term Debt	89
STATISTICAL SECTION	91

CITY OF CENTERVILLE
    Department of Finance   R.J. Bowman
       1011 City Hall   Director of Finance
     Centerville, NJ 08000
      August 15, 19X5

Honorable Floyd Vermillion
Mayor, City of Centerville
Room L115
City Hall Annex
Centerville, NJ 08000

Dear Mayor Vermillion:

The Comprehensive Annual Financial Report (CAFR) of the City of Centerville for the fiscal year ended June 30, 19X5, is submitted herewith. We believe the information, as presented, is accurate in all material aspects; that it is presented in a manner designed to set forth fairly, in all material respects, the financial position and results of operations of the City as measured and reported by the financial activity of its various funds; and that all disclosures necessary to enable the reader to gain an adequate understanding of the City's financial affairs have been included. It is the responsibility of the management of the City to prepare the CAFR.

    To facilitate the understanding of the City's financial affairs, the CAFR is divided into an introductory section, financial section, and statistical section. The introductory section includes a table of contents, a letter of transmittal, and the Certificate of Achievement for Excellence in Financial Reporting. The financial section of the CAFR consists of the independent auditor's report, the general purpose financial statements, and the combining and individual fund and account group statements and schedules. Information included in the statistical section is not part of the City's financial statements although the material is part of the CAFR.

    A basis for preparing the CAFR for the City was the identification of the reporting entity. Various potential component units were evaluated to determine whether they should be reported in the City's CAFR. A component unit was considered to be part of the City's reporting entity when it was concluded that the City had a significant oversight responsibility with respect to the potential component unit. Criteria that were used to evaluate the oversight responsibility of the City included financial interdependency, selection of the governing authority, designation of management, ability to influence operations, and accountability for financial matters.

The CAFR includes all the funds and account groups of the City and the funds of the Centerville School District, Public Housing Corporation of Centerville, Centerville Urban Renewal Corporation, Centerville Flood Control District, and Centerville Transit Authority. Not included in the funds and account groups are the Centerville Museum and the Industrial Development Corporation of Centerville.

Reflected in this report is the extensive range of services provided by the City of Centerville. These basic services include public safety, streets, recreation and parks, health and welfare, and general administration services, as well as the activities of the previously mentioned public agencies and authorities.

Economic Condition and Outlook

The City is located in a metropolitan area that has a robust and diverse economy.

The unemployment rate in the City is well below the national average. In addition, per capita income within the City continues to grow at a rate approximately 15% greater than the national average and well above the rate of growth for the State of New Jersey. By all statistical measures the City and the surrounding communities can be characterized as affluent.

The economic base of the City consists of a healthy balance between service and light manufacturing industries. Over the past seven years, the City has experienced especially strong growth in the high technology and pharmaceutical industries. In general, the City is well positioned for future growth and somewhat protected from a general economic downturn or the loss of a specific enterprise or industry.

The economic growth has placed increased demands on services, but the City has adopted a conservative approach to the expansion of various public services. The general philosophy of the City is that increased revenues from existing taxes and other revenue sources must provide the base for the expansion of public expenditures. As demonstrated over the past six years, the City is committed to this philosophy. As discussed later in this letter, it is expected that certain infrastructure capital assets will need to be replaced or renovated in a 3–5 year period, but it is expected that these capital expenditures will be financed through the issuance of general long-term capital debt that will be repaid approximately over the estimated useful lives of the capital projects.

While the economic environment and public expenditure policies are subject to change and reevaluation, it is anticipated that the City will experience manageable growth that will not be disruptive to the current financial position of the City.

Major Initiatives

At the close of the current fiscal year, the City had virtually completed a new Civic Center that will serve as a convention site and as an entertainment complex. The construction of the center has been financed, for the most part, from intergovernmental grants and long-term financing. When the center is completed, it will further enhance the economic vitality and quality of life of the City and its citizens.

The City has tentative plans to expand significantly recreational and cultural services now offered through the various departments. These plans are consistent with the increasing sophistication and affluence of its citizens. As noted earlier, the increased expenditures that will occur in the recreational and cultural budgets will not result in increased or new taxes, but rather will be financed through expected receipts from the existing tax structure. It is expected that other services will increase to some extent, but these expenditures will be consistent with expected growth in economic activity.

In conjunction with anticipated significant increases in the operating budgets for recreational and cultural services, the City has plans to initiate several capital projects that will accommodate the overall strategy of providing services to a changing citizenry. These expected capital projects include a multipurpose center that will serve as a base for the City's Philharmonic Orchestra and a regional opera consortium. Also, several neighborhood centers are planned for construction to provide recreational activities, including, in some instances, open space for a championship golf course and an expansion of two existing parks.

Although the City anticipates the expansion of some services in the future, the City is committed to providing services that are both effective and efficient. In general, the City provides its services (general government, public safety, streets, recreation and parks, and health and welfare) at cost per capita that is comparable to or below other communities with similar demographic and economic characteristics.

Financial Information, Management, and Control

A detailed understanding of the financial position and operating results of the City is provided in the CAFR. Presented below is a brief description of financial information, management of financial resources and obligations, and control techniques applicable to financial resources, obligations, and information.

Basis of Accounting Basis of accounting refers to when revenues and expenditures or expenses are recognized in the accounts and reported in the financial statements. All governmental funds and expendable trust funds are accounted for using the modified accrual basis of accounting. Their revenues are recognized when they become measurable and available. Expenditures are generally recognized under the modified accrual basis of accounting when the related fund liability is incurred. All proprietary funds and Nonexpendable Trust Funds and Pension Trust Funds are accounted for using the accrual basis of accounting. Their revenues are recognized when they are earned, and their expenses are recognized when they are incurred.

Accounting Systems and Budgetary Control In developing and evaluating the City's accounting control system, consideration is given to the adequacy of internal accounting controls. Accounting control comprises the plan of organization and the procedures and records that are concerned with the safeguarding of assets and the reliability of financial records and consequently are designed to provide reasonable assurance that:

- Transactions are executed in accordance with management's general or specific authorization.
- Transactions are recorded as necessary (1) to permit preparation of financial statements in conformity with generally accepted accounting principles or any other criteria, such as finance-related legal and contractual compliance requirements applicable to such statements, and (2) to maintain accountability for assets.
- Access to assets is permitted only in accordance with management's authorization.
- The recorded accountability for assets is compared with the existing assets at reasonable intervals and appropriate action is taken with respect to any differences.

The definition of accounting control comprehends reasonable, but not absolute, assurance that the objectives expressed in it will be accomplished by the system. The concept of reasonable assurance recognizes that the cost of internal control should not exceed the benefits expected to be derived. The benefits consist of reductions in the risk of failing to achieve the objectives implicit in the definition of accounting control.

All internal control evaluations occur within the above framework. We believe that the City's internal accounting controls adequately safeguard assets and provide reasonable assurance of proper recording of financial transactions.

In accordance with the State Laws of New Jersey, the City has formally established budgetary accounting control for its operating funds. Budgetary control is maintained at the division level by the encumbrance of estimated purchase amounts prior to the release of purchase orders to vendors. Purchase orders which result in an overrun of division balances are not released until additional appropriations are made available through transfer from other accounts either by ordinance of City Council or administrative transfer. Open encumbrances are reported as reservations of fund balances at June 30, 19X5.

Fund Descriptions The accounts of the City are organized on the basis of funds and account groups, each of which is considered a separate accounting entity. The operation of the funds is accounted for by a separate set of self-balancing accounts that comprise its assets, liabilities, fund equity, revenues, and, as applicable, expenditures and expenses. The individual funds account for the governmental resources allocated to them for the purpose of carrying on specific activities in accordance with special regulations, restrictions, or limitations. The funds used by the City are grouped into three broad fund types and seven generic funds as follows:

Governmental Funds These funds are used to account for the programs and activities of the governmental functions of the City.

General Fund: This fund serves as the general operating fund of the City. It is used to account for all financial resources except those required to be accounted for in another fund.

Special Revenue Funds: These funds are used to account for the proceeds of specific revenue sources (other than expendable trusts or major capital projects) that are legally restricted to expenditures for specified purposes.

Debt Service Funds: These funds are used to account for the resources devoted to the payment of interest and principal on long-term capital obligation debt other than those payable from specific governmental funds and Enterprise Funds.

Capital Projects Funds: These funds are used to account for financial resources to be used for the acquisition or construction of major capital facilities (other than those financed by Enterprise Funds).

Proprietary Funds These funds are used to account for ongoing organizations and activities which are similar to those found in the private sector.

Enterprise Funds: These funds are used to account for operations that are financed and operated in a manner similar to private business enterprises where the intent is that costs (expenses, including amortizations and depreciation) of providing goods or services to the general public on a continuing basis be financed or recovered primarily through user charges.

Internal Service Funds: These funds are used to account for the financing of goods or services provided by one department or agency to other departments or agencies of the governmental units, or to other governmental units, on a cost reimbursement basis.

Fiduciary Funds These funds are used to account for assets held by a governmental unit in a trustee capacity or as an agent for individuals, private organizations, and other governmental units and funds.

Trust and Agency Funds: These funds are used to account for assets held by Expendable Trust Funds, Nonexpendable Trust Funds, Pension Trust Funds, and Agency Funds.

In addition to the seven generic funds described above, the City uses account groups to establish accounting control and accountability for the City's general fixed assets and general long-term capital debt. The two account groups are described below:

General Fixed Assets Account Group: This group of accounts is used to account for all fixed assets of the City other than those accounted for in proprietary funds and certain fiduciary funds.

General Long-Term Debt Account Group: This group of accounts is used to account for all long-term debt of the City except debt accounted for in specific governmental funds, proprietary funds, and certain fiduciary funds.

General Government Functions Municipal activities and services are accounted for in the General Fund, Special Revenue Funds, Debt Service Funds, and Capital Projects Funds.

General Fund An excess of revenues over expenditures of $320,000,000, was reported for the fiscal year ended June 30, 19X5. For budgetary comparison purposes, revenues from the General Fund amounted to $1,050,000,000 for fiscal year 19X5, an increase of approximately 2.4% over the previous fiscal year. The sources of revenues for the 19X5 fiscal year are summarized below.

	19X5 Amount	Percentage of total revenues	Increase (Decrease) over 19X4	
Tax revenues	$ 500,000,000	47%	$30,000,000	6.00%
Fees and other nontax revenues	400,000,000	38	5,000,000	1.25
Grants and receipts from other governments	90,000,000	9	(20,000,000)	(22.22)
Other revenues	60,000,000	6	10,000,000	16.67
Totals	$1,050,000,000	100%	$25,000,000	2.38%

The increase in tax revenues resulted, for the most part, from the addition of new commercial properties to the property tax rolls during the year and increased retail activity reflected in gains in the gross receipts tax.

Expenditures from the General Fund amount to $730,000,000 for fiscal year 19X5, an increase of approximately 2% over the previous fiscal year. An analysis of expenditures for the year is presented below.

	19X5 Amount	Percentage of total expenditures	Increase (Decrease) over 19X4	
General government	$292,000,000	40%	$15,000,000	5.15%
Public safety	146,000,000	20	6,000,000	4.11
Streets	36,000,000	5	(5,000,000)	(13.89)
Recreation and parks	58,000,000	8	(3,000,000)	(5.17)
Health and welfare	132,000,000	18	8,000,000	6.06
Other expenditures	66,000,000	9	(7,000,000)	10.61
Totals	$730,000,000	100%	$14,000,000	1.92%

The reduction in expenditures for street maintenance and repairs was due to an unusually high level of payments for overtime that occurred during 19X4. During 19X5, steps were taken to schedule City employees in a manner to minimize overtime and to use private contractors to provide adequate services during certain peak tourist periods.

The reduction in expenditures for other services was due to nonrecurring legal fees that were incurred during 19X4 related to complex negotiations of real estate contracts in which land for the construction of the new Civic Center was acquired.

Special Revenue Funds The Parks Fund and The Parking Meters Fund make up the Special Revenue Funds. These funds had combined revenues of $775,000,000 and expenditures of $640,000,000 for fiscal year 19X5.

Debt Service Funds With the exception of special assessment bonds, revenue bonds, and debt issued by Enterprise Funds, long-term debt is serviced through the Debt Service Funds. During fiscal year 19X5, debt service payments amounted to $685,000,000.

Capital Projects Funds The Capital Projects Funds consist of the Parks Fund and Civic Center Fund. Proceeds of general obligation bond issues are accounted for in these funds until improvement projects or new projects are completed. Completed projects under construction at the end of the fiscal year are accounted for in the General Fixed Assets Account Group.

During 19X5, 15 new or capital improvement projects were begun. General capital expenditures for these projects and other projects under construction at the beginning of the year amounted to $55,000,000. The capital project activities of the proprietary funds are reflected in those respective funds, and are not part of the general capital expenditures of the City.

Proprietary Operations Certain activities of the City are accounted for in Enterprise Funds and Internal Service Funds.

Enterprise Funds: The City's Enterprise Funds are the Airport Fund and the Water and Sewer Fund.

The Airport Fund owns and operates the municipal airport and performs a variety of services for which it charges a fee. Although the City provided a significant amount of start-up capital and capital for expansion at various dates, it does not provide operating subsidies to the Airport. The Airport is a modern facility that has been profitable for the past twelve years. The City is responsible for operating deficits should they arise; however, during the current year the Airport had net income of $8,000,000 after making transfers out of $14,000,000.

The Water and Sewer Fund charges City residents a semiannual fee for the services it provides. The City is responsible for any operating deficits of the Fund. During the current year the Fund had a loss from operations of $12,000,000 which was, for the most part, funded from intergovernmental grants and internal transfers. The net income for the year was $4,000,000. It is expected that similar but decreasing grants and subsidies will be needed for the next four years, until the user rate structure increases to fully cover all costs. For the past three years the revenue structure of the Fund has been incapable of funding operating expenditures because expenditures have increased significantly based on stringent water quality control standards mandated by the State. State grants to cover increased costs arising from the new standards will eventually be phased out over a period ending June 30, 19X9. At that date it is expected that user charges will have been adjusted to a level to cover operating costs and other costs of the Fund.

Internal Service Funds: The Municipal Garage Fund and the Central Printing Fund are the only Internal Service Funds operated by the City. These funds provide repair and maintenance services for automobiles and light trucks owned by various City departments, agencies and authorities, and printing services for various City departments. Each fund bills each governmental unit for the services it renders.

Fiduciary Fund Types The City maintains a Pension Trust Fund, Nonexpendable and Expendable Trust Funds, and Agency Funds.

Pension Trust Fund: The City's pension plan is administered through the Employee-Retirement Trust Fund. Contributions made by employees and the City as well as retirement expenditures are accounted for in the fund.

Nonexpendable Trust Fund: The Employee Loan Fund is accounted for as a Nonexpendable Trust Fund. Contributions made by the City and private contributors provide the basis for making low-interest loans to City employees that have an unexpected need for the funds.

Expendable Trust Fund: The Employee Scholarship Fund is accounted for as an Expendable Trust Fund. Contributions made by the City and private contributors provide the basis for certain education-related expenses incurred directly by a City employee.

Agency Funds: The Payroll Deduction Escrow Fund and the State License Fund are accounted for as Agency Funds.

Debt Administration   The ratio of net tax-supported bonded-debt to assessed valuation and per capita are useful indicators of the City's debt position to municipal management, citizens, and investors. A comparison of these ratios is summarized below.

	19X5	19X4
Net tax supported bonded debt	$2,329,000,000	$2,799,000,000
Net tax supported bonded debt per capita	$124	$127
Net tax supported bonded debt as a percentage of assessed valuation	8.4%	8.5%

The City's latest bond issues, excluding debt issued by component units, were rated as follows:

	Moody's Investors Service	Standard & Poor's
General obligation bonds	A	A−
Water and sewer revenue bonds	A	A

During the current year, debt retirements amounted to $480,000,000, while new issuances amounted to $10,000,000.

Cash Management and Investments   The intention of the cash management system is to limit the amount of funds placed in accounts where low or no interest is paid. Idle cash is invested in various instruments with various maturity dates, depending on the anticipated cash requirements during the period.

The overall strategy of holding deposits and making investments is to expose the City to a minimum amount of credit risk and market risk. All bank balances of deposits as of the balance sheet date are entirely insured or collateralized with securities held by the City or by its agent in the City's name. With respect to risk, investments may be classified as follows:

Category 1   Insured or registered, with securities held by the City or its agent in the City's name

Category 2   Uninsured and unregistered, with securities held by the counterparty's trust department or agent in the City's name

Category 3   Uninsured and unregistered, with securities held by the counterparty or by its trust department or agent, but not in the City's name

The City's investments, other than investments in state investment pools, were classified as Category 1 (62.5%), Category 2 (25%), and Category 3 (12.5%).

Risk Management The City is exposed to a variety of accidental losses and has established a risk management strategy that attempts to minimize losses and the carrying cost of insurance.

Risk control techniques have been established to reasonably assure that the City's employees are aware of their responsibilities regarding loss exposures related to their duties. In a similar manner, risk control techniques have been established to reduce possible losses to property owned or under the control of the City. Furthermore, supervisory personnel are held responsible for monitoring risk control techniques on an operational basis.

The primary technique used for risk financing is the purchase of insurance policies from commercial insurers that include a large deductible amount. The use of a large deductible clause reduces the cost of insurance, but, should losses occur, the portion of the uninsured loss is not expected to be significant with respect to the financial position of the City.

Independent Audit

The financial records, books of account, and transactions of the City and its components for the fiscal year ended June 30, 19X5, have been audited by a firm of Independent Public Accountants, and their opinion is included in the Financial Section of this report.

The financial statements are the responsibility of the City. The responsibility of the Independent Public Accountants is to express an opinion on the City's financial statements based on their audit. An audit is conducted in accordance with generally accepted auditing standards. Those standards require that the audit be planned and performed in a manner to obtain a reasonable assurance as to whether the financial statements are free of material misstatement.

Awards

The Government Finance Officers Association of the United States and Canada (GFOA) awarded a Certificate of Achievement for Excellence in Financial Reporting to the City for its Comprehensive Annual Financial Report for the fiscal year ended June 30, 19X4.

In order to be awarded a Certificate of Excellence, a governmental unit must publish an easily readable and efficiently organized Comprehensive Annual Financial Report, the contents of which conform to program standards. Such reports must satisfy both generally accepted accounting principles and applicable legal requirements.

A Certificate of Excellence is valid for a period of one year only. We believe our current report continues to conform to the Certificate of Excellence Program requirements, and we are submitting it to GFOA to determine its eligibility for another certificate.

Acknowledgement

The preparation of the Comprehensive Annual Financial Report on a timely basis could not have been accomplished without the efforts and dedication of the staff of the Department of Finance. I would like to express my appreciation to my staff and other personnel from various departments, agencies, and authorities who assisted in its preparation. Also, I would like to thank the Mayor and the City Council for their interest and support in planning and conducting the financial operations of the City in a dedicated and responsible manner.

Respectfully submitted,

R. J. Bowman

R. J. Bowman
Director

CERTIFICATE OF ACHIEVEMENT FOR EXCELLENCE IN FINANCIAL REPORTING

Presented to:
City of Centerville

For Its
Comprehensive Annual Financial Report
for the Fiscal Year Ended
June 30, 19X4

A Certificate of Achievement for Excellence in Financial Reporting is presented by the Government Finance Officers Association of the United States and Canada to governmental units and public employee retirement systems whose comprehensive annual financial reports are judged to substantially conform to program standards.

President

OFFICIAL SEAL

Executive Director

This Certificate is for illustrative purposes only. The publisher has not sought nor obtained an actual Certificate of Achievement for Excellence in Financial Reporting from the Government Finance Officers Association.

FINANCIAL SECTION

General Purpose Financial Statements

HOWARD, FINE & HOWARD
CERTIFIED PUBLIC ACCOUNTANTS
#12 Susquehanna Street
Centerville, NJ 08000

Honorable Mayor Floyd Vermillion
and Members of City Council
Centerville, New Jersey

We have audited the accompanying general purpose financial statements of the City of Centerville, N.J., and the combining, individual fund, and account group financial statements of the City of Centerville as of and for the year ended June 30, 19X5, as listed in the table of contents. These financial statements are the responsibility of the entity's management. Our responsibility is to express an opinion on these financial statements based on our audit.

    We conducted our audit in accordance with generally accepted auditing standards. Those standards require that we plan and perform the audit to obtain reasonable assurance about whether the financial statements are free of material misstatement. An audit includes examining, on a test basis, evidence supporting the amounts and disclosures in the financial statements. An audit also includes assessing the accounting principles used and significant estimates made by management, as well as evaluating the overall financial statement presentation. We believe that our audit provides a reasonable basis for our opinion.

    In our opinion, the general purpose financial statements referred to above present fairly, in all material respects, the financial position of the City of Centerville, N.J., as of June 30, 19X5, and the results of its operations and the changes in financial position of its proprietary fund types for the year then ended in conformity with generally accepted accounting principles. Also, in our opinion, the combining, individual fund, and account group financial statements referred to above present fairly, in all material respects, the financial position of each of the individual funds and account groups of the City of Centerville, N.J., as of June 30, 19X5, and the results of operations of such funds and the changes in financial position of individual proprietary funds for the year then ended in conformity with generally accepted accounting principles.

    Our audit was made for the purpose of forming an opinion on the general purpose financial statements taken as a whole and on the combining, individual fund, and individual account group financial statements. The accompanying financial information listed as supporting schedules in the table of contents is presented for purposes of additional analysis and is not a required part of the financial statements of the City of Centerville, N.J. Such information has been subjected to the auditing procedures applied in the audit of the general purpose, combining individual fund, and individual account group financial statements and, in our opinion, is fairly stated in all material respects in relation to the financial statements of each of the respective individual funds and account groups, taken as a whole.

September 15, 19X5   Howard, Fine & Howard
                                            Certified Public Accountants

Combined Statements—Overview

City of Centerville
Combined Balance Sheet
All Fund Types and Account Groups
June 30, 19X5

(in thousands of dollars)

	Governmental Fund Types			
	General Fund	Special Revenue Funds	Debt Service Funds	Capital Projects Funds
ASSETS				
Cash	$122,000	$ 25,000	$310,000	$18,000
Accounts receivable	12,000	13,000	–	–
Taxes receivable	149,000	27,000	–	–
Allowance for doubtful accounts	(18,000)	(4,000)	–	–
Investments	–	150,000	340,000	5,000
Due from other funds	12,000	30,000	70,000	13,000
Interest receivable	2,000	–	30,000	1,000
Inventory	6,000	23,000	–	–
Other (current) assets	–	–	–	–
Restricted assets	–	–	–	–
Property, plant, and equipment (net)	–	–	–	–
Advance to internal service fund	20,000	–	–	–
Other assets	9,000	–	–	8,000
Amount available in debt service fund	–	–	–	–
Amount to be provided for retirement of general long-term debt	–	–	–	–
Total assets	$314,000	$264,000	$750,000	$45,000

90.22 / GOVERNMENTAL GAAP GUIDE

(in thousands of dollars)

	Proprietary Fund Types		Fiduciary Funds	Account Groups		
	Enterprise Funds	Internal Service Funds	Trust and Agency Funds	General Fixed Assets	General Long-Term Debt	Total (memorandum only)
	$ 10,000	$ 2,000	$ 41,000	–	–	$528,000
	33,000	–	14,000	–	–	72,000
	–	–	–	–	–	176,000
	(6,000)	–	(2,000)	–	–	(30,000)
	–	–	506,000	–	–	1,001,000
	7,000	6,000	15,000	–	–	153,000
	–	–	18,000	–	–	51,000
	3,000	9,000	–	–	–	41,000
	7,000	3,000	–	–	–	10,000
	67,000	–	–	–	–	67,000
	143,000	29,000	–	$755,000	–	927,000
	–	–	–	–	–	20,000
	–	–	6,000	–	–	23,000
	–	–	–	–	729,000	729,000
	–	–	–	–	1,600,000	1,600,000
	$264,000	$49,000	$598,000	$755,000	$2,329,000	$5,368,000

	General Fund	Special Revenue Funds	Debt Service Funds	Capital Projects Funds
LIABILITIES				
Vouchers payable	$ 67,000	$ 77,000	–	$ 8,000
Accounts payable	12,000	39,000	–	5,000
Accrued expenses	–	13,000	–	3,000
Due to other funds	77,000	42,000	–	10,000
Deferred revenues	10,000	–	$ 10,000	–
Contracts payable	39,000	–	–	–
Notes payable	–	–	–	–
Payroll taxes payable	–	–	–	–
Advance from general fund	–	–	–	–
General obligation bonds	–	–	–	–
Revenue bonds	–	–	–	–
Mortgage notes payable	–	42,000	–	–
Other liabilities	–	–	11,000	7,000
Total liabilities	205,000	213,000	21,000	33,000
FUND EQUITY				
Contributed capital	–	–	–	–
Investment in general fixed assets	–	–	–	–
Retained earnings				
Reserved for debt retirement	–	–	–	–
Unreserved	–	–	–	–
Fund balance				
Reserved for encumbrances	12,000	13,000	–	5,000
Reserved for inventory	6,000	23,000	–	–
Reserved for debt service	–	–	729,000	–
Reserved for retirement system	–	–	–	–
Reserved for loans	–	–	–	–
Reserved for scholarships	–	–	–	–
Reserved for advance to internal service fund	20,000	–	–	–
Unreserved	71,000	15,000	–	7,000
Total fund equity	109,000	51,000	729,000	12,000
Total liabilities and fund equity	$314,000	$264,000	$750,000	$45,000

The notes to the financial statements are an integral part of this statement.

Enterprise Funds	Internal Service Funds	Trust and Agency Funds	General Fixed Assets	General Long-Term Debt	Total (memorandum only)
$ 3,000	$ 3,000	–	–	–	$ 158,000
5,000	1,000	–	–	–	62,000
10,000	4,000	$ 7,000	–	–	37,000
15,000	5,000	4,000	–	–	153,000
5,000	–	–	–	–	25,000
–	–	–	–	–	39,000
6,000	–	–	–	–	6,000
–	–	2,000	–	–	2,000
–	20,000	–	–	–	20,000
80,000	–	–	–	$2,329,000	2,409,000
21,000	–	–	–	–	21,000
14,000	–	–	–	–	56,000
–	–	6,000	–	–	24,000
159,000	33,000	19,000	–	2,329,000	3,012,000
75,000	12,000	–	–	–	87,000
–	–	–	755,000	–	755,000
7,000	–	–	–	–	7,000
23,000	4,000	–	–	–	27,000
–	–	–	–	–	30,000
–	–	–	–	–	29,000
–	–	–	–	–	729,000
–	–	528,000	–	–	528,000
–	–	24,000	–	–	24,000
–	–	27,000	–	–	27,000
–	–	–	–	–	20,000
–	–	–	–	–	93,000
105,000	16,000	579,000	755,000	–	2,356,000
$264,000	$49,000	$598,000	$755,000	$2,329,000	$5,368,000

City of Centerville
Combined Statement of Revenues, Expenditures, and Changes in Fund Balances
All Governmental Fund Types and Expendable Trust Funds For Year Ended June 30, 19X5

(in thousands of dollars)

	Governmental Fund Types	
	General Fund	*Special Revenue Funds*
Revenues		
Taxes	$ 500,000	$ 400,000
Fees and other nontax revenues	400,000	370,000
Grants and receipts from other governments	90,000	–
Other	60,000	5,000
Total revenues	1,050,000	775,000
Expenditures		
General government	292,000	–
Public safety	146,000	150,000
Streets	36,000	–
Recreation and parks	58,000	490,000
Health and welfare	132,000	–
Educational benefits	–	–
Debt service		
Principal	–	–
Interest	–	–
Capital outlays	–	–
Other	66,000	–
Total expenditures	730,00	640,000
Excess of revenues over (under) expenditures	320,000	135,000
Other financing sources (uses)		
Proceeds from bond sales	–	–
Transfers from other funds	20,000	90,000
Transfers to other funds	(357,000)	(210,000)
Total other financing sources (used)	(337,000)	(120,000)
Excess of revenues and other sources over (under) expenditures and other uses	(17,000)	15,000
(Increase) decrease in reserve for encumbrances and other reservations	(3,000)	(10,000)
Net change in unreserved fund balance for year	(20,000)	5,000
Fund balance–unreserved July 1, 19X4	91,000	10,000
Fund balance–unreserved June 30, 19X5	$ 71,000	$ 15,000

The notes to the financial statements are an integral part of this statement.

	(in thousands of dollars)		
Governmental Fund Types		*Fiduciary Funds*	
Debt Service Funds	*Capital Projects Funds*	*Expendable Trust Funds*	*Total (memorandum only)*
$ 348,000	–	–	$1,248,000
–	–	–	770,000
–	$12,000	–	102,000
9,000	4,000	$ 1,000	79,000
357,000	16,000	1,000	2,199,000
–	–	–	292,000
–	–	–	296,000
–	–	–	36,000
–	–	–	548,000
–	–	–	132,000
–	–	3,000	3,000
480,000	–	–	480,000
205,000	–	–	205,000
–	20,000	–	20,000
–	3,000	–	69,000
685,000	23,000	3,000	2,081,000
(328,000)	(7,000)	(2,000)	118,000
–	10,000	–	10,000
332,000	5,000	3,000	450,000
–	(2,000)	–	(569,000)
332,000	13,000	3,000	(109,000)
4,000	6,000	1,000	9,000
(4,000)	(5,000)	(1,000)	(23,000)
–	1,000	–	(14,000)
–	6,000	–	107,000
–	$ 7,000	–	$ 93,000

City of Centerville
Combined Statement of Revenues, Expenditures, and Changes in Fund Balances—Budget (GAAP Basis) and Actual
General, Special Revenue, and Capital Projects Funds
For Year Ended June 30, 19X5

(in thousands of dollars)

	General Fund			Special Revenue Fund		
	Budget	*Actual*	*Variance*	*Budget*	*Actual*	*Variance*
Revenues						
Taxes	$ 510,000	$ 500,000	$(10,000)	$ 390,000	$ 400,000	$ 10,000
Fees and other nontax revenues	385,000	400,000	15,000	375,000	370,000	(5,000)
Grants and receipts from other governments	94,000	90,000	(4,000)	—	—	—
Other	62,000	60,000	(2,000)	7,000	5,000	(2,000)
Total revenues	1,051,000	1,050,000	(1,000)	772,000	775,000	3,000
Expenditures						
General government	290,000	292,000	(2,000)	—	—	—
Public safety	144,000	146,000	(2,000)	151,000	150,000	1,000
Streets	40,000	36,000	4,000	—	—	—
Recreation and parks	50,000	58,000	(8,000)	485,000	490,000	(5,000)
Health and welfare	135,000	132,000	3,000	—	—	—
Capital outlays	—	—	—	—	—	—
Other	64,000	66,000	(2,000)	—	—	—
Total expenditures	723,000	730,000	(7,000)	636,000	640,000	(4,000)
Excess of revenues over (under) expenditures	328,000	320,000	(8,000)	136,000	135,000	(1,000)
Other financing sources (uses)						
Proceeds from bond sales	—	—	—	—	—	—
Transfers from other funds	18,000	20,000	2,000	85,000	90,000	5,000
Transfers to other funds	(359,000)	(357,000)	2,000	(200,000)	(210,000)	(10,000)
Total other financing sources (uses)	(341,000)	(337,000)	4,000	(115,000)	(120,000)	(5,000)
Excess of revenues and other sources over (under) expenditures and other uses	$ (13,000)	(17,000)	$ (4,000)	$ 21,000	15,000	$ (6,000)
(Increase) decrease in reserve for encumbrances		(3,000)			(10,000)	
Net change in unreserved fund balance for year		(20,000)			5,000	
Fund balance—unreserved July 1, 19X4		91,000			10,000	
Fund balance—unreserved June 30, 19X5		$ 71,000			$ 15,000	

The notes to the financial statements are an integral part of this statement.

(in thousands of dollars)

	Capital Projects Funds			Total		
	Budget	Actual	Variance	Budget	Actual	Variance
	–	–	–	$ 900,000	$ 900,000	–
	–	–	–	760,000	770,000	$ 10,000
	$ 14,000	$12,000	$(2,000)	108,000	102,000	(6,000)
	3,000	4,000	1,000	72,000	69,000	(3,000)
	17,000	16,000	(1,000)	1,840,000	1,841,000	1,000
	–	–	–	290,000	292,000	(2,000)
	–	–	–	295,000	296,000	(1,000)
	–	–	–	40,000	36,000	4,000
	–	–	–	535,000	548,000	(13,000)
	–	–	–	135,000	132,000	3,000
	20,000	20,000	–	20,000	20,000	–
	7,000	3,000	4,000	71,000	69,000	2,000
	27,000	23,000	4,000	1,386,000	1,393,000	(7,000)
	(10,000)	(7,000)	3,000	454,000	448,000	(6,000)
	10,000	10,000	–	10,000	10,000	–
	8,000	5,000	(3,000)	111,000	115,000	4,000
	(1,000)	(2,000)	(1,000)	(560,000)	(569,000)	(9,000)
	17,000	13,000	(4,000)	(439,000)	(444,000)	(5,000)
	$ 7,000	6,000	$(1,000)	$ 15,000	4,000	$(11,000)
		(5,000)			(18,000)	
		1,000			(14,000)	
		6,000			107,000	
		$ 7,000			$ 93,000	

City of Centerville
Combined Statement of Revenues, Expenses, and Changes in Retained Earnings/Fund Balances
All Proprietary Fund Types and Similar Trust Funds
For Year Ended June 30, 19X5

(in thousands of dollars)

	Proprietary Fund Types		Fiduciary Fund Types		
	Enterprise Funds	Internal Service Funds	Pension Trust Fund	Nonexpendable Trust Fund	Totals (memorandum only)
Operating revenues					
Charges and Fees	$197,000	$62,000	—	—	$259,000
Rentals and commissions	23,000	—	—	—	23,000
Contributions—employer	—	—	$ 84,000	$4,000	88,000
Contributions—employees	—	—	42,000	—	42,000
Interest	—	—	38,000	1,000	39,000
Other	11,000	11,000	3,000	1,000	26,000
Total operating revenues	231,000	73,000	167,000	6,000	477,000
Operating expenses					
Personnel services	82,000	33,000	—	—	115,000
Purchase of services	54,000	21,000	—	—	75,000
Materials and supplies	42,000	18,000	—	—	60,000
Depreciation	10,000	3,000	—	—	13,000
Pension benefits	—	—	92,000	—	92,000
Refunds of members' contributions	—	—	5,000	—	5,000
Other	21,000	2,000	3,000	1,000	27,000
Total operating expenses	209,000	77,000	100,000	1,000	387,000
Operating income (loss)	22,000	(4,000)	67,000	5,000	90,000
Nonoperating revenues (expenses)					
Debt service—interest	(8,000)	—	—	—	(8,000)
Grants	15,000	—	—	—	15,000
Other	(10,000)	—	—	—	(10,000)
Total nonoperating revenues (expenses)	(3,000)	—	—	—	(3,000)
Income (loss) before operating transfers	19,000	(4,000)	67,000	5,000	87,000
Operating transfers in (out)	(7,000)	—	—	2,000	(5,000)
Net income	12,000	(4,000)	67,000	7,000	82,000
(Increase) decrease in retained earnings reserved for debt service	(3,000)	—	—	—	(3,000)
(Increase) decrease in fund balance reserved for employee retirement	—	—	(67,000)	—	(67,000)
(Increase) decrease in fund balance reserved for employee emergency loans	—	—	—	(7,000)	(7,000)
Net change in unreserved retained earnings/fund balance for year	9,000	(4,000)	—	—	5,000
Retained earnings/fund balance—unreserved July 1, 19X4	21,000	8,000	—	—	29,000
Retained earnings/fund balance—unreserved June 30, 19X5	$ 30,000	$ 4,000	—	—	$ 34,000

The notes to the financial statements are an integral part of this statement.

City of Centerville
Combined Statement of Changes in Financial Position
All Proprietary Fund Types and Similar Trust Funds
For Year Ended June 30, 19X5

(in thousands of dollars)

	Proprietary Fund Types		Fiduciary Fund Types		
	Enterprise Funds	Internal Service Funds	Pension Trust Fund	Nonexpendable Trust Fund	Total (memorandum only)
Sources of working capital					
Operations					
Net income (loss)	$12,000	$(4,000)	$ 67,000	$ 7,000	$ 82,000
Items not requiring working capital					
Depreciation	10,000	3,000	—	—	13,000
Working capital from operations	22,000	(1,000)	67,000	7,000	95,000
Other sources					
Capital contributions	6,000	2,000	—	—	8,000
Proceeds of bond issue	25,000	—	—	—	25,000
Maturing investments	—	—	70,000	1,000	71,000
Other	5,000	—	—	—	5,000
Total sources	58,000	1,000	137,000	8,000	204,000
Applications of working capital					
Purchase of property, plant, and equipment	21,000	3,000	—	—	24,000
Retirement of debt	11,000	—	—	—	11,000
Acquisition of investments	15,000	—	120,000	6,000	141,000
Other	14,000	1,000	—	—	15,000
Total applications	61,000	4,000	120,000	6,000	191,000
Net increase (decrease) in working capital	$ (3,000)	$(3,000)	$ 17,000	$ 2,000	$ 13,000

Elements of Net Increase (Decrease) in Working Capital

Cash	$ 3,000	$(1,000)	$ (6,000)	$(2,000)	$ (6,000)
Investments	—	—	16,000	—	16,000
Accounts receivable (net)	(3,000)	—	—	1,000	(2,000)
Due from other funds	4,000	3,000	4,000	2,000	13,000
Inventory	1,000	(4,000)	—	—	(3,000)
Interest receivable	—	—	1,000	—	1,000
Other current assets	1,000	1,000	—	—	2,000
Other assets	—	—	1,000	—	1,000
Accounts payable	3,000	—	—	—	3,000
Vouchers payable	1,000	1,000	—	—	2,000
Notes payable	(2,000)	—	—	—	(2,000)
Due to other funds	(6,000)	(1,000)	—	—	(7,000)
Accrued expenses	(3,000)	(2,000)	2,000	1,000	(2,000)
Other liabilities	(2,000)	—	(1,000)	—	(3,000)
Net increase (decrease) in working capital	$ (3,000)	$(3,000)	$ 17,000	$ 2,000	$ 13,000

The notes to the financial statements are an integral part of this statement.

Notes to the Financial Statements

CITY OF CENTERVILLE
NOTES TO FINANCIAL STATEMENTS
FOR YEAR ENDED JUNE 30, 19X5

The accounting methods and procedures adopted by the City of Centerville, New Jersey, conform to generally accepted accounting principles as applied to governmental entities. The following notes to the financial statements are an integral part of the City's Comprehensive Annual Financial Report.

1. SUMMARY OF SIGNIFICANT ACCOUNTING POLICIES

Reporting Entity The City of Centerville was created in 1919 and operates under an elected Mayor/Council form of government. The City's major operations include health services, public safety, fire protection, recreation and parks, and general administrative services. In addition, the City exercises sufficient control over other governmental agencies and authorities that are included as part of the City's reporting entity.

The National Council on Governmental Accounting (NCGA), in order to clarify which organizations, functions, and activities of government should be included in general purpose financial statements, issued NCGA-3 (Defining the Governmental Reporting Entity) in December 1981. The NCGA has been replaced by the Governmental Accounting Standards Board (GASB), but the latter organization has endorsed NCGA-3. In issuing NCGA-3, the NCGA's intention was to provide a basis for making comparisons among units of government or between time periods for a given government, to reduce the possibility of arbitrary exclusion or inclusion of organizations in financial reports, and to enable financial statement users to identify the operations for which governmental entities are responsible. The NCGA concluded that the basic criterion for including an agency, institution, authority, or other organization in a governmental unit's reporting entity is the exercise of oversight responsibility over such agencies by the governmental unit's elected officials. Oversight responsibility is defined to include, but is not limited to:

Financial interdependency When a separate agency produces a financial benefit for or imposes a financial burden on a unit of government, that agency is part of the reporting entity.

Manifestations of financial interdependency include responsibility for financing deficits, entitlements to surpluses, and guarantees of, or "moral responsibility" for, debt.

Selection of governing authority An authoritative appointment is one where the entity's chief elected official maintains a significant continuing relationship with the appointed officials with respect to carrying out important public functions.

Designation of management When management is appointed by and held accountable to a governing authority that is included in the entity, the activity being managed falls within the entity.

Ability to significantly influence operations This ability includes, but is not limited to, the authority to review and approve budgetary requests, adjustments, and amendments.

Accountability for fiscal matters Fiscal authority normally includes the authority for final approval over budgetary appropriations, responsibility for funding deficits and operating deficiencies, disposal of surplus funds, control over the collection and disbursement of funds, and maintenance of title to assets.

There may be, however, factors other than oversight that are so significant that exclusion of a particular agency from a reporting entity's financial statements would be misleading. These other factors include:

(a) *Scope of Public Service*—Aspects to be considered include who the activity benefits and whether it is conducted within the entity's geographic boundaries and generally available to its citizens.
(b) *Special Financing Relationship*—Such a relationship may have been created to benefit the entity by providing for the issuance of debt on behalf of the entity.

Based on the criteria established by NCGA-3, as supplemented by NCGA Interpretation-7 (Clarification as to the Application of the Criteria in NCGA Statement-3—Defining the Governmental Reporting Entity), the reporting entity includes the Centerville School District, the Public Housing Corporation of Centerville, the Centerville Urban Renewal Corporation, the Centerville Flood Control District, and the Centerville Transit Authority.

The City of Centerville's financial statements do not include the Centerville Museum or the Industrial Development Corporation of Centerville. A description of these entities and the reasons for their exclusion from the reporting entity are summarized below.

Centerville Museum

The Centerville Museum was organized in 19X1, and construction of its facilities began the following year on land owned by the city. Currently, the city leases the land to the museum, and this relationship suggests that the museum should be part of the reporting entity. The following factors suggest that the museum should not be included in the reporting entity:

- Contributors to the museum elect all the members of the governing board.
- The governing board is solely responsible for the employment of museum personnel.
- The museum's management is solely responsible for the day-to-day operations of the museum.
- The city is neither entitled to operating surpluses nor responsible for operating deficits of the museum.
- The museum is exclusively responsible for administration of its fiscal affairs.
- The museum is open to the public-at-large and not exclusively for enjoyment of residents of Centerville.

Based on these factors it has been concluded that the City of Centerville has no oversight responsibility for the museum, and therefore the financial statements of the museum are excluded from the reporting entity.

Industrial Development Corporation of Centerville

The Industrial Development Corporation of Centerville was organized in 19X2 to promote and develop commercial and industrial properties, and encourage employment within the city. The following factors strongly suggest that the unit be excluded from the reporting entity's financial statements:

- The corporation's governing board is approved by the mayor, but there is no continuing relationship between the corporation and the city.
- The management of the corporation is selected by the governing board.
- The operation of the corporation is the exclusive responsibility of the corporation's management, and the city has no authority to interfere with these operations.
- The corporation is responsible for its financial affairs including the funding of deficits and the disposition of surpluses.
- The city does not guarantee the corporation's outstanding debt.

Although the city must approve the corporation's issuance of debt and the corporation operates within the geographical boundaries of the city, these factors are not considered significant enough to warrant inclusion of the corporation in the financial statements of the City of Centerville.

Basis of Presentation—Fund Accounting The accounts of the City of Centerville are organized on the basis of funds and account groups, each of which is considered a separate accounting entity. The City has created several types of funds and a number of discrete funds within each fund type. Each fund is accounted for by a separate set of self-balancing accounts that comprise its assets, liabilities, fund balance, revenues, and expenditures/expenses. The individual funds account for the governmental resources allocated to them for the purpose of carrying on specific activities in accordance with laws, regulations, or other restrictions.

The funds are grouped into three fund types and eight generic funds as described below:

Governmental Fund Types These are the funds through which most governmental functions typically are financed. The funds included in this category are as follows:

General Fund This fund is established to account for resources devoted to financing the general services that the City performs for its citizens. General tax revenues and other sources of revenue used to finance the fundamental operations of the City are included in this fund. The fund is charged with all cost of operating the government for which a separate fund has not been established.

Special Revenue Funds These funds are established to account for the proceeds of specific revenue sources other than special assessments, expendable trusts, or major capital projects that are legally restricted to expenditures for specified purposes.

Debt Service Funds These funds are established for the purpose of accumulating resources for the payment of interest and principal on long-term general obligation debt other than those payable from Enterprise Funds and Special Assessment Funds.

Proprietary Fund Types These funds account for operations that are organized to be self-supporting through user charges. The funds included in this category are the Enterprise Funds and Internal Service Funds.

Enterprise Funds These funds are established to account for operations that are financed and operated in a manner similar to private business enterprises, where the intent is that costs of providing goods or services to the general public on a continuing basis be financed or recovered primarily through user charges.

Internal Service Funds These funds are established to account for the financing of goods or services provided by one department to other departments of the City on a cost-reimbursement basis.

Fiduciary Fund Types These funds account for assets held by the City as a trustee or agent for individuals, private organizations, and other units of governments. These funds are as follows:

Pension Trust Fund This fund was established to provide pension benefits for City employees and employees of certain other related governmental agencies. The principal revenue source for this fund is employer and employee contributions.

Nonexpendable Trust Fund This fund is used to account for funds that are to be used for emergency loans to City employees.

Expendable Trust and Agency Funds These funds are used to account for funds that are to be used for educational expenditures incurred by City employees and for funds held in escrow for other parties.

In addition to the three broad types of governmental funds, the City also maintains two account groups as described below:

General Fixed Assets Account Group   This is not a fund but rather an account group that is used to account for general fixed assets acquired principally for general purposes and excludes fixed assets in the Enterprise Funds and the Internal Service Funds.

General Long-Term Debt Account Group   This is not a fund but rather an account group that is used to account for the outstanding principal balances of general obligation bonds and other long-term debt not reported in proprietary funds.

Basis of Accounting   Governmental funds, Expendable Trust Funds, and Agency Funds utilize the modified accrual basis of accounting. Under this method, revenues are recognized in the accounting period in which they become both available and measurable. Licenses and permits, charges for services, fines and forfeits, and miscellaneous revenues are recorded as revenues when received in cash. General property taxes, self-assessed taxes, and investment earnings are recorded when earned (when they are measurable and available). Expenditures are recognized in the accounting period in which the fund liability is incurred, if measurable, except expenditures for debt service, prepaid expenses, and other long-term obligations which are recognized when paid.

All proprietary funds, Nonexpendable Trust Funds, and Pension Trust Funds are accounted for using the accrual basis of accounting. Their revenues are recognized when they are earned, and their expenses are recognized when they are incurred. Interest on revenue bonds, proceeds of which are used in financing the construction of certain assets, is capitalized during the construction period net of interest on the investment of unexpended bond proceeds.

Agency Fund assets and liabilities are accounted for on the modified accrual basis.

Budgetary Data   Formal budgetary accounting is employed as a management control for all funds of the City. Annual operating budgets are adopted each fiscal year through passage of an annual budget ordinance and amended as required for the General Fund, Special Revenues Funds, Debt Service Funds, and proprietary funds, and the same basis of accounting is used to reflect actual revenues and expenditures/expenses recognized on a generally accepted accounting principles basis. Budgets for certain Special Revenues Funds and Capital Projects Funds are made on a project basis, spanning more than one fiscal year. Budgetary control is exercised at the departmental level or by projects.

All unencumbered budget appropriations, except project budgets, lapse at the end of each fiscal year.

Cash The City pools cash resources of its various funds in order to facilitate the management of cash. Cash applicable to a particular fund is readily identifiable. The balance in the pooled cash accounts is available to meet current operating requirements. Cash in excess of current requirements is invested in various interest-bearing securities and disclosed as part of the City's investments.

Receivables All receivables are reported at their gross value and, where appropriate, are reduced by the estimated portion that is expected to be uncollectible. Estimated unbilled revenues from the Water and Sewer Fund are recognized at the end of each fiscal year on a pro rata basis. The estimated amount is based on billings during the month following the close of the fiscal year.

Investments Debt securities are valued at amortized cost since it is generally the policy of the City to hold such investments until they mature.

Due to and due from other funds Interfund receivables and payables arise from interfund transactions and are recorded by all funds affected in the period in which transactions are executed.

Interest receivable Interest on investments and certain receivables are recorded as revenue in the year the interest is earned and is available to pay liabilities of the current period.

Inventories Inventories for all governmental funds are valued at average cost. The purchase method is used to account for inventories. Under the purchase method, inventories are recorded as expenditures when purchased; however, material amounts of inventories are reported as assets of the respective fund. Reported inventories in these funds are equally offset by a fund balance reserve, which indicates they are unavailable for appropriation even though they are a component of reported assets.

Inventories of proprietary funds are valued at the lower of cost (first-in, first-out) or market.

Other assets Other assets held are recorded and accounted for at cost.

Restricted assets Enterprise Funds, based on certain bond covenants, are required to establish and maintain prescribed amounts of resources (consisting of cash and temporary investments) that can be used only to service outstanding debt.

Property, plant, and equipment Fixed assets used in governmental fund type operations are accounted for in the General Fixed Assets Account Group. Public domain (infrastructure) general fixed assets consisting of certain improvements other than buildings, such as roads, sidewalks, and bridges, are not capitalized. Property, plant, and equipment acquired or constructed for general governmental operations are recorded as expenditures in the fund making the expenditure and capitalized at cost in the General Fixed Assets Account Group.

Property, plant, and equipment acquired for proprietary funds is capitalized in the respective funds to which it applies.

Property, plant, and equipment is stated at cost. Where cost could not be determined from the available records, estimated historical cost was used to record the estimated value of the assets. Assets acquired by gift or bequest are recorded at their fair market value at the date of transfer.

Depreciation of exhaustible fixed assets used by proprietary funds is charged as an expense against operations, and accumulated depreciation is reported on the proprietary funds' balance sheets. Depreciation has been provided over the estimated useful lives using the straight-line method of depreciation.

Advances Advances to and advances from governmental funds represent noncurrent portions of interfund receivables and payables. The governmental fund making the advance establishes a fund balance reserve equal to the amount of the advance.

Long-term debt Long-term obligations of the City are reported in the General Long-Term Debt Account Group. Long-term liabilities for certain general obligation bonds, revenue bonds, and mortgage bonds are reported in the appropriate Enterprise Fund.

Pensions The provision for pension cost is recorded on an accrual basis, and the City's policy is to fund pension costs as they accrue.

Fund equity The unreserved fund balances for governmental funds represent the amount available for budgeting future operations. The reserved fund balances for governmental funds represent the amount that has been legally identified for specific purposes. Unreserved retained earnings for proprietary funds represent the net assets available for future operations or distribution. Reserved retained earnings for proprietary funds represent the net assets that have been legally identified for specific purposes.

Revenues and expenditures/expenses Revenues for governmental funds are recorded when they are determined to be both measurable and available. Generally, tax revenues, fees, and nontax revenues are recognized when received. Grants from other governments are recognized when qualifying expenditures are incurred. Expenditures for governmental funds are recorded when the related liability is incurred.

Revenues and expenses of proprietary funds are recognized in essentially the same manner as in commercial accounting.

Property tax revenues Property taxes are levied on July 1 based on the assessed value of property as listed on the previous January 1. Assessed values are an approximation of market value. A revaluation of all real property must be made every seven years. The last revaluation date was January 1, 19X2.

Property taxes are recognized as revenue when they are levied because they are considered to be both measurable and available. Proper allowances are made for estimated uncollectible accounts and delinquent accounts.

Vacation, sick leave, and other compensated absences City employees are entitled to certain compensated absences based on their length of employment. With minor exceptions, compensated absences do not vest or accumulate and are recorded as expenditures when they are paid.

Total Columns The Combined Financial Statements include a total column that is described as memorandum only. Data in these columns do not present financial position, results of operations, or changes in financial position in conformity with generally accepted accounting principles. Interfund transactions have not been eliminated from the total column of each financial statement.

44 / COMPREHENSIVE ANNUAL FINANCIAL REPORT

2. STEWARDSHIP, COMPLIANCE, AND ACCOUNTABILITY

Compliance with bond covenants Certain bond covenants require that the City's total debt, both current and noncurrent, not exceed $3.5 billion. During the fiscal year, the limit was exceeded on two occasions for less than thirty days.

Deposits with financial institutions State statutues require that the City's deposits be collateralized by securities held in the name of the City by the trust department of a bank that does not hold the collateralized deposits. During the year, the City on two occasions permitted a bank to hold securities that collateralized deposits that were held by the same bank.

3. CASH

All bank balances of deposits as of the balance sheet date are entirely insured or collateralized with securities held by the City or by its agent in the City's name.

4. PROPERTY TAXES

The City is responsible for assessing, collecting, and distributing property taxes in accordance with enabling state legislation. Property taxes become a lien on the first day of the levy year and may be paid in two equal installments. The first installment is due on or before April 30 and the second installment, which bears interest at the rate of 6%, is due on or before October 31.

All property taxes are recognized in compliance with NCGA Interpretation-3 (Revenue Recognition—Property Taxes) which states that such revenue is recorded when it becomes measurable and available. Available means due, or past due and receivable within the current period and collected no longer than 60 days after the close of the current period.

Property taxes receivable as of June 30, 19X5, are composed of the following:

90.44 / GOVERNMENTAL GAAP GUIDE

	(in thousands of dollars)	
Year of levy:	General fund	Special revenue fund
19X5	$ 80,000	$14,000
19X4	10,000	1,000
19X3	5,000	
19X2	4,000	
Before 19X2	1,000	
Total property taxes receivable	100,000	15,000
Less allowance for uncollectibles	5,000	
	$ 95,000	$15,000

Most property owners choose to pay property taxes in a single payment on or before April 30 in order to avoid interest charges.

5. INVESTMENTS

Investments made by the City are summarized below. The investments that are represented by specific identifiable investment securities are classified as to credit risk by the three categories described below:

Category 1   Insured or registered, or securities held by the City or its agent in the City's name

Category 2   Uninsured and unregistered, with securities held by the counterparty's trust department or agent in the City's name

Category 3   Uninsured and unregistered, with securities held by the counterparty, or by its trust department or agent but not in the City's name

	(in thousands of dollars)				
	Category			Carrying	Market
	1	2	3	value	value
U.S. government securities				$ 400,000	$ 410,000
Bankers' acceptances		$200,000	$100,000	300,000	305,000
Commercial paper	100,000			100,000	105,000
	$500,000	$200,000	$100,000	800,000	820,000
Investment in state investment pool				301,000	310,000
Total investments				$1,101,000	$1,130,000

6. DUE TO/FROM OTHER FUNDS

As of June 30, 19X5, interfund receivables and payables that resulted from various interfund transactions were as follows:

	(in thousands of dollars)	
	Due from other funds	Due to other funds
General fund	$ 12,000	$ 77,000
Special revenue funds—Parks fund	25,000	24,000
Parking meter fund	5,000	18,000
Debt service funds—General purposes	70,000	
Capital projects funds—Parks fund	4,000	4,000
Civic center	9,000	6,000
Enterprise funds—Airport fund	5,000	6,000
Water and sewer fund	2,000	9,000
Internal service funds—Municpal garage fund	4,000	3,000
Central parking fund	2,000	2,000
Pension trust fund—Employee retirement	12,000	
Nonexpendable trust fund—Employee emergency fund	1,000	
Expendable trust fund—Scholarship fund	2,000	
Agency fund—License fund		4,000
Total	$153,000	$153,000

7. PROPERTY, PLANT, AND EQUIPMENT

Activity for general fixed assets which are capitalized by the City is summarized below:

	(in thousands of dollars)			
	Balances July 1, 19X4	Additions	Deductions	Balances June 30, 19X5
Land	$137,000	$30,000	$ 5,000	$162,000
Buildings	301,000	20,000	15,000	306,000
Equipment	228,000	19,000	25,000	222,000
Under construction	55,000	10,000		65,000
Totals	$721,000	$79,000	$45,000	$755,000

A summary of property, plant, and equipment of proprietary funds is presented below:

	\multicolumn{3}{c	}{Enterprise funds}	\multicolumn{3}{c}{Internal service funds}
(in thousands of dollars)	Airport fund	Water & sewer fund	Total	Municipal garage fund	Central printing fund	Total
Land	$ 40,000	$25,000	$ 65,000	$20,000	$2,000	$22,000
Buildings	72,000	52,000	124,000	13,000	1,000	14,000
Equipment	18,000	6,000	24,000	8,000	3,000	11,000
Under construction	3,000	2,000	5,000			
	133,000	85,000	218,000	41,000	6,000	47,000
Less accumulated depreciation	28,000	47,000	75,000	16,000	2,000	18,000
Net property, plant, and equipment	$105,000	$38,000	$143,000	$25,000	$4,000	$29,000

FASB-34 (Capitalization of Interest Costs) requires that interest expenditures incurred during construction of assets be capitalized. FASB-62 (Capitalization of Interest Cost in Situations Involving Certain Tax-Exempt Borrowings and Certain Gifts and Grants) concludes that constructed assets financed with the proceeds of tax-exempt debt (if those funds are externally restricted to finance the acquisitions of the asset or used to service the related debt) should include capitalized interest only to the extent that interest cost exceeds interest earned on related interest-bearing investments acquired with proceeds of the related tax exempt borrowing. During 19X5, no interest costs were capitalized because interest expenditures related to constructed assets did not exceed related interest revenue.

8. PENSION COSTS

Plan Description

Substantially all full-time employees of the City of Centerville and its related agencies are covered by the City of Centerville PERS. The PERS is the administrator of a single-employer pension plan that was established by the City in accordance with the City charter and state statutes. Although the PERS presents separate financial statements, it is also a component unit (reporting as a Pension Trust Fund) of the City's financial reporting entity.

As of June 30, 19X5, employee membership data related to the pension plan was as follows:

Retirees and beneficiaries currently receiving benefits and terminated employees entitled to benefits but not yet receiving them	6,853
Active plan participants:	
Vested	5,675
Nonvested	32,500
Total	38,175

The pension plan provides pension benefits, deferred allowances, and death and disability benefits. A member may retire after reaching the age of 55 or accumulating 25 years of service in one of the departments or agencies of the city. Benefits vest after 12 years of service. Employees who retire at or after age 55 with 12 or more years of service are entitled to pension payments for the remainder of their lives equal to 2% of their final, five-year average salary times the number of years for which they were employed by the City. The final, five-year average salary is the average salary of the employee during the final five years of full-time employment with the City exclusive of payments for overtime.

Pension provisions include deferred allowances whereby an employee may terminate his or her employment with the City after accumulating 25 years of service but before reaching the age of 55. If the employee does not withdraw his or her accumulated contributions, the employee is entitled to all pension benefits upon reaching the age of 55.

Pension provisions include death and disability benefits whereby the disabled employee or surviving spouse is entitled to receive annually an amount equal to 45% of the employee's final, five-year average salary exclusive of overtime payments. The disabled employee is entitled to receive disability payments for life, while the surviving spouse may receive death benefits for life or as long as the spouse does not remarry.

Employees of the City are required to pay 10.1% of their gross earnings to the pension plan. The payments are deducted from the employee's wages or salary and remitted by the City to the PERS on a monthly basis. If an employee leaves the employment of the City before 12 years of service, the accumulated contributions plus earned interest are refunded to the employee or the employee's designated beneficiary.

The City makes annual contributions to the pension plan equal to the amount required by state statutes.

For the year ended June 30, 19X5, the City's total payroll for all employees and the City's total covered payroll amounted to $457,655,172. *Covered payroll* refers to all compensation paid by the City to active employees covered by the Centerville PERS on which contributions to the pension plan are based.

Summary of Significant Accounting Policies and Plan Asset Matters

The City of Centerville PERS financial statements are prepared on the accrual basis of accounting. Contributions from the City and the City's employees are recognized as revenue in the period in which employees provide services to the City. Investment income is recognized as earned by the pension plan. The net appreciation (depreciation) in the fair value of investments held by the pension plan is recorded as an increase (decrease) to investment income based on the valuation of investments as of the date of the balance sheet.

Investments in securities are valued at current market prices. Corporate bond securities are assigned a value based on yields currently available on securities of issuers with credit ratings similar to the securities held by the pension plan. Unrestricted capital stock securities are assigned a value based on quoted market prices. The estimated value assigned to restricted capital stock securities is based on a multiple of current earnings less an appropriate discount. The earnings multiple is based on current multiples and earnings for companies similar to the securities held by the pension plan.

No investment in any one organization represents 5% or more of the net assets available for pension benefits.

There are no investments in, loans to, or leases with parties related to the pension plan.

Funding Status and Progress

Presented below is the total pension benefit obligation of the City of Centerville PERS. The amount of the total pension benefit obligation is based on a standardized measurement established by GASB-5 that, with some exceptions, must be used by a PERS. The standardized measurement is the actuarial present value of credited projected benefits. This pension valuation method reflects the present value of estimated pension benefits that will be paid in future years as a result of employee services performed to date and is adjusted for the effects of projected salary increases and any step-rate benefits. A standardized measure of the pension benefit obligation was adopted by the GASB to enable readers of the PERS financial statements to (a) assess the City of Centerville PERS funding status on a going-concern basis, (b) assess progress made in accumulating sufficient assets to pay benefits when due, and (c) make comparisons among PERS.

Because the standardized measure is used only for disclosure purposes by the City of Centerville PERS, the measurement is independent of the actuarial computation made to determine contributions to the PERS. The actuarial funding method used to determine contributions to the PERS is explained later in this note.

A variety of significant actuarial assumptions are used to determine the standardized measure of the pension benefit obligation and these assumptions are summarized below:

- The present value of future pension payments was computed by using a discount rate of 7%. The discount rate is equal to the estimated long-term rate of return on current and future investments of the pension plan.
- Future pension payments reflect an assumption of a 5% (compounded annually) salary increase as a result of inflation.
- Future pension payments reflect an assumption of a 2% (compounded annually) salary increase as a result of seniority and/or merit adjustments.
- Future pension payments reflect no post-retirement benefit increases, which is consistent with the terms of the pension agreement.

The standardized measure of the unfunded pension benefit obligation as of June 30, 19X5, is as follows:

Pension benefit obligation:	(in millions)
Retirees and beneficiaries currently receiving benefits and terminated employees not yet receiving benefits	$290.2
Current employees—	
Accumulated employee contributions including allocated investment income	97.4
Employer-financed vested	93.8
Employer-financed nonvested	138.7
Total pension benefit obligation	620.1
Net assets available for benefits, at market	538.0
Unfunded pension benefit obligation	$ 82.1

No changes in actuarial assumptions or benefit provisions that would significantly affect the valuation of the pension benefit obligation occurred during 19X5.

Contributions Required and Contributions Made

Periodic employer contributions to the pension plan are determined on an actuarial basis using the entry age normal actuarial cost method. Normal cost is funded on a current basis. The unfunded actuarial accrued liability is funded over a 30-year period. Periodic contributions for both normal cost and the amortization of the unfunded actuarial accrued liability are based on the level percentage of payroll method. The funding strategy for normal cost and the unfunded actuarial accrued liability should provide sufficient resources to pay employee pension benefits on a timely basis.

Total contributions to the pension plan in 19X5 amounted to $126,000,000, of which $79,632,000 and $46,368,000 were made by the City of Centerville and its employees, respectively. The contributed amounts were actuarially determined as described above and were based on an actuarial valuation as of June 30, 19X5. The pension contributions represent funding for normal cost ($90,000,000) and the amortization of the unfunded actuarial accrued liability ($36,000,000). Contributions made by the City of Centerville and its employees represent 17.4% and 10.1%, respectively, of covered payroll for the year.

Significant actuarial assumptions used to compute pension contribution requirements are the same as those used to determine the standardized measure of the pension obligation.

The computation of the pension contribution requirements for 19X5 was based on the same actuarial assumptions, benefit provisions, actuarial funding method, and other significant factors used to determine pension contribution requirements in previous years.

Trend Information

Historical trend information for the City of Centerville PERS is presented below:

	Fiscal year		
	19X5	19X4	19X3
• Net assets available for benefits as a percentage of the pension benefit obligation applicable to the City's employees	86.8%	81.9%	81.3%
• Unfunded pension benefit obligation as a percentage of the City's annual covered payroll*	17.9%	18.4%	19.8%
• City's contributions to the pension plan as a percentage of annual covered payroll	17.4%	17.3%	17.3%

*Showing the unfunded pension benefit obligation as a percentage of the City's annual covered payroll approximately adjusts for the effects of inflation for analytical purposes.

Ten-year historical trend information is disclosed on pages XX-XX of the City of Centerville PERS separate financial report.

Historical trend information is presented in order for a reader to assess the progress made in accumulating sufficient assets to pay pension benefits as they become payable.

9. CONSTRUCTION AND OTHER SIGNIFICANT COMMITMENTS

As of June 30, 19X5, the City had the following commitments with respect to unfinished capital projects:

Capital project	Remaining construction commitment	Expected date of completion
X4-107-Senior citizen's center	$200,000	June 1, 19X6
X5-004-Police substation	700,000	May 30, 19X7
	$900,000	

10. CLAIMS AND JUDGMENTS

The City participates in a number of federal, state, and county programs that are fully or partially funded by grants received from other governmental units. Expenditures financed by grants are subject to audit by the appropriate grantor government. If expenditures are disallowed due to noncompliance with grant program regulations, the City may be required to reimburse the grantor government. As of June 30, 19X5, significant amounts of grant expenditures have not been audited but the City believes that disallowed expenditures, if any, based on subsequent audits will not have a material effect on any of the individual governmental funds or the overall financial position of the City.

11. LEASE OBLIGATIONS

The City is obligated under certain leases accounted for as operating leases. Operating leases do not give rise to property rights or lease obligations, and therefore the results of the lease agreements are not reflected in the City's account groups. The following is a schedule by years of future minimum rental payments required under operating leases that have initial or remaining noncancelable lease terms in excess of one year as of June 30, 19X5:

Year ending, June 30	Amounts
19X6	$ 20,000
19X7	18,000
19X8	18,000
19X9	15,000
19Y0	10,000
Later years	45,000
Total minimum payments required	$126,000

The following schedule shows the composition of total rental expenditures for all operating leases except those with terms of a month or less that were not renewed:

Minimum rentals	$15,000
Contingent rentals	17,000
Less: Sublease rentals	(4,000)
	$28,000

12. LONG-TERM DEBT

The following is a summary of the City's long-term debt transactions for the year ended, June 30, 19X5:

(in thousands of dollars)

	General obligation bonds	General obligation bonds (Enterprise funds)	Revenue bonds (Enterprise funds)	Mortgage notes (Enterprise funds)
Debt outstanding 7/1/X4	$2,799,000	$70,000	$16,000	$15,000
Additions of new debt	10,000	20,000	5,000	
Retirements and repayments	(480,000)	(10,000)		(1,000)
Debt outstanding 6/30/X5	$2,329,000	$80,000	$21,000	$14,000

Debt outstanding as of June 30, 19X5, consisted of the following:

(in thousands of dollars)

	Interest rate	Maturity date	Amounts Issued	Amounts Outstanding
General obligations bonds				
Serial bonds	7.6%	*	$1,500,000	$1,000,000
Term bonds	8.2%	19Y5	$2,000,000	1,329,000
				$2,329,000
Enterprise fund bonds				
Term bonds (general obligation)	10.5%	19Y6	100,000	$80,000
Revenue bonds	9.0%	19Y2	25,000	21,000
Mortgage notes	10.1%	*	22,000	14,000
				$ 115,000

* Due in installments

Presented below is a summary of debt service requirements to maturity by years:

(in thousands of dollars)

	General obligation		Enterprise funds		
	Serial bonds	Term bonds	Term bonds	Revenue bonds	Mortgage bonds
19X6	$557,000	$108,978	$8,400	$1,890	$3,300
19X7	528,500	108,978	8,400	1,890	3,300
19X8		108,978	8,400	1,890	3,300
19X9		108,978	8,400	1,890	3,300
19Y0		108,978	8,400	1,890	3,300
19Y1		108,978	8,400	1,890	3,300
19Y2		108,978	8,400	22,890	
19Y3		108,978	8,400		
19Y4		108,978	8,400		
19Y5		1,437,978	8,400		
19Y6			88,400		
19Y7					
Total	$1,085,500	$2,418,780	$172,400	$34,230	$19,800

The amount of long-term debt that can be incurred by the City is limited by state statute. Total outstanding long-term obligations during a year can be no greater than 11% of the assessed value of taxable property as of the beginning of the fiscal year. As of June 30, 19X5, the amount of outstanding long-term debt was equal to 5.4% of property assessments as of July 1, 19X4.

On May 15, 19X5, the City was authorized by voter approval to issue the following long-term debt:

<pre>
General obligations bonds:
   Street and curbing improvements   3,000,000
   Landfill acquisition sites   6,000,000
Revenue bonds:
   Airport expansion   1,000,000
                                      $10,000,000
</pre>

As of June 30, 19X5, none of the authorized bonds listed above had been issued.

All outstanding revenue bonds are secured by a first lien on net revenues earned by Enterprise Funds. Net revenues are defined in the revenue bond agreements. The Enterprise Funds are required to establish user fees and rates that will yield net revenues equal to at least 1.3 times the debt service that will become due in the following fiscal year.

13. FUND EQUITY

Reservations of fund balances of governmental funds are created to either (1) satisfy legal covenants that require that a portion of the fund balance be segregated or (2) identify the portion of the fund balance that is not appropriable for future expenditures. Specific reservations of the fund balance accounts are summarized below.

Reserve for encumbrances This reserve was created to represent encumbrances outstanding at the end of the year based on purchase orders and contracts signed by the City but not completed as of the close of the fiscal year.

Reserve for inventories This reserve was created to represent the portion of the fund balance that is not available for expenditures because the City expects to use these resources within the next budgetary period.

Reserve for debt service This reserve was created to segregate a portion of the fund balance account for debt service, including both principal payments and interest payments. The reservation was established to satisfy legal restrictions imposed by various bond agreements.

Reserve for retirement system This reserve was created to restrict the use of all resources contributed to or earned by the Pension Trust Fund. State statutes require that such fund balance be fully reserved.

Reserve for employee loans This reserve was created to restrict the use of all resources contributed to or earned by the Employee Emergency Loan Fund. The restriction was mandated by a donor trust agreement.

Reserve for employee scholarships This reserve was created to restrict the use of all resources contributed to or earned by the Employee Scholarship Fund. The restriction was mandated by a donor trust agreement.

Reserve for advance to internal service fund This reserve was created to represent the portion of the fund balance in the General Fund that is not available for expenditures of the General Fund because repayment by the Internal Service Fund is not expected to be made until two years after the close of the current fiscal year.

Reservations of retained earnings of Enterprise Funds are created by increases in assets restricted for debt service. These increases result from earnings on restricted assets and other interfund transfers to restricted accounts. Earnings on restricted assets are included in net income of the Enterprise Funds. When reserved retained earnings are increased there is an equal reduction to the portion of retained earnings that is unreserved. Specific reservations of retained earnings are summarized below.

Reserve for debt service This reserve was created in conjunction with the issuance of revenue bonds and is funded by initial deposits from the proceeds of such bonds and by transfers from the revenue accounts based on assets held by the Enterprise Funds that are restricted for debt service. The purpose of the reserved retained earnings is to service the revenue bonds.

14. RELATED-PARTY TRANSACTIONS

The City provides certain legal, engineering, and printing services to the Industrial Development Corporation of Centerville (IDCC). Although the IDCC was created by the City and its governing board is approved by the mayor, it is not part of the City's financial reporting entity. Services provided by the City to the IDCC are billed at an amount that will approximately recover the City's full cost of providing such services. This basis of billing has been used by the City consistently over the years to determine the amount of revenues and expenditures/expenses arising from quasi-external transactions.

Total billings for the period amounted to $37,000, and this amount was reported as revenue by the General Fund ($31,000) and the Central Printing Fund (Internal Service Fund) ($6,000) and as an expense by the IDCC. As of the end of the year, an intergovernmental receivable (of $6,000) arising from the services provided to the IDCC was reported by the General Fund ($4,000) and the Central Printing Fund ($2,000).

15. SUMMARY DISCLOSURE OF SIGNIFICANT CONTINGENCIES

Litigation The City is a defendant in a number of lawsuits arising principally from claims against the City for alleged improper actions by City employees, including alleged improper police action, negligence, and discrimination. Total damages claimed are substantial; however, it has been the City's experience that such actions are settled for amounts substantially less than the claimed amounts. The City Attorney estimates that the potential claims against the City not covered by various insurance policies would not materially affect the financial condition of the City.

16. SIGNIFICANT EFFECTS OF SUBSEQUENT EVENTS

On July 25, 19X5, the City issued tax revenue and anticipation notes in the amount of $10,000,000. The interest rate on this debt is 7.4%. The notes will be repaid in fiscal year 19X6 from unrestricted funds, primarily from sales and property tax revenues. The note resolution requires that the City set aside in a restricted fund one quarter of the principal and interest due in the months of September, December, March, and June of fiscal year 19X6. Repayment of notes is scheduled for June 20, 19X6.

Combining Statements

Combining Statements
Governmental Fund Types

City of Centerville
Special Revenue Funds
Combining Balance Sheet
June 30, 19X5

(in thousands of dollars)

	Parks Funds	Parking Meters Funds	Totals
ASSETS			
Cash	$ 20,000	$ 5,000	$ 25,000
Accounts receivable	5,000	8,000	13,000
Allowance for doubtful accounts	(3,000)	(1,000)	(4,000)
Taxes receivable	15,000	12,000	27,000
Investments	80,000	70,000	150,000
Due from other funds	25,000	5,000	30,000
Inventories	8,000	15,000	23,000
Total assets	$150,000	$114,000	$264,000
LIABILITIES			
Vouchers payable	$ 45,000	$ 32,000	$ 77,000
Accounts payable	23,000	16,000	39,000
Accrued expenses	12,000	1,000	13,000
Due to other funds	24,000	18,000	42,000
Other liabilities	22,000	20,000	42,000
Total liabilities	126,000	87,000	213,000
FUND BALANCES			
Reserved for encumbrances	5,000	8,000	13,000
Reserved for inventories	8,000	15,000	23,000
Unreserved	11,000	4,000	15,000
Total fund balances	24,000	27,000	51,000
Total liabilities and fund balances	$150,000	$114,000	$264,000

City of Centerville
Special Revenue Funds
Combining Statement of Revenues, Expenditures, and Changes in Fund Balances
For Year Ended June 30, 19X5

(in thousands of dollars)

	Parks Funds	Parking Meters Funds	Totals
Revenues			
Taxes	$400,000	–	$400,000
Charges and fees	–	$ 370,000	370,000
Other	4,000	1,000	5,000
Total revenues	404,000	371,000	775,000
Expenditures			
Public safety	–	150,000	150,000
Recreation and parks	490,000	–	490,000
Total expenditures	490,000	150,000	640,000
Excess of revenues over (under) expenditures	(86,000)	221,000	135,000
Other financing sources (uses)			
Transfers from other funds	90,000	–	90,000
Transfers to other funds	–	(210,000)	(210,000)
Total other financing sources (uses)	90,000	(210,000)	(120,000)
Excess of revenues and other sources over (under) expenditures and other uses	4,000	11,000	15,000
(Increase) decrease in reserve for encumbrances	(1,000)	(9,000)	(10,000)
Net change in unreserved fund balance for year	3,000	2,000	5,000
Fund balance – unreserved July 1, 19X4	8,000	2,000	10,000
Fund balance – unreserved June 30, 19X5	$ 11,000	$ 4,000	$ 15,000

City of Centerville
Special Revenue Funds
Combining Statement of Revenues, Expenditures, Encumbrances, and Changes in Fund Balances
Budget (GAAP Basis) and Actual
For Year Ended June 30, 19X5

(in thousands of dollars)

Parks Fund

	Budget	Actual	Variance favorable (unfavorable)
Revenues			
Taxes	$390,000	$400,000	$10,000
Charges and fees	—	—	—
Other	5,000	4,000	(1,000)
Total revenues	395,000	404,000	9,000
Expenditures			
Public safety	—	—	—
Recreation and parks	485,000	490,000	(5,000)
Total expenditures	485,000	490,000	(5,000)
Excess of revenues over (under) expenditures	(90,000)	(86,000)	4,000
Other financing sources (uses)			
Transfers from other funds	85,000	90,000	5,000
Transfers to other funds	—	—	—
Total other financing sources (uses)	85,000	90,000	5,000
Excess of revenues and other sources over (under) expenditures and other uses	$ (5,000)	4,000	$ 9,000
(Increase) decrease in reserve for encumbrances		(1,000)	
Net change in unreserved fund balance for year		3,000	
Fund balance—unreserved July 1, 19X4		8,000	
Fund balance—unreserved June 30, 19X5		$ 11,000	

Note: This financial statement is not required by NCGA-1.

(in thousands of dollars)

	Parking Meters Fund			Totals		
Budget	Actual	Variance favorable (unfavorable)	Budget	Actual	Variance favorable (unfavorable)
—	—	—	$ 390,000	$ 400,000	$ 10,000
$ 375,000	$ 370,000	$ (5,000)	375,000	370,000	(5,000)
2,000	1,000	(1,000)	7,000	5,000	(2,000)
377,000	371,000	(6,000)	772,000	775,000	3,000
151,000	150,000	1,000	151,000	150,000	1,000
—	—	—	485,000	490,000	(5,000)
151,000	150,000	1,000	636,000	640,000	(4,000)
226,000	221,000	(5,000)	136,000	135,000	(1,000)
—	—	—	85,000	90,000	5,000
(200,000)	(210,000)	(10,000)	(200,000)	(210,000)	(10,000)
(200,000)	(210,000)	(10,000)	(115,000)	(120,000)	(5,000)
$ 26,000	11,000	$(15,000)	$ 21,000	15,000	$ (6,000)
	(9,000)			(10,000)	
	2,000			5,000	
	2,000			10,000	
	$ 4,000			$ 15,000	

City of Centerville
Debt Service Funds
Combining Balance Sheet
June 30, 19X5

(in thousands of dollars)

	General Purposes	Park Purposes	Civic Center	Totals
ASSETS				
Cash	$100,000	$40,000	$170,000	$310,000
Investments	200,000	40,000	100,000	340,000
Due from other funds	70,000	–	–	70,000
Interest receivable	15,000	5,000	10,000	30,000
Total assets	$385,000	$85,000	$280,000	$750,000
LIABILITIES				
Deferred revenues	$ 10,000	–	–	$ 10,000
Other liabilities	6,000	$ 3,000	$ 2,000	11,000
Total liabilities	16,000	3,000	2,000	21,000
FUND BALANCES				
Reserved for debt service	369,000	82,000	278,000	729,000
Total fund balances	369,000	82,000	278,000	729,000
Total liabilities and fund balances	$385,000	$85,000	$280,000	$750,000

City of Centerville
Debt Service Funds
Combining Statement of Revenues, Expenditures, and Changes in Fund Balances
For Year Ended June 30, 19X5

(in thousands of dollars)

	General Purposes	Park Purposes	Civic Center	Totals
Revenues				
Taxes	$187,000	$ 45,000	$116,000	$ 348,000
Other	6,000	3,000	—	9,000
Total revenues	193,000	48,000	116,000	357,000
Expenditures				
Debt service:				
Principal	320,000	100,000	60,000	480,000
Interest	90,000	15,000	100,000	205,000
Total expenditures	410,000	115,000	160,000	685,000
Excess of revenues over (under) expenditures	(217,000)	(67,000)	(44,000)	(328,000)
Other financing sources (uses)				
Transfers from other funds	218,000	69,000	45,000	332,000
Excess of revenues and other sources over (under) expenditures and other uses	1,000	2,000	1,000	4,000
(Increase) decrease in reserve for debt service	(1,000)	(2,000)	(1,000)	(4,000)
Net change in unreserved fund balances for year	—	—	—	—
Fund balances—unreserved July 1, 19X4	—	—	—	—
Fund balances—unreserved June 30, 19X5	—	—	—	—

City of Centerville
Capital Projects Funds
Combining Balance Sheet
June 30, 19X5

(in thousands of dollars)

	Parks	Civic Center	Totals
ASSETS			
Cash	$ 6,000	$12,000	$18,000
Investments	5,000	–	5,000
Due from other funds	4,000	9,000	13,000
Interest receivable	1,000	–	1,000
Other assets	2,000	6,000	8,000
Total assets	$18,000	$27,000	$45,000
LIABILITIES			
Vouchers payable	$ 3,000	$ 5,000	$ 8,000
Accounts payable	2,000	3,000	5,000
Accrued expenses	1,000	2,000	3,000
Due to other funds	4,000	6,000	10,000
Other liabilities	3,000	4,000	7,000
Total liabilities	13,000	20,000	33,000
FUND BALANCES			
Reserved for encumbrances	2,000	3,000	5,000
Unreserved—undesignated	3,000	4,000	7,000
Total fund balances	5,000	7,000	12,000
Total liabilities and fund balances	$18,000	$27,000	$45,000

City of Centerville
Capital Projects Funds
Combining Statement of Revenues, Expenditures, and Changes in Fund Balances
For Year Ended June 30, 19X5

(in thousands of dollars)

	Parks	Civic Center	Totals
Revenues			
Revenues from other governments	—	$12,000	$12,000
Other	—	4,000	4,000
Total revenues	—	16,000	16,000
Expenditures			
Capital outlays	$ 8,000	12,000	20,000
Other	1,000	2,000	3,000
Total expenditures	9,000	14,000	23,000
Excess of revenues over (under) expenditures	(9,000)	2,000	(7,000)
Other financing sources (uses)			
Proceeds of bond sales	10,000	—	10,000
Transfers from other funds	3,000	2,000	5,000
Transfers to other funds	(2,000)	—	(2,000)
Total other financing sources (uses)	11,000	2,000	13,000
Excess of revenues and other sources over (under) expenditures and other uses	2,000	4,000	6,000
(Increase) decrease in reserve for encumbrances	(3,000)	(2,000)	(5,000)
Net change in unreserved fund balance for year	(1,000)	2,000	1,000
Fund balance—unreserved July 1, 19X4	4,000	2,000	6,000
Fund balance—unreserved June 30, 19X5	$ 3,000	$ 4,000	$ 7,000

City of Centerville
Capital Projects Funds
Combining Statement of Revenues, Expenditures, Encumbrances, and Changes in Fund Balances Budget (GAAP Basis) and Actual
For Year Ended June 30, 19X5

(in thousands of dollars)

	Parks Budget	Parks Actual	Variance favorable (unfavorable)
Revenues			
Revenues from other governments	—	—	—
Other	—	—	—
Total revenues	—	—	—
Expenditures			
Capital outlays	$ 9,000	$ 8,000	$ 1,000
Other	3,000	1,000	2,000
Total expenditures	12,000	9,000	3,000
Excess of revenues over (under) expenditures	(12,000)	(9,000)	3,000
Other financing sources (uses)			
Proceeds from bond sales	10,000	10,000	—
Transfers from other funds	4,000	3,000	(1,000)
Transfers to other funds	(1,000)	(2,000)	(1,000)
Total other financing sources (uses)	13,000	11,000	(2,000)
Excess of revenues and other sources over (under) expenditures and other uses	$ 1,000	2,000	$ 1,000
(Increase) decrease in reserve for encumbrances		(3,000)	
Net change in unreserved fund balance for year		(1,000)	
Fund balance—unreserved July 1, 19X4		4,000	
Fund balance—unreserved June 30, 19X5		$ 3,000	

Note: This financial statement is not required by NCGA-1.

(in thousands of dollars)

	Civic Center			Totals		
Budget	Actual	*Variance favorable (unfavorable)*		Budget	Actual	*Variance favorable (unfavorable)*
$14,000	$12,000	$(2,000)		$ 14,000	$12,000	$(2,000)
3,000	4,000	1,000		3,000	4,000	1,000
17,000	16,000	(1,000)		17,000	16,000	(1,000)
11,000	12,000	(1,000)		20,000	20,000	—
4,000	2,000	2,000		7,000	3,000	4,000
15,000	14,000	1,000		27,000	23,000	4,000
2,000	2,000	—		(10,000)	(7,000)	3,000
—	—	—		10,000	10,000	—
4,000	2,000	(2,000)		8,000	5,000	(3,000)
—	—	—		(1,000)	(2,000)	(1,000)
4,000	2,000	(2,000)		17,000	13,000	(4,000)
$ 6,000	4,000	$(2,000)		$ 7,000	6,000	$(1,000)
	(2,000)				(5,000)	
	2,000				1,000	
	2,000				6,000	
	$ 4,000				$ 7,000	

Combining Statements
Proprietary Fund Types

City of Centerville
Enterprise Funds
Combining Balance Sheet
June 30, 19X5

(in thousands of dollars)

	Airport Fund	Water & Sewer Fund	Total
ASSETS			
Current assets			
Cash	$ 4,000	$ 6,000	$ 10,000
Accounts receivable	8,000	25,000	33,000
Allowance for doubtful accounts	(2,000)	(4,000)	(6,000)
Due from other funds	5,000	2,000	7,000
Inventory	1,000	2,000	3,000
Other current assets	3,000	4,000	7,000
Total current assets	19,000	35,000	54,000
Restricted assets			
Cash on deposit	6,000	2,000	8,000
Investments	12,000	4,000	16,000
Accounts receivable	2,000	1,000	3,000
Sinking fund	20,000	17,000	37,000
Interest receivable	2,000	1,000	3,000
Total restricted assets	42,000	25,000	67,000
Property, plant, and equipment			
Land	40,000	25,000	65,000
Buildings	72,000	52,000	124,000
Equipment	18,000	6,000	24,000
Under construction	3,000	2,000	5,000
	133,000	85,000	218,000
Less accumulated depreciation	28,000	47,000	75,000
Net property, plant, and equipment	105,000	38,000	143,000
Total assets	$166,000	$98,000	$264,000

	(in thousands of dollars)		
	Airport Fund	Water & Sewer Fund	Total
LIABILITIES AND FUND EQUITY			
Current liabilities			
Vouchers payable	$ 2,000	$ 3,000	$ 5,000
Accounts payable	1,000	2,000	3,000
Accrued expenses	2,000	4,000	6,000
Due to other funds	6,000	9,000	15,000
Deferred revenues	4,000	6,000	10,000
Notes payable	1,000	4,000	5,000
Total current liabilities	16,000	28,000	44,000
Long-term liabilities			
General obligation bonds	40,000	40,000	80,000
Revenue bonds	18,000	3,000	21,000
Mortgage notes payable	12,000	2,000	14,000
Total long-term liabilities	70,000	45,000	115,000
Total liabilities	86,000	73,000	159,000
Fund equity			
Contributed capital—municipality	40,000	10,000	50,000
Contributed capital—others	20,000	5,000	25,000
Total contributed capital	60,000	15,000	75,000
Retained earnings—reserved for debt service	5,000	2,000	7,000
Retained earnings—unreserved	15,000	8,000	23,000
Total retained earnings	20,000	10,000	30,000
Total equity	80,000	25,000	105,000
Total liabilities and fund equity	$166,000	$98,000	$264,000

City of Centerville
Enterprise Funds
Combining Statement of Revenues, Expenses, and Changes in Retained Earnings
For Year Ended June 30, 19X5

(in thousands of dollars)

	Airport Fund	Water & Sewer Fund	Total
Operating revenues			
Charges and fees	$117,000	$ 80,000	$197,000
Rentals and commissions	23,000	–	23,000
Other	7,000	4,000	11,000
Total operating revenues	147,000	84,000	231,000
Operating expenses			
Personnel services	45,000	37,000	82,000
Purchase of services	30,000	24,000	54,000
Materials and supplies	20,000	22,000	42,000
Depreciation	7,000	3,000	10,000
Other	11,000	10,000	21,000
Total operating expenses	113,000	96,000	209,000
Operating income (loss)	34,000	(12,000)	22,000
Nonoperating revenues (expenses)			
Debt service – interest	(5,000)	(3,000)	(8,000)
Grants	1,000	14,000	15,000
Other	(8,000)	(2,000)	(10,000)
Total nonoperating revenues (expenses)	(12,000)	9,000	(3,000)
Income (loss) before operating transfers	22,000	(3,000)	19,000
Operating transfers in (out)	(14,000)	7,000	(7,000)
Net income	8,000	4,000	12,000
(Increase) decrease in retained earnings reserved for debt service	(2,000)	(1,000)	(3,000)
Net change in unreserved retained earnings for year	6,000	3,000	9,000
Retained earnings – unreserved July 1, 19X4	14,000	7,000	21,000
Retained earnings – unreserved June 30, 19X5	$ 20,000	$ 10,000	$ 30,000

City of Centerville
Enterprise Funds
Combining Statement of Changes
in Financial Position
For Year Ended June 30, 19X5

(in thousands of dollars)

	Airport Fund	Water & Sewer Fund	Total
Sources of working capital			
Operations			
Net income (loss)	$ 8,000	$ 4,000	$12,000
Items not requiring working capital			
Depreciation	7,000	3,000	10,000
Working capital from operations	15,000	7,000	22,000
Other sources			
Capital contributions	6,000	–	6,000
Proceeds of bond issues	5,000	20,000	25,000
Other	2,000	3,000	5,000
Total sources	28,000	30,000	58,000
Applications of working capital			
Purchase of property, plant, and equipment	9,000	12,000	21,000
Retirement of debt	5,000	6,000	11,000
Acquisition of investments	6,000	9,000	15,000
Other	6,000	8,000	14,000
Total applications	26,000	35,000	61,000
Net increase (decrease) in working capital	$ 2,000	$(5,000)	$(3,000)

Elements of Net Increase (Decrease) in Working Capital

	Airport Fund	Water & Sewer Fund	Total
Cash	$ 1,000	$ 2,000	$ 3,000
Accounts receivable (net)	2,000	(5,000)	(3,000)
Due from other funds	3,000	1,000	4,000
Inventory	–	1,000	1,000
Other current assets	(2,000)	3,000	1,000
Accounts payable	1,000	2,000	3,000
Vouchers payable	–	1,000	1,000
Notes payable	–	(2,000)	(2,000)
Due to other funds	(1,000)	(5,000)	(6,000)
Accrued expenses	(1,000)	(2,000)	(3,000)
Deferred revenues	(1,000)	(1,000)	(2,000)
Net increase (decrease) in working capital	$ 2,000	$(5,000)	$(3,000)

City of Centerville
Internal Service Funds
Combining Balance Sheet
June 30, 19X5

(in thousands of dollars)

	Municipal Garage Fund	Central Printing Fund	Total
ASSETS			
Current assets			
Cash	$ 1,000	$ 1,000	$ 2,000
Due from other funds	4,000	2,000	6,000
Inventory	6,000	3,000	9,000
Other current assets	1,000	2,000	3,000
Total current assets	12,000	8,000	20,000
Property, plant, and equipment			
Land	20,000	2,000	22,000
Buildings	13,000	1,000	14,000
Equipment	8,000	3,000	11,000
	41,000	6,000	47,000
Less accumulated depreciation	16,000	2,000	18,000
Net property, plant, and equipment	25,000	4,000	29,000
Total assets	$37,000	$12,000	$49,000
LIABILITIES AND FUND EQUITY			
Current liabilities			
Vouchers payable	$ 2,000	$ 1,000	$ 3,000
Accounts payable	1,000	—	1,000
Accrued expenses	2,000	2,000	4,000
Due to other funds	3,000	2,000	5,000
Total current liabilities	8,000	5,000	13,000
Long-term liabilities			
Advance from general fund	15,000	5,000	20,000
Total liabilities	23,000	10,000	33,000
Fund equity			
Contributed capital	7,000	5,000	12,000
Retained earnings	3,000	1,000	4,000
Total fund equity	10,000	6,000	16,000
Total liabilities and fund equity	$33,000	$16,000	$49,000

City of Centerville
Internal Service Funds
Combining Statement of Revenues, Expenses, and Changes in Retained Earnings
For Year Ended June 30, 19X5

(in thousands of dollars)

	Municipal Garage Fund	Central Printing Fund	Total
Operating revenues			
Charges and fees	$40,000	$22,000	$62,000
Other	8,000	3,000	11,000
Total operating revenues	48,000	25,000	73,000
Operating expenses			
Personnel services	20,000	13,000	33,000
Purchase of services	16,000	5,000	21,000
Materials and supplies	7,000	11,000	18,000
Depreciation	2,000	1,000	3,000
Other	1,000	1,000	2,000
Total operating expenses	46,000	31,000	77,000
Operating income (loss)	2,000	(6,000)	(4,000)
Retained earnings—unreserved July 1, 19X4	1,000	7,000	8,000
Retained earnings—unreserved June 30, 19X5	$ 3,000	$ 1,000	$ 4,000

City of Centerville
Internal Service Funds
Statement of Changes in Financial Position
For Year Ended June 30, 19X5

(in thousands of dollars)

	Municipal Garage Fund	Central Printing Fund	Total
Sources of working capital			
Operations			
Net income (loss)	$ 2,000	$(6,000)	$(4,000)
Items not requiring working capital			
Depreciation	2,000	1,000	3,000
Working capital from operations	4,000	(5,000)	(1,000)
Other sources			
Capital contributions	1,000	1,000	2,000
Total sources	5,000	(4,000)	1,000
Applications of working capital			
Purchase of property, plant, and equipment	3,000	–	3,000
Other	–	1,000	1,000
Total applications	3,000	1,000	4,000
Net increase (decrease) in working capital	$ 2,000	$(5,000)	$(3,000)

Elements of Net Increase (Decrease) in Working Capital

Cash	$(1,000)	–	$(1,000)
Due from other funds	2,000	$ 1,000	3,000
Inventory	2,000	(6,000)	(4,000)
Other current assets	1,000	–	1,000
Vouchers payable	–	1,000	1,000
Accounts payable	–	–	–
Accrued expenses	(1,000)	(1,000)	(2,000)
Due to other funds	(1,000)	–	(1,000)
Net increase (decrease) in working capital	$ 2,000	$(5,000)	$(3,000)

Combining Statements
Fiduciary Fund Types

City of Centerville
Fiduciary Funds
Combining Balance Sheet
June 30, 19X5

(in thousands of dollars)

	Pension Trust Fund *Employee Retirement*	Nonexpendable Trust Fund *Employee Emergency Loan*	Expendable Trust Fund *Employee Scholarship*
ASSETS			
Cash	$ 15,000	$ 6,000	$14,000
Accounts receivable	—	14,000	—
Allowance for doubtful accounts	—	(2,000)	—
Investments	495,000	3,000	8,000
Due from other funds	12,000	1,000	2,000
Interest receivable	14,000	3,000	1,000
Other assets	2,000	2,000	2,000
Total assets	$538,000	$27,000	$27,000
LIABILITIES			
Accrued expense	$ 4,000	$ 3,000	—
Due to other funds	—	—	—
Payroll taxes payable	—	—	—
Other	6,000	—	—
Total liabilities	10,000	3,000	—
FUND BALANCES			
Reserved for retirement system	528,000	—	—
Reserved for loans	—	24,000	—
Reserved for scholarships	—	—	$27,000
Total fund balances	528,000	24,000	27,000
Total liabilities and fund balances	$538,000	$27,000	$27,000

(in thousands of dollars)

	Agency Funds		
Payroll Escrow	License		Total
$2,000	$4,000	$	41,000
—	—		14,000
—	—		(2,000)
—	—		506,000
—	—		15,000
—	—		18,000
—	—		6,000
$2,000	$4,000		$598,000
—	—	$	7,000
—	4,000		4,000
$2,000	—		2,000
—	—		6,000
2,000	4,000		19,000
—	—		528,000
—	—		24,000
—	—		27,000
—	—		579,000
$2,000	$4,000		$598,000

Account Groups

City of Centerville
Statement of General Fixed Assets
June 30, 19X5

(in thousands of dollars)

General fixed assets		
Land		$162,000
Buildings		306,000
Equipment		222,000
Under construction		65,000
Total general fixed assets		$755,000
Investments in general fixed assets from		
General fund		$383,000
Special revenue funds		112,000
Capital projects funds		
General obligation bonds	$110,000	
Federal grants	80,000	
State grants	41,000	231,000
Special assessment funds		15,000
Donations		14,000
Total investment in general fixed assets		$755,000

City of Centerville
Schedule of General Fixed Assets
(By Function and Activity)
June 30, 19X5

(in thousands of dollars)

	Land	Buildings	Equipment	Total
Function and activity				
General government control				
Legislative	–	–	$ 12,000	$ 12,000
Executive	–	–	10,000	10,000
Judicial	–	–	40,000	40,000
Total control	–	–	62,000	62,000
Staff functions				
General government buildings	$ 50,000	$102,000	23,000	175,000
Community improvements	5,000	18,000	2,000	25,000
Legal and finance	–	–	15,000	15,000
Other	–	–	5,000	5,000
Total staff functions	55,000	120,000	45,000	220,000
Total general government	55,000	120,000	107,000	282,000
Public safety				
Police	70,000	110,000	40,000	220,000
Fire	10,000	20,000	40,000	70,000
Inspection	5,000	10,000	5,000	20,000
Total public safety	85,000	140,000	85,000	310,000
Streets	1,000	12,000	13,000	26,000
Sanitation	2,000	8,000	12,000	22,000
Health and welfare	5,000	13,000	1,000	19,000
Libraries	5,000	12,000	1,000	18,000
Recreation	9,000	1,000	3,000	13,000
Total	22,000	46,000	30,000	98,000
Total general fixed assets allocated to functions and activities	$162,000	$306,000	$222,000	690,000
Under construction				65,000
Total general fixed assets				$755,000

City of Centerville
Schedule of Changes in General Fixed Assets
(By Function and Activity)
For Year Ended June 30, 19X5

(in thousands of dollars)

	General Fixed Assets 7/1/X4	Additions	Deductions	General Fixed Assets 6/30/X5
Function and activity				
General government control				
Legislature	$ 9,000	$ 5,000	$ 2,000	$ 12,000
Executive	8,000	3,000	1,000	10,000
Judicial	35,000	5,000	—	40,000
Total control	52,000	13,000	3,000	62,000
Staff functions				
General government buildings	166,000	10,000	1,000	175,000
Community improvements	22,000	3,000	—	25,000
Legal and finance	10,000	7,000	2,000	15,000
Other	4,000	1,000	—	5,000
Total staff functions	202,000	21,000	3,000	220,000
Total general government	254,000	34,000	6,000	282,000
Public safety				
Police	230,000	10,000	20,000	220,000
Fire	80,000	—	10,000	70,000
Inspection	15,000	7,000	2,000	20,000
Total public safety	325,000	17,000	32,000	310,000
Streets	24,000	3,000	1,000	26,000
Sanitation	20,000	2,000	—	22,000
Health and welfare	18,000	5,000	4,000	19,000
Libraries	16,000	3,000	1,000	18,000
Recreation	9,000	5,000	1,000	13,000
Total	87,000	18,000	7,000	98,000
Total general fixed assets allocated to functions and activities	$666,000	$69,000	$45,000	690,000
Under construction				65,000
Total general fixed assets				$755,000

City of Centerville
Statement of General Long-Term Debt
June 30, 19X5

(in thousands of dollars)

Amount available and to be provided for the payment of general long-term debt		
Serial bonds		
Amount available in debt service funds	$300,000	
Amount to be provided	700,000	$1,000,000
Term bonds		
Amount available in debt service fund	429,000	
Amount to be provided	900,000	1,329,000
Total amount available and to be provided		$2,329,000
General long-term debt payable		
Serial bonds payable		$1,000,000
Term bonds payable		1,329,000
Total general long-term debt payable		$2,329,000

City of Centerville
Schedule of Changes in Long-Term Debt
For Year Ended June 30, 19X5

(in thousands of dollars)

	General Long-Term Debt 7/1/X4	Additions	Retirements	General Long-Term Debt 6/30/X5
Long-term debt				
Serial bonds payable	$1,176,000	$ 4,000	$180,000	$1,000,000
Term bonds payable	1,623,000	6,000	300,000	1,329,000
Total	$2,799,000	$10,000	$480,000	$2,329,000

STATISTICAL SECTION

STATISTICAL SECTION

Information statistics and statistical tables should be included in this section of the Comprehensive Annual Financial Report. NCGA-1 requires that the following statistical tables be presented (unless they are inappropriate based on the reporting entity's circumstances).

- General Governmental Expenditures by Fund—Last Ten Fiscal Years
- General Revenues by Source—Last Ten Fiscal Years
- Property Tax Levies and Collections—Last Ten Fiscal Years
- Assessed and Estimated Actual Value of Taxable Property—Last Ten Fiscal Years
- Property Tax Rates—All Overlapping Governments—Last Ten Fiscal Years
- Special Assessment Billings and Collections—Last Ten Fiscal Years (if the government is obligated in some manner for related special assessment debt)
- Ratio of Net General Bonded Debt to Assessed Value and Net Bonded Debt Per Capita—Last Ten Fiscal Years
- Computation of Legal Debt Margin (if not presented in the General Purpose Financial Statements)
- Computation of Overlapping Debt (if not presented in the General Purpose Financial Statements)
- Ratio of Annual Debt Service for General Bonded Debt to Total General Expenditures—Last Ten Fiscal Years
- Revenue Bond Coverage—Last Ten Fiscal Years
- Demographic Statistics
- Property Value, Construction, and Bank Deposits—Last Ten Fiscal Years
- Principal Taxpayers
- Miscellaneous Statistics

The above statistical tables are not illustrated in the *Governmental GAAP Guide*.

TOPICAL INDEX

ADVANCED REFUNDINGS AND DEFEASED DEBTS
  Accounting standards 40.16
  Computing the required disclosures 40.21
  Debt refunding 62.18
  Disclosure standards 40.19
    Difference in cash flow requirements 40.20
    Economic gain or loss 40.20
  In-substance defeasance 62.17
  Legal defeasance 62.15
AMERICAN INSTITUTE OF CPAS
  Auditing standards board 1.12
  Current status of pronouncements 1.07
  Industry audit guide for state and local governments 1.10
  Statements of position 1.08
ASSETS
  Depreciation 30.11
  Disclosures 30.13
  Escheat property 30.05
  Expendable financial resources 30.01
  Fixed assets 30.07
  Interfund receivables/payables 30.06
  Leased property 30.09
  Materials and supplies 30.01
    Consumption method 30.02
    Purchase method 30.03
  Prepayments and deferrals 30.04
    Allocation method 30.04
    Nonallocation method 30.05
ASSETS OF FUNDS
  Capital projects funds 61.20
  Colleges and universities 81.14
  Debt service funds 62.25
  Fiduciary funds 65.03, 65.12
  General and special revenue funds 60.20
  Hospitals 80.14
  Other nonprofit organizations 82.18
  Pension trust funds 66.12
  Proprietary funds 64.16

BASIC CONCEPTS AND STANDARDS
  Capital projects funds 61.01
  Colleges and universities 81.01
  Debt service funds 62.01
  Fiduciary funds 65.01, 65.09, 65.17
  General and special revenue funds 60.01
  Hospitals 80.01
  Other nonprofit organizations 82.01
  Pension trust funds 66.01
  Proprietary funds 64.01

BASIS OF ACCOUNTING
  Accrual basis 3.02
  Capital projects funds 61.01
  Cash basis 3.02
  Colleges and universities 81.01
  Debt service funds 62.02
  Fiduciary funds 65.01, 65.09, 65.17
  General and special revenue funds 60.02
  Hospitals 80.02
  Illustration 3.08
  Modified accrual basis 3.03
  Other nonprofit organizations 82.02
  Pension trust funds 66.03
  Proprietary funds 64.04
BOND, TAX, AND REVENUE ANTICIPATION NOTES
  Bond anticipation notes 40.05, 67.04
  Tax and revenue anticipation notes 40.05
BUDGETARY ACCOUNTING SYSTEM
  Accounting for the budget 6.04
  Accounting for encumbrances 6.06
    Lapsing appropriations 6.07
    Nonlapsing appropriations 6.09
  Capital projects funds 61.02
  Colleges and universities 81.03
  Debt service funds 62.03
  Fiduciary funds 65.01
  General and special revenue funds 60.04
  Hospitals 80.03
  Other nonprofit organizations 82.03
  Pension trust funds 66.04
  Proprietary funds 64.06
BUDGETARY PROCESS
  Budgeting for fiduciary funds 6.02
  Budgeting for governmental funds 6.02
  Budgeting for proprietary funds 6.01
BUDGETARY REPORTING
  Comprehensive annual financial report 6.13
  General purpose financial statements 6.11
  Minimum reporting standards 6.15
  Reconciling budget and GAAP information 6.15
    Basis differences 6.16
    Entity differences 6.15
    Perspective differences 6.16
    Timing differences 6.16
BUDGETARY SYSTEM AND ACCOUNTS
  Capital projects funds 61.02
  Colleges and universities 81.03
  Debt service funds 62.03
  Fiduciary funds 65.01, 65.09, 65.17
  General and special revenue funds 60.04
  Hospitals 80.03

GOVERNMENTAL GAAP GUIDE / **95.01**

Topical Index

BUDGETARY SYSTEM AND ACCOUNTS
(continued)
Other nonprofit organizations **82.03**
Pension trust funds **66.04**
Proprietary funds **64.06**

CAPITAL PROJECTS FUNDS
  Assets **61.20**
    Classification and disclosure **61.21**
  Basic concepts and standards **61.01**
  Basis of accounting **61.01**
  Budgetary system and accounts **61.02**
    Recording encumbrances **61.03**
    Recording the budget **61.02**
  Expenditures **61.12**
    Capital leases **61.16**
    Classification and disclosure **61.20**
    Interest expenditures **61.15**
    Quasi-external expenditures **61.14**
    Reimbursements **61.14**
  Financial statements **61.30**
    Balance sheet **61.34**
    Combining financial statements **61.34**
    Other financial statements **61.35**
    Statement of revenues, expenditures, and changes in fund balance **61.32**
  Interfund transactions **61.27**
    Classification and disclosure **61.29**
    Operating transfers **61.28**
    Residual equity transfers **61.28**
  Liabilities **61.21**
    Bond anticipation notes **61.23**
    Claims and judgments **61.26**
    Classification and disclosure **61.27**
  Measurement focus **61.02**
  Revenues and other sources of financing **61.04**
    Bond discount **61.07**
    Bond premium **61.07**
    Bonds sold between interest payment dates **61.05**
    Capital grants **61.08**
    Classification and disclosure **61.12**
    Dedicated taxes **61.10**
    Investment income **61.11**
    Proceeds from issuance of long-term debt **61.05**
    Shared revenues **61.10**

CERTAIN NONPROFIT ORGANIZATIONS
  Assets **82.16**
    Collections **82.18**
    Fixed assets **82.20**
    Investments **82.18**
  Basic concepts and standards **82.01**
  Basis of accounting **82.02**
  Budgetary system and accounts **82.03**
  Endowment funds **82.34**
  Expenses **82.12**
    Depreciation **82.16**
    Functional classification basis **82.13**
    Grants **82.17**
    Natural classification basis **82.16**

Financial statements **82.42**
  Balance sheet **82.43**
  Combined financial statements **82.50**
  Statement of activity **82.50**
  Statement of changes in financial position **82.50**
Liabilities **82.21**
  Deferred revenue and support **82.22**
  Deferred taxes **82.22**
  Encumbrances **82.21**
Measurement focus **82.04**
Operating funds—restricted **82.31**
Operating funds—unrestricted **82.24**
Plant funds **82.37**
Revenues and other sources of assets **82.05**
  Capital additions **82.08**
  Contributed materials and facilities **82.11**
  Contributed services **82.10**
  Investment income and realized gains and losses **82.11**
  Pledges **82.09**
  Restricted support **82.07**
  Revenues **82.06**
  Support **82.07**
  Unrestricted support **82.07**
Transfers and interfund transactions **82.23**
  Interfund borrowings **82.23**
  Interfund investment transactions **82.23**

CLAIMS AND JUDGMENTS
Accrual **41.03**
Disclosure **41.06**
Fund balance designation **41.09**
Loss contingency **41.02, 67.08**
Proprietary funds **41.08**
Self-insurance funds **41.08**
Trust funds **41.08**

CODE OF PROFESSIONAL CONDUCT
Rule 203 **1.02**

COLLEGES AND UNIVERSITIES
Agency funds **81.62**
Annuity and life income funds **81.49**
Assets **81.14**
  Inventories and deferred charges **81.14**
  Investments **81.14**
  Plant assets and related liabilities **81.16**
  Plant fund—investment in plant **81.19**
  Plant fund—renewals and replacements **81.18**
  Plant fund—retirement of indebtedness **81.19**
  Plant fund—unexpended **81.16**
Assets held by sponsoring religious groups **81.21**
Basic concepts and standards **81.01**
Basis of accounting **81.02**
Budgetary system and accounts **81.03**
Current fund—restricted **81.35**
Current fund—unrestricted **81.26**
Endowment and similar funds **81.43**
Expenditures **81.11**
  Capital expenditures **81.12**
  Contributed services **81.13**
  Expenditure and transfer classification **81.13**
  Fund balance deductions **81.14**

Topical Index

Financial statements 81.64
  Accounting changes 81.74
  Balance sheet 81.65
  Resources held by others 81.76
  Statement of changes in fund balances 81.65
  Statement of revenues, expenditures, and other changes 81.72
  Supplementary material and schedules 81.72
Interfund and interdepartmental transactions 81.22
  Interdepartmental transactions 81.24
  Interfund borrowing 81.24
  Mandatory transfers 81.23
  Nonmandatory transfers 81.23
Liabilities 81.21
Loan funds 81.39
Measurement focus 81.03
Plant funds 81.55
Revenues and other sources of assets 81.05
  Allocated tuition and fees 81.06
  Endowment income 81.08
  Fund balance additions 81.11
  Governmental appropriations 81.07
  Governmental grants and contracts 81.07
  Independent operations 81.10
  Other revenue sources 81.11
  Pledged tuition and fees 81.06
  Private gifts and grants 81.08
  Sales and services of auxiliary enterprises 81.10
  Sales and services of educational activities 81.10
  Sales and services of hospitals 81.10
  Tuition and fees 81.05

COMPENSATED ABSENCES
Accrual 42.02
Accumulated sick pay benefits 42.06
General Long-term Debt Account Group 67.10
Nonaccrual 42.05
Proprietary funds 42.07
Trust funds 42.07

COMPREHENSIVE ANNUAL FINANCIAL REPORT
Financial section 5.10
  Auditor's report 5.10
  Combining statements—by fund type 5.17
  General purpose financial statements 5.11
    Combined balance sheet 5.12
    Combined statement of changes in financial position 5.13
    Combined statement of revenues, expenditures, and changes in fund balances—all governmental fund types 5.12
    Combined statement of revenues, expenditures, and changes in fund balances—budget and actual 5.12
    Combined statement of revenues, expenses, and changes in retained earnings 5.13
    Disclosures 5.13
    Narrative explanations 5.16
    Notes to financial statements 5.14
  Individual fund and account groups 5.17

  Required supplementary information 5.17
  Schedules 5.18
Statistical tables section 5.19

CONVENTIONAL ACCOUNTING BASIS/MEASUREMENT FOCUS
Capital leases 3.13
Claims, judgments, and compensated absences 3.13
Debt proceeds 3.12
Encumbrances 3.12
Expenditures for servicing long-term debt 3.12
Grants, entitlements, and shared revenues 3.11
Inventories 3.12
Operating expenditures 3.11
Operating transfers 3.14
Other revenues 3.11
Pensions 3.13
Prepayments 3.12
Property tax revenues 3.10
Sales tax revenues 3.11

DEBT SERVICE FUNDS
Assets 62.25
  Classification and disclosure 62.27
Basic concepts and standards 62.01
Basis of accounting 62.02
Budgetary system and accounts 62.03
  Recording encumbrances 62.04
  Recording the budget 62.03
Expenditures 62.13
  Capitalized interest cost 62.21
  Capital leases 62.19
  Classification and disclosure 62.25
  Debt extinguishments 62.15
  Debt refunding 62.18
  In-substance defeasance 62.17
  Legal defeasance 62.15
  Unmatured principal and interest 62.14
  Zero interest-rate bonds 62.23
Financial statements 62.32
  Balance sheet 62.36
  Combining financial statements 62.36
  Statement of changes in fund balance 62.34
  Statement of revenues and expenditures 62.34
Interfund transactions 62.30
  Classification and disclosure 62.32
  Operating transfers 62.30
  Residual equity transfers 62.31
Liabilities 62.27
  Bonds sold between interest payment dates 62.29
  Classification and disclosure 62.30
  Unmatured principal and interest 62.28
Measurement focus 62.03
Revenues and other sources of financing 62.05
  Classification and disclosure 62.13
  Investment income 62.09
  Property taxes 62.05
  Shared revenues 62.08
  Transfers and other sources of financing 62.12

GOVERNMENTAL GAAP GUIDE / **95.03**

Topical Index

DEPOSIT AND INVESTMENT DISCLOSURES
  Book entry systems **31.17**
    Counterparty **31.19**
    Counterparty's trust department or agent **31.18**
    Entity's agent **31.18**
  Deposits **31.03**
    Collateral **31.04**
    Credit-worthiness **31.04**
    Insurance **31.03**
  Financial institutions and broker-dealers as counterparties **31.15**
  Financial reporting standards **31.09**
    Deposit and investment disclosures **31.15**
    Deposit disclosures **31.11**
    Investment disclosures **31.12**
    Legal or contractual provisions for deposits and investments **31.10**
  Investments **31.02**
    Credit-worthiness **31.03**
    Custodial responsibility **31.03**
    Insurance **31.03**
    Registration of ownership **31.03**

DEPRECIATION
  General assets **30.11**
  Restricted grants **30.11**

EXPENDITURES/EXPENSES
  Basis of accounting **20.02**
  Capital projects funds **61.12**
  Colleges and universities **81.11**
  Debt service funds **62.13**
  Encumbrances **20.09**
  Fiduciary funds **65.02, 65.11**
  General and special revenue funds **60.16**
  Hospitals **80.10**
  Interest and principal **20.02**
  Interfund transactions **20.04**
  Measurement focus **20.01**
  Other nonprofit organizations **82.12**
  Pension trust funds **66.11**
  Proprietary funds **64.12**

FEDERAL GOVERNMENTAL FINANCIAL STATEMENTS
  Accounting principles **1.14**

FIDUCIARY FUNDS
  Agency funds **65.17**
    Discretionary agency fund **65.19**
    Dual recording agency fund **65.20**
    Financial statements **65.22**
    IRC Section 457 deferred compensation plans **65.23**
    Pass through agency fund **65.18**
  Expendable trust funds **65.01**
    Assets **65.03**
    Escheat property **65.04**
    Expenditures **65.02**

    Financial statements **65.04**
    Investments **65.04**
    Liabilities **65.04**
    Materials and supplies **65.03**
    Prepayments and deferrals **65.03**
    Revenues and other sources of financing **65.01**
  Nonexpendable trust funds **65.09**
    Assets **65.12**
    Donations **65.11**
    Expenses **65.11**
    Financial statements **65.12**
    Grants, entitlements, and shared revenues **65.10**
    Investment income **65.09**
    Liabilities **65.12**
    Revenues **65.09**

FINANCIAL ACCOUNTING FOUNDATION
  Agreement to establish GASB **1.01**

FINANCIAL ACCOUNTING STANDARDS BOARD
  Pronouncements as authoritative sources of generally accepted accounting principles **1.12**

FINANCIAL STATEMENTS
  Capital projects funds **61.30**
  Colleges and universities **81.64**
  Debt service funds **62.32**
  Fiduciary funds **65.04, 65.12, 65.22**
  General and special revenue funds **60.36**
  Hospitals **80.59**
  Other nonprofit organizations **82.42**
  Pension trust funds **66.16**
  Proprietary funds **64.33**

FIXED ASSETS
  Disclosures **30.13**
  Expendable trust funds **30.09**
  Governmental funds **30.08**
  Nonexpendable trust funds **30.09**
  Proprietary funds **30.09**

FUND ACCOUNTING
  Definition **2.24**
  Number of funds **2.33**
  Types of funds **2.25**

GENERAL AND SPECIAL REVENUE FUNDS
  Assets **60.20**
    Capital outlays **60.24**
    Classification and disclosure **60.25**
    Current assets **60.20**
    Escheat property **60.25**
    Materials and supplies **60.22**
    Noncurrent assets **60.24**
    Prepayments and deferrals **60.23**
  Basic concepts and standards **60.01**
  Basis of accounting **60.02**
    Accrual basis **60.03**
    Cash basis **60.03**
    Modified accrual basis **60.03**
  Budgetary systems and accounts **60.04**
    Recording encumbrances **60.06**
    Recording the budget **60.04**

Topical Index

Expenditures **60.16**
  Classification and disclosure **60.19**
  Debt service payments **60.16**
  Quasi-external expenditures **60.17**
  Reimbursements **60.18**
Financial statements **60.36**
  Balance sheet **60.44**
  Interim financial statements **60.44**
  Statement of changes in fund balances **60.43**
  Statement of revenues and expenditures **60.42**
  Statement of revenues, expenditures, and changes in fund balance—budget and actual **60.36**
Interfund transactions **60.32**
  Classification and disclosure **60.35**
  Interfund receivables/payables **60.35**
  Operating transfers **60.32**
  Residual equity transfers **60.34**
Liabilities **60.26**
  Bond anticipation notes **60.26**
  Classification and disclosure **60.31**
  Current liabilities **60.26**
  Demand bonds **60.29**
  General long-term debt **60.31**
  Tax and revenue anticipation notes **60.26**
Measurement focus **60.03**
Revenues and other sources of financing **60.08**
  Change in accounting method **60.11**
  Change in estimate **60.10**
  Classification and disclosure **60.16**
  Grants, entitlements, and shared revenues **60.12**
  Miscellaneous revenues **60.14**
  Proceeds from issuance of long-term debt **60.15**
  Property taxes **60.08**
  Quasi-external revenues **60.15**
  Sales taxes **60.13**
  Taxpayer-assessed revenues **60.14**

GENERAL FIXED ASSETS ACCOUNT GROUP
  Acquisition of general fixed assets **68.01**
  Capital lease rights **68.06**
  Construction in progress **68.04**
  Depreciation **68.07**
  Disclosures **68.10**
  Disposition and exchange of general fixed assets **68.08**
    Dissimilar exchanges **68.09**
    Similar exchanges **68.10**
  Financial statements **68.12**
  Infrastructure fixed assets **68.04**

GENERAL LONG-TERM DEBT ACCOUNT GROUP
  Advance refundings and defeased debt **40.15**
  Bond anticipation notes **67.04**
  Compensated absences **67.10**
  Debt instruments **67.02**
  Demand bonds **67.06**
  Disclosures **67.15**
    Bond anticipation notes **67.16**
    Compensated absences **67.17**

    Demand bonds **67.16**
    Leases **67.17**
    Loss contingencies **67.16**
  Financial statements **67.17**
  Leases **67.13**
  Loss contingencies **67.08**
  Special termination benefits **67.11**

GOVERNMENTAL ACCOUNTING, AUDITING, AND FINANCIAL REPORTING
  GAAFR 1968 **1.09**
  GAAFR 1980 **1.09**

GOVERNMENTAL ACCOUNTING STANDARDS BOARD
  Interpretations **1.06**
  Pronouncements **1.05**
  Rule-making powers **1.04**
  Statements **1.05**
  Technical bulletins **1.06**

GOVERNMENTAL FINANCE OFFICERS ASSOCIATION
  Certificate of achievement for excellence in financial reporting **1.14**

GOVERNMENTAL FUNDS
  Basis of accounting/measurement focus **3.10**
  Overview **2.25**

GOVERNMENTAL GENERALLY ACCEPTED ACCOUNTING PRINCIPLES
  Authoritative sources **1.01**
  Compliance with generally accepted accounting principles **2.22**
  Principle 1—Accounting and reporting capabilities **2.18**
  Principle 2—Fund accounting systems **2.18**
  Principle 3—Types of funds **2.18**
  Principle 4—Numbers of funds **2.19**
  Principle 5—Accounting for fixed assets and long-term liabilities **2.20**
  Principle 6—Valuation of fixed assets **2.20**
  Principle 7—Depreciation of fixed assets **2.20**
  Principle 8—Accrual basis in governmental accounting **2.20**
  Principle 9—Budgeting, budgetary control, and budgetary reporting **2.21**
  Principle 10—Transfer, revenue, expenditure, and expense account classification **2.21**
  Principle 11—Common terminology and classification **2.21**
  Principle 12—Interim and annual financial reports **2.22**

GRANTS, ENTITLEMENTS, AND SHARED REVENUES
  Disclosures **10.13**
  Fiduciary fund types **10.11**
  Governmental fund types **10.07**
  Proprietary fund types **10.09**

GROUP OF ACCOUNTS
  General fixed assets account group **2.31**
  General long-term debt account group **2.32**

GOVERNMENTAL GAAP GUIDE / **95.05**

Topical Index

HOSPITALS

Assets 80.14
  Cash 80.14
  Long-term security investments 80.16
  Marketable equity securities 80.14
  Property, plant, and equipment 80.17
  Receivables 80.17
Basic concepts and standards 80.01
Basis of accounting 80.02
Board-designated funds 80.48
Budgetary system and accounts 80.03
Consolidated or combined financial statements 80.70
Endowment funds 80.54
Expenses 80.10
  Capital grants 80.11
  Depreciation expense 80.10
  Interest cost 80.13
Financial statements 80.59
  Balance Sheet 80.60
  Statement of changes in financial position 80.67
  Statement of changes in fund balances 80.60
  Statement of revenues and expenses 80.60
Interfund transfers and restricted resources 80.31
Liabilities 80.18
  Accrual of loss contingency 80.20
  Asserted and unasserted claims for health care providers 80.24
  Contingent liabilities 80.19
  Deferred revenue—third-party reimbursements 80.30
  Disclosure of loss contingency 80.22
  General obligation bonds 80.19
  Nontransfer of malpractice risk 80.23
  Other disclosures 80.23
  Revenue bonds 80.19
Measurement focus 80.03
Operating fund 80.34
Plant replacement and extension fund 80.55
Revenues and other sources of assets 80.05
  Charity services 80.06
  Contractual adjustments 80.06
  Donated services 80.08
  Donated supplies and equipment 80.07
  Endowment fund investment transactions 80.08
  Nonoperating revenues 80.08
  Nonprofessional services 80.07
  Other deductions 80.06
  Other investment transactions 80.09
  Other operating revenues 80.07
  Patient service revenues 80.05
  Pledges 80.09
  Provision for bad debts 80.06
  Transfers from restricted funds 80.07
  Unrestricted gifts 80.09
  Unrestricted investment transactions 80.08
Separate trust funds 80.69
Specific-purpose funds 80.50

INTERFUND TRANSACTIONS

Loans and advances 20.04
Operating transfers 20.08
Quasi-external transactions 20.05
Reimbursements 20.06
Residual equity transfers 20.07

INTERFUND TRANSFERS

Capital projects funds 61.27
Colleges and universities 81.22
Debt service funds 62.30
General and special revenue funds 60.32
Hospitals 80.31
Other nonprofit organizations 82.23
Proprietary funds 64.31

JOINT VENTURES

Accounting principles 5.25
Definition 5.25
Disclosures 5.26
Proprietary funds 64.20

LEASES

Lessee accounting 43.01
  Capital leases 43.01
  Contingent rentals 43.07
  Depreciation 43.06
  Disclosures 43.08
  Fiscal funding clauses 43.07
  Operating leases 43.09
  Recording a capital lease 43.03
Lessor accounting 43.11
  Bad debts 43.14
  Contingent rentals 43.16
  Direct financing leases 43.11
  Disclosures—direct financing leases 43.16
  Initial direct costs 43.15
  Operating leases 43.18
  Recording a direct financing leases 43.12
Proprietary funds 43.24
Related parties 43.20
Sale-leaseback transaction 43.21
  Purchaser-lessor accounting 43.24
  Seller-lessee accounting 43.21
Trust funds 43.24

LIABILITIES

Capital projects funds 61.21
Colleges and universities 81.21
Debt service funds 62.27
Fiduciary funds 65.04, 65.12
General and special revenue funds 60.26
Hospitals 80.18
Other nonprofit organizations 82.21
Pension trust funds 66.14
Proprietary funds 64.25

LONG-TERM LIABILITIES

Bond, tax, and revenue anticipation notes 40.04
  Bond anticipation notes 40.05, 67.04
  Tax and revenue anticipation notes 40.05

Debt refunding **62.18**
Demand bonds **40.08, 67.06**
Disclosures **40.29**
Extinguishment of debt **40.14**
General long-term debt account group **40.03, 67.01**
Specific fund liabilities **40.02**
    Nonexpendable trust funds **40.02**
    Proprietary funds **40.02**

MATERIALS AND SUPPLIES
Consumption method **30.02**
Purchase method **30.03**

MEASUREMENT FOCUS
Capital projects funds **61.02**
Colleges and universities **81.03**
Debt service funds **62.03**
Fiduciary funds **65.01, 65.09, 65.17**
Flow of current financial resources (modified accrual basis) **3.06**
Flow of economic resources (accrual basis) **3.05**
Flow of total financial resources (modified accrual basis) **3.06**
General and special revenue funds **60.03**
Hospitals **80.03**
Illustration **3.08**
Other nonprofit organizations **82.04**
Pension trust funds **66.03**
Proprietary funds **64.04**

NATIONAL COUNCIL ON GOVERNMENTAL ACCOUNTING
Current status of pronouncements **1.06**

OBJECTIVES OF FINANCIAL REPORTING
FASB Concepts Statement-4 **2.13**
    Assessing management **2.16**
    Assessing services provided **2.16**
    Comments made by managers **2.17**
    Economic resources and obligations **2.17**
    Resource allocation decisions **2.16**
GASB Concepts Statement-1 **2.02**
    Assessment of accountability **2.05**
    Assessment of potential for providing services and ability to meet obligations **2.07**
    Evaluation of operating results **2.07**
NCGA Concepts Statement-1 **2.08**
    Communications **2.13**
    Financial condition **2.10**
    Legal, contractual, and fiduciary requirements **2.11**
    Organizational and managerial performance **2.12**
    Planning and budgeting **2.12**
    Short-term financial resources **2.10**

PENSION DISCLOSURES
Defined benefit pension plan information **50.02**
    Component units' pension information in the reporting entity's financial reports **50.42**

Employers contributing to cost-sharing multiple-employer PERS **50.38**
Multiple-employer PERS included as a pension trust fund in the employer reporting entity **50.37**
Noncontributing employers **50.44**
Pension disclosures in employer financial reports **50.24**
Pension disclosures in separately issued PERS reports **50.02**
Reporting by nonemployer contributors **50.46**
Single-employer PERS included as a pension trust fund in the employer reporting entity **50.36**
Unfunded pension arrangements **50.45**
Defined contribution pension plan information **50.47**
Employer disclosures **50.51**

PENSION TRUST FUNDS
Assets **66.12**
    Equity securities **66.13**
    Fixed income securities **66.13**
    Insurance contracts **66.13**
    Securities subject to forced liquidation **66.13**
Basic concepts and standards **66.01**
Basis of accounting **66.03**
Budgetary system and accounts **66.04**
Designation of fund balances **66.14**
Disclosures **66.15**
Disclosures as a component unit **66.15**
Expenses **66.11**
Financial statements **66.16**
GASB-4 **66.01**
Liabilities **66.14**
Measurement focus **66.03**
Objectives of pension fund reporting **66.02**
Revenues **66.04**
    Debt securities **66.05**
    Equity securities **66.07**
    Exchange of debt securities **66.07**
        Completed transaction method **66.08**
        Cost pass-through method **66.10**
        Deferral/amortization method **66.09**
    Investment income **66.05**
    Other revenue **66.10**

POSTRETIREMENT BENEFITS
Accounting for certain postretirement benefits **51.01**
Disclosures for certain postretirement benefits **51.02**

PREFERRED ACCOUNTING PRACTICES FOR STATE GOVERNMENTS
Current status **1.11**

PREPAYMENTS AND DEFERRALS
Allocation method **30.04**
Nonallocation method **30.05**

PROPERTY TAXES
Available **10.03**
Deferred revenues **10.04**
Disclosures **10.04**
Measurable **10.01**

Topical Index

PROPRIETARY FUNDS
  Assets 64.16
    Classification and disclosure 64.24
    Interest capitalization 64.17
    Joint ventures 64.20
    Leased property 64.19
  Basic concepts and standards 64.01
  Basis of accounting 64.04
  Budgetary systems and accounts 64.06
  Expenses 64.12
    Classification and disclosure 64.16
    Depreciation expense 64.13
    Quasi-external expenses 64.13
  Financial statements 64.33
    Balance sheet 64.37
    Combining financial statements 64.40
    Segment information—enterprise funds 64.40
    Statement of changes in financial position 64.39
    Statement of changes in retained earnings 64.37
    Statement of revenues and expenses 64.34
  Interfund transactions 64.31
    Classification and disclosure 64.33
    Operating transfers 64.31
    Residual equity transfers 64.32
  Liabilities 64.25
    Classification and disclosure 64.30
    General obligation bonds 64.26
    Revenue bonds 64.27
    Self-insurance internal service funds 64.28
  Measurement focus 64.04
  Revenues 64.07
    Classification and disclosure 64.12
    Grants, entitlements, and shared revenues 64.09
    Quasi-external revenues 64.08

REPORTING BY COMPONENT UNITS
  Component units financial report 5.24
  Discrete presentation 5.23
  Including unit in reporting entity 5.20
  Separate presentation 5.24

REPORTING ENTITY
  Ability to significantly influence operations 4.06
  Accountability for fiscal matters 4.07
    Budget authority 4.08
    Fiscal management 4.08
    Revenue characteristics 4.08
    Surplus/deficit 4.08
  Basic criteria 4.03
  Designation of management 4.05
  Disclosures 4.12
  Evaluation of criteria 4.12
  Financial interdependency 4.03
  GASB research project 4.17
  Other criteria 4.10
    Scope of public service 4.10
    Special financial relationships 4.11
  Selection of governing authority 4.04

REPURCHASE/REVERSE REPURCHASE AGREEMENTS
  Accounting and reporting standards 31.21
  Dollar fixed coupon repurchase agreements 31.22
  Dollar fixed coupon reverse repurchase agreements 31.22
  Dollar yield maintenance repurchase agreements 31.22
  Dollar yield maintenance reverse repurchase agreements 31.22
  Repurchase agreements 31.21
  Reverse repurchase agreements 31.22
  Financial reporting standards 31.09
    Other agreements 31.21
    Reverse repurchase agreements 31.20
    Yield maintenance agreement 31.20
  Repurchase agreements 31.04
    Collateral 31.07
    Credit-worthiness 31.06
    Custodial responsibility 31.07
    Written agreements 31.06
    Yield maintenance agreements 31.07
  Reverse repurchase agreements 31.08

REVENUES
  Financial reporting disclosures 10.15
  Grants, entitlements, and shared revenues 10.06
  Miscellaneous revenues 10.14
  Other financing resources 10.15
  Property taxes 10.01
  Quasi-external transactions 10.14
  Sales taxes 10.05

REVENUES AND OTHER SOURCES OF FINANCING
  Capital projects funds 61.04
  Colleges and universities 81.05
  Debt service funds 62.05
  Fiduciary funds 65.01, 65.09
  General and special revenue funds 60.08
  Hospitals 80.05
  Other nonprofit organizations 82.05
  Pension trust funds 66.04
  Proprietary funds 64.07

SPECIAL ASSESSMENTS
  Capital improvements financed by special assessment-related debt 11.03
    Capital projects funds 11.03
    Debt service funds 11.03
    GFAAG 11.04
    GLTDAG 11.04
  Classification of special assessment debt 11.09
    General obligation debt 11.10
    No obligation to pay debt 11.11
    Obligated in some manner 11.10
  Disclosures 11.19
    Governmental unit not obligated for debt 11.20
    Governmental unit obligated for debt 11.19
  Effective date and transition 11.20
  Enterprise funds 11.16
  Financing special assessments with current resources 11.15
  Governmental liability for debt 11.08
  No governmental obligation for debt 11.13

95.08 / GOVERNMENTAL GAAP GUIDE

Agency fund **11.13**
Capital projects fund **11.13**
GFAAG **11.14**
Services financed by special assessments **11.02**
Special assessment districts as component units **11.19**
Special assessment reserve, guarantee, or sinking fund **11.12**
Statistical tables **11.20**

TERMINOLOGY AND CLASSIFICATION
Expenditures **7.03**
   Activity classification **7.04**
   Character classification **7.04**
   Function (or program) classification **7.03**
   Object class classification **7.05**
   Organization unit classification **7.03**
Fund balance reserve **7.10**
Interfund receivables and payables **7.13**
Operating transfers **7.05**
Prior period adjustments **7.09**
Proceeds from issuance of debt **7.08**
Proprietary funds **7.14**
Quasi-external transactions **7.06**
Reimbursements **7.07**
Reserves and designations **7.13**
Residual equity transfers **7.11**
Revenues **7.03**

OTHER PROFESSIONAL PUBLICATIONS OF INTEREST

1990 MILLER COMPREHENSIVE GAAP GUIDE

The 1990 edition of this highly respected and well-known reference includes every current promulgated pronouncement through late 1989. Arranged by subject matter to bring together related opinions of different dates, this thoroughly cross-indexed guide is a must for the professional accountant who wants to understand new GAAP. Over 1,100 pages. Paperback—$40. Deluxe hardcover edition—$55.

1990 MILLER COMPREHENSIVE GAAS GUIDE

Since its publication in June of 1982, the Miller Comprehensive GAAS Guide has won the acceptance of thousands of accounting professionals. Here, in one handy volume, are all the promulgated and many of the nonpromulgated standards, practices, and procedures which an independent auditor or accountant must apply in the performance of any type of professional engagement. Over 1,400 pages. Paperback—$40. Deluxe hardcover edition—$55.

1990 MILLER ACCOUNTING UPDATE SERVICES

Subscribers to Miller Accounting Update Services can count on keeping up with changes in GAAP and/or governmental GAAP. Within weeks of any official FASB or GASB promulgation you will receive your Update Bulletin—a complete restatement and analysis of the new pronouncement. Each subscription includes one softcover copy of the GAAP Guide or the Governmental GAAP Guide. GAAP Guide Update Subscription—$135. Governmental GAAP Guide Update Subscription—$110.

STANDING ORDER PLAN...All orders include annual replacement editions or Update subscription renewals. Standing orders may be canceled at any time.

SAVE 10%...when you purchase 2 or more of our Guides. Call our toll-free number for more information.

QUANTITY DISCOUNTS...of 23% on all orders for 25 or more copies.

TOLL-FREE ORDERING AND INFORMATION
Call **1-800-543-1918**. In MO and AK, call collect **314-528-8110**.

HBJ MILLER ACCOUNTING PUBLICATIONS, INC.
A subsidiary of Harcourt Brace Jovanovich, Inc.
465 S. Lincoln Drive, Troy, MO 63379